GÉNÉRAL LOUIS DIO

The Wartime Epic of One of Free France's Greatest
Soldiers, 1940–1946

Jean-Paul Michel and Monique Brouillet Seefried

Translator, Jason R. Musteen

Editor, Stephen Ede-Borrett

ASSOCIATION OF THE
UNITED STATES ARMY

Helion & Company
Published in cooperation with the
Association of the United States Army

Helion & Company Limited
Unit 8 Amherst Business Centre
Budbrooke Road
Warwick
CV34 5WE
England
Tel. 01926 499619
Email: info@helion.co.uk
Website: www.helion.co.uk
X (formerly Twitter): @Helionbooks
Facebook: @HelionBooks
Visit our blog at https://helionbooks.wordpress.com/

Published by Helion & Company 2025 in co-operation with the Association of the United States Army
Designed and typeset by Mach 3 Solutions (www.mach3solutions.co.uk)
Cover designed by Paul Hewitt, Battlefield Design (www.battlefield-design.co.uk)

Text © Jean-Paul Michel and Monique Brouillet Seefried 2022
Translation © Jason R. Musteen 2025
Illustrations © as individually credited

First published in 2022 by Bernard Giovanangeli Éditeur (France) as *Le général Dio, Le connétable de Leclerc, 1940-1946*

ISBN 978-1-804517-62-8

British Library Cataloguing-in-Publication Data.
A catalogue record for this book is available from the British Library.

For details of other military history titles published by Helion & Company Limited, contact the above address, or visit our website: http://www.helion.co.uk

We always welcome receiving book proposals from prospective authors.

MIX
Paper | Supporting
responsible forestry
FSC
www.fsc.org FSC® C014540

For Dio, Leclerc and all those who served with the FFL

Contents

Acknowledgements

During our research, we have had the good fortune and the honour to benefit from the help of many people. For the English version of this book, we would first like to thank its outstanding and passionate translator, Colonel Jason Musteen, without whom it would not have seen the light.

We would like to express our gratitude in particular to Pierre Robédat, a former Free Frenchman who fought in the *1re DFL* and who subsequently became close to *Général* Dio. He shared his memories with us to help us better understand the different facets of the personality of this exceptional officer. The French Republic greatly honoured Colonel Robédat in 2023 by elevating him to the dignity of grand' croix de la Legion d'honneur. Sadly, he died before the publication of this book in English. We have also benefited from the memories of several of his old *Régiment de Marche du Tchad* comrades-in-arms, of whom we would in particular like to thank: Henri Auvray, Charles Pégulu de Rovin (deceased), Roger Doré and Robert Bensaïd. Our gratitude goes also to Catherine Massu and Jeanne Penet who have been kind enough to tell us about their meetings with Général Dio. Some descendants of military personnel who fought at his side, such as the members of the Debray family (*Amiral* Michel Debray, his brothers and his sister Marie-Abeille), the prefect Paul de Langlade, grandson of the *général*, Marcel Poualion, son of Maurice Poualion, Jean-René Van der Plaetsen, grandson of *Général* Crépin, Patricia Simic, daughter of a former member of the *501e RCC* and also Sophie Galy-Dejean, daughter of *Colonel* Jean-Pierre Durand-Gasselin, have shared with us documents and memories that have been infinitely precious. The same goes for Colonel Harry Cunningham's grandsons, James and Andrew F. Cunningham.

We cannot forget the members of *Maréchal* Leclerc de Hauteclocque's family, notably his daughter Bénédicte de Francqueville and his two very active grandchildren, Philippe de Francqueville and Isabelle Gevin, as well as Pierre de Waziers and François de Wendel.

We are also indebted to Guillemette de Sairigné, daughter of *Colonel* de Sairigné, Malcy Guichard, daughter of Olivier Guichard, Suzanne Drégi, daughter of Noëlle Brouillet, and René Vial, nephew of René Brouillet for their interest and their help.

Our gratitude goes also to all the people who have welcomed us and have facilitated our research in the following institutions:

The *Service Historique de la Défense*, *Lieutenant Colonels* Vincent Arbaretier and Marcel Joussen, and Géraud Létang,

At the *Centre d'Histoire et d'études des Troupes d'Outre-mer* in Fréjus, *Lieutenant Colonel* Philippe Roudier and Sandrine Crepet,

At the *Musée de l'Ordre de la Libération*, its director, *Général* (*2e Section*) Christian Baptiste; its curator, Vladimir Trouplin; Christine Levisse-Touzé, President of the historical committee; and Julien Toureille,

At the *Fondation de la France Libre*, its president, *Général* Robert Bresse; its historian, Sylvain Cornil-Frerrot; its Secretary, Yvette Quelen-Buttin (unfortunately deceased); and Christophe Bayard,

At the *Fédération National des Anciens de l'Outre-Mer* with its *Président*, *Général* (*2e Section*) Philippe Bonnet and, in particular, Roger Daumas who was *Général* Dio's aide-de-camp,

At the *Musée de la Libération de Paris, Musée du Général Leclerc, Musée Jean Moulin*, with its director Sylvie Zaidman, Pierre Argaw and his two archivists Catherine Decaure and Muriel Leclerc,

At the *Établissement de Communication et de Production Audiovisuelle de la Défense* (ECPAD),

To the *Association du 12ᵉ RC* and in particular Patrick Botte,

To the *Régiment du Marche du Tchad*, its regimental commander, *Colonel* Renaud Merlin, and to his officers.

In the United States, the director of the US Army Center for Military History, Charles H. Bowery, and David W. Hogan (Director of Histories) have been immensely generous towards us. Similarly, in Italy, *Generale* Basilio Di Martino, who was kind enough to share his research with us.

We are also very grateful to the *Fondation Maréchal Leclerc de Hauteclocque* and to its members. Through their enouragement, have allowed us to embark on this wonderful memorial adventure, *Généraux (2ᵉ Section)* Cuche and Anselme. Our thanks go to Christophe Legrand, vice-president in charge of remembrance, for his wise advice and to the whole team of current members of the foundation, in particular *Général (2ᵉ Section)* Éric Hautecloque-Raysz, Véréna Lamy, Roselyne Ettori, Nathalie Martin-Leborgne and Xavier Proy-Bonningues and Guy Aubert.

During a visit in Brittany in the footsteps of Louis Dio, we were received with infinite kindness at the sanctuary of Sainte-Anne d'Auray by its rector, Father Gwenaël Maurey, manager Bruno Belliot, and Cécile Perrochon, responsible for the collections, as well as by *Colonel* Le Ny. Similarly, in Vannes, Christian Chaudré, professor at the Collège Jules Simon, offered us a privileged welcome as did Father Jean-Yves Lesaux, vicar general of the diocese, and Gwenn le Roux, in the historical diocesan archives.

In Rennes, Jean-Noël Cloarec, from the *Association Amélycor* (Lycée Émile Zola) allowed us to find the young precocious lycée student whom Dio was, and the places in which he was formed. Finally, in Coëtquidan, *Général* Patrick Collet and *Lieutenant Colonel* Pierre de Labareyre, director of the museum, welcomed us and offered valuable advice.

We would also like to thank Victor Leray, Emmanuel Rigault, Thibault de Quievrecourt, Bertrand Dias and Émilie Michel, who spontaneously helped us, as well as the enthusiasts of history Pascal-Henry Biwolé, Alain Eymard, Dominique Forget, and Ambrogio Orlando who shared their knowledge with us. Jean-Jacques Brot, Vincent Hommeril, André Rakoto, Stefano Silvestri are also entitled to our gratitude for the introductions they gave us.

Finally, we would like to thank our relatives who have us brought valuable help or provided advice and encouragement. Hoping not to have omitted any of them, or those to which we are indebted, we would like to also express our gratitude to our French editor, Bernard Giovanangeli, and his entire team, who allowed this work to see the light of day. We thank you with all our hearts. Likewise, to the team at Helion & Company, particularly Duncan Rogers who agreed to publish the book and Stephen Ede-Borrett who edited it with great dedication and knowledge. They have helped us bring *Général* Dio to the English-speaking world. Our gratitude also goes to Professor and Chair of War Studies at the United States Army War College, Michael S. Neiberg who wrote the foreword for the English version of this book. We are grateful to Joseph Craig, Director, AUSA (Association of the United States Army) Book Program for introducing us to them. Our thanks are also due to Colonel Gail Yoshitani, Professor and Head of the Department of History at the United States Military Academy, for her support and for recommending to us Colonel Jason Musteen, who completed the English translation of our work.

Translator's Introduction

The task of a translator is simply to convey the words and meaning of the authors. I have had the great benefit of collaborating with Monique Seefried and Jean-Paul Michel, who have generously and kindly reviewed my translations and offered suggestions to help me do that. Yet, I am also a career soldier and a professional historian, which has informed my choices as I worked. Therefore, although the assistance I received from the authors has been invaluable, any errors I have made are mine alone.

In cases where I felt English-speaking readers would need more information or context, I have sometimes modified the words of the original text. For example, I sometimes translated '*le chef de la France Libre*' simply as 'de Gaulle' rather than keeping the literal 'leader of Free France.' In some cases, I have added elaborations into the authors' text. For example, for an officer described simply as a '*polytechnicien*' in the original text, I have translated that as 'a graduate of the École Polytechnique.' When translating direct quotes, I have tried to stay as literal as possible while still conveying the original meaning and style of delivery. In cases where a longer explanation is necessary to understand a cultural reference, I have inserted footnotes that are distinguished from the author's footnotes with the creditation 'Translator's note.'

For the names of locations that have a conventional English spelling, I used that convention: Cameroun as Cameroon, Tchad as Chad, Koufra as Kufra.[1] For locations that lack an English convention, I left them as they appear in French, including diacritical marks, such as Ebuéï. In cases where the original text uses French transliterations of Arabic or other languages, I have kept the French transliteration.

I have kept the proper names of French units in French, but have capitalised them for clarity. Thus, I use *2ᵉ Division Blindée* and *2ᵉ DB* rather than 2nd Armoured Division. However, when not part of a proper name, I have usually chosen to use English. For example, 'an artillery regiment,' rather than 'a *régiment d'artillerie*,' but '*3ᵉ Régiment d'Artillerie Coloniale*.' I made an exception for *groupement* and *groupement tactique* for the sake of clarity; there are several units of varying size and changes over time that would all otherwise be translated as a 'group.' For subordinate units with generic numbered designations, I use English: '1st Platoon' or '6th Company.'

There are many specific words to describe different types of French soldiers, such as *cuirassier*, *chasseur*, et cetera. That is particularly true for indigenous soldiers in the colonial forces: *tirailleur*, *goumier*, *spahi*, *fusilier-voltigeur*, et cetera. I have kept those terms in French but have used English for more standard terms (infantryman for *fantassin*, artilleryman for *artilleur*, sapper or engineer for *sapeur*, et cetera). I have typically kept *méhariste* in French, but in some cases I chose 'camel soldier' when the original text implied an emphasis on distinguishing *méharistes* from their more traditional counterparts in the metropolitan army.

I have kept ranks in their original language, although that sometimes requires further explanation. Many French ranks of equal grade have different terms depending on the branch of the army. French army branches are divided between *armes à pied* (dismounted branches, such as infantry,

---

1   The spelling of the town is variously Koufra in French and Kufra in English. Generally the English spelling has been used throughout. (Editor's note)

engineers, et cetera) and the *armes à cheval* (mounted branches, such as the cavalry, artillery, transportation, and gendarmerie). There are multiple ranks in the French army that are the equivalent of a major in the UK or US: the basic rank is *commandant*, but for a *commandant* commanding a battalion in the dismounted branches, the rank is *chef de bataillon*. The equivalent in the mounted branches is *chef d'escadron*. In conversation, all are typically referred to as 'commandant.' In all cases, I have kept them as they appeared in French. Some NCO and lower ranks in the mounted arms are different from those in the dismounted arms, as well. A *sergent* (sergeant) in the infantry is equal to a *maréchal des logis* in the cavalry, and a *brigadier* in the cavalry is equal to a corporal, not to a brigadier general. There is a rank equivalence chart below that should help.

Finally, although I have used British spelling, I am an American; therefore, some phrases and expressions I have used may be more American than British. I have kept measurements in metric, using kilometres for distance, except in instances where nautical miles were used in the original. In that case, I kept it in miles, adding 'nautical' for clarity. Wherever Celsius was used for temperature, I included a conversion to Fahrenheit in parentheses.

It has been a joy to learn more about *la Division Leclerc* and particularly *Général* Louis Dio. I hope this translation makes them and their epic fight against the Axis Powers more accessible to an English-speaking audience. I would like to thank Monique Seefried for her trust and encouragement, Marna for her love and patience, and Jeff and Kristi McFarland for their generosity and friendship. They have always been my example in that regard.

Colonel Jason R. Musteen, PhD

Abbreviations

A.D.	Artillerie divisionnaire	Division Artillery
AD	Attaché de Défense	Defence Attaché
AEF	Afrique Equatoriale Française	French Equatorial Africa
AFL	Afrique Française Libre	Free French Africa
AMI	Assistance médicale indigène	Indigenous Medical Assistance
AOF	Afrique Occidentale Française	French West Africa
BAO	Banque de l'Afrique occidentale	Bank of West Africa
BET	Borkou-Ennedi-Tibesti	
BG	Bataillon du génie	Engineer Battalion
BM	Bataillon de marche ou bataillon médical (le 13ᵉ BM in the 2ᵉ DB)	Marching Battalion (Provisional Battalion Task Force), or Medical Battalion
BR	Bataillon de renfort	Reinforcement Battalion
BTG	Bataillon de tirailleurs du Gabon	Gabonese Rifle Battalion
CA	Corps d'armée	Army Corps
C.A.1	Compagnie d'accompagnement n°1	
CCR	Compagnie de circulation routière et compagnie de commandement	Traffic Circulation Company and Command Company
CDC	Compagnie de découverte et de combat	Long Range Reconnaissance and Combat Company
CFA	Corps Franc d'Afrique	African Free Corps
CHETOM	Centre d'histoire et d'études des troupes d'Outre-Mer	
CHR	Compagnie hors rang	Headquarters Company
CMIDOM	Centre Militaire d'Information Documentation Outre-Mer	Overseas Military Information and Documentation Centre
CP	PC in French, Post de Commandement	Command Post
DB	Division blindée	Armoured Division
DC	Découverte et combat, abréviation de CDC	Long Range Reconnaissance and Combat
DFL	Division de la France Libre	Free French Division
DI	Division d'infanterie	Infantry Division
DIA	Division d'infanterie Algérienne	Algerian Infantry Division
DMI	Division de marche d'infanterie	Infantry Marching Division (Provisional Division Task Force)
ECPAD	Établissement de Communication et de Production Audiovisuelle de la Défense	Defence Communication and Audiovisual Centre
ER	Emetteur récepteur	Receiver-Transmitter
ESS	État signalétique des service	Personnel Evaluation

FFI	Forces françaises de l'Intérieur nées de la fusion en 1944 des principaux groupes de résistance intérieure française	French Forces of the Interior (created in 1944 by merging the main French resistance groups)
FFL	Forces Françaises Libres	Free French Forces
FFO	Forces Françaises de l'Ouest	French Forces of the West
FTA	Forces terrestres antiaérienne	Army Anti-Aircraft Forces
FTP	Francs-tireurs et partisans: mouvement de résistance intérieure fondé en 1942 par le parti communiste français	Free shooters and partisans; communist resistance movement founded in 1942
GB2	Groupement blindé n° 2	Armoured Group 2
GCFTA	Groupement colonial des forces terrestres antiaériennes	Colonial Anti-Aircraft Group
GER	Groupement d'évacuation et de réparation	[Vehicle] Recovery and Maintenance Group
GI	Soldat américain	American Soldier (Government Issue)
GNB	Groupe nomade du Borkou	Nomadic Group of Borkou
GNE	Groupe Nomade de l'Ennedi	Nomadic Group of Ennedi
GNT	Groupe nomade du Tibesti	Nomadic Group of Tibesti
GSC	Groupe sanitaire de colonne	Column Medical Group
GT	Groupement tactique	Tactical Group
GTD	Groupement tactique Dio	Tactical Group Dio
GTL	Groupement tactique Langlade	Tactical Group Langlade
GTR	Groupement tactique Rémy	Tactical Group Rémy
GTV	Groupement tactique Warabiot	Tactical Group Warabiot
JEUCAFRA	Jeunesse camerounaise française	French Cameroonian Youth
JMO	Journal de marche et des opérations	Operations Journal
JORF	Journal Officiel de la République Française	Official Journal of the French Republic
LRDG	Long range desert group	
OKW	Haut commandement de la Wehrmacht	German Armed Forces High Command
OSA	Officier supérieur adjoint	Deputy Commander / Executive Officer
PAK	Anti-aérien (en allemand)	Anti-Aircraft (in German)
QG	Quartier général	Headquarters
RAC	Régiment d'artillerie coloniale	Colonial Artillery Regiment
RADB	Régiment d'artillerie de division blindée	Artillery Regiment of the Armoured Division
RANA	Régiment d'artillerie Nord-africaine	North African Artillery Regiment
RBFM	Régiment blindé de Fusiliers Marins	Armoured Naval Infantry Regiment
RCA	République Centre-Africaine ou Régiment de Chasseurs d'Afrique (le 12e RCA pour la 2e DB)	Central African Republic, or Regiment of Chasseurs of Africa (Cavalry Regiment)
RC	Régiment de cuirassiers (le 12e RC pour la 2e DB)	Cuirassier Regiment
RCC	Régiment de chars de combat	Tank Regiment

RMSM	Régiment de marche de Spahis Marocains	Moroccan Spahi Regiment
RMT	Régiment de marche du Tchad	Marching Regiment of Chad
RTC	Régiment de tirailleurs du Cameroun	Regiment of Riflemen of Cameroon
RTST	Régiment de tirailleurs sénégalais du Tchad	Regiment of Senegalese Riflemen of Chad
SDN	Société des Nations	League of Nations
TD	Tank destroyer	Tank Destroyer
TO	Transmission order signifie un message militaire	Transmission Order

Table of Comparative Ranks

French Army	French Navy	British Army	US Army
Soldat de 2ᵉ Classe[1]	Matelot	Private	Private
Soldat de 1ᵉʳ Classe	Quartier-Maître de 2ᵉ Classe	Lance Corporal	Private First Class
Caporal, Brigadier	Quartier-Maître de 1ʳᵉ Classe	Corporal	Corporal
Caporal Chef, Brigadier Chef	Second-Maître	Sergeant	Sergeant
Sergent, Maréchal des Logis	Maître	Sergeant	Staff Sergeant
Sergent Chef, Maréchal des Logis-Chef		Colour Sergeant	Sergeant First Class
Adjudant	Premier Maître	Warrant Officer Class 2	Master Sergeant
Adjudant Chef	Maître Principal	Warrant Officer Class 1	Sergeant Major
Major	Major		
Aspirant	Aspirant	Cadet	Cadet, Officer Candidate
Sous Lieutenant	Enseigne de Vaisseau de 2ᵉ Classe	Second Lieutenant	Second Lieutenant
Lieutenant	Enseigne de Vaisseau de 1ʳᵉ Classe	Lieutenant	First Lieutenant
Capitaine	Lieutenant de Vaisseau	Captain	Captain
Commandant, Chef de Bataillon, Chef d'Escadron, Chef d'Escadrons[2]	Capitaine de Corvette	Major	Major
Lieutenant-Colonel	Capitaine de Frégate	Lieutenant Colonel (Navy: Commander)	Lieutenant Colonel (Navy: Commander)
Colonel	Capitaine de Vaisseau	Colonel	Colonel
Général de Brigade	Contre-Amiral	Brigadier	Brigadier General
Général de Division	Vice-Amiral	Major General	Major General
Général de Corps d'Armée	Vice-amiral d'Escadre	Lieutenant General	Lieutenant General
Général d'Armée	Amiral, Amiral de la Flotte[3]	General	General
Maréchal de France	Amiral de France	Field Marshal	General of the Army

1 Soldiers of the two lowest ranks are generally called Soldat, but their actual rank corresponds to their branch and function (Fantasin, Cuirassier, Chasseur, Sapeur, Artilleur, Légionnaire, Goumier, Tirailleur, Spahi).

2 In speaking, all officers of this rank are usually referred to as 'Commandant' regardless of the branch.

3 In 1939, François Darlan was promoted to Amiral de la Flotte, a unique rank created for him. Darlan wore the 5 stars of an Amiral, not the 7 stars of an Amiral de France.

Foreword

My first contact with *Général* Dio dates back to 1955 in Chad: he was the *général* in command of troops in the *Zone de Défense de l'AEF-Cameroun* (Cameroon Defence Zone of French Equatorial Africa). While he inspected my unit, the *Compagnie Saharienne du Moussoro*, he reminisced of his time in command of the *Groupe Nomade du Tibesti* as a *capitaine* in 1938–1940. Walking the terrain with him, I was able to envision in situ his epic African adventure alongside *Général* Leclerc in 1940–1943.

We met again in Paris in 1958, and then I served on his staff in Paris from 1961 to 1963, before becoming his neighbour in Toulon in 1969. He was a retired *général* and I was the commander of the *4ᵉ Régiment d'Infanterie de Marine* (*4ᵉ RIMa.*) The periods spent under his command and our common past as Free French soldiers – me in the *1ʳᵉ Division de la France Libre* – gave us much to talk about.

Graduating from the Military Academy at Saint-Cyr in 1928, Dio chose the *méharistes* (the Camel Corps) of the Colonial Troops. During several tours in Mauritania and French Sudan (present day Mali), he established himself as a true soldier of the Sahara.

Having learnt basic Arabic at Saint-Cyr, he quickly became familiar with different dialects. In an environment where nature and mission are so harsh, it is essential to immerse oneself: the commander, just like the *goumier*, must lead his camel,[1] eat *kessrah*, and sleep in a *faro*.[2]

Dio led several successful counterraids, demonstrating his courage and his leadership qualities and earning two citations. In 1938, as a young *capitaine*, he was given command of the *Groupe Nomade du Tibesti* (in Chad). In that position, he was responsible for all civil and military functions in his territory. In practice, because of the need for grazing areas, *Capitaine* Dio's jurisdiction extended into the northern part of Kanem, the rangeland of the Senusiyya nomads. Therefore, out of concern for the human environment, he worked to build relationships with local leaders. He became intimate with Bey Ahmed,[3] the spiritual leader (or *marabout*) of the Senusiyya, whose *zawiya*[4] and sanctuary are located in Gouro, an oasis on the south-eastern edge of the Tibesti Mountains.

Likewise, he won the confidence of the 'Alifa' of Mao, who was a descendant of the former head of the Kanembu Empire and was still recognised as the 'Commander of the Faithful' and the local leader of Kanem, from whom the Senusiyya received authorisation to use pastureland. The Alifa's

---

1   Contrary to what one might think when looking at photos of *méharistes* perched on their camels, they had to spend half the journey walking in front of their animal, 'pulling' it with a lead rope.

2   A *goumier* is an indigenous Moroccan soldier in the French Army of Africa. *Kessrah* is a semolina flat bread made by the Saharans to accompany their meals, which are cooked under the sand with the fire on top; a *faro* is a sleeping bag made of the skins of sheep or (better yet) jackals.

3   The tribe of this customary chief once 'reigned' over the Fezzan and southern Libya. After the severe repression carried out by the Italians in the 1930s, almost the entire tribe was taken in by Chad, which in 1933 allocated to it the Eguéï, an area rich in pastures north of Kanem, with a capital at Mao. This 700km zone extended from Lake Chad to the Langama cliff in the north. The Bey lived with his siblings between Gouro and Eguéï. It should be noted that Bey Ahmed had retained many supporters in Fezzan and southern Libya.

4   A *zawiya* is a building associated with Sufi Islam that serves as a mosque, school, mausoleum, or some other religious purpose. It could be seen as the 'home' of a religious order or group. (Translator's note)

trust in Dio became so strong that he even allowed Dio to validate and sign *qanuns*, judgements rendered under the customary Islamic sharia law.

At the end of his assignment in the summer of 1940, Dio found himself in Douala, Cameroon, in charge of a detachment of Senegalese tirailleurs.[5] They were intended to sail for metropolitan France as reinforcements, but they were still stuck in Cameroon when the armistice was signed. On the night of 26/27 August 1940, *Colonel* Leclerc arrived by canoe in Douala. During a subsequent meeting held at a logging company, Dio responded to Leclerc, saying: 'Understood, I'll go get my company.' In fact, along with some other officers, he had already developed a plan to take control of Douala. On 27 August at 8:00 a.m., *Colonel* Leclerc was installed as the governor in Douala. The next day, after sending part of Dio's unit to the capital city Yaoundé, Governor Brunot signed '*le ralliement du Cameroun*,' pledging the colony's support for de Gaulle.

Général de Gaulle arrived in Douala on 8 October with about 1,600 Free French who had departed from Liverpool with him on 30 August. *Capitaine* Dio was ordered to take a column from Cameroon into Gabon. The town of Mitzic rallied to de Gaulle on 29 October. Then, on 13 November, after the Foreign Legion and the Cameroon Battalion took Port-Gentil and Libreville, all of Gabon followed. Thus, in two successive territories, it was Dio who opened the path to rally to Free France. At the beginning of December 1940, *Capitaine* Dio accompanied *Colonel* Leclerc to Chad. The *Colonel* was finding himself in a situation with which he was completely unfamiliar. After the death of *Lieutenant Colonel* d'Ornano, Dio became Leclerc's closest adviser. But their early interactions were not smooth. Years later, Dio still spoke with his friend Dronne about the disagreements, and even tempestuous arguments, he had with Leclerc regarding the tactics to be adopted in the Sahara. Leclerc's attitude changed when Dio introduced him to Bey Ahmed. Leclerc immediately grasped the value of 'on the ground' intelligence, and he especially appreciated the importance of the letters of introduction to Ahmed's representatives throughout southern Libya, particularly at Kufra. From then on, there was complete trust between the hard-charging cavalryman and the experienced Saharan. It was Dio who prepared the attack on Kufra with 400 men and 65 vehicles. The tactics of the old desert raids, adapted for a motorised force, led to the surrender of the strongest Italian position in Libya on 1 March 1941.

This first victory for Free France and then the Oath of Kufra marked the beginning of Leclerc's epic, and of his acceptance by the English. Dio led the main element during the attack, and the circumstances of his serious injury, suffered during hand-to-hand combat in a tunnel leading to the fort, speaks volumes about his personal courage. After seven months in the hospital in Yaoundé, he returned wearing the stripes of a *commandant*.

Next, he prepared a series of harassing raids Leclerc ordered against the Italian posts on the Zouar-Sebha-Tripoli axis. '*Colonne Leclerc*' was a motorised *rezzou*, or raiding unit, made up of 1,000 men mounted on 200 vehicles. Dio commanded the heavy element in the engagements of February and March 1942. The success was complete, and after taking Tedjéré from the Italians, he returned with two holes shot through his kepi. Starting at the end of November 1942, the next stage aimed to establish a link with the British 8th Army near Tripoli. The combat force included 2,100 men and 300 vehicles. With the combat trains the total was 4,800 men and 700 vehicles divided into three groups, the largest of which was entrusted to Dio.

It was Dio who first reached Tripoli, where he welcomed *Général* Leclerc on 23 January 1943.

General Montgomery, commanding the 8th Army, considerably reinforced what became *Force L* and entrusted it with covering the southern wing of the attack towards Tunis. With the flying column of the *1re Division de la France Libre*, the strength of *Force L* exceeded 6,000 men.

---

5 A *tirailleur* (rifleman) was an indigenous West African infantryman. (Translator's note)

The combat formation was divided into two groups of more than 1,500 men each, placed under the command of *Lieutenant-Colonel* Dio and of *Commandant* Vézinet, respectively. Dio was in charge of establishing *Force L* at Ksar Ghilane on 23 February. *Force L* stopped German armoured attacks from 4 to 10 March, and Dio was slightly injured during the fighting. In an assessment of the fighting on the evening of the 10th, to which the Royal Air Force largely contributed, Montgomery replied 'well done.' The southern flank of the 8th Army was saved. This little-known episode was the turning point of the war in Tunisia, and Dio was the pivot. The fighting ended on 13 May 1943 with the surrender of Axis forces. While Free French forces had been isolated in Sabratha, Libya, Dio reorganised the *Régiment de Tirailleurs Sénégalais du Tchad* (*RTST*) into the *Régiment de Marche du Tchad* (*RMT*)[6] and became its first commander.

Force L eventually became the *2ᵉ Division Blindée* (2nd Armoured Division, or *2ᵉ DB*). After its inception in Morocco and establishment in England, *Colonel* Dio, while commanding the *RMT*, also received command of one of the three tactical groups comprising the *2ᵉ DB*, the *Groupement Tactique Dio* (*GTD*), which he kept until the end of the war. The *GTD* landed in Normandy on 1 August 1944, and then actively participated in the victorious operations of the French Campaign by liberating Alençon and then Paris on 25 August 1944. At the Kaiserspalast in Strasbourg, which was reached first by a unit of the *GTD* on 23 November 1944, *Général* Leclerc demonstrated quite spontaneously the special connection he felt for his companion from the start. As Dio entered, Leclerc stood up and opened his arms, exclaiming, 'So my old Dio, here we are in Strasbourg; now we can both croak.' The Oath of Kufra was fulfilled.

On 22 June 1945, *Général de Division* Leclerc handed over command of the prestigious *2ᵉ DB* to *Colonel* Dio, who was 37 years old. He soon became the youngest *général* in the French Army.

When the *2ᵉ DB* was dissolved on 31 March 1946, *Général* Dio took command of the territories of southern Tunisia until 1950. He was then assigned to Cambodia from 1950 to 1952 to command the Cambodian Land Forces. He also served as interim High Commissioner of the French Republic in Cambodia. After his tour in Cambodia and training courses for general officers, he experienced what he called 'the happiest period of his life' – command of the Armed Forces of *Zone de Défense de l'AEF-Cameroun* from 1955 to 1957. He received the third star of a *général de division* there and was satisfied when the minister ratified the transformation of the Saharan companies into *Escadrons Sahariens de Découverte et de Combat* (Saharan Long Range Reconnaissance and Combat Squadrons).

Dio was promoted to *général de corps d'armée* at the end of 1958. He wanted to retire so he could devote himself to the health of his wife, but *Général* de Gaulle refused his request. De Gaulle needed his old companion by his side in the troubled times ahead. His knowledge of Africa would make him a valuable adviser. During that period, the Overseas Office (*Bureau Outre-Mer*) was created, directly attached to the Minister of the Armed Forces. The *État-major des Forces Terrestres Stationnées Outre-Mer* (General Staff of the Overseas Land Forces) was also established and placed under Dio's command (*Journal Officiel de la République Française*, 11 April 1940). This was during the period of decolonisation, following the construction of indigenous African armies and retrocession of equipment. There was not an African head of state passing through Paris who did not pay a visit to Dio, who managed everything superbly. With his innovative management of the overseas budget, he had the *Véhicule de Combat Outre-Mer* (overseas combat vehicle) manufactured by Ateliers Legueu Meaux, which was presented and approved by Minister of Defence Pierre Messmer in 1962. It became the *Véhicule Léger de Reconnaissance et d'Appui* (Armoured Liaison,

---

6   A *unité de marche* is a provisional unit created from available units for a specific and temporary task (a task force, in English). It is formed by pulling men from other units to accomplish the specific task. (Translator's note)

Reconnaissance, and Support Vehicle) in use by many armies, including the French Army, today. He participated in a study at Dassault Aviation to develop a support and transport aircraft adapted to African combat that would be capable of remaining on target while firing a heavy gun from the side of the aircraft. The 'Spirale' flew successfully in 1963, but unfortunately funding did not follow. Dio was promoted to *général d'armée*, receiving his fifth rank star in 1965. *Général* Dio ended his career as Inspector General of the Army and retired to Toulon in 1969.

Living next door to the *4ᵉ RIMa*, which I was honoured to command, he took pleasure in participating in regimental meetings and meals. On frequent occasions, ministers or other senior civil or military authorities visited him.

Dio died in 1994. In his will, Dio requested a simple burial without full military honours. But since he did not have a family, his small circle of friends arranged a humble ceremony that included honours.

His intelligence, his foresight, his courage, his humility, his audacity, his concern for others, and his humour made Louis Dio a fascinating character, an exceptional soldier who participated actively in Africa and on metropolitan soil, at the side of *Maréchal* Leclerc de Hauteclocque, at the major stages of this epic which led to the liberation of France. I am particularly happy to make a contribution to the Fondation du Maréchal Leclerc de Hauteclocque in the memorial work it is undertaking concerning *Général* Louis Dio. *Général* Louis Dio, Grand-croix de la Légion d'honneur, Companion of the Liberation, holder of 14 citations, deserves to be better known and recognised in our national history.

Colonel Pierre Robédat, Veteran of the *1ʳᵉ Division de la France Libre (1ʳᵉ DFL)* (1924–2024),
Grand-croix de la Légion d'honneur,
Veteran of the *1ʳᵉ Division de la France Libre* (*1ʳᵉ DFL*),
Platoon Leader in the *4ᵉ Batallion de Marche* (BM4), 2ᵉ Brigade
President of the *Amicale de la 1ʳᵉ DFL* (2013–2018)

Preface

No American newspaper took notice of the Free French seizure of the obscure Libyan oasis of Koufra from the Italians in March 1941. Nor does the event appear in the memoirs of any of the major American politicians and military officers of the time. Even Robert Murphy, the senior American expert on France after the German conquest in 1940, failed to mention it. It is hard to blame them. Then, and even now, the intricacies and complexities of the internecine French political system struck Americans as impenetrable, and Libya was quite far from the imaginations of Americans during what was still a period of legal neutrality.

Koufra nevertheless mattered. There, the French commander, a supremely talented officer living under the *nom de guerre* of Philippe Leclerc, had his men pledge what has become known as the Koufra Oath: 'Swear not to lay down arms until our Colours, our beautiful Colours, fly over the cathedral of Strasbourg.' Leclerc was on his way to becoming one of the great heroes of Free France and a legend in the French Army.

The first officer to join him in his quest to liberate France from the Axis and its Vichy collaborators, *Capitaine* Louis Dio, was not present for the oath. He was recovering in a hospital from wounds sustained leading an attack at Koufra. Nevertheless, he had already become invaluable to Leclerc. Dio had served most of his career in the French Empire in Africa. The knowledge he had acquired there helped Leclerc and Dio to convince leaders in parts of the French Empire such as Chad, Cameroon, and Gabon to reject Vichy and join Charles de Gaulle's Free France. A Free French presence in Africa gave de Gaulle political legitimacy and a power base. Thereafter, African soldiers formed an important component of the Free French Army as it built itself into a credible fighting force. Although no one in 1941 could have predicted it, by 1944 it had become a powerful, if sometimes difficult, ally of the Americans and the British.

Dio remained at Leclerc's side as they built Free French forces from among French troops based in Africa, other Frenchmen who opposed Vichy and found their way to Leclerc, many of them having crossed through Spain, and even some Spanish Republicans. It was a diverse collection of religious beliefs, philosophies, political parties, representing 22 nationalities. Dio's unit, the *Régiment de Marche du Tchad*, became the infantry component of Leclerc's Second Armoured Division (*Deuxième Division Blindée* or *2ᵉ DB* in French military parlance) in August 1943. By then, of course, the Americans were in the war and slowly warming to de Gaulle's Free French movement. Meanwhile, plans for the invasion of Normandy continued to develop. By April 1944 the *2ᵉ DB* was under US command in Yorkshire, training for operations with the Allied armies and receiving supplies from America – the 'Arsenal of Democracy'.

Although Leclerc, Dio, and the *2ᵉ DB* might have become an integral part of Allied plans for Normandy, Allied leaders still did not fully trust de Gaulle. As a result, he did not play a role in the planning of OVERLORD nor did the Allies intend to use the *2ᵉ DB* in the first days, or even weeks, of the Normandy campaign. The only Free French troops to take part on 6 June 1944 were a small number of parachutists and marine commandos under British command. De Gaulle never forgave or forgot this slight to French honour. For years thereafter he refused to attend most of the ceremonies held in Normandy, preferring instead to go to Provence for commemorations of Operation DRAGOON, where his French forces had fought as complete units from the start.

American, British, and French strategic goals, moreover, differed from the start. De Gaulle, Leclerc, and Dio naturally wanted to free their homeland after four increasingly brutal years of occupation. The Allies, especially the British, wanted to move through France and reach the Scheldt Estuary and the River Rhine as quickly as possible. While the two goals were not necessarily incompatible, neither did they overlap perfectly. The British and Americans were perfectly willing to bypass major French cities and towns (including Paris) in order to pursue the Germans more quickly. Nor, given Vichy's repugnant collaboration, had the Americans yet decided whether they wanted to treat France as a liberated country, like Denmark and The Netherlands, or a conquered one like Italy. A full American occupation plan, called AMGOT, was ready for execution if they chose the latter. Some Allied planners hoped to keep the *2e DB* in England for three months after D-Day, or until the Americans, the British, and the Canadians had pushed the *Wehrmacht* back inside Germany itself.

Leclerc and Dio knew that they could not do much to change this painful situation. They also knew that they needed the Americans far more than the Americans needed them. Only the United States had the resources and the willingness to provide the tanks, uniforms, fuel, ammunition, sealift, spare parts, and even food that the rebuilding French armies needed. They therefore sat impatiently in England for almost two months until the Americans finally decided to send them to France in early August to join the American Third Army, then breaking out of Normandy following the Battle of Saint-Lô in mid-July. Once in France, the *2e DB*, with Dio in command of a *groupement tactique* (combat command), fought with great distinction. At the Battle of the Falaise Pocket which began on 12 August, the division decisively defeated the German *9. Panzerdivision*, killing 4,500 Germans and taking more than 8,000 prisoners of war for the loss of 133 killed, 648 wounded, and 85 missing.

Falaise had important consequences for the *2e DB* and its relationship with the Americans. The victory broke German resistance in France and opened the road to Paris, then approaching starvation conditions because the Germans had taken everything they could carry with them as they retreated. For Dio and Leclerc, the long-suffering capital and its brave citizens, then rising up to fight the occupiers, needed their immediate help. For de Gaulle, if the French Army did not come to the aid of the resistance inside Paris, the crisis in the city held out the terrifying possibility of a civil war or political turmoil, due to the communists' desire to seize power. Get to Paris as quickly as you can, he told Leclerc, with or without American permission.

Leclerc was surely willing to follow de Gaulle's orders, but he faced major problems of supply. The Falaise victory proved to the Americans that the *2e DB* could and would fight as hard and as well as any Allied unit in France. But it needed replacements for the 75 armoured vehicles and 750 other vehicles that it had lost, as well as the fuel to make them move. The Americans had precious little of either and even less desire to give what they did have to the French to start what might be a costly urban battle for what Omar Bradley dismissed as a 'prestige' objective. Until the last minute, the Americans still preferred to bypass Paris and hope that the city would fall into their hands once the Germans retreated.

Leclerc and Dio, for obvious reasons, could not accept such a strategy, no matter how desperate their supply problems. Courageous and daring Parisians were fighting the Germans and erecting barricades throughout their neighbourhoods. If the Germans turned on them with full fury, they might destroy Paris and kill Parisians by the thousands just as they had recently done in Warsaw. Leclerc, Dio, and the other officers of the *2e DB* thus began to hoard fuel and supplies in order to prepare for a mad dash into the city. They also began to disobey orders, moving their units closer and closer to the main routes into the capital. Leclerc even considered abandoning the Americans altogether and taking his orders directly from de Gaulle. The *2e DB*'s American corps commander, General Leonard Gerow, grew increasingly frustrated, calling Leclerc 'that miserable man.'

Events moved quickly inside Paris, leading the Americans to belatedly order the *2ᵉ DB* to the city on 24 August 1944. Colonel Dio and his *groupement tactique* had the honour of entering the city the next day through the Porte d'Orléans on its southern edge. Visitors to the site today will find there the Place du 25 Août, the Square du Serment de Koufra, and the Avenue du Général Leclerc. From the Porte d'Orléans, Dio's men drove north, liberating the Gare Montparnasse, Les Invalides, and government buildings on the Seine such as the foreign ministry on the Quai d'Orsay and the Chamber of Deputies in the Palais Bourbon. A second column liberated the Eiffel Tower.

Despite the fears of civil war, revolution, and mass bloodshed, the liberation of Paris happened with remarkably little violence. The American Fourth Infantry Division entered the eastern part of the city at the same time as the *2ᵉ DB*, with Leclerc's nemesis and commanding officer, Leonard Gerow, becoming the first American general to enter the liberated city. For a while, the tensions and mistrust of the previous few weeks evaporated thanks to the ecstasy of the liberation. The next day, Dio and his men greeted Charles de Gaulle at the Place de l'Étoile (now also called the Place Charles de Gaulle) to render military honours to their chief and join him in a triumphal parade down the Avenue des Champs Élysées. Their success, combined with de Gaulle's political acumen, meant that the Americans soon abandoned AMGOT and instead planned for the full restitution and independence of post-war France.

However, inspiring that Paris's liberation had been, the leaders of the *2ᵉ DB* did not see it as the end of their journey. Dio and his men still had an oath to fulfil. They continued to drive east, working more smoothly with the Americans on the operational level while tying themselves ever more closely on the political level to de Gaulle. Dio and his *groupement tactique* participated in the liberation of Strasbourg in November, achieving their goal as they watched the French flag fly over the single spire of the city's magnificent cathedral. 'Well, Dio,' Leclerc said, 'I guess we can kick the bucket now.' But there was work yet to be done. The *2ᵉ DB* had by now become legendary and drove deep into Bavaria, reaching Hitler's famed Eagle's Nest at the end of the war. American units, including the 101st Airborne Division's Easy Company (today made famous by the television series *Band of Brothers*), saw a French flag flying over the building when they arrived. That flag had been with the *2ᵉ DB* since its time in Cairo.

The *2ᵉ DB* moved into quarters near Munich soon after. Leclerc left Europe to assume command of French forces in East Asia for the anticipated final campaign against the Japanese. He personally selected Dio to succeed him as the division's commander. At just 37 years old, Louis Dio was now the youngest general officer in the French Army.

Bringing Louis Dio and the *2ᵉ DB* back into the story helps us understand the American experience in France at the end of the Second World War. We can better see the political and alliance contexts that shaped Allied operations and strategy in 1944 and 1945. The controversies over the liberation and de Gaulle's bitterness over French exclusion from the Normandy landings should also help Americans to see the tensions in Franco-American relations after the war with more empathy for the French side. We should therefore be grateful to Jean-Paul Michel and Monique Brouillet Seefried for giving us such a well-researched and well-written look at the complicated French experience of the war through one of its most fascinating and under-appreciated heroes, *Général* Louis Dio.

Michael S. Neiberg

Chapter 1

Cameroon,
1 April to 29 August 1940

At the end of March 1940, *Capitaine* Louis Dio was in command of the *Groupe Nomade du Tibesti* (*GNT*) in Zouar, Chad, part of French Equatorial Africa, when a memo arrived informing him that he was being reassigned to Fort Archambault.[1] The orders required him to relinquish his command on 1 April and then to proceed to Fort-Lamy where he would report to *Colonel* Marchand, commander of the *Régiment de Tirailleurs Sénégalais du Tchad* (*RTST*). Dio was circumspect, wondering why he was being assigned to Group 1 of Fort Archambault, since it was a training post for new recruits. He was also surprised to have to turn over his command just when it appeared that Tibesti would soon be the front line in the coming war against the Axis forces of Italy and Germany. Then again, he had arrived in Chad in April 1938 and colonial tours typically lasted only two years. He had also not requested an extension for an additional year as he had done in Araouane and Néma, during his last two assignments in French Sudan.[2] He simply agreed to be transferred during the summer just like many other colonial soldiers. He had been in the desert for the past nine years, and his body was worn out, so he had decided against requesting a third year. The life of a *méhariste*[3] is demanding, and lately his body had been sending him some unmistakable signals. Since the end of the Saharan winter, it had been harder to withstand the first heat. He had just succumbed to renal colic, and on his return from a reconnaissance mission in the Aouzou Strip,[4] he joked that he was going to be medically sent home 'for pissing stones.' But Dio loved his job too much to slow down or limit what gave the *Groupe Nomade* its distinct character – life in the field.

Dio sensed that this premature reassignment had to have something to do with the situation in mainland France. But why now, six months after the declaration of war on 3 September 1939? Besides, was it really a war? In Tibesti, no one understood what was happening. Germany and France had declared war on each other but sat motionless on either side of the Rhine as if neither really wanted to do anything. It took six weeks, at best, for newspapers to arrive in Zouar. Through official channels, brief communiqués came by telex or directly by telephone. But in the completely isolated posts like Zouar, radio operators also had an unofficial way of obtaining information – they could pick up international radio on low frequency transmissions. Although it was against regulations, it was possible to receive Radio Paris on short wave late in the evening outside of the regular broadcast times.[5]

---

1   Fonds Leclerc, *Memorandum n°359 of 16.03.40*, boîte 5a, dossier 3, chemise 1.
2   French Sudan is the present day Republic of Mali. (Translator's note)
3   A *méhariste* is a soldier of the colonial camel corps. (Translator's note)
4   Jacques Massu, 'Souvenirs du général Dio', *Caravane*, No. 384, 1994, p.3.
5   Charles Béné, *Carnets de Route d'un 'Rat du Désert', Alsacien de la France Libre, Première époque, 1940–1942* (Raon-l'Étape, Imprimerie Fetzer S.A., 1991) p.44.

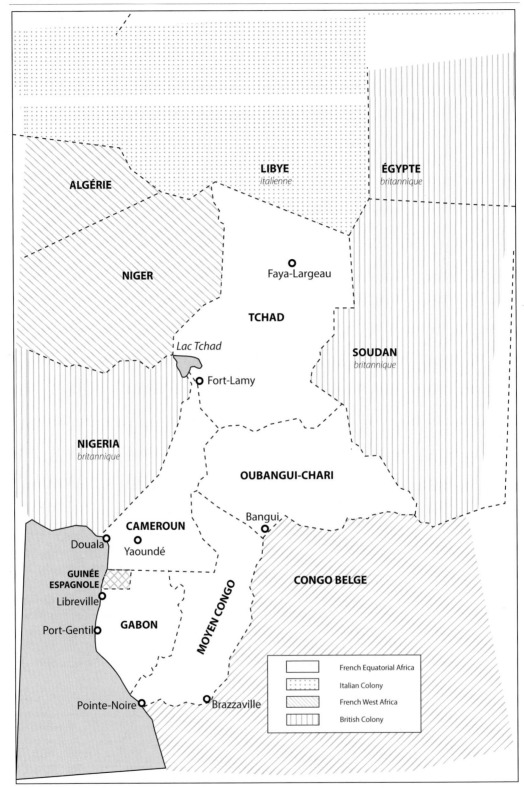

Map 1 French Equatorial Africa Prior to Joining Free France.

As soon as he learnt he would be leaving, Dio went to the oasis town of Bardaï one last time to greet the *Derdé*, the leader of the Toubou people, who had been elected the previous year. Dio liked this new traditional chief, named Oueddei Kichidemi.[6] In his immaculate *djellabah* and *cadmoul* (turban), he cut an impressive figure. A mutual respect led them to limit their words when they met. Men of the desert avoid small talk and communicate everything through their eyes. Dio was honoured with a *diffa* in the *Derdé's* house.[7] He took advantage of his visit to Bardaï to push further north and go as far as Aouzou to meet *Lieutenant* de Bazelaire, who was in charge of the post located on the northern edge of the Tibesti Massif. Aouzou is in a hollow dominated by a plateau that offers an excellent view to the north. The year before, Dio had a ladder built so troops could quickly reach the top of the plateau and avoid a long and difficult climb, which was especially challenging at night.[8] From the top of this plateau, the *choufs* (watchmen) took turns watching the border with the Italians just beyond Kayougué, a camp often occupied by nomads.

Dio had to leave his command on 1 April. The non-commissioned officers and *tirailleurs* could not understand why this beloved leader, this man they respected, was being taken away from them when war had just been declared. According to colonial tradition, Dio devoted several evenings to saying his farewells to his men. There was a small party with the indigenous *tirailleurs*, the great Saras from southern Chad, and the Hadjeraïs ('People of the Rocks' in the local dialect) from the Mongo region. The party ended with the beating of drums. In a quieter event, Dio's *goumiers*, mostly Toubous but including some Goranes and Kredas, wanted to hold one last *diffa* in honour of their leader.[9] Finally, the last evening was spent with the cadre of European troops of the *GNT* and *Capitaine* Jacques Massu's 6th Company. The two *RTST* units in Zouar were strongly united together, and bottles appeared out of nowhere to toast the health of their *capitaine*, a man respected by all.

Dio's official farewell took place the following day, Monday, 1 April 1940, during a very simple military ceremony organised in Zouar, where sections from the two units were drawn up in front of the flagpole. Dio reviewed his men one last time, returning their salute as they presented arms, and then he turned his command over to his first officer, *Lieutenant* Sarazac.[10] Everyone's voices joined in singing *La Marseillaise*, their eyes fixed on the French tricolour floating in the light morning breeze. Like the departing commander himself, the ceremony was a low-key, unassuming affair. Finally, the men all gathered together over refreshments at the end of the simple ceremony. Dio circulated among the groups that gathered around and he shook hands with each of his men. The *méhariste* departed his command with some reassurance and with complete confidence in *Lieutenant* Sarazac. Besides, he knew that *Capitaine* Massu would be there to help and advise him if necessary. As he left, Dio had no idea that fate would quickly lead him back to many of these men again.

With a team reduced to two *goumiers* and six camels, Dio left for Faya-Largeau, 500km from Zouar.[11] He had two personal camels, one of them saddled with a *ralha*, on which he would occa-

---

6   He was the father of Goukouni Oueddei, who would later be President of Chad between 1979 and 1982.
7   A *diffa* is a traditional meal, usually with couscous on the menu, eaten while seated cross-legged on mats on the floor.
8   The ladder built in 1939 on Dio's orders has been known ever since as 'Dio's Ladder.' It was still there as late as the 1960s.
9   The Saras are the largest ethnic group in Chad, representing almost one-third of the population. Hadjeraïs comprise around 7 percent of the Chadian population, while Goranes and Kedas are around 2 percent each. (Translator's note)
10   The first officer is the most senior officer after the commander, in this case *Lieutenant* Sarazac. He was promoted to *capitaine* in 1942 and participated with his *Groupe Nomade* in the Fezzan operations, being the only camel unit in *Colonne Leclerc* in 1943.
11   André Bendjebbar, 'Soldat de Légende', *Du Capitaine de Hauteclocque au Général Leclerc* (Paris: Éditions

sionally sit during the journey. The second was equipped with a *bassour* made of acacia wood and a mat placed on the hump that served as a large luggage rack to carry his kit, which contained his uniforms and some personal belongings, including some books. Like all colonial officers departing their garrison, Dio gave a lot of small items and personal effects to the locals who had served him. Each was honoured to receive a gift from their leader. Accompanying Dio on the journey was Ganaye, his faithful Toubou *goumier*. They had become attached to each other over the years and had developed an enduring mutual loyalty. The small group also included *Lieutenant* Florentin who had taken over from *Lieutenant* Dubut in Bardaï. Having completed his mission, he returned to Faya-Largeau. He walked beside Dio but avoided speaking, aware of Dio's melancholy. Dio felt like he was on his last camel trek. He had no idea what the war had in store for him. He did, however, know what to expect in the short term. The time had come for an officer of his rank and seniority to receive staff training, and he would have fewer opportunities in the future to serve with the line troops. He also figured that motorised vehicles were likely to quickly supplant the camel units. Considering all that, he wanted to be deliberate with his thoughts, and to enjoy one final journey through the desert to which he had devoted the first 12 years of his career.

The relatively flat route ran along the southern edge of Tibesti with no obstacles to slow them down or to hinder their navigation. The small caravan finally arrived on Friday, 12 April 1940, in the large palm groves of Faya-Largeau. Dio had covered the 500km from Zouar in 12 days, or 40km per day. He entered the European quarter with its tricolour flying atop a large mast over the central Place Blanche. The command post of Group 3[12] stood out from its surroundings. That part of the territory, located north of the 13th parallel, represented 40 percent of the area of the Chadian colony, and included the regions of Borkou, Ennedi, and Tibesti (BET). It was the only region of Chad under military administration because it was mainly inhabited by nomadic populations. As soon as he arrived, Dio reported to his commander, *Commandant* Jean Colonna d'Ornano, who enthusiastically welcomed him. Both *méharistes*, they respected and liked each other a great deal. During their conversation, Dio learnt that d'Ornano had also been summoned to Fort-Lamy. The two officers realised that they had been in the colony for two years and sensed that their hasty departure was most certainly linked to the situation in France. Over dinner that night, they speculated about what their near-term fate might be.

The garrison of Faya-Largeau was not going to let one of the leaders of Group 3 leave without organising a military ceremony in his honour. The commander of the *Groupe Nomade du Tibesti* was one of their leaders, so a parade of all the units present in Faya-Largeau was scheduled for early Monday morning, 15 April. *Tirailleurs* liked having these ceremonies at the beginning of the week because it was a good way to start the week. *Commandant* d'Ornano invited Dio to join him for the passing in review. Afterwards, he read an Order of the Day announcing the departure of the *commander* of the *GNT*. After summarising the first part of *Capitaine* Dio's career, the *commandant* then described his missions and activities since 1 December 1938, leading the *méharistes* of his camel unit, emphasising the success of his relations with the local populations. D'Ornano concluded with an expression of his gratitude for Dio's excellent work and wished him good luck in his new assignment at Fort Archambault. Following the ceremony, the 20 Europeans in the cadre at Faya-Largeau and a few local notables gathered for lunch. Before the end of the feast, Dio had the great pleasure of seeing Bey Ahmed, who had arrived directly from his stronghold at Gouro. Dio and the great chief of the Senusiyya had developed a strong bond during their time together.

Complexe, 2000), p.423.

12   Chad was divided militarily into four groups: Group 1 in the southern region of Fort Archambault, Group 2 in the eastern region with Abéché, Group 3 encompassing the entirety of the BET in the north, and Group 4 in the western region with Mao.

The Bey was touched to see this *toubab*[13] speaking in his language. The chief was particularly grateful to Dio for having brokered the agreement which allowed the Senusiyya to graze their camels in the rich pastures of the Eguéï region of Kanem.[14] The tribes of the area north of Lake Chad viewed the Senusiyya as invaders, and they repeatedly resisted their attempts to graze their camels, so Dio had to intervene on several occasions to deescalate the situation.

On 18 April, Dio left Faya-Largeau, taking advantage of a small convoy of Matford trucks headed to Fort-Lamy to complete the 1,000km journey. The trucks were ill-suited to the desert and were barely holding on, but it was the best that was available.[15] It took three days to complete the journey, which, as usual, was slowed down when the trucks passed through the Djourab Desert. It took more than a full day to cross the 110km of this Paleo-Chadian seabed, through the dreaded powdery sand of the Djourab, which the Chadian drivers call *fech-fech*. Vehicles routinely got stuck in it, requiring the soldiers to remove the side panels of the trucks and place them under the wheels to gain traction. In some cases, that was the only way the desert could be crossed, and sometimes that process had to be repeated over and over for several kilometres at a time. Despite the skill of the drivers, the convoy could only drag along at 500 metres per hour.

They reached the village of Koro-Toro at the end of the first day, finally across the Djourab. That night was restorative for the travellers, especially for the team of *tirailleurs* who had spent the day constantly getting the trucks unstuck. From Koro-Toro, the rest of the route to Fort-Lamy would move at a steady pace. The next day, they stopped for lunch in Salal, a village backed up against a small fort. At the end of the second evening, they stopped at Moussoro, which was a large military post with a mess for the officers. There were even rooms with the ultimate luxury – beds. A *méhariste* who is used to sleeping on his *tara* made with palm branches covered with animal skins or on the ground in his *faro* while patrolling the desert, needs several days to get used to the softness of a mattress. Dio, who had become accustomed to these transitions, chose, for the first few days, to lie down at the foot of the bed because sleeping on a mattress caused him excruciating back pain.

Capitaine Dio arrived at Fort-Lamy on 21 April 1940.[16] The capital of the French colony of Chad was a lively and noisy city, despite the still small number of vehicles there. The near constant street noise was unsettling to the camel soldier used to the silence of the desert. He was taken directly to the mess, which was in a building reserved for junior officers. Life at Fort-Lamy was governed by strict rules of hierarchy. Even the dining rooms were segregated by rank, which Dio found a little ridiculous after having just spent two years sleeping in the field with his non-commissioned officers and *tirailleurs*. Before going to bed that night, he remembered to take his dress uniform out of his baggage to give to the boys who would wash and iron it during the night.

Dio was summoned to the office of *Colonel* Marchand, commander of the *Régiment de Tirailleurs Sénégalais du Tchad* on Monday, 22 April. He reported at 10:00 a.m. to the executive officer (XO), who served as the military assistant and controlled access to the commander. Dio had been in that exact spot, following the same formal procedure, when he had arrived two years earlier. At the signal from the XO, he knocked on the *colonel*'s door. Dio entered the door wearing his kepi on his head. On his left was the regimental Colours in a display case. He snapped to attention and rendered an extended salute to the tricolour with its battle honours embroidered on the silk. Then,

---

13   *Toubab* means white man in the local language and originates from the word *toubib*, or doctor, since only whites served as doctors during the colonial period.
14   In 1931, France signed an agreement with the Senusiyya who had been driven out of Libya by the Italians, under the terms of which they handed over their arms to the French administration and, in exchange, received grazing areas to feed their camels.
15   François Ingold, *L'Epopée Leclerc au Sahara, 1940–1943* (Paris: Éditions Berger-Levrault, 1948), p.239.
16   Fort-Lamy was renamed N'Djamena in 1973. (Translator's note)

with a quarter turn to the right, he saluted *Colonel* Marchand, seated behind his desk. He removed his kepi and reported: '*Capitaine* Dio at your orders, *mon colonel.*'

The regimental commander stared at him and replied: 'Hello Dio, relax…. You look tired. And I think you've lost some weight since our last meeting in Zouar.' That meeting was more than six months earlier.

'Yes, *mon colonel*, but it's nothing serious as far as I am concerned, I'm sure it's just a result of the first days of the heat.' The *colonel* then launched into a long monologue explaining to Dio that the *RTST* had to provide several detachments to reinforce metropolitan France. Then he told Dio he would command Reinforcement Detachment Number 3, consisting of a reinforced company of *tirailleurs* which was then part of the 2nd Battalion at Fort Archambault. Due to the crisis in France, *Général* Paul-Louis Husson, commander of French Equatorial Africa (*AEF*), wanted the detachments to depart immediately. However, Marchand managed to delay the departure until the beginning of June, when they would board their ships in Douala. The colonel told Dio not to waste any time at Fort-Lamy and to be on the road to Fort Archambault by the weekend. After issuing his instructions, the *colonel* asked, "What are your questions, *capitaine*?"

Dio immediately responded, "Everything is clear, *mon colonel.*" Marchand then emphasised the importance of the mission – Dio would represent the *RTST* in defending the homeland. Marchand ended the meeting with an exhortation for Dio, telling him that he had full confidence in him, and wishing him good luck. Marchand then dismissed the *capitaine* with a wave of his hand. And with a quick salute, Dio was gone.

Dio had less than four days to prepare for his departure. Faya-Largeau's doctor had scheduled a check-up for him at the hospital at Fort-Lamy. In particular, the doctor had to check his kidneys, which had been giving him problems. His gums were also inflamed, and his teeth hurt with every bite. So, he would need to visit the dentist, as well. He also needed to go to the personnel office for his movement orders, to the treasurer so he could have his pay transferred, and to the adjutant general to update his files. He also had some shopping to do. And some friends assigned to the regimental headquarters asked him to save an evening for them to host a soirée for him. He agreed, even though he found such events rather boring. Although he did not care much for social events, Dio also knew he had to re-socialise and resume the rhythm of a 'normal' life, psychologically, but also physically. Specifically, it was his feet that he had to get back to normal. Stuffing them back into shoes again caused Dio a lot of pain despite his daily routine of brushing his feet with formaldehyde to prevent blisters and injuries.[17]

The next three days passed quickly. It was the first time in a long time that he only had himself to take care of. On Friday, 26 April, Dio departed alone with the small weekly convoy to Fort Archambault. It took more than two days of travel, with occasional difficulty, to complete the next 600km leg of his journey. The two overnight stops were spent in *cases de passage* (traveller's huts). Particular to the Chadian desert at that time, the *cases de passage* were a bit like small mountain shelters that offered travellers the barest essential conditions for spending the night in areas where there were no other options. The huts varied according to circumstances and were generally found in small villages on the route between Fort-Lamy and Fort Archambault. They offered few amenities, but some had a small cooking area and several rooms for sleeping.

Upon arrival at the stopping point, Ganaye would start to prepare dinner with meal packets provided by the quartermaster. Dio filled his pipe and watched the day quickly fade. Once darkness fell, he would wash at the well or the river. Then, *Capitaine* Dio and Ganaye would sit cross-legged together and eat, speaking to each other in the Toubou dialect. The Chadian was aware that he would not be able to follow his leader to France; nevertheless, Ganaye tried to convince

---

17   *Méharistes* generally wore sandals on the hard desert soils and often simply went barefoot in the sand.

him of the advantages of taking him along, anyway. Dio was moved by the gesture of loyalty. After drinking some chai, Ganaye would set up the two *faro* in which they would sleep in a corner of the room. Despite the stifling heat and humidity, Dio could still believe himself to be in Zouar when he lay down for the night.

Arriving at Fort Archambault on the afternoon of Sunday, 28 April, Dio went directly to the garrison mess where a room had been reserved for him. The garrison of Fort Archambault was, at the time, the most populous place in French Equatorial Africa. There were two battalions at the Fort, plus around 1,000 military workers, totalling about 4,000 men, including 50 officers and 150 non-commissioned officers. The large base had two essential missions: the construction of roads and railways, and most important, training the indigenous Chadian troops. It was the recruiting centre for the *tirailleurs* of the *RTST*, who came mainly from the two major ethnic groups surrounding the base. The majority were from the Sara ethnic group which was divided geographically into two enclaves. The first was located around Massénya, south of Fort-Lamy, and the other bordered the southern limits of the territory, near Moundou. The second ethnic group from which recruitment took place was the Hadjeraï. They were located around Mongo (400km north of Fort Archambault) in the rocky area[18] in the centre of the southern part of the territory. Recruitment did not present a challenge in those regions, as many young men volunteered, and donning the uniform of a *tirailleur* was well-regarded among the local people. The soldier's pay, and the prospect of regular meals, were also strong incentives to enlist.

On the morning of Monday 29th, Dio reported to the garrison commander, *Commandant* Callaud, who was in charge of managing the military life of Fort Archambault. Very soberly, Callaud told Dio that his arrival had been expected, and that the commander of the 2nd Training Battalion was waiting for him to take command of the 8th Company, which would form the backbone of Reinforcement Detachment No.3, destined for metropolitan France. *Capitaine* Dio was taken to the commander of the 2nd Battalion, a *capitaine* senior to him. He put his young comrade at ease with a warm welcome, and he immediately told Dio that the battalion would do whatever he needed to make his job easier. The mission awaiting them in France would require a well-trained and seasoned company. Callaud suggested that he meet his future deputy, *Lieutenant* Maziéras,[19] during lunch. Dio quickly linked up with his unit because he knew he would have little time to build it into an effective force. He immediately realised there was a shortage of leadership. To fight in France, he needed more European officers and NCOs. The same was true for the lower ranks of indigenous troops in the platoons of *tirailleurs*. Most of the men did not speak or read French, so the junior officers had to relay orders in the local dialect. Dio's reputation was helpful on both counts. His record as a seasoned *méhariste* with two citations for bravery sparked the imaginations of his young leaders, especially the NCOs. Their mission of going to France to 'crush the Boche' was also attractive to volunteers. Oftentimes, in the evening, small groups of NCOs from other units waited for Dio so they could tell him they wanted to join the 8th Company. Dio took their names and diplomatically requested from their leaders that they be assigned to reinforce his detachment. Dio also successfully convinced the battalion to reinforce him with more French-speaking Chadian soldiers.

---

18   '*Hadjer*' means rock in the Chadian dialect.
19   Alphée Maziéras was a Saint-Cyrien of the Class of 1933–1935 (named for Belgian King Albert I), he was assigned to Northern Cameroon in 1939. Maziéras followed Dio to Gabon and then to Chad for the campaigns of Fezzan where he was twice cited in combat. He was an impulsive and generous southerner, passionate about rugby and Basque pelota. Seriously injured in a motorcycle accident in Faya-Largeau, he could not join Dio and the *RMT* until the autumn of 1944. After only a month in command of the 11th Company of the 3rd Battalion of the *RMT*, he was killed by German artillery on 18 November 1944, in Badonviller, France, at the Bréménil quarries, along with his superior, *Lieutenant-Colonel* de La Horie.

On Friday, 10 May, Germany suddenly invaded The Netherlands, Belgium, and Luxembourg. Everyone at Fort Archambault recognised that the nature of the conflict had changed, and all the European soldiers expressed their solidarity for Dio and his mission. After the waiting game of the 'phoney war,' it was clear the 8th Company was going to be engaged in combat. Leaders from other units let it be known that they would allow volunteers to join *Capitaine* Dio's unit. As a result, the 8th Company was very quickly completed to a much higher level than the other units of the *RTST*. The prospect of returning to fight in France appealed to most of the young leaders. Dio's good reputation was also important. Having noted that 70 percent of the *tirailleurs* were young recruits who had not yet finished their training, particularly shooting and manoeuvring, Dio had the priority for usage of the garrison's firing ranges and the supply of additional ammunition. He wanted to focus on marksmanship. Unlike the *goumiers*, who had hunted since childhood, the *tirailleurs* lacked a natural aptitude with the rifle. He ordered the best riflemen to also be trained on machine guns because Dio knew that machine gun crews had to be quickly replaced in the heat of battle. The firepower of his crew-served weapons was a priority in combat, and complementarity and versatility were crucial assets. The last 15 days were intense in terms of training activities. Dio asked a lot of his officers and NCOs, constantly telling them: 'tough training, easy war'. He took advantage of these moments of intense training to get to know his officers and *tirailleurs* better, both professionally and personally, learning each person's strengths and weaknesses. In return, his men came to understand him as their leader, getting to know his command style as well as his personality. Dio knew how to be demanding, yet familiar at the same time. At the end of the day, when he was satisfied, he took his subordinate commanders to the bar for drinks. Everyone could then decompress and forget all the shouts of correction they had received on the training ground.

While this training was taking place, in May 1940 the fighting in France was at its height. After working hard every day, in the evening the soldiers would turn to the news. Various, often contradictory, reports came over the radio. The radio operators in the garrison tried to pick up Radio Paris directly, but it was becoming less and less audible. However, the German radio broadcast over Radio Seesen, came through, and with alarming news. The Alsatians among Dio's men translated the press releases of the *Wehrmacht*, which announced, 'that a new weapon had been used: the *Fallschirmjäger*, entire battalions of paratroopers.'[20] There were also bombardments of cities in eastern France. On 14 May, the French front broke at Sedan. The Maginot Line was useless.[21] On 17 May, German radio announced that the Allied armies, including the British, were being chased out of Belgium by panzers and Stukas. Clearly things were going terribly wrong, and Dio's European cadre was growing increasingly concerned, and they worried about their families in France. Would they even make it to metropolitan France before the end of the fighting? Would they finally embark just as Rommel's tanks reached Abbeville, encircling the Anglo-Franco-Belgian Army of the North? The Chadian *tirailleurs* had different thoughts. They knew the war was waiting for them, but they had a lot of confidence in the French Army. The prospect of going to see 'the white man's country,' which they had only seen in calendars and books, excited them – and their family were very proud of them.

On Thursday, 23 May, Reinforcement Detachment No.3 was ready. A convoy of 10 trucks departed Fort Archambault towards Bangui, capital of Ubangi-Shari, located nearly 500km due south. The roads were passable because the rainy season (mid-July to mid-November) had not yet broken through the tricky passes. Still, a lot of time was lost in river crossings because ferries

---

20   Béné, *Carnets, Première époque*, p.51.
21   The Maginot Line, built between 1929 and World War II, was a series of fortifications along the borders between Belgium, Luxembourg, Germany, Switzerland, and Italy. It bears the name of André Maginot, Minister of War, who had voted the funds to build it.

could generally only carry one truck at a time. The whole convoy had to wait until the tenth truck was ferried across before it could continue on. The first stop was Batangafou, and the next was a military post just before Damard. The convoy finally arrived on Saturday, 25 May in Bangui. European-style buildings were rare in the capital of Ubangi-Shari. Informed of the arrival of the column, the territorial headquarters worked to prepare acceptable accommodations for the detachment. The heat grew stifling, and the mosquitoes ruthlessly attacked the men, whose bodies were aching from hours of bouncing around on metal benches in the back of the trucks. The latest news from France was not comforting. Operation DYNAMO, the evacuation of the encircled troops from Dunkirk to the UK, began on 26 May. If the French and British forces withdrew from Belgium, would the rest of the French Army be able to restore the situation? It had worked in 1914, with the counterattack on the Marne. Was there another *Général* Joffre in the ranks of the French high command who could stop the Germans?

Reinforcement Detachment No.3 left Bangui on 28 May and headed due east towards Bouar. Bad roads and the need to cross a lot of streams by ferry slowed progress. After passing through the small French garrison at Bouar and then Baboua, the trucks arrived in Cameroon. Next, the large village of Abong-Mbang served as a staging point. The final part of the journey was faster, Cameroon being the most developed part of French Equatorial Africa and endowed with a regularly maintained road network. At the end of the day on 30 May, the convoy entered Yaoundé, the administrative capital of Cameroon. The local military command went out of the way to accommodate the detachment as best as possible. They put them up at Camp Batchinga, which offered accommodations the *tirailleurs* had never known. The leaders gave strict instructions so that the use of bathrooms and the canteen were respected. The Saras were astonished, and morale among the Europeans rose. Even the news from France took a turn for the better. Radio Paris reported that the Allies had recaptured Narvik, in Norway, from the Germans on 28 May.

In Yaoundé, the detachment received its final reinforcements. Soldiers with special skills such as mechanics, radio operators, medical personnel, and administrative staff were typically located at the regimental level. But, to operate autonomously, an isolated infantry company would need those specialists. Finally, the doctor, *Capitaine* Jacques Chauderon,[22] reported to Dio as the detachment physician, along with a supporting medical orderly. Dio was surprised to learn that Dr Chauderon's wife would also accompany them on the trip. The detachment had to reach the port of Douala to embark on the liner *Brazza*, which had been requisitioned when war was declared and had been transformed into a troop transport. Dio was familiar with the vessel, having made the Bordeaux to Pointe-Noire trip on it when he was assigned to Chad in 1938.

They would make the journey between Yaoundé and Douala by train, which was something completely new for the *tirailleurs*. Before they boarded at Yaoundé central station on 1 June 1940, the commander of troops in Cameroon, *Lieutenant Colonel* Bureau, presided over a departure ceremony. The population was invited to show their gratitude to the soldiers going off to fight the 'Boche.' Governor Brunot and other key individuals from the city were there. Women danced and sang to music provided by the police band and the traditional bands with their drums. The crowd cheered the departing soldiers, who swelled with pride before the train finally departed Yaoundé for Douala. Throughout the journey, small armed detachments saluted the men as the train passed through. At the stations of Eséka and Edéa, 'the population thronged to the platforms and the guard rendered honours.'[23] In Douala, however, the welcome planned by the commander-in-chief,

---

22   Dr Chauderon wrote a twelve-page article which is currently in the archives of overseas forces, Centre d'Histoire et d'Études des Troupes d'Outre-Mer (CHETOM) in Fréjus. This is currently the only archival information on Reinforcement Detachment No.3. Boîte 18H296, dossier 2.

23   Jacques Chauderon, p.1, CHETOM, 18H296.

Capitaine Pradier, was spoiled by heavy rain, a herald of the coming equatorial rainy season. Finally, trucks carried the detachment to Camp Bassa on the outskirts of the city. After the hot sand of Tibesti, Dio had to get used to the ubiquitous mud. He lodged with his men, sharing a room with *Lieutenant* Maziéras, while the doctor roomed – with his wife – in a hospital ominously called 'Ambulance Européenne.'

Dio was unfamiliar with the Cameroonian terrain he had just crossed, but he would quickly learn its key features. At the time, Cameroon, under French mandate, had an area of 431,320km2 and a population of '2,500,000 inhabitants, including 2,500 Europeans, among whom were fewer than 2,000 French.'[24] That was larger than the combined population of the three colonies of French Equatorial Africa: Chad, Middle Congo (present day Republic of the Congo) and Ubangi-Shari (present day Central African Republic). Cameroon was experiencing a budget surplus stemming from its export of agricultural products (cocoa, coffee, peanuts, oil, rubber, wood, et cetera) and minerals (tin, gold, rutile, et cetera). Cameroon, which had been a German colony prior to the First World War had been a source of conflict between France and Germany. Some German planters still lived there, and Hitler had demanded the return of the former German colony to the Greater Reich, a move some indigenous Cameroonians favoured. Additionally,

> Cameroon was a strategically important concern. Due to its geographical position, it was the linchpin of Atlantic Africa, and it was also the doorway to the heart of Central Africa through the vast port of Douala on the Wouri Estuary and the two railways that continued inland.[25]

That was the reason Douala was Cameroon's economic capital. Approximately 600 Frenchmen lived in Douala in 1939; they held all the political power, and much of the economic power as well. The country was efficiently administered, 'divided into 17 regions and 46 subdivisions.'[26] The administration was run by about 200 civil servants, including 80 colonial administrators and assistant administrators. The primary services were political affairs, economic affairs, customs, public railways, ports and harbours, water and forests, post offices, public education, agriculture, and sleeping sickness. Apart from the civil and military officials, private society was heterogeneous but powerful. It gathered at the Douala Chamber of Commerce. Most of the activities conducted were dependent upon the busy port. There was also a fairly large community of about 350 missionaries, mostly Catholic, but also some Protestants.

Cameroon was under a League of Nations mandate; therefore, France was not allowed to raise military forces from among the population. Hence, the locally recruited troops, which were supervised by French soldiers, were called police forces. The highest-ranking police officer in Cameroon was not actually a police commissioner. He was *Lieutenant Colonel* Bureau, an 'intelligent and cultured, elegant and affable man'[27] from the colonial era who served all over Africa and the Far East. There were two types of units in Cameroon in June 1940. The native guard comprised 1,060 men, dispersed in small detachments across the 46 subdivisions. That dispersion deprived it of any operational value. Additionally, there was a militia battalion of 624 men supervised by 18 French officers and 48 non-commissioned officers, the same ratio found in the *tirailleur* battalions of Equatorial Africa.[28] It was the militia that was responsible for maintaining order

---

24   André Martel, 'L'A.F.L. support de guerre Français et Allié', *Le Général Leclerc et l'Afrique Française Libre, 1940–1942*, Actes du Colloque International (Paris: Fondation Maréchal Leclerc de Hauteclocque, 1987), p.93.

25   Jacques Michel, 'Leclerc et l'Afrique Noire', *Du Capitaine de Hauteclocque au Général Leclerc* (Paris: Éditions Complexe 2000), p.256.

26   Michel, 'Leclerc et l'Afrique Noire', p.259.

27   Raymond Dronne, *Le Serment de Koufra* (Paris: Éditions du Temps, 1964), p.33.

28   Michel, 'Leclerc et l'Afrique Noire', p.264.

and for defending the territory. One company of the militia was assigned to the city of Douala. The navy maintained two ships in Cameroon: the submarine *Sidi-Ferruch* and a coastal surveillance ship. In addition, to protect the port and its approaches, a colonial coastal artillery battery was set up at Manoka, a large island controlling the entrances to the Wouri Estuary. Finally, the health service was spread across all regions of Cameroon, with experts in tropical medicine who had been trained at Pharo, the remarkable school of military medicine located near Marseille.[29] The head of Cameroon's health service was *Médecin-Colonel* Vaucel. Cameroon's health service, like those in the Middle Congo and Chad, would come to play an important role in rallying the territory to *Général* de Gaulle.

The men who had come from Chad found Douala a lively and pleasant city with a lot of shops that offered a wide choice of products. And the people were welcoming. As in all ports, there was a cosmopolitan atmosphere, with foreigners, soldiers, and civilians intermingling. Douala's nightlife was a favourite. The climate was the only downside for the soldiers of the reinforcement detachment. *Général* Edgard de Larminat, future commander of the *1re Division Française Libre* (1st Free French Division) during the war, later wrote 'the climate in Douala is very debilitating. It is one of the most unpleasant I have ever known: heavy, interminable rains, humidity, heat.'[30] In June, the temperature became more and more oppressive, announcing the rainy season.

At the beginning of June 1940, everyone was focused on the situation in Europe. The news from metropolitan France was once again very worrying, and a great despair seized the Europeans. How was it possible that things had turned so bad in such a short time? The largest French cities were under bombardment – Marseille, Lyon, and Paris. What would happen with Reinforcement Detachment No.3? The evacuation of Dunkirk ended on 3 June. On 6 June, with the collapse of the 'Weygand Line' on the Somme, the defeat of the French Army seemed inevitable. And then *Capitaine Dio* received more bad news, learning by telex from Brazzaville that the *Brazza* had been torpedoed by a German submarine off the Moroccan coast on 27 May.[31] There were no other ships available to take his troops to France.[32] He also learnt that another reinforcement detachment under the orders of *Commandant* Colonna d'Ornano was also stuck in Pointe-Noire for the same reason. He was told to stay put, 'length of the delay unknown.'

Dio decided to continue training the detachment. Since their arrival in Douala, activity had dropped considerably, so he ordered his section leaders to step up the pace. He asked *Capitaine* Pradier, the garrison commander, for time slots on the rifle range. Travel to and from the distant range was done by foot in order to harden the men. Dio knew that idleness was the greatest danger to the morale of the troops. He could tell that the civilian leaders were very concerned about the events in France. Moreover, they seemed to have better information than he was receiving through military channels. Dio and his team met regularly during the evenings at the fashionable

---

29 Created in 1905, this school of the colonial troops health service played an essential role in the health policy of the colonised territories. Taking advantage of the field experience of its colonial doctors, it joined a research laboratory which has become a world standard. Advances in the treatment of malaria and of bacterial meningitis, treatment of epidemics, therapies against plague, cholera, leprosy, and sleeping sickness were developed at Pharo. In 2013, the government decided to close it. The African Continent owes much to this school in terms of health.

30 Edgard de Larminat, *Chroniques Irrévérencieuses* (Paris: Éditions Plon, 1962), p.136.

31 *L'Eveil du Cameroun* of 27 September 1940 relates: 'The *Brazza* of the Chargeurs Réunis [shipping company] was torpedoed by the Germans 80 [nautical] miles north of Vigo. The torpedo exploded in one of the oil tanks. The ship blazed like a torch and sank in 4 minutes. 535 lost and 105 saved. Of these, several died of their wounds, or rather of their burns, on the French warship which picked them up 5 hours later. The *Brazza* was travelling alone and was torpedoed without warning. The news was kept secret for a long time...'

32 Jérôme Ollandet, *Brazzaville, Capitale de la France Libre, Histoire de la Résistance Française en Afrique 1940–1944* (Paris: L'Harmattan, 2013), p.40.

European hot spot, the Lido Bar, to listen to the gossip of the day. His doctor introduced him to another *médecin capitaine* by the name of Laquintinie, who was quite active in a civilian network that was working to continue the fight against the Germans. The network was also strengthening the relationship with British civil administrators, who were in Douala because Britain held the western part of Cameroon under the League of Nations mandate. Laquintinie informed his companions about the events taking place not only in Europe but also in the local territory.

On 10 June, the French government withdrew to Bordeaux; that same day, Italy declared war on France. When he heard that, Dio immediately thought of Tibesti and of his *méharistes* at their post on the Libyan border. He was sickened by the Italian decision for war. The neighbouring country had been on the French side during the second part of the First World War. Now, he knew that the posts he had established on the borders of Chad would soon fulfil their true purpose. Then Dio was further saddened to learn of the German entry into Paris on 14 June. It was beyond comprehension to him and to his officers how quickly it had all happened. Massu wrote, 'the retreat of the army and the collapse of France is incomprehensible, almost disgraceful.'[33] How could such a debacle have happened? They simply did not want to believe it. They were frustrated, feeling guilty for being in Africa where nothing was happening. Like Massu, who remained in Tibesti, Dio was 'surprised to see his *tirailleurs* also preoccupied with the news, following the echo of the events shaking the white world.'[34] Even if the homeland was under the Nazi boot, capitulation was inconceivable. The French colonial empire was immense and must, in his opinion, continue the fight.

Among the local civilian population, opinion was more mixed. At least half advocated for continuing the war so, on 12 June, in the village hall of Akwa, Governor Brunot affirmed his desire to continue the fight alongside the British, '…Cameroon asks Great Britain, in its capacity as a member of the League of Nations, for needed assistance…'[35] But, along with the German or pro-German population, including the indigenous population, there were also businessmen for whom defence of the homeland was not the priority. On 17 June, *Maréchal* Philippe Pétain addressed the French people, 'I have asked the adversary to put an end to hostilities … we wanted to save ourselves the effort; today we have met misfortune. I have been with you in the glorious days. I am and will remain with you in the dark days as the head of government.'[36] Even though the Radio Paris signals were being increasingly jammed, the news spread rapidly in Douala. Discussions quickly turned to Pétain's request for an armistice and what that would mean for the colonies. But the hero of Verdun never mentioned the colonies in his speech.

Due to the proximity of British Cameroon, some among the population of Douala were in the habit of listening to BBC, which was not yet being jammed. On 18 June, the day after Pétain's speech, they listened to *Général* Charles de Gaulle's call to continue the fight over BBC Radio. According to Gilberte Crognier, the wife of a French merchant from Douala, de Gaulle's Appeal was heard, 'and copies were even distributed by Roger Mauclère. A Gaullist movement was organised.'[37] It is noteworthy that the resistance movement first emerged from among the civil servants. Roger Mauclère was the Head of Public Works. *Médecin Capitaine* Chauderon wrote, 'After the shock of 10 May, came the ray of sunshine of 18 June. As soon as it reached us, the situation and our position became clearer. At last, the resistance had a leader, a symbol, a capital, a link with free Europe, and the embryo of a fighting army.'[38]

---

33   Pierre Pellissier, *Massu* (Paris: Perrin, 2003), p.33.
34   Pellissier, *Massu*, p.33.
35   Jean Mouchet, *Leclerc. Débuts méconnus de son historique épopée – Londres – Cameroun* (Provence: Les Éditions du Midi, 1978), p.32.
36   Béné, *Carnets, Première Époque,* p.58.
37   Michel, 'Leclerc et l'Afrique Noire' p.262.
38   Chauderon, CHETOM, 18H296, dossier 2.

The Royal Navy sought to reassure the inhabitants of Douala whenever it could. At the end of May, the Australian armed merchant cruiser HMS *Bulolo* anchored for several days, and the crew arranged on-board visits for the population. The light cruiser HMS *Dragon* docked several times in Douala and the governor went on board, where the crew hoisted a huge French flag and played 'La Marseillaise.' However, after HMS *Dragon* set sail, the French submarine *Sidi-Ferruch* docked. The crew of *Sidi-Ferruch* had remained loyal to Pétain after the armistice. It was a bit of a game of cat-and-mouse between the two navies trying to avoid confrontation.

Meanwhile, events were moving fast in Europe. The armistice with the Germans was signed on 22 June 1940, and a separate one with the Italians on 24 June. The ceasefire took effect on 25 June. Yet Pétain still made no mention of the colonies, or the fate reserved for the ex-German possessions in Africa.[39] *Maréchal* Pétain addressed the French people again on 25 June to present the conditions of the armistice that his government had just signed. Since Radio Paris was no longer being jammed by the Germans, everyone could listen. At last, he spoke to the expatriates in the colonies:

> The war was lost in metropolitan France. Should we have prolonged it by fighting in our colonies? I would be unworthy of remaining your leader if I had agreed to shed French blood to prolong the dreaming of a few Frenchmen who are ignorant of warfare. I did not want to place myself or my hope outside the soil of France.

The *maréchal* was obviously targeting *Général* de Gaulle by calling him a dreamer, even a megalomaniac, and continued:

> I was no less concerned about our colonies than about the metropole. The armistice safeguards the ties which unite the colonies to France. France has the right to expect their loyalty.[40]

After the uncertainty of May and June, the situation became clearer in everyone's mind. There were two choices available, and each person had to make up their own mind. To follow *Maréchal* Pétain and accept the armistice was the path of prudence and legality. Following the unknown *Général* de Gaulle, who was calling for resistance, was tempting, but it was risky on many levels. In Cameroon, there was one other consideration that could influence everyone's decision. That was the British, who were firmly resolved to continue the fight with the motto 'Victory or Death.' British Cameroon was a stone's throw from Douala, and the immense British colony of Nigeria was just beyond. Relations between the two colonies, particularly in the commercial sector, were still active. Britain had a Consul in Douala, Colonel Miles Clifford, and many French colonists spoke English, more so than in the other colonies. Choosing the Free France option was perhaps easier there than anywhere else. After Pétain's speech, the civilian population of Douala became increasingly divided. Gilberte Crognier reported the thoughts of Governor Brunot's wife: 'The Governor is like a father who has three sons: one for de Gaulle, another for Vichy, and the other who keeps his thoughts quiet.'[41] The political leaders and certain heads of services observed a relative neutrality by avoiding taking a position. Such was the case with Governor Brunot, who was caught, 'between local pressures and his duty to obey the legal state.'[42] Despite his inclination towards Free France, he dared not take the plunge yet. It was difficult for him to manage, especially since the governor of French Equatorial Africa, Pierre Boisson, soon rallied to Vichy.

---

39   Jacques Fourneau, *Témoignage d'un administrateur en poste*, CHETOM 18H42.
40   Béné, *Carnets, Première époque,* p 60.
41   Michel, 'Leclerc et l'Afrique Noire', p.260.
42   Michel, 'Leclerc et l'Afrique Noire', p.261.

For the military, the situation was clearer. In Brazzaville, *Général* Husson had little sympathy for the young *Général* de Gaulle, and he also opted for Vichy in August. The legalists, soon to be called Pétainists, were recruited from among the senior cadre, many of whom had fought in the First World War. They were those who had the most to lose by choosing disobedience. Under French Penal Code the consequences of Article 75 were clear: 'Any Frenchman who maintains intelligence with a foreign power .... will be guilty of treason and punished by death...' This sentence also included the confiscation of property and military degradation. To clearly show its determination, and to set an example, the Vichy government had *Général* de Gaulle sentenced to death in absentia. The military tribunal of Clermont-Ferrand presided over by *Général* Frère issued the verdict on 27 July. In contrast to the senior cadre, the younger soldiers were not adherents of the cult of the hero of Verdun, and they had less to lose by choosing adventure and disobedience. For Massu obedience was not even an option: 'There was no more power ... for us, authority no longer existed! France was ruined! .... Ass over head!'[43] They refused to submit as part of a vassal state. Admittedly, they chose not to fight back, but they did not believe they were incapable of doing so. For the young colonials of the AEF the choice was simple, it was simply a matter of, 'rallying to this unexpected leader who told us that France had lost a battle but not the war, and that if we joined him, we would finally be able to fight.'[44] Dio agreed with Massu. He was shocked to learn that the government in Vichy had, as early as 25 June, asked Félix Eboué, the Governor of Chad, to withdraw the French garrisons from Tibesti and to hand them over to the Italians.[45] Fortunately he firmly refused.

The choice of disobedience, which Dio forged in Douala during the summer of 1940, was clearly a result of his career with the *méharistes*. Massu later stated that it was easy for a *méhariste* to make such a decision. 'Saharan life is a stripped-down life; we see only the main issues. When it comes to making a difficult choice, it's easier to decide in the desert than in the comfort of civilised life.'[46] Another characteristic of the *méharistes* was their independence of mind. It is therefore not surprising that 'the *méhariste* esprit de corps, which views autonomy as a mark of prestige, rejects the strict application of military regulations.'[47] But Dio was in command of, and responsible for, a detachment of men. Overall, he knew all his men would follow him, including his cadre of European leaders. During mealtimes, he could hear the thoughts that the NCOs shared with each other, but he wanted to avoid dragging them into a dead end. He knew his decision as the commander of the detachment should not just be a personal choice. Most of his subordinate commanders were young and without family responsibilities. Therefore, confiscation of their property in France, which would certainly happen if they chose dissidence, would not be too costly to them. There was also career development to consider. For those who were active – those civil servants who were only limited by age – Dio would let them make up their own mind. He had to be careful not to drag them into some hopeless adventure. Therefore, he needed to understand better the intentions of this *Général* de Gaulle and measure whether the risk was acceptable for them. He was reassured to learn that, on 27 June, the British officially recognised de Gaulle as the leader of the Free French, determined to continue the fight at their side.

Dio was also concerned about the state of mind of his *tirailleurs*. Their sense of honour was wounded by the announcement of the military defeat in France. They simply could not understand

43   Alain-Gilles Minella, *Entretiens avec le Général Massu, le Soldat Méconnu* (Paris: Éditions Mame, coll. 'Trajectoire', 1993), p.93.
44   Minella, *Entretiens*, p.92.
45   Gérard Ingold, *Général Ingold, Figure de la France Libre* (Paris: Challenges d'Aujourd'hui, 1995), p.38.
46   Minella, *Entretiens*, p.95.
47   Géraud Létang, *Mirages d'une Rébellion. Être Français Libre au Tchad (1940 – 1943)*, Thèse de doctorat en histoire, Institut d'Études Politiques de Paris (2020), inédit, p.163.

how the 'strongest army in the world' had fallen before the enemy in such a short time. What they feared most was being 'ridiculed by the women of their villages in the bush, when the military authorities sent them back to their homes.'[48] Dio did not feel that he could tell them it was all over before firing even a single shot. That was an important factor for him that what they considered to be the British before deciding which way to lead his detachment. In fact, he had a plan B if things were to go wrong in Douala. The fight could continue by joining the British troops in Nigeria to the west.

Douala was increasingly agitated by the tensions emerging within the three groups: Vichy, Gaullist, and the hesitant. *Lieutenant* Maziéras and *Médecin Capitaine* Chauderon often met with *Médecin Capitaine* Laquintinie, who was one of the rare soldiers to openly stand with the pro-Gaullist group of Mauclère. He kept Dio's small team informed of events among the civil circle in Douala. In that period of uncertainty, the announcement of the tragedy of Mers-el-Kébir[49] on 3 July 1940, struck the Gaullists as a catastrophe. That tragedy, in which more than a thousand French sailors died, swayed many of the hesitant towards Pétain. Vichy, stressing what they considered the British treachery of Mers-el-Kébir to be, wanted to regain the initiative in the colonies. Governor Boisson then took up the cause of *Maréchal* Pétain, who appointed him governor of the *AEF* and the *AOF*. Boisson departed for Dakar, leaving *Général* Husson in Brazzaville with civil and military powers over *AEF*-Cameroon. From that moment, it was clear that the Gaullists had less and less space to manoeuvre. In Douala, the Vichyites hurled accusations at the hesitant: for them 'true patriotism consists in returning as soon as possible to mainland France to associate more closely with our unhappy compatriots … in the unconditional, almost mythical confidence they have in the *Maréchal*.'[50] According to them, dissidence was only a pretext to continue 'the nice little colonial life.'

According to *Médecin Capitaine* Chauderon, the *Forces Françaises Libres* (or *FFL*, Free French Forces) were called 'Raving Libertarian Madmen.'[51] Nevertheless, around 10 July, a public meeting was organised by Governor Brunot. The meeting began with a minute of silence in tribute to the French sailors. Then he gave the floor to the British Consul, whom he had invited. The Consul cleverly focused his remarks on the economy to reassure settlers and traders. Great Britain would supply the territory and undertake to sell local products. The meeting ended with the singing of 'La Marseillaise' followed by an unambiguous 'God save the King,' Chauderon noted.[52]

Vichy was informed of events in Cameroon and decided to react. On 20 July, *Contre-amiral* Charles Platon, representing Pétain's government, arrived by plane.[53] Platon had distinguished himself at Dunkirk by commanding the evacuation of the French contingent to England. During his travel to the Palais du Gouvernement, he choked back his anger at seeing British sailors moving about in town. During his stay, he visited the entire French administration in Cameroon, summoned the directors, and gave them his instructions. The Vichy representative realised that the situation in Cameroon was not a simple one and that the Gaullist dissidents were numerous.

---

48   Béné, *Carnets, Première époque*, p.63.
49   Following the armistice of 22 June 1940, the British feared that the French naval squadron based at Mers-el-Kébir, in Algeria, would rally to Pétain's France and subsequently fall into German hands. Therefore, the British destroyed the squadron, which had refused to comply with their ultimatum to depart to the French West Indies, scuttle themselves, or get interned in a neutral country. Churchill commented, 'This was the most hateful decision, the most unnatural and painful in which I have been concerned.'
50   Chauderon, CHETOM, 18H296.
51   Chauderon, CHETOM, 18H296.
52   Chauderon, CHETOM, 18H296.
53   In September 1940, Charles Platon became Minister of the Colonies, and he favoured collaboration with Nazi Germany. He was shot in August 1944 by the French communist resistance organisation, *Francs-Tireurs et Partisans*.

When he left on Saturday, 27 July, he was not only shocked to see the aircraft hangar adorned with French and British flags, but also to find a committee led by Mauclère waiting for him. Mauclère gave him a firm speech, without mincing any words. He ended his solemn declaration by looking him straight in the eye: 'On behalf of French Cameroon, conquered from the *Boche* with French, English, and Belgian blood, we declare our desire to remain Free French Cameroon; we indignantly reject any attempt to force a *fait accompli* on us from Bordeaux or Vichy or Berlin, and we further fiercely refuse with determined will, to serve under the swastika.'[54] He could not have been more clear or direct. The text of Mauclère's speech was sent to *Général* de Gaulle and to the British Consul in Douala. Nevertheless, Platon was unimpressed by this local determination. Back in Vichy, he advocated for strong measures which were quickly disseminated in Cameroon. On 28 July, Governor Brunot let it be known that, by order of the Admiralty, access to the port of Douala would henceforth be forbidden to British ships.[55] It was a serious pronouncement. Great Britain had received the League of Nations mandate over the western part of Cameroon and so was a de facto partner of France, which administered most of the territory. The decision to prohibit access to the port of Douala therefore violated the terms of the League of Nations mandate. Additionally, although diplomatic relations with Great Britain were severed on 7 July, Britain was not officially an enemy of Vichy France. Moreover, Churchill, focused as he was on his fight against Nazi Germany, left *Général* de Gaulle in an awkward position until 1942. But *Amiral* Platon's hatred for the British after Mers-el-Kébir was unrestrained.

On Tuesday, 30 July, the leader of Free France sent a message to the colonies via the BBC. Despite Nazi efforts to jam the London radio, de Gaulle's advertised address to the residents of the colonies was heard. It is quite possible that *Capitaine* Dio listened in carefully. The *général*, a refugee in England who was unknown to Dio, seemed to him more and more credible. He agreed with de Gaulle's analysis that the war would become global and that the colonies could play a role in the reconquest of France. On 1 August, the submarine *Sidi-Ferruch* landed once again in Douala with Inspector of the Colonies Huet on board. He had come to take charge of purging the administration.[56] Huet was greeted on the quay by about 20 Gaullists displaying French and British flags. The commander of the submarine was furious to see the emblem of a country in a state of war with the French admiralty and he made it known.[57] At the beginning of August, the European population of Douala was completely divided between the legalists and the dissidents, between the Pétainists and the Gaullists. Events followed one another a bit like a game of ping pong, each day bringing events favourable to one side, counterbalanced the next day by an event from the opposite side.

At the end of July, *Lieutenant Colonel* Bureau, commander of the Cameroonian troops, went to Brazzaville to meet *Général* Husson. On his return on 2 August, he agreed to meet a group of pro-Gaullists led by Mauclère, who offered the leadership of the movement to him. Bureau categorically refused. The senior officer even warned them that in the event of a coup, he would be followed by all the active officers present in Cameroon and would be obliged to 'subdue' any dissident movement. But on the same day, around 4:30 p.m., 'the colonel, in front of all the soldiers, specified that *Général* Husson's attitude was to put up passive resistance to orders from Vichy, without openly declaring himself against it...'[58] Dio, who was present, and who was informed of the content of the previous meeting with the civilians, was disappointed with the turn of events. In front of the civilians, *Colonel* Bureau remained firmly on the legal side. In front of his military

---

54   Mouchet, *Leclerc,* pp.34–35.
55   A. Rogez, *Douala 1940 juillet-août,* boîte 15, dossier 1, chemise 6.
56   Jean-Christophe Notin, *Leclerc, le Croisé de la France Libre* (Paris: Éditions Perrin, 2015), p.72.
57   Rogez, *Douala 1940.*
58   Rogez, *Douala 1940.*

subordinates, his speech was quite different. For Dio, two things were clear: Bureau was less sure of his subordinates than he claimed, and he was indecisive. The *colonel* had the same attitude as the governor, claiming not to want to shed French blood.

The presence of Inspector of the Colonies Huet compelled the colonial officials to implement the terms of the armistice in Cameroon.[59] Governor Brunot communicated directives he received from Vichy. However, lacking courage, he limited his remarks to economics alone when he addressed the civil society of Douala.

It was presumably in that context that Dio made his personal decision. *Médecin Capitaine* Chauderon stated that one 'fine day, *Capitaine* Dio went to the English Consulate to ask for permission to perhaps serve in the British Army if things went wrong.' He and Maziéras followed Dio's example and also received authorisation.[60] In taking that path, Dio had definitively chosen the honourable side – that of fighting, but also of disobedience by refusing to join those who collaborated with the Nazis. He did not yet know if he would involve his detachment in the adventure. He hesitated to make a decision that would commit his men. For the moment, his education, his Christian faith, his ethics, and his great sense of humanity prevented him from deciding for himself as commander of his unit. He understood that his reinforcement mission for metropolitan France was no longer valid. But then what could he do, stuck in port? Dio still belonged to the *Régiment de Tirailleurs Sénégalais du Tchad*. Had he been forgotten by Fort-Lamy? He suspected that *Colonel* Bureau had asked *Général* Husson to keep his unit in Cameroon, being the only one in the territory that was operational. Dio had shown complete neutrality so far, in his words and his relationships. Taciturn, he was apparently content to watch the protagonists of both camps without taking sides.

Vichy, clearly perceiving the local internal resistance and having identified those who did not accept the armistice, transferred individuals to break up the group of pro-Gaullist resistance fighters. Thus, at the beginning of August, *Médecin Capitaine* Chauderon was abruptly transferred to the *Assistance Médicale Indigène* and was therefore forced to leave the reinforcement detachment. Dio was disappointed because he had become friends with the energetic and capable doctor. He was sickened by the methods of the Vichy administration. Consequently, Chauderon and his wife left for Dschang, in Bamileke territory, the so-called 'Auvergne of Cameroon.' Yet the post had the advantage of being close to British Cameroon and the Bamenda border crossing in case he decided to continue the fight with the British.

On Sunday 4 August, the submarine *Sidi-Ferruch* left the port of Douala. According to reservist *Lieutenant* Rogez, some submariners hanging out at the beach had explained why the day before: the war between Britain and Germany would benefit France because it would weaken the two adversaries.[61] All the arguments from the Pétainists were good, even the most twisted of them! The same day, the British Consul declared, 'that all measures had been taken to welcome Frenchmen in Nigeria.'[62] Faced with pressure from Vichy and this invitation from the British, many of them then decided to join the British Army in Nigeria via British Cameroon. That was the start of a movement that would very seriously reduce the active pro-Gaullist forces on the ground. On Tuesday, 6 August, *Lieutenant* Rogez, accompanied by *Lieutenant* Bonnet, took a boat to reach Tiko where they were warmly welcomed.[63] Rogez went the next day to Victoria, capital of what

---

59   Rogez, *Douala 1940*.
60   Chauderon, CHETOM, 18H296.
61   Rogez, *Douala 1940*.
62   Rogez, *Douala 1940*.
63   *Lieutenant* Rogez would finally be sent to the Gold Coast (Ghana) to join a battalion of Senegalese *tirailleurs* under the orders of *Commandant* Parant who was preparing to act in Cameroon. At the time of departure, the Senegalese *tirailleurs* deserted en masse, tired of the procrastination and behaviour of the

was then British Cameroon, and there he met three French officers wearing British uniforms. He realised that the British wanted to swell their ranks rather than risk an operation in Cameroon under French command. He took measures to warn those who were still in Douala to stay there. In fact, the situation deteriorated sharply there, and Vichy seemed on the verge of winning the game. 'Around mid-August, we learnt startling news, the appointment of a new governor, Mr Annet, and Colonel Claveau as the new military commander.'[64] The two leaders of the territory thus paid for their indecision. Governor Brunot had not resolved to cut off contact with the British Consulate in Douala and *Colonel* Bureau had also taken a wait-and-see approach. Vichy wanted to bring the recalcitrant territory back into line.[65] Hearing that news left the supporters of Free France in despair. Considering the game lost, many chose to join those who had already gone over to the British.

On 27 August, there were only 11 trustworthy people left in Douala, gathered around Mauclère.[66] The handful of resisters decided that they would be more useful where they were. According to Jean Mouchet, 'it was at this time that a cable was sent to *Général* de Gaulle in London, confirming and urgently requesting a leader.'[67] In London, as in Victoria, officials were aware of the need to do something. There was a window of opportunity that should be seized. Dio was also aware of the deteriorating situation in Douala. He realised that it would be difficult to act once the new administration was in place. As far as he was concerned, he had already made his decision. He was bolstered in his choice when he heard news coming from Chad and the Belgian Congo that restored his morale. He learnt that Vichy had asked Fort-Lamy on 13 August to appoint an Italian-speaking officer to accompany an armistice commission which was scheduled to visit. *Colonel* Marchand's response was scathing: 'not a single volunteer in Chad to accompany an Armistice Control Commission but many to reject it.'[68] In addition, a *colonel* from Léopoldville in the Belgian Congo led an African committee of Free France. He distributed a leaflet on 23 August that concluded with the statement: 'the men of overseas France will simply remake France, despite a government held captive by the enemy.'[69]

If his personal choice was clear, Dio was still torn as the commander of a detachment of almost 200 men, and he could not bring himself to abandon them.[70] So, should he make them cross the border with all their weapons and baggage? If he did, he had no means to carry out such an exfiltration from Douala to British Cameroon either by road or by sea. He was unsure of the environment he was in, and he had no confidence in *Colonel* Bureau since the recent events. *Capitaine* Pradier, the local garrison commander, seemed as undecided as his chief. Dio often discussed it with his deputy, *Lieutenant* Maziéras. The two men were rather gloomy on Monday, 26 August 1940. They had a drink at dinner, and then went to bed as the rain intensified, making a terrible noise on the sheet metal roof of their building.

---

new commanders and they wanted to return home. A unit was formed with the remaining personnel. They did not arrive in Douala until 30 August and thus too late. Rogez would serve during a large part of the conflict at the Manoka battery. (André Rogez, *Douala 1940 July-August*, Fonds Leclerc, boîte 15, dossier 1, chemise 6).

64   Mouchet, *Leclerc*, p.36.
65   Michel, 'Leclerc et l'Afrique Noire', p.262.
66   Michel, 'Leclerc et l'Afrique Noire', p.263.
67   Mouchet, *Leclerc*, p.37.
68   Béné, *Carnets, Première époque,* p.78.
69   Poualion, private collection.
70   In 1944 Leclerc would evoke this case of conscience, saying: 'it is true that when I made my decision to leave, I was alone, I no longer had command and consequently I was freed from the responsibility of leadership. The problem of conscience and of abandoning my troops did not arise,' Compagnon, Jean, *Leclerc, Maréchal de France,* (Paris: Flammarion, 1994), p.357.

I, 27 August 1940, Douala (Cameroon)

On that day, the fates of *Commandant* (soon to be *Colonel*) Philippe Leclerc and *Capitaine* Louis Dio intersected in Douala.[71] From then on, the two officers would never be separated from each other. It was the beginning of what remains one of the greatest epics in the history of France. All the works on Leclerc have described this historical episode with more or less precision, using the accounts of participants to try to describe it as faithfully as possible. Among the 24 companions of Leclerc who arrived by canoe with him, *Commandant* Hettier de Boislambert,[72] *Capitaine* Tutenges, *Lieutenant* Denise, and *Lieutenant* Quilichini recorded their versions of the event either directly or through an intermediary.[73] There were also local witnesses.[74] And then, of course, there were those close to Leclerc, his comrades-in-arms who described that day, such as Massu, Compagnon, Troadec, Ingold, Salbaing, Merle, and a number of others.[75] There are also writers and historians who have searched the available archives and sometimes found documents that shed additional light on the existing evidence collected.[76] It is important to consider this historic day and in particular the meeting which took place around 3:00 in the morning on Tuesday 27 August 1940. The meeting had been planned on 18 August in Lagos, the capital of Nigeria, where *Général* de Gaulle's envoys (*Commandant* Leclerc, the civilian Pleven, and *Capitaine* Hettier de Boislambert)[77] had met with *Colonel* de Larminat who was then on the way to London. They had recently been ordered to try to reach French Equatorial Africa and Cameroon, and they had carte blanche. 'Do whatever is best where and when it would be possible' were de Gaulle's instructions. They were split between the colonies: Pleven was sent to Chad, where he was joined by *Commandant* Colonna d'Ornano, who arrived from Brazzaville on 22 August. Chad was the territory with the easiest situation. In fact, the Governor of Chad, Félix Eboué as well as *Colonel* Marchand, commander of the *Régiment de Tirailleurs Sénégalais du Tchad*, had already publicly

---

71   Leclerc arrived in London with the rank of *capitaine*. He was promoted to *commandan*t by de Gaulle, certainly due to the mission he entrusted to him in Africa, but also because Leclerc was, at the time, the only graduate of the *École de Guerre* who rallied to the leader of Free France in London.

72   Claude Hettier de Boislambert, *Les Fers de l'Espoir* (Paris: Plon, 1978), p.216.

73   The testimony of Boislambert is covered in most works but it is short (he would very quickly leave Douala on the orders of de Gaulle to go first to Pointe-Noire then to Dakar, to prepare to bring the *AOF* over to Free France. He was taken prisoner during the failed attempt to rally the *AOF*). The versions of events written by Tutenges and Denise, other witnesses, agree with each other on the facts. Quilichini confided in his friends Vézinet and Guillebon. His version is similar to that of these other two comrades.

74   Gilberte Crognier, who later became Leclerc's secretary in Cameroon, or Jean Mouchet, the depot manager at Yaoundé station. This was also the case for Raymond Dronne, administrator of the colonies in Cameroon mobilised as a lieutenant at that time. He was not present in Douala but he knew the environment well. This was also the case of Charles Béné, who, as a radio operator, was able to collect confidential information which he thought to write down.

75   Works noted in the bibliography.

76   Like Notin, Levisse-Touzé, Corbonnois, Bergot, Destrem, Croidys… (see bibliography). Let us also quote the RP Engelbert Mveng (Engelbert Mveng, SJ, 'L'œuvre de Leclerc au Cameroun et la contribution des Camerounais à l'effort de guerre', *Le Général Leclerc et l'Afrique Française Libre, 1940–1942,* Actes du Colloque International (Fondation Maréchal Leclerc de Hauteclocque, Paris, 1987), pp.59–72. who collected the testimony of Lucas Atangana, agent of the great Chief Ewondo, Charles Atangana. A Cameroonian Saint-Cyrien, class of 2002, Pascal-Henry Biwolé wrote his thesis '*Le Ralliement et l'Œuvre de Leclerc au Cameroun,*' (inédit) which is very useful in examining these moments in the common history of France and Cameroon.

77   Leclerc, who had just been promoted to the rank of commandant by de Gaulle, was appointed leader of this team. His codename was Sullivan. René Pleven is a Malouin, an intrepid businessman who twice escaped German clutches like Leclerc. Hettier de Boislambert, a great traveller who knew Equatorial Africa well, was passionate about hunting, like Leclerc.

expressed their support for de Gaulle. In contrast, the case of Middle Congo appeared more diffi-cult. *Général* Husson, commanding all the forces of French Equatorial Africa, was there and he was a convinced Pétainist. *Colonel* de Larminat, just arrived from Léopoldville, was chosen for that difficult mission. Leclerc opted for Cameroon. Why? Leclerc explained it by saying, 'it was necessary to affirm that although it was under a [League of Nations] mandate, the territory was completely and profoundly French.'[78] He did not offer other reasons, but it is quite possible that he was also responding to a personal resentment against the Germans because Cameroon was a former German colony. He certainly had not forgotten the insult of being taken prisoner in June 1940.[79] Economically, Cameroon was the richest, or at least it was the least poor, of the *AEF* territories. It would therefore be better able to support the Free French war effort. Politically, the situation was confused, since it was a divided colony between the French and British.

Leclerc sent Boislambert to British Cameroon to meet the French from Douala. On his return, he reported that the middle-aged French there were mostly legitimists while the younger residents wanted to continue to fight alongside the British. His observation was true not just among the administration and the army, but also in civil society, as well. There were also a large number of undecideds who were waiting to see how things would develop. This was also true among the educational community, which was mostly a wait-and-see group. The clergy also remained unde-cided, even though the Bishop of Yaoundé, *Monseigneur* Lemaignoux, was rather legalist. On 24 August, en route from Victoria,[80] Leclerc was in British Cameroon, just a few dozen kilometres across the Wouri Estuary from Douala in the small banana port of Tiko. Based on the informa-tion he had, Leclerc understood that he had to act. Vichy, stressing the British 'treachery' of Mers-el-Kébir, wanted to regain the initiative in the colonies. The successors of Governor Brunot and *Colonel* Bureau had just received their assignment orders. Governor Annet and *Colonel* Claveau were expected within the next 48 hours.[81] Moreover, the submarine *Sidi-Ferruch* had just left Douala and was due to be replaced by the submarine *Poncelet* in the next few days. It would be wise to take advantage of the time until then because Leclerc knew it would be difficult to convince naval officers to join the Gaullist cause. A majority of them had chosen to remain legalists since the trauma of Mers-el-Kébir. He needed to get ahead of the Vichyites by ensuring that Mauclère's pro-Gaullist movement did not wither. Their ranks had already thinned since the beginning of August when 35 of them joined up with British Cameroon in the course of just a few days. There were only around a dozen trustworthy and determined members left in Douala.

On 25 August, Leclerc decided to act. 'Let's go,'[82] he declared, without waiting any longer for the arrival of *Commandant* Parant's detachment of 300 Senegalese *tirailleurs* from the Gold Coast (present day Ghana). He resolved to leave with just the reduced team he had from the personnel present in British Cameroon.[83] Besides Boislambert, he had four officers who had joined him in

---

78   Notin, *le Croisé*, p.71.
79   Leclerc never forgot the contemptuous remarks of the German officer towards him and towards France in general when he was taken prisoner in June 1940. He called on his paternity to escape from captivity: 'what say you from a nation where you no longer have to defend your *Vaterland* (Fatherland) because you have six children? …nation in decadence…go away.' Jacques-Napoléon Faure-Biguet, *General Leclerc* (Paris: Plon, 1948), p.19.
80   Limbé in present day Cameroon.
81   Notin, *le Croisé*, p.75.
82   Hettier de Boislambert, *Fers de l'Espoir*, p.215.
83   8 officers: Colonel Philippe Leclerc, *Commandant* Claude Hettier de Boislambert, *Capitaine* Émile Tutenges, *Lieutenants* Henri Fougerat, Robert Quilichini, François Denise, Jean Son, Aspirant Marcel Penanhoat (reserve officer, a banana planter by trade).
     • 7 non-commissioned officers: *Adjudant Chef* Henri Drouihl, *Maréchal des Logis Chef* René Bezagu, *Sergents* Philippe Fratacci, Henri Frizza, Armand Civel, Léon Lacroix, *Maréchal des Logis* Jacques de Bodard

Victoria: *Capitaine* Tutenges, *Lieutenants* Fougerat and Quilichini who arrived from Dahomey (present day Benin), and *Lieutenant* Denise who arrived from Togo. Leclerc then selected 16 soldiers from among Tiko's French Cameroonian 'refugees,' including two officers who knew Douala well: *Lieutenant* Son and *Aspirant* Penanhoat. They informed their new leader that the senior military officer in Cameroon was *Lieutenant Colonel* Bureau, officially the chief of police. They felt it would be appropriate for Leclerc's rank to be at least equivalent to Bureau. Whether or not it would help the mission succeed, Leclerc immediately decided to promote himself to *colonel* so he would outrank Bureau. In the French Army of 1940, the rules regarding rank and subordination were quite formal. The officers would thus be much more reassured in doing their duty if they were following a superior officer. *Capitaine* de Boislambert immediately ripped the three stripes of a *capitaine* from the left sleeve of his jacket and had one sewn on each of Leclerc's sleeves, who thus became a *colonel*.[84] Boislambert sewed the remaining third stripe on his own right arm, thus becoming a *commandant*… at least on one sleeve![85] The other members of the group laughed at his expense, watching him try to hide his left arm behind his back in the first few hours after landing in Douala.

What was Leclerc's analysis of the military situation in Douala? From information received locally, the militia company did not appear to present any major problem. *Capitaine* Pradier, the local commander in Douala, was waiting to see how things turned out, just like much of his chain of command in Yaoundé. The small coastal surveillance vessel present in Douala would also not pose a problem because the Gaullists took it upon themselves to win over the young *Enseigne de Vaisseau* Thibeaudeau who commanded it. He promised he would rally to Free France when the time came. Leclerc had two concerns, though…

First was the coastal defence of Manoka, commanded by *Capitaine* Crépin, a colonial artilleryman and *polytechnicien* (graduate of the École Polytechnique). Crépin's heavy artillery could deny access to the port of Douala to any vessels. Therefore, the recommendation to Leclerc was to infiltrate at night in light canoes tucked up against the opposite bank of the river to avoid detection.

The second concern was even more serious for Leclerc. How would the company of *tirailleurs* from the *RTST*, that had been waiting to embark for France since June, respond to his landing in Douala? The unit of nearly 200 men intended to reinforce the army in mainland France was a well-trained and well-led company made up mostly of Chadians selected at Fort Archambault. 'There was a solid company of *tirailleurs*, commanded by *Capitaine* Dio, a well-known bush fighter who had recently arrived from Chad; success or failure ultimately depends upon him.'[86] Leclerc knew that Dio was a *méhariste* brought in from Chad where he had commanded the *Groupe Nomade du Tibesti*. He also knew, from *Commandant* Colonna d'Ornano, who had been Dio's commander at Faya-Largeau, that Dio was not a pushover. He was a man of few words, and slow to trust others. Leclerc had also heard that the Gaullist civilians in Douala had tried in vain to sound out this *capitaine* and had not yet won him over. Dio was obviously an active officer who was firmly bound to the duty of discretion. He was not in the habit of confiding in civilians, especially with regard

---

- 9 junior enlisted soldiers: *Caporal Chef* Fernand Thevenet, *Caporals* Henri Arnal, Paul Laumonier, Jacques Martin, Henri Hugues, *Reverend Père* Dehon (Priest of Mvolye who was forbidden to say mass by his superiors because 'at each of his homilies …. he railed against traitors and cowards who had sold their country to the Nazis.' (Biwolé, *Le Ralliement*, p.40), *Soldats* Noël Lavigne, Eugène Mercier, Ernest Moser.

84 Leclerc quickly advised de Gaulle of this ruse but the leader of Free France, who needed men of this calibre, confirmed Leclerc's rank of *colonel*, on a temporary basis. He was a *capitaine* when he arrived in London, promoted to *commandant* by de Gaulle – a month later, he was a colonel.

85 Compagnon, *Leclerc*, p.145.

86 Pierre Croidys, *Notre Second Bayard – le Général Leclerc – Grand Soldat – Grand Chrétien* (Paris: Édit. Spes, 1950), p.64.

to his political opinions. At the time, French soldiers did not even have the right to vote. But Mauclère and his team did not know that Dio had visited the British Consulate in July, nor that he had signed a contract to continue the fight in the British Army if the situation in Cameroon turned out badly for the Gaullists.

As an experienced soldier, Leclerc knew he would need Dio's company to take the city of Douala. He perfectly understood the importance of this *méhariste capitaine*, and he knew that the success of his mission depended upon Dio's decision. Leclerc was no match for such a detachment, his companions in the canoes being armed only with pistols. Leclerc carried a note placing Dio 'at the top of the list of personalities to be temporarily placed under house arrest after flattering him.'[87] Boislambert received the same orders.[88] Leclerc later recalled, on 27 June 1943 in Tripolitania:

> …that he had been warned that everything depended on an officer who kept his opinions to himself and confided in no one. We only knew that he had his company well in hand, that he had distributed ammunition to it, and that he was ready to intervene. His name was Dio.[89]

The personalities of these two *capitaines*, Crépin and Dio, with whom Leclerc had to come to terms, were therefore well known to him. They were young, both 32 years old. They might be more inclined than others to accept his proposals. But, above all, Leclerc knew that they were each responsible for a unit of nearly 200 men with cadres of commanders. Therefore, they had to think before making a decision, and overall they had to assess the consequences for their soldiers so as not to drag them into a hopeless adventure.

Émile Tutenges, who was with Leclerc in Tiko on 26 August, remembered that at about 8:00 a.m., 'we boarded a boat on which there was a British naval officer responsible for taking us to the limit of territorial waters, where there were three canoes waiting for us.'[90] The 16-metre-long canoes made from the trunk of okoume trees slid silently through the water, allowing them to pass by unnoticed. They were the perfect choice for Leclerc, who wanted to avoid being criticised for having arrived in the 'foreign baggage trains' of a boat belonging to His Royal Majesty. The 24 'dissident' soldiers were split up among three canoes.

Starting at the end of the afternoon, they rowed in silence for 20km to reach the port of Douala. A heavy tropical rain suddenly began to fall, helping the infiltration by reducing the risk of being detected from the coast. The men very quickly found themselves completely soaked in the bottom of the canoe. Navigation through the many meandering channels of the estuary took longer than expected and then the tidal shift slowed their progress even further, and the canoes lost sight of each other. It had been expected. There was a member of the team in each canoe who knew Douala well and was responsible for guiding the team to the meeting point in the house of a pro-Gaullist Frenchman. They sent a message to the owner of the house, a man named Dr Mauzé, who was one of the main leaders of the dissident movement in Douala.[91] The canoes landed in scattered order on

---

87   Notin, *le Croisé*, p.78.
88   Compagnon, *Leclerc*, p.148.
89   Christian Girard, *Journal de Guerre, 1939–1945, Témoignage de l'aide de camp de Général Leclerc de Hauteclocque* (Paris: L'Harmattan, 2000), p.84.
90   Fonds Leclerc, *Mémoire du colonel Tutenges, premier compagnon du Colonel Leclerc*, boîte 5a, dossier 2, chemise 2.
91   There remains great uncertainty about the location of the meeting. Many books mention the hut of a forester named Sill. The colonial administrator, Raymond Dronne, was not present, but in his first book he mentions Sill's hut but in the second, he says he carried out checks and was convinced that the meeting took place at Mauzé's. Leclerc himself, in a story he told at the end of 1943 during a dinner, mentioned Dr Mauzé (Christian Girard, *Journal de Guerre, 1939–1945, Témoinage de l'aide de camp Leclerc de Hauteclocque*, Paris: L'Harmattan, 2000, p.89).

the quays of the port, which had been deserted due to the tropical rain. Leclerc's canoe was the first to arrive at around 2:00 a.m. near the Nassif house in Akwa. He landed in the dark night against some logs and fell into the water along with Boislambert. It was an inauspicious start, made worse by the fact that the expected welcoming committee was nowhere to be seen. Completely soaked, Leclerc immediately asked the guide on his canoe to take him to the meeting place.

The team of eight men left the banks of the Wouri in the dark and climbed towards the Centennial Church. Continuing on, they soon arrived in front of a large colonial house. The guard approached from behind the gate, worried to see white people in the middle of the night. They asked him to inform his boss of their arrival. The doctor quickly arrived and explained that the message announcing their arrival had just reached him. He hurriedly brought in the eight soaked men from the first boat. Leclerc introduced himself and asked the doctor to arrange a meeting at once. Mauzé complied and immediately telephoned his Gaullist companions, who arrived one by one. Among the first to arrive was Mauclère, the director of public works and the leader of the pro-Gaullist movement in Douala. He was followed by Sill the forester, Peux the chief administrator of the colonies, Le Breton the doctor, Mascart the customs agent, Taillandier, Arnaud, de Suarez, Schoofs, Rogez, Lechnardt, Guillery, Baudon, Morand. After rushed greetings, Leclerc addressed them and quickly explained his purpose. *Lieutenant* Son had devised a detailed plan to seize the key points of the city.[92] The civilians were stunned to learn that such a small team intended to take the city that very night with so little means. In the meantime, the members of the other two boats arrived. Even with their arrival, the group of about 20 men seemed laughable to the civilians present. Mauclère and his companions tried to dissuade Leclerc from immediate action. Mauzé added that 'this arrival was premature and that he had already put together a plan.'[93] He pointed out that his plan was different from theirs and he proposed to postpone the operation for a week. Leclerc was unmoved, saying that he was there, and he would stay there. One of the participants then brought up the troops in the garrison. How would they react? He mentioned specifically the company of Chadian *tirailleurs*, which was the only real military force present in the town. Leclerc then realised that there were no soldiers present in the room, except those who had arrived with him. So, he asked that this *capitaine* who he had heard about be invited to join them, along with other officers, as soon as possible.[94] Mauclère, 'the master of the house, therefore telephoned Capitaine Dio's command post, asking him to join him immediately because he had something important to tell him.'[95] He also sent messengers to those who had not openly shown their opposition. While they waited for their arrival, the newcomers were offered a bite to eat.

Awakened, Capitaine Dio quickly got dressed and 'grabbed his revolver to arm himself…' later saying, 'I was suspicious …. in truth, I'll admit that I thought it was a set-up by the Vichyites!'[96]

Leclerc waited for the arrival of the officers, particularly Dio, and asked Lieutenant Son, who knew Dio, to let him know as soon as he arrived. The aviator *Lieutenant* François Goussault was the first to join them, and he greeted Leclerc. They already knew each other and exchanged a few words. *Médecin Capitaine* Laquintinie arrived next. Finally, two other officers appeared. *Lieutenant* Son gestured to Leclerc, who stepped forward to face them. They stood to attention and saluted the young *colonel*. Shaking hands with Leclerc, they introduced themselves, giving their rank and

92   Biwolé, *Le Ralliement*, p.45.
93   Fonds Leclerc, *Note du colonel Denise sur le ralliement du Cameroun à la France Libre, le 27 août 1940,* boîte 5a, dossier 2, chemise 1 Colonel Denise.
94   Notin, *le Croisé,* p.77, Tutenges (Boîte 5a, dossier 2, chemise 2), Compagnon citing testimony of Denise (Compagnon, *Leclerc,* p.147). Biwolé, (*Le Ralliement,* p.49, note 1) summarises this passage as follows: 'they were afraid of the company of Capitaine Dio, whom we had then gone to find in order to convince him.'
95   Croidys, *Notre second Bayard*, p.65.
96   René de Berval, 'Le Colonel Dio', *Caravane*, 26, 1945, p.31.

name: *Capitaine* Dio and *Lieutenant* Maziéras. Like many others who met Leclerc for the first time, Dio was immediately taken by his gaze. As soon as he arrived, his blue eyes somehow hypnotised Dio.[97] Colonial administrator Raymond Dronne met Leclerc two days later and wrote 'that look, that face, the intensity of his gaze, those eyes, that radiance. Natural authority emanated from him.'[98] *Général* Compagnon added: 'in the years to come, that look would strike all those who were to see it for the first time.'[99]

Next to arrive were other officers, including *Enseigne de Vaisseau* Thibaudeau. Leclerc began his second address, this one to the military men in the room. He quickly told them about *Général* de Gaulle and the mission he had received from him, explaining why Africa was being called upon to play a pivotal role in the plans for Free France. He frequently looked *Capitaine* Dio over, 'feeling that he was the one who had to be convinced, and that his support would win the others.'[100] He also brought up the British and the role they could play. He revealed the 'Lagos plan' regarding the *AEF* and told them that Chad would certainly join them once he spoke to them. Leclerc noticed that the *capitaine* straightened up slightly, even if for the moment his face still masked his feelings. Dio learnt that his former commander, *Commandant* Colonna d'Ornano, was at that moment in Fort-Lamy with Pleven to overthrow Chad. He also learnt that *Capitaine* Delange, assistant to d'Ornano in Faya-Largeau, was going to help Larminat in the attempt to win over the Middle Congo. He realised that those brothers-in-arms whom he held in high regard had joined de Gaulle without hesitation. How could it be otherwise here? He was convinced by what he heard. His regiment, the *Régiment de Tirailleurs Sénégalais du Tchad*, would naturally be on the front line in Chad, but also in the Middle Congo because his units would be responsible for enforcing the terms of joining Free France. In a way, his regiment's role revealed the path forward. While reflecting on it, the *méhariste* listened to the young *colonel* as he shared the broad outlines of the plan to seize Douala. Leclerc ended on a martial tone by saying that he had arrived and that he intended to stay there. Then softening, he addressed the officers and asked, 'Gentlemen, do you agree?' Up to that point, *Capitaine* Dio had not let anything show, but in his heart of hearts, he was impressed. The energy that flowed from this man and his strong and coherent words had completely won Dio over. He thought this was finally a leader who knew what he wanted! Leclerc's last question went unanswered. None of the young officers present dared to answer the *colonel* directly, waiting instead to hear from Dio. He was their spokesperson, the *méhariste* with two combat citations, 'a man known in the Colonies.'[101] But Dio remained silent. So, Leclerc turned to him: 'And you Dio, what do you think?' Dio rose, and answered slowly, 'I'm with you, *Colonel*, I'll go get my company.'

'Well then, welcome, *Capitaine* Dio. I am glad to have you with me, because I was told: if Dio is with you, you will certainly succeed; but if he is against you, you'll have a very difficult time.'[102]

97   'The essence of his physical person is in his eyes.' (J. N. Faure-Biguet, *Le Général Leclerc*. Paris: Plon, 1948, p.33).

98   Raymond Dronne, *Carnets de Route d'un Croisé de la France Libre* (Paris: Éditions France-Empire, 1983), pp.41–42.

99   Compagnon, *Leclerc*, p.151.

100   Jacques de Guillebon, *Leclerc le Victorieux, 1902 – 1947* (Paris: Fondation du Maréchal Leclerc de Hauteclocque, 1954), p.43.

101   Notin, *le Croisé*, p.78.

102   Compagnon, *Leclerc*, p.147. The course of Leclerc's meeting with Dio, as described here, derives from three eyewitnesses: *Capitaine* Tutenges, *Lieutenant* Denise, and *Lieutenant* Quilichini, as recounted in Guillebon's work. Vézinet describes the meeting as follows: 'The two men weighed each other with their gaze, then Leclerc, after explaining the mission he received from *Général* de Gaulle, simply said to Dio: 'Are you marching?' – 'I'm marching,' was the answer' (Adolphe Vézinet, *La 2ème DB, Gal Leclerc*. Paris: Arts et Métiers Graphiques, 1945, p.170). Pierre Croidys has a similar version: 'Are you marching with us, *Capitaine* Dio? We want to chase the Boche out of France!' Leclerc told him. Without hesitation the old bush fighter

With Dio on his side, Leclerc knew that he had just won the support of everyone – civilians and soldiers alike. Guillebon wrote, 'with a leader like Dio and men like his, the authority of *Colonel* Leclerc was unquestioned.'[103] No one disputed it after that. 'He quickly reassigned the missions and concluded, 'Gentlemen, it is 4:30 a.m. You still have an hour before daylight to act. Let's go! I'm counting on you.'[104] André Gambourg wrote, Leclerc, 'this 'dissident' would meet under precarious circumstances another officer and rally him to his patriotic company …. The officer in question, who would change the destiny of France was named Dio.'[105]

Dio was completely won over by Leclerc's personality. He had a perfect understanding of the situation he found when he arrived at Mauzé's house, later writing to Dejouy: 'That night, when *Colonel* Leclerc landed in Douala with a handful of filthy men, I was the one in control of the situation; I could have thrown him back in the water, locked him up, or helped him. After he spoke to us and I looked him in the eyes, I took the last option, simply by intuition.'[106] And what did Dio mean by intuition? According to Dejouy, 'a man like that perceives before analysing, feels before perceiving, and already he has taken action. A good head on his shoulders, a solid mind, but a heart that leads the way, sharpened in the sand of the desert. There is an infallible sixth sense in these exceptional men.'[107]

It was 27 August and Dio was with Leclerc from that date forward, conquered by his 'slick mouth,' as he said in the plain soldier's speech he used in those days. 'Such was Dio. Rough manners and a character of absolute loyalty.'[108] During their first meeting, Leclerc and Dio 'understood each other and knew that in the future each could count on the other.'[109] Leclerc's saga would now begin.

At around 5:00 a.m., Maziéras, Dio's second in command, escorted Leclerc and Boislambert to the military camp. The guards and sentries had just been replaced by *RTST tirailleurs* on *Capitaine* Dio's orders. Dio welcomed them and led them to the offices of the garrison commander. *Capitaine* Pradier,[110] representing *Lieutenant Colonel* Bureau, was caught off guard as he was getting out of bed. He had been woken a few hours earlier to take part in the meeting at Dr Mauzé's but had threatened to arrest the Free French envoy. He was senior in rank to Dio but was nevertheless impressed by Dio's notoriety and demeanour. Therefore, Pradier immediately made himself available to Leclerc and even had a meal served on site to his 'guests.' In short order, the company of *tirailleurs* assembled outside, under arms, and awaited orders. A *tirailleur* company had four combat platoons and a command section. Each combat platoon was divided into three squads of a dozen men, each squad comprising two fire teams, each fire team led by a *caporal*. Reinforcement Detachment No.3 had additional European cadre attached because of its planned departure for metropolitan France, so each platoon was led by a European, as were most of the squads. It was therefore completely different from the militia company at the camp, not only in quality of leadership, but also in equipment and training. This company could therefore be divided into many small

replied: 'There's nothing I want more! (Croidys, *Notre second Bayard,* p.65). Boislambert's version is shorter and does not mention the dialogue between the two men.

103 Guillebon, *Leclerc,* p.35.
104 Notin, *le Croisé,* p.78.
105 Fonds Leclerc, André Gambourg, '*Le destin de la 3e Cie du Tchad*', boîte B1, dossier 3, chemise 1.
106 Jacques Dejouy, *Les grandes certitudes* (Saint-Brieuc: Éditions Vu de France, 1993), p.73.
107 Dejouy, *Les grandes certitudes,* p.73.
108 Erwan Bergot, *La 2 ème D.B.* (Paris: Presses de la Cité, 1980), p.15.
109 Berval, 'Colonel Dio,' p.31.
110 Pradier was curiously promoted to *commandant* shortly thereafter. As a result, this led him to write Dio's personnel evaluation at the end of 1940. He described his role as '… at the head of the local movement to rally to Free France, hosted *Général* de Gaulle's envoys on 27 August' (*Capitaine* Dio's *bulletin de notes* in 1940, Musée de l'Ordre de la Libération).

detachments led by men capable of following directions and accomplishing a mission The *tirailleurs* in the company were young men who were taller than the average Cameroonian. With their cheeks scarified according to the tribal traditions of southern Chad, they cut an impressive figure. Well armed and highly disciplined, they obeyed only their immediate leader. They were trained and imposing.

By 5:30 a.m., they were ready to launch the operation.

'Dio immediately formed patrols, had roaming guards relieved, and secured the guard posts at the military camp.'[111] Simultaneously, in accordance with *Lieutenant* Son's plan that they had agreed to at Dr Mauzé's house, he assigned a detachment of *tirailleurs* to each of the teams responsible for seizing the key points of the city. The teams split up and wove their way through the city streets. It was nearly dawn, and a radiant sun would soon rise after the night's tropical storm. Dio held onto detachments made up exclusively of soldiers who would deal with the most sensitive objectives, such as the Gendarmerie, the Central Police Station, and Customs House, as well as the departure of the Dibamba ferry from the Wouri to Edéa and to Bonabéri. The unit of gendarmes quickly rallied to *Lieutenant* Quilichini and offered its assistance.[112] The customs officers would be a little trickier because Languilhem, one of their leaders, was a convinced Pétainist. He was, therefore, put under surveillance. The airport was entrusted to *Adjudant Chef* Henri Drouihl, the aviator with four aerial victories during the First World War. The seizure of civilian targets proceeded as planned. The post office was not open yet, and a cordon of *tirailleurs* was set up to prevent its opening. Then the station was occupied and the telephone lines cut.[113] The New Bell radio, the Treasury, and the *Banque de l'Afrique Occidentale*, suffered the same fate. The important services of Water and Forest, Public Works, Public Instruction, Agriculture, and Sleeping Sickness were also soon occupied. Buildings of the city services were also neutralised before they opened. Unlike the delegate of the governor of Douala, the mayor voluntarily rallied to Free France.

A team of military doctors including *Capitaines* Laquintinie and Le Breton was responsible for going to the homes of those known to be in opposition.[114] It was a delicate mission, but it was made easier by the presence of Chadian *tirailleurs*. Those Doualans who opposed Free France lost all desire to resist once they jumped out of bed and saw those giants with *chechias*[115] on their heads. As expected, *Mr* Manger, the head of the *Compagnie Française de l'Afrique Occidentale*, refused his support, but he did not put up any resistance. Only one pro-German businessman tried to sound the alarm, and it went badly for him. Dr Le Breton struck him down with a perfectly aimed blow that broke his jaw.[116] It turned out to be the only act of violence in what Vichy referred to as a coup d'état.

All those in opposition were immediately gathered together in Camp Batchinga and put under guard. They were very quickly repatriated to the *AOF* and then to France. Meanwhile, *Colonel* Leclerc continued to work, settling into the *Palais du Gouvernement*, where he got organised.

---

111 Maya Destrem, *L'Aventure de Leclerc* (Paris: Éditions Fayard, 1984), p.94.

112 Mouchet, *Leclerc*, p.47.

113 Gilberte Grognier, 'Extraits du journal tenu à Douala', *Le Général Leclerc et l'Afrique Française Libre, 1940–1942*, Actes du Colloque International (Paris: Fondation Maréchal Leclerc de Hauteclocque, 1987), document No. 8, p.576.

114 It should be noted that the civil and military health service of Cameroon rallied en masse to Free France, following in the footsteps of the illustrious *Médecin-Général* Adolphe Sicé who would exercise the functions of High Commissioner for Free French Africa in Brazzaville. *Médecin Capitaine* Jean Laquintinie contracted sepsis in Faya-Largeau while operating on the wounded of Kufra and died on 5 March 1941 in Yaoundé. He was made Companion of the Liberation, and the main hospital of Douala still bears his name.

115 A *chechia* is a short, box-like hat from the Maghreb that is similar to a fez, but less rigid. They are worn by *tirailleur* units. (Translator's note)

116 Notin, *le Croisé*, p.78.

Dr Mauzé became his *chef de cabinet*,[117] *Capitaine* Tutenges, his chief of staff. With the help of Gilberte Crognier, whom he recruited as secretary, Leclerc summoned the editor-in-chief of *L'Eveil*, Charles van de Lanoitte. He asked him to put up 300 posters in the city announcing to the population the seizure of power by *'France Combattante'* (Fighting France).[118] Later in the morning, he declared Douala in a state of siege, again with posters. That proclamation ended with *'Vive le Cameroun Libre'* (Long Live Free Cameroon).[119] In his memoirs, de Gaulle summed up this seizure of power with a bit of humour: 'Leclerc, who had become, as if by magic, *colonel* and governor, occupied the Palais du Gouvernement with ease.'[120]

Militarily, two urgent decisions had to be taken. First, the *colonel* asked Tutenges to go to Manoka to contact *Capitaine* Crépin, commander of the coastal battery. Tutenges left along with a European *sergeant* and a combat group. Crépin agreed to rally to Leclerc, with his battery, 'after having granted himself a symbolic period of reflection' to spare his men.[121] Next Leclerc called for *Lieutenant* Quilichini. He asked him to go to Yaoundé to try to convince *Lieutenant Colonel* Bureau to come to Douala. He hoped the task would be eased by the fact that the two men had known each other during their time in Indochina. At the end of the morning, Leclerc gathered the population at the Palais du Gouvernement. Respectful of local customs, Leclerc received traditional leaders and Cameroonian notables, specifically, 'the important leaders Marc Eteme, Paraiso, Bell, Belote Akwa, members of the *JEUCAFRA* [*JEUnesse CAmerounaise FRAnçaise* – French Cameroonian Youth] Paul Soppo Priso, Rodolphe Tokoto, and Ebongue.'[122] At 11:00 a.m., a large crowd formed in front of the building, whites and blacks mixed together. The colourful African crowd came from the neighbourhoods to see 'the man who came from beyond the river,' as they called Leclerc in the Douala dialect. Leclerc delivered a speech in which he, 'invoked the honour of the inhabitants of Cameroon' …. 'Free' Cameroon and gave 'the assurance of the resumption of economic life.'[123]

Meanwhile, *Capitaine* Dio inspected all the points held by his men. He asked them if there were any problems, took necessary corrective measures, and arranged for a rotation of troops.

In the afternoon, Leclerc asked Dio to pick up a challenging visitor arriving from Yaoundé at the New Bell train station. It was Inspector General of the Colonies Huet, commissioned by Vichy to bring Governor Brunot to his senses. Huet had returned from his mission and would then depart Cameroon from Douala on the submarine *Sidi-Ferruch*. *Capitaine* Dio picked him up early in the evening when he got off the train and then escorted him, politely but firmly, to the Palais du Gouvernement to present him to the *colonel*. Huet quickly cut Leclerc off, calling him an adventurer. So, Leclerc sent him to join the other Vichyites at Camp Batchinga on the outskirts of the city.

On Leclerc's orders, *Lieutenant* Quilichini had departed on the afternoon of that eventful 27 August for Ongola la Grande (another name for Yaoundé). Using a *draisine*,[124] it took about five hours to cover the 300km between the cities. It was a delicate mission. Quilichini knew that *Lieutenant Colonel* Bureau, commander of the Cameroonian Police Force, liked him, but it had been several years since they had seen each other. Along the way, Quilichini met the regular train from Yaoundé to Douala that carried Inspector General Huet, but he was unaware that Dio would pick up the high-level official a few hours later at the station.

117 Biwolé, *Le Ralliement*, p.51.
118 Compagnon, *Leclerc*, p.148.
119 Mouchet, *Leclerc*, p.49.
120 Charles de Gaulle, *Mémoires de Guerre. L'Appel, 1940–1942*, (Paris: Éditions Plon, 1961), p.95.
121 Notin, *le Croisé*, p.80.
122 Biwolé, *Le Ralliement*, p.51.
123 Biwolé, *Le Ralliement*, p.52.
124 A *draisine* is a small motor-powered vehicle specially equipped to transport personnel and equipment along a railway. They are mainly used for track maintenance.

Jean Mouchet, the station manager at the Olézoa-Si station at the entrance to Yaoundé, had cut the telephone wires further up the line on the recommendations of young pro-Gaullist officers. Quilichini ditched the draisine at the small station near the Catholic mission, deciding not to take it any further to avoid alerting the Pétainists. Jumping down from the cart, *Lieutenant* Quilichini was surprised to be greeted by a colonial *lieutenant*. His name was Laigret, head of military intelligence on the Yaoundé general staff, and one of the leaders of the opposition to Vichy. After brief introductions, he led Quilichini directly to the chief of police. To maintain secrecy, the meeting was held at the Hôtel Bellevue. 'Who is this Leclerc?' was the first question Bureau asked after listening to the young *lieutenant*.[125] He was intrigued and agreed to go immediately to Douala. Returning to the *draisine*, they left for Douala early that night. Bureau and Quilichini finally arrived at the Palais du Gouvernement at 1:00 in the morning. Before presenting Bureau to Leclerc, Boislambert first received him. With firm cordiality, he explained that if wanted to keep his job, he had only one choice, shocking Bureau with a *fait accompli*. Then he was taken to Leclerc, who also spoke directly. Leclerc told Bureau that the BBC had just announced that Chad had gone over to Free France. Bureau agreed to join the Gaullist cause, 'rather relieved not to have had to make a decision.'[126] He warned Leclerc that the situation in Yaoundé had become tense since Inspector General Huet's departure. He recommended sending troops as quickly as possible to extinguish any plans from among the Vichy supporters. Leclerc told him that a plane would fly over Yaoundé the next day, dropping leaflets.[127] He also informed him that *Capitaine* Dio was relieving his company of *tirailleurs* with local troops in Douala and preparing them for action. The company should be ready to leave the following day by train.

Thus ended this memorable day of 27 August 1940, the true starting point of Leclerc's saga. The fact that it all took place without firing a single shot and without the loss of life makes it all the more extraordinary. The only act of violence of the day was a single punch to control one agitated man. The vast majority of the African and European populations spontaneously joined Free France. Leclerc's seizure of power in Douala has gone down in history as an extraordinary success because of an audacity of action that surprised even Churchill himself. Any time a member of his cabinet advised caution during the war, Churchill never hesitated to recall the example of the 25 men who took Douala and with it, all of Cameroon. With Chad, Cameroon, and soon the Middle Congo to rally to Free France as well,[128] 27 August was the midpoint of what history would call the 'three glorious days of 26, 27, and 28 August' (*Les Trois Glorieuses*).[129] Father Maurice Cordier, who became one of the chaplains of the *2e DB*, knew the men who were involved very well. He summarised 27 August 1940 as:

> …the rallying of Cameroon, given to Leclerc as his first mission, was due to the meeting of two men: it was *Capitaine* Dio, irresistibly seduced by Leclerc's influence, who went with his company to shake the doubt and the apathy of those who hesitated … That instant infatuation was atypical of the future Général Dio.[130]

125   Mouchet, *Leclerc*, p.56.
126   Biwolé, *Le Ralliement*, p.51.
127   Mouchet, *Leclerc*, p.62.
128   From the Belgian Congo, Larminat took power in Brazzaville with the help of Reinforcement Battalion No.4 of the *RTST*, under the command of *Commandant* Delange, which had been stuck there since the beginning of June.
129   In France, *Les Trois Glorieuses* can also refer to the three days of the July Revolution of 1830 that replaced the Bourbon King Charles X with the Orléans King Louis Philippe. (Translator's note)
130   Maurice Cordier and Roger Fouquer, *Le Général Leclerc, ou se Commander à Soi-Même* (Paris: Éditions Desclée de Brouwer, 1990), p.52.

Leclerc would never forget that day of 27 August and he recognised the crucial role played by Dio in the success of this 'coup d'état of Douala,' as de Gaulle would call it in his memoirs. Shortly before his death, Leclerc wrote a letter to Dio, saying 'without him, the 2ᵉ DB would never have existed.'[131]

II, 28 August 1940: Dio's Capture of Yaoundé

Taking Douala was the first step. The economic capital of Cameroon had turned, but Yaoundé, the administrative capital, had yet to join Free France. Leclerc decided to entrust Dio with the mission. Leclerc himself later recounted during a dinner in Sabratha, on 27 June 1943, 'While the arrests continued in Douala, Dio and his company took the train to Yaoundé where Governor Brunot remained undecided.'[132]

On Wednesday, 28 August, Dio urgently set up a marching unit (*unité de marche*) with a substantial backbone of *tirailleurs*, but also integrating as many European commanders as possible. Leclerc asked him to coordinate the whole operation, particularly the neutralisation of the Vichyites to prevent the local situation from degenerating.[133] Dio was unsure what he would find waiting for him in Yaoundé. He wanted to keep control of the situation at all costs, and he had great confidence in his *tirailleurs* and his European cadre. To assist him in his mission, Dio brought along *Capitaine* Gardet and *Lieutenant* Quilichini, departing on a commandeered train late in the morning. He obviously lacked a travel permit, which was usually required because the route was a single track over much of the distance between Douala and Yaoundé. Nevertheless, all went well with the railway officials when the train stopped at the main stations at Edéa and then at Eséka. In the latter station, a reservist *lieutenant* named Raymond Dronne introduced himself and offered his services. Dronne commanded a company of the Cameroon Police Force that was assisting with the construction of the Douala-Yaoundé road. Despite the unit's lack of military training, Dio nevertheless decided to accept the reinforcements. Dronne was quick to get his men on board so they could get the train moving again. Once on board, the men dozed off, lulled by the slow progress of the train as it crossed through the forest.

The train stopped near the small station of Otélé, but rather than moving again after the usual few minutes, it sat still at the station. Something was wrong. The station master, as a diligent public servant, refused to allow the unscheduled train to depart.[134] As he obstinately stood in front of the engine, *Capitaine* Dio had to calm his subordinates who intended to settle the incident rather undiplomatically. With a little trouble and a little firmness, though, they got the train moving again. It was not until the end of the afternoon that the train, crowded with troops, arrived at the small station of Olézoa-Si, three kilometres from the central station of Yaoundé. *Lieutenant* Laigret, the same man who had welcomed *Lieutenant* Quilichini the day before, was waiting on the platform. This time, he was surrounded by about 20 young officers and non-commissioned officers from the garrison who would serve as guides for the arriving troops. They quickly split into different detachments and set off for their objectives. Under *Capitaine* Dio's direction, *Capitaine* Gardet and a reinforced detachment took charge of the military camp while *Lieutenant* Dronne and his company moved into town. The squads set up on the main intersections and deployed their

---

131 This letter was probably destroyed by Dio himself before he died. But before it was destroyed, *Colonel* Robédat, who was very close to Dio, personally read it in Toulon.
132 Girard, *Journal de Guerre*, p.84.
133 Mveng, SJ, *Leclerc au Cameroun*, p.62.
134 Mouchet, *Leclerc*, p.64.

machine guns.[135] As they had done in Douala, they attacked the station, the *Postes, Télégraphes, et Téléphones*, and the Palais du Gouvernement. The chief of police, a notorious Pétainist, was absent, and the police station fell without resistance. *Capitaine* Gardet took a reinforced detachment towards the military camp located on the outskirts of the city, and once he arrived, things moved quickly. The commander of one of the companies in the camp, a *capitaine* named Huet (the same name as the senior Vichy official) immediately offered his service to the Gaullists.[136] Simultaneously, the units that remained hesitant were quickly neutralised because 'Gaullist officers had previously stolen the bolts out of their weapons, rendering them ineffective.'[137] Units that rallied to the Free French then joined in the capture of the key points in the city. Dio, accompanied by Quilichini, moved immediately to the Palais du Gouvernement. He introduced himself and 'made Governor Brunot accept the situation.'[138] The governor, like *Lieutenant Colonel* Bureau, was relieved at the turn of events, and cooperated without qualms. Dio could then subdue the authorities who held Pétainist sentiments. Mayor Guilloux, the administrator of the Yaoundé Chauleur region, and the police commissioner were among them. Dio ordered their capture without violence, which was taken care of during the night.

Faced with the rapid turn of events, the traditional chiefs met at the home of Charles Atangana, senior chief of the Ewondos, the main ethnic group in central Cameroon. It is likely that Dio's knowledge of the importance of chiefdoms in Africa is what led him to go to see them, reassuring them and announcing that Leclerc would arrive in Yaoundé the next day. On 28 August 1940, '*Capitaine* Dio took control of Yaoundé as easily as Leclerc had taken Douala.'[139]

III, 29 August 1940: Leclerc's Arrival in Yaoundé

On the morning of 29 August, the city returned to calm as the military presence in the streets lessened. Everyone seemed relieved. Leclerc could finally arrive on his famous *draisine*. As in Douala, it was tremendously popular, with a crowd waiting for him on the station square. Leclerc did not forget anyone in his thanks, which were particularly aimed at the old wise Cameroonians, the traditional chiefs, who had come to meet him. They joined him immediately. They, too, were fascinated by this man with the steely gaze who pierced the eyes of those who saw him. But above all they wanted to entrust their destiny to Free France, which had rejected the Nazi boot. The Cameroonians knew the Germans, and they knew that indigenous Africans like them were considered *Untermenschen*[140] by the regime in Berlin.

In more good news, the colonial administrators spread throughout the regions were rallying en masse: 'out of forty-eight colonial administrators, heads of the regions of Cameroon, only two of them categorically refused to join.'[141] The vast majority of the local populations followed suit. Dr Chauderon noticed this at the end of August when he was in a small village in the Dschang region in Bamileke country. The interpreter translated the chief's speech as: 'mo docto, when you see 'zénéralé de Gaulle' you tell him that we are all behind him as I am behind you.'[142] At noon on the

---

135   Each of these infantry squads consisted of 10 men led by a *sergent*.
136   Mouchet, *Leclerc*, p.56.
137   Biwolé, *Le Ralliement*, p.55.
138   Victor Giraud, *Leclerc, Maréchal de France* (Éditions Spes: Paris 1952), p.35.
139   Croidys, *Notre second Bayard*, p.66.
140   Subhuman.
141   Biwolé, *Le Ralliement*, p.57.
142   Chauderon, CHETOM, 18H296.

29th, Cameroon had completely rallied to Free France. Those in opposition were neutralised and no longer presented a threat, and so they were allowed to leave the territory.

In less than 72 hours, Cameroon had rallied to Free France without a shot being fired. From London, de Gaulle said only: 'Cameroon has just made a good decision and set a magnificent example. This example will soon be followed by the whole Empire.'[143] With Chad (26 August), the Middle Congo (28 August), and Ubangi-Chari (29 August), de Gaulle had recovered part of the African Empire and gained a starting point for the reconquest. Free France, which was until then only a concept born in London, had become a tangible reality in the eyes of the world, with men and territories. A part of the French Empire had refused to accept the capitulation and answered the call sent out by an unknown *général* on the BBC, exactly 70 days earlier. 'The collective area of those territories was six times the size of metropolitan France.'[144] Magnanimous, the victors allowed those who wanted to leave the territory to sail for metropolitan France or to the *AOF*.

Leclerc, who had appointed himself commander of the troops, was then able to devote himself to his second role, that of governor. In his proclamation of the evening of 29 August, he announced the new path to follow: 'a shared task unites us: all our forces, all our feelings must be concentrated on its realisation.'[145] Leclerc already had his team in mind. Among the soldiers who supported him, there was one who had a special place. It was the great *méhariste*, a man of action rather than words, and a great leader of his men. Leclerc asked *Général* de Gaulle to promote Dio. The two men understood each other at their first meeting, and a deep mutual trust had grown to unite them. Leclerc knew he could count on such an officer and Dio knew that Leclerc was a leader who attracted success. They would be together until the final victory. Dio became the 'constable'[146] of Leclerc. He would be in all the battles to come, and it was to him that Leclerc would entrust his division in the summer of 1945. According to him, no one else could be more worthy of it.

For Cameroonians, the story of Leclerc arriving by river, welcomed by that great silent *méhariste*, and winning over the territory without violence, is mythical or even a miracle. The storytellers with their *mvet*[147] would even set it to music. More than three generations later, traditional Cameroonian folklore, shared over a meal with friends, still recalls 'the man who came from beyond the river.'[148]

---

143 Fonds Leclerc, Charles de Gaulle, Journal Eveil du Cameroun du 7 Sept 1940, boîte U.

144 Croidys, *Notre second Bayard,* p.66.

145 Fond Leclerc, Tutenges.

146 In French, 'constable' (*connétable*) does not imply a police officer, as it might in English. The word derives from the 'count of the stables,' and was the title of the supreme commander of the French Royal Army from the eleventh through to the seventeenth centuries. The *Connétable de France* (Constable of France) served as the lieutenant to the King and was the highest-ranking of the officers of the crown. Dio's position as 'constable of Leclerc,' therefore implies that he was Leclerc's chief subordinate and right-hand-man. (Translator's note)

147 *Mvet* is a seven-stringed lyre.

148 Author's personal experience.

Chapter 2

Gabon,
1 September to 27 November 1940

After all the excitement of the previous days, local society was able to return to its normal routines on Sunday, 1 September 1940. In French Equatorial Africa, Sundays were special, in accordance with the Christian traditions that determined the rhythm of life at the time. Families put on their Sunday clothes and went to church. Men and boys were grouped on the right side of the church, while women, with their daughters and young children, were on the left. They enthusiastically sang Gregorian chants, creating a sort of competition between the two groups. After leaving church, women rushed to their stoves to prepare Sunday lunch, the best meal of the week. Men gathered outside for small group discussions while children played and shouted all around them. It was an opportunity to meet up with friends. On that particular Sunday, there was no rain, which was rare during that period, but the sky was threatening. The humidity was high, and people's clothing was stained with sweat. The rainy season was in full swing.

Capitaine Dio went alone to the cathedral in Douala. Religion was a strictly personal matter for him, and he scrupulously separated the practice of his faith from his professional life. As he left the cathedral, he stopped to pack his pipe with tobacco and observed the mixed society, with whites and blacks united. He realised, ultimately, that the customs in Douala were the same as those back in Vannes. He thought of his mother in Brittany who was surely going through the same ritual on that Sunday morning. At that very moment, she was most certainly at Saint-Pierre Cathedral in Vannes, in the heart of the city on rue Chanoines. He imagined her in the aisle on the right side, near the Sainte-Anne chapel, just beyond the baptismal font. That had been her usual seat ever since she placed Louis under the protection of the patron saint of Brittany. The stained-glass window of the chapel depicts the pilgrimage of Sainte-Anne d'Auray, the most important site of atonement in Brittany. Each year on 26 July, the Feast of Saint-Anne, Madame Dio participated in High Mass followed by the solemn procession of the devotional statue from the basilica to the Breton War Memorial. Sited on a prominent piece of terrain, the memorial was erected in honour of 240,000 Breton soldiers who died in the First World War. Dio's older brother, Daniel, was certainly celebrating mass in the chapel of Saint-Yvi Collège in Pontivy, where he had been a professor of philosophy since 1937.

Dio's thoughts of his native Brittany soon faded, though. As he returned to the Palais de Gouvernement, he reflected on the events of the past few days. He had returned from Yaoundé on Thursday, 29 August, with *Colonel* Leclerc. During the train journey to Douala, the *colonel* had questioned Dio about his availability. Leclerc spoke frankly, looking him straight in the eyes, telling him that he needed officers like him and he wanted him on his team. Naturally, Dio had agreed on the spot. Since their first meeting at Mauzé's, his intuition drove him to follow this *colonel*, in whom he saw a leader. Dio liked *Colonel* Leclerc, with his 'almost unbearable steel blue

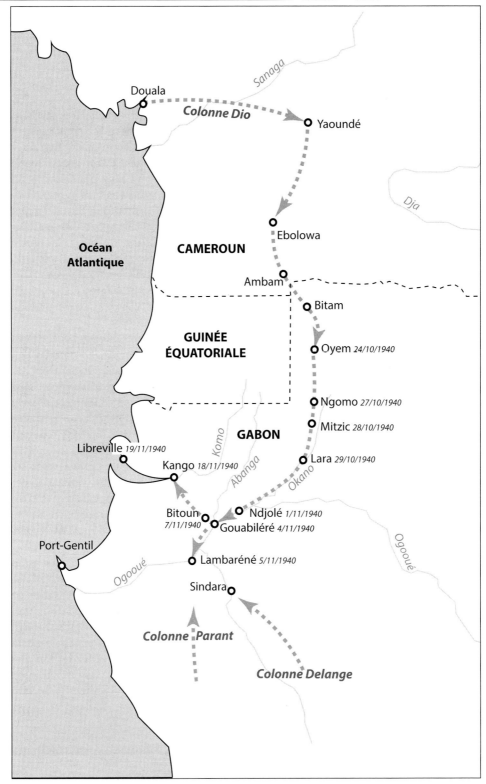

Map 2 The Role of the Column Dio in the Rally of Gabon.

gaze,'[1] especially his determination and his skills of synthesis. Everything was clear and precise with Leclerc. The cavalryman inspired trust from the very beginning, and he was simple and direct. Nor was he motivated by selfishness or personal gain; instead, his actions were always for the common good.

Likewise, Leclerc immediately sensed that the Breton *capitaine* was a reliable and loyal man. He had already tested him twice in Douala and Yaoundé, where he witnessed his effectiveness in action. He knew that he was a leader of men, and it was clear that his subordinates gladly served under his command. Leclerc particularly appreciated the way Dio fulfilled the mission entrusted to him in Yaoundé. Dio left on 28 August, and in less than 24 hours, he brilliantly organised the city's rally to Free France. When he arrived in the capital on 29 August 1940, Leclerc found the situation perfectly managed at all levels. The governor was waiting for him, opponents had been neutralised, the military had rallied en masse, and the traditional leaders had brought the population over to de Gaulle. All of this was accomplished without a single shot fired, just as in Douala. At that point, Leclerc did not yet know the colonial *méharistes* very well, in fact, Dio was the first one he had met. Leclerc was unaware that, in that particular part of the army, the junior officer was alone responsible for managing all issues – military as well as administrative, judicial, and cultural. A great ability to adapt to any situation, combined with razor-sharp relational skills, was the mark of *méhariste* officers. Dio was precisely the officer Leclerc needed, and he wanted to bring him into his circle of trusted individuals. Moreover, he liked Dio's personality – he was a calm and modest officer who was naturally easy to get along with.

Before arriving at the Douala train station, Leclerc instructed Dio to report to his chief of staff, *Capitaine* Tutenges, to be assigned a room. On the afternoon of 30 August, Dio moved into the headquarters of the Cameroonian troops, next to the Palais de Gouvernement. On Saturday 31st, he learnt from *Lieutenant* Maziéras that a message had arrived from Fort-Lamy that morning. Signed by the *RTST* commander, *Colonel* Marchand, it required the 8th Company, which formed the backbone of Dio's Reinforcement Detachment Number 3, to return to Fort Archambault as soon as possible. The Chadian territory was on the front lines, with the Italians to the north and Vichy troops from Niger to the west. A repositioning of military forces within the *RTST* was underway throughout the territory, so Dio understood that it was a reasonable request. The remainder of *Commandant* Parant's Gold Coast battalion (Ghana) had just arrived in Douala. All the French cadre who had joined the British in recent weeks were also returning. Cameroon was by far the most populated of the colonies of the *AEF*. Therefore, there were plenty of leaders and men available. Such not the case in Chad. So, Dio planned to talk to *Colonel* Leclerc the next day to seek permission for *Lieutenant* Maziéras to escort the company to Fort Archambault and rejoin his regiment.[2]

Leclerc called a meeting on Monday, 2 September, asking his chief of staff to gather the key officers at 9:00 a.m. Tutenges informed Dio that the meeting would take place at the Palais du Gouvernement. Leclerc was very busy with his functions as High Commissioner, yet he arrived precisely on time and got straight to the heart of the matter. He began with an update on the situation in the *AEF*. After Chad and Cameroon, Middle Congo rallied on 28 August through the efforts of *Colonel* de Larminat and *Commandant* Delange. Ubangi-Shari, after some reluctance, also finally rallied on 30 August. Unfortunately, the same could not be said for Gabon, the last colony in the *AEF* that had not rallied to Free France. Governor Georges Masson had informed de Gaulle by telegraph on 29 August of his decision to join him. But on 1 September he reversed

---

1   Michel Chauvet, *Le Sable et la Neige, 'Mes Carnets dans la Tourmente,' 1939–1945* (Paris: Éditions du Petit Véhicule, 1996), p.100.

2   This company would form part of the *3e Battalion de Marche*, which would later be engaged in February 1941 in Eritrea and subsequently in Syria and Libya (1942) under Commandant Garbay's command.

his decision and 'declared his attachment to High Commissioner Boisson in Dakar.'[3] This turna-round, Leclerc explained, was certainly due to pressure exerted by Vichy on the governor. In fact, Air Force *Lieutenant Général* Tétu and several Glenn Martin bombers had just arrived in Libreville from Dakar, as well as the submarine *Poncelet*, the dispatch vessel *Bougainville*, and the banana boat *Cap des Palmes* carrying two companies of Senegalese *tirailleurs*.[4]

If Gabon, sitting in the heart of the *AEF*, remained loyal to Vichy, it would constitute an unacceptable threat to Free French forces, particularly with the presence of the port and the Libreville airfield. 'Gabon was an abscess that needed to be lanced, no matter how painful the operation might be.'[5] Leclerc told the assembled group that operations against Gabon would have to be carried out soon. Général de Gaulle would make the decision. He explained that the purpose of the meeting was to consider what initial measures they needed to take – to be ready – if the leader of Free France asked them to fight in future battles. The *colonel* reminded them that many Europeans in the territory wanted to fight and 'let their weapons speak.' In response to that expectation, Leclerc had given his tentative agreement to the creation of a legion of volunteers from Cameroon as soon as he arrived.[6] But the *colonel* was aware that the meagre structure was insufficient for the future battles that would have to be fought across the African Continent.[7] He invited the participants to share their ideas on a possible future military organisation for Cameroon. One officer pointed out that the status of the police forces in Cameroon was regulated by the League of Nations, which prohibited any military use. Leclerc retorted that Cameroon was at war and that it was no longer bound by peacetime rules. Another officer then proposed that they set up a military unit from the existing police and indigenous guard units. He pointed out that their leadership was composed of cadre from the colonial troops. It would be quite easy to group them together to form a regiment. Leclerc approved of the idea. He added that in terms of resources, there were already 'external' units that had just arrived, not to mention the numerous reservists available. One of the participants then suggested that a historical unit of Cameroon be recreated, referring to the *Régiment de Tirailleurs Sénégalais du Cameroun*, which was created in 1915 and then disbanded in 1925. Leclerc thought it was a great idea but asked that the designation 'Senegalese' be removed from the historical title. The new unit would therefore be called the *Régiment de Tirailleurs du Cameroun (RTC)*.[8] Leclerc, as usual, wasted no time and signed the order creating the *RTC* the same day.[9]

---

3   Compagnon, *Leclerc*, p.169.
4   Larminat, *Chroniques,* p.195.
5   Dronne, *Carnets de Route,* p.49.
6   Marcel Poualion, son of Maurice Poualion, had his father's 'act of voluntary enlistment to the *Légion du Cameroun*,' dated 27 August, on which he registered under number 30. In the enlistment, he 'solemnly undertakes to serve Free France, free from any constraint, to carry out all the missions entrusted to me, to fight with all the allies of Free France, against all its enemies until final victory.'
7   The *Légion des Volontaires* consisted of 3 platoons: (1) an active platoon with volunteers under 43 living in Douala who could devote at least a third of their time; (2) a reserve platoon capable of reinforcing the active platoon in the event of a military operation (3) a propaganda platoon. The leader chosen was *Capitaine* Haugou. The *Légion* would always remain limited both in quality and size. Personnel from the active platoon would later reinforce the military units engaged in Gabon in October and November 1940. Subsequently, several non-commissioned officers left to be integrated into Leclerc's units or into the Free French *Battalions de Marche*. (Taken from *Cameroun Libre*, 21 September 1940.)
8   Part of the *RTC* would be committed to Gabon in the coming weeks. Subsequently, it served primarily as the training body of numerous Free French *Battalions du Marche* (*BM4*, *BM5*, and *BM9*), and participated in the establishment of *BM13* and *BM14*. It was a very important role for Free France. It was dissolved at the end of 1945, its mission complete. The unit insignia for the *RTC* was produced in 1942 and bears the motto '*j'y suis, j'y reste*' (I'm here, I'm staying here), in memory of Leclerc's statement on 27 August at Mauzé's house. R. Villeminey and J. J. Marquet, *Insignes et Historiques des Formations Indigènes de l'Infanterie Coloniale* (Château-Chinon: Presses de l'Établissement d'Impression de l'Armée de Terre, 2004), pp.164–165.
9   Biwolé, *Le Ralliement,* p.83.

Dio had not said a word, so before closing the meeting, Leclerc asked for his opinion. Dio responded that the organisation of the *RTST* in Chad could serve as a model for the *RTC*, and that he was ready to assist those assigned responsibility for the new unit. He pointed out that it would be necessary to quickly establish a training centre in Cameroon so that the instruction provided would be uniform and focused solely on military skills.[10] Dio concluded by asking the *colonel* if he could see him privately after the meeting. Leclerc ended the meeting and, while the two walked to Leclerc's office, he listened as Dio told him of the *RTST*'s request to recall the 8th Company. Leclerc quickly agreed to return the unit to Fort Archambault as soon as possible. As Dio left the Palais du Gouvernement, he thought he would be working on the reorganisation of Cameroonian military forces. However, that would not be the case; Leclerc had not yet read Dio's evaluation, but he sensed that he was not suited for paperwork. The situation in Gabon weighed heavily on him. Leclerc did not like being forced into reacting to circumstances, always wanting to take the initiative instead. Therefore, things were about to move very quickly for Dio.

What did Gabon represent in 1940? With an area of 267,000 square kilometres, about half the size of metropolitan France, the little-known colony was particularly underpopulated. Out of a population of only 350,000 inhabitants, the majority lived near the sea, in Libreville and Port-Gentil.[11] Disease, ethnic conflict, and a difficult geographic environment were all obstacles to population growth. For a long time, foresters said that while crossing through Gabon, there was twice as much chance of encountering an assala elephant as a man.[12]

In early September 1940, *Colonels* de Larminat and Leclerc consulted with each other. They decided to launch exploratory detachments on the access routes leading to Libreville. There were two possibilities to reach Lambaréné and then Libreville by land:

- In the north, coming from Cameroon, a vehicular route to Mitzic, and then a forest trail to Lambaréné via N'Djolé.
- In the south, starting from Dolisié in the Middle Congo, a vehicular route towards Fougamou and Sindara, and then forest trails to Lambaréné.

As Larminat later explained:

Initially our plan was to rally through persuasion. Our detachments pushed forward. When they encountered a post, they negotiated and tried to convince. The leaders on both sides were young officers, often classmates, who more or less knew each other, and were ultimately driven by the same feelings. If the opponent resisted, we deployed our force to the point where we could act decisively. At that moment, the stupidity of the situation became apparent – Frenchmen fighting each other because some wanted to fight Hitler and others blindly obeyed instructions that they didn't agree with. It was beyond common sense.[13]

---

10   The training camp was set up very quickly. It was located 80 kilometres from Yaoundé, on the right bank of the River Sanaga, a location chosen by *Capitaine* Dronne with the assistance of *Médecin Capitaine* Chauderon, the former doctor of Dio's Reinforcement Detachment Number 3. The concern at the time was to find a location that offered protection from the tsetse fly, which carries the terrible sleeping sickness. The camp, officially opened in February 1941, and was named Camp d'Ornano in homage to the man who had just given his life in Murzuk. Chauderon, CHETOM, 18H296, dossier 2.

11   Larminat, *Chroniques*, p.192.

12   Assala is the local name given to the elephants that inhabit the forests of Gabon. They are characterised by their small size and solitary nature. Very well adapted to the environment, this species survives more easily than the savannah elephant because it is protected by the forest.

13   Larminat, *Chroniques*, p.193.

On 3 September Leclerc again gathered the military leaders of the territory. Dio was back in the same meeting room as the day before. The *colonel* explained that in coordination with Brazzaville, they would act in Gabon. It was not an act of war but rather 'attempts to rally [the population] on the periphery of Gabon.'[14] The goal was to persuade young officers serving in the territory. The recent events in Yaoundé and Brazzaville encouraged them to initially prioritise that approach. Then Leclerc assigned missions. He appointed Dio to establish a small battalion-sized marching unit to penetrate into Gabon through Cameroon.[15] '*Capitaine* Dio, who was unperturbed by any extraordinary task, and who was surrounded by a legend of bravery in Chad, found it natural that Leclerc would send him to conquer Gabon, which had remained attached to France since the armistice.'[16] *Capitaine* Dio had to move quickly to create the marching unit he would lead. The 'indigenous guard' forces scattered throughout the territory would be regrouped and trained for military operations. As a result, they could not be immediately engaged in Gabon. He decided to use the militia battalion, which had one company in Douala and two companies in Yaoundé. For the time being, Dio kept the 'militia' structures within the marching unit, so that it would be available for immediately action in Gabon.

In addition to that detachment, Dio received the brand-new platoon of the *Légion des Volontaires du Cameroun*. But he was unsure whom he should assign to command it. The solution presented itself on 4 September. That morning, *Lieutenant* Maziéras arrived at the Palais du Gouvernement, where Dio had set up a small command post. Dio saw Maziéras approach and salute him. "Not leaving yet, *lieutenant?*" he asked. "No, *mon capitaine*, we're having some difficulties gathering the trucks necessary for the return to Fort Archambault." he replied. Then, continued, "Besides, I've come because I don't want to leave any longer." Dio immediately raised his head, nervously exhaled a puff of pipe smoke, and interrogated him with his gaze, "I want to stay with you, sir.... I found a volunteer officer to escort the company back to Chad." Initially, Dio was irritated to have to reconsider what he had already decided with Leclerc. But at the same time, he was touched by this gesture of loyalty from the *lieutenant* with whom he had worked so closely during the last five months. "You're pissing me off, Maziéras! Get the company ready to depart. I'll give you an answer tomorrow. Dismissed."

The *lieutenant* knew his *capitaine* well, and he could see in his eyes that there was hope for a positive answer that was hidden by Dio's words. Maziéras left with confidence. And indeed, the next day, Dio appointed him to command the platoon of the *Légion des Volontaires du Cameroun*. He also immediately decided to place a company in Ambam, a village near the border with Gabon to avoid any surprises, since the intentions of the Vichy forces in Libreville were still unknown. Dio sent the 6th Company of the militia from Cameroon, under the command of *Lieutenant* Liurette, to Ambam without delay. Its mission was to emplace a platoon of 30 men on the N'Tem, the river that delineates the border between Cameroon and Gabon, to monitor any activity to the south. They crossed the river by ferry. In the following days, the 7th Company of the militia, under the command of *Lieutenant* Bertaut, was positioned in Ebolowa, the area just beyond Ambam. Leclerc's first phase of the plan, called 'Preliminary Actions,' could then start.[17] From southern Cameroon, the plan consisted of carrying out three successive preliminary actions to gather information on the Vichy units positioned in the northern region of Gabon and to sound out the leaders

---

14   Compagnon, *Leclerc*, p.169.
15   A *unité de marche* is a provisional unit created from available units for a specific and temporary task (a task force, in English). It is formed by pulling men from other units to accomplish the specific task. (Translator's note)
16   Croidys, *Notre second Bayard*, p.67.
17   *FFL: Note du commandement militaire du Cameroun Français/ 3° bureau n°74/3 'opérations menées en zone forestière par les troupes du Cameroun signée Lieutenant-Colonel de Tournadre, Commandant militaire.'*

of those units. They were not acts of force, but rather 'political' actions that took place between 5 and 17 September.

On 5 and 6 September, *Lieutenant* Liurette was sent into Gabon to make contact with Vichy forces that might be there. He was alone in his vehicle, but accompanied by the civil administrator, Allouard, Chief of the Ambam subdivision. He went twice to Bitam, a Gabonese village about 10 kilometres from the border and adjacent to Ambam on the Cameroonian side. It was there that *Capitaine* Gourvez, commander of the 2nd Company of the *Bataillon de Tirailleurs du Gabon* (*BTG*), had established his command post. Gourvez suggested that he and his unit might potentially join the Free French, and he authorised the two men to travel the roads freely. From 9 to 13 September, *Commandant* Gardet, commander of the 2nd Battalion of the *RTC* and commander of the garrison in Yaoundé, was ordered to continue the persuasion operation to rally as many Vichy units as possible. On 9 September, he left Yaoundé by car, without troops. On the 10th, he picked up *Lieutenant* Liurette and Administrator Allouard along the way. In Bitam, *Capitaine* Gourvez remained undecided. However, *Lieutenant* Lamour, the company's second in command, pledged his support for Free France. The NCOs appeared indifferent, waiting to follow their leader's orders. Gardet was authorised to go to the provincial capital, Oyem, which he reached at 9:00 p.m. Then he tried, unsuccessfully, to contact Administrator Brizon. He finally met him on the 11th, continuing his progress towards Mitzic. But Brizon flatly refused any allegiance to Free France, even giving orders to 'cut off all communication north and south of Oyem.' Consequently, *Commandant* Gardet's vehicle was stopped at a roadblock of felled trees 48km north of Mitzic. He asked the detachment protecting the roadblock if he could meet with their *capitaine*, *Capitaine* Baylon, who commanded the 1st Company of the *BTG* at Mitzic. However, Baylon 'refused to rally to Free France until the military commander of Gabon, *Commandant* Raunier, either rallied or was arrested.'[18] So, *Commandant* Gardet was forced to retrace his steps to Oyem.

On 12 September, Gardet rallied the entire population of the town. He relieved Administrator Brizon[19] of his duties and replaced him with a reserve *capitaine* named Martocq. Taking advantage of *Capitaine* Gourvez's understanding, and with the cooperation of *Lieutenant* Lamour, he brought in a combat group from Ambam from Liurette's company to hold the capital. Then *Commandant* Gardet returned to Cameroon. He met *Capitaine* Dio at the Eking ferry and updated him on his activities of the past two days. Dio was then tasked with carrying out the third phase of Leclerc's Preliminary Actions Plan. From 11 to 16 September, Leclerc ordered Dio to carry out a political-military operation similar to the previous two.[20] The only difference being that he would be accompanied by a detachment of 30 legionnaires from Cameroon commanded by *Lieutenant* Maziéras (whose continued service Dio easily obtained from Leclerc). The first two persuasion operations had established contacts, provided knowledge of the position of the opposing camp, and had taken the capital of Oyem. Dio had to try to go at least as far as N'Djolé, and if possible, as far as Lambaréné, using persuasion. But, if necessary, he might also have to use a little coercion in the form of his troops.[21] In coordination with a column leaving from Middle Congo, the ultimate objective was to rally the troops in Lambaréné to the Gaullist cause. It would then be possible to

---

18   *FFL*, Tournadre.

19   Brizon eventually joined Free France in mid-September, once he had crossed into Cameroon.

20   Dio's service record (*L'État Signalétique des Services*) establishes the beginning of his engagement in the Gabonese campaign as 9 September 1940. SHD, Dossier Louis Dio, 14 Yd 1759.

21   The distance from Bitam (Gabonese border post) to N'Djolé (first objective assigned to Dio) is 520km. Along the route, Oyem is at kilometre 100 then Mitzic at kilometre 220. From N'Djolé, Lambaréné can be reached by the Ogooué River over a distance of 100km.

invest Libreville by land to compel Governor Masson and *Général* Tétu to abandon their ambition of keeping Gabon in the hands of the Pétainists.[22]

In Bitam, Gourvez's company of the *Bataillon de Tirailleurs du Gabon* continued to hold the crossing points, keeping the ferries operational at Eking, Kye, and Meyo. The provincial capital of Oyem had been reached, its administrator neutralised and replaced. However, the 1st Company of the *BTG* under *Capitaine* Baylon was still blocking the road to Mitzic. On 12 September, Dio arrived in Bitam and had a serious discussion with Gourvez. Dio knew how to be persuasive with his comrade. The report states that he 'strengthened the position taken by *Capitaine* Gourvez to rally [to Free France].' Following the meeting, his company definitively switched to the Gaullist camp. Dio and Maziéras continued their progress southward and passed Oyem. At 10:00 p.m., they were stopped by the same roadblock that *Commandant* Gardet had found 48km north of Mitzic. It had been reinforced to a depth of over two kilometres and was held by a detachment under the command of *Sergent Chef* Bardet. During the night, Dio ordered his personnel to destroy the obstacle with axes and saws. Faced with such determination, the *sergent chef* retreated before dawn. On the morning of 13 September, progress could resume.

Dio sped up his small detachment because he realised that *BTG* units to his front were trying to destroy the bridges north of Mitzic. His acceleration prevented them from carrying out their mission, and they retreated in the face of the Free French advance. On the outskirts of Mitzic, a 'monumental wooden barrier' had been erected, with a platoon of *fusiliers-voltigeurs* to defend it.[23] Dio contacted *Capitaine* Baylon, whom he knew from their time together as classmates at the military academy of Saint-Cyr. The two officers spoke for three hours until they reached an arrangement between old friends from the Pol Lapeyre promotion.[24] Baylon agreed not to oppose Dio's progress to N'Djolé and back, and he reiterated his promise to rally as soon as his superior was arrested. Baylon believed the cause of Free France was just, but he would not disobey his leader as long as that leader remained the legitimate authority. His sentiment is a good illustration of the intellectual and moral complexity experienced by some officers at the time.

Colonne Dio resumed progress and continued during the night of 13/14 September. Despite further obstacles, the column captured the ferry 28km from Mitzic before it could be destroyed, and then after crossing the gap, got back on the trail heading south. On the morning of 14 September, the convoy arrived at a bridge under repair, guarded by a platoon under the command of *Lieutenant* Hervouet. N'Djolé was only 30km away to the southwest. *Capitaine* Dio boldly decided to impose himself on the young *lieutenant*, who was impressed by the tone of his voice, his appearance, and his arguments. Dio asked him to go to N'Djolé and to bring him back information on the situation there. Despite his opposition to Free France, Hervouet obeyed. When he returned, he told *Capitaine* Dio that N'Djolé was held by *Lieutenant* Duvauchelle's platoon, which had come from Libreville and was reinforced by 16 local guards. Hervouet warned him not to expect any kind of allegiance. Nevertheless, Dio continued on his way. The bluff worked.

Upon arriving in N'Djolé, *Capitaine* Dio's small column realised that the platoon had retreated. They found themselves on the banks of the Ogooué, a tumultuous river that crosses Gabon from

---

22   Georges Masson, Governor of Gabon since August 1938, initially pledged his allegiance to Free France, but switched to Vichy under pressure from the influential Apostolic Vicar Louis Tardy and a good part of the European community. After agreeing to mediate the negotiations between the two camps during the surrender of the territory, he killed himself on the ship taking him back to France.

23   FFL, Tournadre.

24   Since 1829, graduating classes (referred to as 'promotions') at Saint-Cyr have adopted a name, which often comes from a battle or a famous Frenchman. Dio and Baylon were in Saint-Cyr's 113th Promotion (1926–1928), named for *Lieutenant* Pol Lapeyre of the *5e Régiment de Tirailleurs Sénégalais*, who was killed in the Moroccan Rif War in 1925. (Translator's note)

east to west and allows easy access to the city of Lambaréné. Large barges normally used for transporting goods were available; however, it was raining and visibility was almost zero. After considering it, Dio abandoned his plan to go to Lambaréné. He lacked the manpower to subdue a garrison that included several combat platoons, while he only had one. He settled on the left bank of the Ogooué and planned to hold the position, which would serve as a starting point for future action against Lambaréné. After a night of reflection, he realised that this was not a good plan either. He did not have the means to hold an isolated post 520 kilometres from the Cameroonian border. Where would he find food, not to mention ammunition if he had to engage in combat? Considering everything, he was in a bad position because the Mitzic company had still not joined him. He feared that his old Saint-Cyr comrade would receive firm orders from Libreville. So, he decided to fall back to Oyem to establish his forward base. Even though his temperament pushed him forward, *Capitaine* Dio always took time to reflect before acting. On 15 September, he got the column back on the road, and headed in the opposite direction. He crossed the *BTG*'s position near Mitzic without difficulty, and the convoy reached Oyem in the afternoon of 16 September.

Dio and his men were exhausted after five busy days in the forest with short nights of sleep. But two items of good news awaited them: A platoon of the *BTG*, consisting of 20 men from Libreville led by *Lieutenant* Buttin, had joined Free France, and had arrived in Bitam the day before. The second was the arrival of the first detachment of the 8th Company of the militia, composed of 40 *tirailleurs* under the orders of the colonial administrator, Reserve *Lieutenant* Raymond Dronne. The new arrivals would allow Dio to strengthen the defence of Oyem and thus have a solid advanced base in Gabonese territory.

With that, the preliminary action phase came to an end, and the result was generally positive. They had made important contacts and identified the necessary interlocutors. Half the opposing force had rallied. Reconnaissance missions conducted to just outside N'Djolé had gained valuable knowledge of the terrain with which they could plan future manoeuvres. In his report to Leclerc, Dio emphasised the difficulties ahead. He drew the *colonel*'s attention to the fact that the terrain favoured the side on the defensive. The numerous waterways blocking the route deep into Gabon would be difficult obstacles to overcome given the weak and antiquated means available. If the crossing sites were defended with force, progress would be delayed even more. After Mitzic, the roads diminished into a simple forest trail. Additionally, the rainy season was in full force, so movement would be particularly difficult and slow. After letting Dio speak, the *colonel* informed him that the Middle Congo had also dispatched a column, under the command of *Commandant* Parant, that was moving by foot towards Lambaréné. On 15 September, the column had managed to seize Mayumba by surprise. The Vichy military command in Gabon was outraged by all the movements in Gabonese territory and considered them as acts of war.

Leclerc had already planned the next phase of the operations but needed de Gaulle's agreement to take forceful action. Consequently, he asked Dio to prepare a detachment to be able, on order, to carry out an offensive operation in Gabon. The objective was to capture Lambaréné by conducting a coordinated pincer action with Parant's column advancing from the Middle Congo. Once they broke through the lock of Lambaréné, the two columns could then attack Libreville. Leclerc also approved of Dio pre-positioning the detachment in Oyem.

At the same time, Leclerc asked Dio to take protective measures against Spanish Guinea to avoid any surprises. Indeed, the military intelligence section[25] in Brazzaville had reported that Spanish Guinea could become a threat to Free French troops positioned in the north of Gabon. Vichy and Madrid might potentially have signed agreements. There was a potential that enemy troops, including Germans, could land in Bata, the capital of the small Spanish colony. Leclerc

---

25   Also called the S2 or 2nd Section (*2e bureau*).

did not seem to believe in the threat but still asked Dio to take appropriate measures. Dio felt honoured to receive his orders directly from Leclerc and to have been chosen for the complex mission. He would be in command of a combined arms battalion, despite being only a *capitaine*. Dio had only one objective in mind: to prove himself worthy of the trust that Leclerc had shown him by appointing him to such a command.

Dio returned immediately to Ambam, the last Cameroonian village before the border with Gabon, where he set up his command post. His first decision was to establish a defensive position facing Spanish Guinea. Waterways were the main infiltration routes in that forested region. At the north-eastern border of Guinea, two major rivers caught his attention, the N'Tem and the Kye. The rivers were possible infiltration routes into southern Cameroon and northern Gabon where his troops were stationed. As a result, he organised a defensive system consisting of two lines. He had the 2nd Company of the *BTG*, which had joined him a few days earlier and was commanded by *Lieutenant* Lamour, but he wanted to avoid that company from having to engage other units of the *BTG*. In addition, the 6th Company of the Cameroonian militia under *Lieutenant* Liurette and the *Groupe Franc* of the *Légion des Volontaires du Cameroun*, under the command of the faithful *Lieutenant* Maziéras, would complement the defence system.[26] The first line would consist of outposts responsible for monitoring the infiltration routes coming from Spanish Guinea. The second line, called the 'line of resistance,' would consist of blocking positions designed to halt any progress. To reinforce the line of resistance, 100 workers assigned to Dio carried out extensive terrain defence work construction during the stationary period.

Leclerc came to see Dio, and then wrote to Boislambert on 21 September: 'Dio is facing major difficulties but manoeuvring well. There are about 200 Germans now in Spanish Guinea. You can see that the situation continues to be challenging.'[27] While the defensive works were being carried out, Dio formed and assembled the future *batallion de marche* that was planned to attack Lambaréné and then Libreville. The initial attack position for the detachment would be north of Oyem, in Gabonese territory. The detachment would be composed of:

A command element: Dio selected *Lieutenant* Buttin, promoted to *capitaine* on 25 September, as his deputy.[28] Buttin had come from Libreville and would be useful due to his knowledge of the territory. Radio contact would be maintained through an ER 26 (radio transmitter-receiver, model 26), which could reach Douala or Brazzaville, even from the heart of the thick virgin forest.

The 4th Militia Company with three platoons of *fusiliers-voltigeurs*,[29] under the command of *Lieutenant* Bruzeaux, with *Lieutenant* Bonnet as his deputy.

A detachment from the 6th Militia Company with two platoons, under the command of *Lieutenant* Liurette, assisted by the veterinarian *Sous Lieutenant* Mandon.

A detachment from the 14th Company (formerly the 8th Company) under *Lieutenant* Dronne, with *Lieutenant* Schrimpf as his deputy, consisting only of a reinforced platoon.

The *Groupe Franc* of the *Légion des Volontaires du Cameroun*, commanded by *Lieutenant* Maziéras.

---

26   The *Groupe Franc de la Légion des Volontaires du Cameroun* consisted of a 30-man platoon.
27   In a handwritten letter: Biwolé, *Le Ralliement*, p.82.
28   ESS (*État signalétique des services*) Buttin, archives privées.
29   The old names of the 'police forces' of Cameroon are used here although the *1er RTC* was officially created on 10 October in Douala during a large ceremony presided over by de Gaulle, which included an official presentation of colours.

In total, the detachment included 68 Europeans, 350 indigenous soldiers, and 100 labourers required for the defensive phase. The labourers would be replaced by 300 indigenous porters at the beginning of the offensive phase.[30] Nearly 40 trucks were mobilised for the movement to Mitzic. Beyond that, progress by motor vehicle would quickly become impossible, so they would have to dismount and continue on foot, in single file (*en colonne*). That is why the designation used in official reports for the battalion that left Cameroon was *Colonne Dio*. *Lieutenant* Dronne described his commander, *Capitaine* Dio, saying at that time,

> The first impression he gave was that of a gruff-looking adventurer. His language was coarse. Instead of a cane, he carried a thick, short cudgel made from the trunk of a coffee tree with carved figurines at one end – a fine example of indigenous art.[31] He had an irreverent motto: 'No mercy for the balls.' I quickly realised, though, that this rough exterior concealed a heart of gold, with a lot of sensitivity and refinement. The Breton *capitaine* was a sincere Christian (his brother was a 'rector' somewhere in his native Brittany); he neither hid nor flaunted his convictions; he simply lived them. He was a warrior, trained in the austere school of the Saharan *méharistes*, and therefore not very talkative. Once you got to know him, you felt a connection and esteem for him. He was a bit like a prickly pear, which hides soft flesh under a spiky exterior.[32]

Dronne's beautiful metaphor is a perfect description of the complexity of Dio's character. Dio was 32 years old, still young. Like everyone else, he would grow, but one trait that would not change was his sense of humour. He loved making jokes and puns and tricking others with a confusing demeanour. His playful side remained with him throughout his career.

On 24 September, Dio informed Leclerc that he was ready to move towards Lambaréné when ordered. However, he also pointed out the weaknesses of his detachment. It was made up solely of infantry who lacked combat experience, and its commanders were young officers, some of whom were reservists. The companies were under the command of *lieutenants* rather than *capitaines*, as called for in regulations. Furthermore, he lacked supporting troops: he had no artillery to support the infantry's manoeuvres, nor engineers to assist in crossing the rivers. He also lacked reconnaissance and liaison elements. Finally, there was no medical support. Dio concluded his brief assessment by making several requests for reinforcements. *Colonel* Leclerc, recognising the validity of the requests, promised to do his best to assist him.

While awaiting the order to begin the attack, Dio ordered intense training for his troops. The militia troops had to quickly become regular riflemen. The focus was on marksmanship and basic platoon-level manoeuvres for two types of tactics: secure forward movement and reduction of isolated resistance. Dio's deputy, *Capitaine* Buttin, was personally responsible for the training. Buttin knew that the only way to prepare the troops was constant drill. The scenarios were repeated over and over again until actions became reflexive, everyone executing their part mechanically.

It was also important to realise that the Gabonese equatorial forest was a very difficult and demanding environment for conducting operations. For *Général* de Larminat, 'the oppression of the great forest .... is much more difficult than the Saharan desert, more debilitating and nerve-wracking.'[33] The stifling heat, day and night, combined with persistent humidity, lack of sunlight

---

30 Workers and porters were provided by the villages to develop the land or carry loads and were paid for their work.
31 Dio described this stick in an article he wrote in 1949 for *Caravane* No. 89, April 1949, p.14. According to him, Leclerc did not have a cane when he arrived in Douala. Copying the custom of British officers, Dio offered him 'a stick of my making, made from a coffee plant, with polished and regular knots.' This anecdote illuminates the attachment that already existed between the two officers at that time. Having lost the stick shortly after, Leclerc bought a simple cane in a shop in Douala.
32 Dronne, *Carnets de route*, pp.50–51.
33 Larminat, *Chroniques*, p.191.

under the canopy, aggressive fauna, including insects and mosquitoes, and the constant noise quickly took a toll on morale. The ground was like a sponge with mud that clung to feet, making movement challenging. The dangerous marsh called *poto-poto* could swallow an entire vehicle. Numerous rivers served as obstacles to progress. Bridges were rare, and crossings usually made by ferry.

Meanwhile, events taking place thousands of kilometres away in another theatre of operations had a direct impact on Dio's battalion. On 23 September, de Gaulle was defeated in Dakar. A Free French expeditionary force led by de Gaulle, with the support of the Royal Navy and consisting of 2,000 men, attempted to land in Dakar. The Vichy navy and the Governor of French West Africa, Boisson, repelled them with artillery fire. This 'rejection of the Appeal of 18 June' significantly delayed Leclerc's planned offensive in Gabon.[34] Shaken by the failure in Senegal, de Gaulle had no intention of repeating it in Gabon. The leader of Free France, still in shock, arrived in Douala by boat on 8 October. Leclerc welcomed him as he stepped off the gangway of the Free French ship *Commandant Duboc*. Fortunately, the enthusiasm shown by the indigenous Gabonese population towards de Gaulle boosted the morale of the '*l'Homme du 18 Juin*'.[35] Leclerc accompanied him on his tour throughout Cameroon and Chad.

As a result, the Gabon operation temporarily took a back seat. However, Leclerc quickly finessed it back to the forefront. With the help of Larminat, who sent telegrams from Brazzaville also encouraging action in Gabon, Leclerc gradually convinced de Gaulle to consider that a Vichy territory in the heart of Free French Africa was unacceptable. Leclerc tried to persuade him to approve the advance of the two columns from Cameroon and Middle Congo. In fact, that plan had already been in progress since mid-September, when Dio and Parant entered Gabon. De Gaulle was not best pleased to learn that the columns were already moving, because he felt like his hand was being forced. However, Leclerc finally persuaded de Gaulle to order the attack at the end of October. Compagnon wrote, '... upon arriving in Cameroon on 5 October .... de Gaulle realised that Leclerc already had elements under Dio's command engaged in the north of Gabon. His choice and decision were therefore not entirely free, and it was with reluctance that he decided to carry out the operation.'[36]

The additional month of delay allowed Dio's battalion to complete its tactical training and raise its operational proficiency. It also afforded Dio an opportunity to strengthen the battalion. De Gaulle landed in Douala with an expeditionary force of nearly 2,000 men (some with experience in the Norwegian campaign), with weapons and equipment.[37] Dio's personnel requests could therefore be partially fulfilled from those troops. *Colonne Dio* received various reinforcements throughout the month of October. The first to arrive, around 10 October, was the medical team under *Médecin Lieutenant* Orsini. He and his small team of medics and five ambulances would provide medical support to the detachment. A group of vehicles from Support Company Number 2, under the command of *Lieutenant* Soulé-Susbielle, including a 37mm gun and two 81mm mortars, led by Sergent Peschaud,[38] joined Dio around 20 October.[39] Next, a motorcycle detach-

---

34   Notin, *le Croisé*, p.85.

35   Ever since de Gaulle's Appeal of 18 June 1940, over BBC radio from London, he has been known as *l'Homme du 18 Juin*' (the Man of 18 June). (Translator's note)

36   Compagnon, *Leclerc*, p.605.

37   The corps was composed of Colonel Monclar's *1er Régiment de la Légion Étrangère* (French Foreign Legion), the *14th Demi-brigade de la Légion Étrangère*, a battalion of marine riflemen, a company of tanks, and units of engineers and artillery.

38   Mobilised in French Cameroon in 1940, Philippe Peschaud 'deserted' to the British. As a non-commissioned officer, he joined *Colonne Dio* in Gabon as chief of the mortar section. After an internship at the Colonna d'Ornano Military School in Brazzaville, he was assigned as an *aspirant* in Chad in April 1942. He served in traffic control within the *2e DB*. He later followed Leclerc to Indochina and became the very capable president of the *Association de la Maison des Anciens de la 2e DB* (2nd Armoured Division Association) from 1967 to 1998.

39   Some works mention the presence of a 75mm artillery battery under the orders of *Capitaine* Laurent Champrozay. Note 74/3 contains no mention of such a unit. We do not accept its presence for two reasons:

ment from the Foreign Legion consisting of 15 motorcycles, a sidecar, and a 3-ton truck, under *Adjudant* Tartière, joined the column on 28 October.[40] Finally, a platoon of tanks[41] commanded by *Lieutenant* Volvey from the *1ʳᵉ Compagnie de Chars de Combat* was scheduled to reinforce the column later. Dio was glad to have the mortars, which could support the infantry if necessary, and also the engineers to assist his force in the difficult movement. The motorcycles could provide him with a fast means of transportation and for scouting. Before launching into the deep Gabonese forest where the column would quickly become isolated, the medical support was crucial. Dio was, however, a bit more sceptical of the ability of the tanks to operate in the terrain they would have to move through.

On 24 October 1940, *Capitaine* Dio received the order to advance. His assembly area was in the Oyem region. Faced with the threat posed by Spanish Guinea, he left only the company from the *BTG*, which allowed him to pick up the two platoons of *Lieutenant* Liurette's 6th Company, which were on surveillance duty on the border with Guinea.

Note 74/3 from the operations section of the Military Command of French Cameroon on 21 April 1941, signed by *Lieutenant-Colonel* de Tournadre, allows us to trace the daily actions of *Colonne Dio*,[42] which have previously been either unknown or little known. Therefore, the text of the note is presented here in italics. When necessary, it is followed by additional explanations that illustrate the difficulty of the tasks that Dio and his column would have to accomplish.

> **24 October 00:00:** *depart from Oyem in trucks towards Mitzic (116km)*
> - *35km north of Mitzic, stop by road blocks several kilometres deep.*
> - *08:00, search for enemy contact and begin clearing, slow progress under fire from Pahouin partisans armed with trade rifles, often perched in trees along the road, mostly invisible, always elusive.[43]*
> - *16:00, make contact at the village of Ngomo (28km north of Mitzic) where elements of the BTG are entrenched and protected by the destruction of 5 bridges.*
> - *At 20:00, the convoy rejoins the main group.*

When he received the order to depart, Dio had not yet received the Foreign Legion motorcyclists or the tanks from the *1ʳᵉ Compagnie de Chars du Combat*. However, he had been reinforced with a support detachment that could assist with mobility. He could give the engineers two types of missions: clearing obstacles such as the roadblocks, and repairing damaged bridges or ferries. They departed in the middle of the night. Dio prioritised the element of surprise by deciding to start the movement at night because he knew night operations were not usually favoured in Africa. The

---

First, it is hardly likely given the nature of the mission. Artillery is a heavy terrain saturation weapon, and its use is inconsistent with the spirit of Dio's mission of rallying the territory to Free France. Second, on a technical level, it is not possible to use indirect fire systems with the lower trajectory of 75mm canons in the forest. Preferable to artillery, the higher trajectory of light 81mm mortars could, if necessary, support infantry in open areas around villages over a short distance.

40   *Ordre de mission n°1.278/3 de la 14e demi-brigade de Légion Étrangère du 27 octobre 1940, signé colonel Monclar, de son vrai nom Magrain-Verneret.*

41   French Hotchkiss H39 light tanks manufactured in 1935, weighing 12 tons, with a crew of two men and having a range of 129km. Armed with a 37mm gun and a 7.5mm machine gun. This tank company was the initial element of the future *501e RCC*, one of the three armoured regiments of the *2e DB*.

42   FFL, Tournadre.

43   Pahouins are a forest-dwelling people present in several countries of Central Africa. Here, he refers to the Fang ethnic group of Gabon. Trade rifles, also called *poupou*, are rifles that Europeans distributed to indigenous populations in the nineteenth century for self-defence and hunting. They were single shot black powder weapons, which were often modified over time. They also sometimes existed in completely artisanal versions.

first roadblock, 35km from Mitzic, was held only by some indigenous snipers who took shots from the tree line at the soldiers tearing down the obstacles. Leclerc's chief of staff, Tutenges, stated that *Colonne Dio* 'was soon harassed by snipers perched in the trees of the Gabonese forest.'[44] The village of Ngomo was held by Vichy forces, most likely belonging to *Capitaine* Baylon's company. Dio refused to engage in combat first, knowing he was facing other Frenchmen. 'We did not want to be the one to attack and jeopardise the chances of them rallying.'[45] Despite having military superiority, he would first negotiate to try to persuade his opponents to rally or to at least let him pass. If that failed, he had planned to overrun the opponents' positions to encourage them to retreat.

25 October: *engagement in Ngomo.*
- *11:00, Brigadier Robert (engineer from Support Company 2) is slightly injured by a partisan.*
- *13:30, Sergent Jacques Félix, from the 14th Company, is severely injured while securing the rear of the detachment.*

Brigadier Robert had his 'chest shot through from one side to the other.' *Médecin Lieutenant* Orsini operated on him on a table, but he lacked anaesthesia to give to the wounded NCO. The operation lasted an hour, the patient conscious the entire time without uttering a single complaint. Miraculously, he survived, and after the war, he became a renowned ethnobotanist. Based on that experience, a surgical truck later joined the column.[46] *Sergent* Félix was injured while he was at the rear of the detachment, meaning that Vichy sympathisers allowed the column to pass them by while they hid in the dense virgin forest. Dio would remember that guerrilla tactic in the coming days.

26 October: *fighting outside of Ngomo, attempt flanking manoeuvre by the resistance in the high forest;*
- *11:00, gunfire and heavy firing of automatic weapons.*
- *14:00, on the eastern flank of the detachment, a fierce engagement between Lieutenant Bonnet's section and a strong enemy patrol that had moved to within 30 metres from the aid station. The medical personnel, entrenched, participate in the fight.*
- *21:30, gunfire at the outposts. Indigenous corporal Gombe from the company is lightly injured.*
- *23:00, the fighting intensifies at the outposts, very intense firing from automatic weapons.*
- *23:30, Indigenous corporal Braye from the 6th Company is brought to the aid station in very serious condition (lumbar region) and died from his injury.*

The Vichy supporters were initially not fooled. At 11:00, the *BTG* troops opened fire on a group of Dio's infantry who, having outflanked the village, tried to attack it from the side. However, the Vichy troops overran Dio's position and arrived in his rear, hitting the aid station. Dio's men, including the medical personnel, were forced into a hasty defence against the Vichy troops.

These two actions revealed to Dio the toughness of the adversary he faced. If he launched a daytime frontal assault, the losses were likely to be high on both sides. Therefore, he waited for nightfall to resume the attack on the village, assigning the mission to *Lieutenant* Liurette's 6th Company. *Capitaine* Dronne, who witnessed the action, mentioned another incident that was left out of the operational report: Vichy planes flew over Dio's column and, 'dropped bombs, which

44   Fonds Leclerc, Tutenges, p.6.
45   Dronne, *Carnets de Route*, p.50.
46   Dronne, *Carnets de Route*, p.53.

fell near the road …. and sank into the muddy ground. Most of them failed to explode.[47] Larminat also mentioned the presence of three American-made Glenn Martin planes, which Dakar had sent to Libreville to reinforce the territory.[48] This aerial attack might have taken place during this period when the Vichyites did everything they could to stop *Colonne Dio* before it reached Mitzic. The operational report evidently omitted to mention it due to its insignificant outcome.

Lieutenant Volvey and his reinforcing tank platoon also arrived on that day. The platoon consisted of three H39 tanks, a Humber command vehicle, a motorcycle platoon (equipped with British Matchless motorcycles) under the command of *Aspirant* Tresca, and three logistics trucks. The *lieutenant* pushed the motorcycles ahead of his tanks, which followed 24 hours after the motorcycles. When Dio and Volvey first met, 'the *capitaine* was wearing baggy *sarouel* pants with dirty feet in dirty sandals. He wiped his hand across his foot before shaking hands with the *lieutenant*, who did not appreciate the old *méhariste* joke.'[49] Dio's mischievous welcome was a bit of a 'haze,' to remind his young comrade that he was reinforcing a colonial unit. Traditional greetings were somewhat different in the French cavalry of that time! Leclerc also welcomed the young officer in a mocking manner when he told him before his departure to Gabon: 'For men who have taken Narvik, seizing Lambaréné is no big deal!'[50]

27 October:
- *15:00: occupation of the village of Ngomo, evacuated hastily by the enemy.*
- *19:00: Colonel Leclerc arrives.*

The village was finally occupied in the afternoon. Dio, who lost two men during the night, did not want to take excessive risks. To break the deadlock, he ordered several flanking movements to catch his adversary completely off guard. But that took some time, allowing the enemy to retreat before being surrounded. Leclerc arrived in Ngomo early in the night. The Hotchkiss tank platoon also arrived that night after an eventful evening of navigating the muddy trails during the rainy season, along with numerous river crossings on ferries or bridges. The bridges in that part of Gabon were made of wood and were designed to support trucks weighing 4 to 5 tons, not 12-ton tanks!

28 October:
- *Resume movement towards Mitzic*
- *10:00, enter into Mitzic, evacuated by its garrison whose troops retreat to Libreville via a forest trail.*
- *Organisation of the pursuit led by Lieutenant Schrimff (sic) and a combat group from the 14th Company.*
- *During the pursuit, the Vichy troops lose:*
  Killed: two tirailleurs
  Prisoners: Lieutenant Hervouet who rallies to Free France shortly after
  Sergent Chef Levasseur
  12 tirailleurs
- *- 18:00, arrival of the convoy and the surgical ambulance*

47   Dronne, *Carnets de Route,* p.54.
48   Larminat, *Chroniques,* p.197.
49   Pierre Quillet, *Le Chemin le plus Long. Chronique de la Compagnie de chars de combat du Général de Gaulle, 1940–1945* (Paris: Maisonneuve et Larose, 1997), p.171.
50   Quillet, *Le Chemin le plus Long,* p.156.

In the few volumes written on the campaign in Gabon, the capture of Mitzic remains the highlight of *Colonne Dio*'s actions. Dronne notes that the arrival of the Hotchkiss tanks must have frightened the Vichy garrison.[51] Some commentary emphasises Dio's slowness, demonstrating an excessive caution. Tutenges wrote that Leclerc felt that Dio was 'stalling.'[52] Referring to Leclerc, Notin wrote 'Dio's prudence in Mitzic annoyed him. Furious, he personally went to attack the village only to discover that it had been abandoned.'[53] Leclerc's impatience as a leader and his desire for decisive action is a well-known fact.[54]

Dio was in a tough position between his direct superior and the directives of the higher command of the *AEF*. The instructions he received from Brazzaville stated: 'We must avoid offensive engagement with detachments of the adversary at all costs.'[55] Upon arriving at Mitzic, and considering what had happened in Ngomo, Dio ordered patrols to widely flank the city to the north and south. The delay clearly annoyed Leclerc. Dronne, who was with Dio at Mitzic, related an anecdote demonstrating the low quality of the units made available to Dio. One platoon, led by a reserve *lieutenant*, who was a veterinarian by profession, got lost in the forest during the flanking manoeuvre to bypass Mitzic. Going in circles, the flanking platoon returned without realising it and found itself facing the friendly position set up to the north of Mitzic. Both sides believed they were confronting enemy troops, and a fratricidal fire fight ensued for several minutes. Dio and Dronne had difficulty stopping the fight. Miraculously, there were no casualties.[56] Hearing the gunfire, *Lieutenant* Hervouet of the *BTG*, tasked to defend the city, realised that he would soon be surrounded. After destroying the post, he decided to discreetly withdraw.[57] But before the flanking patrols could report the adversary's escape, Leclerc decided to enter the area on foot. Hervouet had just withdrawn. Dio then decided to engage in a pursuit, believing he had a good chance of catching up with him. The main goal was to neutralise Hervouet's platoon which had delayed Dio's column with its tenacious defence.

After spending more than 24 hours with Dio, Leclerc came to understand the difficulties of the terrain and the relative weakness of his units, and he realised that the attack would take time. 'Leclerc understood that the small columns moving slowly through the Gabonese forest would not be able to converge on … Libreville.'[58] Moreover, if the enemy fought as tenaciously as it had at Mitzic, losses would be high on both sides. He also realised that the tanks he sent were clearly unsuitable in the forest environment. Up to Mitzic, the route was passable for trucks and armoured vehicles, but after Mitzic, the route descending into the forest to N'Djolé was barely usable.

29–30 October:
* *Cantonment in Mitzic, reconnaissance patrols towards La Lara.*

La Lara is a village located between Mitzic and N'Djolé, situated where the Lara River flows into the Okano River. 100km further south, the Okano then empties into the Ogooué. By sending reconnaissance troops to La Lara, Dio wanted to gather information about the presence of *BTG* troops as well as the condition of crossing sites.

51   Dronne, *Carnets de route*, p.55.
52   Fonds Leclerc, Tutenges, p.6.
53   Notin, *le Croisé*, p.90.
54   Leclerc arrived in a Lysander piloted by *Sergent Chef* Lignon, 'who had got lost and had 'wandered' for a long time in the equatorial forest' (Jean de Pange, *lettre à Dronne, du 18 juin 1965*).
55   Notin, *le Croisé*, p.89.
56   Dronne, *Carnets de route*, p.54.
57   Archives FFL, Raymond Dronne, 'La douloureuse affaire du Gabon en 1940', *Carrefour*, 1965.
58   Compagnon, *Leclerc*, p.170.

Upon returning to Douala, *Colonel* Leclerc addressed the Cameroonian population, announcing that:

> *Capitaine* Dio's forces occupied Mitzic on the morning of Monday, 28 October. On the 29th, his leading elements had already reached La Lara. The enemy mounted serious resistance on 26th and 27th, reinforced by the dense forest, the destruction of numerous bridges, and the use of roadblocks. Confronted by the zeal of our troops, a general panic broke out: units of European troops fled through forest trails to the west and southwest. The scattered African soldiers in the bush had already started to rally to our side on the 29th. A soldier from the 6th Company was killed. *Sergent* Jacques Félix was shot through the lung, but his life seems to have been saved. *Brigadier* Robert was shot and slightly wounded in the shoulder. The actions and morale of everyone involved were splendid. Among other captured documents, one order instructs Vichy troops to resist in place and another one directs the enemy to prioritise Europeans when they fire.[59]

31 October:
- *03:00, departure by truck to N'Djolé. Lieutenant Dronne ensures the security of Mitzic with a section of fusiliers-voltigeurs.*
- *At La Lara, repair of the ferry damaged by the enemy.*

Less than 200 kilometres separated Mitzic from N'Djolé. Dio left Dronne in Mitzic with a detachment. He wanted to avoid threats to his rear and to keep the route back to Cameroon open for medical evacuations and supplies.

1 November:
- *around 03:00, occupation of N'Djolé without fighting.*

Colonne Dio covered nearly 200km in 24 hours, which was particularly remarkable considering the state of the roads during the rainy season and the fact that part of the movement was made at night.

2 November:
- *preparation for the movement towards Kango.*
- *fortification of N'Djolé.*

Leclerc followed the progress by radio from Douala. Impatient, he always thought the advance was too slow. On 2 November, Leclerc had just convinced de Gaulle to simultaneously land troops in Libreville. With the failure of Dakar still in his mind, the leader of Free France had initially refused. According to Notin, 'He did not want a second failure that would condemn him in the eyes of the Allies.'[60] Nevertheless, aware that the situation in Gabon had to be resolved without delay, he reluctantly agreed. To launch this joint service operation, Colonel Leclerc waited for Lambaréné to fall. It was preferable to launch the offensive on Libreville without having to worry about an attack from that direction, as well.[61]

---

59   Christine Levisse-Touzé et Julien Toureille, *Écrits de Combat* (Paris: Sorbonne Université Presses, 2023) p.158.
60   Notin, *le Croisé*, p.90.
61   Didier Corbonnois, in collaboration with Alain Godec, *L'Odyssée de la Colonne Leclerc, Les Français Libres au combat sur le front du Tchad, 1940–43* (Paris: Histoire & Collections, 2003), p.19.

- *Colonne Parant besieges Lambaréné.*
- *Dio's detachment maintains contact with Parant, protecting it from the north by opposing the arrival of reinforcements sent from Libreville.*
- *mission: move down the Ogooué, hold the confluence of the Abanga, the village of Gouabiléré, crossroads of routes to Libreville – Mango – Lambaréné and Lambaréné – N'Djolé – Mitzic.*
- *Reconnaissance of the trail towards Kango.*

Simultaneous to *Colonne Dio*'s advance from the north, the *AEF* command sent *Commandant* Parant's column from the Middle Congo to Lambaréné. Parant, leading a remnant of the battalion of *tirailleurs* stationed in the Gold Coast, had only arrived in Douala on 30 August. The *tirailleurs* had been redistributed among the different units of the Cameroonian forces while *Commandant* Parant was sent to Brazzaville on de Gaulle's orders to reinforce his staff. Once there, Parant was given the mission to organise a column from the Middle Congo to first take Lambaréné and then the capital, Libreville. His objective was the same as Dio's. On 16 September, *Commandant* Parant boldly flew to Mayumba, the post of the Vichy forces located furthest south in Gabon. Mixing firmness and persuasion, he rallied the small garrison through negotiation. Then he moved along trails to the post of Fougamou, about a hundred kilometres from Lambaréné, and rallied it in the same way. Joined by *Commandant* Delange's *1ᵉʳ Bataillon de Marche*, *Colonne Parant* arrived in front of Lambaréné on 10 October. The city is located on an island in the middle of the River Ogooué, allowing the well-organised Vichy troops to establish a strong defence. Too weak to attack alone, Parant had to resign himself to waiting for Dio's arrival so they could take the city by force. Arriving in N'Djolé on 1 November, the column coming from Cameroon would attempt to hold the path near the village of Gouabiléré (at the confluence between the Ogooué and Abanga) to cut off the route between Lambaréné and Libreville. River boats equipped with 37mm guns and machine guns had been detected, so holding the path at Gouabiléré would also interdict movement down the Ogooué.[62] Kango is located at the south-eastern end of the Gabon estuary, while Libreville lies on its north-western bank. Kango controls access to Libreville from the interior and was therefore the objective for both columns once Lambaréné fell.

3 November:
- *Leaving Lieutenant Liurette's company and the motorcycle detachment at N'Djolé, Capitaine Dio and the rest of the detachment embarks on pinnaces.*
- *The Groupe Franc of the Légion du Cameroun forms the advance guard.*
- *One platoon positions at the confluence of Abanga/Ogooué while a strong reconnaissance patrol occupies the village of Evoungoung, 15km from Gouabiléré.*

From N'Djolé, *Colonne Dio* would move first by river on pinnaces and then on foot to Libreville. The vehicles would have to be left behind, so from N'Djolé the column was composed exclusively of infantry, but Dio was reinforced with 300 indigenous porters to carry the supplies, mainly food and ammunition. Dio always tasked *Lieutenant* Maziéras as the vanguard, leading the way at the head of the column. He had become the man Dio relied on. Since Fort Archambault, he had come to know him well and he shaped him under his command. In addition, the 'Cameroonian legionnaires' who made up Maziéras' unit were mostly Europeans from Douala. They were well adapted to the equatorial environment but above all, they were highly motivated.

---

62 This flotilla was made up of three pinnaces: *Falaba*, *Mandji* and *Oviro* and a tugboat: *Provence*. Mengone, Barthélémy Ntoma, *La Bataille de Libreville*, ed. L'Harmattan, 2014, p.36.

4 November:
- *09:00, all available elements reach the village of Evoungoung, north of which is an opposing indigenous compagnie de marche reinforced by a strong European element.*
- *09:05, bursts of machine gun fire to the south of Evoungoung against the rear of the detachment. An opposing patrol loses 8 prisoners, including 1 European, 1 machine gun, and ammunition.*
- *09:30, new contact with a patrol led by an aspirant [Permon?], who is mortally wounded.*
- *12:00, the enemy attacks north of Evoungoung but is repelled, leaving one European killed and 1 machine gun on the field.*
- *17:00, return of the Groupe Franc that went on patrol southwest of Evoungoung.*
- *18:00, departure to Gouabiléré.*

True to the tactic adopted in the previous days, Dio advanced at night and seized Gouabiléré on the night of 4/5 November. By holding the village of Gouabiléré, *Colonne Dio* stopped all supplies and reinforcements coming from Libreville by land. The Vichy troops found Lambaréné's isolation unacceptable. Therefore, they sent the 'indigenous *compagnie de marche*' to oppose Dio's progress. 'The Vichy commander of Libreville had launched a column to oppose the Cameroonian and Congolese 'invaders.' Composed of Europeans and Senegalese with no experience of the country, it had a lot of difficulties.'[63] Dio knew that he had to hold the road leading to Libreville at all costs. For the first time in the campaign, the fighting was intense. On 4 November, Dio abandoned the strategy of persuasion that had been used so far against the loyalist troops. It was the only day when, militarily, he considered that he was facing 'enemies' and no longer 'adversaries.' As a result, the Vichy losses were relatively heavy. For the defenders of Lambaréné, the military situation was hopeless. With the 'Gaullist dissidents' in control of the crossroads leading to Lambaréné, their surrender became inevitable. They knew they could no longer be reinforced or supplied from Libreville (by land) or Port-Gentil (by river), and they could resist attacks coming from both the north (Dio) and the south (Parant) of the city only with great difficulty.

5 November:
Link up with Colonne Parant in Lambaréné.

The two columns linked up on the Ogooué, a navigable river in the region. *Capitaine* Dio, with a light detachment aboard two pinnaces, joined *Colonne Parant*. Larminat wrote: 'Lambaréné fell, just as *Colonne Dio*, after two months of persuasive and complicated operations from the Cameroon border, made contact.'[64] As planned, with the arrival of elements from *Colonne Dio*, the garrison of Lambaréné raised the white flag. *Colonne Parant* then took the city, having the honour of being the first to enter Lambaréné. But it was undeniable that the surrender was enabled by *Colonne Dio*. 'Lambaréné gave in …. after the unexpected arrival of *Colonne Dio*.'[65] Furthermore, Parant credited 'Dio's detachment of the Cameroonian troops' for the capture of Lambaréné in his report to *AEF* command.[66] *Général* de Gaulle sent a telegram to Parant on 6 November:

> I embrace you and congratulate you, *Lieutenant-Colonel* Parant, governor of Gabon. Congratulations from me to all those under your command, especially Commandant Dio.

63   Archives FFL, Dronne, 'Affaire du Gabon', *Carrefour*, 1965.
64   Larminat, *Chroniques,* p.199.
65   Notin, *le Croisé,* p.94.
66   Archives FFL, TO n°79 du 5.11.40 du Commandant Parant au Gouverneur général Brazzaville. TO indicates a military message, from the English 'Transmission Order.'

Tell your troops that they have served well. It is for France that they have fought and won at Sindara, Mitzic, N'Djolé, Lambaréné. Now we must complete the success.'[67]

That is how the leader of Free France promoted the two column commanders, who learnt of their promotion by telegram.

Upon learning of the capture of Lambaréné, Leclerc immediately launched the combined operation towards Libreville, clearly demonstrating the important role played by his two columns. 'On 5 November, the *Savorgnan de Brazza*, on which Leclerc embarked, and the *Fort-Lamy*... set sail.'[68] D-Day in Libreville was set for the 8th.

6 November:
Rest in Gouabiléré where news arrives of the capture of Lambaréné and the retreat of the opposing compagnie de marche to Kango.

The majority of *Colonne Dio*, under the command of Maziéras, remained in Gouabiléré, maintaining radio contact with Lambaréné, Douala, and Brazzaville. After setting up its wire antennas in the trees and orienting them in the right direction, the transmitter received Morse code messages intended for it. Unable to oppose *Colonne Dio*, the indigenous *compagnie de marche* retreated towards Libreville, allowing Maziéras to adopt a lighter security posture. The operations note described 6 November as a 'day of rest,' when in fact, it was more reconditioning of personnel and equipment rather than literal rest. The priority was to maintain the weapons that had been strained in such a humid environment. It was also necessary to wash both individual and collective equipment. Finally, each soldier would then be able to clean themselves, to eat, and to sleep.

7 November:
- *Through Bifoun (village), Lake Nguéné, the Boukoue (river), Dio's detachment sets off for Kango in order to reestablish contact with the compagnie de marche.*
- *Arrival at Bifoun.*

After the 'day of rest' and Dio's return to Gouabiléré, the column resumed its advance on foot. The thick Gabonese forest trails only allowed for movement in single file, so the column stretched out a considerable distance. Depending on the nature of the terrain, it could cover 10km to 25km per day. The axis of advance reoriented to face generally west towards Kango, the gateway to Libreville.

8 November:
Stationary at Bifoun. Search for intelligence.

9, 10, 11 November:
- *Stationary on the road 70km from Kango, reconnaissance on Lake Nguéné.*
- *The fall of Libreville was announced to the detachment.*

Having landed north of Libreville on 8 November, the Free French landing force commanded by Leclerc pushed *Général* Tétu's Pétainist forces back to the airfield. The formal surrender of the city was signed on 9 November at 11:00 p.m.[69]

---

67   Gaulle (de), *L'Appel*, p.311.
68   Notin, *le Croisé*, p.94.
69   Notin, *le Croisé*, p.97.

12, 13, 14 November:
Stationary at the Polidori logging camp (18km east of km 70). Preparation for river navigation.

Foot movement through the Gabonese forest was exhausting for the soldiers. Logging camps were used to 'regain strength.' Additionally, the column took every opportunity to travel by river to conserve the men's strength.

15 November:
Departure at 09:00. Embarkation on Lake Nguéné, upstream on the Abanga River. Cantonment at the Saussy logging camp, end of navigation.

16 November:
Foot movement through the forest from 09:00 to 23:39 along the 'Telegraph' trail. Stationary at the Sinquin logging camp.

Dio had to tell the men to speed up so they would arrive at Librevile on time. Walking through the forest for 14½ hours was an extraordinary challenge, and he had to motivate his men to arrive at the forest camp during the night.

17 November:
Departure at 11:00. Arrival at 18:00 at the dock on the Bakoué River where the detachment stops.

The movement to the dock on the River Bakoué, which would carry them to Kango, was fortunately a short one. The city had fallen and there was no longer any Vichy resistance remaining.

18 November:
- *Embark on the pinnaces.*
- *13:00: Arrival at Kango, evacuated by the opposition.*
- *23:00: Departed Kango.*

The distance between Kango and Libreville is about 100km. The movement was done by trucks on a terrible road, which explains the delays in reaching the capital.

19 November:
- *06:00: Arrival in Libreville.*
- *19:00: Embark on the transport 'Nevada' heading to Douala.*

Colonne Dio would have only stayed a very short time in Libreville.

21 November:
- *13:00: Disembark in Douala.*

It took 42 hours to reach Douala by sea, which gave the men some time to recover from the fighting and accumulated fatigue of the past month. Dronne described the health problems caused by the prolonged stay in the Gabonese forest: 'We had to deal with *cros-cros*, these ugly crater-like wounds on the legs, get rid of parasites, treat numerous cases of malaria, take care of the itching caused by those tiny damned *'moutes-moutes'* gnats that attack you in tight battalions at dawn and dusk.'[70] Dio's men landed in Douala on the 21st and were met with jubilation by the population. The European inhabitants were present, rushing to admire in particular 'the *Légion du Cameroun* which included the heads of many families from Douala and Cameroon.'[71] Dio thought about the men he left behind in N'Djolé (Liurette's company) and Mitzic (Dronne's detachment). He ordered Dronne to stay a few more weeks. Following the fighting, 'most of the black troops fled and hid in the forest …. If good order is not quickly restored, people will have nothing left to eat.'[72] Dronne's new mission was, 'to reassure the population, reintegrate them into their villages, put them back to work…'[73] It took until mid-December to settle things down.

Colonne Dio's Gabonese campaign thus came to an end. Once Gabon rallied to de Gaulle's side, French Equatorial Africa and Cameroon represented the first homogeneous territorial bloc of Free France. From then on, it was referred to as *Afrique Française Libre* (*AFL*, Free French Africa), from which the Gaullist troops would be able to begin, alone or with the British and eventually the Americans, the reconquest of France. It was a great victory for Free France. 'Free French Africa brought de Gaulle legitimacy, territory, and administration, making Free France no longer a movement but a government.'[74] Jean Lacouture said with more wit that 'de Gaulle had ceased to be a squatter on the banks of the Thames.'[75]

However, the Gabonese campaign saw Frenchmen fighting each other. As a result, despite the victory, Free France did not advertise it much. The newspaper in Douala, *L'Éveil du Cameroun*, referred to the landing in the capital as 'police operations carried out in Libreville.' On the other side, Vichy highlighted the losses caused in fratricidal fighting against 'dissidents.' Despite the propaganda, the combat losses were actually relatively low: 26 killed on the Vichy side and seven on the *FFL* side. However, as Notin wrote, 'the truth is that Gabon was much more than a police operation; it was a fratricidal war, the victory of which cannot remove the bitter taste.'[76]

Commentary on the campaign is scarce. Most studies gloss over the events, especially the role of the two columns that advanced from Cameroon and Middle Congo. For many, the two columns were a partial failure. Even de Gaulle, certainly misinformed, wrote that 'these lingering and painful fights offered no solution.'[77] Those works that recount the campaign in Gabon mainly focus on the joint landing operation in Libreville on 8 and 9 November 1940. The two columns are barely mentioned, but the operations report, found in the archives of the Fondation de la France Libre, gives Dio and his men the recognition they deserve as actors in the success of the Gabonese campaign. *Colonne Dio* carried out a true military operation. For example, no other study has distinguished that *Capitaine* Dio's operation was in two phases. The first, conducted from 11 to 16 September, was a mostly political phase in which he sought to rally loyalist military forces through persuasion. That phase was an immediate success, as Dio, with a few men and without using force, managed to rally a complete company of the *BTG* and the population of the city of Oyem, and to establish his military presence in this provincial capital of northern Gabon.

Contrary to what has been written, he did not spend three months in stagnation. The purely military operations were carried out from 24 October to 5 November, covering more than 500km to Lambaréné. Considering the extreme difficulties of moving through the Gabonese equatorial forest with very limited means, this achievement is admirable.

---

70   Dronne, *Carnets de Route*, p.61.

71   Journal *Eveil du Cameroun* du 27 nov. 40.

72   Journal *Eveil du Cameroun* du 27 nov. 40.

73   Dronne, *Carnets de route*, p.58.

74   Éric T. Jennings, *La France Libre fut Africaine* (Paris: Perrin, ministère de la Défense, 2014), p.11.

75   Jean Lacouture, *De Gaulle. 1. Le Rebelle, 1890–1944*, (Paris: Éditions du Seuil, 1984) p.435.

76   Notin, *le Croisé*, p.98.

77   Gaulle (de), *L'Appel*, p.115.

Furthermore, Dio, faithful to his orders, and above all faithful to his soldier's ethics, did everything he could to limit the losses in a battle against other Frenchmen.[78] Knowing that *Capitaine* Baylon was Dio's military academy classmate at Saint-Cyr, we can understand the moral dilemma he experienced. As Messmer mentions, other Free French officers abstained altogether: '*Colonel* Monclar and several officers – including Lamaze – refused to take part in the operation, relying on the text of their enlistment which specified that Free French would never be obliged to fight against other Frenchmen.'[79] This was not the case for Dio. It is important to note that in 12 days, Dio fulfilled his mission: the arrival of his detachment on the outskirts of Lambaréné forced the garrison to surrender after resisting for 26 days against Parant. It is true that the two columns did not participate in the attack on Libreville, but Leclerc waited for the fall of Lambaréné to launch his landing force from Douala on 5 November. He did not want to take the risk of investing Libreville without neutralising the threat from the forces coming from within Gabon. Nearly 30 percent of Gabonese troops were outside the capital to face the 'invaders' from Cameroon and Congo. Those troops were therefore not in Libreville to oppose the landing force of the Free French.

The moral impact of the campaign against Vichy troops in Libreville also deserves to be highlighted. They were certainly aware of the two columns advancing on the capital. From the end of October, they watched increasing parts of Gabonese territory rally to Free France. Once Lambaréné fell, only the western part of Gabon remained loyal to Vichy. After Free French troops landed in the north of Libreville, Vichy held only about 10 percent of the territory. The non-commissioned officers and *tirailleurs* of the Gabonese forces realised that momentum was no longer on their side. Their morale was at its lowest on 8 November during the landing of the Free French forces. Proof of this is that the fighting at the Libreville airport was brief, lasting only a part of the day on the 9th. Dronne noted that '*légionnaires* and *tirailleurs* leapt into the assault and quickly gained control of the situation.'[80] During the night, the demoralised Gabonese troops simply stopped fighting. During talks between the representatives of the two sides, Leclerc's chief of staff *Commandant* Tutenges heard *Colonel* Claveau, commander of the Gabonese ground forces, confess that 'he had been forced to stop fighting because his troops had fled.'[81] It is therefore certain that the advance of the two columns contributed to the rapid success of the landing force in Libreville and to the decline in morale among the Vichy soldiers.

Leclerc was pleased with the way Dio had worked in Douala and Yaoundé at the end of August. Therefore, he chose the *méhariste capitaine* to command the column from Cameroon. With a size equivalent to a combined arms battalion, a *commandant* would normally have been assigned to command it.[82] Leclerc had several *commandants* at his disposal in early September, for example Gardet and Pradier, however, he deliberately chose Dio. It was a delicate mission for two reasons. First, it involved leading an operational column made up of poorly trained personnel, generally under-supervised and under-equipped, and in a very difficult environment. Leclerc knew that Dio was a leader of men and that he would be able to motivate them. The other difficulty lies in the fact that they were confronting a French adversary who had to be spared as much as possible. Leclerc expected Dio to have a highly tuned management style that could combine the power of

78   De Gaulle ordered that the operation be carried out with an emphasis on permanently 'maintaining communications with the adversary inviting him to an honourable surrender, one which would safeguard life and, to the extent possible, personal liberty.' (Notin, *le Croisé*, p.91.).

79   Pierre Messmer, *Après tant de Batailles…, Mémoires* (Albin Michel, 1992), p.37.

80   Archives FFL, Dronne, '*La douloureuse affaire du Gabon en 1940*,' Carrefour 1965.

81   Fonds Leclerc, Tutenges, p.8.

82   A combined arms battalion is a unit made up of several arms or branches of service: artillery, cavalry, infantry, engineers, communications, et cetera.

persuasion with gaining the upper hand over his opponents. Indeed, both of them knew that if there were heavy casualties, it would discredit Free France. Dio had to constantly reconcile the safety of his men while demanding the utmost discipline from them. On this front, *Capitaine* Dio had been completely successful. The losses in his ranks were minimal compared to the gains achieved on the battlefield. The losses of his adversary were also limited. In terms of command, *Capitaine* Dio gained one important lesson – he learnt in Mitzic that sometimes during combat he had to personally force destiny. Without knowing whether the adversary had left the area, Leclerc risked entering the village first, allowing for the subsequent pursuit and neutralisation of the adversary. As the leader of the column, Dio was certainly embarrassed by that, but when circumstances require it, the leader must step up personally to break a stalemate. Dio would remember this lesson for the future, and he would demonstrate it on many occasions, especially in Kufra, very soon.

The Gabonese campaign strengthened Leclerc's respect for *Capitaine* Dio. He appreciated his resourceful subordinate who followed his orders while also being able to take initiative. Dio became his trusted man. From there on, Dio remained one of Leclerc's most faithful comrades-in-arms, always entrusted with leading Leclerc's main effort all the way to Berchtesgaden in 1945.

Dio's evaluation report for the Gabon campaign contains the following assessment: 'Returned promptly to Gabon, took command of a column, marched on Libreville through the interior, and for two months in the most difficult terrain, methodically and cautiously led his troops, pushing the enemy back step-by-step and taking one line of resistance after another.'[83] In addition, Dio received a commendation for his action in Gabon, despite instructions given by de Gaulle,[84] Dio's citation read:

> Commanding the column tasked with retaking Libreville through the Gabonese forest, he demonstrated the finest military qualities during long and difficult operations. He successively occupied Oyem, Mitzic, N'Djolé, and Kango, establishing a connection with friendly elements from the south and accomplishing his mission with minimal losses.[85]

This citation was presented at Brazzaville, the capital of Free French Africa. Leclerc wrote nothing about Dio during the Gabonese campaign, but there is no doubt that he was the one who intervened for de Gaulle to promote him to *commandant* after the capture of Lambaréné. Upon landing in Douala, Dio was pleased to learn that his promotion to temporary *commandant* was backdated to 6 November.

Dio's fate was attached to that of Leclerc from then on. What would their next step be? Would this young *colonel* who rallied two colonies to Free France in three months stay in Cameroon? Indeed, Leclerc was performing well in his secondary role as governor of the territory. He was respected by the entire administration and the Cameroonian population. His reforms were heading in the right direction, and *Général* de Gaulle noticed his extraordinary energy and his managerial talent. But Free France had enough administrators and not enough military leaders of his quality. Therefore, in Libreville on 12 November, just after the fighting ended, the leader of Free France 'informed Leclerc of his transfer to the command of military forces in Chad .... *Général* de Gaulle had foreseen the exceptional war leader he could become. On the Italian Sahara and Tripolitania, he opened wide the doors of French victory for [Leclerc].'[86] Chad was the only

---

83   SHD, Dio, 14 Yd 1759.

84   De Gaulle wrote in his memoirs that at the end of the operation, 'I announced, with general agreement, that no citation would be awarded for this unpleasant occasion.' (Gaulle, (de), *l'Appel*, p.116).

85   *Ordre de la Libération, ordre général No. 32 du général supérieur des Forces de l'AFL du 27.3.41.*

86   Verdier, Henri, 'Le rôle du Colonel Leclerc dans la Constitution de l'Afrique Française Libre', *Le Général Leclerc et l'Afrique Française Libre, 1940–1942,* Actes du Colloque International (Paris: Fondation Maréchal

territory of Free French Equatorial Africa (*AEF*) that shared a border with the Italian enemy to the north and the Vichy adversary to the west. He showed him a map of Fezzan and Tripolitania, saying, 'now there is this and this,' pointing to the region of Kufra in the east and the region of Fezzan to the west. Leclerc later said, 'I have never received such a brief directive that I followed with such conviction.'[87]

Despite an initial moment of disappointment due to leaving his dual civil-military functions in Cameroon, Leclerc understood the objective de Gaulle gave him. 'Chad, which *Général* Mangin had once called the 'keystone of the African system,' would serve as a starting base for French and Allied units.'[88] It was the point of departure from which Free France could enter the fight and assert itself as the true France, the one on the side of victory. 'It was the sword of Free France .... planted in the soft belly of the Berlin-Vichy axis.'[89] The situation made it a territory of high military value for Free France. Leclerc, in a letter published on 27 November, addressed the inhabitants of Cameroon: '*Général* de Gaulle informed me in Libreville that I am leaving Cameroon. In the face of the higher interest, I reluctantly obeyed, and today I come to say goodbye to you.'[90] He stayed one more month in Cameroon to consolidate the administrative and governmental reforms he had initiated, as well as to pass on instructions to his successor, Pierre Cournarie. He bid his official farewell in Douala on 21 November and in Yaoundé on 22nd.

Commandant Dio arrived in Douala from Gabon on 21 November, the same day as Leclerc's farewell. Nevertheless, Leclerc managed to find time in his schedule for a one-on-one meeting with Dio. The *colonel* informed him that he would be taking command in Chad, and he asked Dio to join him, knowing full well what Dio's response would be. Compagnon wrote that Leclerc chose: *Capitaine* Dio, promoted to *commandant*, whose strength he recognised the moment he arrived in Douala and during the Gabon campaign, and who possessed a deep knowledge of northern Chad, where he long commanded the *Groupe Nomade du Tibesti*.'[91] There was a scarcity of senior officers at the time. The High Commissioner of Free French Africa, *Général* de Larminat, needed many 'four-stripe'[92] officers to take command of the future *bataillons de marche* (*BM*)[93] that would soon be engaged in the Levant. In the same 'category' as Dio, there were other strong officers such as *Commandants* Delange (*BM1*), Garbay (*BM3*), Bouillon (*BM4*), and Gardet (*BM5*). Among this group, Leclerc chose the recently promoted commandant to accompany him to Chad, having been able to bring with him only 'a few officers including Dio and Quilichini.'[94] Dio knew all that. He was once again honoured by Leclerc's trust in him. Just as on 27 August at Dr Mauzé's house in Douala, the *méhariste capitaine* did not hesitate to follow the young *colonel* who understood his loyalty and initiative.

Leclerc took advantage of his short meeting with Dio to give him a special mission. He handed Dio a telegram from Brazzaville dated 19 November 1940 that announced the impending arrival of the *Cap Olomo* in Douala. The British cargo vessel was carrying six 25mm anti-tank guns

Leclerc de Hauteclocque, 1987), p.57.

87   Verdier, 'Le rôle du Colonel Leclerc', p.57.

88   Ingold, *Général Ingold*, p.53.

89   Notin, *le Croisé*, p.100.

90   Fonds Leclerc, *Journal l'Eveil du Cameroun du 27 novembre 1940*.

91   Compagnon, *Leclerc*, p.214.

92   Larminat was speaking of *commandants* (majors), whose insignia of rank is four gold or silver stripes, and *lieutenant colonels*, whose insignia of rank is four stripes alternating between gold and silver. (Translator's note)

93   These *Bataillons de Marche*, were created from the available troops of the *AEF* to go to Syria, then to Egypt to assist the British. The battalions formed the *1re Division Française Libre* (*1re DFL*), which would later distinguish itself within the *1re Armée Française*.

94   Dronne, *Carnets de route*, p.62.

and ammunition destined for Chad, and the *colonel* asked Dio to ensure the arrival of the equipment. Dio quickly completed the mission. On a simple piece of yellow paper, pretentiously titled 'Mission Order,'[95] Dio wrote: '*Légionnaire* Poualion is responsible for collecting and transporting the expected anti-tank equipment and ammunition by sea to Fort-Lamy, destined for the territory of Chad. Douala, 23 November 1940. For *Colonel* Leclerc and *p/o* of *Capitaine* Dio. Signed: Dio.'[96] The handwritten document demonstrates the strong bond that had already formed between the two men. Leclerc relied implicitly on Dio. Dio was no longer just his right-hand man in operational matters; he had become a valuable deputy on whom he automatically entrusted all types of missions. By signing on behalf of Leclerc, with the addition of '*p/o*,' (by order of), Dio's note illustrates the unity between the two officers. Dio signed as *capitaine* even though he was already a *commandant*. This was either an error on his part or his official promotion orders had not yet reached his unit.

It should be noted that the French forces were in want of everything at the time. There was still no official stationery with a formal letterhead, nor was there a dedicated service to collect and transport war materiel. Dio entrusted this mission to '*Légionnaire*' Poualion, a French expatriate mechanic who lived in Douala in 1940. Having joined the *Légion des Volontaires du Cameroun* upon Leclerc's arrival, he accompanied Dio to Gabon with Maziéras' company. Shot in the left leg on the Ogooué on 3 November, he received the citation:

> Courageous *légionnaire*. Tasked with carrying out a mission between N'Djolé and Lambaréné; the only European on board a canoe, he managed to cross enemy lines under automatic weapon fire, which shot numerous holes through his boat and caused his paddlers to desert.[97]

Dio spotted the 40-year-old in Gabon, recognising that he was resourceful and had a local network that opened a lot of doors. Dio could rely on him. Like Leclerc, Dio had the gift of knowing how to surround himself with capable people. He would not regret his choice because Poualion would soon save his life. The two men would not part ways until the defeat of Nazi Germany in 1945.

Dio was happy at the thought of returning to Chad, where he would once again operate in the desert with his *méhariste* companions and his beloved *RTST*. The *Régiment de Tirailleurs Sénégalais du Tchad* was the first unit to fully rally to *Général* de Gaulle, along with the entire territory of Chad. On 27 August 1940, the leader of Free France awarded the Order of the Empire to Chad.[98] Dio was particularly proud of the role played by the *RTST* in rallying Cameroon, Middle Congo, and Ubangi-Shari. It can also be hypothesised that the rally in Gabon did not happen peacefully because 'it was the only territory where the *RTST* was not present.'[99]

---

95   Poualion family private collection. It is indeed Dio's signature and handwriting.
96   Corbonnois, *L'Odyssée de la Colonne Leclerc,* p.156. Collection privée famille Poualion.
97   *Ordre Général No.12 du 5 février 1941 du Général de Larminat*, collection privée famille Poualion.
98   This was the first citation signed by the leader of Free France: 'Despite a particularly dangerous military and economic situation, the territory of Chad refused to subscribe to a shameful capitulation and decided to continue the war until the victorious end. Through admirable resolution, [Gabon] showed the path of duty and showed the way to recovery to the entire French Empire.' Gaulle, (de), *l'Appel,* p.289.
99   Létang, *Mirages,* p.190.

Chapter 3

Chad and Kufra,
26 November 1940 to 7 March 1941

Leclerc arrived at Fort-Lamy on November 25, accompanied by *Capitaine* Quilichini. He met with his leaders, issued his orders to them, and then most likely flew to Faya-Largeau with Larminat at the end of November.[1] He chose 2 December as the date to officially take command in Chad. The date was not a random choice. For graduates of l'École Spéciale Militaire de Saint-Cyr (the French military academy of Saint-Cyr) 2 December is '2S,' the anniversary of the Battle of Austerlitz.[2] Each year at the camp at Coëtquidan, Saint-Cyr's first battalion commemorates Napoléon's greatest victory. Leclerc liked using dates as symbols of significance.

Alongside his command of all military forces in Chad, which included the air force and the health service, Leclerc was also the commander of the *RTST*. It was a large unit of the colonial army, comprising 6,500 men, the majority of whom were African; only 450, or 7 percent of the regiment, were European. The *RTST* was deployed in around 30 posts over an area of almost 1.3 million square kilometres, an area almost two and a half times the size of mainland France.

Naturally, *Commandant* Dio followed Leclerc to Chad. Compagnon wrote, 'soon, he would call for Dio, who had just finished the Gabon campaign.'[3] Dio had become Leclerc's trusted man. In addition, the former commander of the *Groupe Nomade du Tibesti* knew the northern borders of Chad better than just about anyone. Dio's orders indicate 26 November 1940 as his effective date of assignment, while his service record notes that he 'arrived in Lamy' on 8 December, a discrepancy of 12 days. Dio stayed in Cameroon for a few more days to settle his personal affairs and complete the round of formal departure requirements. The health service also most certainly would have summoned him to the Yaoundé hospital for a medical check-up after his prolonged period in the Gabonese forest.

Dio's journey to Chad was by road. There were two routes that reached Fort-Lamy, depending on the season. During the first half of the year, the direct route through Cameroon was possible on an axis due north via Yaoundé – Ngaoudéré – Garoua – Maroua – Fort-Lamy, stretching approximately 1,000km. During the rainy season that route became unpassable, necessitating a much longer journey of 1,776km through Oubangui-Chari: Yaoundé – Bertoua – Baboua – Bozoum – Doba – Bongor – Fort-Lamy. The longer route took six days in five stages, and it was the one Dio

---

1   Compagnon, *Leclerc*, p.180, note 2.
2   The academic calendar year at the French military academy runs from October to July, with each month corresponding to a letter of the name Austerlitz, which took place on 2 December 1805. Using that format, A is for October, U for November, et cetera through to Z for July. August and September are months of leave and are therefore not represented. In the 'Austerlitz calendar,' December is signified by the letter S; therefore, 2 December is written as '2S.' (Translator's note)
3   Compagnon, *Leclerc*, p.185.

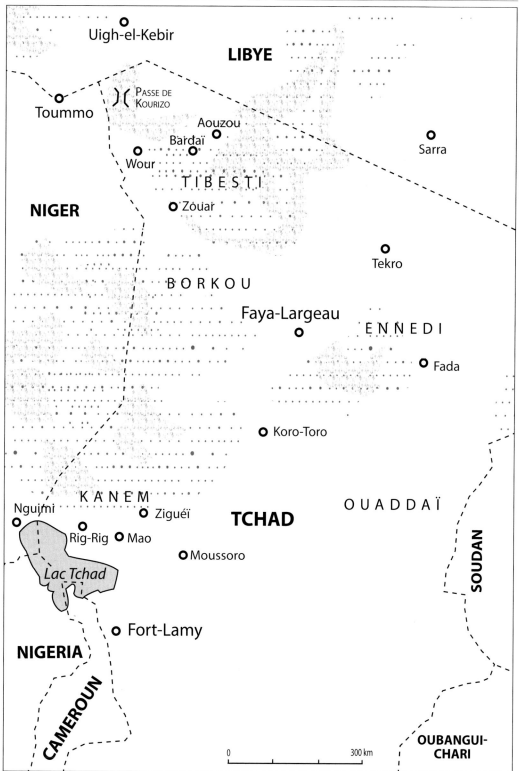

Map 3 Northern Chad.

took. He travelled in the company of a British officer named Lieutenant George Mercer Nairne,[4] who presented himself to Dio upon departure from Yaoundé on Tuesday, 3 December 1940. The young officer of His Gracious Majesty spoke excellent French and was assigned as a liaison officer to Leclerc's staff at Fort-Lamy. During 'the long overland journey that I made with *Commandant* Dio,' Mercer Nairne learnt what the '2S' commemoration was about and what the date represented for Saint-Cyriens. Dio certainly noticed that the young British officer was wearing the cap badge of his regiment, the Royal Scots Greys, which includes the battle honour 'Waterloo.' Fortunately, the two officers had a sense of humour. They became close during those six days of travel spent in each other's company.[5] Arriving in Fort-Lamy on Sunday, 8 December, Dio noted that the town was already livelier than the one he had passed through in May. Was Leclerc's recent takeover the cause? Dio headed straight to the officers' mess with Lieutenant Mercer Nairne, settling into the rooms booked for them.

The next day, Dio went to military headquarters. In Chad, Leclerc did not hold the office of governor, as he had in Cameroon. The Palais du Gouvernement was occupied by Pierre-Olivier Lapie, appointed governor by de Gaulle in December. Dio presented himself to the *RTST* chief of staff, *Capitaine* de Guillebon, requesting a meeting with *Colonel* Leclerc. Guillebon informed him that the *colonel*'s time was taken up with various inspections. He promised to find a slot before Leclerc's scheduled departure on 16 December for a long tour of the posts in Borkou-Ennedi-Tibesti. While waiting for the meeting, *Commandant* Dio made his rounds to the various staff sections and assessed the general atmosphere among his acquaintances at the *RTST* headquarters. He asked to see the documents Leclerc had posted since taking command on 2 December. He paid particular attention to the telegram Leclerc sent to all *RTST* posts on 3 December, especially noting the last sentence of the short message: 'We are pursuing a single goal together: …preparation to defend ourselves as well as to attack, under the orders of *Général* de Gaulle.'[6] The verb 'attack' had not been used in Chad for a very long time. It sounded like a wake-up call for the soldiers serving in the territory. 'A telegram which woke us from our moral slumber,' noted the head of the radio station of the *Groupe Nomade du Borkou*.[7]

A few days later, *Colonel* Leclerc wrote a memo laying out his views on command. For a second time, he raised the possibility of offensive action, despite the difficulties the *RTST* faced. Therefore, he required 'the instruction and training of leaders and men …. in manoeuvre and offence.' He set the tone for his leaders: 'prudent initiative, supported by regulations, will never be criticised.'[8] Leclerc's writings were no surprise to Dio, and he liked what he read. He nevertheless wondered what the offensive action Leclerc had been talking about since his arrival would be. During his visit around the staff sections, the *commandant* listened attentively to the comments of the officers and non-commissioned officers, particularly those concerning *Colonel* Leclerc:

4   George John Charles Mercer Nairne Petty-Fitzmaurice, descendant of ancient Scottish lineage, was the liaison officer seconded to *Colonel* Leclerc in 1941–1942. He participated in the first part of the Kufra operation, being with Major Clayton during the Italian ambush of the LRDG. Parachuted into France in 1944, he later became a minister in the British government (1962–1964). Under his title of 8th Marquess of Lansdowne, he was president of the Franco-British Society from 1972 to 1983. He was named a *Commander* of the French *Légion d'Honneur.*

5   Description of the trip made in 1987 by the former British liaison officer who became Lord Lansdowne: Lord Lansdowne, 'Leclerc, Chef de Guerre',' *Le Général Leclerc et l'Afrique Française Libre, 1940–1942,* Actes du Colloque International (Paris: Fondation Maréchal Leclerc de Hauteclocque, 1987), p.238.

6   Compagnon, *Leclerc,* p.195.

7   Béné, *Carnets, Première époque,* p.134.

8   Compagnon, *Leclerc,* p.196.

The officers found it bitter to see a unit like theirs entrusted to a man who was just a *capitaine* yesterday, and even worse, a cavalryman, and one who presented himself as such by continuing to wear his silver stripes.[9].... In addition, some were irritated by the fact that *Lieutenant Colonel* d'Ornano, a very capable officer who had been on site for a long time, had not been appointed instead. Surely, he was more qualified than this incompetent young man from London.[10]

Dio understood their annoyance but told them to give it time. Leclerc was a meticulous officer, even sometimes legalistic, but overall, he was a formidable leader in the field. Dio saw that firsthand in Cameroon and Gabon. The NCOs were the most upset about their new commander, also preferring that *Lieutenant Colonel* d'Ornano take over from *Colonel* Marchand. They explained to Dio that the first memo Leclerc signed concerned the triviality of dress and discipline in the mess. Moreover, they added, the directive was not even enforced. Indeed, *Capitaine* Troadec, Leclerc's aide-de-camp, noted on 3 December that 'd'Ornano, no doubt upset at not having had command of the *RTST*, came to the mess yesterday in shorts and a short-sleeved shirt .... I think we will soon find out what transpired between Leclerc and him.'[11] In fact, *Lieutenant Colonel* d'Ornano became deputy commander of the *RTST*. Dio was pleased to greet him, finding him to still be the cheerful officer he was at Faya-Largeau the previous May. Without offering any details, he hinted to Dio of a project he was setting up with the British.

Colonel Leclerc finally received *Commandant* Dio for a one-on-one dinner during the week. Leclerc was a believer in informal dinners which allowed him to continue working in a more relaxed atmosphere. After a polite short exchange on the conditions of Dio's arrival at Fort-Lamy, the new *colonel* commanding the *RTST* explained his short term objective: to prepare to attack the Italians. He briefly recounted his meeting with de Gaulle, who asked him to quickly join the British in the conflict. Leclerc added that it would be good to carry out offensive actions as quickly as possible because he had learnt that the heat in those latitudes would prohibit all large-scale operations after April. Then, he gave his quick analysis concerning the *RTST* that he had discovered since his arrival, emphasising the areas of progress to be made. Dio implicitly understood that the *colonel* was not quite satisfied with what he found at Fort-Lamy. Leclerc spoke of his second in command, *Lieutenant Colonel* Colonna d'Ornano, and told him that he was happy to be able to benefit not only from his knowledge of the men of the regiment but also of the entire BET region, which bordered the Italian territory. That could prove very useful if Mussolini's troops went on the attack. Leclerc explained to him that there was also a threat in the west that he would particularly like to guard against – the Vichy troops in Niger. He wanted to know what their disposition would be in the short term. Would they take advantage of Leclerc's offensive against the Italians in the north to attack from the west? Notin writes: 'Before undertaking any major action, you must secure your rear. One of Leclerc's first concerns was to discover Niger's intentions.'[12]

Before Dio could speak, Leclerc suddenly told him, quite bluntly, that he was thinking of him for the border mission. As such, he planned to entrust him with command of Group 4. He added that his previous experiences in Kanem would help him execute that mission. In 1938, Dio had spent six months as commander of the 4th Company in Mao, the capital of Kanem Province where the unit was deployed. In addition, as commander of the *Groupe Nomade du Tibesti*, Dio

9   The five stripes of rank of a *colonel* in the infantry are gold, while those of the cavalry and other mounted branches are silver. Leclerc would change his stripes later. (Translator's note)

10   Adrien Dansette, *Leclerc* (Paris: Éditions J'ai Lu, Flammarion,1952), p.79.

11   René Troadec, 'Extraits du Journal', *Le Général Leclerc et l'Afrique Française Libre, 1940–1942*, Actes du Colloque International, (Paris: Fondation Maréchal Leclerc de Hauteclocque, 1987), p.584.

12   Notin, *le Croisé*, p.107.

had maintained regular contact with the military authorities of Niger as part of the Niger-Chad border framework. Leclerc was surprised to learn that before the war Tibesti was included in an operational zone called *Commandement des Confins de l'AOF* (French West African Border Command), under the orders of a French *général* based in Zinder.[13] Leclerc knew there was still contact between the French leaders in Chad and in Niger, despite the two territories having taken opposite political sides. Leclerc could not accept such communication. Although he did not believe the Pétainists were capable of attacking, he feared that their propaganda would undermine the morale of the young *RTST* officers and therefore wanted to prohibit any individual exchanges. He specified that *Commandant* Dio would be the only officer from Chad authorised to communicate with the Vichyites in Niger.

On 31 December, Leclerc wrote to de Gaulle that the Vichyites had set up a defensive system and that they were targeting his personnel in Chad with propaganda. Leclerc said, 'this rather ugly method can always annoy the weak. I therefore instructed Dio, their immediate neighbour, to take all measures: he was authorised to speak with them, to write, to accept appointments, to drag everything out at length.'[14] In his letter Leclerc pointed out the approach taken by *Colonel* Garnier[15] in Niger who wrote a personal letter to *Lieutenant* Sammarcelli, stationed at Rig-Rig in Kanem, saying: 'You should know that the *Maréchal's* [Pétain's] policy is the only one that can save France at this time… I am a patriot from Lorraine. … Have you considered that to thwart Pétain's efforts would bring revolution and Bolshevism to France?'[16]

Commandant Dio was not particularly enthused by the *colonel's* decision to assign him to Group 4. He believed the mission risked becoming a sort of 'Tartar Steppe,'[17] while he awaited a hypothetical attack coming from Niger. And, assuming it actually happened, he would have to fight against Frenchmen again, which he absolutely did not want to do. The Gabonese experience left him with a bitter taste. He preferred to participate in the main action in the north against 'real' enemies and to find his *méhariste* friends. He avoided mentioning anything to Leclerc, but he thought about it a lot. Destrem summarised Dio's state of mind after learning of Leclerc's decision: 'Obsessed by a possible attack from the Vichyites in Niger, he sent Dio north of Fort-Lamy to Mao, in a position that blocked the only road from Niger. Dio chafed like a louse at the idea of perhaps still having to fight against the French, even though he had already done so in Gabon.'[18] Nevertheless, he did not argue, he simply indicated that he would do his duty and accomplish the politico-military mission. Leclerc was grateful to Dio for not complaining and appreciated his attitude.

One can speak freely in a climate of trust, so the conversation between the two men during dinner went well. Leclerc mentioned the problems of behaviour and discipline among the central portion of the regiment at Fort-Lamy and suggested that it needed to be taken back in hand. He was also concerned with the high number among the European cadre who took on administrative tasks while the ratio of officers & NCOs to soldiers was dangerously low in the *tirailleur* units. He believed there should be at least one European 'officer' for every 10 indigenous soldiers. He also mentioned the reluctance of some to accept him as commander of the *RTST*. He did not specifically mention the colonial officers and NCOs, but Dio understood his meaning. Perhaps Leclerc wanted

---

13   Zinder was the capital of the former French colony of Niger.

14   Gaulle (de), *L'Appel*, p.332.

15   *Colonel* Garnier was the military commander of Chad until April 1940 and therefore knew almost every officer on the other side of the border.

16   Notin, *le Croisé*, pp.107–108.

17   *The Tartar Steppe*, or *Il Deserto dei Tartari* was a 1940 Italian novel written by Dino Buzzati. The novel tells the story of a young officer who passes his life guarding a lonely and untested border fortress. (Translator's Note)

18   Destrem, *L'Aventure de Leclerc*, p.115.

to establish his authority too abruptly at first. Inevitably, a 'war of the buttons,' the exacerbation of the differences between branches of the army, for example between cavalrymen and colonial troops, would resurface. 'Leclerc imposed his will with less ease in Chad than he did in Cameroon.'[19] It was a culture shock for which neither the cavalryman nor the colonials were prepared. For Troadec, 'Leclerc, energetic, is a little short on tact in his [exercise of] command.'[20] In the cavalry tradition, it was inconceivable to accept 'the slovenliness and carelessness to which certain soldiers abandon themselves, without even caring about it, through a sort of Chadian snobbery.'[21] Conversely, the colonials did not understand a leader who, upon his arrival, 'on 2 December, signed a memo about uniforms,'[22] while they waited for a leader who would lead them into battle. Leclerc's own uniform, bearing the attributes and distinctive insignia of the cavalry, particularly exasperated the non-commissioned officers. Colonial troops were not used to 'cohabitating' with metropolitan troops, they looked more to the Ministry of Colonies than to the Ministry of War, and they were not happy seeing their commander in a blue uniform with silver braid.

An anecdote from this period clearly illustrates that Leclerc was not yet accepted by the colonial cadres. A young *sergeant* named Brousse, serving at Faya-Largeau, made a bet with his peers that he would bring Leclerc to attention, in front of him, a colonial non-commissioned officer. A few days later, a meeting took place in the meeting hall of Place Blanche, in the presence of the *colonel*. As it was about to end, the *sergeant* suddenly stood up and began singing *La Marseillaise*. Leclerc was forced to rise with the entire assembly and stand at attention. Of course, the young NCO was ultimately reprimanded by Leclerc, but he won his bet. 'At the evening meal Brousse was the hero of the day,' said one of his fellow non-commissioned officers.[23]

Confronted by these challenges, Leclerc even admitted to de Gaulle in a letter of December 1940, 'I sometimes want to give everything up.'[24] It is perhaps one of one of the only times in which Leclerc expressed such low morale. Dio listened to Leclerc during the dinner and had hardly spoken until then. But when Leclerc brought up his difficulties with certain *RTST* officers, the *méhariste* officer diplomatically tried to explain the state of mind of his colonial colleagues. He praised the cadre from the three *groupes nomades* operating in northern Chad. Then he quickly introduced Leclerc to his brothers-in-arms: *Capitaines* Sarazac in Tibesti, Poletti in Borkou, and Barboteu in Ennedi.[25] They were the ones who could best advise him on the specificities of that part of the territory. Dio also took the opportunity to discuss the important role of local chief-doms. He recommended that Leclerc contact the leader of the Senusiyya, Bey Ahmed en Nacer, who rallied to France when the Italians expelled him from Fezzan in 1931. Dio explained that the Senusiyya populations that remained in Libya were always loyal to their leader. They could become allies against the Italians, Dio explained. He added that Bey Ahmed had a brother, Abd el Jellil ben Sif en Nacer, who had not agreed to surrender his weapons to the French 'roumis' upon arriving in Chad, unlike his elder brother had. He preferred to take refuge in Egypt even though the Senusiyya *zawiya* was located in northern Chad, in Gouro, 100km due north of Faya-Largeau, at the foot of the eastern slope of Tibesti.[26]

---

19   Compagnon, *Leclerc*, p.203.
20   Troadec, *Le Général Leclerc et l'Afrique Française Libre, 1940–1942*, Actes du Colloque International, p.584.
21   Dansette, *Leclerc*, p.79.
22   Dansette, *Leclerc*, p.79.
23   Béné, *Carnets, Première Époque*, p.159.
24   Notin, *Le Croisé*, p.106.
25   Fernand Barboteu was in the same graduating class as Dio at Saint-Cyr, named for *Sous Lieutenant* Pol Lapeyre.
26   Gouro was a small, fortified village, the sacred place of the Senusiyya, where their ancestors are buried. The Senusiyya come from a Sufi brotherhood created in Mecca in 1837 to oppose the advance of Westerners in North Africa. They are located in Fezzan, southern Cyrenaica around Kufra and northern Tibesti. King

Dio received his assignment as commander of Group 4 on 13 December 1940 and returned to the Chadian province that he knew so well. Kanem is a large region of 120,000 square kilometres with a provincial capital at Mao. Its limits are the Nigerian border to the west, Lake Chad to the south, the Fort-Lamy-Faya-Largeau axis to the east and Djourab to the north, the bottom of the Paleo-Chadian Sea. The town of Mao, then populated by a few thousand inhabitants, is located more towards the southern part. The region is populated by several ethnic groups. In Mao, the Kanembous dominate, but there are also Toubous and Goranes, and to the north are the Dazas. This relative ethnic diversity is partly explained by the fact that Kanem was a region of transit, coveted for its pastures. This area, called Eguéï, extended from Ziguéï, a small town 80km north of Mao, to Kichi-Kichi. All the camels from the *groupes nomades* came to rebuild their humps in Eguéï. It was the same for the animals of Bey Ahmed's Senusiyya. An agreement was signed, authorising him to benefit from these vast expanses of pasture. Kanem is home to one of the oldest royalties on the African Continent. Created in the eighth century, the hereditary Kingdom is ruled by a divine-right sultan, commonly called Mao's Alifa.[27] The Zezerti dynasty of the Kanembou ethnic group has reigned since the Kingdom's creation.[28] This authority administers around 5,000 villages and 76 tribal chiefs. It holds judicial powers and issues *canouns* within the framework of sharia law. Dio made sure to visit that customary authority on the day after his arrival. They knew each other well. The *méhariste* spoke in classical Arabic with the Sultan, who was honoured that his visitor could address him directly without the help of an interpreter.

Dio remembered the meeting he had with Leclerc concerning his mission. Although Leclerc did not believe the Vichy forces would attack Chad from Niger, he could not risk the possibility and wanted to confirm his belief before attacking the Italians to the north. Therefore, Leclerc asked Dio to establish a defensive position on the border as quickly as possible. He also wanted to stop the propaganda from Zinder that was targeting his *RTST* officers. The method used by the Vichyites was the 'incessant sending of letters and telegrams that alternated tenderness, threats, good and especially bad news from families, and promises of sensational revelations.'[29] To discourage those 'bandits under Hitler's orders,' Leclerc wanted Dio to become their one and only interlocutor.[30] Dio was arguably not an impartial choice to lead the mission. Leclerc wrote to de Gaulle on 31 December: 'the Libreville coup had panicked the Vichyites; they were convinced that operations against Niger and Dahomey would follow.'[31] Dio was the only officer in Chad at that time who had fought against Vichy troops during the Gabonese campaign. Officials and soldiers stationed in Zinder could not ignore the fact that Dio had inflicted losses on them at Mitzic and Lambaréné. As a result, 'the trench of blood which now separates Capitaine Dio's battalion from the troops in Niger will also serve to dissuade Vichy from taking action or hoping to succeed through negotiation.'[32] Hence the importance of assigning Dio to command of the border region.

The new commander of Group 4 decided to resolve the problem of communication between the two territories immediately. He knew most of the *RTST* officers in positions of command on the border with Niger, and he knew he could trust them. It would be sufficient to simply give them

---

Idriss I of Libya (Mohamed Idris El-Mahdi El-Senoussi), who reigned until he was deposed by Gaddafi in 1969, was a Senussi.

27 The Sultan of Kanem is called 'The Alifa of Mao' because his name was Alifa Ali.

28 The Sultan of Kanem keeps in his residence sets of European armour that date from the Crusades: mail, helmets, and armour. He says that his ancestors fought against the Crusaders. (Testimony of Colonel Pierre Robédat, September 2019).

29 Létang, *Mirages*, p.234.

30 Notin, *le Croisé*, p.108.

31 Gaulle (de), *L'Appel*, p.331.

32 Létang, *Mirages*, p.235.

clear instructions. During his visit to Zouar, he learnt that Leclerc had criticised *Capitaine* Massu, commander of the Tibesti subdivision, for maintaining communication across the border. He reprimanded Massu, telling him, 'If they don't open their eyes, you have to think of your ex-comrades as enemies.'[33] Dio asked Massu to fill him in on what had transpired. Massu explained that, 'From 12 to 20 October, I made contact at Wour, on the western edge of the massif, with *Lieutenant* Aune of the *Groupe Nomade de N'Guigmi*, who promised he would meet up at Tibesti in the event of an operation.'[34] But Massu did not understand why there should be any concern about his own resolve because, 'There should be nothing to fear from [one who has made] an irrevocable decision.'[35] For example, he told Dio that *Commandant* Nicloux, serving in Bilma, contacted him,

> Shortly before the arrival of Leclerc, to let me know that *Général* Cornet was arriving by plane. I had no doubt that this was an attempt to convince me to join Vichy! But to this message, delivered by camel, and confirmed on the scheduled date with the prescribed radio transmission: 'Are you ready to receive 50 litres of oil?' I answered honestly: 'affirmative but do not guarantee their return.' A plane and a *général* seemed to me a good catch for the still embryonic Free French Forces![36]

Dio was convinced that the young *RTST* officers were not fooled by Vichy propaganda. Still, he sent a message to all border posts strictly prohibiting anyone from maintaining or responding to any requests coming from Niger. He informed them that he would be the sole point of contact for the Vichy troops. He therefore required them to direct all contact requests coming from Niger to him.

It was then time to contact the Nigerien military authorities as Leclerc had requested.

In Zinder, on the opposite side of the border, *Général* Cornet commanded Vichy troops on the Niger-Chad borders. His chief of staff was *Colonel* Garnier, who had been the military commander of Chad barely eight months earlier, and he knew Louis Dio very well. It was Garnier who had signed Dio's evaluation for the year 1939, ending with the assessment that Dio was a 'war leader who could be counted on in the most difficult times at the head of a unit.'[37] Consequently, *Commandant* Dio did not delay in offering to meet with *Colonel* Garnier. The meeting, and those that followed, took place on the shores of Lake Chad.[38] Dio adopted a polite but resolute attitude with *Colonel* Garnier. In coordination with Leclerc, he allowed intelligence to pass through the lines that was designed to demonstrate their great resolve. Accordingly, he disclosed details on part of the defence system to Garnier. Besides, he knew that in a territory crisscrossed by nomads, information would circulate and would be hard to hide anyway. To impress his contact, Dio also mentioned the British ships that regularly brought weapons into Douala and Pointe-Noire which then moved directly to Chad during the dry season. Leclerc wrote to his Saint-Cyr classmate, Kersauson, stationed at the Allied headquarters in Egypt: 'in Zinder, above all, great fear of seeing us attack, always the result of the immediate strength of Libreville …. Garnier was given the mission of 'converting' Chad.'[39] On this last point, Dio explained to Garnier that his scheme had been exposed. He demanded that he stop, or else Dio would consider it an aggressive act against his troops. He made it clear that the Free French of Chad were determined on an armed response

33   Jacques Massu, *Sept Ans avec Leclerc* (Paris, Librairie Plon, 1974), p.12.
34   Massu, *Sept ans*, p.13.
35   Béné, *Carnets, Première Époque*, p.104.
36   Massu, *Sept Ans*, p.12.
37   SHD, rating report, Dio, 14 Yd 1759.
38   Notin, *le Croisé*, p.108.
39   Notin, *le Croisé*, p.108.

to any attack. The result was immediate. Solicitations towards young *RTST* officers ceased at the beginning of 1941. Dio's plans of deterrence were clearly working well.

In parallel with these negotiations, and in accordance with Leclerc's orders, Dio took defensive measures against Niger to avoid being surprised. He followed *Colonel* Leclerc's orders to the letter regarding this mission.[40]

PERSONAL NOTE TO *COMMANDANT* DIO

1. The group being the only one in direct contact with Niger, must be able to:
    *   Either stop any Vichy offensive
    *   Or to exploit for propaganda and direct intervention any mistake of the adversary that allows progress towards the west to be resumed. The preparation and execution of this advance must remain the final objective

2. MEANS
    *   4th – 16th Companies
    *   20th and 21st Mounted Companies
    *   *Groupe Nomade du Kanem*
    *   Artillery Section No. 5
    In addition, *Commandant* Dio, exercising civilian authority:
    *   Will have complete freedom to raise and employ potentially useful supporters. Armament and credit requests will be made for this purpose.
    *   Will establish the group primarily for propaganda purposes. *Lt* Panède will be assigned to that role.

3. DEFENSIVE MISSION
    In the event of an attack, the defence will include
    *   Fixed points: Rig-Rig, Mao, Moussoro, on which the OT [organisation of the terrain] will be pushed to the maximum extent, which will be defended with no thought of withdrawal but never in a passive manner [nighttime patrols and surprise attacks, adaptation of the defence to the adversary's manoeuvres].
    *   Actions on the flanks, rear, and on the adversary's line of communication designed:
        *   to slow down and stop his progress
        *   to fully exploit any hesitation
        *   to clear fixed positions
    All mobile elements of Gr 4 will be devoted to these actions and will be trained for that purpose from now on day and night.

4. OFFENSIVE MISSION
    The assessment of the general situation or the adversary's mistakes can provide an opportunity to advance towards the west, an opportunity which must be seized, after authorisation from the military commander of the territory (except in cases of absolute emergency).
    For this purpose, Commandant Dio is authorised to maintain and develop contacts with elements in Niger, by any means deemed useful, subject to personally directing and

---

40   This undated document, handwritten by Leclerc (authentication by Christine Levisse-Touzé), was found in Général Dio's file at the Musée de l'Ordre de la Libération. Unpublished, it is reproduced here in full.

controlling these relations.

5. INTELLIGENCE
    Commandant Dio will arrange for intelligence collection within his group in liaison
    with the *SR* [intelligence service] of Fort-Lamy (*SELA*)

6. LIAISON AND COMMUNICATION
    Command Post Groupe Mao
    Additional resources: 1 radio, 2 pick-ups
    Push link up instructions with aircraft

The purpose of the note was to order *Commandant* Dio to defend against a potential attack from Niger. However, it reads almost like an operations order rather than personal instructions. The *colonel* went into tactical details that should normally have been Dio's responsibility. The document is full of lessons on Leclerc's way of operating and clearly illustrates his temperament and his tactical spirit. Leclerc saw the defence only as a means to return to offensive action, including bypassing and flanking actions. It was a tactic he would use a few weeks later against the *Sahariana* of Kufra. He favoured manoeuvre and surprise, and was determined to seize the initiative from his enemy. Leclerc asked Dio to 'establish the group primarily for propaganda purposes.' At the time, 'propaganda' was used in today's sense of 'communication.' So, far from being secret, the defensive preparations had to be clearly known to the adversary so as to dissuade the Pétainists of Niger from attacking Kanem. In typical military usage, a personal note like this was developed in consultation with the person for whom it was intended, and Leclerc certainly spoke to Dio about what he envisioned. The modes of action recommended in the instruction were not foreign to the *méhariste* Dio. The principles of surprise, manoeuvre and initiative were favoured in his branch of the Army. In 1932, in the French Sudan, it was these factors that allowed Dio's detachment to completely neutralise a dangerous *rezzou* at Ksaib.

The two officers obviously had the same tactical concept of ground combat. It was all the more surprising since they were both trained in schools that, at the time, strongly advocated the defence. The construction of the Maginot Line was proof that the offensive strategy, in force during the First World War, had been resolutely abandoned. How could these two officers have been so impervious to the teachings of their time and take the opposite view of the lessons they were taught? From this 'Personal Note to *Commandant* Dio' emerges the rejection of the principle of any form of static defence. Leclerc in Morocco and Dio in French Sudan had understood and adopted the two main tactical factors of success: surprise and speed. In this, they had intellectually assimilated du Guesclin's short maxim 'No attack without surprise.' The cavalier and the colonial camel soldier were on the same wavelength when it came to planning military actions. That like-mindedness allowed Dio to always understand Leclerc's manoeuvres; he could sometimes even anticipate them.

Dio followed his orders, constructing defensive positions on the axis leading into Niger. To expedite the work, he had to hire local labourers, working through the Alifa of Mao to recruit them. The traditional chief was the only one capable of finding the right balance between the different local ethnic groups because the workers hired by the French military were well paid and the jobs highly sought after. Dio ordered defensive works to be built in Rig-Rig, the Chadian village closest to the Nigerien border, entrusting the mission to *Lieutenant* Sammarcelli, the commander of the outpost in that small village of the Kanem region.

The pace sped up at the end of 1940. Despite Dio's relative isolation, his friends in Tibesti kept him updated on events. On 16 December, Leclerc, accompanied by *Lieutenant Colonel* d'Ornano, brought together commanders from the units along the Chadian borders at Faya-Largeau. Then he revealed his plan for the future operation: they would attack the two Italian posts of Kufra and

Aouenat on the French Sudanese border, and they would do so before the hot season. The next day, 17 December, in Zouar, he ordered *Capitaine* Sarazac, Dio's successor in command of the *GNT*, to lead a camel-mounted reconnaissance to the Italian post of Tedjéré located in Fezzan. On 18 December, returning to Faya-Largeau, Leclerc ordered *Commandant* Hous, leading Group 3 of the BET to reconnoitre for a route from Ounianga-Kébir to the Italian border that could be covered in vehicles. The orders astonished the Chadian colonials. When he learnt of it, Massu exclaimed: 'This plan is madness! None of us will come back from this.'[41] After a moment of surprise, some went as far as to wonder if this young cavalry *colonel* was actually serious. Is this 'some adventurous fantasy of an inexperienced metropolitan?'[42] On 5 January, *Capitaine* Poletti, commanding the *Groupe Nomade du Borkou*, a veteran *méhariste*, said to his men: 'This *Colonel* Leclerc wants to send us against the Italians with our camels. This is insane! He also wants to attack the Italian post of Kufra with a motorised column. He doesn't seem to know much about the terrible conditions in which such operations could take place.'[43]

Lieutenant Colonel d'Ornano was also worried about the plan, which Leclerc developed without much consultation. D'Ornano had his own short-term project that he was very keen on – the expedition to Murzuk with the British. In November 1940, de Gaulle had accepted the principle of *RTST* participation 'to the greatest extent possible in the operation prepared by the English in Fezzan.'[44] D'Ornano had been the one who proposed the possibility of joining in a raid on Murzuk with the British Long Range Desert Group (LRDG). He negotiated with Major Clayton, leader of the patrol, for French participation in exchange for a fuel supply in Cayougué, north of the Aouzou Strip, on the border with Fezzan. But Leclerc had officially opposed the project during the meeting on 17 December and d'Ornano, surprised, had not publicly flinched. But, since then, he skilfully took advantage of every opportunity when he was alone with the *colonel* to convince him to reconsider his decision. He explained to him that it might be useful to experiment with a motorised raid like the one planned by the LRDG before attacking towards Kufra. Along with the camel raid on Tedjéré, it would provide Leclerc with two sets of beneficial lessons. The *colonel* finally relented. He realised the advantages offered by this opportunity and, on 21 December, authorised d'Ornano to 'commit French troops to Murzuk without providing further explanations.'[45] There was also another reason for his change of heart. He perceived that the officers of the *RTST*, in particular the *méharistes*, were reserved if not reluctant about their future plan of operations against Kufra. It was true that Leclerc had not yet demonstrated anything to them other than his harsh tone and inflexibility. However, he knew the respect the *RTST* officers had for d'Ornano. Leclerc needed his help, and he had also just received 'advice' from Larminat which made him think. The High Commissioner took the liberty of reminding Leclerc that he had to rely on his subordinates by telling him 'your role is not to command a combat patrol. Don't break organic links. This is what you want to do yourself, but you must give it to your subordinates.'[46] Leclerc rose from the rank of *capitaine* to that of *colonel* in a few weeks. Larminat, older than him and certainly informed, advised him to let his subordinates do their jobs.

Dio followed it all from a distance. Like his brothers-in-arms from the BET, he doubted that Leclerc fully understood the challenges of the Kufra plan. But Dio knew Leclerc and knew that by avoiding confronting him head-on, it was possible to make him reverse a decision. At the end

41   Compagnon, *Leclerc*, p.198.
42   Dansette, *Leclerc*, p.85.
43   Béné, *Carnets, Première époque*, p.149.
44   TO No. 772 of 8 November 1940.
45   Notin, *le Croisé*, p.114.
46   Notin, *le Croisé*, p.109.

of 1940, he was often at Fort-Lamy, which was not far from Mao. It was the most passable route in Chad at that time.

Along with some of the more measured officers, Dio tried to explain to his commanding officer the difficulties of the operation, given their resources and timeline. Dio relied on Jacques de Guillebon, the graduate of the École Polytechnique and Leclerc's trusted chief of staff, who was also alarmed by the plan. 'On his own initiative, Guillebon drew up an assessment of the situation.'[47] The *capitaine* pulled out of his filing cabinet a document dated September 1939 that already mentioned Kufra. 'A note was drawn up by the colonial staff on the possibility of a French column conducting offensive actions … on the Faya – Kufra axis. The study was the basis for the creation of the company set up in Faya.'[48] The note provides for '1,000 men, 190 vehicles, 100,000 litres of petrol, 20 tons of food, 110 tons of water' in order to take Kufra.[49] The resources deemed necessary in 1939 far exceeded anything they had available in northern Chad at the beginning of 1941. In Chad, at that latitude, April is the latest possible time to conduct military operations. Helped by Dio, Guillebon argued for a postponement of the attack, highlighting the dearth of resources. A motorised raid of that magnitude seemed impossible to them. The *RTST* had very few trucks, and those that were available were unsuitable for the desert. However, the biggest challenge, in terms of preparation, was in logistics. The Chadian north is several thousand kilometres from the ports of Douala and Pointe-Noire, from which they could receive supplies. 'Simply put, it would take 800 litres of petrol to transport 200 to Chad.'[50] It was also important to remind Leclerc of the resources[51] that *Generale* Graziani's Italians gathered in 1931 to take Kufra from the Senusiyya when the latter 'had [only] a maximum of 500 rifles and a few machine guns …, no aviation nor artillery.' They pointed out to Leclerc that Graziani had written candidly in his book *Roman Peace in Libya,* that: 'This operation is the fruit of meticulous preparation rather than simple, but dangerous, improvisation.'[52] But Leclerc was immovable. He wanted to respect de Gaulle's orders to get Free French forces into combat as quickly as possible, and Leclerc did not want to wait until the end of 1941 to do so. He knew that time was running out and that he had to launch his operation no later than February, before the extreme heat prevented it. On 26 December, London received a telegram from Fort-Lamy specifying that, 'If contacts are favourable, a major motorised and *méhariste* operation would be carried out on Kufra.'[53] The die was cast. Remaining loyal to their commander, Dio and Guillebon accepted the principle that 'with Leclerc, we first set the objective, and then we figure out the means to achieve it.'[54] Dio had to admit that this way of doing things in Cameroon and Gabon had turned out rather well. Therefore, it was better to help than to obstruct. He and Guillebon adopted that attitude at Fort-Lamy in the face of the iron will of Leclerc, who often repeated: 'don't tell me it's impossible.' So, Leclerc's subordinates pulled out the 1939 plan and began to adapt it to the means they had at their disposal.

During a trip to Fort-Lamy at the end of December, *Commandant* Dio signed his evaluation for the year 1940 which ended with:

---

47   Notin, *le Croisé,* p.103.
48   Compagnon, *Leclerc*, pp.197–198.
49   SHAT, Étude de l'état-major des colonies du 25 septembre 1939, 1K239 (4).
50   Notin, *le Croisé,* p.103.
51   3,000 men, 7,000 camels, 300 trucks, a squadron of armoured vehicles, and an artillery section, according to François Ingold, *L'Épopée Leclerc au Sahara, 1940–1943* (Paris: Éditions Berger-Levrault, 1948), p.26.
52   Ingold, *L'épopée,* p.27.
53   Notin, *Le Croisé,* p.107.
54   Notin, *Le Croisé,* p.103.

Promoted to *Chef de Bataillon* at the end of these operations [Gabon], *Commandant* Dio, above all a man of action, departed at the end of the year for Chad to resume the fight against the Italians. A fine war leader, having considerable influence over his subordinates and his troops. Calm and composed, bold, but thoughtful. Officer of the greatest valour and bright future. To be used in garrison only when it is not possible to do otherwise. One of the best men among the colonial officers of Free France.[55]

Dio especially appreciated the penultimate sentence, knowing it was written by the officer who, in Douala on 27 August, refused to go to the meeting at Mauzé's house to welcome Leclerc. But all armies need 'pencil pushers,' he thought with a smile as he signed the evaluation.

On Wednesday 1 January 1941, Dio was in Mao to celebrate the New Year. For the soldiers in Chad, the new year promised to bring hope, which had been lacking a year earlier. With the arrival of their young *colonel*, they understood that they would finally be able to fight the Italians. They hoped to have their 'revenge for the shame of the armistice of Villa Incisa, an armistice with an Italian military that had not even come close to defeating the French Army of the Alps' in 1940.[56] The officers were of course concerned about the conditions, but they were all eager to begin the fight. The personnel of Group 4 on the Chad-Niger border understood that they risked missing the fight, but they were somewhat comforted by Leclerc's message of 21 December assuring 'that those who remain armed, standing guard on all our borders, need not worry; their turn will come.'[57] Dio managed to maintain the morale of his few troops by keeping them occupied with the construction of their defences, alternating with extensive training in the field, especially at night.

At the beginning of 1941, two combat missions departed from Tibesti almost simultaneously. On 5 January, *Capitaine* Sarazac and *Lieutenant* de Bazelaire left It Alafi in the direction of Tedjéré, in southern Fezzan. Their small detachment was made up of the best elements of the *Groupe Nomade du Tibesti*, including two officers, one non-commissioned officer, 25 *tirailleurs*, 19 *goumiers* and 70 camels. Their objective was the Italian post of Tedjéré, 400km away. On 6 January, *Lieutenant Colonel* d'Ornano, with *Capitaine* Massu, *Lieutenant* Eggenspiller, two non-commissioned officers, and five *tirailleurs* departed in the vehicles of Major Clayton's LRDG from Kayougué, north of Aouzou. Their objective was Murzuk, another large Italian garrison located 800 kilometres from the Chadian border.

On returning from their mission, the *méharistes* of the *GNT* had travelled approximately 1,000 kilometres. Although all the men and animals made the journey, they were exhausted. Having ceded the element of surprise, they failed to take the Tedjéré fort. However, the raid on Murzuk caused significant destruction on the Italians. Yet, the victory was unfortunately overshadowed by the death of *Lieutenant Colonel* d'Ornano, who was killed during the assault.

Leclerc quickly absorbed the tactical lessons of the two operations. Concerning Tedjéré, he wrote:

The importance of this reconnaissance lies in the fact that it was carried out by an entirely *méhariste* detachment. It underlines the current difficulty of the offensive use of these units …. The disparity between the range and the speed of the *méhariste* versus motorised elements is quite evident; in summary, although they are useful for defence and surveillance of the mountain ranges of the northern regions of Chad, the *groupes nomades* have a limited offensive capacity. They could, however, still provide service as support, reinforcements, or relief of the motorised detachments.[58]

---

55   SHD, Dio, 14 Yd 1759.
56   Romain H. Rainero, 'L'Italie et la campagne saharienne de Leclerc' in Christine Levisse-Touzé (ed), *Du Capitaine de Hauteclocque au Général Leclerc* (Paris: Éditions Complexe, 2000), p.340.
57   Béné, *Carnets, Première Époque*, p.144.
58   Fonds Leclerc, *Rapport concernant l'activité des FFL du Tchad en janvier et février 1941*, signé Leclerc du 10 mars 1941, boîte 6a, dossier 2, chemise 3.

In contrast, the raid on Murzuk proved to everyone that vehicles could suitably replace camels in desert offensives. The goal of the raid was not to take Murzuk but to create insecurity among the Italian garrisons of Fezzan. That was accomplished. Vehicles could cover twice as many kilometres in the same time as camels. Additionally, they were much less vulnerable to aircraft due to their better mobility. Finally, after a simple refuelling, vehicles are ready to be driven again. Camels, after 1,000 kilometres at such a pace, need several months to rebuild their humps.

These two full-scale exercises unfortunately signalled the end of the *méhariste* troops in offensive action. Leclerc had a keen understanding of that, having seen it for himself. No *méhariste* could blame him for subsequently loading the *groupes nomades* on trucks, as he would soon do. Massu, returning from Murzuk where he had been slightly wounded, admitted: 'after two years of crossing the desert on camels, my motorised initiation in the desert was dazzling.'[59] Dio was the first to be convinced and knew how to get the message across to the few who were 'nostalgic' for the great *méharées* (camel treks) of the beginning of the century. Nevertheless, he was proud of 'his' GNT which had returned in full force. In 1942 and 1943, he would suggest that Leclerc use it during the offensives in Fezzan.

Lieutenant Colonel Colonna d'Ornano's death was felt deeply in Chad. Among his companions, he would always be remembered as the first Free Frenchman from Chad to give his life. He became legendary among the French cadre in Chad, and his legend then spread throughout Free France after some well-organised 'propaganda' carried his story out through Brazzaville. He was presented as the first hero of Free France. In the Middle Congo and Cameroon, new training schools emerged under his name, and the details of his career reiterated by everyone as an example. Cited for bravery four times during the First World War, he served as a *méhariste* in Algeria, Mauritania, and Morocco. In 1937 he took command of Group 3 in Chad. 'His extreme height, his magnificent face, the ease with which he wore the desert uniform … and an enthusiasm that flowed through his crude speech, and his sometimes-colourful humour. He was a devoted and cheerful leader, whom others naturally obeyed,' was Massu's description of d'Ornano.[60] He also had a profound impact on Dio, who certainly copied some of his behavioural traits, particularly in his subordinate relationships. Just like d'Ornano, Dio maintained informal and direct relationships with his subordinates during his command positions throughout the war. Paradoxically, by addressing them in such a direct way, he showed them consideration and esteem. Regardless of where one sat in the hierarchy, every relationship within a brotherhood of arms was important, much like every link of a chain. A leader had to have a strong personality and great charisma for that type of command to be accepted. D'Ornano and Dio could afford such relationships, forged in the harsh environment of the desert.

D'Ornano's death deprived Leclerc of a second in command with whom he was beginning to get along well. 'Faced with this fact, there can only be one response: grit your teeth and avenge him,' Leclerc commented in a letter to Guillebon.[61] On the eve of his offensive against Kufra, the loss deprived him of an adviser and of an intermediary with the colonial officers. *Général* Compagnon summed it up well: 'It was also a loss for Leclerc, who found in him an intelligent deputy who knew the terrain and the men of Chad very well.'[62]

Leclerc departed on 16 January for Faya-Largeau, which he chose to become the hub of operations. The *colonel* quickly realised that he was missing a trusted adviser at his side to help him prepare the attack on Kufra. He then realised that Dio would be perfect to replace d'Ornano.

59   Massu, *Sept Ans*, p.28.
60   Massu, *Sept Ans*, p.15.
61   Notin, *Le Croisé*, p.115.
62   Compagnon, *Leclerc*, p.209.

Leclerc was able to measure Dio's 'toughness ever since his arrival in Douala and throughout the Gabon campaign, and he was aware of Dio's deep knowledge of northern Chad, where he had long commanded the *Groupe Nomade du Tibesti*.'[63] The *méhariste* officer knew the desert, particularly that northern part of Chad which would serve as the base of departure. He also had the respect of all the *méharistes* and leadership of the *RTST*. Was he not the first *RTST* officer to have returned to combat? 'It was in Gabon that the *RTST*'s baptism of fire took place.'[64] Leclerc's decision was quick. He summoned Dio to Faya-Largeau. To continue the mission against Niger, an officer would be assigned as interim commander of Group 4 at Mao. In the event of specific threats coming from Niger, Leclerc had a solution. He wrote to *Général* de Gaulle: 'If Niger becomes offensive, which is always possible, I will call on the *Bataillon* Bouillon *de Maroua*.'[65] That unit, which became *4e Bataillon de Marche*, was training in Maroua, a town in northern Cameroon, 200km from Fort-Lamy.

On the way to Faya-Largeau, Dio took a small team from the cadre of Kanem: *Lieutenant* Sammarcelli, *Adjudant* de Bodard, and *Caporal* Collin, who was an expert on wells in the desert. A plane was made available, and they arrived in Faya-Largeau on 20 January.[66] Faya-Largeau had become a veritable hive. Place Blanche, in the centre of the garrison, was clogged with vehicles. Leclerc set up his command post in the department chief's residence, a large, low building of immaculate whiteness. He was pleased to see *Commandant* Dio arrive. This pleasure was also shared by the colonial officers and NCOs who were there. 'Dio, who accompanied Leclerc in his new command, was reassuring to the *méharistes* of Chad.'[67] The veteran camel soldier quickly found Ganaye, the devoted Tibesti *goumier* who had been at his side since 1938. The Toubou guide was dear to Dio, and he was simultaneously an adviser, an interpreter, a bodyguard, and a servant. He was very courageous and formidable with a rifle in his hand, like many men of his ethnic group.

Dio understood Leclerc's expectations when he immediately gave Dio the mission of organising and preparing the 'modest means available to them, which were actually relatively considerable given the shortage existing in Chad.'[68]

He invested himself completely in the preparations for the attack on Kufra. As a good desert specialist, he learnt about the geographical and physical environment of Kufra, the particularity of which is its isolation. Ingold quotes Émile-Félix Gautier, a specialist in Saharan issues, who wrote in the 1923 book *The Sahara*:

> It is a unique situation in the entire Sahara. Kufra is almost exactly in the geographical heart of the Libyan desert. In whatever direction one moves, one must cross 400 to 500 kilometres of nothingness to arrive at an inhabited region. This 500-kilometre halo around Kufra is almost unexplored. It is by far the largest blank spot on the entire Saharan map.

Ingold adds,

> The Kufra Oasis itself occupies the bottom of an elongated basin (Wadi Kufra) approximately 50 by 20 kilometres. This basin includes six oases. El Giof with 2,500 inhabitants is the largest centre of the Kufra Oasis. Dominating El Giof to the north is the El Tag massif, the crown.[69]

63   Compagnon, *Leclerc*, p.214.
64   Létang, *Mirages*, p.216.
65   Fonds Leclerc, *Correspondance de Gaulle-Leclerc*, boîte 2, dossier 1, chemise 2.
66   Dio's personnel file states: 'departed Mao on 20 January 1941 for operations in Kufra.'
67   Notin, *le Croisé*, p.102.
68   Compagnon, *Leclerc*, p.214.
69   Ingold, *L'Épopée*, pp.14–15.

The six oases are called El Giof, Buma, Buema, Zurgh, Tleilib and Tallab. Water is abundant, extracted from numerous wells with an average depth of only six metres. But temperatures in the basin can become extreme and reach 60° Celsius (140° Fahrenheit) in the shade.

Historically, Kufra was an ancient Toubou citadel, which was conquered by the Muslims in the eighteenth century. 'It was a holy city after the installation of the Mahdi-es-Senousi.'[70] At the beginning of the twentieth century, Kufra was the centre of resistance for that ethnic group, 'a sort of Mecca of the Senusiyya, it had resisted the French in 1913 during Brazza's conquest of Central Africa.'[71]

The Italians took Kufra in 1931. *Generale* Graziani, who commanded the troops, wrote about the conquest of Kufra in *Roman Peace in Libya*: 'We can affirm, without fear of being contradicted by anyone, that the occupation of Kufra by force is the largest Saharan operation that has ever been carried out, as desert operations,' adding, 'These same Frenchmen cannot claim to compare themselves to us.'[72] Kufra included a well-equipped airport that facilitated west-east flights between Italy and Ethiopia, and was therefore an important post within the Italian colonial empire. The airport facilities were located between the village and the fort, which was built on a piece of ground called El Tag. The 'Fort of El Tag [the crown], a perfect square of 150 metres on each side, placed on a rocky outcropping, is a choice location.'[73] The Kufra Oasis is 1,000km from Faya-Largeau. Attacking it required an enormous logistical preparation with limited resources available in Chad. With determination, Leclerc meticulously prepared the operation with Dio's assistance. His energy became contagious. Little by little, Leclerc drew the most obstinate men to his side and moved things along. 'Faya-Largeau became the central focus in Chad, where troops destined for the next task massed, one after the other. From there, constant convoys set out to transform the post at Ounianga, 250km to the northwest, into a huge warehouse.'[74]

Dio dispelled concerns and responded positively to those who still doubted Leclerc. He expressed to them the qualities of the *colonel* whose courage, determination, and tactical judgement he came to appreciate in Gabon. He promised them that everything would get better with time. Guillebon also advocated for Leclerc among his peers. He wrote: 'Sceptics yesterday, we all let ourselves be ignited by his enthusiasm… Taking Kufra became the fixed idea.'[75] It was not Leclerc's intent to take Kufra, though. As he wrote to de Gaulle on 31 December:

> I do not intend to take it, but we will do maximum damage to the air base and other organisations outside the fort. For a workforce of 200 useful fighters, I will be obliged to take 70 vehicles, given the great distance of the raid and the significant consumption of our trucks, which are in no way made for this sport. Whatever the difficulties, we will go, and we will succeed.[76]

Dio provided unfailing support, particularly in the area of logistics. He knew how to travel in the desert and was therefore better able to prepare the necessary conditions for vehicles to replace camels. Unfortunately, the regiment was equipped with Matford trucks, which were under-powered and lacked the ability to carry a load in sand. In 1941, they were on their last legs. The same was true of the Lafly S15 trucks with semi-inflatable tyres that towed the 75mm guns. Both types of vehicles were particularly unsuitable for the operation. Fortunately, Leclerc managed to have 'vehicles

70   CHETOM, L.V. Bertarelli, *Libia* (Milano, TCI, mars 1937).
71   Notin, *Le Croisé*, p.104.
72   Ingold, *L'Épopée*, p.27.
73   Notin, *Le Croisé*, p.113.
74   Notin, *le Croisé*, p.108.
75   Compagnon, *Leclerc*, p.198.
76   Fonds Leclerc, *Correspondance de Gaulle-Leclerc*, boîte 2, dossier 1, chemise 1.

assigned to the *RTST* [that were] initially intended for the *Brigade Française d'Orient*.[77] They were 1½-ton Bedford trucks, made in England, which had taken part in the Norwegian campaign with the Foreign Legion. The 26 appropriated vehicles would arrive in time to equip the *RTST* mounted company just before departure to Kufra. Because of their high mobility in desert areas, the vehicles would be less affected than the Fiats and Spas used by the Italian Saharan companies. Responding to the emergency, the *AEF* command in Brazzaville had 30 Ford trucks delivered to the *RTST*. Although new, the Fords raised concerns among experts because they had high pressure tyres with a small diameter, which might cause difficulties when operating in sandy areas.

Despite the reinforcements, the *RTST*'s supply of trucks was barely enough to transport the operational units of the attack column. Solutions had to be found that would ensure the transport of supplies (fuel, ammunition, and food), medical support, and maintenance. Civilian vehicles called 'caouadji trucks,'[78] were requisitioned[79] and quickly militarised. That essentially consisted of cutting down the cabs and removing the doors to allow the crews to see and fire in all directions, including for aerial surveillance. Dio personally took charge of equipping the column's vehicles. The load weights had to be calculated as accurately as possible. The *méharistes* practised this strict organisation of logistics at crew level. Dio had sand removal plates made from 200-litre petrol drums to be hung on the sides of the trucks. In the absence of barrels, palm tree trunks called 'kékés' did the trick. He welded exterior equipment racks to hang baggage and *guerbas*.[80] Even with the modifications, the column of vehicles still lacked a military appearance, but functionality is what mattered. Everything was weighed and assessed, anything superfluous was eliminated. Ceccaldi, who helped Dio with the modifications, summarised it:

> It was necessary to cut the roofs of the cabins to allow the automatic weapons to fire in all directions. Machine gun mounts were installed, and the truck bodies reinforced. All this in record time and with delirious enthusiasm. The whole thing undoubtedly gained in effectiveness, but without losing its precarious and hand-cobbled appearance.[81]

The men's supplies were also reduced. Dio provided each staff with the *méhariste* food ration: dried bananas and dates, dried meat, pasta,[82] and some canned goods. Met with grimacing from some of the Europeans pulled from office jobs, he told them, good-humouredly, that they could supplement their rations with what they found on site.

To write the operations order, Leclerc's officers divided up the tasks. They established the four usual sections of a general staff: personnel (S1), intelligence (S2), operations (S3), and logistics (S4). The different paragraphs of the order were developed from partial information taken from land and air reconnaissance. From 13 to 27 December, *Commandant* Hous discovered a vehicular route between Ounianga-Kébir and Le Rocher Noir on the Libyan border. The route would therefore pass through Tékro (the last French fort with a permanent water point), La Roche de Tomma, the Jef-Jef Plateau and Le Rocher Noir. The border was approximately halfway, 500km, between Faya-Largeau and Kufra. For the journey into Libyan territory, aerial reconnaissance made it possible to identify two known points leading into the Kufra Oasis: the Ma'atan as-Sarra (the Well of Sarra)

---

77   Létang, *Mirages,* p.259.
78   *Caoudjis* or *caouadjis* were trucks used by local traders. (Translator's note)
79   Ingold, *L'Épopée,* p.86.
80   *Guerbas* are goatskin bags used to hold water reserves. (Translator's note)
81   Roger Ceccaldi, 'Koufra, Souvenir de l'Artilleur', *Le Général Leclerc et l'Afrique Française Libre, 1940–1942,* Actes du Colloque International (Paris: Fondation Maréchal Leclerc de Hauteclocque, 1987), p.431.
82   This pasta was a 'greyish boiled macaroni that was the exclusive food of the troops… *Major* Dio called it 'the macaroni of friendship." (Croidys, *Notre Second Bayard,* p.86.)

and Djebel Sherif, a distinctive mountain. *Lieutenant* Corlu listed the difficulties of the journey that the French troops in Chad would face:

> The column will follow the route: Faya – Ounianga – Kébir – Tékro, and then Kufra; it involves passing through the Bénenbèche threshold, a series of steep hills separated by very soft beds of sand, crossing a triple line of cliffs, crossing a rocky plateau strewn with sharp stones that destroy tyres, then the reg, flat as a billiard table, sometimes compact sand, sometimes black stones, the route runs along notable massifs [Djebel Sherif, Bréhéra] and then Kufra appears from a great distance, announced by the Gara-Touila, a splendid landmark reminiscent of Mont Saint-Michel.'[83]

On 25 January, Major Clayton's two patrols from the Long Range Desert Group arrived at Faya-Largeau from Zouar, where they had spent time recuperating with Massu after their raid on Murzuk. The LRDG's commander, Major Bagnold, also arrived at Faya-Largeau from Egypt. Leclerc organised a small military ceremony at Place Blanche to honour the British allies.[84] After the ceremony concluded, Bagnold and Clayton met with Leclerc and Dio. Dio was quite interested in the techniques and equipment of the special unit which allowed it to operate so well in the desert. Major Bagnold, an officer-explorer who was unusual in many respects, had been travelling the desert since the 1930s. He had developed 'two key innovations for those who want to travel in a Saharan environment: the solar compass and a system of sand removal by using rigid plates.'[85] Equipped with 'Chevrolets without a cab, doors, or windshield, fitted with very wide tyres, they manoeuvre with great ease.'[86] The LRDG was a formidable tool, likened to a 'sort of over-armed, over-equipped swarm of bees.'[87]

Dio took careful note of everything he saw and heard while meeting with the two British officers.[88] He discovered during the meeting that Bey Ahmed's brother, Abd El Jellil ben Sif en Nacer, had been a part of the LRDG patrols. The British took him along with them in their baggage 'in order to incite the populations of Fezzan to revolt.'[89] Dio met with him and tried to engage him in conversation, but the sheikh was very reserved and appeared to be guarded. Seeing that, Dio was happy to be able to arrange a meeting between Leclerc and his brother, the much more cooperative Bey Ahmed. 'Leclerc would speak with him and get information. The Fezzani refugees would provide very useful guides when the time came.'[90] At Dio's request, Bey Ahmed agreed to write an introductory note for the local chief of the Kufra Oasis so the troops from Chad would receive a warm welcome. Leclerc took it with him. Dio had no trouble convincing Leclerc of the need to

---

83 Jean-Marie Corlu, 'Causerie' (*Eveil du Cameroun*, 26 May 1941). Publication of a talk given at the Bellevue Hotel in Yaoundé.

84 Ingold, *L'Épopée* p.85.

85 Létang, *Mirages,* p.250.

86 Ceccaldi, 'Koufra, Souvenir de l'Artilleur', p.433.

87 Notin, *Le Croisé*, p.114.

88 He would have certainly had this meeting at Faya-Largeau in mind many years later when he came up with the specifications for creating the prototype *véhicule léger de reconnaissance et d'appui,* or *VLRA* (light reconnaissance and support vehicle) used by the French Army as well as many African armies. The *VLRA* is a family of multifunctional vehicles launched by Ateliers Legueu Meaux in the early 1960s. The vehicles were built by the *Ateliers de Construction Mécanique de l'Atlantique* in Saint-Nazaire. Called 'desert camel,' the President of the Republic uses one every 14 July during the Bastille Day parade down the Champs Élysées. It is still in use in the French Army as of 2024 and was even adopted by the British SAS for use in Afghanistan.

89 Notin, *le Croisé*, p.114.

90 Compagnon, *Leclerc,* p.204.

rely on local populations. Like the British, he believed that the Senusiyya leaders would also ally with him against the Italians.

Leclerc's initial intention was to carry out a raid on Kufra similar to that of Murzuk, causing as much damage as possible in the area, particularly to the airfield. The operations report signed by *Colonel* Leclerc dated 15 March 1941 is the primary source from which the story derives.[91] Only specific information regarding *Commandant* Dio, taken from other sources, has been added. This warrants clarification because some versions of the mission to Kufra derive from this single source.

The composition of the column formed for the raid on Kufra was:

- Staff: *Colonel* Leclerc, *Commandants* Hous (commander of Group 3) and Dio (reinforcement), *Capitaine* de Guillebon (chief of staff) and Captain Mercer Nairne (British liaison officer),
- Two platoons of the mounted company, under *Capitaines* Rennepont[92] and Geoffroy,
- Two sections of the *Groupe Nomade de l'Ennedi* under Capitaine Barboteu, reinforced with the European cadres of the *Groupe Nomade du Borkou* of Capitaine Poletti as well as *Lieutenants* Sammarcelli (Kanem) and Corlu (Tibesti),
- Two sections of the 7th Company of the *RTST* (Faya-Largeau), under *Lieutenant* Fabre,
- Two groups of 81mm mortars, with *Lieutenant* Dubut of the 6th *RTST* Company,
- A section of 75mm mountain (artillery) under the orders of *Lieutenant* Ceccaldi,
- A section of Laffly armoured cars under the orders of *Adjudant* Detouche,
- A combat train with supplies, medical section, and maintenance, under the orders of *Lieutenant* Combes, *Médecin Capitaine* Mauric and *Capitaine* Parazols, respectively.

Approximately 90 wheeled vehicles made up the attack column,[93] which was further reinforced with Major Clayton's LRDG patrol of 24 well-equipped and well-armed vehicles. Finally, a Blenheim bombing group under the orders of *Commandant* Astier de Villatte was assigned to support the attack column if necessary. Lysander and Potez 29 aircraft from Chad were in support. The column comprised 101 Europeans and 301 indigenous Africans, an unusually high proportion of Europeans. In the units of *tirailleurs sénégalais*, a ratio of Europeans approaching 10 percent was typically considered satisfactory. For the Kufra attack column, it was 25 percent. This ratio was achieved by drawing on European cadres from units not participating in the operation. It was also obtained by taking European administrators out of their offices. Sedentary administrative tasks could be, according to Leclerc, carried out by local staff or contracted staff, such as expatriates or the wives of Frenchmen. Finally, a number of '*Légionnaires Volontaires du Cameroun*,' such as Marcel Poualion, followed Dio to Chad.

The order for the departure from Faya-Largeau was issued on 27 January 1941. *Lieutenant* Sammarcelli led the vanguard with two vehicles, preceding the bulk of the column by several days, to reconnoitre and mark the 1,000-kilometre route to Kufra. With *Aspirant* Lami responsible for navigation, the small detachment had to find the right route and relay information on the enemy, particularly air activity, via long-range radio. The day before departure, Major Clayton, commanding the LRDG patrol, obtained Leclerc's approval to precede the column by a day to Djebel Sherif, 100 kilometres short of Kufra. The attack column arrived on 28 January at Ounianga-Kébir, 210 kilometres from Faya-Largeau. 'The Ounianga-Kébir post was built on a

---

91   Fonds Leclerc, *Rapport d'opérations Koufra,* boîte 6a, dossier 2, chemise 2b.
92   Pierre de Hauteclocque (alias Rennepont) was the son of Wallerand de Hauteclocque, the brother of Leclerc's father. He was, therefore, Leclerc's first cousin. The *nom de guerre* 'Rennepont' was part of his mother's maiden; she was born Françoise du Croquet de Saveuse de Pons Rennepont.
93   Corbonnois, *L'Odyssée de la Colonne Leclerc,* p.157.

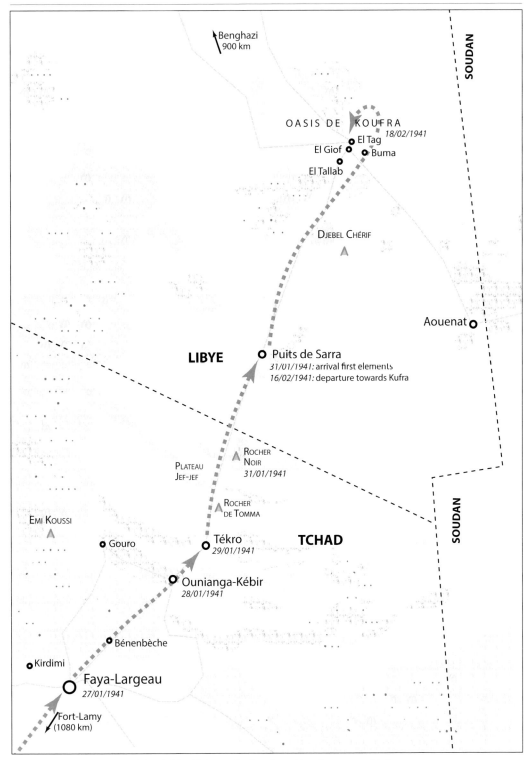

Map 4 The Colonne Leclerc from Faya-Largeau to Kufra.

rocky peak which overlooked a splendid lake 25 to 30 kilometres in circumference. The water of the lake was salty, but, strangely, on all sides small streams brought fresh and very clear water.'[94] This French post was chosen to be the logistics base of the operation. For several weeks, fuel had been carried in by trucks and camels and stored there. A landing strip had been built near the post, making it the forward base for Chadian aircraft. The column left the next day after refuelling.[95] It arrived 100 kilometres further north at Tékro, the last fortified French post before the border, held by *Sergent* Vandal and a few *tirailleurs*. In the middle of the desert, it was the last permanent water point in Chadian territory before the column continued the march northwards.

As expected, the British Bedfords overcame the off-road difficulties with relative ease. However, the French Matfords and American Fords struggled, getting stuck in the sand and breaking the gearboxes. Dio was responsible for gathering up and pushing the stragglers so that the column could reconstitute at each night stage. 'The terrain was difficult and the temperature, which was hot during the day and very cold at night, was challenging.'[96] The thermometer reached as high as 60° Celsius (140° Fahrenheit) during the day and approached zero in the middle of the night. The convoy arrived with great difficulty on 31 January at Rocher de Toma.[97] Leclerc then decided to send *Commandants* Hous and Dio with the detachment of the *Groupe Nomade de l'Ennedi* towards the Ma'atan as-Sarra, within Libyan territory. The well was the only water point located between Tékro and Kufra.

At the end of the day, a radio communication from Sammarcelli's detachment informed Leclerc that Clayton's patrol had been attacked on 30 January by *Capitano* Francesco Mattioli's '*Sahariana di Cufra*'[98] and its planes, at the Djebel Sherif pass. Several vehicles were damaged and Major Clayton had been taken prisoner. The operations order he carried was almost certainly recovered by the Italians. The hoped-for surprise would therefore no longer be possible, so the remainder of the LRDG patrol retreated to the Ma'atan as-Sarra. Additionally, Sammarcelli's detachment also retraced its steps having been spotted by Italian planes 90km from Kufra at Djebel-el-Bub.[99] Finally, in more bad news, Dio reported to Leclerc that the Ma'atan as-Sarra was unusable. The Italians had blocked it with stones and a dead camel, making it impossible to refill the column's water supply as planned. Faced with these setbacks, Leclerc decided to leave a detachment to unblock and guard the well while the bulk of the column under *Commandant* Hous, assisted by Dio, withdrew to Tékro to await orders. *Maréchal des Logis-Chef* Collin who came with Dio from Kanem was a well digger.[100] He would take charge of clearing the well, which was not a simple task, due to its large size: 64 metres deep and 1.2 metres in diameter. Leclerc also asked the detachment to set up a makeshift airfield. Leclerc then decided to move forward personally towards Kufra to find out more for himself. The wildest rumour was circulating about the size and armament of the Italians. He would reconnoitre the oasis with the two platoons of the mounted company,

94   Béné, *Carnets, Première époque*, p.201.
95   The trucks in the column consumed on average 100 to 150 litres of fuel per 100km. Ingold, *L'Épopée*, p.260.
96   Roger Ceccaldi, 'Koufra, Souvenir de l'Artilleur', *Le Général Leclerc et l'Afrique Française Libre, 1940–1942*, (Paris: Actes du Colloque International, Fondation Maréchal Leclerc de Hauteclocque, 1987), p.437.
97   The operations report gives the date 3 February, which must be a typographical error, as confirmed by the rest of the story. Fonds Leclerc, boîte 6a, dossier 2, chemise 2b: Rapport d'opérations Koufra, 15 March 1941.
98   Basilio Di Martino, *Scenari Sahariani Libia, 1919–1943, la via italiana alla guerra nel deserto* (Roma: Ufficio Storico Stato Maggiore Difesa, 2021), pp.191–194.
99   Ceccaldi illuminates the relatively little-known exploit of this young officer, who was the first to open the way to Kufra, without a map or information of any kind. Roger Ceccaldi, 'Koufra, Souvenir de l'Artilleur', p.428.
100 The following November, this *méhariste* NCO contracted rabies when he was bitten by his dog, which had previously been attacked by a rabid hyena. He died in excruciating pain at the end of 1941.

equipped with Bedford trucks with a range of 1,000km. That reconnaissance detachment included 60 European and 30 indigenous troops. A vehicle from Clayton's patrol, the '*Manouka*,' equipped for navigation in the desert, remained with the detachment. Leclerc agreed to allow the remainder of the British LRDG patrol to return to Egypt. He only asked them to pass through Djebel Uweinat to confirm or deny the presence of Italians in the small post 150km to the southeast on the border with Sudan. *Lieutenant* Corlu joined them, returning shortly thereafter with news that Mussolini's troops had abandoned the post. On that same day in northern Libya, British forces under General Archibald Wavell pushed Graziani's Italians into retreat towards Tripolitania.

Before leaving for the Kufra Oasis, Leclerc ordered the aviators on 2, 5, and then 10 February, to bomb Fort El Tag and the Buma airfield, located nearby, to test the morale of the Italians at Kufra. The air attacks failed to produce the desired destruction since the Blenheim bomber was ill-suited for such a mission. Nevertheless, it all kept the pressure on the Italians. Advancing only at night to protect themselves from planes and maintaining radio silence, Leclerc's personal reconnaissance detachment cautiously approached the Kufra Oasis on the evening of 7 February. Leclerc's men moved into the village of El Giof at night. The first Sanusi they encountered told the *degaullisti* that the Italians withdrew into the fort every evening to spend the night. Contact could then be made with local leaders, including the chief of El Giof, to whom they gave Bey Ahmed's written 'introduction.' Leclerc thus ensured the support of the local population. Meanwhile, the platoons destroyed the only aircraft on the airfield, as well as its facilities, including the direction-finding and weather stations. Once done, Leclerc gave the order to withdraw before daybreak. During its return towards Chad, the detachment was strafed and bombed by three Italian *Ghibli* planes, which inflicted some losses among the French.[101] Nevertheless, the column managed to recover four survivors from Clayton's patrol who had travelled 300km on foot with very little water.

Colonel Leclerc, after a brief flight to Faya-Largeau, decided to resume the initial plan and attack towards Kufra with the column that was waiting at Tékro. He personally identified the route and saw the layout of the objective – enough to satisfy him for a renewal of the attack.

Curiously, before leaving, the *colonel* decided to separate from *Commandant* Hous by giving him a mission in Tibesti. The commander of Group 3, Hous was a tactically competent officer. Regardless, as the only senior officer remaining in the column with Leclerc, *Commandant* Dio became his de facto deputy for the second phase of the attack. It appears that Leclerc had thus indicated his preference for Dio. This had already been the case in Gabon when he was appointed to command a battalion even though he was only a *capitaine*.

Leclerc was in a hurry to complete the mission to Kufra. The hot season was approaching, and the vehicles had sustained some damage; some of the trucks were no longer operable. It was necessary to reduce the heavy loads. It was at that moment that it was decided to only take a single 75mm artillery piece, which would reallocate weight for more ammunition. The total strength of 400 men remained essentially the same. It was divided into 250 combat troops and 150 men for support. The column was armed with 26 automatic rifles, four machine guns, two 37mm guns, four 81mm mortars, and a 75mm gun transported by a Chevrolet truck and equipped with 400 shells.

The attack column departed Tékro for the north on 14 February and arrived at the Ma'atan as-Sarra on 16 February. There, the soldiers in the column found the small detachment guarding the well with the two Laffly armoured cars and a reserve of petrol. Collin had cleaned out the well, enabling the column to re-water,[102] and an expedient airfield had been established. Leclerc

---

101 The aircraft were Caproni Ca.309s, small biplanes made in Italy and armed with twin 8mm machine guns and light bombs. They received the nickname *Ghibli*, meaning desert wind.

102 This version is contested: the well could also have been cleared out after the capture of Kufra by *Lieutenant* Gourgout. (Ceccaldi, 'Koufra, Souvenir de l'Artilleur', p.435).

decided to move forward again as he had during the earlier personal reconnaissance. He wanted to eliminate the Saharan company that had caused so much damage to Clayton's LRDG. These *sahariane*[103] were motorised Saharan companies developed by the Italians for combat in desert areas. 'There were six *sahariani* (sic) in 1940, and each *sahariane* [sic] included between 76 and 187 men mounted on 15 to 20 vehicles, with an autonomous range of 600km, and reserves of one month of food and five days of water.'[104] Ingold described a *sahariana*: 'the composition of a Saharan motorised company was as follows: a *méhariste* platoon, a Saharan motorised platoon (transport trucks, armoured cars), an aviation section with three aircraft, and a *Fezzanais* platoon on foot.'[105] The vehicles were Spas, trucks with very large diameter wheels. They were not very fast, but they could go just about anywhere. That *sahariana* was in a way the guard dog of the fort of Kufra. Thanks to its planes it could detect any approaching enemy column and ambush it. Clayton's case was a little different, as it was the radio broadcast from one of the British vehicles that had alerted the Italians.[106]

Progress resumed on 17 February. Leclerc took command of the vanguard detachment composed of the two platoons of *Capitaines* Rennepont and Geoffroy. The objective was to move quickly and discreetly to Kufra. They knew the route. *Commandant* Dio led the bulk of the column, following three hours behind Leclerc's advance guard.

> The infantry was placed under the orders of *Commandant* Dio, the former *méhariste* and great desert specialist. *Capitaine* Poletti was his deputy. This 'heavy' column was made up of the *Groupe Nomade de l'Ennedi* (*Capitaine* Barboteu), the 7th Company of the *RTST* based in Largeau (*Capitaine* Florentin), the artillery (*Lieutenant* Ceccaldi), and the health service (*Capitaine* Mauric).[107]

Having entered Libyan territory, French troops were then in the area likely to be patrolled by Italian Ghibli planes and Savoia bombers.[108] Very strict instructions were given to each vehicle crew prohibiting all movement from sunrise until mid-afternoon. The Italian planes returned to their base quite early, allowing the French column to resume around 4:00 p.m., travelling mainly at night. During the day, troops had to take care to position themselves to prevent being detected by the enemy planes. *Commandant* Dio and *Capitaine* Poletti taught each crew how to position their vehicle to best take advantage of the shade of high ground or vegetation. They also taught them how to erase tyre tracks several hundred metres from their position. Finally, anything that might shine had to be covered, particularly vehicle windshields. They were instructed to freeze when aircraft passed overhead and above all not to shoot. *Méharistes* knew the art of blending into the desert landscape.

The vanguard's Bedford trucks progressed without difficulty. However, the vehicles in the main column lagged behind, despite the efforts of Dio and his subordinate leaders. On 18 February, late in the afternoon, Leclerc arrived at the southern edges of the Kufra Oasis. He moved well beyond the fort of El Tag on the east, planning to approach it from the north. Following the advice of the Senusiyya chief of El Giof, he was able to approach undetected through the vegetation and

---

103 The companies were called *sahariane* and the soldiers who comprised them were *sahariani*.
104 Dominique Lormier, *C'est Nous les Africains, l'Épopée de l'Armée Française d'Afrique 1940 – 1945* (Paris: Calmann-Lévy, 2006), Ed. Kindle, loc. 1311.
105 Ingold, *L'Épopée*, p.53.
106 To avoid being detected, one must stop using the radio (a practice the military calls 'radio silence') to avoid being discovered by an opposing radio direction-finding station.
107 Béné, *Carnets, Première Époque*, p.188.
108 Savoia-Marchetti SM.82, triple-engine monoplane transport and bombing aircraft, long range but very slow.

the folds of the terrain. Arriving north of the fort, he surprised the *Sahariana* stationed there and immediately attacked. Leclerc manoeuvred his two platoons using voice commands, completely surprising the Italians and forcing them to fall back. Geoffroy's platoon remained north of the fort to prevent the Italians from slipping away while Rennepont pursued the *Sahariana*. The next morning, 19 February, seven *Ghiblis* arrived to support the *Sahariana*. The Italian planes circled overhead, continually attacking the French. Nevertheless, the Italian company on the ground was forced back a second time.

Rennepont's platoon pursued the Italians for 150 kilometres, which left the second platoon in a difficult situation. Given the meagre means available to the platoon, it was feared that the Italians would be able to break out of the fort. Leclerc reached Dio over the radio, telling him to move quickly and help neutralise Fort El Tag. However, the vehicles in the main column, delayed in thick sand, advanced slowly towards the village of El Giof. Dio decided to move out ahead of the column so he could reach Leclerc and identify the best route of advance. He could then also develop a plan of attack based on the terrain as the first elements arrived. Once Dio arrived at El Giof, he began looking for Leclerc. *Commandant* Dio[109] recounted:

> After having occupied the airfield, the *carabinieri* barracks, and the *Sottozona* [administrative building] during the night, I set out on the morning of the 19th in Parazol's[110] Humber [truck], looking for the *général*[111] on the rocky plateau of El Tag. Two or three *Ghibli* were circling in the sky constantly strafing Geoffroy's detachment, which was watching the fort's exits. The movements of those wicked planes forced Parazols to stop and camouflage his truck in the ravine, the scene of the fight the day before…. Once the danger had passed, we set off again and finally found the *général* with *Capitaine* de Guillebon, halfway up a peak from where he observed the final flight of the Italian Saharan Company, crushed a second time.[112]

Leclerc and Dio then moved into the local village, which was hidden from view of the fort. Dio reported to his *colonel*: 'My 'circus' is stuck in the sand on the edge of the palm grove not far from here. I received your order to hurry but it was the best I could do.'[113] *Lieutenant* Corlu recounted the sequence of events:

> The mobile elements having been liquidated, the fort and its garrison remained. But where was our artillery that everyone was already counting on? Rightly judging it imprudent to venture his equipment into a 14km area as flat as a billiard table, the leader of the detachment [Dio] decided to wait for night to avoid the constant planes. The *colonel* absolutely wanted his 75, so he ordered *Commandant* Dio to hurry forward. The latter, who had not slept for 36 hours, accepted the mission but providentially found Kufra's only horse, which was grazing on cabbages in the garden. It was the personal mount of the fort commander. He jumped on

---

109 'La première canne de Koufra', *Caravane*, 89, avril 1949, p.14. This article is not signed by Dio, but it is written in the first person and the story is located after an article written by him.

110 This officer was in charge of the vehicle repair teams.

111 For Dio, and all the veterans, when they spoke of their leader, it was '*Général* Leclerc.' This was so true that even after Leclerc was elevated to the dignity of *Maréchal*, they did not call him '*Maréchal* Leclerc' but rather, '*Général* Leclerc, *Maréchal de France*.' But here, at the beginning of the summer of 1941, Dio is wrong, because Leclerc was still a *colonel*.

112 Louis Dio, 'L'audace raisonnée du Général Leclerc', *Caravane*, No. 89, April 1949; p.14; 'La Première canne de Koufra', *Soldats de Leclerc, récits et anecdotes 1940–1946* Fondation Général Leclerc de Hauteclocque, Maréchal de France (Paris: éditions Lavauzelle, 1997), p.41.

113 Jean-Julien Fonde, 'Koufra: la victoire d'une volonté,' *La Cohorte* 79 (juillet 1983) p.6.

it and paraded for 1,000 metres at the foot of El Taj [sic][114] paying no attention to the firing directed at him. Sand shot up on all sides, the beast was upset at the whistling of bullets and took off at a gallop. It was a fierce pursuit out to the maximum range of the weapons. Upon arriving at his destination, *Commandant* Dio admitted 'That was a close one! They must not have liked me taking Morechini's jackass.'[115] But the brave beast in question made sure the artillery could arrive, despite the attacking planes, giving the fort a foretaste of the sauce that it would be eaten with.[116]

The horse anecdote even appears in Leclerc's report of the operation, which illustrates the importance he attached to it:

> Around 12:00 p.m. on the 19th, Colonel Leclerc was at El Giof with *Commandant* Dio, the latter having arrived ahead of his vehicles which were struggling against the sand in the SE basin of El Giof. A native brought the horse belonging to the *capitano* in command of the area. *Commandant* Dio mounted it and, met with numerous weapons from the fort, galloped back to his vehicles which he managed to bring to El Giof that night.

Leclerc obviously appreciated the panache of Dio's somewhat crazy act, which certainly could have ended very badly. *Commandant* Dio, who was an excellent rider, remembered the episode of Mitzic, where Leclerc entered alone into the village that had just been abandoned by the enemy. He wanted to prove to him that he was also capable of setting such an example for his men. The story remained famous within the *2ᵉ DB* and contributed to Dio's reputation among the younger soldiers in particular. The one who least appreciated it was Ganaye, the Toubou *goumier*, who saw his leader in such a dangerous situation, but was unable to be at his side.

Once the main force of the attacking detachment had arrived with the artillery, the siege of the fort could begin.

> Dominating the surrounding area on a spur of Djebel-el-Bub, the Italian Fort El Taj (sic) was an imposing fortress, 150 metres square, with walls four metres high, flanked by bastions topped with guns and machine guns. The citadel commanded respect with the unexpected appearance of its mass perched on the peak of a rocky cape. No one could move within 1,500 metres around it without being subjected to covered machine gun fire, and the visual range from the fort was extended by the observation post in one of the pylons of the wireless radio. Any vehicle leaving the *djebels* [mountains] which border the Kufra basin within a radius of 15km would be immediately spotted by the observers in the fort.[117]

Nevertheless, the Italians in the fort could no longer count on the *sahariana*, their guard dog outside, nor on their air force. The Italians had confused two Lysander liaison planes and a Free French medevac Potez for fighter planes when the three planes landed 15 kilometres from the fort on an 800-metre-long emergency runway south of Ez Zurgh. Thereafter, no Italian plane would dare to venture into the area. The military situation on the Libyan coast had also turned against the Italians, who had just lost all of Cyrenaica. The new developments changed the situation. Initially, Leclerc wanted simply to carry out a raid on Kufra, only destroying the installations,

---

114 Fort El Tag was the name of the Italian fort.
115 Mario Moreschini was the Italian commander of the Saharan Company.
116 Corlu, 'Causerie.'
117 Corlu, 'Causerie.'

as he had written to *Général* de Gaulle on 31 December 1940. *Général* de Larminat, who was in contact with Leclerc, wrote to de Gaulle on 26 February, that 'it is impossible to think of removing Kufra by force.'[118] In fact, Leclerc's resources, which numbered around 250 fighting men, were incapable of seizing a fort occupied by equal or even greater forces. Tactically, a ratio of three to one is usually necessary to successfully attack a prepared defensive position. But, even with the ratio militating against an attack, Leclerc had a hunch that he could certainly achieve more than he had originally bargained for. In consultation with Dio, he decided to remain and carry out actions aimed essentially at undermining the morale of the Italians. The French therefore began to carry out deception operations. For example, 'vehicles arrived with their headlights turned on, stopped three thousand metres from the fort, turned off their headlights, turned around, left again in another direction with headlights on, stopped at the same distance... and did this all night. This tactic gave the impression of an army on the march.'[119]

Along with deception, Leclerc's men also harassed the Italians with artillery fire and with raids during the night. *Lieutenant* Ceccaldi's 75mm Schneider mountain gun fired an average of 20 to 30 rounds per day.[120] The 1928 canon was not made for the intense heat, and the recoil brake constantly leaked. The commander of the unit, a non-commissioned officer named Grand, had to continually refill it with nitrogen. The artillery piece normally had an effective range of more than four kilometres. But, in this case, it had to move closer because 'the truck carrying the observation and aiming instruments had not yet arrived.'[121] Some of the Kufra accounts mention that Ceccaldi adjusted the firing location to make the Italians believe that the French had several guns. Ceccaldi himself provides the actual answer: 'During the operation, we often changed position. Contrary to what people say, it was not to give the impression of heavy artillery; rather, it was to escape the machine gun fire which impacted all around us because we were on particularly open terrain.'[122] At night, Ceccaldi's artillerymen moved closer to the fort to increase their accuracy. They knew the arrangement of the buildings inside the walls of the fort from aerial photos. Ceccaldi's well-placed shots were devastating to Italian morale. *Lieutenant* Dubut's 81mm mortars also contributed to the harassing fires, shooting from the palm grove north of the fort. Regarding the fire on the fort, Corlu says:

> The artillery, fired at irregular times and at an unpredictable cadence, created a mental tension which increased and eventually overcame the defenders. Ten shots in the morning, three in the afternoon, five or six separate shots at night, the next day a double regime, in the meantime mortar fire on the ancillary defences made life unpleasant inside the fort.[123]

The second form of harassment was raids on enemy positions, which were conducted only at night. The Italians had built trenches running from the fort out to the bastions, which were equipped with firing points.[124] Leclerc described this advanced defensive system in the operations report: 'In addition to the fort itself, the plateau which surrounded it was filled with numerous covered

---

118 Notin, *Le Croisé,* p.125.
119 Philippe Etchegoyen, *Une Ombre dans la Nuit* (Paris: Les Éditions la Bruyère, 1992), p.37.
120 Characteristics: 4,100m range, projectile weight of 6.5kg, muzzle velocity of 270m/sec, rate of fire of 20 rounds/min, and weight of the entire piece, 400kg.
121 Ceccaldi, 'Koufra, Souvenir de l'Artilleur', p.438.
122 Ceccaldi, 'Témoignage de l'Artilleur de Koufra', *Le Général Leclerc et l'Afrique Française Libre, 1940–1942,* Actes du Colloque International (Paris: Fondation Maréchal Leclerc de Hauteclocque, 1987), p.299.
123 Corlu, 'Causerie.'
124 These trenches are easily visible in the photos taken by *Lieutenant* Daruvar during the summer of 1941 from the observation tower that also served as a radio antenna. (Photos, FML)

locations for automatic weapons that were linked by telephone, supporting a well-thought-out fire plan.' These defensive works made it possible to protect the fort at night. Yet determined infantry could attack in the blind spots at the foot of the fort, moving under cover of darkness. Therefore, the troops of the *RTST* focused their harassment actions against those external Italian defensive positions. According to Corlu:

> These actions were carried out with reduced manning. They consisted of eliminating the occupants of a small post, possibly taking the post itself or luring Italian patrols, and then surprising them with an ambush. These particularly tricky actions worked really well – without taking any losses ourselves, our surprise attacks hit all the enemy's posts, inflicting casualties, especially among the Europeans.[125]

A good number of the French leaders present around Fort El Tag were *méharistes* who were used to often travelling at night with their camels to avoid the heat of the day; they were therefore well prepared to carry out night operations. These 'surprise attacks were carried out by the *méharistes* on the exterior strong points of the fort.'[126] The Italians decided to completely deploy their external defence system in order to loosen the French grip, which allowed the French harassment to intensify. 'On 22 February we noticed some commotion. The Italians evacuated the fort to disperse into the rocks surrounding it where solid bastions were built, connected to each other by telephone, and equipped with provisions; a defensive arrangement at least as serious as the fort itself.'[127]

Dio decided to personally participate in one of the surprise attacks, unusual for someone of his rank and position. Certainly, Dio was still young, having not yet turned 33. He sometimes forgot his rank and acted like the *lieutenant* he was in Sudan and who wanted to prove everything, first to himself, but also to his men and his commander. 'We're going to show him what we can do!' 'him' was of course Leclerc.[128] That was what he said as he gathered his team during the evening of Monday, 24 February 1941. Selecting his men, he first chose *Lieutenant* Corlu[129] to assist him. The young *méhariste lieutenant* immediately endeared himself to Dio, who appreciated the circumstances of his joining Free France. Next, he chose *Maréchal des Logis* Poualion, the *Légionnaire Volontaire du Cameroun* who acted so remarkably in Gabon and who had not left Dio since then. Obviously, Ganaye was there, as well. Finally, three *tirailleurs* were selected from among those of the 7th Company from Faya-Largeau. At the start of the night, the small team set off towards the bastion they had identified. They dropped their equipment. The officers were simply armed with revolvers, their pockets full of hand grenades. The other team members had only their rifles and a few magazines of ammunition. They were fortunate in having a dark night. As they approached the Italian bastion, they dropped to the ground and continued moving forward at a crawl to avoid awakening the enemy sentries in their trenches. *Lieutenant* Corlu recounts:

> Surprised five metres from the low wall, the *commandant* saw two silhouettes rise up, almost touching him. Two shots were enough. Then jumping into position he threw all his grenades in quick succession. At that moment the Italians reacted and wounded the two officers who,

125 Corlu, 'Causerie.'
126 Notin, *Le Croisé*, p.124.
127 Corlu, 'Causerie.'
128 Notin, *Le Croisé*, p.125.
129 Graduate of Saint-Cyr (promotion du Tafilalet, 1931–1933), Jean-Marie Corlu (1912–1944) commanded the *Groupe Méhariste d'Agadès* (Niger) in 1940; refusing to accept defeat, he managed to travel the 700 kilometres on camel to neighbouring Nigeria and he placed himself at the disposal of Leclerc, who assigned him to the *Groupe Nomade du Tibesti*.

no longer able to continue fighting, returned surrounded by *tirailleurs*. That was when a Cameroonian *légionnaire* did an amazing thing. This non-commissioned officer, who was posted a little behind, heard the small group returning. He recognised his two officers and then saw that they were injured. He had to stay where he was so he could cover the movement. A few minutes later an Italian patrol passed, following the traces of blood left by our two wounded. *Maréchal des Logis* P... knowing the *commandant* was incapable of walking quickly and for a long time, saved him by attracting attention to himself. He made noise with his rifle and his canteen, he coughed, and he ran off in the opposite direction. As he expected, the whole patrol pursued him, but he had a head start and after a while he hid himself in a half-blocked well that he providentially found along the way. The patrol moved on without seeing him, so he remained still all night. The next day when he looked up he realised that he was in the middle of an open area under fire from the fort. He remained patient, kept watch all day, and returned in the evening, asking for news of his *commandant*, whom he had saved by his risky actions.'[130]

In his report, Leclerc described it in these terms: 'patrols and surprise attacks are carried out almost every night.' The most daring was the work of an 8-hour patrol which penetrated the heart of the Italian position, *Commandant* Dio and *Lieutenant* Corlu were unfortunately injured there. Massu also recounted the fight: 'As part of the siege of Kufra, on the night of the 25th he [Dio], along with 4 men, carried out a surprise attack with a revolver and grenades on a strongpoint where 35 Italians were entrenched. He put 10 out of action, but was wounded and evacuated by plane...'[131]

Commandant Dio was seriously wounded in the lower abdomen, legs, and torso by grenade fragments and was bleeding profusely. *Dr* Mauric did his best to stop the bleeding, but he lacked the necessary environment to operate in sanitary conditions. *Lieutenant* Corlu was less seriously injured, although he had received numerous shrapnel wounds to both legs. The doctor asked *Colonel* Leclerc for authorisation to carry out an emergency medical evacuation for Dio. Dio was fortunate because the 'old dilapidated Potez 29' plane, called the medical 'limousine,' was pre-positioned in Kufra the day before.[132] Mauric took *Commandant* Dio and *Lieutenant* Corlu on board.[133] After stopping at the Ma'atan as-Sarra, the 'limousine,' piloted by *Lieutenant* de Goujon de Thuisy, reached the Ouninga-Kébir logistics base.[134] The medical infrastructure at the base was insufficient to treat the two officers, so Dio and Arnaud were then transported first to Faya-Largeau, then later to Fort-Lamy,[135] in an Italian Caproni three-engine plane.[136] An American film crew captured Dio's arrival on a stretcher at Fort-Lamy airport.[137] It is moving to see *Commandant* Louis Dio, bearded and shaggy, looking haggard, lying on his stretcher with his *commandant's*

130 Corlu, 'Causerie.'
131 Massu, 'Souvenirs du général Dio', p.3
132 Jean de Pange, lettre au Colonel Dronne, CHETOM 18H283 No. 31, p.16.
133 *Caravane* No. 48, 25 août 1946, p.3: in an article on Corlu, Dio wrote that he was 'evacuated on the same plane.'
134 Pange (de), lettre au Colonel Dronne, CHETOM, 18H283 No. 31, p.16.
135 Corbonnois, *L'Odyssée de la Colonne Leclerc,* p.164.
136 The Caproni Ca.133 is an Italian triple-engine aircraft manufactured in 1935. It was taken from the Italians in Haifa on 20 September 1940 and transformed into a transport aircraft.
137 A short film from the series 'Outtakes from 'March of Time' Newsreels, 1934 – 1951' in the 'March of Time Collection, 1934 – 1951,' at the US National Archives and Records Administration (NARA, 'Fighting French'/Local Identifier MT-MTT- 929 OO) shows 'wounded arriving by plane from recent operations.' Among them, 'Major Dio, one of Kufra's heroes.' NARA offers an online version of this film that also shows *Général* de Gaulle arriving at Fort-Lamy and welcomed by *Colonel* Leclerc, then reviewing the troops with General Spears, and other images of this visit to Fort-Lamy: https://catalog.archives.gov/id/149274148.

jacket on his stomach, on top of the bandages. He tried to greet the large number of officers who had come to welcome him, but his face betrayed his suffering.

Without air medical evacuation, Dio would have died in the Kufra Oasis because land evacuation would not have been possible.[138] He also owed his life in part to *Maréchal des Logis* Poualion for his important role, which was confirmed by the citation the NCO received from the army corps:

> Kufra operation from 7 to 28 February 1941 – Very brave non-commissioned officer. Participated on 25 February in a night attack against a strongly defended position. At the moment of disengagement, realising that his wounded leader was going to be found by an enemy patrol, remained behind alone, attracting the pursuers in another direction; remained all day in observation near enemy positions and rejoined the following night, bringing back good intelligence. This citation includes the award of the 1940 *Croix de Guerre* with star. Signed by Larminat. Fort-Lamy, 12 March 1941. For certified extract, Colonel Leclerc, Military Commander of Chad. With signature.[139]

Maréchal des Logis Poualion received his *Croix de Guerre* in a ceremony at Fort-Lamy on 20 September 1941. Dio and Poualion showed mutual affection and would be together throughout the war. Employed in his specialty as a mechanic, the NCO remained close to *Groupement Tactique Dio* within the *2ᵉ DB*.

The episode remained a difficult subject for Dio, not only because of the serious wounds, which caused problems for him in the future, but mainly because he missed out on participating in the victory of Kufra with Leclerc. Five days after his injury, Dio missed the pleasure of being alongside Leclerc and his comrades-in-arms when they invested Fort El Tag on 1 March 1941.[140] He was not there to see Leclerc's incredible bluff when he literally forced the door of the fort open and seized the initiative from the Italians.[141] He also did not have the honour of witnessing the Oath of Kufra on 2 March, on the fort's parade ground. He would have liked to hear the 'boss' pronounce those now-legendary words that provided their direction for the next three years: 'Let us swear not to lay down our arms until our Colours, our beautiful Colours, once again float over Strasbourg Cathedral.' Daring to pronounce this oath just nine months after experiencing the greatest defeat in the history of the French Army was crazy, Dio thought from the depths of his hospital bed. He also learnt that the harassment tactics paid off and caused the Italians' nerves to break down. The evidence is in a remark made by the Italian *capitano* who commanded the fort. *Lieutenant* Corlu asked, 'Why did the Italians surrender despite having superior armament to us and a year's worth of supplies? *Capitano* Colonna explained the reason to us. Invited to dinner by the *colonel* after our entry into the fort, the [Italian *capitano*] ate with great appetite and said: 'Finally, the first quiet meal in twelve hours.'"[142]

---

138 Dio spoke about his injury several decades later. He told *Colonel* Robédat in the 1970s, that he 'owed his life to Ganaye and the pilots.' According to Dio, it was Ganaye who pulled him from the Italian bastion and carried him on his back. Ganaye, despite his height and small build, was *'gaoui'* (strong). Dio obviously forgot to mention *Maréchal des Logis* Poualion, whose role had also been crucial.

139 Military document from the private collection of the Poualion family.

140 Ingold, *Général Ingold*, p.64.

141 Leclerc recounted this episode with a bit of humour. To Mrs Ingold who asked him during a dinner how he managed to take the fort of Kufra, he replied: 'It was very simple, Madame, the door of the fort was open, so I drove in.' Ingold, *Général Ingold,* p.64.

142 Corlu, 'Causerie.'

Commandant Dio regretted having to leave his brothers-in-arms before victory. His companions were also sad to see him leave the fight. *Lieutenant* Ceccaldi, chief of artillery, wrote:

> During one of them [the patrols], *Commandant* Dio, wounded, was evacuated by plane to Fort-Lamy. We are very saddened by this. We love this old *blédard*[143] whose manners are sometimes brusque but whose orders are always thoughtful and judicious. We met back up with him in Fezzan where I was still part of his tactical group. His great experience in the desert would still be useful to the *colonel*.[144]

In strategic terms, Kufra was certainly a limited victory, but its impact was nevertheless considerable. It was the first French victory led by Frenchmen from French territory. Its impact was significant in France and the Empire, particularly among the military, hesitating between legality in Vichy and the hope of Free France. De Gaulle telegraphed his congratulations to *Colonel* Leclerc from London on 3 March: 'The hearts of all French people are with you and with your troops. *Colonel* Leclerc, I congratulate you on their behalf on the magnificent success of Kufra. You have just proven to the enemy that he is not finished with the French Army.'[145] He ended his telegram with, 'I embrace you,' an atypical familiarity from de Gaulle. The military victory resonated as hope in France and throughout the world. One must remember that at that time, Nazi forces were moving rapidly from success to success, while the USA still remained neutral, and the Soviet Union was still allied with the Germans. The Gaullists in London spread the word about this first victory of the French Army. Michel Chauvet, a young Free Frenchman training in England, wrote: 'the successful operation in Kufra was broadcast widely on London radio and in English newspapers.'[146]

For the Italians, the loss of the fort had a catastrophic impact on the morale of their troops in southern Libya. For the British, fighting in Egypt, Kufra freed them from a threat on their southern flank and offered them a prime stopover for their air transit between AOF and Egypt-Sudan.[147] For the future *2ᵉ DB*, the *Serment de Koufra* (Oath of Kufra) would remain the driving force and motivation of Leclerc's 16,000 men, from Utah Beach to Strasbourg.[148] Finally, the victory of Kufra had a significant impact on the command of Chad's troops. Filled with admiration for their leader, all the colonial leaders of the *RTST*, who had previously been sceptical of Leclerc, unanimously adopted him. *Capitaine* Poletti, on his return, completely changed his opinion of Leclerc, 'of whom he now spoke with great respect. The exceptional courage of the *Colonel* had touched the depths of the heart of the old adventurer. He was especially struck by Leclerc's great audacity by seizing El Tag.'[149] In combat alongside them, Leclerc also abandoned his formalism on

---

143 A *blédard* is a person from a small village in North Africa, or a soldier stationed there. The word derives from 'bled,' slang for a remote village in the Maghreb. (Translator's note)

144 Fonds Leclerc, Ceccaldi, *Lecture of 4 October 1997* in Rambouillet, boîte 6a, dossier 2, chemise 2.

145 Compagnon, *Leclerc*, p.224.

146 Chauvet, *Le Sable et la Neige*, p.99.

147 The defence of Kufra was entrusted to *Capitaine* Barboteu, commander of the *GNE*. De Gaulle made the post available to the British, who then established it as a base of departure for their LRDG patrols. Until 1943, they carried out deep raids on the Italian-German rear causing great damage. After the war, a French section of the *RTST* permanently occupied the fort at Kufra until 15 November 1955, at the request of King Idriss of Libya. Additionally, the radiomen realised that Kufra was an incomparable radio crossroads, allowing them to monitor the Middle East and Africa. So, a valuable listening post was installed there. The last 'commander' of the fort was *Lieutenant* Demaison of the *1er Escadron de Découverte et de Combat de Moussoro*. Testimony of *Colonel* Pierre Robédat in 2019.

148 The daughter of a former member of the *2e DB* wrote: 'The sworn oath of Kufra was above all a commitment to never renounce one's ideals, whatever the cost.' Testimony from a letter retrieved by the author.

149 Béné, *Carnets, Première époque*, pp.199–200.

uniforms. He accepted that his soldiers were arrayed in a variety of uniforms. In complete want of everything, they adapted their clothing to the climate where the temperature differences between day and night were considerable. *Lieutenant* Ceccaldi described himself, 'barefoot, in a bad khaki sweater, unshaven, a scarf on my head as a hat' when he presented himself to the Italians at Fort Kufra who wanted to see the devil of a gunner who caused them so much destruction.'[150]

The *marsouins* of the *RTST* noticed with pleasure that Leclerc had adopted their uniform.[151] 'Leclerc himself sported a *marsouin* jacket with a double row of buttons and a long *djellaba*.'[152] Indeed, Leclerc quickly abandoned his blue cavalry kepi, to the great joy of the young non-commissioned officers who preferred to see him wearing a colonial helmet. Jean Compagnon wrote: 'With the war and the African heat, Leclerc would become less 'voracious.'[153] He became more understanding and more tolerant regarding formal discipline, because when it came to mental discipline, he required total adherence.'[154] Leclerc thus became '*le Patron*' (the boss) for all his men, whether in garrison or in field operations. What was Dio's role in bringing about this transformation of attitudes among the colonial leaders? Two direct witnesses wrote: 'during Leclerc's entire African adventure, particularly at the beginning, *Commandant* Louis Dio was the *général*'s guarantor with the 'colonials,' who were *a priori* reticent towards a 'metro' officer, especially one who came from the cavalry.'[155] There is no question that Dio's influence in Chad was crucial at that time. The prestige he acquired in Douala and Gabon was a routine conversation in the mess halls. After Kufra, Dio had no problem telling the men, 'You see, I told you that this colonel was the man for the job!' It was from Kufra that the mutual devotion between the *RTST* leaders and their *colonel* grew. In 1953, Dio wrote:

> The troops of Chad had seen their young *colonel* at work and now gave him their admiration and their boundless confidence that he would make them better than the sum of their parts and worthy of him. He could now ask them anything: under his orders nothing was impossible.[156]

With the total commitment of each of the men of the RTST behind the soon to be *Général* Leclerc,[157] the epic could continue. The men who had taken part in Operation Kufra returned to their units filled with justifiable pride. On 7 March 1941, Leclerc wrote the following summary:

> On 2 March at 8:00 a.m., the French colours were raised over the fort of El-Tag, taken from the enemy after 10 days of combat. With this victory, the *Régiment de Tirailleurs Sénégalais du Tchad* showed everyone that France had not been defeated and that its army was determined

---

150 Ceccaldi, 'Koufra, Souvenir de l'Artilleur', p.440.

151 '*Marsouin*,' or porpoise, is a nickname for French naval infantry soldiers. Initially the colonial forces belonged to the navy (*La Marine Royale*, later *Marine Nationale*). They were called *troupes de marine*, responsible for discipline on board ships. They were compared to the porpoises that often accompany the ships. Gunners in the French Navy are nicknamed *Bigors*, derived from the command '*Bigue Hors!*' given on French royal navy ships, meaning 'run out' the guns (push the guns out of their gun ports prior to firing).

152 Notin, *le Croisé*, p.111.

153 In the slang of Saint-Cyr, 'voracious' describes members of the cadre whom the cadets judge to be too rigid and formal.

154 Jean Compagnon, Jean, 'Instructeur et formateur,' pp.165–176, in Christine Levisse-Touzé (ed), *Du Capitaine de Hauteclocque au Général Leclerc* (Éditions Complexe, 2000), p.174.

155 Roger Pons and Jean Lucchési, *AFL review*, 288, 4th Quarter 1994, 'le général Louis Dio, ancien président national de l'AFL, p.60.

156 Dio, '2 mars 1941, Koufra', *Caravane*, No. 134, April 1953, pp.1–2.

157 Leclerc was promoted to général de brigade in August 1941.

to fight on until the final victory. The importance of this feat of arms will be keenly felt first by our brothers-in-arms, then by our allies, and finally by our compatriots who remained under the yoke of the enemy, or cowardly resigned to defeat. My first duty is to thank everyone who made this success possible. I bow before the graves of *Caporal Chef* Derque and *Tirailleurs* N'Doonon and Digueal, who gave their lives for *la Patrie*. I thank *Chef de Bataillon* Dio, *Lieutenants* Arnaud and Corlu, *Sergent-Chefs* Bourre, Briard, Griselly, and Habert, *Caporal Chef* Kerleo, *Soldats* Deraet and Ulrich, *Caporals* Boulbogol and Kossibay, *Tirailleurs* Assoum, Gomai, Gleke, Kladom, Tetaina, and Tougoungar who shed their blood at Kufra.[158]

---

158 Fond Leclerc, *Ordre du Jour 7 mars 1941*, boîte 7, dossier 1, chemise 1.

Chapter 4

Fezzan 1,
6 March 1941 to 12 March 1942

Following his serious wounding at Kufra, *Commandant* Dio had been in the Fort-Lamy hospital since the end of February 1941. His wound was causing him a great deal of pain, and he was not improving. He could barely even move. Dio, a man of action who loved the wide-open desert more than anything, was also suffering emotionally in his confinement to a small hospital room. On 5 March, he learnt that *Médecin Capitaine* Jean Laquintinie had died at the Yaoundé hospital. A victim of his duty, he had contracted septicaemia in Chad while operating on the wounded of Kufra, which he did right until the last moment. Dio knew the medical officer well, and they had spent a lot of time together in Douala before Leclerc's arrival. Laquintinie was one of the rare soldiers who immediately rallied to the Gaullist movement with Mauclère and Dr Mauzé. He also kept Dio and his team updated on events in Douala. Dio was saddened by the death of a true comrade-in-arms, one who was a year younger than himself.

Fortunately, Dio could receive visitors at the Fort-Lamy hospital. Among them, the short but regular visits from *Colonel* Leclerc were good for him. Leclerc was concerned about the health and morale of his deputy and took every opportunity to pay him these short visits. He kept him informed of the repercussions of Kufra on the international level and discussed the future with him. He also told him that he had officially relieved him of command of Group 4, effective of 6 March. On 12 March, the *colonel* came to see him again to read a citation he had just signed concerning him. It was the highest distinction in an Order of the Army:

> [This] Officer set an example to all with his bravery and energy. On 25 February, responsible for leading a surprise attack on an advanced blockhouse at Kufra, he insisted on being the first to approach the enemy position. Wounded by a grenade, he nevertheless managed to kill two of his adversaries and put the others to flight. Returned to our lines under his own power despite his injuries.

The citation promoted him to *chevalier* in the order of the *Légion d'honneur* and included the award of the 1940 *Croix de Guerre* with palm.[1] The cross of a *Chevalier* of the *Légion d'honneur* was presented to him on 18 March 1941 on his hospital bed, most certainly by Leclerc himself, who wanted to reward the man who had become his most loyal operational assistant. Dio only attached a relative value to decorations even though this was the fourth citation he was receiving for combat. At the time, such an attitude made him exceptional among the officers of his generation. What Dio remembered above all was that Kufra was the third time he had fought alongside

---

1 SHD, Dio, 14 Yd 1759, *OG (ordre général) No.25 du Général commandant supérieur des Forces de l'A.F.L., 18 Mars 1941.*

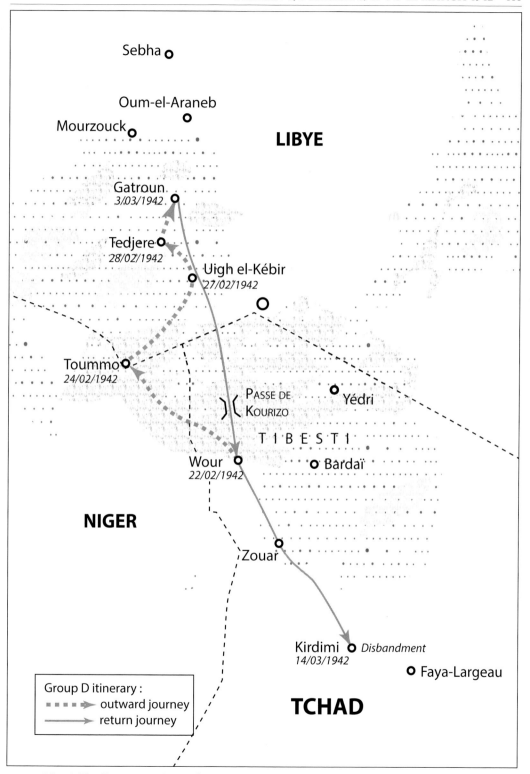

Map 5 The Groupement Dio in the Fezzan 1 Campaign (22 February 1942 to 14 March 1942).

Leclerc, after Douala and Gabon. He was the only one to have accompanied him in all three theatres of operations that were the prelude to his epic. From then on, the two officers were united, in good times and in bad.

Additionally, *Général* de Gaulle decided to award *Commandant* Dio the *Croix de la Libération* by decree of 14 July 1941. Forty years later, when the organisation of the Order of the Liberation asked him: 'What value did you attribute to the *Croix de la Libération* at that time?' Dio responded: 'I never thought about it. I had something else to think about, or rather [something else] to do.'[2] His response may seem a little hard to believe, since the decoration is so highly prized. It symbolised the commitment of the Free French who were particularly deserving and recognised as such by the leader of Free France. Its rarity made it valuable. In the protocol establishing the precedence of decorations, the *Croix de la Libération*[3] *is placed just below the red-ribboned Légion d'honneur.* During ceremonies, many *Compagnons de la Libération*, as they are known, made a show of wearing it above the 'red.' Leclerc particularly appreciated the motto inscribed on the reverse of the medal *PATRIAM SERVANDO, VICTORIAM TULIT* (By serving the Fatherland, he achieved victory). *Colonel* Leclerc was also awarded the *Croix de la Libération* for the victory of Kufra in March 1941, receiving it from *Médecin-Général* Adolphe Sicé[4] at Fort-Lamy on 20 September 1941. Dio should have received it on the same day. In a message to de Gaulle,[5] Sicé explained that he was unable to present it to Dio, as Leclerc had asked him to do, because Dio was not at Fort-Lamy on that date.

For *Commandant* Dio, the dark succession of bad news continued on 15 March when he learnt that *Lieutenant Colonel* André Parant had died at Yaoundé hospital from his injuries. He was another officer who had been close to Dio. They might have known each other in Cameroon because Parant's battalion was supposed to support Leclerc's landing in Douala. However, he arrived three days late, so it was in Gabon where they crossed paths. Parant led the column that left Middle Congo to subdue the Vichy forces, and they cooperated in taking Lambaréné by force. Subsequently, de Gaulle appointed Parant as Governor of Gabon, a territory of the *AEF* that had been forcibly attached to Free France. On 7 February 1941, while carrying out his new civilian functions, Parant was seriously injured in a plane accident in Bitam, on the Gabon-Cameroon border. As with Laquintinie's death, Dio's hospitalisation prevented him from attending the funeral of yet another comrade-in-arms. Moreover, his own recovery was not progressing well. In mid-March, the health service decided to transfer him to the Yaoundé hospital, as the Fort-Lamy hospital lacked sufficient capacity to treat him.

Against his will, Dio was sent back to Cameroon, a territory he left only three months earlier. Being further in the rear, the wounded in Yaoundé received fewer visitors. *Capitaine* Dronne, who

---

2   Order of the Liberation, Dio file, *Questionnaire destiné aux Compagnons de la Libération.*

3   Ending in 1946, *Général* de Gaulle awarded 1,061 crosses, to 1,038 people, five municipalities and 18 combat units. The last *Compagnon de la Libération*, Hubert Germain, was buried in the crypt of the Mont Valérien memorial on 11 November 2021, in vault no.9, surrounded by the 15 vaults of other companions who rest there. They are all fighters killed in 1940, 1941, 1943, 1944 and 1945, of all ranks including resistance fighters, three indigenous *tirailleurs*, and two women. The companion cities are Nantes, Grenoble, Paris, Vassieux-en-Vercors and Ile-de-Sein. Four units belonging to the *2e DB* are *Compagnons de la Libération*: *Régiment de Marche du Tchad*, the *501ᵉ Régiment de Chars de Combat*, the *3ᵉ Régiment d'Artillerie Coloniale*, and the *1ᵉʳ Régiment de Marche de Spahis Marocains.*

4   Dr Adolphe Sicé was born in Martinique in 1885, received his medical degree in 1911, and attended the tropical medicine course at the École de Pharo in Marseille. He served as a military doctor in Morocco prior to the First World War and then in France during the war. He remained in the colonial army in the interwar period and rallied to de Gaulle in 1940. Promoted to *général*, he was appointed High Commissioner of Free French Africa in July 1941. (Translator's note)

5   A telegram from *Médecin-Général* Sicé explained: 'I presented the Cross of Liberation to *Colonel* Leclerc at Fort-Lamy. Did not accept Leclerc's request to hand over the Cross of Liberation to *Commandant* Dio, who had no means of transport.' (Order of Liberation, dossier Dio, 1622/HC of 21.9.41).

was still serving in Cameroon at that time, was one of his rare visitors. With his talent for words, the colonial administrator turned *capitaine* spoke of his hospital visits with his former leader in Gabon:

> Several of us had gone to visit the seriously injured *Commandant* Dio, who had been evacuated to Cameroon. During a patrol under the walls of Fort Kufra, an Italian grenade, one of those terrible grenades that detonate on impact with the ground, exploded between his legs. We couldn't help but think of his motto during the Gabonese escapade: 'No mercy for the balls.' He also thought about it and wondered if his injury might have been a divine judgement.[6]

Another of Dio's visitors in Yaoundé was *Capitaine* Buttin. He had been assigned to Gabon and had spontaneously rallied to Dio while he was forming his column in October 1940, becoming his deputy throughout the operation. The two men liked each other. Thanks to a small pocket planner[7] from the year 1941 on which Buttin occasionally noted his schedule, it is possible to follow some of Dio's activities during that difficult period of his life. Buttin visited Dio for the first time at the Yaoundé hospital on Monday, 17 March. For that day, he wrote in the planner: 'saw Dio. Wound is much worse than was known. But he is in good spirits and expects to be quickly back on his feet to return to the fight.' The Breton officer did not want to show his young comrade how poorly he was doing, even though his morale was low. During the week, Buttin worked in the new training centre of the *1er Régiment de Tirailleurs du Cameroun* established by Dronne and located 70km from Yaoundé. He was among the cadre of the *5e Bataillon de Marche*. Buttin saw Dio again at the beginning of April. By then, Dio evidently could leave the hospital for a few hours because Buttin noted: 'lunch at G…'s house with Dio, who is still full of enthusiasm despite his wounds. What a difference between him and G…! He seems like a frank and upright man, full of vitality and courage. I am proud to be his friend.' On Sunday 13 April, Buttin wrote that he went to mass with Dio. In the following week, Buttin's planner tells us that a *Lieutenant Colonel* Antoine, sent by *Général* de Gaulle, visited all the wounded and sick in the hospital.

On Thursday 17 April, Buttin's planner mentioned that 'Dio left for Douala and Fumban.' The care provided in Yaoundé yielded good results, so the hospital released him for a period of convalescent leave, which the military called *PATC* (*permission à titre de convalescence*). Dio was glad to stop over in Douala for the opportunity to see some friends again. Fumban is one of the oldest cities in Cameroon, dating from 1394. Located 250 kilometres northeast of Yaoundé in a high plateau region, it is the capital of the Bamum Kingdom. Dio was put up in the house of a planter named Brugeaux, who must have had a hand in rallying Cameroon to Free France. Buttin joined Dio on Sunday, 27 April in Fumban, with some planter friends. Buttin noted that Dio would be leaving the region on 20 May. He would certainly have had an appointment in the following days with the doctor at the Yaoundé hospital. He had to undergo an examination to determine if he was fit to return to service and, if so, under what conditions. There is no record of this medical examination in the archives, but the health service evidently accepted *Commandant* Dio's return to duty, yet also required him to hold a more or less sedentary job. It also must have ordered him to remain assigned to the Fort-Lamy area where there was a hospital. This was obviously not what Dio wanted, preferring instead to 'return to the fight.' But the health service always has the last word, requiring the unit to respect duty restrictions. It turned out not to be a problem, though,

---

6   Dronne, *Carnets de Route,* p.70.
7   The planner was kindly lent to the authors by his wife, Madame Yvette Buttin-Quelen, who would later become the esteemed secretary of the *Fondation de la France Libre.*

because operational activities in Chad came to a halt in May. Béné explains it beautifully: 'With the month of May 1941, the Chadian border entered the cycle of 'summer wintering,' an obligatory break due to the climatic conditions particular to this central part of the African Continent.'[8]

On 27 May, the *commandant* obtained his discharge papers from the Yaoundé hospital. From 28 May, he would resume his service with the *RTST* in Chad. He hit the road in a pick-up truck in the company of *Capitaine* Combes. During the journey, Dio made a new friend. In the journal *Caravane*,[9] Dio himself recounts the circumstances of the meeting:

> We spent a night in Berberati, on the border of Cameroon and Ubangi; the next morning, as we were leaving, a sort of black cocker spaniel that was wandering around the camp jumped into the cab of the pick-up and energetically refused to be dislodged. I really like dogs, and this little creature seemed very nice; we took him in. This brave dog belonged (at least, in principle) to a Capuchin father from the Berberati mission, very warmly known in the region, he was known as 'Father Rasputin,' because of his magnificent black beard. I therefore baptised my little companion Rasputin. This name stuck with him.[10]

In 1941, the Catholic holiday of Pentecost fell on Sunday, 1 June. Dio arrived in the Chadian capital just before the Pentecost weekend and settled into the mess where a room was waiting for him.

In the days that followed, Dio gradually regained his bearings in Chad. During his first discussions in the *RTST* headquarters, Dio discovered the letter that Leclerc wrote to the *RTST* leaders dated 31 March. After Kufra, the *colonel* very quickly perceived that an unhealthy climate was taking hold among the officers and non-commissioned officers. This was mainly among those who had not participated in Kufra, which was the vast majority of them (three-quarters of the 500 European cadre present at the time), who were feeling down. 'Things were not going well in *La Coloniale*.'[11] Leclerc understood those who asked themselves questions like: 'When will we leave? When will we fight? Why did 'X' leave and not me? We came here to fight, not to train…'[12] Leclerc decided to write a letter to all of them to try to respond to that mood. He began the letter by asking himself questions to which he provided answers. The first question was: 'Where are we?' He said that if the *AEF* was a more difficult region than others, it had the merit of being part of Free France. To the question, 'Why are we there?' he replied that it was a question of life or death for the Fatherland. Then he reassured those who had not yet been engaged because, 'There will be enough combat for everyone before our colours fly again over Strasbourg Cathedral.'[13]

The second part of his letter revolved around the verb 'to hold.' It put them on notice. They would need moral and physical strength to last and to hold out in the war, as their elders had done in the trenches. He did not want to lie to them about the long term. It would certainly be a long war. It would be difficult, as living conditions were challenging and separation from loved ones would become more and more of a heavy burden. Leclerc's words to his men were truth. He did

---

8   Béné, *Carnets, Première époque*, p.233.

9   *Caravane* is the journal of the *2e DB*. It began publication in 1944 and continues today with four issues per year. (Translator's note)

10 Dio, 'Quand le Général Leclerc dédicaçait des photographies à Raspoutine', *Caravane* No.89, April 1949, p.26.

11 Destrem, *L'Aventure de Leclerc*, p.143.

12 Destrem, *L'Aventure de Leclerc*, p.83.

13 This is the first time that Leclerc referred to the Oath of Kufra. He perceived that this image of the flag with the Cross of Lorraine flying in Alsace would become a strong symbol in the minds of all his soldiers and transcend them. Destrem, *L'Aventure de Leclerc*, p.145.

not call on blood, sweat and tears as Churchill did to his people in May 1940, but the spirit was the same. Then, he appealed to their pride by evoking their status as Free Frenchmen: 'From a historical point of view, we are already all great Frenchmen...' He ended the letter with an exhortation: 'In the meantime, hold on! Hold for as long as it takes. Final victory is certain and is worth all the sacrifice.'[14]

Dio appreciated the straight truth. He also appreciated its form and style. Leclerc had clearly lost the 'stuck-up' side[15] that he had when he arrived at the *RTST* on 2 December 1940. His letter was now full of humanity, recognising the difficulty of separation from loved ones and showing concern for the soldiers' living conditions. In December 1940, when Leclerc took command and created tensions, Dio knew he would adapt, in every sense of the word, to the new environment.

Dio was pleased to find *Capitaine* de Guillebon at the Chadian military headquarters. The brilliant and pleasant *polytechnicien*[16] had demonstrated during the Kufra campaign that he knew how to fight as well as manage the daily life of a staff. A solid friendship linked the two colonial officers. Prioritised on Leclerc's schedule, the *colonel* received Dio on Tuesday 3 June during a one-on-one dinner. The reunion between the two men was not exuberant but it was strong: a virile handshake and a pointed look were enough. Dio noticed that his commander was wearing the patch of the colonial troops on his sleeve. Dio stayed quiet about it, but would learn a little later the story behind the *colonel*'s adoption of the distinctive insignia.[17] Knowing the medical restrictions imposed by the health service, the *colonel* inquired about the convalescent's health. Leclerc then caught Dio up on what had happened since his evacuation to Yaoundé. As usual, the *colonel* went straight to the point throughout his remarks. Kufra belonged to a page in the past and he no longer talked about it. He was already entirely focused on the next mission, one that *Général* de Gaulle had set for him in Libreville back in November 1940. 'The book is open to the pages of Fezzan.'[18] Leclerc wanted to take advantage of the 'summer wintering' to implement what he called the 'lessons of Kufra.' He told Dio that he wanted to work in three particular directions: the cadre of leaders, organisation of the units, and equipment. Leclerc explained to Dio that he intended to use the mounted company to establish units that resembled the Italian Saharan companies. To do so, they needed more vehicles adapted to the desert. He hoped that the countless requests he had addressed to Brazzaville or London would soon be followed up. He raised the subject with de Gaulle during his visits to Fort-Lamy from 23 to 26 March and again on 6 May. De Gaulle promised to do what was necessary with the British, on whom Free France depended, particularly for equipment.

Leclerc changed the subject to talk about personnel. He seemed a little embarrassed to broach this subject because he knew of Dio's attachment to the indigenous soldiers, whether they were *tirailleurs* or *goumiers*. He told the *commandant* that, in his opinion, given what he experienced in Kufra, the *AEF tirailleurs*, 'are unfortunately not very suitable for this form of modern combat.'[19] Leclerc, obviously, would prefer North African soldiers, having been able to appreciate their qualities in Morocco. He further told Dio that the only way to compensate for the weakness would be to increase the quota of Europeans within the *tirailleur* units. He made a request to de Gaulle that he direct European volunteers to Chad. Dio was not entirely convinced by this approach, having

14   Destrem, *L'Aventure de Leclerc*, p.146.
15   Troadec *Le Général Leclerc et l'Afrique Française Libre, 1940–1942*, Actes du Colloque International, p.584.
16   Graduate of the *École Polytechnique*.
17   On 15 April, Leclerc went to Zouar to give his instructions to *Capitaine* Massu, head of the Tibesti subdivision. Massu recounts: 'During the meal that followed, I asked the *colonel* to accept our insignia with the naval anchor. This 'cavalier' is, in my eyes, a hundred times worthy of it.' (Compagnon, *Leclerc*, p.236).
18   Compagnon, *Leclerc*, p.231.
19   Létang, *Mirages*, p.284.

fought with African *tirailleurs* since 1932. Nevertheless, he remembered the evaluation he received from *Colonel* Garnier in 1939 reproaching Dio for his 'lack of esteem for the indigenous Chadians in comparison with those of Mauritania where he previously served.'[20] Obviously he had been a victim of the same feeling as Leclerc when he first arrived in Chad, but things had changed over the past two years. It was true that motorisation and the use of heavy weapons had changed the nature of combat. Wanting to avoid confronting Leclerc, Dio nevertheless reminded him that in Kufra, 'many Frenchmen were [also] not quite up to the task. Fortunately, the officers among the cadre were fine.'[21] He also pointed out that Cameroonians, for example, were capable of taking on small responsibilities such as driving and maintaining vehicles or manning the radios. The Sara or Hadjeraï *tirailleurs* of the *RTST* were perhaps less capable of taking initiative, but they were very loyal, faithful, and could be courageous when they had confidence in their immediate superior. Dio believed that with training and drill[22] it was possible to transform them into good fighters. Leclerc ended the debate, but it would undoubtedly come up again between the two of them.

Leclerc next turned to the international situation. In the Libyan theatre, Rommel's counter-offensive in March and early April threw the British back to where they had started at the end of 1940, and on 27 April the front was once again on the Egyptian border. Only the city of Tobruk in Cyrenaica resisted the Germans. According to Leclerc, the British were paying for their sudden change of priorities. To help Greece, Churchill had stopped Wavell's offensive in Libya at the end of February. If they had continued their efforts in Libya, Tripolitania could have been conquered by British troops. That would have allowed Leclerc to commit to Fezzan after Kufra, to 'accompany' the British advance on a southern axis. 'If the English had continued their offensive towards Tripolitania, I would have acted at Fezzan even with exhausted and insufficient means.'[23] But now, having entered the hot season, the front between the British and Germans in North Africa had stabilised. It was obvious that an attack by the Free French of Chad to conquer Fezzan was contingent upon the resumption of a British offensive westward, along the Libyan coast.

The Syrian theatre of operations also troubled Leclerc – a lot. On 7 May, French *Amiral* François Darlan opened the Syrian airfields to Hitler, meaning that front would require an urgent dispatch of men and equipment. The *AEF* would be the main provider. The creation of *bataillons de marche* for Eritrea, Syria, Ethiopia, and Libya would take men and equipment that might otherwise have been available to Leclerc. On 2 June, de Gaulle appealed solemnly to French troops in Syria to avoid fighting other Frenchmen. *Général* Dentz, a convinced Vichyite, refused to listen.[24] During the fratricidal fighting in Syria, the tension between *l'Afrique Française Combattante* (Fighting French Africa) and the territories held by Vichy was at its peak. As a result, the Chad-Niger border once again became a threat. Leclerc downplayed the prospect in his letter to de Gaulle in December 1940. However, he ordered Dio as commander of Group 4, to resume defensive measures on the only axis between the two territories, between Mao and Nguigmi. But the contact that *Commandant* Dio had with his former superior, *Colonel* Garnier, led him to believe that Niger had adopted a resolutely defensive attitude towards Chad. The Vichyites were convinced that the Gaullists had sent Dio to the border to repeat what he did in Gabon. Leclerc, with a small smile on the corners of his lips, told Dio how he was perceived by the Niger troops.

20   SHD, Dio, 14 Yd 1759, notation 1939.
21   Notin, *le Croisé*, p.124.
22   Drill consists of learning through repetition until each person's movements become reflexive actions – minimising the effects of fear or stress. It is mainly used in a military context.
23   Compagnon, *Leclerc*, p.231.
24   When the fighting stopped on 10 July 1941, the Syrian Campaign had caused 1,060 deaths among *Général* Dentz's men and 800 among *Général* Legentilhomme's *FFL*. It was no comparison with the losses in Gabon (around 30 killed), which at the time had been blamed on Leclerc.

An article dating from May 1941, coming from the Vichy Secretariat of State for War and entitled 'Overview of Dissidence' discussed Dio's role in Gabon. He was presented as a dangerous psychopath who 'executed with his own hand a French *sergent* who had used an elephant hunting rifle to defend himself... [and] released from prison the commander of the scuttled submarine *Sidi-Ferruch* who then shot himself with his revolver.' During his meetings with *Colonel* Garnier, commanding the Niger-Chad borders, Dio is said to have threatened: 'if you attack us, I will come and fight you with five times more pleasure than I did against the Italians...I now have the taste of blood.' The Vichyites concluded with 'acts and words of a madman undoubtedly to whom a prolonged stay under the tropical sun has made him lose all common sense.'[25] Dio had succeeded, beyond all expectations, in creating an aura of fear around himself. It also demonstrates the state of psychosis to which some Vichyites had evolved in justifying their lack of commitment to the Gaullists. Nevertheless, *Général* de Gaulle remained worried about Niger. *General* Erwin Rommel's advance into Egypt at the end of April 1941 and the meeting between Darlan and Hitler in Berchtesgaden on 11 May made him think that Niger could threaten Chad. According to *Général* de Gaulle, it was possible that the Germans could invade the *AEF* from Vichy bases in *AOF*. Thus, de Gaulle asked the British to open up meetings with the French in Chad so they could establish operational rules for coordination in the event of an attack. Leclerc told Dio that General E. B. B. Hawkins, commander of Nigeria's military forces, had therefore contacted him to invite him to a meeting in Kano the following month.

Leclerc had placed the northern borders of Chad under surveillance. With Rommel's advance in Cyrenaica, the Italians might want to take revenge on Kufra from Fezzan. They had well-equipped Saharan units, supported by aviation, which were capable of conducting raids in northern Chad. The Franco-Italian Rome Agreement signed by Pierre Laval in January 1935 had returned the entire Aouzou Strip to the Italians, but the transfer had not yet happened. It could motivate the Italians, anxious to regain a little credibility in the face of the *degaullisti*. Leclerc informed Dio that he had given Massu responsibility for the surveillance. Massu, 'responsible for Tibesti, reorganised his system in Bardaï, Aouzou, and Wour, and closed some of the passes. Surveillance of this area would be permanent.'[26]

Then Leclerc abruptly raised the question of Dio's role in the short term. He reminded him that he had to be seen by a medical commission in September to decide on his fitness for service. If his disability rate was greater than 20 percent, the *commandant* would no longer be able to remain in a combat unit like the *RTST*. In the meantime, he had to be spared so that he could recover. From the outset, the colonel told him that he would not send him to the north. Leclerc offered for Dio to remain with him at Fort-Lamy to assist primarily in two areas. First, Dio would be his direct adviser on everything concerning Niger. Having established the mission last December, no one was better suited than Dio to do so. The second area he wanted to entrust to Dio was the reorganisation of the motorised units. In that area, Dio would work in close coordination with *Capitaine* de Guillebon who closely supervised the territory's vehicles. He wanted to establish something functional with the means they had available. Saving the best for last, Leclerc revealed his plan for Dio's assignment: he would create for him the position of garrison commander of Fort-Lamy. That function did not exist until then, with the commander of the *RTST* de facto assuming the role. Noticing the lack of enthusiasm in Dio's eyes, he immediately asked him to look into the defence of the city and to propose adjustments that needed to be made. Leclerc made Dio read a note that

---

25   Fonds Leclerc, *Aperçu sur la dissidence* (Extrait du Bulletin d'information No.3) May 1941, box 7, folder 2, file 1.

26   Jean Delmas, 'Le Général Leclerc et la contribution de l'Afrique Française Libre aux opérations', *Le Général Leclerc et l'Afrique Française Libre, 1940–1942*, Actes du Colloque International (Paris: Fondation Maréchal Leclerc de Hauteclocque, 1987), p.157.

de Gaulle had just sent to him from Cairo: 'Organise the defence of all your airfields, even those in the south. In Crete, it was through paratroopers and transport planes that the Germans won the game.'[27]

It should be noted that the position of Fort-Lamy garrison commander does not appear on any of Dio's service records. It is Dio's evaluation, signed by Leclerc, that reveals the assignment he entrusted to Dio during the summer of 1941.[28] Under normal circumstances, he should not have assumed such a position until the reform commission had ruled on his medical condition. However, the particular circumstances of the Free French in 1941 and the voluntary nature of *Commandant* Dio's service meant that normal procedures were not completely followed. But if he did not respect the procedures, Leclerc nevertheless respected their spirit by holding back his wounded *commandant*.

Coming out of his one-on-one with Leclerc, Dio could not help but smile inwardly. He thought back to his evaluation from 1940 that said Dio should be used, 'in garrison only when it is not possible to do otherwise.'[29] Leclerc probably had not read it when assigning him to be garrison commander of Fort-Lamy. Dio had to acknowledge that the events of the past six months had changed his life. Even if he did not appreciate that type of position, Dio, conscientious and disciplined, dived into his new assignment with determination.

The garrison commander is responsible for everything relating to military regulations in the garrison. The commander was responsible for discipline, housing, security, the reception of transient troops, the distribution of duties, service relations between units – all of which were administrative functions in which *Commandant* Dio had never really invested until then. He was also the preferred contact for civil partners such as the governor, mayor, police commissioner, et cetera. The aim was to relieve the *RTST* and its *colonel* of all these administrative burdens. Leclerc also instructed Dio to study the defence of the city. That is what first caught the attention of the ex-*méhariste*.

Fort-Lamy was founded on 29 May 1900 by Émile Gentil, a colonial explorer and was the namesake of Port-Gentil in Gabon. Initially, it was a simple French post, but becoming a centre of commerce due to its location, a town quickly developed there, on the right bank of the River Chari, near the confluence of the Rivers Chari and Logone. It was named Fort-Lamy in memory of *Commandant* François Lamy, who died during the Battle of Kousseri on 22 April 1900. Kousseri is a border town in Cameroon, close to Fort-Lamy. The defeat of Sultan Rabah's Army by Lamy's French column marked the beginning of France's conquest of Chad. Prior to the Second World War, Fort-Lamy remained small, with around 20,000 inhabitants. Upon his arrival, *Sergent* Béné described it:

> Fort-Lamy had nothing of a great African capital. We were rather disappointed when we saw a large bare square where black children were playing ball, a bazaar like we had seen in Bangui…, indigenous women squatting while selling fruit and fish on which a swarm of flies were hovering. On our way to the military camp, where the administrative district was also located, we came across houses for Europeans, low constructions, almost all identical, with a stained white colour. Further on, the 'Governor's Palace,' which was in fact just a residence a little larger than the others. In the indigenous neighbourhoods, with poorly maintained low huts, we were constantly assailed by a swarm of children who either asked us for a cigarette,

---

27   Fonds Leclerc, boîte 8A, dossier 1, chemise 1.
28   Berval, 'Colonel Dio', p.32, specifies 'as soon as he recovered, he was named garrison commander of Fort-Lamy.'
29   SHD, Dio, 14 Yd 1759.

or offered to bring their sister after dark. Going towards the river bank we met fish sellers because fishing was one of the main activities of the indigenous population of Fort-Lamy. The women wore multi-coloured dresses or loincloths or simply dressed in black, their hair was braided and rubbed with rancid butter, making big shiny tails.[30]

Until then, Dio had only passed through Fort-Lamy, so he was still unfamiliar with the city. But as the garrison commander, he needed to know all the districts. The city was growing more and more lively. From Cameroon and Middle Congo, large logistical deliveries arrived daily. The two ports of Douala and Pointe-Noire were operating at full capacity and unloaded materiel which then moved by train, road, and waterway. Chad and Fort-Lamy became the central point of convergence of the war economy for Fighting French Africa. 'Fort-Lamy was changing visibly. It would soon have 50,000 inhabitants. Playgrounds, sports grounds, mosque, Catholic church, bank, hotel for travellers, hospital, souks…'[31]

Dio needed to quickly assess the needs for the defence of the city. The River Chari flows 100 kilometres further north into Lake Chad. It is a vast expanse of endorheic water (a closed water system with no connection to the ocean) with an area of 1,350 square kilometres. Besides Chad, three other territories border the lake: Cameroon, Nigeria, and Niger – with the longest waterline. Although the lake is shallow, it could still be a route of penetration from Niger. Therefore, the garrison commander had to plan works to defend his banks and oppose any landing coming from Niger by river. The protection of central buildings was another point of vulnerability to check. That involved providing combat posts around the governance district to control access. Finally, the airport was another sensitive point in the defence of the city; a lot of work was needed at the Fort-Lamy airport. Dio noticed that the airport was not entirely enclosed by a wall; access onto the airstrip was therefore very easy. The new garrison commander also noticed the enormous fuel reserve made up of 200-litre drums lined up in the open next to the buildings. The airport's anti-aircraft defence was almost nonexistent. A few old machine guns were deployed around battle posts built with sandbags. It needed to be reinforced and outfitted with 40mm Bofors guns. But these were still rare in Chad, and he had to prioritise the northern detachments which were facing an Italian air force that was greatly superior in numbers.

Dio invested himself completely in the defence mission. Leclerc was clearly satisfied because he mentioned in Dio's 1941 evaluation, that the garrison commander, 'established and carried out a judicious defence plan for the city.'[32]

With respect to the defences facing Niger, *Commandant* Dio asked for an update of the work he had initiated back in January. Accompanied by Léon-Marie Le Nuz, his successor as commander of Group 4, he asked to visit the defensive posts on the line from Mao to Rig-Rig leading to the Nigerian border. He decided to propose a third line of defence near Massakori. It would not be permanently activated and would only be armed in the event of an attack by land.

Colonel Leclerc had to meet with Major General Hawkins to coordinate with the British in Nigeria. In preparation, Leclerc and Dio met several times to decide together which questions they would need to ask their British counterparts. The meeting took place in Kano on 22 July 1941.[33] Leclerc was accompanied by *Capitaine* Langlois, designated as his liaison officer, and arrived with the following questions:

30   Béné, *Carnets, Première Époque*, pp.26–27.
31   Destrem, *L'Aventure de Leclerc*, p.150.
32   SHD, Dio, 14 Yd 1759, livret militaire.
33   Fonds Leclerc, *Procès-verbal d'une conférence à Kano le 22 juillet 1941*, boîte 7, dossier 2, chemise 3.

- What would the attitude of the British be if Germans enter Niger?
- What would the attitude of the British forces in Nigeria be if Niger attacked the western flank of Chad while Leclerc's troops were on the offensive in Fezzan?

Then he set out his two counterattack plans depending on the season:

- During the rainy season: the French attack would use the axis north of Lake Chad: Mao/Rig-Rig/N'Guigmi. The goal would be to attract the Vichyites while the British attacked Zinder.
- Outside of the rainy season: the Free French attack would use a southern axis passing through Cameroon: Fort-Lamy/Maiduguri/Potiskum/Nguru. The objective would be the capture of Zinder by a pincer action with the British.

At the end of the meeting, the following coordination measures were taken:

- Since the Vichyites and the Free French wore the same uniform, Leclerc would mark his vehicles with a distinctive sign,
- An exchange of liaison officers would take place between the two staffs,
- An aviation coordination code would be transmitted,
- The refuelling of Chadian vehicles would be ensured by the British,
- Leclerc would provide six guides with knowledge of Niger and the Zinder region.

Even though General Hawkins clarified that an attack on their part in Niger was subject to the agreement of his government, Leclerc returned from the meeting satisfied. He passed on the results to Dio, who was responsible for the defence. On 14 August, Dio had a letter signed by Leclerc that listed the approved decisions from the Kano meeting. Dio continued to plan operations towards Niger accounting for different eventualities. The next meeting would take place in October in Fort-Lamy.

On 22 June, the news of Nazi Germany's attack against the USSR stunned the cadre of the *RTST*. For Dio, it was good news. The resources Hitler would have to devote to that conquest would prevent him from strengthening his position in Africa. Moreover, *Général* de Gaulle's prophecy was coming true; the war would become global.

The third area Dio was responsible for in that summer of 1941 was the reorganisation of the motorised units. The lessons of Kufra demonstrated that operations in the desert required motorised units (replacing camels) that were fast, mobile, and largely autonomous. They had to be adapted to the Saharan environment to favour speed and surprise, the two watchwords of the cavalryman Leclerc and the *méhariste* Dio. Dronne explained it: '... in the Saharan war, more than in any other war, manoeuvre is of paramount importance. Broad overwhelming manoeuvre will surprise an already fixed enemy in his flanks and rear. It was through manoeuvre that the Saharan company of Kufra, although more powerful, was defeated.'[34] But this did not exclude manoeuvre by the infantry; the fight had to be carried out alternately by mounted and dismounted troops, as evidenced by Operation Kufra.

Dio was fully invested in the project. He believed that the *RTST* was lagging behind and needed to evolve. He understood that the *méhariste* had to adapt his mount for modern combat in desert areas. But he wanted to ensure that the long-accumulated experiences of the *méharistes* were taken into account during this profound reorganisation of the *RTST* units. He had to find a compromise

---

34   Dronne, *Le Serment de Koufra*, p.92.

between what was feasible and what was possible. The Italian Saharan companies offered an ideal example. They had a 'square' structure, consisting of four platoons: two vehicle-mounted Saharan platoons, a dismounted platoon, and an aircraft platoon with two *Ghibli* planes. They were equipped with SPA and Fiat 634 trucks, adapted to the desert and armed with 20mm guns and heavy machine guns. However, the Free French understood they lacked the means for such an organisation. The LRDG model could not be copied, either; their equipment and structure allowed them to hit the enemy's rear, but not to take and hold ground.

Following Dio's recommendations, *Colonel* Leclerc adopted a new type of unit – the '*compagnie de découverte et de combat*' (Long Range Reconnaissance and Combat Company), the *CDC*, which everyone would eventually simply call the *DC*. Long range reconnaissance includes gathering intelligence on the terrain, avenues of approach, and of course the enemy. Given the lack of vehicle protection, combat was based on manoeuvre, which had to be prioritised. The *DC* could not allow itself to be fixed by the enemy. In addition to these two basic missions, the *DC* had to be able to carry out security missions, for example, moving as the vanguard of a heavy unit or protecting the flank of the unit when it attacked. Coordination was the subject of a lot of discussion between Dio and Leclerc. French Army culture favoured a triangular structure, which was often dictated by shortages. Each company would therefore include three platoons. Unfortunately, the lack of resources and personnel in 1941 did not allow them to build three homogeneous sections per company. There would therefore be two true sections per platoon and one command section. Sections consisted of four vehicles. Each truck had four to eight men constituting a crew, a new structure in the *RTST*. Men 'live together constantly, more united, more mutually supportive even than the crew of a boat. They live, fight, and die together. They constitute the basic cell. Each crew must be able to show initiative and to fend for itself.'[35]

The British Bedford trucks received prior to Kufra had been sufficiently modified, but only around 15 remained in good condition. After many requests to the British, Leclerc obtained American Ford or Chevrolet commercial trucks[36] with powerful engines and a performance comparable to that of the Bedford. Yet the soldiers still had to 'tinker' with them a bit, as they had done before Kufra. Dio gave them his instructions from a distance. 'The forward cabs were sawed off ....[and] mounts installed so the heavy weapons could fire.'[37] The sides of the trucks were redesigned to hold equipment and to add sand removal plates made from old 200-litre petrol drums. They also added a new feature. Using the fibrous husk of palm trees, they made camouflage nets to conceal the trucks, primarily from aircraft. The camouflage was rolled up on the sides of the truck and could be unrolled in just a few seconds. They also hung food and supplies on the exterior sides of the trucks, including the famous '*méhariste* sausage.' 'When a Saharan kills a gazelle, he cuts the legs without skinning them and hangs them on the side of his camel while he travels. The legs dry out, harden, and keep wonderfully.'[38]

The armament was a mixture of weapons. Despite requests, few crew-served weapons arrived. French arms such as the model 24–29 machine gun were not suitable for sandy areas, and the Hotchkiss machine guns were worn out. Therefore, they used the weapons captured from the Italians in Kufra. The loot in Fort El Tag included four 20mm guns, three Breda 12.7mm machine guns, 18 heavy machine guns, and 32 Fiat-34 machine guns. Some of those weapons were mounted on the *DC*'s trucks, as long as they still had ammunition. The old 75mm artillery pieces remained but they were no longer reliable, the recoil brakes leaking under the effect of the heat. The only new

---

35   Dronne, *Le Serment*, p.95.

36   In the United States, they had been used as milk trucks. Dronne, R., *Carnets de Route*, p.104.

37   Dronne, *Le Serment*, p.94.

38   Dronne, *Le Serment*, p.97.

weapons they received were a 40mm Bofors anti-aircraft gun and a 25pdr (114mm) gun, delivered by the British. Considering the missions planned, and the equipment and the weapons available, the two *DC*s had to increase their ratio of Europeans to at least two or three per crew. Leclerc and Dio agreed on the selection of the commanders for the two units, which would become the spearhead of the troops in Chad. The *1ʳᵉ DC* was entrusted to *Capitaine* Massu. He participated in the Murzuk raid, and he knew Tibesti and its outlets perfectly. The *2ᵉ DC* went to *Capitaine* Geoffroy who performed remarkably well at Kufra at the head of a motorised platoon. *Capitaine* Pierre de Rennepont, who commanded the company brought to Kufra, left the regiment. His fussy behaviour had annoyed the *RTST* leadership, so Leclerc made the decision and sent his cousin back to the '*13ᵉ Demi-Brigade* of the Foreign Legion, where he would play an active role in the vast El Alamein offensive.'[39] Although Rennepont was trained in Saumur in the same cavalry culture as Leclerc, he failed to understand, as his cousin had, that in Chad he would have to adapt to the new human environment and not the other way around.

The *1ᵉ DC* was equipped with Bedfords and Italian SPAs while the *2ᵉ DC* was equipped with Chevrolets. Both were augmented with additional European cadres; sections were exclusively led by officers and often platoons were led by *capitaines*. Dio, who knew all the officers and many non-commissioned officers well, selected the leaders for those positions. The 1st Platoon of the *1ʳᵉ DC* was led by *Lieutenant* Dubut, 2nd Platoon by *Lieutenant* Gourgout, and 3rd Platoon by *Lieutenant* Tommy-Martin. In the *2ᵉ DC*, 1st Platoon was led by *Capitaine* Maziéras, who had been Dio's deputy in Douala. The 2nd platoon was led by *Lieutenant* Eggenspiller, and the 3rd by *Capitaine* Alaurent. The weapons within the platoons were completely disparate. Attached to makeshift mounts in the trucks, they consisted of a choice of a 37mm gun, a 20mm Oerlikon, a 20mm Breda, a 12.7mm Breda machine gun, a 13.2mm and an 8mm Hotchkiss, a 13.2mm twin MAC, and the 24-29 machine gun. In addition to these direct fire weapons, the *DC*s were equipped with 60mm or 81mm Brandt mortars in each platoon. In its dress, its weapons, and its vehicles, the unit resembled a guerrilla troop more than a regular army.

Contrary to the calm usually reigning during the extremely hot summer period, things were hopping at every level in the Chadian capital. Leclerc expended a lot of energy and put a lot of pressure on those around him. But fortunately, there were also some touching moments. When Dio arrived from Cameroon with his cocker spaniel, Rasputin, the little dog was immediately adopted by members of the general staff, including *Colonel* Leclerc. Arriving with Dio every morning at the regimental headquarters, Rasputin went around the offices to greet the *colonel*, the chief of staff, and *Capitaine* Quilichini.

> So many times I heard, without seeing him, the *général* greet the arrival of his little visitor with a jovial 'hello Rasputin!' The *général* tolerated a lot of his pranks, including his annoying habit of watering the walls and the table legs. One day, having smelled the new katembourou (horse antelope) skin boots that the *général* had ordered for himself, Rasputin made a few preparatory movements under the desk and then demonstrated his disapproval by hiking an irreverent leg at them. Far from getting angry, though, the *général* found the whole thing funny and laughed heartily.[40]

Leclerc, a Picardy hunter, naturally appreciated dogs and also, more surprisingly, wild animals. During an inspection, a colonial administrator offered him a young lion. To everyone's amazement,

---

39   Notin, *le Croisé*, p.133, note.*

40   Dio, 'Quand le Général Leclerc dédicaçait des photographies à Raspoutine', *Caravane* No.89, April 1949, p.26.

Leclerc accepted the 'gift.' He took it with him to Fort-Lamy and entrusted it to *Sergent* Butelot, his standard bearer. The young beast was named Doude (meaning lion in the Sara language). Doude became the darling of the garrison to the fury of Rasputin, who barked furiously at him, but always from a distance! As an adult, one night, Doude broke his chain, entered Leclerc's room, and came within a few centimetres from his face to sniff him. It was a rude awakening. In the middle of the night, Butelot and Leclerc tried unsuccessfully to catch the lion for more than two hours. Doude thought it was all a game, but concerned that the lion might run into town, Leclerc, with a broken heart, was forced to kill him. Doude's tanned skin was then made into a rug and placed in the house. Leclerc said to his officers: 'I'll show it to my sons. They won't be able to say that I haven't been to Africa.'[41]

As part of the inner circle, Dio had the chance to rub shoulders with this simple man, who showed the affection of a good father towards his family. It would be the only time that Dio lived in daily and permanent contact with Leclerc for an extended period. They spent more than seven months together, allowing Dio to better understand Leclerc's personality, and deepening his appreciation for his *chef*. Dio found the analysis of *Général* Valluy, who succeeded Leclerc in Indochina in 1946, very accurate about this extraordinary leader: 'His faults added to his prestige: brusque because he was shy, cold because he was sensitive and caring, demanding of his subordinates because he was scrupulous in his convictions. He was singular and uncompromising in his action, indifferent to changing moods, fatigue, risks; overcoming personnel and material obstacles, he charged forward… and he won.'

On 14 July 1941, Free France proudly celebrated its first Bastille Day at Fort-Lamy and at all its other posts. In Africa, the national holiday was a day of jubilation for everyone, civilians and soldiers alike. It was a day of no work, with ceremonies, parades, and the presentation of decorations. The next day, 'the evening news bulletin broadcast by Brazzaville announced that *Général* de Gaulle had, among other promotions, elevated *Colonels* Leclerc and Koenig to the rank of *général de brigade*.'[42]

Leclerc, believing that his advancement was too rapid according to the normal regulations, wanted to hide it from his subordinates and continued wearing the stripes of a *colonel*.[43] He wrote to de Gaulle, 'I should only be promoted after success.'[44] But he did not realise that radio operators, especially in the isolated posts, listened to the news every evening. Therefore, everyone knew about the *colonel*'s promotion. The soldiers of Chad were proud of it. A *général* at the head of the *RTST*! Later they learnt that Leclerc donated the difference in salary he received as a *général* to the charitable needs of the regiment. Nobody said anything but everyone appreciated it. It was during this period that Dio, whom Leclerc increasingly admired, learnt that Vichy had discovered who Leclerc was.[45] Informed of Leclerc's true identity by Vichy officers from Cameroon and Gabon whom Leclerc had magnanimously allowed to return to metropolitan France, a 'court-martial at Gannat stripped [*Capitaine* Philippe de Hauteclocque] of his French nationality on 16 June.' This same court, 'on 11 October, sentenced him to death for crimes and manoeuvres against the unity

---

41   François Ingold and Louis Mouilleseaux, *Leclerc de Hauteclocque* (Paris: Éditions Littéraires de France, 1948), p.65.

42   Béné, *Carnets, Première Époque*, p.242. The official decree appointing him as a temporary brigadier general was signed on 10 August 1941.

43   He agreed to use his new rank when he returned from the first Fezzan campaign. Until then, his men would continue to call him *colonel*.

44   Notin, *le Croisé*, p.145.

45   Philippe de Hauteclocque had taken on the *nom de guerre* of Leclerc to protect his family, which was living under German occupation. After the war, he incorporated the name into his own, becoming Philippe Leclerc de Hauteclocque. (Translator's note)

and protection of the homeland.[46] Dio sensed worry in Leclerc, who was certainly thinking of his family, all of whose property would be confiscated. But the *colonel* remained imperturbable. Outwardly, he showed nothing. Rather than weakening his resolve, it was strengthened.

Throughout the summer and fall, *Colonel* Leclerc often went to the north to check on the equipment and the build-up of the logistics base. This involved pre-positioning reserves of fuel, spare parts, and food in the northern reaches of Chad, particularly at Wour, a small post located opposite the Libyan border to the north-west of the Tibesti Massif. Dronne called that period 'a laborious pause which was used to strengthen combat resources and to prepare.'[47] Everyone worked, including the Italian prisoners, who were put to work after the seizure of Kufra.

> Immediately distributed to the workshops of Faya-Largeau and Fort-Lamy, they showed themselves to be model workers who contributed greatly to the repair, modification, and equipping of the vehicles. The French in Chad did not really see them as enemies. Most often the contacts were rather cordial. The 30 or so Italians employed at Largeau were practically in semi-freedom. On Sunday evening there were passionate Franco-Italian football matches on Place Blanche in Faya-Largeau.[48]

During the fall Leclerc put pressure on his men, but even more so on his superiors in Brazzaville and London. Dio witnessed the occasionally incendiary messages that came from Fort-Lamy. On 26 August, *Général* de Gaulle returned to Brazzaville to celebrate 'the three glorious days' recalling the rallies of August 1940. Fort-Lamy also celebrated the first anniversary with enthusiasm. A parade was organised and the gate of 'Camp Kufra' was inaugurated. All this was done to maintain everyone's morale, especially the soldiers who were impatiently waiting to get into the battle. That evening, as everyone gathered in the mess, Dio and Leclerc exchanged glances. That was all it took for them to remember 27 August 1940 in Douala where it all began. They preferred to keep the memory to themselves. So much had happened since then!

Bad news came at the beginning of September with the announcement of the departure of *Général* de Larminat for the Levant. He was replaced by *Médecin-Général* Sicé. A good bond united Leclerc and Larminat. They often formed a united front to convince or influence de Gaulle's decisions. It would be harder for Leclerc with a doctor at the head of the *AFL* military command, especially since relations between Leclerc and Governor Lapie in Chad were not in good shape. Leclerc's aide-de-camp, *Capitaine* Troadec, called Lapie an 'operetta governor'[49] hardly in keeping with the colonial mentality. The tense relationship between the two leaders complicated their efforts to achieve the common goal. Civilians, who are used to having all the prerogatives at their disposal in times of peace, do not always appreciate the powers given to the military in times of war. Leclerc was consumed with the actions he had to take and insisted that everything had to be directed towards the war effort. Governor Lapie did not entirely share that vision. As the commander of the garrison, Dio was able to realise that, having had to establish frequent contacts with the governor and his departments.

Fortunately, there was also some good news. The announcement of the upcoming arrival of around a hundred American commercial trucks on the next chartered ship delighted Dio. The *chef*'s pestering paid off. It was a great relief because the three *groupes nomade* were still using their camels. Leclerc, after asking Dio's opinion, decided that the *Groupe Nomade du Borkou*

---

46   Notin, *Le Croisé*, p.147.
47   Dronne, *Le Serment* p.92.
48   Béné, *Carnets, Première Époque*, p.235.
49   Notin, *Le Croisé*, p.144.

(*GNB*) would be the first to receive trucks. It was a logical choice because camels had better mobility than trucks in mountainous Tibesti, so keeping a camel-mounted *Groupe Nomade* there made sense. Consequently, *Capitaine* Poletti, commanding the *GNB*, received 15 Chevrolet trucks with Cameroonian drivers in civilian clothes in early October. All the personnel of the *Groupe Nomade* understood that the arrival of the vehicles meant they would lose their camels and become a truck-mounted company. With some sadness, the *méharistes* worked to militarise their new mounts. Geoffroy's *2ᵉ DC* was also equipped with Chevrolet trucks. The combat units would then have vehicles more adapted to the desert. They would also have Cameroonian drivers who had received a quick driving course, although their military training was almost nonexistent. 'All were Christians. Most knew how to read and write, and some spoke very good French.'[50] They were always cheerful.[51] Some were even heroic: 'such as the crew that was lost between Koro-Toro and Zouar. They were finally found after a three-week search; all had died of thirst. Near the desiccated bodies, a note was hung; scribbled in pencil, it contained this simple sentence: if you don't come in two days, we are dead. *Vive la France.*'[52] With Cameroonians driving the vehicles, it was possible to assign Europeans to combat and specialist positions. But relations with the *tirailleurs* and *goumiers* were difficult. The Cameroonian drivers considered the others to be savages while the *Toubous* spat on the ground when they passed a Cameroonian. The commanders had to ensure that tensions between them did not escalate.

Other good news was the regular arrival of European reinforcements at Fort-Lamy. The movement had been growing since the beginning of summer. At Zouar, Dio fittingly greeted five *méharistes* who arrived in May from Colomb-Béchar, Algeria. They broke 'all distance records to reach Free France, travelling, sometimes on foot, sometimes on camelback, nearly eight thousand kilometres.'[53] Perhaps less physically demanding than that, still other volunteers 'escaped from France (many Bretons among them), Frenchmen from the *AOF*, escapees from Germany, and even 34 relegated former prisoners from Guyana'[54] continued to arrive throughout the year 1941.[55] These men were all received by Leclerc or Dio, sometimes by both, who assigned them where they were most needed. The quality of these men, particularly moral and ethical, was not always the highest. Leclerc did not concern himself with such considerations, telling Dio, 'In a pinch, we can make soldiers out of thieves. We can never do so with cowards.'[56]

On 2 September, Dio had an appointment at Fort-Lamy hospital to appear before the reform commission. He was a bit nervous in front of the doctors, knowing that if his disability was assessed to be higher than 20 percent, he would have difficulty remaining in a combat unit and holding an operational command assignment. He could not see himself in an administrative job like his father, who spent his whole life as an administrative officer. The maxim 'like father like son' is perhaps not always accurate. The reform commission ruled: 'total disability 19 percent – disability less than 20 percent.'[57] Dio was happy to announce to Leclerc that same day that he was 'fit for service.' The *colonel* still did not want to rush things. He knew that Dio was impatient to return to the north, but he was also aware of Dio's state of health. There was no hurry because he was still

50 Dronne, *Carnets de Route*, p.105.
51 'They had composed a song exalting their own merits: we are the good ones, the good drivers of General di Gaulle, di Gaulle.' (Dronne, *Serment de Koufra*, p.97).
52 Dronne, *Le Serment*, p.97.
53 Béné, *Carnets, Première Époque*, p.235.
54 After serving his prison sentence, a condemned prisoner had to remain in forced residence in Guyana for the same number of years as the sentence he had served in prison. Those former prisoners were then called *relégués* (relegates).
55 Destrem, *L'Aventure de Leclerc*, p.151.
56 Destrem, *L'Aventure de Leclerc*, p.151.
57 SHD, Dio, 14 Yd 1759, extrait des pièces du livret administratif (ESS: état signalétique des services).

needed at Fort-Lamy to complete the transformation of the *RTST*. No one knew the people and the environment of Chad as well as Dio. His advice, always marked by common sense and pragmatism, was reassuring to Leclerc. In Dio's evaluation for the year 1941, signed on 23 September, Leclerc ended his assessment with: 'Beneath a somewhat rough exterior hides a great deal of feelings, a tenderness and a camaraderie appreciated by all. In summary, an exceptionally good leader, capable of exercising any command.'[58] Leclerc perceived his deputy's personality clearly. He overlooked his direct language, which was often graphic and sometimes crude. He understood that in fact, Dio's way of expressing himself was a screen that hid his great sensitivity. In addition, he realised that the Breton's sometimes 'rough' behaviour, far from repelling his subordinates, made him an undisputed leader. It was a quality that allowed him to adapt to all types of command. In his assessment, Leclerc confirmed the consideration and esteem he felt for his subordinate.

Finally, towards the end of October, Leclerc sent Dio back to the north, tasking him with corralling a foreign delegation.[59] Massu wrote: 'On 29 October, he [Dio] accompanied an American delegation on a brief visit to Zouar that was escorted by *Colonel* Carretier and was interested in defence. He thus gave us the joy of seeing him again, and he left us a few bottles, drunk to his health by the officers of Zouar, including the *méharistes*.'[60] *Colonel* Carretier was the head of the *AEF* air force. The American delegation, led by Colonel Harry Cunningham, was there to see the airfield. Leclerc tried to impress the Americans, who could provide him with equipment and weapons. He rolled out the red carpet for them and put his deputy at their disposal. Dio was happy to return to his beloved Tibesti. He had the habit of never arriving empty-handed whenever he went to the field. He knew all too well the pleasure of having a good drink with friends when you have been drinking natronated water for months. But Dio also came personally to inform Massu of his new position: '*Commandant* Dio was coming to tell Massu of his change of assignment. He would hand Zouar over to *Capitaine* Vézinet and take command of a new unit. Leclerc had just decided to create the *compagnies de découverte et de combat*.'[61] The fact that it was Dio who informed Massu is evidence that he had invested a lot alongside the *colonel* in the creation of the new units. The appointment of Massu to the key position was certainly due to the esteem in which Dio had held him since 1938.

In mid-November, Leclerc informed Dio of his new assignment, which they must have already discussed. The *colonel* decided to create a new post in Tibesti. The large mountain range in the northwest of Chad is like a balcony overlooking Fezzan, and it would be the launching point for the attack against the Italian colony. Up to that point, Tibesti had been placed under the responsibility of two *capitaines*, Vézinet and Sarazac. The former commanded the 6th Company and administered the civilian populations in the Tibesti region. He had just been assigned to this position and was based in Zouar. The latter commanded the *GNT*, a *méhariste* unit which, by definition, had no permanent base, controlling the nomadic populations and monitoring the zone of action. As part of the preparation for the attack towards Fezzan, Tibesti would become an important logistical staging base in the coming weeks. Fuel reserves would be scattered along the axes leading to the north. Soon the complete units would arrive with their equipment. It was therefore appropriate to strengthen the command of this area by creating a *Groupe Tibesti* under the orders of a senior officer with authority over the troops located there. Leclerc assigned Dio to that new position. He needed a leader to strengthen the system that was being built – a leader who knew the region intimately, a leader recognised by the men there,

---

58   SHD, Dio, 14 Yd 1759, dossier de notations de Dio.
59   Dispatch from the American Consul to Léopoldville, 20 October 1941, https://history.state.gov/historical-documents/frus1941v02/d517 (accessed 15 May 2020).
60   Massu, 'Souvenirs du général Dio', p.3.
61   Pellissier, *Massu*, p.45.

and a leader who would faithfully execute the plans they had developed together during the summer at the *RTST* headquarters.

Commandant Dio 'took command of the *Groupe du Tibesti* on 30 November 1941.'[62] Arriving at Zouar, in the middle of the Tibesti region, Dio received a situation update on Fezzan, with details of the Libyan province. Fezzan is bordered to the north by the province of Tripolitania, to the south by Chad and Niger, to the west by Algeria, and to the east by the province of Cyrenaica. It is a vast territory equal in size to all of France, located in the southwest of Libya. The province is dotted with oases in which the Italians had built fortified posts. Between the oases are all the characteristics of Saharan terrain: the *djebel* (mountain), the *reg* or *sérir* (flat and stony expanse), the *hamada* (rocky high plateau), the *ramla* (sand dune) with portions of dreaded *fech-fech* (powdery sand). At that time, the local population was estimated at 40,000 people throughout Fezzan. From Chad, any advance north-westward would move through four main lines of oases. The first line was made up of the oases of Uigh-el-Kébir and Ouaou-el-Kébir, on either side of Djebel Domazé. Tedjéré, Gatroun, Oum-el-Araneb and Tmessa made up the second line of Italian posts. The third line was made up of Sebha, the cultural capital of Fezzan, and Murzuk. Finally, Brack in the centre and Ghat on the Algerian border, represented the fourth and last line. In addition to the presence of Italian troops, reinforced by Fezzanese auxiliaries (*askaris*) in the posts, three Saharan companies were operating in Fezzan ready to intervene with their aviation.'[63] The bases of the three *sahariane* were Sebha, Murzuk, and Ghat, garrisons that each had a military airport. Tedjéré, Gatroun, and Brack had makeshift landing fields. The distances were vast; 1,000km separated Zouar, the departure base for the Free French, from Brack, which was the most remote Italian post in Fezzan.

Having assisted in their preparation at Fort Lamy, Dio knew the composition of the different components of the ground forces that Leclerc wanted to commit to Fezzan. In mid-November, tensions increased in Tibesti. Time was running out because the British CRUSADER counter-offensive had been launched on 18 November.[64] General Auchinleck received orders from Churchill to renew the British attack, advancing westward along the Libyan coast from Cyrenaica towards Tripolitania. The Free French from Chad would be coordinated with the British advance. By mutual agreement, the signal for the attack would be given when the British reached the Gulf of Sirte which is at the same latitude as the western outlets of Tibesti. Thus, by coordinating their two attacks, the Allies would prevent the Italo-German headquarters from switching forces from one theatre to another. The presence of a British liaison officer with Leclerc allowed him to maintain an excellent relationship with his British counterpart, General Claude Auchinleck. Leclerc followed the evolution of the British progression day by day to ensure he would not be late in launching his attack. He personally joined his tactical headquarters on 2 December in Zouar.

Pre-positioning of troops at their respective departure bases was completed by the beginning of December. Everything was done with the greatest discretion. Vehicle movements were planned 'before 9:00 a.m. and after 3:00 p.m. to avoid being spotted by the Italian air force.'[65] Due to the range limits of their aircraft, the Italians could only fly over the north of Tibesti in the middle of the day. Consequently, the French camouflaged their vehicles and remained immobile during the midday window.

On 7 December 1941, the news of the Japanese attack on the American naval base at Pearl Harbor was relayed by all radios, stunning the troops in Chad. This surprise attack led the US to

---

62   SHD, Dio, 14 Yd 1759, extrait de l'ESS.
63   Ingold, *L'épopée*, p.52.
64   'CRUSADER' was the code name for the British counterattack (18 November –30 December 1941) launched by the British 8th Army under the orders of General Auchinleck, against the Italo-German forces in North Africa.
65   Destrem, *L'Aventure de Leclerc*, p.162.

immediately enter the war against Japan and, a few days later, against the Axis forces of Germany and Italy. De Gaulle's prophecy of 18 June 1940 was thus fulfilled. In the name of Free France, de Gaulle quickly declared war on Japan the following day. It was high time since the Japanese had occupied Indochina since 23 July. This news aroused great hope in the hearts of the Free French. Far from their families, often without news from home, they hoped that the enormous American industrial potential would allow them to shorten the war. Like his comrades from Chad, Dio also thought of his family, of his mother, alone in Vannes. He was unable to give her any news, and he knew she must have been worried.

At the end of December, Leclerc was still waiting for the British offensive to reach Tripolitania so he could launch his attack. He laid his initial plan out in a letter addressed to *Général* Serres dated 22 December: '...my thousand fighters will be well armed. Known enemy: five times more numerous, with a network of around 10 concrete forts and aviation. The aviation will be my most dangerous adversary.'[66] Then Leclerc discussed his 200 vehicles, which would infiltrate through the Kourizo Pass to arrive at Uigh-el-Kébir. He expounded on his plan: 'Once Uigh is reached, I will move up to Gatroun, which I will even try to seize; creation of a rear base. I will then move on to Oum El Araneb which I will also try to seize to establish a forward base.'[67] Leclerc was planning a true invasion of Fezzan to coincide with the British offensive along the coast.

After the Kufra operation, Leclerc and Dio appreciated the threat posed by the small *Ghibli* planes of the Italian *sahariane*. Therefore, the general staff released a document on 10 December entitled 'Some Principles of Manoeuvre and Service in the Field' signed by Leclerc.[68] In the first paragraph, Leclerc established the instructions to be adopted during an air attack. The most important point remained opening fire only with careful deliberation to conserve ammunition. Additionally, he prohibited shooting while moving, and firing only 'one weapon out of two' when stationary. He then specified to 'not forget that the most effective response remains passive defence, particularly when stationary: camouflage and avoid marked points.' In the second paragraph he defined the principles of 'some probable missions.' In the last paragraph entitled 'significance given to some missions' he gave instructions in particular on behaviour to adopt towards local populations, such as, 'life in the country: use indigenous resources but avoid upsetting local inhabitants (pay as much as necessary); unit commanders will initially receive sums of money for this purpose.'[69]

On 23 December, Italian planes bombed Zouar. Even though the attack caused only minimal damage, it showed that the Italians remained aggressive. It also restored some of the edginess of combat among the men, who were itching with impatience after a long period of idleness.

The Christmas and end-of-year celebrations took place in an atmosphere of combat. No festivities were authorised, and no travel was permitted. The nights of 24 and 31 December, 1941 were celebrated at crew level (four to eight men), with a little wine or tafia[70] being the only improvement on otherwise ordinary days. Father Basset, a missionary in Cameroon and chaplain of the expedition, said mass, but only in Zouar.

The British 8th Army counter-offensive progressed slower than planned. General Auchinleck succeeded in loosening the siege of the city of Tobruk which his troops had heroically held for eight months. However, on Churchill's orders, he had to send part of his forces to the Far East to oppose the Japanese. As a result, the attack in North Africa stalled. By the end of January 1942,

---

66   *Le Général Leclerc et l'Afrique Française Libre, 1940–1942*, Actes du Colloque International (Paris: Fondation Maréchal Leclerc de Hauteclocque, 1987), Lettre Leclerc, document 6, III, p.566.

67   *Le Général Leclerc et l'Afrique Française Libre, 1940–1942*, Lettre Leclerc, document 6, III, p.567.

68   Fonds Leclerc, *note 46/CC signée Leclerc du 10 décembre 1941 sur les principes de manœuvre*, boîte R, dossier 2, chemise 1.

69   Fonds Leclerc, *note sur les principes de manœuvre*, boîte R, dossier 2, chemise 1.

70   Tafia is an alcohol made from sugar cane molasses.

the forces of Chad realised that the planning for a coordinated Anglo-French attack on two axes was going to be cancelled. And then, on 21 January, Rommel launched his counterattack at El Agheila, located between the two Libyan provinces of Tripolitania and Cyrenaica, pushing the 8th Army back towards Egypt. 'As if to show that he had not forgotten the French, two days earlier, *Hauptmann* [Theo] Blaich's Heinkel 111 bombed the Fort-Lamy runway.'[71] Leclerc's aide-de-camp, *Capitaine* Troadec, explained: 'The *DCA* was not ready. Result: a 60,000-litre aircraft fuel depot, which the aviators had not dispersed and camouflaged, despite Dio's numerous requests when he was in charge of the close defence of Fort-Lamy with me, was set on fire.'[72] The former garrison commander at Fort-Lamy was certainly angered by the news and probably railed against the airmen at the airport.

The British, under the pressure from the armoured vehicles of Rommel, 'the Desert Fox', retreated to El Gazala, 200km west of the Egyptian border.

The offensive as planned by Leclerc was no longer feasible. He had to bring his subordinates together to consider the options available to them. Invading Fezzan alone was no longer possible. Should they stop everything and wait for better options? Dio, along with the other officers, sensed the men's impatience to go into battle. While they had been deployed on the ground for many weeks in precarious conditions, it would be difficult to admit to them that the fight had been postponed. Great frustration was likely to arise in the ranks, particularly among those who had been waiting since 1940 to get into battle. Abandoning any idea of combat would be a blow to the morale of the soldiers. Kufra was almost a year in the past; it was hardly possible to make them continue to wait for even more months. Something had to be done. The units were ready. So were the logistics, which had required considerable efforts over many months. An officer then brought up Murzuk and the example of the LRDG carrying out a hit-and-run raid using speed and surprise. Leclerc immediately latched onto the idea, which suited his temperament. All the *méharistes*, Dio first and foremost, were won over. For once, they would reverse the roles, they would be the main effort for the *rezzou*.

On 1 February, Leclerc presented his plan to de Gaulle for the raid, which had the advantage of showing Churchill that they could 'do without British coordination.'[73] De Gaulle gave Leclerc the green light on the 4th. To avoid the summer heat, no time could be wasted. Nevertheless, faithful to his principles, Leclerc gave himself and his subordinates the necessary time to prepare a 'simultaneous attack on ten posts in Fezzan after a silent and dispersed approach.'[74] Before launching the detachments, careful preparation and coordination was essential. That would involve synchronising each of the planned offensive actions in advance in order to guarantee surprise. Once the troops were launched over an area 800 kilometres deep, they could no longer modify the plan. Leclerc led the preparations with the help of Dio and a few other *méharistes*, including Massu. Massu and *Lieutenant* Eggenspiller were the only officers who knew Fezzan as far as Murzuk. The routes and terrain were studied down to the smallest detail to properly plan the timing for each detachment. They planned three axes to start the attack in order to surprise the Italians at several places simultaneously. Previous reconnaissance made it possible to rough out the routes, all of which had traditionally been camel routes but had never been used by motor vehicles.

The central route, via the Kourizo Pass, was the shortest route into Fezzan but a 1935 Italian report deemed it impassable for vehicles.[75] The western route through Toummo was the most well

71   Notin, *le Croisé*, p.153.
72   Fonds Leclerc, René Troadec, *Journal du Capitaine Troadec du 10 mars 42 au 1er novembre 42*; *Rapport sur Bombardement de Fort-Lamy par un avion allemand 23 janvier 1942*, boîte A, dossier 2, chemise 1.
73   Notin, *Le Croisé*, p.154.
74   Notin, *Le Croisé*, p.153.
75   Ingold, *L'Épopée*, p.126.

known and was used by the LRDG during their return from Murzuk. It was also the longest route, extending into the northern part of Niger. Finally, the eastern route passed through Bardaï and ended at Yédri, a small town in the north of the Aouzou Strip. The eastern and central routes would require discreet work to backfill certain passages so they could be used by vehicles. In other places, 'doormats' would have to be built across the dry wadis to avoid getting stuck in the sand. This involved reinforcing the sandy base under the wheels with palm branches. Dio, as commander of *Groupe du Tibesti*, supervised the coordination of the 'road work' as well as the link between the units deployed around Zouar and Leclerc's staff.

To prioritise speed and surprise, it would be necessary to reduce the forces engaged in the hit-and-run raid by almost half. It was decided to create seven autonomous operational detachments, which together would come to be known to history as '*Colonne Leclerc*.'

- The main attack group consisted of the *GNB*, artillery, and a medical detachment, under the orders of *Commandant* Dio. Leclerc would get into the habit of designating Dio to command the most powerful detachment or to lead the decisive action. Ever since Douala, the two men brought each other luck, and there was no reason to believe that it would change.
- Hous would command a detachment of two *DC* platoons.
- Four mobile sections of 10 vehicles each, including Section A under *Capitaine* Geoffroy, Sections B and C under Guillebon, and D under Massu.
- *Capitaine* Sarazac's *Groupe Nomade du Tibesti* with their camels. Dio insisted that a *méhariste* unit be present in the column. It still had a role to play. In any case, there were not enough vehicles to motorise all the units.
- Each detachment had an autonomous combat train with supply trucks (fuel, ammunition, and food).
- The aviation would perform reconnaissance and light bombing missions: 'four Lysanders, four Glenn-Martins, two Potez medevacs, and one Potez 540.'[76]

'With 450 men for 144 vehicles, the ensemble was slightly larger than what had been committed to Kufra.'[77] In fact, at the beginning of 1942, *Colonne Leclerc* was only 30 percent larger in materiel than the Kufra detachment. But it had many more vehicles with better mobility in the sand and with greater autonomy. More important, it was led by a larger number of Europeans, who represented around half of the total force. The heavy machine guns on each vehicle provided excellent firepower, particularly for small-scale engagements. An autonomous operational procedure was adopted, inspired by *méhariste* units and usage: decision making was left to the leader of the detachment and self-sufficiency to each crew. Dio's touch was evident in the reorganisation, and the leaders were very confident. When the American Colonel Cunningham told Leclerc that it was 'suicide' to depart under such conditions, he 'burst out laughing: 'he who risks nothing, gains nothing!'[78]

Colonel Leclerc,[79] always attached to the symbolism of dates, decided to coordinate the attacks[80] so that the various Italian posts were attacked on 1 March. It was his way of reminding the Italians

---

76   Dronne, *Le Serment,* p.103.
77   Notin, *Le Croisé,* p.154.
78   Notin, *Le Croisé,* p.154.
79   He still refused to be called général.
80   The operations order assigned the missions between the detachments:
- Section A, by the eastern route, go as far north as possible and take cover at the Brack and Sebha crossroads.

of the anniversary of the capture of Kufra. So that each detachment could be in place at its objective on the anniversary date, the first detachment set off on 17 February, in accordance with a tightly synchronised plan.

On 20 February 1942, *Commandant* Dio joined his group, which was waiting for him in Wour, in the northwest of the Tibesti Massif. 'The region of Wour was grandiose, of infinite, indescribable beauty. The post, unoccupied at that time, was perfectly preserved. It was at the bottom of the Enneri Woudouy Wadi. Despite being dry, the wadi was nevertheless full of greenery, palm trees, and thalas.'[81] The *Groupement d'Attaque Dio* was made up primarily of the *GNB* mounted on 15 Chevrolet trucks and two Bedfords, led by *Capitaine* Poletti,[82] who would also act as Dio's deputy throughout the '*razzia*' on Italian territory. Poletti was in his fifties and was a veteran of the First World War. He was also a very experienced *méhariste* and a former NCO who had been promoted to the officer ranks during the fighting in Mauritania.

The *Groupement d'Attaque Dio* included an artillery unit equipped with a 4.5-inch British howitzer served by the efficient artillery duo from Kufra – *Lieutenant* Ceccaldi and the gun captain *Sergent* Grand. The two friends exchanged their old 75mm gun, which was on its last legs, for newer and more powerful equipment. It was the only heavy weapon in *Colonne Leclerc*. Supporting the howitzer, five Chevrolet trucks carried men and equipment, including 100 rounds of ammunition. Dio's medical detachment was led by *Médecin Capitaine* Mauric, the same man who, in Kufra, had saved Dio's life by evacuating him. It was no coincidence that the attack group was made up of men who had a shared history with Dio. Like Leclerc, Dio liked to surround himself with men with whom he had a special bond.[83] Likewise, those who had served under him before wanted to remain with him. Thus, he welcomed Bey Ahmed, with a few *goumiers*, into his group. The old Senusiyya chief, driven out of Fezzan in 1931, would be helpful in establishing contacts with the local populations, especially with the *askari* soldiers of Fezzan who had been incorporated into the Italian ranks. Lastly, *Groupement Dio* had a combat train under the command of *Lieutenant* Wormser with five Matford trucks, carrying supplies of fuel, ammunition, and food.

The departure from Wour took place on the morning of 22 February.[84] *Groupement Dio* made a short trip to a fuel resupply point called depot 'W' to top up the vehicles before entering Fezzan. A little before noon, Leclerc arrived with his command post made up of seven vehicles, a mixture of Bedfords, Chevrolets, and Fords. The *colonel* was in a pick-up with *Capitaine* Quilichini and

---

- Sections B and C: on the itinerary is 'act on Tmessa, Zuila, Oum-el-Araneb, possibly on Traghen.' Dronne, *Serment de Koufra*, p.103.
- Section D: 'in the vanguard of *Groupement Dio* via the Toummo route; after Uigh-el-Kébir, probe towards Oum-el-Araneb and possibly Traghen.' Dronne, *Serment de Koufra*, p.103.
- *Détachement Hous*: via Kourizo, attack Tedjéré.
- *GNT*: patrol and cover in southern Fezzan.
- *Groupement d'attaque Dio*: via Toummo, attack the Gatroun post.

81   Béné, *Carnets, Première Époque*, p.261. This work by Charles Béné serves as a guide for the detailed description of the operations carried out by *Groupement Dio* throughout the operation. *Caporal Chef* Béné was the group's radio operator and therefore a privileged witness who was always close to *Commandant* Dio.

82   The motorised version of the *GNB* included:
- Three sections of around 20 *fusiliers-voltigeurs* under *Adjutant* Ferrano, *Aspirant* Le Calvez and d'Abzac.
- A section of two Hotchkiss machine guns and an 81mm mortar,
- The radio element of *Caporal Chef* Béné, equipped with a Ford V8 1500 truck,
- Maintenance element of *Sergent* Brousse.

83   *Maréchal des Logis* Poualion would not be part of *Groupement Dio* as he wanted after Gabon and Kufra. A mechanical expert, he was employed in the 4th Section of Motorised Company 4, which was still a part of the *Colonne Leclerc*.

84   The Operations Report of 18 March 1942 signed by *Commandant* Dio served as a reference regarding the chronology of operations carried out by his group. Fonds FMLH, dossier Robédat.

Lieutenant Troadec. Two communications trucks followed with *Capitaine* Duault, and then a truck with the British liaison officer, Major Barlow. Behind them were the trucks of the aviation liaison officer, *Capitaine* Morel; the engineering officer, *Capitaine* Guérin; and the maintenance truck for repairs. Leclerc would move with *Groupement Dio*. During lunch, the two officers toured the crews and chatted with the men. *Caporal Chef* Béné met Leclerc for the first time, describing the colonel's uniform as: 'huge *sirwal* pants, woollen military jacket, a simple soldier's cap with thin colonel's stripes.'[85] Dio was in the same uniform but wore a kepi, as did Poletti and *Lieutenant* d'Abzac.[86]

Leclerc and Dio shared the men's rations, which consisted of 'drinking natronated water that tasted like petrol, eating biscuits, and snacking on smoked meat and dried dates.'[87]

The column set out again in the afternoon towards the west, reaching the Sobozo Pass between two rocky *garas*[88] in the evening. The border with Niger was close.

The next day, 23 February, the column moved northwest. At midday, an Italian plane flew over the group at high altitude, but fortunately, the vehicles had stopped at 9:00 a.m. and set up their camouflage. They resumed movement at 3:00 p.m. Having crossed the Reg, an immense flat and stony expanse, the vehicles could continue without problem. *Commandant* Dio stopped the column before nightfall, slightly ahead of his march plan. The bivouac was set up to the east of Emi Fezzan, a vast rocky peak. 'The whole region had a lunar appearance, not a bit of greenery, nothing but sand, stones, and from time to time a pile of large rocks.'[89] On 24 February, progress was slowed by the *fech-fech*, which the Cameroonian drivers and their passengers dreaded. *Fech-fech* is a terrible sand with the consistency of flour in which the trucks frequently became stuck. The wheels sank until the body rested on the ground. Soldiers would then have to dig under the wheels and slide plates under them to get the vehicle out. Very often it would just get stuck again shortly afterwards. Some parts of the journey required the use of the plates along the entire length of the *fech-fech*. It was exhausting for everyone. Progress was obviously very slow and fuel consumption increased.

Despite the difficulties, the column arrived in sight of the Toummo mountains at the end of the evening. The Toummo is a *djebel* with scree of black stones and an inhospitable appearance. It has several characteristics. First, it was the point of intersection of the borders of Chad, Niger, and Fezzan. It was, therefore, a well-known crossing point for caravans and it was prudent not to stay there for too long, at the risk of being spotted. It was also one of the rare watering holes in the region. The crews took just enough time to fill the *garbas*[90] hung on the sides of their trucks. To get away from the crossing point, Dio made them travel around 15km before stopping the column for the night's bivouac. That evening, in enemy territory, they used *méhariste* methods to form 'square' by simply lining their vehicles up on four sides to face all directions. On 25 February, the column of vehicles from *Groupement Dio* reached the north of Djebel Ati, which they bypassed to the east, in a place that offered many small *garas* for camouflage from aerial observation. The next day, out of caution, Dio decided to slow the progress. It was an advance to contact with the objective in sight. They had to be careful not to take the wrong route, especially since a sandstorm had picked up. They had to choose a route that most importantly concealed their approach with either small

---

85   Béné, *Carnets, Première Époque*, p.266.
86   Some of the colonial officers imitated Dio and wore their kepi instead of the heavy helmet during combat, including those of the *2e DB*. It was certainly out of form of defiance that they did it, but Leclerc went along with it. Béné, *Carnets, Première Époque*, p.275.
87   Béné, *Carnets, Première Époque*, p.267.
88   A *gara* is a conical mound with a truncated summit, evidence of a long-eroded landscape.
89   Béné, *Carnets, Première Époque*, p.267.
90   Water bag made of animal skin.

rises in the terrain or with thala trees.[91] In the early evening of 26 February, they reached the *garas* of Cingé. They had travelled around 650km to get to this point.

Colonne Dio remained on site during the 27th. *Commandant* Dio informed his subordinate commanders that Massu's section had been advancing in the vanguard since they left Wour. Massu received the mission to seize the Italian post of Uigh-el-Kébir, which was the planned assembly area on which the advanced logistics post was to be set up. He had first to neutralise the Italian *chouf*[92] that monitored the southern ingress before the alarm could be raised. The *chouf* was on a rocky height to their front, called Domazé, which overlooked Uigh-el-Sérir. Taking advantage of the lack of visibility caused by the sandstorm, Massu, assisted by his *goumiers*, managed to surprise 'two Italian *méharistes* squatting near their saddled animals.'[93] When questioned, they divulged their entire warning system. Eight Italian *méharistes* were on Uigh-el-Sérir,[94] a position located further north. With that information, Massu then captured the second *chouf* by surprise before it could raise the alarm with the post of Tedjéré. The post of Uigh-el-Kébir, located near Uigh-el-Sérir, could then be seized; there were no Italians there. *Groupement Dio* and *Groupement Hous*, as well as the *Groupe Nomade du Tibesti* met on 27 February at Uigh-el-Kébir as planned. Bey Ahmed questioned the Italian prisoners taken at Uigh-el-Sérir, loosening their tongues. 'The interrogation made it possible to clarify the Italian system: the garrison of Gatroun had been reduced to a small section of *askaris*; however, a *méhariste* company was based in Tedjéré.'[95] In consultation with Dio and Hous, Leclerc swapped the mission of the two units. Dio, who had the larger group, would attack Tedjéré and Hous would have to seize Gatroun.

Lying in foxholes dug in the sand, the men had difficulty falling asleep. It was freezing cold and their *burnous* and *faro* were barely sufficient to keep them warm. Many of them understood that the next day would be their first day of combat. The tension among the crews was palpable.

The forward logistics base was set up in Uigh-el-Kébir, with one of the platoons from the GNT responsible for monitoring it. The second platoon was attached to *Groupement Dio* for the attack on Tedjéré. The Italian post was fortified and powerfully defended, and it included a makeshift airstrip. On 28 February, *Groupement Dio* headed for Tedjéré, 70 kilometres to the northwest. The commandant intended to arrive at the objective around 4:00 p.m. to confirm its layout and draw up a plan of attack. Initially, there were no problems with the route, but progress slowed. The distances between vehicles closed to avoid losing contact with Ceccaldi's 'heavy' artillery section. The weather grew worse, as the stifling and blinding sandstorm continued. All the men wore scarfs around their heads, which they pulled down over their nose and mouth. The terrible conditions were ultimately a benefit, though, because it meant the Italian *Ghiblis* would either fly less or be less effective when they did fly. Around 4:00 p.m., when the column was about 20km from Tedjéré, the leading vehicles suddenly found themselves facing a wall of sand: 'the famous '*ramla*'[96] well known to camel caravans. No one had ever approached it in vehicles.'[97] *Commandant* Dio began first, unleashing the full power of his Ford pick-up. About halfway up the slope, the wheels started to slip and the vehicle sank in the sand up to the body. *Caporal Chef* Béné with his

91   The *thala*, *éthel* in French, is a Saharo-Arabic tree from the tamarisk family. It grows two to five metres high and has rough bark and small scaly leaves. It is relatively preserved from local populations because its wood releases a lot of smoke when it is burnt.

92   *Chouf* is a lookout post in Arabic.

93   Dronne, *Le Serment*, p.104.

94   *Kébir* means 'big' and *Sérir* 'small' in Arabic.

95   Jean-Noël Vincent, *Les Forces Françaises Libres en Afrique, 1940–1943* (Service Historique Armée de Terre, 1943), p.278.

96   *Ramla* means 'sand dune' in Arabic.

97   Béné, *Carnets, Première époque*, pp.270–71.

Ford radio truck tried to pass behind the *commandant*'s pick-up but with the same result. Dio then stopped the column at the bottom of the *ramla*. With Poletti, he decided to form a 'railway' with the metal sheets of all the vehicles on which the trucks could progress without getting stuck in the sand. After exhausting work lasting more than an hour, they had completed the rail, allowing the first vehicles reach the top of the dune. Getting back down the other side was no problem except to remember to always keep the vehicle on the axis of the slope to prevent it from overturning. Night had already fallen when at 7:00 p.m. all the vehicles that had finally made it over regrouped on the northern slope of the *ramla*.

The column had to travel the remaining 20 kilometres to Tedjéré in blackout to prevent being spotted. With all lights turned off, though, progress slowed considerably. Fortunately, the sandstorm weakened during the night and the moon shone through. Dio's truck, guided by Ganaye at the head of the column, reached the Tedjéré airstrip around 11:00 p.m. It was a simple strip with no infrastructure, and empty petrol cans marked the landing area. Dio ordered Béné to set up his radio equipment to transmit a message. From the start, radio silence had been strictly imposed to avoid being discovered by Italian direction-finding stations. On the day of the attack, 1 March 1942, radio silence could finally be broken. Dio reported the situation and the difficulties encountered in five lines to Leclerc, who remained at Uigh-el-Kébir. The station transmitted in text and required power generation provided by the '*ragonot*'[98] operated by two riflemen. To avoid being spotted by the Italian fort which was in direct view of the radio vehicle, Dio and Poletti held up a blanket to hide the light of the handheld lamp necessary for Béné to transmit the message.

Suddenly, a white rocket rose from the Italian fort. Had they heard the sound of the engines after they had formed square? Did the Italians spot the group? The men all froze and held their breath. The night was cold with an icy breeze. The silence was heavy. Suddenly 'the light of the moon faded more and more. Yet there was not a single cloud in the sky! Then the night became completely dark. It was a total lunar eclipse!'[99] The special event greatly troubled the indigenous soldiers who believe in superstitions. The eclipse was quite a dire omen for the Fezzanais *askaris* stuck in the fort! On the other side, it was interpreted as a favourable sign of destiny for the 'Chadians' on that first anniversary of the victory of Kufra. After a few hours of sleep, before daybreak, *Commandant* Dio gave the order to move all the vehicles to a palm grove three kilometres northeast of the fort. Immediately after parking the vehicles, the soldiers erected camouflage over them. For some, that involved unfolding the nets and cutting a few palm branches to break up the shapes of the vehicles. For others, it consisted of erasing tyre tracks upstream of the palm grove with palm branches. To deceive possible aerial reconnaissance, Commandant Dio's truck made several trips back-and-forth to another nearby palm grove. As the sun rose, so did the sandstorm. From their palm grove, the men of *Groupement Dio* could vaguely make out the blurred silhouette of the fort at Tedjéré. Caporal Chef Béné tried in vain to contact the colonel's command post. Yet once again there was no response. To check his equipment, he easily established contact with Hous's detachment, which was just outside of Gatroun. Béné reported back to the commandant that his radio worked fine. Using binoculars, Dio tried to determine the exact configuration of the fort, particularly looking for the exits and the possible approaches.

At 8:00, they heard the noise of a plane engine approaching from the north. Everyone froze. A *Ghibli* appeared and flew over the fort and then directly above the palm grove in which the group was camouflaged. Despite his low altitude, the pilot noticed nothing out of place, confirming to the Frenchmen that they had also not been spotted by the occupants of the fort.

---

98   The '*ragonot*' is a portable crank generator manufactured by the Ragonot company, also called *gégène* in military slang.

99   Béné, *Carnets, Première époque*, p.275.

The sandstorm weakened around 11:00 in the morning and visibility improved, allowing a clear view of the fort. The entrance gate faced the palm grove. Through his binoculars, Dio saw *askaris* carrying out cleaning chores in front of the entrance. It was then that *Adjudant* Ferrano's section intercepted and captured two Italian *méharistes* who were coming from the north and heading towards Tedjéré. These *askaris* turned out to be delivering two bags of mail. Béné recounts how these two soldiers were questioned by 'an old Fezzanais, with a short white beard, wearing a sort of cap and a large djellaba …. I had noticed him several times either in Dio's car or Poletti's. I took him for an old Fezzanais guide. It was in reality Bey Hamed (*sic*), the religious leader of the Senusiyya of Chad.'[100] Valuable information was collected on the enemy in Tedjéré. In addition to the men of the garrison, an entire Italian nomadic group, the *Meharisti dello Sciati*, was currently in the fort. The mail bags also contained the garrison's pay for the month of March, which the Italians were expecting. On a specific question from Dio, the prisoners informed him that the garrison camels were accustomed to grazing to the west of the fort, near the local village. The question was not trivial; rather, it was the instinct of a *méhariste*! And thus he learnt the direction the Italian *méharistes* would take if they decided to leave the fort. That was enough for Dio to launch his attack.

Dio summoned Poletti and Ceccaldi, ordering the latter to open fire on the fort with his gun precisely at noon. *Lieutenant* d'Abzac's section remained in place in an overwatch position. The two sections of the *GNB* with Dio and Poletti would infiltrate 'towards the post from the north-west, using the excellent cover provided by the palm trees, dunes, and tufts of éthel.'[101] Ceccaldi's first shot set off a battle in the fort. Ceccaldi, assisted by his deputy, *Sous Lieutenant* Pons, and *Sergent* Grand, the gun captain, had already proven his expertise as an artilleryman in adjusting fire on a fortification exactly a year ago. The British gun they used was a 4½ inch gun, greatly superior to the old 75mm they had at Kufra. It was also the first time using that calibre in the region. The succession of the falling shells was quick, and the situation soon became untenable for the occupants inside the fort. The previous night's lunar eclipse disturbed many *askaris*. For the *méharistes*, accustomed to wide-open spaces, the four walls of the fort were a trap. It did not take much for the Italians to decide it was time to get out of the fort. When the Italian troops began to pour out of the fort, the Free French who spilled in from the northwest arrived right on their heels.

Commandant Dio, at the head of *Aspirant* Le Calvez's section, pursued closely, engaging in combat. The Italians reorganised and offered a fairly strong resistance. Despite the losses, taking advantage of nightfall, some of them managed to escape. They left around 10 dead on the ground, including *Tenente* Meneghetti, who commanded the Tedjéré platoon. On the French side, *Goumier* Tiouli Elleni[102] was killed and six were injured, including two seriously: *Sergent* Ferry, hit in the shoulder and *Caporal* (medic) Mahamat, in the thigh. *Médecin Capitaine* Mauric treated them immediately. Back in the palm grove where they were parked at the start of the night, everyone realised that *Commandant* Dio had been amazingly lucky. He was unhurt even though 'an Italian bullet had passed through his old kepi.'[103] During the night, a coded telegram was sent to Leclerc's CP to report on the events of the day of 1 March 1942.

The next morning, in the freezing dawn, Dio and Poletti wondered if the fort was still occupied. The sandstorm which had started to blow again made it impossible to see if the Italian flag was still flying. Dio wanted to resume shooting before launching his men towards the fort because it was necessary to cross completely open ground to reach it. But Ceccaldi could not see

---

100 Béné, *Carnets, Première Époque,* p.278.
101 Ingold, *L'Épopée,* p.146.
102 Tiouli Elleni was *Capitaine* Poletti's *goumier*-guide. Ganaye, Dio's, was saddened by the loss of his *Toubou* friend.
103 Béné, *Carnets, Première Époque,* p.281.

through the sandstorm to observe the impact of his shells. Dio sat thinking, a quarter cup of coffee in his hand, surrounded by men who were all dirty, unshaven, and whose faces betrayed fatigue. Suddenly they heard the noise of an engine. It was Leclerc's truck. The *colonel* got out and approached with his cane. 'With long strides, Commandant Dio went to meet him. His ragged kepi, his eight-day beard and his dirty and rumpled clothes contrasted strangely with our always clean-shaven leader.'[104]

The *colonel*, having received no news due to his faulty radio, had decided to leave Uigh-el-Kébir in the middle of the night of 1 March to see what was happening in Tedjéré and then in Gatroun. His vehicle followed the tracks made by *Groupement Dio* and in turn stumbled on the *ramla*, where he had to deal with the same difficulty scaling the dune. He had not slept all night and was not in a very good mood. It was the first time since Kufra that he had not assumed direct command of the troops. For this operation, he tried to leave his subordinates alone, confining himself to the responsibilities of his rank, namely the coordination of the whole. But in Uigh-el-Kébir, alone and without news, his temper took over. He needed to be at the heart of the action rather than behind it. Dio explained the events of the previous day and the questions he had been asking himself that morning: 'I didn't have enough men to surround the oasis and at the same time guard the vehicles. The Italians had to flee that night. I formed a patrol to go and see.'[105] Leclerc approved and, without delay, headed straight towards the fort with only a cane for a weapon, to the great amazement of those present. On the fly, Dio designated *Sergent Chef* Thuilliez's group to serve as his escort and joined Leclerc, followed by Poletti. Ceccaldi and everyone else were stunned, realising the risk they were taking if the Italians were still in the fort. The artillerymen quickly prepared to fire in case they needed to protect an assault in the open, led by a dozen 'infantrymen' consisting of all their leaders.

The group arrived at the entrance to the fort without the slightest problem. The Italians had already evacuated. 'The position was empty, but large pools of blood indicated that Ceccaldi's shells had caused casualties there.'[106] Two sections of the *GNB* then entered the fort. *Lieutenant* d'Abzac, at Dio's request, had the honour of hoisting the French flag with the Cross of Lorraine on the mast of Fort Tedjéré. Ingold recounted the scene: 'Upon its capture, on 1 March 1942, *Lieutenant Colonel* Dio had a large tricolour flag raised to the highest point of the fort at Tedjéré, mockingly defying the Heinkel reconnaissance planes.'[107] Indeed, they had barely finished the impromptu ceremony when the sky hummed with the passage of two bombers, an Italian Savoia and a German Heinkel marked with the black *Luftwaffe* cross. They passed over the fort without dropping their bombs. However, the Frenchmen heard them machine-gunning the northern palm grove where *Lieutenant* de Bazelaire's *GNT* platoon arrived during the night. Miraculously, nobody was injured in the attack. Small bombs, dropped in the sand, lost a large part of their explosive blast effect.

The fort had been invested by the *tirailleurs* and, 'to reward the *tirailleurs* and encourage them for other operations, they were allowed to take anything they wanted.'[108] They were only interested in fabrics and clothing to take back to their villages. The 'harvest' in Fort Tedjéré was excellent because the Italians had fled so quickly without worrying about grabbing any personal effects. The cooks shared the food left by the Italians: pasta, cans of tuna, canned goods, dehydrated vegetables, spices, and even mineral water, all of which was a great improvement on the usual rations of the Free French of Chad.

---

104 Béné, *Carnets, Première Époque*, pp.282–83.
105 Destrem, *L'Aventure de Leclerc*, p.164.
106 Béné, *Carnets, Première Époque*, p.283.
107 Ingold, *L'Épopée*, p.163.
108 Béné, *Carnets, Première Époque*, p.285.

Shortly thereafter, they entered the village adjacent to the fort where Bey Ahmed received the adulation of the indigenous villagers when they recognised him. They also gathered valuable information on the Italians which would prove useful later. Shouts suddenly arose, and *tirailleurs* appeared escorting an Italian officer. He was an Italian medical captain, surrounded by large *Saras tirailleurs*, and scared to death. He explained that he was a doctor, passing through Tedjéré. When the French attacked, he found refuge in the village with *Capitano* Brachietti, commander of the *Meharisti dello Sciati*, whose arm had been torn off at the shoulder by shrapnel. He had been abandoned there by his men, who fled on camels. *Dr* Mauric helped his Italian colleague treat the Italian officer.

Leclerc wanted to leave immediately for Gatroun, but Dio dissuaded him, telling him that he was in contact with *Groupement Hous* by radio. If a serious or unforeseen event had taken place in Gatroun, they would have been notified. He advised him to rest before taking the road together at nightfall to avoid the Italian planes. Leclerc saw the common sense in the recommendation and agreed with Dio. The departure order having been set at 6:00 p.m., everyone found a little corner to recover with a few hours of sleep. At the scheduled time, they departed towards Gatroun, 70km away. Leclerc rushed to the head of the column with his tactical CP. Dio left *Lieutenant* de Bazelaire at Tedjéré to search for any fugitives, to destroy all the ammunition and small arms found in the fort, and then to destroy all the installations. The young *méhariste* officer recovered the 40 camels left by the Italians as well as the bags containing the monthly pay for the Italian *méharistes*. The two Schwarzlose machine guns and the four machine guns recovered in Fort Tedjéré were loaded into the trucks of the group's combat train. *Caporal Chef* Béné remained on site with his radio to provide a means of communicating with Bazelaire's platoon and to take care of the two wounded Frenchmen.

Groupement Dio's column reached the post of Gatroun in the middle of the night, finding the *colonel*'s tactical CP already there. Leclerc, who arrived first on the night of 2/3 March, found no one there and the Italian post smouldering. In the morning, contact was established with *Groupement Hous* which joined them and reported on their events. Fort Gatroun was taken by surprise on 28 February, thanks to the decisive action of *Lieutenant* Dubut who entered the post with *Caporals* Garcia and Névot on foot and took it by surprise in broad daylight.[109] After burning down the post, Hous stationed his unit near a *gara* 25 kilometres to the west to avoid the planes which were sure to search for it. On 3 March, French forces briefly concentrated at Gatroun, with the *colonel*'s CP, *Groupement Dio*, *Groupement Hous*, *Capitaine* Sarazac's *GNT*, and Massu's section all consolidating there.[110] Massu was unable to seize Oum-el-Araneb[111] and had to retreat in the face of a complete *Sahariana*, greatly superior in force to him. Leclerc decided to immediately reengage the Italians. After making contact with them, however, he was forced to withdraw on 6 March, agreeing that the enemy was indeed too powerful.

---

109 *Caporal* Garcia, who had participated in the Kufra operation, received the *Croix de la Libération* for his action under *Lieutenant* Dubut. A high-level athlete when war was declared, Névot took part in the Narvik operation then, winning in Chad, was in all the battles with Leclerc until 1945. After leaving the service, he moved to the United States and became the coach of the American Olympic fencing team. In the 2000s, he returned many times to the *RMT* and had a statue made to the glory of the Chadian *tirailleurs*. This statue is situated in the Dio Quarter of Meyenheim (68) where the *RMT* is stationed. For many years, he remained the only 'survivor of Kufra.' He died in 2019, at the age of 100.

110 A famous photo taken at the makeshift Gatroun airfield shows Leclerc in profile in the centre, Poletti is on the left with his hand on his kepi, and Dio is on the right facing the camera. None of the officers are wearing the same uniform. Dio is bearded, in a short-sleeved shirt with large pockets, shorts, a shapeless kepi on his head, and a cigarette in his left hand. In the background are a Lysander liaison plane and a Bedford truck.

111 *Oum-el-Araneb* means 'the mother of rabbits' because there are many of these little Saharan hares in the palm grove.

Meanwhile, *Groupement Dio* was ordered to retreat to Uigh-el-Kébir on 3 March. The *ramla* of Tedjéré was crossed more easily than on the way out. Then, the group was the first to leave towards Chad via the central route through the Kourizo Pass. Although it was the most direct route, it was not the easiest. Some challenging passages had been built up to make it easier for vehicles to cross. The column advanced slowly but surely until about 50km from the border when they reached the 10km section of *fech-fech*. It took hours of gruelling work, each crew doing its best to move forward. Men and vehicles were put to the test. 'The frames were starting to come apart and take on a slight V shape. All the steering wheels already had more than half a turn of play in them.'[112] Nevertheless, the column soon reached the foothills of the Tibesti range. They were back in Chad. Security measures against planes were lifted, tension subsided, and the bivouacs became lively again.

On 14 March 1942, all the units that had participated in the Fezzan 1 operations of 1941–1942 returned to Chad. The units went directly to their usual base areas. *Groupement Dio* disbanded in Kirdimi. *Commandant* Dio wanted to review all the assembled personnel, believing it important to say something to each of the comrades-in-arms with whom he had just spent almost a month of combat. *Caporal Chef* Béné remembered the moment: 'To the Europeans, gathered in line, he shook hands while saying a few words to each. When he arrived at me, the last in rank, he congratulated me on the good functioning of my radio and told me that he was immediately nominating me for the rank of sergent.'[113] In his operations report dated 18 March, Dio recounted the essential parts in the history of the operation, emphasising the lessons he drew from them. He was preparing for the future. For routes, he recommended the one passing through Kourizo, while finding a way around the *fech-fech*. Furthermore, he advised avoiding the *ramla* north of Tedjéré by going around it to the east. He then described the best way to approach and attack the fort of Tedjéré. He ended on the positive: the personnel, materiel, and the howitzer were completely satisfactory. As usual, Dio limited himself to the essentials. Everything was precise and concise, without any superfluous remarks. In two pages, he captured all the important points to remember for the future operations he was planning.

For his part, Leclerc published an Order of the Day on 17 March to summarise the results of Operation Fezzan 1 and to thank the participants:

> Four fortified posts were taken, more than 50 prisoners captured, several large fuel depots and ammunition burnt, numerous automatic weapons taken away, as well as three planes destroyed. Three flags, including one torn by our bullets, were taken and will take their place in the regiment's hall of honour, opposite that of Kufra. These results are due to the audacity and bravery of the fighters, but also to the hard work of all those who assisted them. We are not yet ripe for slavery. *Vive la France*.

The Order of the Day was signed for the first time: '*Général* Leclerc.'[114]

Beyond the military assessment itself, Fezzan 1 was a formidable training scenario for the Free French of Chad. They gained confidence in their leaders, in their equipment, and in their combat procedures. The operation allowed them to conduct a full-scale test on the terrain of future engagements and to learn how to avoid the traps that motor vehicles were susceptible to fall into in the Sahara. 'Great training was accomplished and experience of motorised warfare in the desert gained.'[115] The last sentence of Leclerc's Order of the Day: 'we are not yet ripe for slavery' had to resonate harshly in the ears of the Frenchmen in the *AOF* who had accepted the German yoke.

---

112 Béné, *Carnets, Première Époque*, p.333.
113 Béné, *Carnets, Première Époque*, p.336.
114 Béné, *Carnets, Première époque*, p.337.
115 Compagnon, *Leclerc*, p.261.

Across the globe, Allied forces did not have many victories to celebrate at the start of 1942. In the north of Libya, the British had just retreated once again in the face of Rommel's counterattack. The Germans repelled violent Russian counterattacks in the Donetz region. Japan continued its expansion in southeast Asia and was threatening Australia. Consequently, the Allied press shone a light on the Fezzan operational theatre. It published numerous press releases on the victorious raid that Chadian troops inflicted on the Italians in the south of Fezzan. From that moment, Leclerc began to be known to the whole world, including his enemies.

Upon his return from Fezzan, Leclerc wore the two stars of a *général de brigade*.[116] *Capitaine* de Guillebon discovered in the quartermaster's store of the Ouaou-el-Kébir fort some silver-white metal stars – Italian collar tab insignia.[117] These stars did the trick. The 'standard bearer, Butelot, made a *chechia*[118] for him with a cardboard visor' to serve as a kepi, on which he attached the stars.[119] The circumstances in which this kepi was presented to Leclerc are not known. In accordance with military tradition, the homemade hat was probably given to him 'by surprise' by a small committee of officers after a meeting, or a big speech, or during an informal drink in the hall of honour. The most senior person would then make a brief speech to tell the 'boss' how proud his subordinates were of the promotion. Dio or Hous, the two commandants, could have made the speech. The (Italian) stars were the first stars that *Général* Leclerc would wear.[120] In addition to the kepi, other stars they had found were 'remounted 'French style' on a piece of black cloth; from March 1942, they adorned the jacket of the victor of Kufra.'[121] Leclerc agreed to wear them because he considered that his promotion was now warranted. He was no longer the unit commander he was in Kufra; he became the actual leader of an operational theatre, in command of land and air forces. The scale had changed. He proved to himself, first of all, as well as to his men, that he had the ability to be a *général*. The leader of Free France had previously sent him a message: 'The victorious operations carried out under your command in southern Libya are a complete success. *Général* Leclerc, you and your glorious troops are the pride of France.'[122]

Leclerc was already preparing the Fezzan 2 operation. To that end, he placed his trusted man at the centre of Chadian operations to prepare the attack on Libya and Tunisia. Memorandum No.71/CSO, dated 12 March 1942,[123] named *Commandant* Dio as deputy of Group 3 and garrison commander of Faya-Largeau. The note was broadcast while the troops were still on their way back. During the operations carried out together in Tedjéré or Gatroun, Leclerc must certainly have revealed the new assignment to Dio and explained to him the reason for it.

---

116 In the French system, two stars indicate a *Général de Brigade* (brigadier general), which would be one star in the US system. There is no one star rank in the French system; thus, French *générals* wear one more star at each rank than their US counterparts. However, the French also do not have a six-star rank. The equivalent of an American 5-star General of the Army is a 7-star *Maréchal de France*. (Translator's note)

117 Corbonnois, *L'Odyssée de la Colonne Leclerc*, p.91.

118 A *chechia* is a short, box-like hat from the Maghreb that is similar to a fez, but less rigid. They were worn in *tirailleur* units. (Translator's note)

119 Notin, *le Croisé*, p.157.

120 At the Cercle de Brazzaville on 28 August 1942, during the second anniversary of the 3 Glorious Days, a charity auction was organised for the *FFL*. Leclerc agreed to have a pair of his stars made with *bersaglieri* insignia put up for auction. They brought in 12,110 francs. Fonds Leclerc *Journal du Capitaine Troadec*, p.30.

121 Corbonnois, *L'Odyssée de la Colonne Leclerc*, p.91.

122 Compagnon, *Leclerc*, p.261.

123 SHD, Dio, 14 Yd 1759, ESS.

Chapter 5

Fezzan 2,
12 March 1942 to 26 January 1943

On 18 March Dio read the memo reassigning him from Zouar to Faya-Largeau. On that day, his duties as commander of the *Groupe du Tibesti*, which he had taken on at the end of November 1941, thus came to an end. He remained there for a little over three months. Leclerc had placed him there to supervise the build-up and preparations for the offensive in Fezzan, which had been very well executed. Dio personally learnt several lessons from the operation, which is how he ended his operations report. Leclerc had explained to him at Gatroun that Operation Fezzan 1 was a training scenario, and he issued his orders for the future. To prepare for the next attack, Faya-Largeau had to become Chad's operational centre. To achieve that, Leclerc needed Dio's presence there. Therefore, he appointed him deputy of Group 3, with the specific responsibility of garrison commander. It was a duty Dio had enjoyed performing at Fort-Lamy during the previous summer. Leclerc asked him to take all necessary measures to make Faya-Largeau capable, both operationally and logistically, of receiving additional units. He made it clear to Dio that the job would be temporary. He counted on him to instil in the personnel the energy necessary to get back to work once they returned to their units, to ensure that the operation that had just ended was not considered as an end in itself, but rather only as a step on the path of reconquest. As had become routine in their exchanges, Leclerc ended his monologue by asking Dio for his thoughts. Dio replied that he completely understood the plan and gave his 100 percent support. But he also drew his *patron*'s attention to the fatigue of some of the leaders among the colonial troops who had been on the borders of Chad since 1938. 'The length of their stay, and the harshness of the climate weigh heavily on the men,' and he added that more men died, 'in the stifling rooms of hospitals than on the battlefields.'[1] Personally, Dio was able to benefit from the leave forced on him following his injury, but he perceived physical and psychological fatigue among the officers and NCOs. It would be prudent, during the 'summer wintering' period, to take measures to give them an opportunity to catch their breath. He added that some would need medical care, particularly dental care. Leclerc thanked him for drawing it to his attention – he would think about it and study what could be done.

From Kirdimi, Dio went straight to Faya-Largeau. He asked that his footlocker, which was still in Zouar, be forwarded to him as quickly as possible. In the meantime, he was 'camping in the premises' of Group 3. He was under the orders of *Commandant* Hous, with whom he worked during the first part of Operation Kufra, although he did not really know him. He had heard some young officers, including Massu, did not think too highly of him. Was it because he had succeeded d'Ornano, who had led them to that judgement? Dio thought that might indeed have been the reason. The Massu affair, which broke out in the days that followed, would raise big questions for

---

1   Dronne, *Le Serment*, p.117.

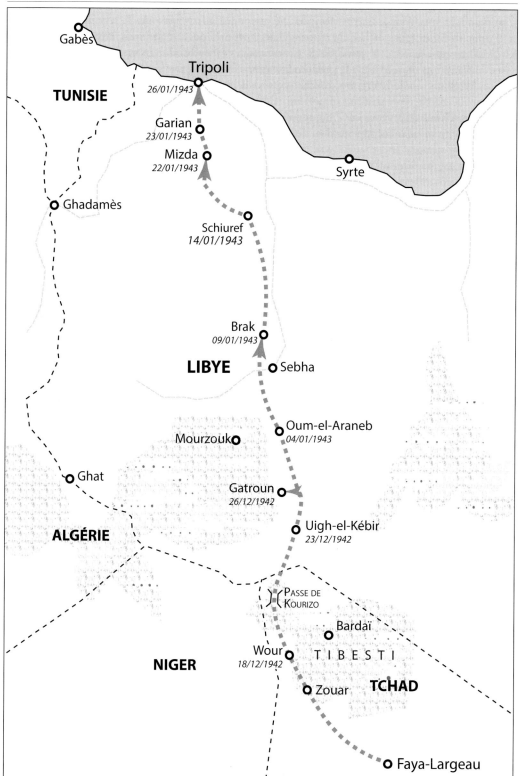

Map 6 The Groupement Dio during Fezzan 2 and Tripolitania (18 December 1942 to 26 January 1943).

Commandant Dio. Massu had performed the rearguard mission for the Fezzan operation under very difficult conditions.[2] When he returned late, he found piles of administrative paperwork that required urgent answers. It came from *Commandant* Hous, commanding Group 3, who even asked him to immediately provide proposed citations following the battles. That was too much for Massu. With his whole being, he directly expressed his irritation to *Commandant* Hous, saying that he believed there were more important things that needed to be done and that in any case, 'everyone had only done their job.'[3] Hous complained directly to *Général* Leclerc, who was uncompromising with breaches of hierarchical discipline. He summoned Massu, who was told that 'I was not thinking straight and that he was transferring me to the troops of the Levant.'[4] '*Lieutenant* Dubut, a platoon leader of Massu's *1re DC*, was also 'dumped' in Fada.'[5] Faced with this injustice, two other platoon leaders of the *1re DC* requested, and obtained, a transfer – along with a disciplinary sanction. *Commandant* Dio was disappointed to find such a poor relationship situation in Faya-Largeau. As deputy to *Commandant* Hous, he would have to ensure the restoration of a more peaceful atmosphere within Group 3.

The newly promoted *Général* Leclerc regularly visited Faya-Largeau by plane for inspections and to inquire about any problems encountered in the build-up of forces in northern Chad. On Sunday 29 March, Troadec noted in his diary, 'The général left by plane for Faya. He found Dio there, sorting out the final details of the campaign.'[6] He then officially announced that men who had stayed in Chad for more than two years would be granted leave. Reception facilities were set up in Cameroon and Middle Congo as well as in South Africa. Poletti, one of the oldest officers in terms of time in theatre, was surprised to be asked in May to go to South Africa for a rest. As with Poletti, all the colonials who had arrived in Chad in 1939 were invited to go for rest and recovery during the summer. Dio appreciated that the *général* had acted on his comments concerning the fatigue of some of his subordinates. Above all, he appreciated that Leclerc never omitted to implement what he recognised to be prudent. At his level, Dio instructed the various unit commanders to organise a rotation to send their *tirailleurs* on leave. Their return to their village at least every two years was stipulated in their recruitment contract. *3e Bataillon de Marche* was either unable or unwilling to respect this clause, so it had to be dissolved.[7] This system of rest and recovery would prove very beneficial, especially since 'in Borkou, the summer of 1942 was exceptionally torrid. For several weeks, an average temperature of 55° C (131° F) in the shade was common.'[8] Charles Béné, newly promoted to the rank of *sergent*, was 85km southwest of Faya-Largeau in Kirdimi, when he recorded this meteorological observation.

On 25 March, de Gaulle named Leclerc commander-in-chief of all troops in Free French Africa with Brazzaville as its headquarters. Initially, the *général* expressed his incomprehension at being appointed to Brazzaville. He replied to de Gaulle 'that there is nothing to do in Brazza, where

---

2   His patrol would suffer four deaths during this phase, as many as all the other units combined.
3   Fonds Leclerc, *Massu, Letter to Farret*, boîte B9A, dossier 1, chemise 5, 01.
4   Massu, *Sept Ans*, p.63.
5   This is the same officer who took Fort Gatroun by surprise a few days earlier.
6   Fonds Leclerc, *Journal du Capitaine Troadec*, p.1.
7   BM3 was created in Chad in October 1940, primarily from Dio's reinforcement company from Douala. Commanded by *Commandant* Garbay, former commander of *Groupe Nomade de l'Ennedi*, BM3 arrived in Anglo-Egyptian Sudan in January 1941. It participated in operations in Eritrea with the British and the victory of Cub-Cub on 14 February 1941. Then in June, BM3 was engaged in Syria with the *1re Brigade Française Libre*. In April 1942, it participated in operations in Libya with the *2e Brigade Française Libre*. In the fall of 1942, realising that their return to Chad was not on the agenda, the Chadian *tirailleurs* mutinied. Returning to Fort-Lamy, the BM3 was disbanded.
8   Charles Béné, *Carnets de Route d'un 'Rat du Désert,' Alsacien de la France Libre, Seconde époque, 1942–1945* (Issy-les-Moulineaux: Elsevier Masson, 1999), p.8.

there is nothing but offices.'[9] He knew that the atmosphere between the Governor-General, Eboué, and the High Commissioner, Sicé, was abysmal. He did not want to waste his time dealing with quarrels of egos which, for him, was nonsensical in the current situation. But the leader of Free France persisted in his idea. Even if he did not like it, Leclerc was bound to obey and his loyalty to his leader mandated it. He therefore agreed to move to Brazzaville, but he kept a watchful eye on Chad. He knew that the next battle would start there. For him, that objective had to remain a priority. The *général* organised a ceremony for his departure from Chad on 10 April: 'Leclerc summoned his key officers before his departure for Brazza, so there is a wild crowd in Lamy. Saturday 11 April 42 – Lunch at the *général's* with all the *chefs de bataillon*.'[10] Dio travelled from Faya-Largeau with *Commandant* Hous for the occasion.

Leclerc did not leave Fort-Lamy with part of his staff until 23 April. But he left what he called his command post (CP) in the Chadian capital with Guillebon, newly promoted to *commandant*. Clearly, although situated in Brazzaville, Leclerc would continue to command Chad by relaying through Guillebon. Troadec, his aide-de-camp, describes the organisation of the command thus, '...in Brazza, the staff directing all the services, commanded by Bernard, – in Lamy, a CP directing the troops and commanded by Guillebon, – Dio commands the northern troops, – Leclerc, whom I will accompany, will be on the move as much as possible. Quilichini, who comes from Brazza, will make the liaisons.'[11] Surprisingly, in this extract from his diary, Troadec mentions Dio instead of *Commandant* Hous, who was the actual commander of the troops located in northern Chad at the time. Leclerc was pleased to have assigned Dio to Faya-Largeau, which he did before he knew of his future appointment in Brazzaville. He knew that with Dio his directives would be implemented and strictly enforced in spirit and, if necessary, with the share of judicious initiatives expected of a subordinate. This situation suited everyone, especially Dio. He did not see himself coming under the orders of any *général* other than Leclerc. 'Dio, the *blédard*, who considered Saumur to be a school for idiots, had been enlightened when he saw Leclerc's blue and direct gaze.'[12] This was a feeling shared by all the soldiers from Chad. They now felt bound by the Oath of Kufra and, in their eyes, only Leclerc had the legitimacy to lead them to Alsace.

During the first month after his arrival, Dio was mainly occupied with the development of the area of Faya-Largeau. He had small mud-brick buildings erected all around the famous Place Blanche. This square owes its name to the colour of the lime which is regularly applied to the walls of the surrounding buildings as well as to the gravel borders which partly delineate the parade ground around the flagpole. These small buildings would make it possible to bring together the personnel of the different services that would be located in Faya-Largeau and they would thus be close to the command. To ensure accommodation for the cadre and soldiers of the expected new units, he had a second camp built to the west of the palm grove, near the camp of the transportation company. He also established a technical support zone north of Faya-Largeau. After the first Fezzan campaign, a large number of vehicles needed serious maintenance and some even needed almost complete reconstruction. Parts were cannibalised from inoperable trucks and used to put less damaged vehicles back into operation. Dio was also building vehicle storage parks. 'Motorised Company No. 4 (*CA 4*) located in

9   Fonds Leclerc, *Journal du capitaine Troadec,* p.1.
10   Fonds Leclerc, *Journal du Capitaine Troadec,* p.2. The general rank of *Commandant* (4 stripes) has different names, depending on the branch of the Armed Forces. A *commandant* in the infantry is a *chef de bataillon,* a *capitaine de corvette* in the navy, and a *commandant* in the air force. They are all usually referred to simply as '*commandant.*'
11   Fonds Leclerc, *Journal du Capitaine Troadec,* p.1.
12   Destrem, *L'Aventure de Leclerc,* p.181.

Kour-Kour'[13] was under the orders of *Capitaine* Dubois.[14] A significant arrival of new equipment and vehicles was then expected in the ports of Middle Congo and Cameroon. Indeed, following the Japanese attack, American industry was operating at full capacity for the Allied war effort. Materially, the troops of Chad were receiving brand-new trucks, in particular Fords with a 3-ton payload, 'equipped with sand tyres with a large surface area.'[15] These trucks, originally intended for transporting livestock, would, once militarised in French style, become formidable desert 'warships.' Dio also began the construction of a huge munitions depot a significant distance from the town. He had underground bunkers built according to various types of ammunition. He took advantage of the palm grove so that the structures could go unnoticed from the air. Finally, having learnt the lesson of the bombing of the fuel pad at the Fort-Lamy airport in January, he had trenches dug to store the 200-litre barrels of petrol. Two sites were prepared, one next to the military airfield and the other near the technical support zone. Part of the work was carried out by local labour. Small civil companies from Fort-Lamy were called upon. An engineering works section was also set up once the earthmoving equipment arrived.

During each of his visits, Leclerc would visit the construction sites in progress. He was satisfied to see the transformation of the area. In April, while passing through Faya-Largeau, Leclerc took Dio aside and told him that Commandant Hous was going to leave Chad. He was assigned to Garoua in northern Cameroon to command the group. On 1 May 1942, Dio, having become Leclerc's right-hand man, was designated to take command of Group 3. Dio had foreseen this outcome ever since the sad events of 'the Massu affair'. Moreover, Massu had not left for the Levant as planned, staying in Chad instead. After a period in Brazzaville where he was able to rest and have his teeth treated, Massu was assigned to Kanem, facing Niger. It seems that Leclerc was let in on what had really happened to Massu and Dubut. As usual, the *général* acted and Dio was relieved to hear it. He was also happy, at a personal level, to become the leader of Group 3 and to have free rein. Territorially, the command extended over 40 percent of the total area of Chad, with responsibility for the three regions of Borkou, Ennedi, and Tibesti. The area, in which nomadic populations lived, was equal in size to that of metropolitan France and was managed by three *groupes nomades*, one per region. The other major peculiarity of Group 3 was the fact that the military was in charge of the civil administration in areas where local populations had a nomadic majority. Dio therefore combined the office of military leader and regional prefect, which is what made the command of Group 3 such an important assignment. The appointment demonstrated the great esteem in which Leclerc held Dio. He liked him, not just as a military leader, but he also liked him personally. Twice during the first half of 1942, Leclerc had the opportunity to demonstrate the attachment he had to this officer who had served him loyally since the first day of his arrival in Cameroon. On 7 April, Troadec wrote in his journal that Leclerc asked him to stay with him as aide-de-camp, promising 'that he would let me join Dio for the next campaign.'[16] Leclerc therefore considered service under Dio's command to be a reward for a junior officer. It was a wonderful indirect tribute! On 9 June 1942, Leclerc was invited to Léopoldville by the Belgians to give a 'talk' on the latest Fezzan operation. Twice he mentioned Dio.[17] While describing the fighting of February 1942, Leclerc could not help but digress about his comrade in-arms by relating with empathy Dio's role in Douala in 1940 and in Kufra in 1941. A second time, Leclerc spontaneously mentioned Dio's kepi, pierced by a bullet in Tedjéré. He thus demonstrated his admiration for his courageous

---

13 Kour-Kour is the indigenous name for the vast palm grove of Faya-Largeau.
14 Béné, *Carnets, Seconde Époque*, p.33.
15 Béné, *Carnets, Seconde Époque*, p.9.
16 Troadec, *Le Général Leclerc et l'Afrique Française Libre, 1940–1942*, Actes du Colloque International, p.590.
17 Fonds Leclerc, *Conférences de Leclerc, Causerie Léopoldville du 9 juin 1942*, boîte 21b, dossier 1, chemise 1.

deputy who did not hesitate to fight hand-to-hand with the Italians. It was on 1 June 1942 that Leclerc presented the *Croix de la Libération* to Dio, most certainly at Faya-Largeau during one of his visits.[18] This decoration, awarded by de Gaulle by decree of 14 July 1941 for his action at Kufra, should have been presented to Dio on 20 September 1941 at the same time Leclerc received his, however, his unavailability because of his wounds prevented it.

In Faya-Largeau, the leader of Group 3 continued the mission entrusted to him, namely the operational preparation of the Free French troops of Chad. In this context, the reinforcement of heavy weapons, particularly artillery, had become a priority. Dio depended upon boats arriving in Douala or Pointe-Noire. But on 10 May 1942, another supply route was opened up. Dio received the following order: 'The *capitaine* commanding *CA4* [Motorised Company No.4] will prepare a convoy which will bring from Wadi Halfa to Faya fifty tons of ammunition, two twenty-five pounder guns, and four Italian forty-seven [millimetre] guns.'[19] The mission, which was entrusted to *Capitaine* Dubois[20] was extraordinary, carried out over 2,000km between Chad and British Sudan, without a means of navigation and in areas for which there were no maps. It was an essential mission because it provided the French troops in Chad with artillery that was sufficiently powerful to support the next offensive operation. On 25 May *Commandant* Dio reviewed the detachment of 40 vehicles on the Place d'Ornano.[21] The column left the same day and returned on 8 July, with the prescribed heavy weapons. On their return, Dio warmly greeted the small, commendable team that had completed what was a truly exceptional journey, considering the means available at that time.

On the international level, the summer of 1942 was not going well for the Allies. On 27 May Rommel's *Afrika Korps* attacked northern Libya, throwing the British back towards Egypt. To cover the retreat of the British 8th Army and to prevent it from turning into a rout, *Général* Marie-Pierre Koenig's *1re Brigade Française Libre* settled in Bir Hakeim. Its mission was to hold for at least 10 days. The brigade held for 16 days, earning Bir Hakeim the name 'Verdun' of Libya. But, even though he managed to take the French position on 12 June, Rommel, with his momentum stalled, missed his chance. The British reorganised near the cliffs of El Alamein, thus saving Alexandria. In Russia, the *OKW* (*Wehrmacht* High Command) announced the fall of Sevastopol on 1 July. All this information reached the posts in Chad from two different sources. German-speaking radio operators, like Béné, listened to German radio and retransmitted small news bulletins to their comrades. The other way was to listen to BBC, and even Radio Paris, broadcasts on wireless sets. The French cadre had got into the habit of meeting in the evening around a radio and commenting on the news. Whenever he could, Dio joined in these informal gatherings, which gave him an opportunity to clearly assess the morale among his men.

On 3 July 1942, Leclerc arrived once again in Faya-Largeau. The advance of the *Afrika Korps* was worrying him. On Friday 29 May, Troadec had already noted in his journal that 'from what we hear at Faya, the 3rd Italian *Saharan* is moving in our direction. Dio will know how to properly welcome them.'[22] Military intelligence mentioned the presence of German units in Fezzan. In

---

18 SHD, Dio, 14 Yd 1759, extrait ESS, corroborated by General Duval in L'Ancre d'Or, n°283 Novembre-Décembre 1994.

19 Robert Dubois, 'Raid Logistique au Soudan Anglo-Égyptien', *Soldats de Leclerc* (Paris: Éditions Lavauzelle, 1997), p.57. Wadi Halfa is on the Nile in what was then the Anglo-Sudan. The 25pdr Mark II or QF 25pdr gun was a modern weapon designed to replace the 4½ inch gun dating from the First World War. The British gave Leclerc a great gift.

20 Capitaine Dubois was nicknamed 'von Kéké' in reference to the palm tree trunks that the crews of the motorised companies threw under the wheels of their vehicles when moving through the sand.

21 Place Blanche, located in the centre of Faya-Largeau, was renamed Place d'Ornano in honour of the first Free Frenchman of the *RTST* to die in combat.

22 Fonds Leclerc, *Journal du Capitaine Troadec*, p.8.

London, there were even concerns that an Italo-German attack on the northern border of Chad was being considered in retaliation for the last raid in Fezzan. Leclerc ordered Dio to put Tibesti in a state of defence – Dio knew exactly what Leclerc wanted. He still remembered the terms of Leclerc's instructions for the defence of Kanem from January 1941. 'Dio knew that Leclerc demanded an 'active' defence. He did not want a wall we would brace ourselves behind. On the contrary, he advocated a 'mobile, active, offensive defence.'' [23] Very quickly, Leclerc realised that Dio understood what he was telling him to do. He stopped pressing the point, and took the plane back to Brazzaville, reassured to have someone there who was on the same wavelength. [24] Dio summoned the two officers in charge of Tibesti: Vézinet, head of the subdivision, and Sarazac, commander of the *GNT*. He explained to them what the defensive system Leclerc had in mind would consist of:

- Lines of defence prepared in depth with firing positions, and the establishment of reserve fuel and ammunition depots,
- Blockades on the routes with alternating obstacles and mines,
- Permanent surveillance consisting of mobile patrols and '*choufs*' at the top of the peaks,
- A reserve element in the Bardaï region 'at the handle of the fan'[25] made up of a platoon from Geoffroy's *1re DC*. This element will have located axes that allow rapid vehicular movement on the two possible directions of attack: west coming from Korizo, or east coming from Yédri,
- An artillery element with 75mm mountain guns, positioned at Bardaï.

On 14 July 1942, de Gaulle named *Lieutenant Colonel* François Ingold military commander of Chad. A 48-year-old colonial officer, he had been wounded twice during the First World War. A very professional man of duty, he suffered the pain of losing one of his sons in 1941 while he was serving in the Free French Air Force. He would be very loyal to Leclerc and would not take offence at the latter's regular presence in Chad. Furthermore, the understanding with his leader of Group 3 would be perfect. Not being a *méhariste*, Ingold would have total confidence in Dio to command the northern Chadian borders.

Leclerc came to inspect the entire defence system of Tibesti at the beginning of August. Accompanied by Dio, he appeared reassured by the measures taken. With this arrangement, French troops could not be surprised. They would always be able to alert the majority of units in place along the Chadian borders with sufficient time to repel an enemy attack. 'Under the leadership of Dio and Vézinet, Largeau and Zouar became strongholds.'[26] In the end, however, the defensive posture proved to be unnecessary.[27] Commanded by General Bernard Montgomery, the British 8th Army stabilised the situation at the end of the summer. The Italo-German forces were experiencing great difficulties, particularly with logistics, and no longer had the capacity to relaunch the offensive along the coast, and even less so in Fezzan.

---

23   Dronne, *Le Serment*, p.120.
24   On that date, Troadec mentions this short visit as follows: 'The dates are ripe. The *général* is enjoying himself.' (Fonds Leclerc, Troadec, *Journal du Capitaine Troadec*, p.24.) He loved the fruit of the date palm and during operations practically only ate dried dates.
25   The military expression '*à la poignée de l'éventail*' (at the handle of the fan) refers to an area from which there are several possibilities, generally axes, on which to manoeuvre.
26   Ingold, *Général Ingold*, p.81.
27   The threat was nevertheless justified. 'Germany planned *Wehrmacht* action as far as the equator and had published articles and sketches on the region of Tibesti, Ennedi, Fort-Lamy, Abéché. In Berchtesgaden, Leclerc found maps of central Africa with shaded areas to be occupied in 1943.' Ingold, *Général Ingold*, p.257.

But the threat still existed on the western flank of Chad. Would the Vichy troops in Niger remain neutral in the face of Chad's military activities or, would they take advantage of them to attack or, at least, hinder them in their undertakings? At de Gaulle's request in London, coordination meetings with the British in Nigeria had resumed. On 7 July, Leclerc received Major General Edward Hawkins[28] at Fort-Lamy for a coordination meeting concerning Niger. At the end, Leclerc asked Dio to give him a report on the Vichy units in northern Niger. For future operations against Fezzan, the Free French would certainly need to take the westernmost route, that of Toummo. This was the route used by *Groupement Dio* in February. However, that route passed through Niger for several tens of kilometres. They did not want to force a confrontation with the Pétainist troops before committing against the Italians.

Many informal contacts persisted between the *méhariste* troops in both camps since many of them knew each other, they had often been classmates. Some had chosen dissidence, others had not. Circumstances greatly influenced those respective choices. It was, for example, easier for a single person to choose dissidence than it was for someone responsible for a family. Hierarchical rules were also often decisive. The senior officers of Niger, most of whom were devoted to an unwavering cult of *Maréchal* Pétain, exerted very strong pressure on the choice of the younger officers. Faced with the increase in regular defections of officers of the rank of *lieutenant* in Niger, the Governor of the *AOF*, Boisson, asked to place reliable people in the border areas to stop departures towards Free France. Leclerc was well informed of this and wanted to find out about the state of mind of those on the other side. So, Dio asked the *méhariste* officers of Tibesti to discreetly probe their counterparts. Mainly, they wanted to know whether they would let the Chadian columns pass if they crossed through the northern end of Niger. An internal document from the garrison commander of Agadez, *Commandant* Gilles, dated June 1942, shows the deep unease experienced by many officers serving in Niger. He described his peers,

> …all swing; many hesitate; some, the least thoughtful or the most ambitious ones driven by the spirit of adventure, leave and go to either Chad or Nigeria. More than a flagrant crime – we do not leave our post – there is a total error in this attitude: never in the course of its history has France been rescued from a catastrophic situation by foreigners. It was within herself that she always sought and found the means and the path to her salvation.[29]

A deep dismay in fact dwelt within those officers. They sought to justify their choice against the Gaullists. Several informal contacts were made on the ground between young French *méhariste* officers from the Niger-Chad borders. The patrols would meet for a few minutes around the same well. From the various contacts established, it appeared that the Pétainist troops in Niger would not confront the Gaullists. There was disagreement between the two camps, but not hatred. Dio, who knew perfectly the codes of the *méharistes*, was convinced of that. And that is what he reported to Leclerc.

The summer continued with the build-up of Leclerc's operational force with Dio serving as conductor of the orchestra. All orders, decisions, or adjustments went through him. However, tensions or misunderstandings could sometimes arise between Leclerc and Dio. Thus, on 21 August, the *général* wrote a letter to the *commandant* informing him of the discouragement of the *intendant* of Chad[30] following the numerous remonstrances coming from Faya-Largeau. Group 3 criticised the support branches for their slowness in honouring their orders and ensuring the

---

28   Hawkins was the general officer commanding British troops in West Africa.
29   CHETOM, boîte 18H149, monographie du poste militaire d'Agades – juin 1942.
30   Responsible for troop support.

transport of personnel returning from leave. From Brazzaville, Leclerc wrote to Dio: 'Let us be in complete agreement on this point of view. Your role is obviously to request from headquarters everything you need. But be careful to pass on the complaints of grumbling subordinates like all good Frenchmen. We have made a considerable effort from a supply point of view. We must not discourage the people who provided it.'[31] *Commandant* Dio responded in a handwritten note on 23 August. He recognised that the letters exchanged with the support branches had certainly not been sufficiently respectful. 'I apologise for bothering everyone with various requests…. forgive me for my anger, whatever anyone says, it's the only way to get something.'[32]

Clearly Dio recognised that the manner of his requests was not satisfactory, but that it was sometimes necessary. Leclerc was no fool; he had personally used the same approach when he was preparing Operation Kufra by harassing the general staff in Brazzaville. Deep down, he completely approved of Dio even if, as commander of the *AEF*, he had to take care of his senior subordinates such as *Intendant* Dupin. On the document he used for his talk in Léopoldville in June, he wrote in his own hand next to Dio's name: '… leader who never has to push his subordinates but, rather, has to hold them back. One of the greatest satisfactions of command.'[33] This was what Leclerc appreciated the most about Dio. Moreover, after the admonitions, he took care not to offend the recipient of his letter, ending thus: 'My best to Rasputin and believe, my dear Dio, in my very faithful friendship.'[34] This is not typical language used in military correspondence between a commander and his subordinate. Leclerc mentioned Dio's little dog, which brightened up work at the general staff during the summer of 1941. Actually, Dio had left his dog Rasputin at Fort-Lamy in November 1941 when he was transferred to Zouar. The animal had been entrusted to the *général's* standard bearer. But when he accompanied the *général* to Brazzaville in March, the dog was left behind. In Faya-Largeau, with living conditions permitting, Dio decided to bring the 'cocker bastard' along. In April, helpful airmen brought Rasputin back to his master, but the cocker spaniel was no longer in good health. He unfortunately died in November, a day when Leclerc happened to be present at Faya-Largeau. Leclerc was very saddened to learn of the little mascot's death, and the *général* immediately dedicated the two photos of Rasputin that Dio retained: 'one from 14 July 1941… where (Rasputin), howling next to the *général*, faces the *nouba*[35] playing 'Aux Champs.' On the second, Rasputin parades with the greatest seriousness, ten steps in front of the Colours of the *Régiment du Chad*.'[36]

Tensions could also arise within the units. They were often due to rapid changes in organisation and structure. Dio had to adjudicate over several of them. That was his role. One arbitration particularly caught his attention and made him smile inwardly. This took place within the *Groupe Nomade du Borkou*. This unit, under the command of *Commandant* Poletti, an inveterate *méhariste*, received replacement personnel during the summer. Among them was *Capitaine* Dronne, a reservist who had gained experience during the Gabon campaign with Dio. He was nobody's fool, and often expressed his opinions directly and forcefully. He was a valuable man who helped Leclerc when he arrived in Cameroon. Leclerc recognised that and brought him to Chad. The *GNB* received the order to leave its post at Kirdimi to position itself on the site of Zouré,

31   Fonds Leclerc, *Correspondance 42 entre Leclerc et Dio, 21 août 1942,* boîte 8a, dossier 1, chemise 1.
32   Fonds Leclerc, *Correspondance 42 entre Leclerc et Dio, letter from Dio dated 23 August 1942,* boîte 8a, dossier 1, chemise 1.
33   Fonds Leclerc, *Conférences de Leclerc, causerie Léopoldville du 9 juin 1942,* boîte 21b, dossier 1, chemise 1.
34   Fonds Leclerc, *Correspondance 42 entre Leclerc et Dio, letter from Dio dated 23 August 1942,* boîte 8a, dossier 1, chemise 1.
35   A *nouba* is military music from the North African regiments of the French Army.
36   Louis Dio, *Soldats de Leclerc* (Paris: Lavauzelle, 1997), p.4; 'Quand le Général Leclerc dédicaçait des photographies à Raspoutine', *Caravane* No. 89, Avril 1949.

on the northwest edge of Tibesti. It was a column of 27 overloaded trucks heading towards the Libyan border. The *GNB* was complete with its combat train – supply trucks filled with fuel and ammunition. Air protection measures had to be taken because the region was being over flown by Italian planes. When evening arrived, *Commandant* Poletti found a bivouac location and ordered the traditional *méhariste* square to be formed for the night. This system consists of gathering all the vehicles in the centre of a square made up of four lines of defence. Dronne did not agree with the formation because he rightly believed that 'trucks full of fuel and ammunition, pressed against each other, constitute a prime target for the enemy; it would only take one of them being hit for all of them to explode and burn.'[37] But Poletti refused to listen, bringing up his combat experience in Mauritania. Dronne kept his calm but decided to tell Dio about it at the first opportunity. The reservist officer concluded philosophically: 'Experience is like Aesopian language; it is capable of [teaching] both the best and the worst [lessons].'[38]

Dio knew how to relax the atmosphere of his teams when necessary. He loved to play jokes, especially on his visitors. One of them remained in the memory of several of his subordinates: Dio, entertaining staff from outside Chad for dinner, claimed as seriously as possible that the heat of Faya-Largeau caused the circumference of the head to increase slightly. While everyone was eating, a few accomplices inserted newspaper into the band inside of each guest's kepi. When everyone left the mess at the end of the meal, they were all astonished to notice that when they put their hats back on, they no longer fitted! Dio's joke made everyone laugh out loud.

On 15 September, de Gaulle came to inspect Faya-Largeau, accompanied by Leclerc. Dio, responsible for northern Chad, welcomed them as they got off the plane, a twin-engine US Lockheed named *Koufra*. The leader of Free France was experiencing difficult times in his relations with the British. He felt marginalised by his 'ally' who did not consider it useful, for example, to warn him of the British military operation in Madagascar, a French colony. He could not travel as he wished because his movements were subject to the goodwill of Churchill. Indeed, 'this was the only trip made by de Gaulle to the *AEF* during the summer of 1942.'[39]

De Gaulle took advantage of his visits to Africa to re-energise himself through contact with the soldiers of Free France and the local populations, who were always enthusiastic during his visits. The visit to northern Chad proceeded at a leisurely pace. Leclerc, commander of troops in the *AEF*, was happy to show the work accomplished during the summer to the leader of Free France and the progress made in the increase in operational power of the various units. De Gaulle was reassured by what he saw and heard. 'At Faya, de Gaulle [said he] admired the appearance of the troops who paraded magnificently.'[40] On his return to London, he wrote to Leclerc: 'I was extremely satisfied with my inspection of the forces under your command… The enemy has not yet learnt the value of the French colonial army.'[41] That message warmed the heart and increased the enthusiasm of all the soldiers who had been preparing tirelessly for several months. On 29 September, good news was announced by the Reuters agency. The USSR recognised Fighting France. All Free French were proud when they learnt of Stalin's decision. 'This seems to prove that the important successes achieved by the arms of Free France, on land, at sea and in the air, are recognised for their due merit.'[42]

37 Dronne, *Le Serment*, p.119.
38 Dronne, *Le Serment*, p.120.
39 Compagnon, *Leclerc*, p.283, note 1.
40 Fonds Leclerc, *Journal du Capitaine Troadec*, p.34.
41 Compagnon, *Leclerc*, p.284.
42 Béné, *Carnets, Seconde Époque*, p.47.

But then, Dio learnt he had been stripped of his nationality on 9 October 1942.[43] Having been one of the prominent officers during the Gabon campaign, it could not be otherwise. Vichy was vengeful. A military court-martial was expected to soon sentence him to death *in absentia* for treason, followed by confiscation of all his property. He had nothing personal in mainland France, but he hoped that his mother in Vannes would not be worried on his account. On 10 October, more comforting news reached him. He learnt from Leclerc that the latter had just signed Note Number 90 promoting him to *lieutenant colonel* following the decision taken by *Général* de Gaulle on 25 September 1942.[44] Dio was surprised by the promotion. *Capitaine* in September 1940, he had advanced two steps in rank in just two years. His *patron* had followed an even faster progression since he had advanced three grades in the same period of time. The circumstances were, of course, very exceptional for both men. Within the normal framework of advancement, in 1942, Leclerc would still have been a *commandant* and Dio would certainly have still been a *capitaine*, given his previous evaluations where he had often been criticised by those who disliked him. His behaviour, sometimes judged as atypical by his seniors, certainly did not destiny him to follow a career path with high potential.

Dio continued to supervise everything in Faya-Largeau and Zouar, not neglecting any area. He knew, in particular, that logistical preparation would guarantee the success of the future operation just as much as operational training would. To support a motorised column like the one being prepared, hundreds of thousands of litres of fuel, and hundreds of tons of food and spare parts were required. An oversight or an estimating error could cause a disruption in the units' supplies and they would then be forced to stop on the spot.

November 1942 remains the pivotal month in the history of the Second World War. After the uncertainties of the summer, the fortunes of war seemed to turn for the first time to the advantage of the Allies. The Germans got bogged down in Russia, stumbling at Stalingrad. The Japanese began to retreat in the Pacific under pressure from the Americans, who had rebuilt their fleet. In Libya, General Montgomery's British 8th Army resumed the offensive at El Alamein and Rommel's *Afrika Korps* began to lose ground.

In North Africa, Operation TORCH took place on 8 November, in which Anglo-American forces landed in Morocco and Algeria, under the supreme command of Lieutenant General Dwight D. Eisenhower. Vichy troops initially tried to oppose the operation, but were forced to surrender, the *Armée de l'Afrique du Nord* and then that of the *AOF* finally rallied to the Allies. That meant that Niger no longer represented a threat on the western flank of Chad. The Germans, in response to the Allied landings of November 8, invaded Tunisia on 16 November. With a large reinforcement of armoured vehicles, they took Gabès on 19 November and 'now control the entire coast, from Bizerte to the Gulf of Sirte.'[45] Prior to that, on 11 November, Hitler had launched 'Fall Anton,' the plan for the occupation of all French territory. There was no longer a free zone in mainland France.

In Chad, the Free French troops were ready. The final preparations at the end of the summer allowed them to calmly wait for the offensive to begin. 'This month of November 1942 is the crucial month. Général Leclerc's troops are in place around the natural fortress of Tibesti; They impatiently await the order to depart for the great trek which, through the desert and Fezzan, will lead them to the sea and then to the European Continent.'[46] During that month, *Lieutenant Colonel* Dio 'presided over the ceremony of 11 November. Addressing the garrison gathered at

43   SHD, Dio, 14 Yd 1759, Note 567-C, signed 'Colonial Intendant of 2 Cl Fourquet'.
44   Ordre de la Libération, dossier Dio.
45   Béné, *Carnets, Seconde Époque,* p.71.
46   Dronne, *Le Serment,* p.124.

Place Blanche, he said that our entry into the fight was near.[47] On 14 November, Leclerc was at Faya-Largeau and the next day was at Kirdimi, where the *GNB* was stationed. He went around the mess to 'verbally explain the operation order.'[48]

With the fighting about to resume, how had the two belligerents prepared during the hot period? The Italians learnt their lesson from the raid suffered in February-March 1942, and completely revised their defensive tactics. That made Ingold say: 'Our offensive action in the spring of 1942 had struck, as if with a sickness of neglect, everything that was built up – buildings, *bourjs*,[49] perimeter walls.'[50] The Italians understood that a defensive system based on isolated forts was doomed to failure. Powerful artillery would overcome that type of defence. Their new tactic consisted of developing the terrain preferably on higher ground, near their posts. They built trenches, shelters, bastions. 'These new positions…were completely buried'[51] to protect against the effects of artillery and they were reinforced with barbed wire and minefields. 'During this period, in approximately three weeks, a single platoon of engineers, with the assistance of mixed teams of miners and infantrymen, laid minefields at Hon, Zella, Sebha, Brak, Murzuk, Umm el Araneb, Tmessa, Gatrun, Uau el Chebir, Ghat. At Hon in particular, where 12,500 mines were used, the minefield extended for almost 8,500 metres with a depth of approximately 300 metres.'[52] In addition, all Italian posts were reinforced with artillery to be able to respond to the French guns. In terms of personnel, each post was made up of 'around 100 nationals, 10 to 15 officers, 150 *askaris*.'[53] *Generale* di Martino described the Italian forces in South Fezzan,

> The forces in the Libyan Sahara amounted to a little less than 6,000 men at the end of October 1942 (251 officers, 334 non-commissioned officers, 2,502 Italian soldiers, 2,721 Libyan soldiers), with 28 L6 light tanks, 10 armoured cars, 72 anti-tank guns, 83 x 20mm guns, 50 artillery pieces of various calibres and an assortment of 382 vehicles, of which 157 were ineffective.[54]

Fortunately, Leclerc's troops were well informed about the Italian change in tactics. Nothing escaped the aerial reconnaissance carried out by an aviation unit soon to be named the *Bretagne* aviation group. Consequently, the French also made major modifications during the summer of 1942, following the lessons of the Fezzan 1 raid. The first concerned the size of the units making up the column forming in northern Chad. 'To embark on this conquest, *Général* Leclerc gathered 4,735 men and 787 vehicles.'[55] Compared to the 500 men engaged during the previous operation, the size of this new operation, called GRATUITY changed enormously. Next, *Commandant* Crépin, a *bigor*[56] newly arrived in Chad, was tasked with building artillery commensurate with the objectives set.[57] Leclerc wanted to keep this coastal defence specialist in Manoka. Crépin threatened

---

47   Béné, *Carnets, Seconde Époque*, p.58.
48   Béné, *Carnets, Seconde Époque*, p.59.
49   A *bourj* or *burj* is a tower in Arabic. (Translator's note)
50   Ingold, *L'Épopée*, p.163.
51   Ingold, *L'Épopée*, p.164.
52   Di Martino, *Scenari Sahariani Libia, 1919–1943*, p.308.
53   Ingold, *L'Épopée*, p.164. The nationals were the Italians. The *askaris* were Libyan auxiliary troops recruited locally.
54   Di Martino, *Scenari Sahariani Libia, 1919–1943*, p.306.
55   This figure considers all the personnel involved, including support. Vincent, *Les Forces Françaises Libres en Afrique*, p.290.) Corbonnois discusses the figures for the combat units: 500 Europeans and 2,800 *tirailleurs* (Corbonnois, *L'Odyssée de la Colonne Leclerc*, p.161).
56   Marine (colonial) artilleryman. (Translator's note)
57   Crépin was a graduate of the École Polytechnique and an officer of the colonial artillery. He was in command

to join the Foreign Legion so that Leclerc would agree to his request: 'I want to fight.'[58] Thanks to him, and the arrival of equipment, the capability and the power of the artillery fire tripled. Finally, Chad's air forces were organised. The *Bretagne* group was created, capable of supporting ground troops due to the creation of two squadrons. The first, called *Rennes*, was equipped with five Lysanders and could carry out reconnaissance, intelligence, and key leader transport missions. The second squadron, named *Nantes*, with five Blenheims and three Glenn-Martins, was capable of bombing enemy objectives and also of transporting troops.

Considering the number of soldiers engaged, the cadre of Europeans increased. For example, the number of Europeans in the two long range reconnaissance and combat companies was 65 percent. It was 15 to 20 percent in *tirailleur* infantry units, which was a high rate for such a unit. The Europeans who reached Chad during the summer were escapees from France and North Africa or those who had arrived from England. They were trained either in England or in Brazzaville. But many were French expatriates living in Africa who were mobilised as reservists. At that time, an estimated 30 percent of the European population of the African territories of the AEF and Cameroon became reservists. This is an enormous proportion and was detrimental to the functioning of those territories. Dronne, Troadec, and Lantenois are successful examples of reservists who provided great service within the Chadian troops. Dio particularly appreciated that category of the cadre and subsequently maintained a great friendship with many of them.

With trucks arriving in large numbers, drivers also needed to be trained. The recruitment of Cameroonian drivers who were required to be civilians, called 'cameloubs' by the *tirailleurs*, was intensified during the summer. 'Their numbers increased from 840 in 1941 to 1,189 in 1942.'[59] Although the training of drivers in response to the increase in vehicles was planned, that of guides did not follow suit. Ingold notes that 'for the operations of Fezzan 1942–1943, the number of guides was clearly insufficient given the relative magnitude of the resources.'[60] He adds that their training was complicated by the difficulty they had in moving from guiding camels to guiding vehicles. Finally, logistics were the subject of the command's efforts. During the preparation phase, 'the large civilian transport companies' fleet of trucks in Equatorial Africa had been requisitioned. It was with these 500 civilian trucks that supplies and various materiel were transported from the south and from Fort-Lamy and Largeau to the successive forward bases.'[61] Military means of transportation were used, when the time came, to 'organise efficient logistics over a range of 1,000km.'[62] It was also necessary to change mentalities. By definition, *méharistes* were almost autonomous due to their mounts and the simplicity of their needs, and as a result, logistics was almost an afterthought for the desert soldiers. It was different for motorised units of the period, in which 30

---

of the Manouka base in Douala when Leclerc arrived in Cameroon. At Leclerc's request, he reorganised the coastal defences of the ports of the AEF and Cameroon. Having fulfilled that mission, at his request, he joined Leclerc's forces. Ingenious, he designed the mounting of the 40mm Bofors gun on a Ford truck chassis. He was the highest-ranking artilleryman. He remained, until 1945, the commander of Leclerc's artillery. Dronne gives the following juicy portrait: 'Everyone calls him Dudule. Polytechnicien, very competent artilleryman, very knowledgeable, remarkable weapons technician, very hardworking, very conscientious, very meticulous, a bit of a grouchy bear, both shy and brusque, feared at the time by his subordinates who did not yet know him well. A man with a heart, as people who don't seem to have one often are. The more we know him, the more we like him.' (Dronne, R., *Serment de Koufra*, p.155). In 2018, his grandson, Jean-René Van der Plaetsen, wrote a remarkable book about his grandfather *La Nostalgie de l'Honneur* (le Livre de Poche) which received four prizes including the *Prix Interallié*.

58   Destrem, *L'Aventure de Leclerc*, p.182.
59   Jennings, *La France Libre fut Africaine*, p.134.
60   Ingold, *L'Épopée*, p.176.
61   *Soldats de Leclerc, Sept Ans*, p.74.
62   Vincent, *Les Forces Françaises Libres en Afrique*, p.287.

percent of the personnel and 70 percent of the vehicles were devoted to logistical support, demonstrating the importance of logistics in the operation. Dio ensured that this was well understood by his comrades who had recently swapped their camels for Bedfords.

Since the beginning of November, those at Faya-Largeau had been listening with great attention to the evening press bulletins concerning the British progress. General Montgomery's British 8th Army began its offensive on 28 October at El Alamein. On 20 November, it entered Benghazi, the largest port in Cyrenaica. Yet, although the Germans gave ground in the face of British pressure, progress was slow. It had even been halted in front of El Agheila since 25 November. Montgomery 'is a methodical and careful man; he takes few risks, makes his moves and advances quite slowly.'[63] The Free French, waiting in Tibesti, knew that their departure was subject to the British advance. Leclerc determined the conditions with General Hutchinson in mid-November at Fort-Lamy: 'The arrival of French troops in the region of Uigh-el-Kébir must coincide as best as possible with the launch of the British attack starting from the transversal of El Agheila, that is to say the entry into Tripolitania.'[64] The measure of coordination described left Dio perplexed, as the coordination between two mobile forces is particularly difficult to manage. To be at Uigh-el-Kébir, in Libyan territory, when the British arrived in Tripolitania, would require anticipating their progress in order to launch the Tibesti columns at the right time. Dio estimated that a period of one week would be necessary to make it out of Tibesti, penetrate into Fezzanais territory, take Uigh-el-Kébir, and establish the departure base to support the offensive. His remarks were passed on to the British command. General Alexander, senior commander in the Middle East, promised to provide eight days' notice to his French allies, 'informed that this is the time you need to make a movement to this point from Zouar.'[65] With all these risks in mind, Leclerc, with his officers, decided to build an operational plan based on three hypotheses:

1)   the British attack is too rapid for all the forces of Chad to be in place,
2)   the British attack is on schedule and the French troops are prepared to coordinate in good conditions,
3)   the British attack fails at the start of the year.

It would be the second hypothesis which ultimately proved to be the correct one.[66]

Leclerc reminded his subordinates of what de Gaulle had told him: 'your operation will be carried out under exclusively French command, from French territory, and with French troops.'[67] It was a political decision. De Gaulle wanted Fezzan to be conquered solely by Frenchmen so that he would be able to place the territory under the administration of Free France. It was a major political issue for him. In Algiers, he had not been recognised by the Americans, who chose to deal with Giraud and Darlan.

---

63   Compagnon, *Leclerc*, p.289.
64   Compagnon, *Leclerc*, p.289.
65   Destrem, *L'Aventure de Leclerc*, p.180.
66   Consequently, Leclerc based his manoeuvres on the following organisation:
     Groupement D (*Lieutenant Colonel* Dio) responsible for the main effort, will have the following missions:
     1st Stage: take Uigh-el-Kébir to establish the advanced base,
     2nd Stage: attack and seize Oum-el-Araneb,
     Later do the same in Sebha.
     Groupement G (*Capitaine* Geoffroy) responsible for a diversion in the enemy rear,
     Groupement M (*Lieutenant Colonel* Delange), during the first part defend Uigh-el-Kébir then besiege to the key posts that have been bypassed,
     The advanced base of Uigh-el-Kébir entrusted to the orders of *Commandant* Vézinet,
     Aviation: bomb Murzuk and Sebha, targeting the Italian planes.
67   Destrem, *L'Aventure de Leclerc*, p.182.

What was the main objective on which Leclerc built his manoeuvre to take Fezzan? It was built on a conviction acquired during Fezzan 1. On 3 March 1942, in Gatroun, Massu reported to him that he had had to retreat before the Italian *sahariane* at Oum-el-Araneb. Leclerc then wanted to see the location himself. Taking the risk of delaying the withdrawal of his columns, he went to verify a hunch he had acquired while listening to Massu. What he actually saw at Oum-el-Araneb convinced him that it was indeed the strongpoint of the Italian system in Fezzan. Therefore, when launching his attack nine months later, his idea of manoeuvre was simple: to conquer Fezzan, the main effort must target the post of Oum-el-Araneb. 'Dio, with the most substantial forces, will move straight towards Oum-el-Araneb as quickly as possible, bypassing intermediate defences such as Gatroun, which other follow-on units will reduce.'[68] Leclerc 'sniffed out' the enemy system like the experienced hunter he was. He was a great tactician, and he had the 'constable' to whom he would entrust the achievement of his main objective to bring down Fezzan. For two years, he had entrusted challenging missions to the man he met opportunely when he had arrived in Cameroon.

To compose his *Groupement D*, *Lieutenant Colonel* Dio had the privilege of selecting the units that would be part of it. The *GNB* had become his favourite unit since Operation Fezzan 1. He liked Poletti and all of his leaders, who had converted to vehicles.[69] The *GNB* had been strengthened to include three infantry sections, a heavy support section with mortars, anti-aircraft and anti-tank guns and machine guns, a medical section, and a maintenance section. That represented 30 Europeans for 202 indigenous troops and 27 vehicles. Two specialist *sergents*, Béné in communications and Brousse[70] in maintenance, completed the manpower.

Next, Dio chose the *1re DC*, commanded by Massu's successor, *Capitaine* Farret. He joined the group with two platoons that had been augmented with vehicles and heavy weapons. Each *DC* platoon had become a formidable combat tool. *Capitaine* Combes commanded the first. The second was under the orders of *Capitaine* Troadec, who had served as Leclerc's aide-de-camp up to that point. As Leclerc had promised him, he had obtained his 'exit ticket' to serve in a combat unit under Dio's orders. A young *lieutenant* of the *spahis* named Christian Girard, who had arrived from London, succeeded him as aide-de-camp to the *général*. The 12th Company of the *RTST* would be the second infantry component of *Groupement D*. Formed in 1941, it was made up around a cadre who had escaped from France, and had embraced motorisation into its tactical operation. It was commanded by *Lieutenant* Perceval,[71] who, after being wounded during the action, would be replaced by *Capitaine* Corlu. This unit also included *Lieutenant* Batiment, an Alsatian, and *Sergent* Vourc'h. This motorised company was structured like the *GNB* and also included a heavy support section.

For his artillery element, replacing Ceccaldi,[72] Dio chose *Commandant* Crépin. The *méhariste* had great confidence in this colonial artilleryman whom he had met in Douala. Crépin did not have much of a sense of humour, but he was a solid officer, very capable with artillery fire and also very courageous. Crépin had three artillery sections (*SA*). The SA 15 *bis*, based in Moussoro,

68   Compagnon, *Leclerc*, p.298.
69   They left their camels permanently with *goumiers* and *bellah* to provide the backbone of the new *Groupe Nomade du Kanem*, which was created to monitor the border with Niger.
70   Dio liked this *sergent*, with his Parisian street urchin temperament, who managed to bring Leclerc to attention during the Kufra period. In addition, despite his young age, he was an outstanding radio repairman who found solutions to all breakdowns.
71   In his book, Perceval summarises his meeting with Dio as follows: 'Very good guy' (André Perceval, *Sur les Chemins de l'Audace*, Paris: Presses du Groupe Cilaos, 2000, p.79).
72   In the summer of 1942, Ceccaldi, the artilleryman of Kufra and of Operation Fezzan 1 with Dio, was sent to the Middle East to be trained on British equipment. He found himself, against his wishes, in Bir Hakeim. Having participated in the fighting, he was taken prisoner and detained in Italy. He managed to escape and rejoin French troops to resume the fight.

was equipped with two 75mm field guns under the orders of *Lieutenant* Jeannot. SA 11, based in Faya-Largeau, was equipped with the formidable 4½-inch howitzer under the orders of *Lieutenant* Allègre. The SA 28 anti-aircraft artillery section, equipped with the 40mm Bofors gun mounted on a Canadian Ford 41, was commanded by *Lieutenant* Messiah. Each piece was specifically responsible for ensuring the anti-aircraft defence of the two infantry units.[73]

For the medical support of *Groupement D*, the head of section Number 1 of *Groupe Sanitaire de Colonne No.2* (*GSC No.2*) could only be *Médecin Capitaine* Charles Mauric. He and Dio had become close and had been with each other since Kufra. A great deal of progress had been made since then: Mauric now had two ambulances and six trucks, one of which was equipped with an operating room! The combat logistics train of *Groupement D* was made up of 65 trucks to ensure the necessary supplies over a distance of 1,000km. Finally, *Groupement D* would be initially followed by the 2nd Company of the *RTST* and a section of four Herrington armoured cars.[74] Those two elements would be responsible for defending the forward base of Uigh-el-Kébir, and thus they would remain there. Bey Ahmed asked Dio if he could be a part of his group. At the head of a *harka*[75] *of several dozen rifles, he wanted to participate in the battles to liberate his region. But places were limited in the packed vehicles. Dio convinced his old friend instead to return to his traditional mount and join the GNT which* would be engaged on camels. *Capitaine* Sarazac was in fact once again in the game. He was responsible for monitoring the area around the forward base of Uigh-el-Kébir. Bey Ahmed would be useful to him in his communications with the local populations and obtaining information on the Italian troops. *Groupement D* was the spearhead of *Colonne Leclerc*. It was to Dio that the *général* entrusted the achievement of his main objective – the destruction and capture of the post of Oum-el-Araneb.

The units of *Groupement D* final assembly area was in Tibesti. On 17 November, the 12th Company based in Mongo departed for Zouar. On the 18th, the *1re DC* and the *GNB* left Faya-Largeau and Kirdimi to move towards the North. *GSC No.2*, did not leave Fort-Lamy until 30 November. The 650-kilometre trip from Zouar to Uigh-el-Kébir would not be easy. The distance between Zouar and Kourizo is approximately 400km, and then another 250km within Libyan territory to reach Uigh-el-Kébir. Progress would be difficult because the routes were all camel trails and were in no way designed for vehicles. Numerous obstacles punctuated the axis of advance, particularly the *fech-fech* zones feared by the crews. In addition, the movement would have to be done largely at night to avoid the Italian *Ghibli* and Savoia planes.

For the movement, *Groupement D* was divided into four detachments: the first, composed of the *1re DC*, was under the orders of *Lieutenant Colonel* Dio, the second – the *GNB* – was under *Commandant* Poletti, the third under *Lieutenant* Perceval was 12th Company, and the fourth – the logistics – under the orders of the most senior officer. This division was carried out mainly for security reasons. It was important to avoid detection by the Italians for as long as possible and a column composed of fewer vehicles could camouflage itself more easily to escape enemy aerial reconnaissance. *Groupement D*, comprising more than 100 vehicles, was spread out over two assembly areas from which the attack would be launched. The combat element was in Zouré, 50km from Zouar, while the logistics element was in Meurzo, 15km from Zouar. These two areas were chosen by Dio because they could be more easily camouflaged: they consisted of, 'rock masses falling steeply into the ground covered with vegetation made up of thorny shrubs…'[76]

---

73   This composition of the operational part of *Groupement D* is taken from preparatory order no. 637/3S of Nov. 15, 47 modified by memo no. 52/K of Dec. 4. 42, both signed 'Dio'. (FMLH documents)

74   In one of these armoured cars was the son of *Maréchal des Logis-Chef* Debeugny, killed on 9 March 1942 in Gatroun by Italian planes. This 17-year-old young man convinced Leclerc to include him into the column, on the same armoured gun truck commanded by his father.

75   Armed guard.

76   Ingold, *L'Épopée*, p.181.

Note No.672/3S of 22 November 1942, signed by Dio, defined 'a timetable of principle' for the four detachments.[77] The note ends with specific measures related to movement. Vehicular movement was prohibited between 9:30 a.m. and 2:00 p.m., the usual time slot for Italian reconnaissance flights. Camouflage measures to avoid aerial observation were reiterated: systematic sweeping of tyre tracks at stopping points, removal of all windshields and vehicle windows, an immediate halt in the event of an overflight, no shooting at planes to avoid being detected, radio silence, et cetera. The four detachments were to avoid stopping in the area of Wour, which was heavily monitored. Crossing the Kourizo Pass had to be done at night. The first detachment was responsible for clearing mines from the pass in advance.[78] This stage being 400km from the start, refuelling would take place in hidden depots which were to be pre-positioned. Then, the first detachment would have to find a bypass route to avoid the stretch of *fech-fech* in Libyan territory at kilometre 200, in the Morozidié region.[79] The timetable for moving *Groupement D* between Tibesti and Uigh-el-Kébir called for six stages. A 12-hour spread between the detachments allowed for the first detachment of the group to arrive at the objective on D+6 and the fourth on D+8.

It was December 1942. All the units had been ready since the third week of November and were pawing impatiently in the Tibesti Massif. Even if living conditions were easier for many, the wait became long and boredom set in, which is never good for a soldier's morale.[80] On 8 December, Capitaine Dronne, Poletti's deputy, wrote: 'This morning, arrival of *Lieutenant Colonel* Dio, my former column commander in Gabon, under whose orders we are placed and whom I like.'[81] Many soldiers impatiently thought that if the group leader joined them in Zouré, it meant that the time for departure was approaching. On the evening of 13 December, news from the BBC suddenly lifted the spirits of all the men. Montgomery relaunched his offensive the day before in Cyrenaica. Everyone again hoped for an imminent departure. This became a certainty on 16 December with *Général* Leclerc's arrival at Zouré. Accompanied by *Lieutenant Colonel* Dio and *Colonel* Ingold, Leclerc quickly inspected *Groupement D*. The departure would not be long. The same day, *Groupement G* received the green light to start. It was the only unit taking the eastern route, starting from Bardaï and passing through Yédri before entering Libyan territory. Its route was the longest, hence its early departure. On 18 December, 1942, in accordance with the plan, *Lieutenant Colonel* Dio gave the signal for the first detachment to depart under his command. This subunit included *Capitaine* Farret's *1ʳᵉ DC* with its two platoons, a 75pdr and half of Dio's command post. The second detachment was made up of the *GNB* which was, with the *DC*, the only unit with experience during Fezzan 1. It was completed by the second 75 of Jeannot's section and the rest of Dio's CP. The third detachment was made up of half of the 12th Company with the howitzer and half of the logistics train (supply trucks), in which *Maréchal des Logis* Poualion rode. Finally, the fourth detachment included the other half of the 12th Company and the rest of the logistics, including the medical section of *Dr* Mauric.

The first day of movement was difficult. Had the Cameroonian drivers lost control? The transit of the Zouarké, the Taosur Threshold,[82] and the Enneri Tao were known to be challenging areas

77   Fonds Leclerc, dossier Robédat.
78   Mines had been placed in the area at the beginning of the summer by Tibesti units as part of the defence of the massif against possible Italian infiltrations.
79   The detachments had difficulty crossing the area when they returned from Operation Fezzan 1, leaving a bad memory for all the crews.
80   The climate in Tibesti was more pleasant, and the nights were cool; the presence of *gueltas* offered men the pleasure of drinking soft, non-natronated water. (*Gueltas* are shallow pools of water that evaporates slowly, being in the shadow of high cliffs. Some even have fish.)
81   Dronne, *Carnets de Route*, p.128.
82   The passage was made with palm branches to prevent the wheels from sinking into the sand of the dry riverbed, the Enneri Tao. The dry watercourse could also be called a wadi.

for vehicles to cross. Teams of labourers were deployed on difficult passages to facilitate the progress of heavily loaded trucks. On 19 December 1942, after departing at 3:00 a.m., the column reached the Kourizo Pass around 9:00 a.m. This sandy passage 'between two large hillocks of blackish rocks' close to the border with Fezzan is menacing.[83] As soon as they arrived, some of the men of the *Ire DC* methodically began to clear mines from the path and the surrounding area. Meanwhile, others opened the passage by tearing down the stone walls which had been built as obstacles. Dio had aircraft look outs installed at a high point to raise the alarm in the event of an enemy plane flying over. The men who were required to work during daylight were instructed to lie down and stop moving. At the end of the afternoon, the vehicle odometers indicated 380 kilometres – time to refuel each vehicle. So, the buried petrol drums came out of their hiding place.

It was 5:00 p.m. when Dio ordered Farret to resume moving. Heading due north, the route passed by the foot of the rocky peak of Morozidié and, from there, branched off due west. The notorious *fech-fech*, a passage of around 20km long, was located there. Odometers indicated they were 180 kilometres from Kourizo. On the evening of 20th, Dio stopped the convoy just before the *fech-fech*. What could they do? Finding a route around it would take time. He observed the staggered arrival of the 1,500kg Bedford trucks from the *DC* platoons. They were over-powered trucks, lightweight and equipped with wide, low-pressure tyres. The crews were very experienced. So, he decided to give it a try. He asked Farret to nominate the best crew and to deflate the vehicle's tyres to half the recommended pressure. The mission was simple: cross the powdery sand smoothly while avoiding turning. The Bedford dug a deep furrow but progressed at low speed without getting bogged down. Then, Dio directed the other trucks to stay in the ruts dug by the first. Little by little, the sand settled under the deflated tyres; the underbodies of the vehicles levelled the area between the two wheels, widening and solidifying the ruts. A technique for crossing the *fech-fech* was thus born in the darkness of 20/21 December 1942. It was bitterly cold in the middle of the night in that part of the Saharan Desert and the *méharistes* who had brought their *burnous* did not regret it. The Sara *tirailleurs* and the Cameroonians had never experienced such intense cold. They suffered in the backs of vehicles, huddled together and wrapped in their blankets. *Capitaine* Dronne's *goumier* summed up this painful situation as follows: 'There's some warmth for the freezing cold.'[84]

On 21 December 1942, Dio arrived in sight of Domazé, the *djebel* overlooking Uigh-el-Kébir. The idea was to surprise the Italian *chouf* in order to prevent it from raising the alarm, as Massu had done successfully in February. But a sandstorm was blowing, and visibility was poor. Massu's *goumiers* had been able to approach the lookout post without being detected, but that was not the case any longer. The problem was to precisely determine its location. Dio then decided to cordon off the entire area to intercept the *chouf* team during its withdrawal. But he did not have sufficient personnel to form an airtight seal, so he decided to wait for the second detachment of the column commanded by *Commandant* Poletti. When Poletti arrived on the evening of 22nd, Dio explained his idea for the manoeuvre. Dio, with the *Ire DC*, would outflank the Domazé from the west to be able to cut off the *chouf's* withdrawal route as the *GNB* advanced towards it. He set 8:00 p.m. as the time for *Commandant* Poletti to resume movement. During the night of December 22/23, Dio and the flanking detachment encountered 'bastard territory,' in Dio's words.[85] The cordon was not completely closed when, at 8:00 p.m., the *GNB* advanced towards the *chouf*, which hastily retreated. In February, the pair of lookouts had travelled by camel. In December, the Italians, having learnt their lesson, equipped them with a vehicle. The *chouf* slipped through the cracks. Dio

---

83   Béné, *Carnets, Seconde Époque*, p.79.
84   Dronne, *Carnets de Route*, p.137.
85   Dronne, *Carnets de Route*, p.141.

was furious; he pursued in vain for 30 kilometres. Now, the alert was raised throughout Fezzan. As a result, Dio ordered radio silence lifted – secrecy was no longer necessary. *Colonel* Ingold joined him during the night with his CP. He was accompanied by the British Captain Carter who had to ensure liaison with the 8th Army. A patrol of five LRDG vehicles, whose members were all Rhodesian nationals under the orders of Lieutenant Henry, served as his escort.

23 December and the following days would be rest days, involving repairing, checking, and maintaining equipment. Refuelling and reprovisioning of water and food were done at night. The first convoys of logistics trucks arrived with the third detachment on the night of December 23. Everything was planned well and so far everything was going according to plan. The establishment of the forward base at Uigh-el-Kébir under *Commandant* Vézinet began once the trucks of the logistics train arrived. The radio operators realised that radio activity was intense on the Italian side beginning on 23 December. Fezzan was being put on alert. Indeed, the reaction did not take long. The enemy sent aircraft to the area, and starting on the morning of the 24th, reconnaissance planes strafed the water collection detachment around the only well in the region but inflicted no injuries. They returned again that afternoon, but without further success.

Around 2:00 p.m., Dio and Ingold went to welcome *Général* Leclerc who had come to spend Christmas Eve with his men. His Lysander landed on a makeshift runway, marked by vehicles, about 15 kilometres from Domazé. The location chosen to establish this landing zone was different from that of Fezzan 1. The Italians would not spot this new location. It was very cold that Christmas night. *Lieutenant* Girard described the Christmas dinner of the leaders around Leclerc as: 'an old box of chestnuts found by miracle in my luggage gives us the illusion of a feast, but they were neither hot nor cold.'[86] General Montgomery did not forget his allies: 'At midnight a message reached them from the 8th Army, carried by a British soldier from the Rhodesian patrol: 'Merry Christmas! Wishes of victory to *Général* Leclerc.''[87] The Christmas Eve celebration in Libyan territory did not last long. Each crew remained grouped together and discussions quickly wound down.[88] Everyone was eager to find their hole in the sand so they could slip into their *faro* to warm up. Before going to sleep, the soldiers gave a thought for their distant families on that night of the Nativity. Many of them had not received any news for two years.

Leclerc left on the morning of 25 December 1942. He gave Dio, in the presence of *Colonel* Ingold, his final instructions: 'the progress on Umm-el-Araneb will be as rapid as possible. Reconnaissance of Gatroun, which required passing by Gatroun, should delay progress as little as possible. Its particular aim would be to note the presence or absence of motorised elements.'[89] On the morning of 25 December 1942, a Savoia bombed the *GNB* location in several passes. The crossfire of the 40mm Bofors gun and the 13.2mm machine gun forced him to gain altitude to drop his bombs. That led to reduced precision, and there were no losses on the French side. *Groupement D* left Uigh-el-Kébir at 4:00 p.m. Dio left part of the 12th Company behind to protect the base while waiting for the bulk of the troops to arrive. The first objective was Gatroun, and then Oum-el-Araneb. The formation was: 'at the front, the two platoons of the *Ire DC*, followed by the *GNB* and its artillery, then part of the 12th Company .... finally *Lieutenant Colonel* Dio, *Colonel* Ingold and his small staff, with the British patrol.'[90] Just at the moment of departure, while the camou-

---

86   Girard, *Journal de Guerre*, p.37.
87   Ingold, *Général Ingold*, p.98.
88   According to Général Ingold's son, it was that evening that *Général* Leclerc said to his father: 'Ingold, you will have to write the story of our campaigns.' (Ingold, *Général Ingold*, p.97). Ingold was already known at the time for his talents as a writer. Additionally, Dio affectionately nicknamed him 'the writer' according to Pierre Robédat.
89   Ingold, *L'Épopée*, p.190.
90   Dronne, *Carnets de Route*, p.147.

flage was folded away, two Italian Savoia bombers arrived to bomb and strafe the column as it moved. Luckily, despite the precision of their shots, there was only some slight material damage and punctured tyres. The three Lysanders of the Free French Air Force, present on the makeshift field, took to the air and frightened away the two bombers. The column reformed and after repairs, resumed the advance. Around 5:00 p.m., the vehicles were moving on a large, completely flat *reg* when a new Savoia appeared. The pilot manoeuvred to align with the column's axis of advance. 'At a simple sign from our column leader, our vehicles, quickly on the hard flat ground, cut away sharply to the right and left of the line of the possible bombardment.'[91] Italian planes were now close to their bases and could appear at any time of the day. Fortunately, the French had already taken the aerial threat into account and their training allowed the crews to take responsive actions which limited damage. In addition, the effects of the Italian bombs were limited due to the sand.

The bivouac during the evening of 25 December 1942 was in the folds of a *gara*. It was a short and very cold night. *Lieutenant Colonel* Dio ordered the departure for 3:00 a.m. It was necessary to take advantage of the moon, which allowed progress without having to worry about the Italian planes which had been sticking like flies to *Groupement D* since Christmas. At sunrise on December 26, the vanguard of the column could make out the palm grove of Gatroun. Dio sent Combes' platoon, accompanied by LRDG vehicles, to probe the Italian fort. The mixed Franco-Rhodesian patrol was greeted by intense fire from heavy automatic weapons. The Italians were clearly ready to fight. Meanwhile, Dio posted the bulk of the column 20km east of Gatroun, taking advantage of a *gara* to better camouflage it. He wanted to avoid providing a target for the planes. He asked *Capitaine* Combes to continue probing the fort from several directions. The goal was to force any Italian motorised elements that might be there to expose themselves. The enemy was content to shoot anything that moved. Dio believed he had accomplished the mission; there was obviously no *Sahariana* in the region. He ordered his patrol to join the main body of the detachment. While it was moving on a flat sandy area, two Savoia bombers and five Fiat CR.42 fighters attacked it. It was a sort of deadly game of chicken. Fortunately, the vehicles did not have a roof, which allowed clear observation of the sky. The game consisted of spotting the plane, which aligned itself with the vehicle's direction of movement, then giving the driver the signal to change direction at the last moment. That helped avoid bombs, or bullets from the plane's machine guns. It required tremendous composure to execute the manoeuvre precisely in time. Unfortunately, two Bedfords overturned after turning too suddenly to change direction under the aerial attack. A *tirailleur* was shot and wounded, but the only fatality was in a truck accident. On the Italian side, a Fiat fighter plane appeared to have been hit by heavy machine gun fire. When the planes withdrew, the patrol of *Capitaine* Combes and the LRDG were scattered over several kilometres because of the aircraft avoidance manoeuvres carried out by each crew. The patrol reformed and rejoined the rest of the group. Combes was giving his verbal report to Dio when a Savoia bomber, which had been tracking them, bombed the entire group. It was met with heavy fire from the 40mm Bofors guns and only made one pass. Night soon fell. The French troops would be able to breathe easier.

The mechanics took advantage of the darkness to try to put the two damaged trucks back on their wheels. The one in the worst condition was left behind, but they took as many parts from it as they could, before abandoning it. After brief equipment checks, *Lieutenant Colonel* Dio gave the order to depart at 10:00 p.m. He planned to drive all night. With all lights out, progress in column was made easier by the light of the moon. Driving was particularly tiring, as drivers could not relax their attention without risking hitting the vehicle in front, should it stop or get stuck in the sand. In the early morning of 27 December, *Groupement D* arrived in the Gara Massu

---

91   Béné, *Carnets, Seconde Époque*, p.89.

region.[92] The group advanced in three columns abreast on the hard and flat ground. This was a method to limit damage if the planes returned. They would be forced to choose one of the three columns. It was barely 7:00 a.m. when a Heinkel displaying the black *Luftwaffe* cross on its side and under its wings flew over the French troops. It circled around the advancing columns but did not attack. Then it headed back north to alert its colleagues. Their return would not be long. Dio had the group stationed at the foot of Gara Massu to allow each crew to find a rock behind which to camouflage themselves. The nets were pulled to try to prevent aerial observation. Dio decided to go to reconnoitre a route to reach the palm grove of Umm-el-Sachir, located a few kilometres away, which would offer better camouflage possibilities for all the vehicles. He left with a small element of the *DC*. He had hardly left the rocks when the Heinkel returned with four Fiat fighters. Immediately the planes rushed towards the small column in order to destroy it. The French crews were desperate and turned quickly at the last moment. The open terrain made the avoidance manoeuvres possible. The planes realised that there was better 'game' at the stationary trucks, so they returned to the Gara Massu, where they attacked the entire group. The two trucks equipped with Bofors guns had their outriggers[93] out and were firing continuously. Enemy planes had to gain altitude and, in doing so, lost accuracy. The battle lasted 20 minutes. A British LRDG vehicle was hit and was on fire. Two Rhodesians were injured, one seriously wounded in the chest. On the French side, only light injuries were reported, including *Sergent* Tritchler of the *GNB*.

The Italian planes needed to refuel and rearm, so Dio took advantage of the opportunity. He sent a radio message at 11:30 a.m., ordering the group to move towards him. The column quickly left its position and followed the tracks left by Dio's vehicles. The palm grove was five kilometres away. The palm trees of Umm-el-Sachir provided excellent camouflage possibilities for all of the vehicles. The crews were experienced; having hardly even come to a stop, the men jumped from their vehicles, some unfolded the nets and others swept the tracks away. The whole group could then take a breather. The aerial attacks were a severe test of nerves, and many of the men fell asleep at the base of the trucks. In the afternoon, two bombers and their fighter escort returned. Men unconsciously tucked their heads into their shoulders. Yet they soon realised that the explosions from the bombs were not coming from their own positions, but rather from the position they had held that morning. The German and Italian aviators were relentless, dropping all their munitions on empty sand.

The sandstorm picked up and visibility dropped. Night began to fall and the invasive cold stole in. Dio summoned all of the element leaders to his CP vehicle. 'A little before nightfall, *Lieutenant Colonel* Dio gave the order to leave the palm grove and regroup on the hard *reg* because, apparently, we must be ready at dawn to cross the *ramla* of Oum-el-Araneb, [which is] considered as difficult to cross as the *ramla* of Tedjéré the previous year.'[94] A patrol was sent to try to find the best place to approach the obstacle. The objective was not very far away and Dio ordered the departure for 3:00 a.m. 'True winter weather, freezing wind. The drivers, poorly protected, without gloves, had their hands frozen to their steering wheels.'[95] Around 4:00 a.m., the vehicles arrived in front of the immense sand dune. In the event, it turned out to be easier to cross than expected. A few vehicles got stuck in the sand, but all made it out before sunrise.

---

92   Its true name was Gara Magedoul, but it was renamed Gara Massu after Fezzan 1. It was the place where Massu had to retreat in the face of an Italian *sahariana*.

93   The trucks carrying the 40mm Bofors guns were equipped with outriggers that extended on either side of the truck behind the cab. To fire the gun, the outriggers had to be extended and the truck then lifted on jacks to provide a stable firing platform. (Translator's note)

94   Béné, *Carnets, Seconde Époque*, p.94.

95   Dronne, *Carnets de Route*, p.154.

Groupement D then settled in the palm grove of Méséguin, about 15km from the village of El Hammera, located at the foot of the *gara* of the same name. Patrols of the *1re DC* went out on reconnaissance. At 9:00, just as *Groupement D* had settled in, 'the characteristic noise of enemy aircraft engines was heard.'[96] Two Savoias and four Fiat fighters tried to find the *degaullisti*. Unfortunately, in violation of their orders, 13.2mm machine guns started firing, revealing the group's location to the Italian planes. An hour later, they returned and released their arsenal of bombs. Fortunately, the effects were largely neutralised by the sand. At midday, a vehicle alert was given by the artillery spotters. Around 20 vehicles coming from the Hammera *gara* were heading towards the palm grove where the French were set up. An Italian *sahariana* attacked with its SPA trucks, with their huge tyres and 20mm and 47mm guns. The Italians were sure of themselves. They assumed that the French were still lightly armed as they had been during Fezzan 1. The Italian *capitano* supported his ground attack with his *Ghibli* planes. In linear battle formation, the *sahariana* advanced on bare and flat ground towards the palm grove in which *Groupement D* firmly awaited them. Dio was with the *DC*. He waited for the Italians to get closer before taking them on, only the anti-aircraft weapons came into action against the planes so as to prevent them approaching the French positions. Suddenly, without having received the order to open fire, the 75mm guns of the artillery fired on the *sahariana*. After an adjustment, their shots become precise and destroyed an Italian vehicle. When the Italians realised that they were facing artillery, they chose to hastily retreat. 'The Italians turned around and fled towards the *gara*. Our infantry weapons barely fired; the enemy was too far away.'[97]

Dio ordered Combes' platoon in pursuit. By the time they had removed the camouflage from the vehicles and left the palm grove, the Italians had a good lead and had disappeared behind the Hammera *gara*. They left behind one killed and one wounded in a car equipped with a 20mm gun. Dio railed: the fire was opened too early and the opportunity to inflict heavy losses on the *sahariana* was missed. Why did the gunners open fire? Crépin explained to Dio that he was at the lower end of his firing range. He could not have engaged the Italians if he had let them approach within 2,500 metres. However, this first real contact would be decisive for the future. The Italians had not realised the nature of the French equipment, particularly the presence of powerful artillery. Their morale 'took a hit' because, until then, they were convinced they had technological superiority over their adversary. Throughout the afternoon, Italian planes circled in waves above the French positions, which were now well located. Duels took place between the fighter planes and the operators of the anti-aircraft weapons. *Sergent Chef* Labrevoix, commander of the Bofors gun, distinguished himself by facing, with admirable courage, the dive of the Fiat fighters. Fortunately, the losses were insignificant compared to the weapons deployed and the quantity of bombs and bullets fired from both sides. Dronne summed up the day, 'It takes kilos and kilos of shrapnel to kill one man.'[98]

The night was used to relocate. Dio chose a position five kilometres from the village of Hammera. The Oum-el-Araneb region included many small palm groves suitable for camouflage. He looked for a way to approach the Italian positions. He knew, following Operation Fezzan 1, that the Italians had established dug-in positions around their forts. They had likely done the same thing at Oum-el-Araneb, and it was therefore necessary to find out exactly what their defensive system was. Once known, it would then be time to choose the best place to effect the siege of the Italian position. Therefore, Dio sent out reconnaissance patrols. The nights of 29 and 30 December were used to strengthen the position around Oum-el-Araneb. In the early morning, the greatest pleasure

96   Béné, *Carnets, Seconde Époque*, p.97.
97   Dronne, *Carnets de Route*, p.156.
98   Dronne, *Carnets de Route*, p.157.

for the men was to hear the Italian air force in the distance. 'Each time it attacked our positions [that we had] occupied the day before because, after we left, the tracks in the sand had not been erased like those of the new location that we just occupied.'[99] Dio tried to move out from the north. Unfortunately, he came up against a *sebkra*[100] that prevented him from progressing in that direction.

Dio was forced to retrace his steps. The only access to Oum-el-Araneb was in Hammera. Throughout the day, the planes tried to find where the '*degaullisti* devils' might be. They randomly bombed, hoping for a response that would allow them to detect the location of the group. But very strict orders were given and nobody fired. On 31 December 1942, the group turned around during the night and repositioned into the palm grove of Hammera, in an assembly area southwest of the fort of Oum-el-Araneb. At the end of the afternoon, *Général* Leclerc arrived in his vehicle, escorted by Lavergne's platoon. It would have been too risky to arrive by plane with the Italian planes dominating the air. Leclerc came to spend the end of 1942 with his men. New Year's Eve of 1942 was as sad as Christmas Eve had been. The men tried to warm themselves to sleep. Many dreamt of what the new year would have in store for them.

In the early morning of 1 January 1943, Dio ordered the *GNB*, the most experienced infantry unit, to approach the enemy positions on foot. The vehicles were left at the village of Hammera. Only a few trucks equipped with heavy weapons followed to support the advance of the infantry. Dio was with the lead section, that of *Lieutenant* Le Calvez. They were joined a few minutes later by Leclerc himself. Impatient, Leclerc pushed the men forward, grumbling: 'We're getting nowhere, it's [like] the fighting of '39.'[101] Suddenly, the sound of an aircraft was heard. 'The Adriens again,' thought all of Leclerc's *tirailleurs*. But this time, it was two Blenheims from the Free French Air Force that came to bomb the Italian positions at *Colonel* Ingold's request. The bombardment had two benefits: to make the Italians keep their heads down, and to precisely locate their buried defensive lines. 'The smoke and dust from the explosions allowed us to locate the Italian positions exactly.'[102] The sections of the *GNB* took advantage of the aerial attack to get closer. As they approached the last sandy ridge, they were met with heavy weapons fire and 77mm artillery shells. They were now in contact, although stopped 1,600 metres from the first Italian lines. The siege would begin. Leclerc and Dio exchanged a furtive glance suggesting: 'Shall we start Kufra again?' Commandant Crépin was at the helm, directing the fire of the artillery. His firepower, with two 75mm guns and the howitzer, was three times greater than that deployed at Kufra by Ceccaldi. He settled on a small dune which served as an observation post (OP). The guns were deployed several hundred metres behind his position. The duel could begin. The Italians did not hold back, raining a barrage of fire on the OP with their 47mm and 77mm guns. The Italian 77mm guns were very precise. Fortunately, the shells buried themselves deep in the soft sand of the dune before exploding, losing much of their effectiveness. During the exchanges, '*Colonel* Dio had his pants torn by a shell from a 77 which burst between his legs.'[103] Dronne, who was not very far away, heard Dio shout: 'Obviously, those bastards are after my b...s.'[104] Dio would be forced to go for treatment to the village of Hammera where the medical aid station was located.[105] There he found

---

99   Béné, *Carnets, Seconde Époque*, p.98.

100 A *sebkra* or *sebkha* is a kind of salt marsh, covered with a small hard crust which is completely unsuitable for vehicles.

101 Dronne, *Carnets de Route*, p.165.

102 Dronne, *Carnets de Route*, p.165

103 Girard, *Journal de Guerre*, p.39.

104 Dronne, R., *Serment de Koufra*, p.152.

105 The story of this injury is mentioned in a more graphic way: 'A *commandant*, who has since become a *général*, had his pants torn by a piece of shrapnel. The thing in itself would not have been strange if this *commandant*

his friend, *Dr* Mauric, still performing well in that environment. This time the injury was not serious, or at least not serious enough, to evacuate Dio, and he would be able to return to combat at the head of his group.

2 January passed similar to the previous day. The *GNB* and the artillery occupied the same positions. Crépin thundered his guns regularly as described by Cunningham, the US liaison officer: 'Dio's guns, commanded by Commandant Crespin [sic], using air photos taken by French bombers, fired with great effectiveness on the enemy position.'[106] The French shots seem to have caused damage in the Italian camp. Indeed, the Italians stopped firing back. 'Singular thing, the Italians are silent. Not a bullet, not a shell. After yesterday's avalanches of fire, absolute calm today.'[107] Dio learnt from *Groupement Geoffroy*, which was north of Oum-el-Araneb, that the *sahariana* had slipped away during the night. Dio took that as a good sign. As was the case in Kufra, the Italian position, isolated, would not last long under artillery fire. He decided not to rush things. He could decide to attack the enemy positions, but that could be costly in human lives. In any case, he had to wait for the bulk of the troops and the supplies. His group could not advance without replenishing fuel and ammunition. To achieve the objective, all he needed to do was fix his enemies in place and then continue to bludgeon them.

The nights at the beginning of the year were terrible for soldiers coming from Chad: 'Ink-black night; an icy mist, a nasty drizzle, you would have thought you were in Brest on the worst days of winter.'[108] Bodies suffered from the cold, particularly the *tirailleurs* who found climatic conditions they were not used to. In the middle of the night, a loud explosion rang out from the Italian side. The next day, they learnt that it was three *askaris* who had stepped on a mine while attempting to desert. On the morning of 3 January, the situation remained unchanged. During the night, *askaris* crossed through the lines to surrender. They were interrogated by the artillerymen to find out the precise locations of important objectives that could be targeted. The information bore fruit. In the afternoon, Crépin ordered the howitzer to open fire and its 114mm calibre was very efficient. At the firing of the third round, a loud explosion was heard from among the Italians and then a fire broke out. Crépin certainly hit his target, either an ammunition depot or a fuel reserve. Crépin also targeted the radio station, which was the nerve centre for the besieged position. It was the only link connecting it to the Italian forces. They later learnt that he succeeded in destroying the communications and therefore completely isolating the Italian post. It was now practically abandoned, no more *sahariana*, no more planes, and now no more communications. It is terrible for morale to feel alone!

Dio sensed that the Italians would not last long. To keep the pressure on them, he organised harassment patrols during the night. These patrols were to approach the enemy lines and attack them with grenades to maintain pressure, a tactic that had worked well at Kufra. On the night of 3/4 January, *Capitaine* d'Abzac volunteered to move up to goad the enemy's front lines. During the second part of the night explosions and gusts were heard. On the morning of 4 January, the situation was calm. Dronne noted that no Italian plane had shown up for two days. Poletti responded that they only paid attention to the bad things.[109] *Capitaine* d'Abzac,

---

had not become angry. In Kufra he had received a wound which had violently insulted his manhood. So, this time, he bellowed that the Italians, not content with having taken his potency, also wanted to take away his ability to sit down. But he said it in technical terms.' Christian Berntsen and Robert Soulat, *Un Viking chez les Bédouins* (Paris: Gallimard, 1957), p.135.

106 Harry F. Cunningham, 'Sahara, The Fighting French March to Tripoli', *Infantry Journal*, October 1943, p.33.

107 Dronne, *Carnets de Route*, p.170.

108 Dronne, *Carnets de Route*, p.169.

109 Dronne, *Carnets de Route*, p.172.

with Le Calvez's section, did not return from his night excursion. This young, spirited officer wanted to prove his courage because, during the capture of Tedjéré a year earlier, circumstances gave his section a rather secondary role. This time, he advanced, at the end of the night, so close to the Italian lines that he found himself blocked when the new day dawned. He was too close to the Italians, so he could no longer retreat. His *goumiers*, using the local dialect, communicated with the *askaris*. 'One of our Fezzanais *goumiers*, old Bouchnaff, called out to his African brothers, the *askaris* in the service of the Italians.'[110] He told them that the French would treat them well and that they would be released immediately. Several *askaris* left their positions and presented themselves to the French with arms raised. Brought before Dio and Ingold, an *askari* non-commissioned officer was assigned to return to the Italian post and request that an Italian officer with a white flag come and introduce himself. Security would be guaranteed. At 3:00 p.m., an Italian *capitano* named Lamberto Gerami, preceded by an *askari* carrying a white flag, came out of the Italian lines. Dio and Ingold came forward to demand an immediate unconditional surrender. The *capitano* hesitated and asked for a delay. He returned shortly after and 'declared that he had decided for '*resistancia*' [sic].'[111] Dio, true to his word, let him go but was furious. 'Dio fumed: we're going to pound them.'[112] The Italians were finished. What was their game? Shortly after 4:00 p.m., Dio ordered Guillebon, who had replaced Crépin after he had gone to set up a gun on the west side, to fire a salvo of shells at the post. The shooting had barely stopped when Dio was informed that more than 50 Italians were standing and waving white handkerchiefs. His response was not long in coming: 'In the name of G**: is there a white flag on the observation post? No? Well then, let Guillebon keep shooting! What is this behaviour? F*** them! A few moments later a huge white flag flew over the observation post.'[113] Oum-el-Araneb capitulated. The radio operator noted 'It was 4:30 p.m. when Dio sent me a message for all units: 'cease fire'.[114]

Il Duce's soldiers marched out of their position in column, officers at the front. D'Abzac rushed in and took charge of them. 'In front of the columns of prisoners, he ordered, 'Attention!' then, 'forward.' The two columns set off, officers at the front; well dressed, well equipped, they look almost dashing.'[115] There were around 300 of them, including 100 Europeans. They became prisoners, some enthusiastically so, happy that the war was ending for them under such circumstances. They were almost elegant in their uniforms.[116] Dronne noted the paradox: 'Next to them, we are pathetic, ragged; we are more like vagabonds than soldiers. The prisoners look at us with bewilderment.'[117] The Italian prisoners were ill at ease because they had heard terrible things about the *degaullisti*: 'Bloody murderers and stranglers pushing hordes of cannibalistic Negroes in front of them. At first glance, our appearance and our clothes did not reassure them. What a fright they must have had!'[118] The same phenomenon had occurred in Kufra. Dio decided to regroup the Italians in the old fortified post where they would spend the night before being evacuated to Chad. The *askaris* were searched to check that they were not carrying any weapons and were then immediately released. They could return home. Night was falling. Dio asked Dronne to stay with

---

110   Dronne, *Carnets de Route*, p.173.
111   Ingold, *L'Épopée,* p.199.
112   Girard, *Journal de Guerre,* p.39.
113   Girard, *Journal de Guerre,* p.40.
114   Béné, *Carnets, Seconde Époque,* p.104.
115   Dronne, *Le Serment,* p.157.
116   *Général* Ingold wrote, 'In front of the victors with burnt faces, cracked and bleeding lips, worn uniforms with sometimes odd details, ... they were a perfumed, pomaded, and elegantly equipped vanquished men, who, on the evening of the surrender, lined up and then silently paraded.' Ingold, *Général Ingold,* p.96.
117   Dronne, *Carnets de Route*, p.176.
118   Dronne, *Carnets de Route*, p.180.

a group from the *GNB* in the Italian position 'to prohibit anyone from entering or leaving; guard the weapons, ammunition, food, equipment, which will be counted tomorrow.'[119]

Dronne kept one of the two Italian *capitani* with him, *Capitano* Luigi Pavesi, from northern Italy. The Italian offered a real meal to the reservist French *capitaine*, delighted at the opportunity. The officers' mess was comfortable. His Italian host even found him a bottle of wine. They spent the evening together like old friends. Pavesi told him that the post included two companies: his own company and a Libyan infantry company of heavy machine guns, as well as a 77mm artillery battery commanded by Lamberto Gerami. He also told him that the Free French Air Forces had destroyed most of the Italian planes and the ground installations on 2 January in Sebha. That explained the absence of planes in the sky since that date. Finally, he confirmed that the French artillery fire had caused a lot of casualties and material damage; 50 percent of the 77mm guns and the radio station had been neutralised.

5 January 1943 was a day dedicated to reconstituting the units and inventorying the Italian post. Functioning weapons and ammunition were carefully collected; some weapons, such as the Italian 81mm mortars, fired the same ammunition as the French equivalent. The results were impressive: four 77mm guns, two 65mm mountain guns, two 47mm guns, two 20mm Breda guns, two 81mm mortars, and numerous machine guns. Food, canned goods, pasta, dried vegetables, and parmesan cheese were distributed among all units. Water was abundant in Oum, and men could wash, shave, and change their clothes. They even found carrots in the palm grove – it was a joy for the Europeans to rediscover the flavour of that vegetable. 'It was by crunching raw carrots sprinkled with mineral water that we celebrated this first victory of the second Fezzan campaign.'[120]

Groupement D could be satisfied with this first result, which was achieved under difficult conditions. Everyone experienced their baptism of fire and overall, everyone performed well. However, Dio was not entirely happy with the operation. Mistakes were made, particularly in coordination. He thought back to the *chouf* of Uigh-el-Kébir, who was able to raise the alarm, and to the machine gunners who had opened fire on planes that had not yet spotted the *Groupement*. The delays taken in approaching the Italian position of Oum-el-Araneb stuck in his throat. The column lost two days stuck in the marshy *sebkra* that had been rendered impassable by the torrential rains of the previous weeks. Leclerc had let him lead, not wanting to interfere with his command. A perfectionist, Dio had realised the complexity of commanding a combined arms unit of this size. He was not yet 35 years old, and he had not completed the training courses provided for senior officers. He thus gradually discovered the difficulties of such a command. He promised himself that in the future he would not routinely rush into the firefight along with his leading elements. His role sometimes required more perspective. Dio was not the only one who objectively analysed the lessons to be learnt from the previous days. With his usual verve, Dronne wrote: 'Apart from Leclerc, Dio, and maybe one or two platoon leaders from *DC*, we all did stupid shit. Fortunately for us, the Italians did as well, but even more and bigger.'[121]

For this operation, Leclerc had made the capture of the Italian post of Oum-el-Araneb his main objective which 'was to precipitate the rout of all the enemy garrisons.'[122] And, indeed, as he had predicted, the Italian posts of Fezzan collapsed one after the other, like a house of cards. From 6 January, Gatroun fell under the action of *Capitaine* Sarazac's GNT. On 8 January, *Capitaine* Guéna's company from Commandant Massu's *1er Bataillon de Marche* returned to Murzuk without opposition; the Italians had abandoned the place. It was the same for *Groupement Delange* which

119 Dronne, *Carnets de Route*, p.176.
120 Béné, *Carnets, Seconde Époque*, p.107.
121 Dronne, *Carnets de Route*, p.169.
122 Massu, *Sept Ans*, p.75.

entered Sebha, the capital of Fezzan, without fighting. The day before, 7 January, Alaurent's platoon of the *2ᵉ DC* seized Brack, deserted by its occupants. The platoon had departed on Dio's orders. As Dronne explains: '*Lieutenant Colonel* Dio assigned most of the available resources to the *DC* platoons. From 2 January, 48 hours before the occupation of the Italian position, he sent Alaurent's platoon to scout far away towards the north.'[123] As a good disciple of Leclerc, Dio, like a chess player, always considered the next move. He emptied his fuel reserves to allocate them to Alaurent and gave him the autonomy necessary to advance to the north.

Still in Oum-el-Araneb, *Groupement D* was waiting for its resupply. Dio was pawing impatiently. Like Leclerc, he was eager to resume progress to the north. He felt that, 'we must not let them [the Italians] retreat quietly. We have to hurry them, harass them, poke them in the ass, jostle them, we have to turn their retreat into a stampede and a rout.'[124] *Capitaine* von Kéké (Dubois) did his best to organise the supply chain, but the combat troops moved too fast and the logisticians could not keep up with the advance. Nearly 1,000km had been covered since Zouar. Leclerc managed to convince the Americans, through the US liaison officer, Colonel Cunningham, to provide his troops with a Douglas C3 which 'brings fuel and ammunition on the outward journey and takes the wounded and prisoners on the return. To do it well, we would need around ten of these aircraft.'[125] On 7 January, the C3 unloaded the barrels of fuel they needed to finish refuelling all the vehicles.

In the early morning of 8 January, *Groupement D* resumed the northwards advance. It was urgent to get to Brack, 300 kilometres away, held until then by *Capitaine* Alaurent with his platoon of 60 men and 12 Chevrolet trucks. Alaurent, having received the order to resume his movement towards Schiuref, had only left a patrol from his platoon behind. The progress of *Colonne Dio* was made difficult by the route but also by the state of the vehicles, which had suffered greatly since the start. In the afternoon, vehicles passed by Sebha without stopping. Delange's *Groupement M* was in the process of entering the city. Bivouac for the night was set up at 8:00 p.m. after covering only 150 kilometres during the day. That was not fast enough for Dio's liking, but at the same time he knew that the men were doing their best. Numerous mechanical problems delayed progress and the column of vehicles had to remain grouped together.

On 9 January, progress was further complicated by an area of sand dunes in which the heavily loaded trucks regularly got stuck. The column was only 20 kilometres from Brack when it had to stop for the night. On the horizon stood an immense *gara* that resembled the Rock of Gibraltar. Dio left the column under the orders of his deputy, *Capitaine* Verdier and, with the two platoons of the *Iʳᵉ DC*, he rushed towards Brack, taking *Commandant* Crépin with him. The aim was to reinforce as quickly as possible the elements of Alaurent's platoon left at Brack and to prepare for the arrival of the *Groupement*. Fort Brack stood majestically on a *gara* north of the palm grove. It was an old Turkish fortress next to which the Italians had built a beautiful barracks. The construction was immense. The commander of the patrol that had been left there was happy to welcome Dio. He told him that everything in the fort was intact; the Italians had not destroyed anything when they left and the weapons and ammunition were available. In the middle of the vast interior courtyard of the fort, there was a large stock of mineral water. This led the *GNB* radio operator to say: 'the Italians preferred to leave it there for us, certainly understanding that, for months, we had only been drinking foul water smelling of natron or petrol.'[126]

---

123 Dronne, *Carnets de Route*, p.183.
124 Dronne, *Carnets de Route*, p.182.
125 Dronne, *Carnets de Route*, p.183.
126 Béné, *Carnets, Seconde époque*, p.113.

From the evening bulletin, Dio learnt that Leclerc, following de Gaulle's instructions, was installing a French administration throughout Fezzan. '*Lieutenant Colonel* Delange is designated to administer the military territory of Fezzan.'[127] Administrator Lami, whom Delange took with him, was ready to organise the occupation of the large territory. The British tried to send administrative liaison officers. 'Leclerc thanked them and dismissed them. *Général* de Gaulle had telegraphed: 'Fezzan is France's part in the Battle of Africa.''[128] On the morning of 10 January 1943, the bulk of *Groupement D* reached Brack. Dio gave orders to organise the occupation of the interior of the Italian post. Occupying the *askaris'* barracks, the men were all surprised to be accommodated in conditions that many had never known before. They would be able to sleep in a bed. The leaders had rooms. All the men were happy to abandon their rations and eat Italian style.

Late in the morning, Leclerc landed in a Lysander at Brack. He was not in a good mood. He found that the groups' slow progress had allowed the Italians to withdraw in good order. He wanted to take advantage of the Italian rout and prevent them from reorganising. Dio explained the condition of the vehicles to him. The progress of the column had been disrupted by the countless breakdowns that had occurred. Leclerc received a telegram from General Alexander which read: 'An advance, even by small parties, on Sebha and Schiuref, and Mizda could be of great help to the 8th Army.'[129] He asked that the French provide cover on his southern flank. The *général* looked at a map with Dio and analysed the situation. Brack was the northernmost piece of terrain in French hands, and had the particularity of being situated at the intersection of three axes:

- Towards Ghadamès, on the Algerian border 800km northwest of Brack,
- Towards Hon, 300km northeast of Brack. This city could make it possible to ensure the junction with the British of the 8th Army who continued their offensive to the north, along the coast,
- Towards Tripoli, via Schiuref (330km from Brack) and then Mizda (580km away), via a due north axis.

To act quickly in all these directions, they decided to split *Groupement D* and *Groupement G* to launch more mobile and agile detachments, made up of light vehicles in better condition.[130] Additionally, all posts south of Brack were under the control of the Free French with the exception of Ghat. This Italian garrison in the rear had to be neutralised. Located 560 kilometres southwest of Sebha, it was close to the Algerian border. Leclerc would plan an airlift operation for Ghat.

11 January was dedicated to preparing the detachments that would be sent out. Mechanics selected reliable vehicles and made the usual modifications. Dio organised his thoughts and issued his orders. For the mission to Ghadamès, the departure time of which would be given later, he designated *Capitaine* d'Abzac, who had shown great enthusiasm as detachment leader since the start of the operation. His detachment would include Hébert's section of the *GNB* and *Lieutenant* de Bagneux's platoon from the *2ᵉ DC*, which was under the orders of *Groupement M*. It would be

---

127 Ingold, *L'épopée*, p.208.
128 Dronne, *Carnets de Route*, p.193.
129 Ingold, *L'épopée*, p.213, note 1.
130 These detachments would be created from the *DC* platoons which had so far shown their effectiveness. The missions were distributed as follows:
   Groupement D was responsible for reconnaissance of the axis towards Tripoli, which would be the axis of main effort, and that towards Ghadamès. It was reinforced by Alaurent's platoon which belonged to *Groupement G*,
   Capitaine Geoffroy's *Groupement G* was in charge of the axis towards Hon to ensure liaison, if possible, with the British 8th Army.

supported by *Sous Lieutenant* Lamodière's 75mm gun. The reconnaissance detachment to Mizda would be made up of the usual two platoons of the *1re DC*, under Combes and Troadec, with *Capitaine* Farret at their head. In addition, it would have a 75mm field gun and a 47mm anti-tank gun.

On 12 January 1943, *Lieutenant Colonel* Dio left Brack on the central axis leading to Tripoli at the head of his detachment. Alaurent's platoon preceded him. Alaurent captured Schiuref, located more than 300km from Brack. Then he was attacked by a column of Italians coming from Hon, which he managed to repel. During the day of 12 January, Leclerc made a risky move on Ghat. He considered that the Italians could surrender easily and planned an aerial operation. He sent *Lieutenant* Mahé's Blenheim, followed by the Caproni carrying a section of Massu's *BM1*.[131] Initially, Mahé was responsible for attracting the attention of the Italians and then having the Caproni land so that the section could invest the Italian fort. But the Blenheim was greeted by a hail of gunfire. It was clear that the operation could not be carried out in the face of such unusual determination from the Italians. Finally, Leclerc asked the Vichy *méharistes* of Hoggar to seize Ghat. Their commander, *Capitaine* Mougenot, seized the fort on 24 January. Moving on the eastern axis on 13 January, *Lieutenant* Eggenspiller led his platoon, named 'Alsace', into Hon, which had been occupied since the day before by the British. The junction was therefore established with the British 8th Army, halfway between Brack and the sea.

On 14 January, Dio arrived in Schiuref. He had covered 400km in a day and a half, taking good vehicular routes. The terrain becomes less rugged as one moves north, so the road network was of better quality than that which they had experienced in Chad. Alaurent's platoon was on site with *Capitaine* Geoffroy.

On 15 January, Operations Order No.5 reached Dio:[132]

1) Mission:
   a) seize Mizda while trying to capture as many personnel and materiel as possible;
   b) push a platoon in liaison towards Tripoli immediately after the entry of British troops.
2) Disposition:
   Groupement G: with Alaurent's platoon plus one gun. Proceed along the immediate edges of the Schiuref-Mizda road, making contact with resistance, reducing it if possible and, in all cases, showing maximum activity.
   Groupement D: three platoons of *DC* plus two guns will use the road to the south of El Gheriat and then advance through the western region of the road to attack Mizda or at least blocking it from the north. If off-road movement is impossible, *Groupement D* will take the road, limiting the flanking manoeuvre from the north, which is still to be sought, to local manoeuvres. In this case, Lieutenant-Colonel Dio will take command of the two groups.
3) As soon as Mizda is occupied, the platoon will be pushed towards Garian ready to link up with Tripoli as soon as possible. The departure order will be confirmed via telegraph by the colonel.

When they received the order, Dio and his officers looked at the map: El Gheriat is about 100 kilometres from Schiuref and is in a depression. Mizda backs onto a mountainous area called Djebel Nefoussa, 156 kilometres from El Gheriat. Garian is 85 kilometres north of Mizda and 100 kilometres from Tripoli. They understood that the main objective was Mizda, which must be

---

131 This Kant was the same plane that had transported the wounded *Commandant* Dio to Fort-Lamy in 1941.
132 Ingold, *L'Épopée*, pp.216–217.

a strongpoint held by the Italians. They were asked not to attack frontally but to try to outflank Mizda to take the enemy's position from the rear. For this, *Groupement G* had to remain on the central axis to create a diversion and draw the attention of the Italians. The manoeuvre consisted of finding a route near El Gheriat, west of the axis on the El Homra *hamada*,[133] to arrive at Mizda from the north. This type of plateau is covered with hard sand, so vehicular movement would be relatively simple. Dio understood that he had to use that axis of advance to outflank Mizda and surprise the Italians defending in the city. He also perceived that it was politically imperative for a French element to arrive in Tripoli with the British. At least one *DC* platoon had to demonstrate that the Free French actively participated in the Italian rout and the withdrawal of the *Afrika Korps*. Dio had three superb units that were very experienced by that point. Their morale was soaring, the Sara and Hadjeraï *tirailleurs* and the Toubou and Senussis *goumiers* all wanted to get at the Germans. The Italians, called '*Adriens*' by the *tirailleurs*, no longer had the right to their respect because many of them had surrendered without fighting. They noted that *Général* Leclerc liked the enemy's flags. So, they would try to capture some to decorate the *RTST*'s *Salle d'Honneur* (trophy room) at Fort-Lamy. *Capitaines* Combes, Lavergne, and Troadec were quality officers. They felt good about Dio, whom they admired for his past, his understanding of the desert, and his ability as a trainer of men. They did not want to disappoint him. Troadec, the reservist, wanted to be up to par, particularly with regard to the *général* who authorised him to leave his post as aide-de-camp.

On 17 January 1943, while Dio and his men were preparing for Schiuref, *Général* de Gaulle's communiqué came out, congratulating the troops of Chad and their leader for the qualities they had demonstrated, which 'Provide …. for the world new proof of the value of our arms when they are entrusted to leaders worthy of France.'[134] Reading those congratulations from the leader of Free France warmed everyone's hearts. At the same time as the congratulations, de Gaulle sent very precise instructions from London to each of the general officers that demonstrated his gift of anticipation and his determination to never allow himself to be guided by events. First, he asked Leclerc to fight alongside the British 8th Army in the future battle in Tunisia. Then he planned how Free French forces should be organised once French troops in Africa united under a single command. They would consist of three large units under the command of *Général* de Larminat: an infantry division under Koenig, a light mechanised division under Leclerc, and a brigade of special troops under *Colonel* Lelong.

Dio and all his men awaited the departure order. They were ready. If Leclerc kept them there, it must have been due to a coordination problem with the British. The officers thought with a smile of *Général* Leclerc who had previously believed that they were not moving fast enough, accusing them of waging 'a war of 1939.' To ensure the flank guard against the British contingent to the south, it was obviously necessary to keep pace with them. But Montgomery did not want to make a mistake. He was methodical and that worked for him. In any case, the British allies had become essential if Free France wanted to continue to exist on a military level. The Free French were for the moment 'epic tramps,' according to Malraux, equipped in a rag-tag manner. To fight the Germans, they needed modern equipment that only their allies could provide to them.

The men had been stamping their feet in Schiuref for 24 hours. They were tired of disassembling and cleaning their weapons as all good soldiers do when there is nothing else to do. They were only 450 kilometres from the Mediterranean Sea. It was the short-term dream of all the Frenchmen to see this body of water again. France lay on the other side of it. The indigenous Chadian soldiers also wanted to see the sea that Europeans talked about. Was it really wider than Lake Chad?

---

133 A *hamada* is a high, rocky plateau with no vegetation.
134 Ingold, *L'Épopée*, p.212.

Finally, the departure order came by radio on the evening of 18 January. On the morning of the 19th, *Groupement D*, with the three platoons of the *1ʳᵉ DC*, left Schiuref, maintaining intervals of several kilometres between each platoon. After having covered around 30 kilometres, Dio stopped the platoons and told them to camouflage themselves according to a very extensive system to avoid being spotted by enemy aviation. He asked *Capitaine* Farret to form a light patrol composed of four of the 1½-ton Bedfords. With his 750kg pick-ups, Dio wanted to have light vehicles capable of travelling on all terrain without problems. With this motorised patrol, he headed west to reach the El Homra *hamada*. He wanted to see if the plateau was accessible to vehicles and if it offered acceptable possibilities to continue progress. After an hour of driving, the plateau was in sight. It was easily accessible to vehicles. Once at the top, 'an immense flat and very drivable expanse then opened up.'[135] Over the radio, he ordered *Capitaine* Farret to join him with the entire group starting at 4:00 p.m. Aircraft security instructions were once again applied: no vehicular movement between 9:00 a.m. and 4:00 p.m. Once the bulk of the column arrived, the advance could resume towards the north. The ground, consisting of rocky soil and hardened sand, allowed them to maintain a good pace. On the *hamada*, life is rare: there were no people, only a few gazelles and cheetahs. The bivouac was set up shortly after dark, adopting a triangular arrangement for the night, with the base forward, orienting northwards.

On 20 January, at 3:00 a.m., they began moving again. At 9:00 a.m., they reached the northern edge of the *hamada*. Mizda was still 80km to the northeast. Dio decided to stop, and the camouflage nets were unfolded. Then he had to find a passage to get off the plateau. Near where the group was located, the descent was blocked by a cliff. Two vehicles left to look for a route down. The *colonel* asked them to be discreet – the enemy absolutely must not detect this outflanking manoeuvre. In the middle of the afternoon, the reconnaissance found a path built by the Italians. At 4:00 p.m., the column of vehicles set off and followed the two guide vehicles. Everything went well and at nightfall, the three platoons and the artillery section with its two 75mm guns found themselves at the bottom of the cliff. Dio estimated that he was then 60km from Mizda. What to do? Getting even closer could lead to coming across a *chouf* which would raise the alarm. It was best to stay where they were and to rest. Dio decided to resume the movement in the middle of the night to arrive at Mizda just before dawn, which would be the best time to surprise the sentries.

At midnight on 21 January, as a very pale moon rose, the advance resumed in successive platoons: Lavergne in the lead, followed by Troadec, and then Combes. The night was cold and damp. The leading vehicles suddenly fell onto a path and stopped. Dio arrived shortly thereafter. It was certainly the route linking Mizda to Ghadamès. He decided to follow it. The path became steeper and steeper, following an *enneri*, the Fessanon, enclosed between sheer cliffs. Progress continued through the night. Everyone was on their guard because it was a real 'widow-maker.' Around 4:30 a.m., 'the leading vehicle collided with a low wall blocking the path at the top of an almost vertical cliff.'[136] Immediately a hellish fire broke out on the other side of the low wall and rockets were fired. Shots fired at night are obviously not aimed and are fortunately less effective. Dio ordered the first patrol of Lavergne's platoon to fall back to take shelter behind a small *gara*. The Italian 47mm and 20mm guns sprayed the path intensely. In addition to the darkness, the wadi was bathed in thick fog that further limited visibility. Dio then tried to outflank the Italian defences. He ordered Lavergne to try to climb the cliff to take it from behind. Troadec received the same order for the cliff located on the other side of the wadi. The steep walls prohibited any manoeuvre on foot for the two platoons.

135 Ingold, *L'Épopée*, p.218.
136 Ingold, *L'Épopée*, p.219.

At first light, Dio realised that the bulk of the group had, in fact, entered the enemy lines. 'Lavergne's half-platoon advanced in the *garas*, entirely mixed up with the Italians, who could not even be distinguished from the French through binoculars.'[137] The situation was confused, Lavergne's and Troadec's platoons were in contact within the enemy defensive line. They could no longer move, but they also prevented the Italians from doing so, either. Dio only had Combes' platoon to manoeuvre with, so he sent it in search of a route to bypass the enemy defensive system from the north or the south. Once the reconnaissance was carried out, the platoon leader realised that it was impossible to do so in vehicles. Dio, meanwhile, brought his artillery into action behind the position. An Italian 47mm gun was destroyed. Troadec easily repelled an Italian counterattack. Meanwhile, Lavergne fired on three trucks of *askaris* who had arrived as reinforcements, turning them back. The situation remained unchanged for the rest of the day.

Dio waited until nightfall to resume the offensive. During the day, he did not want to risk losses in such an intertwined system. When night fell, he ordered each platoon to form small groups to harass the Italian positions. A fine, cold rain began to fall; the darkness was total. Whenever the Italians sensed that the *degaullisti* were approaching their position, they fired sporadically. There was great confusion on both sides. The French noticed that enemy responses were becoming less and less strong. In fact, the Italians were taking advantage of the night to pull back. That was what Lavergne and Troadec observed at first light, despite a fairly dense fog which had fallen throughout the wadi. Dio came to the scene to see that the path was clear. The personnel remounted their vehicles, which had been grouped together. The doctor reported that there were miraculously only minor injuries among the soldiers, and that they were all able to return to their posts after treatment.

Around 8:00 a.m. on 22 January, the column set off with Troadec's platoon in the lead, proceeding cautiously, as the Italians could ambush the group, whose presence was now known. Indeed, less than four kilometres from Mizda, the first vehicles were suddenly greeted by heavy fire. The Italians had set up a buried position similar to that of Oum-el-Araneb on a height dominating the route, next to the fort of Mizda. Dio was perplexed. Since the launch of Operation Fezzan 2, this was the first time that the enemy had demonstrated such ferocity in the face of the Chadian troops' advance. The Italian artillery unleashed a violent fire on the platoons. One of their guns, well camouflaged on the right of the path, had the entire French formation under its fire. On Dio's orders, Farret had his 'two 75s, commanded by *Lieutenant* Pons, a young candidate at [the École] Polytechnique in 1940 who had interrupted his studies to enlist in the Free French forces, brought into action.'[138] Pons engaged in a duel with the Italian piece and soon silenced the enemy gun.[139] Dio gave orders to manoeuvre against the enemy position, fixing it under fire in order to outflank and destroy it by an assault. Suddenly, heavy weapons and mortar fire was heard south of the position, aimed at the Italian positions. It was coming from Alaurent's platoon, which had moved along the southern route, coming from Schiuref. Used as a diversion from the flank attack led by Dio, he arrived in front of Mizda, the Italian troops having retreated before him. Facing French fire coming from the south and west and threatened by the infiltration of infantry who were moving towards their position, the Italians withdrew at midday towards Garian, a town 85km north of Mizda.

---

137 Ingold, *L'Épopée*, p.220.

138 Dronne, *Le Serment*, p.169.

139 Later, Pons went to see the famous artillery piece that he had neutralised. Dronne tells us that he noticed with astonishment that his 75mm shell had hit the muzzle of the opposing gun… an extraordinary shot which led the young mathematician to calculate the probability of such a shot. Dronne, R., *Serment de Koufra*, p.170.

At 3:00 p.m. the first vehicles from *Groupement Dio* entered Mizda, to find that the Italians had abandoned their wounded and dead. Immediately, Dio sent Combes' platoon to follow the Italians on the northern route to deny them any respite. Meanwhile, the town was searched by the other two platoons, which would be joined by Alaurent. The population, concerned about the noise of the fighting, had only been coming out into the streets little by little since the firing had ended. The locals were surprised to see these poorly dressed *Francesi*, with trucks that looked like Christmas trees, having overcome the Italians. The notables came to introduce themselves to Dio and invited him to settle into a good military residence. He learnt that the commander of the Tripolitania-Fezzan sector, *Generale* Mannerini, had used it as his command post, which explained the pugnacity that the Italians showed during the previous hours.

Once again the spoils of war were good. The Italians had not destroyed anything when they left. Dio was happy to list in his evening report to Leclerc the heavy weapons, ammunition, fuel, and food that would be recovered, reducing the supplies that would need to be transported across a logistical line of more than 3,000 kilometres. The few Alsatians in the detachment noted with joy that there were stork nests in the area. The sight of these emblematic birds brought them closer in thought to their native region.[140] Combes, who set out in pursuit of the Italians, advanced around 50 kilometres. At nightfall, Dio told him to settle on favourable ground for the night to prevent the Italians from returning. For his part, Dio decided to bivouac in Mizda. It was necessary to gather all the materiel abandoned by the Italians together to prevent the population from using the stock of weapons or supplies. From Brack, where he established his CP, Leclerc sent the following communiqué on the 24th: 'After a fierce struggle, the motorised troops of *Lieutenant Colonel* Dio seized, on 20 January, a very strongly held enemy position covering Mizda …. The next day, our troops occupied Mizda. The enemy fled, left his dead, his wounded, and substantial arms and supplies on the ground.'[141] During the same day, 22 January, *Capitaine* d'Abzac left Brack to probe the famous oasis of Ghadamès located on the triple border of Libya, Algeria, and Tunisia. D'Abzac covered the 800 kilometres in two and a half days. On 26 January, with Bagneux's platoon[142] and the *légionnaires* of Fort-Saint belonging to the Vichy French troops from southern Algeria, he seized Ghadamès, which the Italians had just abandoned. Then on 29 January, on orders, he seized Sinaouen, 150km north of Ghadamès.

Dio departed Mizda on the morning of 23 January, and swiftly joined Combes' platoon with the platoons of Troadec and Lavergne. He left *Capitaine* Geoffroy and Alaurent's platoon in Mizda. Their progress towards the town of Garian, 85km away, was slowed by surrendering Italians. It was necessary to disarm all of these soldiers, for whom the war was over. The *askaris* were released immediately. The Free French arrived in Garian around 5:00 p.m. Elements of the British 7th Armoured Division were ahead of them by only two hours. Contact was established between the two element leaders. The British asked Dio not to advance any further because they were still fighting the Germans at El Azizia, an important crossroads south of Tripoli. In fact, the British did not look favourably on the Gaullist presence in Tripolitania, an area reserved for them. 'The British saw this as confirmation of de Gaulle's quasi-imperialist ambitions on Libya.'[143] But Dio did not forget the last part of his orders, which provided for bringing at least one platoon into Tripoli. It was important that the French be seen during the liberation of the capital of Libya. Also,

---

140 The Alsace region of France is notable for the storks that build large nests on rooftops and other high places. The storks migrate between northern Africa and Europe, so the nests in Mizda were quite likely made by the same birds found in France during the warmer months of the year. (Translator's note)

141 Levisse-Touzé and Toureille, Écrits de *Combat*, p.426.

142 Geoffroy Rosset's book, *Itinéraire d'un Compagnon de la Libération, Geoffroy de Bagneux, duc de Ghadamès* (Paris: L'Harmattan, 2018) tells the story of the capture of Ghadamès.

143 Notin, *le Croisé*, p.188.

without warning his British counterpart, Dio decided on 24 January, shortly before nightfall, to leave the platoons of Combes and Lavergne in Garian and to depart with Farret and Troadec's platoons in the direction of Tripoli. For the first time, vehicles were driving on a metalled road and the Cameroonian drivers appreciated the comfort it provided. Dio's detachment was stopped by British forces near El Azizia, and he spent the day of 25 January there. On the 26th, before the break of day, he once again left his British 'guardians' behind.

There were 50 kilometres of road left to reach Tripoli. Fighting raged in the northwest, and they had to pass through the British lines. They were flown over by British planes. They had to stop several times. At 11:00 a.m., they entered the southern suburbs of the Libyan capital, which had just fallen into Montgomery's hands. The port was devastated by bombing. Dio and his men crossed the city and continued their progress towards the north, 'because what they wanted, what they desired, was to see the sea. The sea that beats the coasts of Provence with the same rhythm. It suddenly appeared to them, at the entrance to the castle of Tripoli, all blue, a violent blue like it is in Cannes, Nice, and Marseille.'[144] The Europeans were moved while the Chadian *tirailleurs* were impressed – they had never seen such an immensity of water in their lives. They went to soak their feet on the beach. The population drew closer to them, wondering who these strange soldiers were, black and white, who were not in British uniforms. The detachment was impressive in its diversity. 'Superb in their rags – some wear helmets, others kepis, some in shorts, others in long pants, some wear *serouals*, others *burnous*, all were in shirts that were dirty to the point of disgusting – in their strange, creaking vehicles, decorated with *gerbas*, palm fronds, nets, armed with heavy machine guns, guns, sometimes bearing the inscription 'Chad' in chalk…'[145] When they understood that they were Free French, they were quickly surrounded and applauded with cries of '*Francesi, Degaullisti*.' Dio and his team quickly felt oppressed in the streets in the middle of such a noisy crowd. It was too stark after the calm of the desert. The British they met also greeted 'those damned Frenchmen from Chad'[146] with 'Hi Free French.' It was surprising for Dio's detachment to encounter, among the British troops, other Frenchmen, those 'from Koenig's Division, whose embryo they had seen leaving Chad at the end of 1940.'[147] These other Free Frenchmen belonged to the *Bataillon d'Infanterie de Marine du Pacifique* which was part of the vanguard of General Montgomery's 8th Army.[148] Dio decided not to linger in town. 'Their mission 'to represent as quickly as possible the French forces fighting from Chad in Tripoli' had been fulfilled.'[149]

Dio was informed over the radio that Leclerc would land in Tripoli late in the afternoon and that he had to welcome him. Dio smiled inwardly, recognising that his leader always wanted to be in the front line. He inquired with the British, who told him that the only field that had just reopened was in Castel Benito, about 20 kilometres on the southern outskirts of the city. The small detachment went there and parked in a small eucalyptus grove on the edge of the airfield, which was littered with many destroyed Italian and German planes. At 4:00 p.m., Leclerc was all smiles when he walked out of his Lockheed plane with his hand outstretched towards Dio, Farret, and Troadec. He simply told them, 'Well done.' A photo captured this historic moment. Leclerc is in

---

144 Ingold, *L'Épopée,* p.223.
145 Destrem, *L'Aventure de Leclerc,* p.193.
146 Notin, *le Croisé,* p.191.
147 Notin, *le Croisé,* p.190.
148 'The *1re DFL* had not participated in the British advance. It was still resting somewhere near Tobruk. Only the *Bataillon d'Infanterie de Marine du Pacifique* remained in contact with the enemy, yet without being engaged in a major operation. Nevertheless, France was already represented, with the entry into action of a commando company of the French SAS, the 2nd Company, formed and trained in Egypt, with only French personnel. It was the first French unit attached to the British 8th Army to enter this territory occupied by the Italo-Germans.' (Béné, notebook, pp.130–131).
149 Ingold, *L'Épopée,* p.224

profile, smiling, his cane in his left hand. He wears his famous *chéchia* kepi,[150] a colonial coat, and boots.[151] Dio is in the centre, a cigarette in his mouth, wrapping his scarf around his neck. He is turned towards Troadec who is in profile on the left and who seems to be talking to him. The former aide-de-camp wears a garrison cap and is also warmly dressed. Troadec had just experienced hours of intense operations with Dio. Leclerc was happy to find these two men for whom he had respect and friendship. The *général* was expected by Montgomery. Dio accompanied him with his and Farret's pick-ups as an escort. The *général* met the commander of the 8th Army 'in his office truck, in the middle of an empty space surrounded by the headquarters tents.'[152] and 'after a forty-minute meeting, they both came out telling stories and laughing loudly.'[153] 'The contact was excellent, the future of *Colonne Leclerc* was assured. After leaving Montgomery, Leclerc found Dio, accompanied by Farret and Troadec. Everyone, for a moment, contemplated the sea…'[154]

The Fezzan 2 campaign thus ended on 26 January 1943. The victory was total. It was a just reward for two years of total commitment and work. The campaign was carried out at a hellish pace. 'Everything happened so quickly that the tail of our columns did not have time to cross the border before the head had already reached Tripoli.'[155] The Frenchmen covered 3,500 kilometres of desert filled with obstacles and blocked by the enemy in less than five weeks. The plan put together by Leclerc and his deputies was bold. 'Since he could not bring up all his troops at once due to a lack of trucks, he was going to launch a small echelon of attack forward …. with the understanding that the rest of the troops would follow as soon as possible.'[156] This attack echelon was essentially made up of *Lieutenant Colonel* Dio's *Groupement D*. It was to him that Leclerc entrusted the mission of taking Oum-el-Araneb, the main objective on which everything rested: '…for the conquest of Fezzan, it was on Oum-el-Araneb that Leclerc decided to carry his effort. Dio, with the most substantial forces, will stand upright' on this Italian fortress, by relying, once again, on speed and surprise.'[157] Leclerc knew that Dio was the officer best suited to fulfil that type of mission. After Cameroon, Gabon, Kufra, and Fezzan 1, he entrusted him with the principal role of leading the tactics he chose. For *Colonel* Ingold, Dio then became 'Leclerc's great constable.'[158]

After Oum-el-Araneb on 4 January, Dio was not entirely satisfied with the way in which the operation had been carried out at his level. Conversely, in Tripoli on 26 January, he was proud of the work accomplished by his group, which perfectly fulfilled its flank-guard mission in support of the 8th Army. 'The *Daily Telegraph* editorial states (speaking of the French): it is a marvellous success. Their advance lightened the left flank of the 8th Army in pursuit of Rommel.'[159] He was aware that sometimes *la Baraka*[160] served them well, notably at Oum-el-Araneb when the sand neutralised the effects of the Italian shells falling in their immediate vicinity. That sense of pride was rightly shared by his men who would be able to take a well-deserved rest and improve their lives, thanks to the provisions taken from the Italians. In addition, this region of Tripoli is a wine-producing area and 'it's the first time in a long time that the guys from Chad have had unlimited

---

150   The one crafted for him by his standard bearer, Butelot, after Uigh-el-Kébir, in March 1942. It was a *tirailleur*'s *chéchia*, covered with a sleeve of khaki calico fabric, to which were attached a visor as well as two Italian stars. It had the appearance of a European kepi.

151   Corbonnois, *L'Odyssée de la Colonne Leclerc*, p.91.

152   Compagnon, *Leclerc*, p.297.

153   Girard, *Journal de Guerre*, p.44.

154   Compagnon, *Leclerc*, p.297.

155   Destrem, *L'Aventure de Leclerc*, p.184.

156   Destrem, *L'Aventure de Leclerc*, p.184.

157   Compagnon, *Leclerc*, p.298.

158   Ingold, *Général Ingold*, p.100.

159   Ingold, *L'Épopée*, p.224, note 1.

160   In Islam, *Baraka* or *Barakah* is the divine blessing of Allah. (Translator's note)

wine, which everyone knows is dear to the heart and throat of every Frenchman.'[161] Dio would join his men during those evenings, where, after the fight, the men communed in the pride of a duty accomplished, Europeans and tirailleurs, united in this brotherhood of arms that can only be built after living through such momentous events together. These men from Chad formed a single unit, *Colonne L*.

It was during that period that 'the insignia of the *RMT*[162] *(formerly RTST)* was distributed to all those who participated in the second and final Fezzan campaign. The artillerymen who participated in the campaign preferred to wear the insignia of the *RMT* over their own.'[163] *Général* de Gaulle cited the mobile columns of Chad in the Order of the Army:

> Admirable troops who, under the command of a leader of exceptional valour, *Général* Leclerc, have perfectly and victoriously prepared and executed a series of offensive operations in Italian Libya against a highly organised enemy, and in the harshest terrain and climatic conditions on the globe, inflicted heavy losses on the Italians, took more prisoners than they counted of men themselves, destroyed or took more equipment than they had.[164]

For his part, Dio received a corps level citation for the Fezzan 2 and Tripolitania campaign: 'Commander of a principal group engaged in Fezzan and Tripolitania, particularly distinguished himself during the operations that led to the capitulation of Oum-el-Araneb and the capture of Mizda.'[165] Dio felt that a page had been turned. He perceived that there would be no returning to Chad for him. He remained very attached to the territory in which he had served continuously since 1938 – with the exception of six months in Cameroon-Gabon. But in Kufra, Leclerc had set the goal. Chad would very quickly become part of the past. Strasbourg Cathedral was still far away, but it was in that direction that they would forge their future.

---

161 Dronne, *Le Serment*, p.173.
162 The *BM3* insignia badge made in Damascus strongly inspired the design of that of the *RTST* made later in Cairo in 1941 and which would become that of the *RMT*. It brings together the same three symbols (navy anchor symbolising the colonial forces, a camel's head for the *méharistes* and the Cross of Lorraine for Free France). Villeminey et Marquet, *Insignes et Historiques des Formations Indigènes*, pp.164–165.
163 Fonds Leclerc, *JMO du 3e RAC*, p.86, boîte O1, dossier 2, chemise 1.
164 Paul Moynet, *L'Épopée du Fezzan* (Office Français d'Éditions, Algiers, 1944), p.61.
165 SHD, Dio, 14 Yd 1759, ESS, citation 26 mars1943, signée Leclerc 1 janvier 1944.

1926-1928. Dio at Saint-Cyr
(Musée de l'Officier de
l'Académie Militaire de
Saint. Cyr-Coëtquidan)

November 1932. Dio (in pith helmet) and his *goumiers* near Taoudeni in French Sudan. (Colonel J-P Durand-Gasselin Collection)

October 1940. Ferry crossing in Gabon. (Poualion Collection)

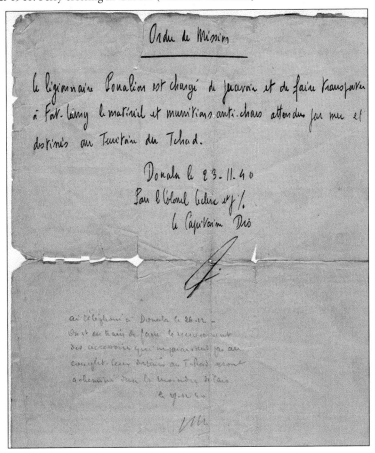

23 November 1940.
Mission Order signed by
Dio and issued to Poualion.
(Poualion Collection)

177

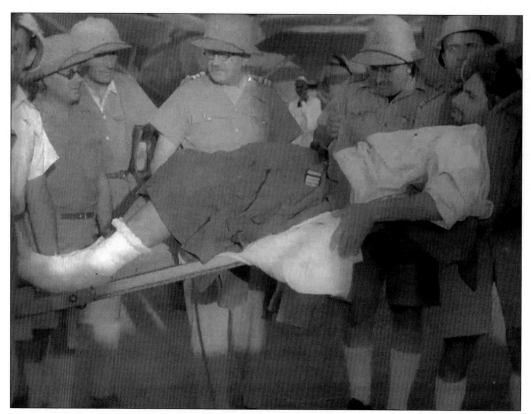

End of February 1941. Dio Arriving at Fort-Lamy after medical evacuation from Kufra. (NARA)

3 March 1942. Poletti, Leclerc, and Dio (from left to right) at Gatroun, Fezzan. (Fonds Leclerc)

January 1943. Troadec, Dio, and Leclerc at Castel Benito in Tripolitania (from left to right). (Fonds Leclerc)

Spring 1943. Dio presents his pennant of command to the *Brigade de Marche du Tchad* at Sabratha in Tripolitania. (G. Chauliac Collection)

End of 1943. Dio and his officers at Témara, Morocco. From left to right: Lavergne, Perceval, Sarazac, Dio, Massu, Corlu, Florentin. (Ploux-Vourc'h Collection)

7 April 1944. *Général* de Gaulle speaking to *Colonel* Dio (in helmet) at the end of the ceremony in Skhirat, Morocco. (ECPAD Collection)

24 June 1944. During Exercise KESTREL in England, from left to right: Massu, Corlu, Baylon, Dio, Vézinet, and Farret. (NARA)

24 August 1944. *Adjudant* Poualion, behind the wheel of his Jeep, having a difficult time working his way through the jubilant crowd in the suburbs of Paris. (Poualion Collection)

26 August 1944. *Général* Leclerc and *Colonel* Dio waiting for *Général* de Gaulle under the Arc de Triomphe. (ECPAD Collection)

27 February 1945. Dio and his *caporals* present the stripes of a *caporal honoraire* of the *RMT* to the US General Haislip at Vergaville en Moselle. (Dimand Collection)

28 March 1945. *Général* Leclerc pins the *Croix de Guerre* on the streamer of the *RMT* flag at Loches. (CMIDOM Collection)

May 1945. Leclerc and Dio with the commanders of the howitzer section of the 1st Battalion at Reichling in Germany. (Musée de l'Ordre de la Libération)

May 1945. *Colonel* Dio with his driver in Germany. (Fonds Leclerc)

22 June 1945. Dio in a lively discussion with *Commandante* Conrad, commander of the *Rochambelles*, at Fontainebleau. (Doctor Krementchousky Collection)

22 June 1945. Change of Command of the *2ᵉ DB*: *Colonel* Dio takes command and salutes *Général* Leclerc. (ECPAD Collection)

1 August 1945. General Haislip revues the troops before presenting the US Presidential Unit Citation to the *2ᵉ DB* at Fontainebleau. (Fonds Leclerc)

18 March 1946. *Général* Dio and Edmond Michelet, *Ministre des Armées,* during the inaugural ceremony of the *Maison de la 2ᵉ DB.* (ECPAD Collection)

Spring 1946. *Général* Dio with the staff of GB2 at Saint-Germain-en-Laye.
First row, left to right: *Commandant* Debray, *Colonel* Rouvillois, Dio, *Lieutenant Colonel* Fieschi. *Capitaine* Dehen is the second from the right of the standing officers. (Dehen Family Collection)

1 August 1946. *Général* Dio presents the *GB2* to *Général* Leclerc at Saint-Germain-en-Laye on his return from Indochina. (Fonds Leclerc)

27 August 1969. Michel Debré, *Ministre de la Défense*, presides over the retirement farewell ceremony of *Général d'Armée* Louis Dio, in the court of honour at Les Invalides. (ECPAD Collection)

Chapter 6

Tunisia,
27 January to 15 May 1943

On 27 January 1943, *Lieutenant Colonel* Dio was at Castel Benito south of Tripoli, having regrouped the four *découverte et de combat* (long range reconnaissance and combat – *DC*) platoons with which he led the last battles of the Free French of Chad in Libya. They settled on a large Italian airfield which was beginning to be attacked by the 'big boys' of the British 8th Army. Leclerc's 'Chadians' were impressed by the colossal means available to this arriving armada. Dio awaited orders from Leclerc, who would spend three days in Tripoli with the 8th Army's commander, General Montgomery. The French *général's* aide-de-camp describes the English officer as, 'small with a large nose, greying hair, smart and friendly air.'[1] 'Monty' was a suspicious man who did not open up easily, especially with strangers. It was similar for the French *général*, who usually tended to be wary of the British, but, surprisingly, the two hit it off immediately.[2]

On 28 January, Dio joined Leclerc in Tripoli, on the 3rd floor of a seafront building. The *général* confided to him the broad outlines of his discussions with the British general staff and the decisions that had been taken. Montgomery was visibly impressed by Leclerc's column and favourably received Leclerc's request to continue fighting alongside him.[3] Leclerc's argument was simple: 'We will probably not be of interest to you, given your very great means, but we ask you to use us, because it is necessary, it is necessary for France.'[4] The British general even agreed to Leclerc's request to partially equip the French troops coming from Chad. Integrated into the Allied forces, they would be reinforced by external elements to constitute *Force L*. The primary mission would be to guard the flank of the British 8th Army on the west side. The *général* read to the *lieutenant colonel* the message he had just sent to de Gaulle:

> Montgomery will employ us in future operations and will take responsibility for our supply of petrol, food, and auto parts starting on 10 February. ... The probable missions, which cannot be specified by radio, take into account the Saharan nature of our resources. ... The combat force employed will be approximately 2,500 men, which is all forces on site except those

---

1 Girard, *Journal de Guerre*, p.44.
2 This was not the case with *Général* de Larminat, who 'exasperated the British with his mania for always challenging [them]; he exasperated them all the more because most of the time he was right.' (Dronne, *Carnets de Route*, p.207). This explains why the *1re DFL* was only engaged in the last phase of the Battle of Tunisia, which always surprised Dio, who knew the operational value of the *bataillons de marches*.
3 Two days earlier, Leclerc received a secret note from Général de Gaulle specifying: 'my intention is that the French fighting forces participate to the greatest extent possible in the battle alongside the 8th Army.' (Vincent, *Les Forces Françaises Libres en Afrique*, p.319).
4 François Ingold (Gal), *Ceux de Leclerc en Tunisie, Février-Mai 1943*, (Paris: Office Français d'Édition, 1945), p.8.

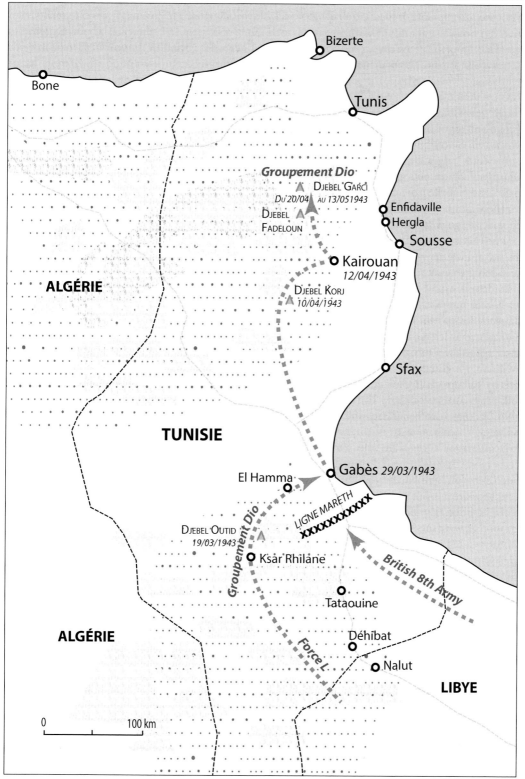

Map 7 Groupement Dio during the campaign of Tunisia.

necessary for the occupation of Fezzan. If I have reached an agreement with Montgomery, it is because I am on the job and have a small number of personnel, therefore not excessively increasing the problems of transport and supplies. I therefore believe it is prudent, as far as my current strength is concerned, to stick to this agreement.[5]

Immediately, Leclerc asked Dio where the units that will constitute *Force L* could be grouped. They were spread throughout Fezzan and Tripolitania. Dio, who had covered much of the area, suggested that Leclerc deploy the units in and around Mizda. Sufficiently far from the coastal strip, this central position would not interfere with the deployment of the 8th Army. Mizda had sufficiently large military buildings and would be able to ensure the water supply for such a group of units. Located on a good vehicular road, it would permit the resumption of the advance towards Tunisia when the time came. It would also be an important link with Chad, via Sebha, Oum-el-Araneb, and Uigh-el-Kébir. Leclerc endorsed this proposal and asked Dio to go quickly to Mizda to welcome and organise the arrival of the units of the future *Force L*.

For Dio, the priority was to find fuel for the vehicles – he estimated the requirement at 10,000 litres.[6] Additionally, the vehicles' tyres were in terrible condition. Punctures were becoming more and more frequent. Driving on the stony *regs* of the north of Fezzan had led to premature wear. The British would have to meet this specific need. Dio managed to find enough from the British to fill the tanks of his vehicles enough to reach Mizda, 180km from Tripoli. The British seemed satisfied to see him liberate the area where the support of the 8th Army was located. Dio and the *DC* platoons left Castel Benito on 1 February 1943. The column took the road due south to El Azizia and then to Garian. It was a real asphalt road! Then, a good vehicular route took them to Mizda at the end of the afternoon. The men knew the town and headed towards the barracks. They were pleased to find *Capitaine* Geoffroy and Alaurent's platoon, which had remained to guard the buildings and particularly the equipment and supplies left by the Italians. Accompanied by the two *DC* commanders, Farret and Geoffroy, Dio visited all the city's buildings so he could allocate space to the different units of *Force L* that would assemble in Mizda. With the information he received from Leclerc, he summarised the composition of the force, which was equivalent to a light motorised brigade. He estimated a force at approximately 2,500 men and 350 vehicles, which should be distributed throughout the city, and then he made sure there were sufficient supplies and support.[7]

In addition, the British command planned at some future date to assign to Leclerc the French units that were serving within the British Army, which had been called the Flying Column.[8]

---

5   Vincent, *Les Forces Françaises Libres en Afrique*, p.319.
6   Girard, *Journal de Guerre*, p.45.
7   Units from Chad included:
     the three *Groupes Nomades* (*GNT, GNB*, and *GNE*) which were by then all motorised,
     the 2nd Company of *BM1*,
     the 12th Company of the *RTST*,
     the two *DCs*,
     a unit of armoured cars,
     Crépin's artillery, composed of the following assets:
     field artillery with 2 x 25pdr guns, the 114mm howitzer, and 5 x 75mm guns,
     artillery: two 40mm guns and one 25mm gun,
     artillery: the former Cameroonian company was being equipped with British guns,
     medical support, maintenance, and resupply.
8   The flying column consisted of:
     Commandant Rémy's reconnaissance unit from the *1er RMSM* with 315 personnel,
     Divry's tank company equipped with the British Crusader tank comprising 153 men. It was this company
        which provided a platoon to *Colonne Dio* during the fighting in Gabon in November 1940.

Succeeding *Colonne Leclerc*, which had always been autonomous until then, *Force L* was integrated into an Allied army. For the first time since the end of 1940, Leclerc had a tactical commander at his side to whom he had to report. But this *Force L*, which could be compared to a light brigade, did not adopt the usual structure of subordinate battalions. It retained a strictly operational task-focused organisation. Leclerc wanted his troops to keep 'their Saharan spirit'[9] by maintaining great flexibility with the *groupement* (approximately 300 to 600 men) or the detachment (100 to 200 men). Thus, depending on the terrain and the mission, operational units (task forces) could be created at short notice depending on circumstances. The smallest basic unit remained the crew, which had worked quite well thus far.[10] Dronne describes this structure as:

> Now, the men, white and black, are well oiled [machines]. In each truck, they're used to living together. Even the Cameroonian drivers, poorly accepted at the beginning, ended up mixing and getting along well with the *tirailleurs* from Chad. Each crew constitutes a team in the full sense of the term: a group of men who unite their efforts for a common goal and who are on the same wavelength.[11]

On 2 February 1943, Dio and his deputies received news that delighted them all. On the Russian front, *Generalfeldmarschall* Friedrich von Paulus's 6th Army had capitulated at Stalingrad. The turning point seen at the end of 1942 was confirmed, the Axis forces crumbled and began their descent into hell. The same day, Leclerc received a telegram from de Gaulle, confirming the orders of 17 January, which provided directions for the future of *Force L*. 'I hope that you will be able to have, one day, under your orders, a mechanised division comprising, at first, a long range reconnaissance regiment equipped with armoured cars, a demi-brigade of tanks, a demi-brigade of mechanised infantry, and a towed artillery regiment with two groups.'[12] This telegram demonstrates that de Gaulle already had the idea of entrusting Leclerc with a predominantly armoured unit. Leclerc and his *méharistes* had proven that they excelled in a fight of speed and manoeuvre.

Units coming from Fezzan gradually arrived in Mizda. Everyone found their place in the beautiful 'settlement with real houses. The Italians are not extraordinary fighters, but they are champions in masonry.'[13] For the French who had lived in Tibesti for years, it was the first time that they saw homes that reminded them of their own country. Béné wrote: 'the Italian residences with their small gardens made me dream of images of France.'[14] On 10 February, all units were regrouped at Mizda, and on 14 February *Force L* was officially established. *Colonne Leclerc*, composed solely of troops from Chad, thus became an international brigade, with a strong French majority, but also with Britons and Greeks.

In addition, Montgomery acceded to Leclerc's requests by reinforcing him with foreign units, namely:
a British engineering company (80 men),
a Greek squadron in jeeps (155 men, mostly officers),
artillery (12 guns 40mm).

9   Ingold, *Ceux de Leclerc*, p.12.
10 This particular structure acquired during the fighting in the desert was unique to the *2e DB*, giving it exceptional operational cohesion: 'To have, for so many days, months and years, lived in the desert, on their vehicles, men and officers have acquired habits, acquired traditions of equality, solidarity, and mutual trust born from the hours spent together, in a total community, in constant intimacy in the narrow confines of the vehicle, eating from the same bowl, sleeping side by side in identical 'faros', sharing the same labours, the same worries, the same sufferings, the same dangers – and the same death.' (Jean d'Esme, *Les Nomades de la Gloire, l'Épopée de la Division Leclerc* (Paris: Les Publications Techniques et Artistiques, 1944), pp.228–229.
11 Dronne, *Carnets de Route*, p.199.
12 Levisse-Touzé and Toureille, *Écrits de Combat, 2 février 1943*, p.432.
13 Dronne, *Carnets de Route*, p.200.
14 Béné, *Carnets, Seconde Époque*, p.132.

Leclerc decided to form two basic groups which would be reinforced by the remaining units depending on the missions or the circumstances of the action. The first, *Groupement D* (Dio), included *Capitaine* Farret's *1re DC*, the *GNB* of *Commandant* Poletti, *Capitaine* Corlu's 12th Company of Chad, a squadron of armoured cars and artillery under *Commandant* Crépin, and CA4. It was the most experienced combined arms group of *Force L*, made up of infantrymen and light armoured vehicles, artillery, and support units. The different components of this group had fought together since the end of 1941. Their cohesion of the *Groupement* under Dio's command was tight; in Leclerc's mind, it would be his shock group. The second group, *Groupement V*, was under the orders of *Commandant* Vézinet. Vézinet was a reservist who came to Leclerc's attention through his calm demeanour and his tactical sense during the previous operation, during which he had commanded the forward logistics base of Uigh-el-Kébir. The group included the two *Groupes Nomades* of Tibesti and Ennedi, the 2nd Company of *BM1*, and artillery.

Falling under British command, Leclerc's troops were therefore supported at all levels by the 8th Army. All the men, including Leclerc, would be provided with British uniforms. 'The English therefore deliver us new clothing, battle dress,[15] shirts, British army shorts, boots, and leggings for the main part.'[16] The *tirailleurs* were particularly happy to wear closed shoes for the first time which 'hurt their feet, but tough luck; with a good pair of shoes, you look good and you're warm.'[17] The 'epic tramps' finally became, through their uniforms, soldiers worthy of a national army. Dronne wrote with humour, 'we are no longer a horde of rag-bags.'[18] Consequently, carelessness in uniform would no longer be permitted. Echoing a directive from Leclerc, Dio demanded that his men shave every day and wear the regulation uniform.

Living conditions were also improving: 'Our food supply …. is enhanced with canned goods (including the famous bully beef), chocolate, and English cigarettes.'[19] Dried dates and smoked meat were quickly abandoned.

The British were also making great efforts in materiel. On vehicles that had travelled more than 4,000km from Chad, they replaced numerous engines (around 30 new engines were delivered to the French troops) and equipped the vehicles with complete sets of new tyres. The maintenance units were given spare parts. Unit vehicles would thus be able to take on a second operational life.

In respect to tactical equipment, *Colonne Leclerc* had two notable shortcomings in confronting the German troops: it had no engineering units and few anti-tank weapons. Therefore, the British reinforced the groups with engineering units intended primarily to facilitate mobility in mined areas. For anti-tank weapons, Montgomery equipped *Force L* with 16 x 2pdr guns.[20] Leclerc immediately decided to form an anti-tank company of six guns with the Cameroon mounted company. But he also ensured that each of the infantry companies was equipped with two guns, allowing them to confront armoured vehicles. They were invited to exchange their Italian 47mm guns towed by the old Fiats for British two-pounders mounted on new trucks. British instructors came to train the gunners and gun captains on the new weapon. The British also reinforced *Force L* with British anti-aircraft units. They provided the groups with a command vehicle equipped with a ground-to-air radio: thus they could be in direct contact with planes that were working in support of the ground forces.

---

15   The khaki battle dress in warm cloth consisted of long trousers, a short jacket stopping at the belt, a helmet, boots, and canvas gaiters.
16   Béné, *Carnets, Seconde époque*, p.132.
17   Dronne, *Carnets de Route*, p.208.
18   Dronne, *Carnets de Route*, p.208.
19   Béné, *Carnets, Seconde époque*, p.132.
20   This means that the guns fire shells weighing two pounds each, a modern weapon with greater range and penetration power.

In terms of communications, *Force L* also upgraded to more modern equipment by receiving portable radios 'working only in voice and powered by a large black battery box,'[21] and including whip antennas. The new equipment would allow troops engaged in areas inaccessible to vehicles to remain in radio contact, which they could not previously do, being in a way 'attached' to their vehicle.

The British also carried out tactical training exercises with the French. Until then, the Chad troops had been exposed to very little danger from mines. The Italians only used them in front of their defensive positions. It was different with the Germans, who used a lot of anti-tank and anti-personnel mines. The roads, tracks, and areas in front of the German positions were riddled with the terrible *Tellerminen 42* anti-tank mines; flat mines that tanks or trucks detonated when they drove over them. These mines were particularly treacherous, especially in sandy areas. The pressure from the first vehicle was not sufficient to trigger the mines in the sand; instead, the mine sank little by little into the sand. Bad luck would eventually get one of the following vehicles, driving in the tracks of the others in accordance with their instructions. To counter the technique of having a heavy vehicle pass in front of the column to destroy the mines, the Germans invented notch mines: 'They pushed the refinement by using notch mines, (sometimes more than one dozen of these notches), a very effective system for immobilising a column of vehicles in two or more sections. Each time a vehicle passed a notch was released, but the explosion did not occur until the eighth or tenth vehicle.'[22] The Germans also used leaping anti-personnel mines, the *Schrapnellminen 35*.[23] Their effects were particularly devastating within a several metre radius. The Nazi troops were masters in the art of booby-trapping homes, corpses, weapons... The British trainers demonstrated these different types of equipment and simulated the most common booby-traps so Leclerc's Chadians could become fully aware of the new danger. Dio insisted that, in addition to leaders, drivers and *tirailleurs* be made aware of the danger of these mines and that very precise instructions on how to deal with them be issued.

Finally, on the administrative level, 'unity of action with the English was confirmed on 13 February by the conversion of our French franc *assignats* into British military pounds.'[24] Dressed, equipped, and led by the British, the Free French of Chad felt like new men.

During this period of learning and training, Dio took the opportunity to catch up on his administrative tasks. A note signed by him as commander of *Groupement D*, in Mizda on 11 February, called 'Ukase,' required his unit commanders to send him proposed citations for the Fezzan 2 operation that they had just completed.[25] His note was very clear about citations, demonstrating that he was a leader who was very concerned about his subordinates. He knew that injustices in this area were sometimes committed and he wanted to avoid them. Therefore, he drew up for his officers a list of the various cases for approving a proposed citation. He did not forget the support personnel, such as radiomen or mechanics, who 'contributed indirectly but undeniably to the success of the operations.'[26]

---

21   Béné, *Carnets, Seconde époque*, p.131.

22   Fonds Leclerc, *Souvenirs du Docteur Charles Mauric*, boîte I, dossier 2, chemise 3.

23   *Schrapnellminen*, or S-mines mines were triggered by the pull of a trip wire connected to one of three metal prongs protruding from the ground, the rest of the mine being buried. An explosive charge lifts the mine about a metre off the ground, and then it detonates in the air. The Americans nicknamed it the 'Bouncing Betty.'

24   Béné, *Carnets, Seconde époque*, p.133.

25   Fonds Leclerc, dossier Robédat. This administrative document, which was humorously named in a non-regulatory manner 'Ukase' (meaning 'decree' in Russian) by Dio, was addressed to: *1re DC, GNB*, 12th Company, *CA4*, and *Commandant* Crépin. It confirms the composition of *Groupement D*, which is sometimes presented with a different structure and composition, depending on the work. Subsequently, the *Groupements D* and *V* would undergo profound changes in their composition, depending on the missions entrusted by Leclerc to his two direct subordinates.

26   Fonds Leclerc, dossier Robédat, *note du 11 février 1943, signée par le commandant du groupement D*.

On the afternoon of 15 February, Leclerc, as usual, brought together his key subordinate commanders. He informed them of the upcoming campaign in Tunisia alongside the British 8th Army, which would attack the Mareth Line with armoured units, while *Force L* protected its left flank. This time they would be fighting Germans, who would be more aggressive than the Italians. Everyone would need to respect the directives and instructions given. To conclude, Leclerc discussed his last contacts with the *Armée Française d'Afrique du Nord*. According to him, senior officers were more difficult to win over because 'they won't forgive *Général* de Gaulle for having been right.'[27] In contrast, the NCOs and the troops seemed more willing to fight alongside them.

At mess in the evening, the leaders asked *Lieutenant Colonel* Dio to tell them about the Mareth Line. Having served as a *lieutenant* in the south of Tunisia, he knew the area on which this second Maginot Line had been built between 1936 and 1940 to defend Tunisia against Italian Libya. Unfortunately, like its big sister, this defensive line only covered part of the territory to be defended. It was near the town of Mareth, halfway between Médenine to the south and Gabès to the north and was built on the Matmata Massif. It was 45 kilometres long, and made up of 40 infantry casemates, eight large artillery casemates, and 15 command posts. To delay the advance of the British 8th Army, it had just been rearmed by the *Afrika Korps* with anti-tank and anti-aircraft guns, reinforced with 100,000 anti-tank mines and 70,000 anti-personnel mines. But it did not go as far as the Grand Erg Oriental (the Great Eastern Sand Sea), whose sand dunes were impassable to vehicles. There was a passage left open in the western part of the Mareth Line, near Ksar Rhilane, where it could therefore be bypassed.

By mid-February 1943, *Force L* was ready. The men were eager to grapple with the German troops; although they were anxious, they were itching to measure themselves against the Nazis. Morale was high within *Groupement D*. They had just received 20 days of food and enough fuel to travel 800 kilometres. The first elements of *Force L* left Mizda on February 18. *Groupement D*, bringing up the rear, left in two detachments on 21 and 22 February. The first objective was Nalut, near the Tunisian border, where *Force L* would assemble. They advanced on a real road, and from the start, Dio adopted intervals between vehicles to protect against an aerial attack. The region had become calm again, and the grain fields, vineyards, and fruit trees they passed were reminiscent of the south of France. 2,000 years after the Romans, the Italians returned to this region and managed to rebuild a flourishing agricultural country in just a few years. 'The Arab invasion had made it a desert. The Italians had successfully undertaken to restore it to its ancient splendour.'[28] The column crossed Tripoli at midday without stopping. The city was calm, and the inhabitants waved at the column. For them, the war was over, and they did not seem to complain about it.

On 24 February, *Groupment D* arrived in full at Nalut, a tourist town built on a high cliff, that includes a large underground living area. Located halfway between Tripoli and Ghadamès, its population is predominantly Berber. The vanguard of *Force L* and *Groupement V* had already left Nalut, advancing towards the north. They reached Ksar Rhilane on 22 February. Upon arriving, *Groupement Dio* learnt that on the previous day, six Stukas had attacked *Groupement V* while it was on the move, killing around 15 men.[29] In Nalut, the men of *Groupement D* discovered curious

27 Dronne, *Carnets de Route,* p.203.
28 Dronne, *Carnets de Route,* p.204.
29 Among the dead was the commander of the *Groupe Nomade de l'Ennedi, Capitaine* Orel, who, stationed in Niger at Dirkou, had crossed Niger by camel to reach Chad in 1940. According to *Dr* Mauric, the Germans had found the solution to the sandy soils which reduced the effects of the bombs when they impacted the ground. 'I learnt that the bombs we received …. had a metal rod whose end touched the ground first and triggered the explosion. This technique made the shards level, horizontal.' (Fonds Leclerc, *Souvenirs du Docteur Charles Mauric*). If the Italian planes had bombs like that, they would have caused many more losses

little cars called jeeps, operated by thick-bearded men. It was the small detachment of the Greek *Escadron Sacré* (Sacred Squadron, but usually translated as 'Sacred Band' in English) which came to place itself at Dio's disposal.[30]

On 26 February, *Groupement D* crossed the Tunisian border at Déhibat. Maximum air protection measures were taken during travel, maintaining the distances between vehicles. At the end of the day, the column arrived at the small palm grove of Remada. The men were quite surprised to see that a French flag was flying over the resplendent white military post! They were greeted by a *sergent chef* from the *Armée d'Afrique* wearing a white *seroual* and a light blue kepi leading *goumiers* in blue *burnous*. The bivouac was set up for the night in this small French village. During a link up, the vehicle of *Capitaine* Corlu, commanding the 12th Company, hit a mine. Corlu was wounded and had to be evacuated. Dio appointed *Capitaine* d'Abzac to replace him in command of the company.

On the 27th, they left early for Bir Amir (the red well), 60km away. The well is located at the start of the corridor that extends between the modest Matmata Massif to the east and the ocean of large sand dunes constituting the Grand Erg Oriental to the west. *Général* Leclerc and his CP were there; he waited for *Lieutenant Colonel* Dio so that he could give him his orders. As planned, the 8th Army charged *Force L* with guarding its west flank during its attack on the Mareth Line. To do this, the French had to set up at Ksar Rhilane, to the west of the end of the German defensive system. The Force's primary responsibility was to oppose any German outflanking manoeuvre which could take the British forces from the rear. The *général* reminded Dio of the safety instructions regarding mines, confirming that the region was riddled with them and that British engineers were working to open routes. All units would have to use the cleared and marked routes. Movement would require more time to clear all the vehicles in a column. In addition, in the face of the aerial threat, travel at night was preferred.

Groupement D, in the rearguard, awaited at Bir Amir for its marching orders. They arrived during 2 March. The group's objective was the village of Chermessa via Foum-Tatahouine. Foum-Tatahouine, well known to the Foreign Legion due to the disciplinary battalion it kept there before the war, is a palm grove and crossroads of routes throughout southern Tunisia. Dio knew the region well; he had served there in 1929 in a unit based in Médenine. They progressed slowly, reaching the village of Chermessa at the end of the afternoon. Options for camouflage were limited, so Dio placed his group in the shelter of a hill to the south of Ksar-Hallouf. On 3 March, *Lieutenant Colonel* Dio, escorted by a small detachment of Greeks from the Sacred Band, decided to move ahead of his group to prepare for the reception of the units upon their arrival at Ksar Rhilane. He left command of the group to *Commandant* Poletti. They began movement in the early evening of a dark night, with all lights turned off. They slowed down considerably due to the mines. Suddenly, along the way, a huge explosion sounded. *Médecin Capitaine* Chauliac's truck had hit a *Tellermine*. The truck was unrecoverable, but miraculously there were no injuries reported among the crew members. The *toubib* and his team, like veteran travellers, had taken care at the outset to place sandbags on the floorboards. Still shocked but unhurt, they jumped into another vehicle and progress resumed. It took all night to cover barely 50 kilometres. By the time they reached Ksar Rhilane in the early morning, they were completely exhausted from a night of sleepless tension.

---

in the ranks of French troops during the Fezzan 1 and Fezzan 2 campaigns.

30   This squadron consisted of a cadre of officers under the orders of *Syntagmatarchis* (Colonel) Christodoulos Tsigantes. This 'great friend of France, graduate of our École de Guerre…had also fought in the ranks of the French Army during the First World War.' (Béné, *Carnets, Seconde époque*, p.137). They reformed the unit that had been created in 371 BCE, by 300 young Theban patriots to defend ancient Greece. Like their glorious ancestors, the men of this 'Sacred Band' were fierce fighters, not hesitating to sacrifice themselves when the mission required it.

Dio welcomed his men and, without delay, took the unit commanders with him to reconnoitre the different assigned locations. It was important for the coherence of a defensive system that each unit understand its position relative to the others. Next, the group commander took his subordinates forward of the positions that had just been assigned to them. It was also essential for them to see what the enemy could see when they arrived at the positions. Ksar Rhilane is 'a wide, shallow basin of sand and rock, slightly undulating, where a few scattered tufts of grass and a few thorny bushes grow. It is the obligatory crossing point between the Grand Erg and the mountain, at the point where the Mareth Line stops. The Germans let this important strategic location be taken by Leclerc. It is obvious that they will try to take it back.'[31]

The Romans had already perceived the importance of Ksar Rhilane, the easternmost of the Tunisian oases, and they had built a post to control it. Vague remains still bear witness to their tactical sense. This is why it was called *ksar* ('castle' in Arabic). In the past, there must have been a small town. Today, nothing remains. The sand has covered everything. Dio and his subordinates noticed a lot of activity at the position. The units of *Groupement V* were setting up and digging in[32] their vehicles with picks and shovels. There was no time to waste because the vanguard of *Force L* had been in increasing contact with the Germans in recent days. *The Afrika Korps* was in the process of concentrating significant resources in Wadi Hallouf (meaning 'wadi of pigs,' or more precisely of wild boars) about 40 kilometres from Ksar Rhilane. The defensive system adopted by Leclerc was an arc, with its back to the dunes of the Grand Erg. Thus, the enemy could not outflank it from the north or the south, the sand prohibiting any movement of vehicles. The Germans would therefore be forced into a frontal assault. An element of the *1re* DC, reinforced by Greek jeeps, patrolled to the front of the defensive system, monitoring all the northern outlets as far as Djebel Outid, 30km away. The units making up the arc-shaped system of Ksar Rhilane, spread out from north to south over approximately two kilometres, were in order: the 12th Company, the *GNE*, the 2nd Company, the *GNB*, the *2e DC*, and the *GNT*. The artillery was to the rear of the lines with the command post.

Dio familiarised himself with the system on 4 March. He had the opportunity to read, at the end of 1942, the lessons of the Battle of Bir Hakeim. He knew that the infantrymen of the *1re Division Française Libre* were able to hold out for several days against German planes and armour by undertaking a significant amount of work moving dirt. Men and vehicles had to be literally buried to be protected from the deluge of fire that was sure to fall on them. Only the heavy weapons were elevated to ground level.

Camouflage was essential so the enemy could not surround the defensive position. Dio had confidence in his crews, which had become experts at blending into the desert. It took an enormous amount of work for the crews to dig vehicular fighting positions in stony and rocky terrain like that of Ksar Rhilane. Fortunately, British sappers provided valuable assistance, particularly in the rocky areas, which had to be dynamited. The men clearly understood what was at stake: 'for the desert runners ... riding in trucks that were on their last legs, poorly equipped, poorly armed, an engagement against the armoured vehicles of the *Afrika Korps* represented an adventure of a new dimension. A wager. A gamble.'[33] Thus, the days of 5 to 7 March were exclusively devoted to defensive work. The defences of each position were refined. Dio advised those who were in the sandy areas to support the walls of their fighting position with sand removal panels from the vehicles.

---

31 Dronne, *Carnets de Route,* p.213.

32 'Digging in.' The French verb 'embosser' means to moor a ship in such a way as to hold it in a specific direction. In the army, it suggests digging vehicles in below the level of the ground to protect them from the effects of artillery while allowing them to fire facing a very specific direction. (Translator's note)

33 Jacob, François, *La Statue Intérieure* (Paris: Éditions Odile Jacob, 1987), p.147.

Twice a day, at 10:00 a.m. and 3:00 p.m., a small enemy reconnaissance plane, a Fieseler *Storch*, flew over the entire area, attempting to identify the position of *Force L*. When it did, the instructions were to stop moving. On 8 March, an NCO who was monitoring the area with binoculars, noticed two men and a donkey at the bottom of a distant wadi. Dio sent out one of his four Greek jeeps, and the two men, two Arabs, fled as they approached. They were immediately shot down with machine guns. The donkey was loaded down with a pack full of *Tellerminen*. The two Arabs were laying mines. 'Now we understand why our cars are hit in places where they passed without incident the day before.'[34]

During the day, Dio was informed that the *général* was departing in a Bedford, having been summoned to Montgomery's CP. The sounds of combat resonated in the distance: it was the vanguard of the *1re DC* and the Greeks who were harassing the German positions beyond Djebel Outid. Leclerc returned in the afternoon of 9 March in the Lysander plane that Montgomery had made available to him. The *général* immediately summoned his three key subordinates: *Colonel* Ingold, *Lieutenant Colonel* Dio, and *Commandant* Vézinet. He sent everyone else out of the CP. First, he told them that Rommel was ill and had left Tunisia the day before. *Generaloberst* Hans-Jürgen von Arnim was commanding the troops of the *Afrika Korps*, and the Italian *Generale* Giovanni Messe remained the commander of the Tunisian theatre. Next, he told them that British intelligence anticipated a German attack on Ksar Rhilane the next day. The enemy force, made up of 60 armoured vehicles and as many trucks, was grouped at Wadi Hallouf. Montgomery advised Leclerc to fall back on Bir Amir, waging a mobile defensive battle. But the French *général* countered, recommending that he stay put. Leclerc knew that his defensive positions at Ksar Rhilane were completely prepared, and withdrawing across such terrain against Messerschmitts and Stukas could prove dangerous. Montgomery, having in mind the pugnacity of the French who had held the defensive position at Bir Hakeim, acquiesced to Leclerc's arguments. Leclerc only asked for priority of support from the Royal Air Force during the attack. Concluding the meeting, Leclerc directed his three subordinates not to inform anyone about the next day's fight. 'He wanted the men to sleep peacefully and be fresh and ready when the shock came.'[35] They would let them know at dawn. Dio agreed with his opinion. The advance guards deployed to the north of the position would prevent any surprises during the night.

On 10 March 1943, the day of the German attack, Dio had the men of his group woken around 4:00 a.m. He told his subordinates that a German motorised armoured group was going to attack them that morning. Everyone had to be at their combat post, taking measures to ensure that they were all supplied with enough water and food to spend the day without moving. The orders were clear: 'resist in place. Open fire only on orders from the *général*.'[36] The tension grew. At 6:20 a.m., the sounds of combat clearly reached the men of *Force L* waiting at Ksar Rhilane. The *1re DC* under Capitaine Savelli fell back in front of around 40 German armoured vehicles advancing towards the south. It was the reconnaissance group (*Aufklärung Abteilung*) 'of *Major* Luck, which had been reinforced with a company of tanks from the *15. Panzerdivision*, a company of 75 *PAK* guns, and a section of two 100mm mortars.'[37] The withdrawal of *Force L*'s vanguard was conducted in good order.

Around 7:00 a.m. the German armoured vehicles came within sight. They headed north of *Force L*'s position, facing the 12th Company, advancing slowly and accompanied by infantry. The armoured vehicles fired at random, seeking a response that would reveal the French

34   Dronne, *Carnets de Route*, p.216.
35   Girard, *Journal de Guerre*, p.50.
36   Béné, *Carnets, Seconde Époque*, p.152.
37   Vincent, *Les Forces Françaises Libres en Afrique*, p.322.

positions. Dio assessed the lead elements, 1,500 metres from d'Abzac's men, who would receive the force of the attack. At that moment, a wave of 30 Junkers 87s ('Stukas') flew over, strafing and bombing. Most of the bombs fell to the rear of the well-buried vehicles. The anti-aircraft weapons remained silent. The Germans on the ground were concerned not to find any opposition in front of them. They hesitated and moved in small bounds, sensing a trap. Leclerc waited until the last moment so that opening fire caused as much damage as possible not only to the armoured vehicles but also to the infantry who accompanied them. 'Finally, the order came by radio – short, brutal, just one word, 'fire.' All the guns, the 75s, the howitzer, the Bofors – ours and those of the British – the 2-pounders, the Italian 47s, the mortars, the automatic weapons began to roar. Our shells hit the mark.'[38]

Just a few minutes after the fire broke out, it was the RAF's turn to take action. Around 40 British aircraft attacked the German armour and infantry who were in the open. Vehicles burst into flames in an indescribable commotion. The first *Afrika Korps* offensive on the northern position was stopped by 8:00 a.m. The Germans retreated, taking their dead and wounded with them. Dio fumed about not having armoured vehicles. He could have exploited the German withdrawal and turned it into a rout. But the 'soap boxes' (the name given by the *tirailleurs* to their trucks) that they had, as well as the Greeks with their jeeps, were no match. Leclerc and Dio believed there was more to come. The enemy, having stumbled to the north of the position, would try to get at it from another direction.

Leclerc, faithful to his tactic of never standing idly by, sent *Lieutenant* Bagneux's patrol to the south of the positions. The patrol was attacked by German troops who, taking advantage of the terrain, infiltrated towards the southern position of *Capitaine* Sarazac's *GNT.* Crépin's artillery had just enough time to turn its guns in their direction. As had happened earlier in the morning, the ground attack was preceded by the attack of around 10 Stukas. The Germans advanced quickly, and their first vehicles entered Sarazac's defences. The situation was becoming critical. Once again the RAF planes appeared. The British Air Support Officer attached to Leclerc's CP brought in air support right on time. Half a dozen armoured vehicles were hit and exploded, and once more, the Germans turned back.

It was noon. The Germans quickly got back into order and stubbornly tried to overcome the resistance from the *Gaullisten.* Having failed in the north and south, they concentrated their attack on the centre of the French defences. It was the *GNB*'s turn to receive the brunt of the attack. Dio had just relayed the order to them to defend in position. At 3:30 p.m., the assault was once again preceded by a German aerial bombardment which, although not effective, forced the defenders to keep their heads down, which allowed the German armoured vehicles to approach. A German armoured car penetrated into the *GNB*'s defence but was stopped with a grenade. German infantry approached. The fight was heading for a bayonet assault when, suddenly, the British planes with their red, white, and blue roundels rushed towards the Germans in the open, once again inflicting heavy losses. The defenders had regained the upper hand with the intervention of the British planes and exerted a hellish fire on the Germans who had no solution but to withdraw, leaving their dead and numerous burning armoured vehicles behind.

Although the ground fight had stopped, a formidable fighter duel took place in the sky between the British Spitfires and the German Messerschmitt 109s.[39] The French soldiers emerged from their holes and applauded the exploits of their Allied comrades every time a German plane fell or exploded in mid-flight. The aerial combat lasted until 6:00 p.m. At nightfall, the men of *Force L*

---

38   Dronne, *Carnets de Route*, p.218.
39   John Watson and Louis Jones, *3 Squadron* at *War* (D.A.F. Squadron Association, Carlingford, New South Wales, 1959), p.122. NB other sources give the British aircraft as Curtis Tomahawks.

were proud of the victorious day, particularly those of *Groupement D* who had twice received the main attack from enemy armour. Leclerc and Dio were beaming: their first fight against the Germans had ended in victory. The two officers were naturally more inclined towards the offensive, but they had just proven that they also knew how to defend. 'The position had been prepared and organised in a remarkable way, with the swinging of shovels and picks. Sweat saves blood.'[40] Leclerc immediately wrote an Order of the Day for his troops:

> The *Boches* wanted to take Ksar Rhilane. They attacked with around 50 armoured vehicles. The troops of Chad, assisted by their British and Greek comrades, inflicted a clear defeat on them and caused them to suffer serious losses. The first contact with the *Boche* was a victory, the others will be too. *Vive Général* de Gaulle! *Vive la France!*[41]

The same evening, at 10:00 p.m., Leclerc was proud to show Dio, Ingold, and Vézinet a short message from Montgomery, saying 'well done,' and ending with 'bravo.' The French had held out without falling apart or panicking, but three times, *Force L* was saved by the last-minute intervention of the RAF. *Capitaine* Sarazac acknowledged that by saying: '*Force L* owed its salvation only to the repeated intervention of the RAF. Otherwise, it would have been our total destruction, which is what the Germans were looking for.'[42] The grateful Frenchmen tried to find out about the aviators who had got them out of difficult situations. They learnt, thanks to the British who were with them, that three units had intervened, two English and one Australian. The RAF's 112 Squadron, responsible for protecting ground attack aircraft against German fighters, was equipped with Spitfires. They were the ones who, at the end of the evening of 10 March, put on the spectacle of a gigantic aerial battle against the German Messerschmitt 109s. Two types of planes attacked the *Afrika Korps*. The British tank buster Hurricanes of 450 Squadron targeted the tanks, whose armour they penetrated with their twin 40mm cannon. The Australian Curtis P40 Kittyhawks of 3 Squadron mainly took care of the lightly armoured cars and trucks. Australian Kittyhawk pilots were renowned for their boldness. Their highly manoeuvrable aircraft allowed them to get as close as possible to their target, leaving him no chance. One pilot, Arthur Dawkins, attacked a large truck located at the rear of the German formation at the end of the day. He was so close to his target when it exploded that he passed through a cloud of debris. His plane seemed to be hit and was only able to reach his airfield with difficulty. Once back on the ground, the pilot was surprised to discover that his air intakes were completely blocked by razor blades! Dawkins deduced that he had destroyed a truck from the German PX.[43] Another Australian pilot attacked a fuel truck so low that the blast damaged the tail of his plane and forced him to make an emergency landing.

The victory of Ksar Rhilane proved decisive for the rest of the fighting in Tunisia. Not only did it prevent the enemy from flanking the 8th Army as intended, but 10 days later it would allow the 8th Army to bypass the Mareth Line through this same passage where it had stopped the Germans. Montgomery later presented Leclerc to King George VI, with, 'it is thanks to him that I was able to take the Mareth Line.'

Dio was very satisfied with the day. Having asked his immediate subordinates for a situation update at the beginning of the evening, he realised that his losses were relatively low considering the fighting they had endured. Only *Sergent* Vigouroux of the *GNB* and his two *tirailleurs* had been killed while fighting a German armoured vehicle. During the final attack, *Capitaine* Dronne

40   Dronne, *Carnets de Route,* p.223.
41   Ingold, F., *Ceux de Leclerc en Tunisie,* p.33.
42   Béné, *Carnets, Seconde époque,* p.158.
43   The PX, or post exchange, is a small store where soldiers can obtain small personal items.

was seriously injured by British planes while trying to signal the position of the French lines to them using flags.

Freed of any threat on his flank, Montgomery attacked the Mareth Line on 12 March. Heavy fighting took place for several days. The casemates, built by the French before 1940, resisted both artillery shelling and British air attacks. The British attack was beginning to stall. So, Leclerc suggested to Montgomery that he outflank the Mareth Line through the Ksar Rhilane Passage, which he still held. The German defensive line would crumble if it were bypassed. Convinced, Montgomery then asked Leclerc to facilitate the breakthrough of General Freyberg's New Zealand Army Corps. The Germans held Djebel Outid, 30km north of Ksar Rhilane, and had mined the access points. The French therefore had to take this massif, which the Germans used as an observation post and a fixing point. *Groupement D* was designated for this mission, which consisted of seizing Djebel Outid and then covering the right flank of the New Zealand Army Corps during its attack. The group's composition was modified to account for the nature of the mission as well as the availability of men and materiel.[44]

Groupement D departed Ksar Rhilane on 19 March at 1:00 a.m. The night was clear, and progress was easy. Throughout the journey, the men could see the losses suffered by the Germans on 10 March. On either side of the road, charred armoured vehicles, trucks, and artillery pieces were abandoned. Shortly before 2:00 a.m., while crossing Wadi Bel-Krecheb, one of the vehicles got stuck in the sand. The crews dismounted to put metal sheets under the wheels while others went off to satisfy the call of nature. In quick succession, two explosions rang out. The dismounted elements triggered two 'bouncing bettys.' The toll was heavy, seven dead in total.[45] Dio shouted his anger loudly into the night because he hated losing men that way. He was furious at them for not having been able to anticipate the Machiavellianism of the Germans, who had obviously anticipated that the vehicles would get stuck in the sand while crossing the wadi, and then mined it with *Schrapnellminen*. He gave very firm orders prohibiting anyone from dismounting without his approval.

Progress cautiously resumed and vehicles drove in the tracks of those to their front. The column arrived at a small pass overlooking an immense wadi behind which stood Djebel Outid. With his subordinates around him, Dio explained his tactical manoeuvre on a map unfolded on the hood of his vehicle. Given the configuration of the rocky massif to be seized, he decided to attack it simultaneously with two detachments, one predominantly armoured detachment from the west and the other with infantry from the east. It was 5:00 a.m. when the units assembled in their designated areas. The attack would begin precisely at 6:00 a.m. Crépin deployed his artillery pieces slightly behind the pass. Everything unfolded just as in training: no excitement, no shouting, everyone in their place knowing what they had to do. Dio had gained experience and perfectly controlled

---

44   Dio took under his orders:
  the *GNT*, still commanded by Sarazac who, although wounded at Ksar Rhilane, wanted to remain at his post,
  the 2nd Company of the *RTST* under the orders of *Capitaine* Wagner,
  the armoured car squadron under the orders of *Capitaine* Savelli,
  an artillery detachment under the orders of *Commandant* Crépin, including the 25pdr battery, the two 75mm mountain guns, reinforced with 5½-inch British guns and the half battery of 6pdrs from the 73rd Anti-Tank Regiment,
  a detachment of the Flying Column, composed of two armoured car platoons with *Lieutenant* Troquereau and *Capitaine* Divry's tank company.
  a small detachment of British engineers,
  four jeeps from the Greek Sacred Band.

45   The dead were: *Lieutenants* Gué (RTST) and Colin (*RMSM*), *Adjudant Chefs* Urbani and Morellou, and *Spahis* Bonnard, Romano, and Savary.

the command of the combined arms group. The amalgamation took place spontaneously within the group, not only with the *spahis* but also with the foreign detachment commanders. The group had an air support vehicle that Dio positioned alongside his vehicle. Ever since the battles at Ksar Rhilane, everyone understood the benefit of excellent coordination with the RAF Hurricanes and RAAF Kittyhawks.

Suddenly, several explosions were heard in the distance, and then a few seconds later, more explosions – even closer – rang out in front of Dio's and Crépin's position. The German artillery began firing, having undoubtedly spotted the group's preparations for attack. Immediately an artillery duel began. Crépin calmly gave his orders to the different detachments under his command.

The attack began at 6:00 a.m., as planned. Dio requested fighters above his position to prevent the Germans from sending their Stukas after his tanks and infantry, who were climbing the rocky massif in the open. Progress was difficult but uninterrupted on each side of the massif. Around 8:00 a.m. the first infantry reached the top of the massif. 'The Germans, in order to avoid the risk of being completely surrounded, withdrew from the *djebel*.'[46] *Groupement D* held Djebel Outid and sent patrols towards the north to secure the German defensive system. The path was clear for Lieutenant General Bernard Freyberg's New Zealand Army Corps, which could launch the 2nd New Zealand Division, the 8th Armoured Brigade, the 1st King's Dragoon Guards, and three artillery regiments towards El-Hamma, a town about 30 kilometres west of Gabès. Montgomery wanted to encircle the elements of the *Afrika Korps* holding the Mareth Line. A speed race was underway. *Général* Leclerc's aide-de-camp wrote: 'We left Ksar-Rhilane …. mixed with the New Zealand Army Corps which was rushing from south to north. It was a huge bullfight. Hundreds of trucks were driving at full speed on several parallel tracks.'[47] By quickly taking the natural linchpin of Djebel Outid, Dio and his group allowed Montgomery to launch his encirclement manoeuvre. Once again, the role of the French was decisive.

Leclerc came under the orders of General Freyberg, commanding the New Zealand Army Corps. Leclerc's mission was as a flank guard for the corps, to the east with *Groupement D* and to the west with *Groupement V*. From 20 to 23 March, *Groupement D* matched the speed of the corps while protecting it on its right flank. Crépin received artillery reinforcements. The mission was going smoothly. Evidently, the *Afrika Korps* understood what Montgomery was doing and decided to withdraw. Only the *Luftwaffe* periodically attacked Allied units to hinder their progress. The group's anti-aircraft artillery, with its Bofors, managed to shoot down a Stuka in the evening of 22 March, causing an immense clamour in the ranks of the group's soldiers.

Freyberg's corps advanced to the south of the Matleb massif. This *djebel*, located southwest of Gabès, overlooks the two axes leading west towards El-Hamma and east along the coast towards Gabès. Its summit is located on Hill 354. The massif blocked the New Zealand Army Corps' advance. So Leclerc proposed, and Montgomery agreed, to take the key position with the units of *Force L*. In truth, the French *général* was disappointed at having only been employed as a flank guard, which was more of a secondary security mission. He wanted to prove to the British the tenacity and operational value of the Free French. *Groupement V* was designated to seize Hill 354 with an infantry attack. The *RTST tirailleurs* and their officers demonstrated their courage by attacking uphill into hand-to-hand combat. During the fighting, *Capitaine* d'Abzac was shot in the forehead and killed. As with the other colonial officers, he wore his garrison cap to lead the assault. He certainly became too easy a target for German snipers. Since Kufra, the colonial officers of Chad had, like Dio, distinguished themselves by going into combat wearing that hat,

---

46   Béné, *Carnets, Seconde époque*, p.163.
47   Girard, *Journal de Guerre*, p.51.

which was typically reserved for ceremonies. Leclerc himself respected this somewhat crazy eccentricity displayed by his colonials. In Gatroun, Dio had his kepi pierced by a bullet. D'Abzac, an audacious young officer who had accompanied him in all the battles since 1941, did not have the same luck on Hill 354. Once the Matleb was taken by *Groupement Vézinet*, Freyberg's corps could then launch its attack towards El-Hamma and Gabès.

Groupement D still had the mission of guarding the New Zealanders' flank. On 29 March in the middle of the afternoon, Dio entered Gabès, shortly after the New Zealanders, 'to the warm welcome of the people.'[48] Gabès was the first major French city liberated with the participation of the Free French. 'The welcome in Gabès is the welcome of liberated France to Frenchmen who, only a few days earlier, fought for this deliverance …. the city is suddenly covered with tricolour flags.'[49] Dio's men did not suspect then that they would experience such scenes of popular jubilation later and throughout their epic advance until 1945. On Sunday, 4 April, Dio and Leclerc attended a mass organised by the city in tribute to the soldiers who had died to liberate it. Leclerc's men were moved to see that 'the young singers in the church choir all wore a small Cross of Lorraine on their white tunics.'[50]

The Mareth Line had fallen. The British wanted to attack towards the north as quickly as possible so as not to give the Italo-German troops time to organise themselves on another defensive line. Tunis was still 310km away as the crow flies. Montgomery launched his attack on the night of 5/6 April with Mezzouna as his objective. *Force L* had come under the command of Lieutenant General Brian Horrocks' British X Corps and was responsible for the flank guard on the west of the 8th Army. The *RMSM* led *Force L* with the two *groupements* behind it in support. On 9 April, the *spahis*[51] of *Chef d'Escadron* Roumiantzoff, upgraded with Crusader medium tanks, 'whose French crews wear black berets,'[52] seized Mezzouna with the British. 'The enemy only fought a delaying operation with small all-arms detachments, relying on a large network of mines.'[53]

During this dynamic phase, small detachments were formed from the two groups that occasionally intervened against points of enemy resistance. On the Bedour Pass, southwest of Fatnassa, *Capitaine* Troadec neutralised a German section on 9 April. The same day, Roumiantzoff's detachment occupied the crossroads of the Sfax-Sbeitla road. On 10 April 1943, *Groupement Dio* and *Groupement Vézinet* relieved a British armoured division in the Djebel Korj Massif north of Fatnassa and set up a defence there. Dio remained on site for 48 hours, allowing the group to rest, maintain its weapons, and repair its equipment. On the 12th, he resumed his advance and entered Kairouan, the religious capital of Tunisia, behind Morel-Deville's squadron of *spahis*.

On 13 April, *Général* Leclerc assembled *Force L* near El-Alem, 10 kilometres north of Kairouan. '*Force L*, still subordinate to the 4th Light Armoured Brigade, must engage in Djebel Fadeloun, between Sidi Nadji and Enfidaville.'[54] The region is dominated by Djebel Garci, which was firmly held by the Germans. This massif, several peaks of which exceed 400 metres, is one of the strong points on which the Italo-Germans rebuilt a defensive line near Djebel Zaghouan.

To capture Djebel Garci, Montgomery asked Leclerc to accompany the 4th Indian Division's attack. *Groupement Dio* was tasked with seizing one of the intermediate peaks of the massif, Hill

48   Vincent, *Les Forces Françaises Libres en Afrique*, p.326.
49   Ingold, F., *Ceux de Leclerc en Tunisie*, p.49.
50   Béné, *Carnets, Seconde Époque*, p.180.
51   These cavalrymen, who were part of the Flying Column, constituted the first tank company of Free France which had fought in Norway, Gabon, and at El Alamein, most recently in the Médenine region. It would form the core of the future *501e Régiment des Chars de Combat* of the *2e DB*.
52   Béné, *Carnets, Seconde Époque*, p.183.
53   Vincent, *Les Forces Françaises Libres en Afrique*, p.327.
54   Vincent, *Les Forces Françaises Libres en Afrique*, p.328.

121. The group was made up of seasoned infantry units, namely the *2ᵉ DC*, and the 2nd and 12th Companies of the *RTST*. The formation Dio adopted for the attack was triangular, with the base forward: the 2nd Company and the *2ᵉ DC* in the lead, with the 12th Company in support. At 10:30 p.m., on the night of 19/20 April, Dio's infantry began their mission towards the summit, silhouetted against the moon. Progress was relatively discreet, and the enemy did not seem to have detected it. Suddenly, 500 metres from the objective, a green rocket from the enemy positions rose into the sky, followed by an artillery barrage. The *tirailleurs* picked up their pace despite the explosions surrounding them. Automatic weapons began to fire. To encourage the attackers, 'a long 'oulouhoulou,' soon echoed by all the *tirailleurs* of the forward units, as well as by the unit in the second echelon' could be heard.[55] The war cries terrified the German defenders, who abandoned their position. Dio's men secured the objective and established a hasty defence to repel possible enemy counterattacks. Unfortunately, the Indian division only partially succeeded in securing the objectives assigned to it, putting the French in a difficult situation. The French position was harassed by incessant artillery fire, forcing the men to quickly dig in once again. Dio obtained reinforcements: 'anti-tank guns and British 25pdr batteries, Rogez's mountain battery of 75s, a section from the *GNE*, and, on the 24th, a section of tanks from Rémy's squadron, and British liaison and observer teams.'[56] The enemy clung to their positions and firmly held their line of defence.

The 8th Army and *Force L* could not advance any further. From Libya, they had just carried out an offensive of several hundred kilometres over difficult terrain. Men and equipment were running out of steam. General Alexander, commanding officer of the British 18th Army Group, became aware of this. To seize Tunis, he decided to outflank this last line of resistance from the west, in concert with the Americans. The 8th Army remained as a fixing point in front of the enemy German defence. On Djebel Garci, *Groupement Dio* received orders to maintain contact with the enemy. Dio could not fall back, and harassment fire caused losses in the French ranks. From 20 to 27 April, Dio lost 6 men killed and 31 wounded. Despite the extreme fatigue of his men, he managed to maintain morale in the ranks. He regularly visited the positions to chat and share a ration with the men. He took steps to improve the food supply. He learnt that the *1ʳᵉ Division Française Libre* with the *BM4* and *BM5* of the 1st Brigade was on his right.[57]

On 6 May 1943, Operation VULCAN was launched, the British 1st Army attacked in the direction of Medjez-el-Bab to Tunis, bypassing the Italo-German defensive system on Djebel Zaghouan. As he had done in Tripoli, Leclerc insisted that Chadian troops be present during the first hours of the capture of the Tunisian capital. On the evening of 8 May 1943, Tunis was liberated by the 19th French Army Corps from Algeria. 'Leclerc believes it would be cruelly unfair if the flag with the Cross of Lorraine was not immediately present in this French-speaking capital of North Africa.'[58] He immediately sent a detachment of 10 vehicles of *tirailleurs* under Ingold's orders. Largely flanking from the west, they reached Tunis on the morning of the 10th. They were 'welcomed with enthusiasm by the Tunisian population, who shouted as they passed: '*Vive* de Gaulle! *Vive les Sénégalais!*''[59]

The fighting in Tunis was over for all the belligerents, but the same was not true at Djebel Garci. The Axis forces still held their positions against the 8th Army and *Force L*. The Italian

---

55   Ingold, *Ceux de Leclerc,* p.70.
56   Ingold, *Ceux de Leclerc,* p.71.
57   Serving in *BM4* was the young *Sous Lieutenant* Robédat, who had his baptism of fire at Takrouna alongside *Groupement Dio*. However, he and Dio would not know each other until much later (Testimony of Colonel Pierre Robédat in 2019).
58   Béné, *Carnets, Seconde Époque,* p.199.
59   Ingold, *Ceux de Leclerc,* p.74.

generalissimo, Giovanni Messe, commanding the forces in Tunisia, did not sign the capitulation until 12 May. And it was not until the next morning that Dio received the flash message from General Alexander announcing, 'the unconditional capitulation of the Axis troops with an immediate cessation of fighting.'[60] This end of the fight delighted everyone, particularly the British units attached to the French. Colonel GBS Hindley, Commanding the Royal Artillery's 73rd Anti-Tank Regt, New Zealand,[61] fully attached to *Force L* since 1 April 1943, and having fought with *Groupement D*, 'confidentially asked his general to henceforth be attached 'to people who fear God.' It was wonderful praise, in a humorous form, of valorous French warriors.'[62]

For *Groupement Dio*, it was the end of a positional warfare that they disliked. 'This kind of positional warfare, fixed in our positions, obviously did not suit the troops of Chad.'[63] The various units still had to participate in the disarmament and internment of 2,000 Italian and German prisoners in their sector before being able to descend Djebel Garci on 14 May. Dio and his men then moved south to *Force L*'s assembly area, in a green valley near Djebel Fadeloun. The units were temporarily set up among the olive trees. In the short term, everyone benefited from this unusual calm. Since December 1942, the men had been engaged in the battles of liberation for Fezzan and then Tunisia. The tension was constant. The road was long: 'a nice trek from Largeau: 3,600 kilometres' according to the odometers of the old Bedfords.[64] They all enjoyed a well-deserved rest after 5 uninterrupted months of tension. The atmosphere became happy and relaxed again, but Leclerc and his immediate subordinates remained attentive to their future concerns. They knew very well that a page had just been turned. What would the future of *Force L* be? What should they do with this composite operational unit whose particular structures were no longer suited to a traditional military unit? The operational organisation into *groupements* no longer had any reason to exist. What role would *Général* de Gaulle give to *Général* Leclerc in the continuation of the fight for liberation? The African Continent had just been completely liberated, but France was still occupied. The Oath of Kufra had set a goal: 'Strasbourg. For those in Chad this was the essence of their mission. Their goal. Sacred. They lived, they suffered, they were ready to die to keep the famous oath, launched in Kufra by 'the boss,' *Général* Leclerc.'[65]

Dio and his men knew they would experience a new phase. But they did not know what it would be. Personally, Dio was rewarded for the Tunisian campaign with a division-level citation: 'Perfectly led his group in the attack and capture of an enemy position, asserting once again during this action, his value as a leader and his personal qualities of bravery.'[66]

60 Béné, *Carnets, Seconde Époque*, p.201.
61 Corbonnois, *L'Odyssée de la Colonne Leclerc*, p.168.
62 Giraud, *Leclerc*, p.45.
63 Béné, *Carnets, Seconde Époque*, p.194.
64 Chauvet, *Le Sable et la Neige*, p.237.
65 Bergot, *La 2 ème D.B.*, p.15.
66 SHD, Dio, 14 Yd 1759, ESS.

Chapter 7

Sabratha-Djidjelli, 16 May to 15 October 1943

On 16 May 1943, at the end of the long and hard fighting that had ended three days earlier, *Lieutenant Colonel* Dio was in Tunisia with all the units of *Force L*, at the foot of Djebel Fadeloun, 30 kilometres north of the town of Kairouan. The men were exhausted from sleepless nights, the condition of their food, and above all by the nervous tension. They had been in action since the end of 1942. Although the men were taking advantage of the much-needed period of rest, Leclerc and his immediate subordinates could not afford to relax. They had decisions to make concerning their future, especially as relations with *Général* Giraud deteriorated. Giraud, a 5-star *général d'armée*, commanding the troops in North Africa, was favoured by the Americans, particularly President Roosevelt. They did not want to hear about de Gaulle, a mere 2-star *général de brigade*[1] who was very protective of French sovereignty, refusing 'any foreign interference in purely French affairs.'[2] Leclerc held *Général* Giraud in esteem and was thus disappointed by the turn of events. Giraud was acting in a petty manner because 'his arguments are based only on vanity – 'I am the only leader because I am the most senior.''[3] *Général* Leclerc often confided in Dio, Guillebon, and Vézinet. He told them about his conversations with de Gaulle and Larminat, and he did not hesitate to ask them for their opinion. He informed them on 14 June of de Gaulle's decision to transform *Force L* into the *2ᵉ Division Française Libre* (*2ᵉ DFL*), 'a very pompous name for the meritorious *Force L*.'[4] Indeed, *Force L* represented only a brigade in terms of strength,[5] only one-third of a division. Leclerc asked Ingold, who was based in a building in Tunis, to recruit volunteers. The fame of the Chadian troops was beginning to be known in Tunisia and many young Frenchmen wanted to join the Free French.

On the 17th, through British channels, the units of *Force L* learnt that a major victory parade was being organised for 20 May. All units that participated in the Tunisian campaign, French (both the *Armée d'Afrique* and Free French) and foreign (UK, US, and Greek), would parade through the streets of Tunis. Dio's men greeted the news with enthusiasm; they immediately began to clean their vehicles and to pull their uniforms out of their footlockers. 'The *tirailleurs* cleaned their Sunday

---

1 In the French system, the insignia of rank for a *général d'armée* is 5 stars, which is the equivalent of a US 4-star general. American leadership defaulted to Giraud, who was much more senior in rank to de Gaulle. Giraud had been captured by the Germans in 1940, escaped, and returned to France. He remained loyal to Pétain after his return, but later agreed to support the Allied invasion of North Africa, at first demanding to be the overall Allied commander before finally agreeing to serve as commander of French forces under Eisenhower's overall command. (Translator's note)

2 Béné, *Carnets, Seconde époque*, p.216.

3 Girard, *Journal de Guerre*, p.66.

4 Notin, *le Croisé*, p.204.

5 A division is usually made up of three brigades comprising approximately 4,000 to 5,000 men each.

chechias and carefully folded their red belts.[6] Unfortunately, the euphoria was short-lived. On 19 May, Giraud's staff decided at the last moment that the parade of French troops would take place on foot in ranks of nine. That type of military parade requires a lot of rehearsals to be done well. Given that requirement, Leclerc justifiably refused outright to participate. Finally, a compromise was found with the help of the British. *Force L* would participate in the motorised parade reserved for foreign troops, but would be limited to 20 vehicles, only two crews at most per company and service. *Commandant* Vézinet was appointed to lead the representation. Dio convinced Leclerc to allow a volunteer cadre in dress uniform to attend this parade, scheduled for the beginning of the afternoon. Packed into two Ford trucks to make the 100 kilometres separating them from Tunis, they left on the morning of 20th. 'We were dropped off around noon in front of the recruitment office set up since 9 May by *Colonel* Ingold.'[7] The officers of *Force L*, dressed in British uniforms, were not welcomed as they expected by the population. They were stared at politely without being recognised as French. They anonymously attended the imposing parade opened by a large contingent of more than 4,000 men from the North African troops,[8] then the American and finally the British. The British were considerate enough to have their contingent in the parade led by the 20 vehicles representing the troops of Chad and the Flying Column. 'After an hour and a half of infantry, our good old long-range reconnaissance and combat vehicles appeared. They were a big hit. Loud cries of *Vive de Gaulle* rose as they passed.'[9] *Sergent* Michel Chauvet was one of the spectators. After the parade on foot, he saw 'our vehicles arrive, shabby, bullet holes everywhere, making a noise like scrap metal, equipped with various weapons. Not a single soldier had the same uniform, but this is when the crowd went wild, where they sang the *Marseillaise*. This parade is our reward in front of these people who offer their thanks to us.'[10] *Général* Giraud presided over the parade from the official stand along Boulevard Gambetta where the parade took place. The British General Alexander and the American General Eisenhower were at his side, surrounded by numerous other French and Allied generals. The Free French, in third place, were represented by *Générals* de Larminat, Koenig, and Leclerc. Only Larminat remained for the lunch that followed. The Free French leaders who came to attend the parade were disappointed by their exchanges with their counterparts from the *Armée d'Afrique* when leaving Tunis. 'We had just realised that here we were not considered as liberators; if anything [we were seen as] Frenchmen in English clothes.'[11]

Lieutenant Colonel Dio did not want to attend this parade. He knew Tunis. But mostly he was very disappointed with the turn of events in recent days. While Nazi Germany had just suffered its second great defeat after Stalingrad, why could the French not unite? He did not understand the position of the *Armée d'Afrique* and especially of its commander, *Général* Giraud who, supported by the Americans, would not agree to join the Gaullist movement. Would all the efforts made over the past 3 years, all the deaths suffered in their ranks, be thrown away by personal conflicts? Rather than going to see the parade, Dio preferred, at Leclerc's request, to prepare the movement of the new division to Hergla, south of Enfidaville. The area is located on the coast, in the Gulf of Hammamet, 50 kilometres north of Sousse. Dio no longer held an operational command, becoming a staff officer once again. The units of his group were returned to the orders of the *capitaines* commanding them.

On 21 May, the new *2ᵉ DFL* moved a dozen kilometres away to settle in Hergla with no problems. The next day, '*Général* de Larminat published an Order of the Day by which he took command

---

6   Béné, *Carnets, Seconde époque*, p.206.
7   Béné, *Carnets, Seconde Époque*, p.207.
8   The troops who had remained loyal to the Vichy government until the Allied landings.
9   Girard, *Journal de Guerre*, p.69.
10   Chauvet, *Le Sable et la Neige*, p.237.
11   Béné, *Carnets, Seconde Époque*, p.209.

of the group of Free French divisions.'[12] Leclerc, now in command of a division, received his third star on 25 May from de Gaulle. But, considering his advancement too rapid, he once again refused to wear the third star of his rank as a *général de division*.

The commander of the *2e DFL* took the first steps to restructure his units. *Capitaine* Savelli's *RTST* armoured car squadron 'is attached to the *1er RMSM* where it is named 4th Squadron.'[13] It made the division more consistent, with the infantry units all grouped together. The communications units were also reorganised, with *Capitaine* Dubut in command of this technical unit. *Commandant* Crépin was confirmed in his role as commander of the artillery and began to reorganise the various units that remained after the departure of the British reinforcements that had been placed at his disposal. But the biggest challenge of the *2e DFL* remained the recruitment of soldiers to supplement its numbers. The office in Tunis was running at full capacity. Young *pieds noirs*[14] from Tunisia and Algeria, escapees from France and, more and more often, deserters from the *Armée d'Afrique*, came knocking at the doors of these Free Frenchmen whose fame was growing. 'With Leclerc's troops, they found a different atmosphere, the camaraderie between everyone with the halo of a past of victories.'[15] This was too much for the Giraudists who could not accept this haemorrhage from their ranks any longer and accused the Free French of 'poaching.' At the end of May, the *2e DFL* learnt 'that a decision from *Général* Giraud's staff in Algiers prohibits us from staying in Tunisia. We were receiving our subsistence from the British, we just had to stay there.'[16] Leclerc himself wrote 'Giraud kicked us out.'[17] The same went for their sister division, the *1re DFL*. Dio and all the other leaders around Leclerc were furious. They considered that sending them back 'to Tripolitania, which they had so gloriously conquered and where they returned as exiles,' had all the makings of a punishment.[18]

However, on the political level, the situation was taking a favourable turn. While they blocked de Gaulle in London, the Anglo-Americans realised that the populations in North Africa mainly supported the Gaullist movement. 'On 1 May 1943, during the Labour Day parade, workers in major Algerian cities chanted: we need de Gaulle.'[19] In mainland France, internal resistance only recognised the Man of 18 June. The Allies, but especially the Giraudists, were ultimately forced to go through de Gaulle. They invited him to Algiers on 30 May, where Churchill came in person to find a solution. At the end of tough negotiations between de Gaulle and Giraud, the latter submitted politically to the leader of Free France. On 3 June, the French Committee for National Liberation was created, bringing together the Gaullist and Giraudist movements into a single entity.[20] Unfortunately, the merger between the troops of Free France and those of North Africa was not yet on the agenda. The *2e DFL* therefore had to leave Tunisia and return to Libya. Fortunately, the British agreed to continue to feed and resupply the Free French. General Brian Horrocks' British X Corps would provide that support. In coordination with Horrocks, the two Free French divisions planned to settle as close as possible to the Tunisian border, in Zuara for the *1re DFL* and in Sabratha for the *2e DFL*. Sabratha is 60km west of Tripoli and 100km from the

12   Fonds Leclerc: *JMO du 1er RMSM, du 07/06/41 au 02/01/1946, en date du 22 mai 1943*, boîte D1.
13   Fonds Leclerc: *JMO du 1er RMSM, en date du 25 mai 1943*, boîte D1.
14   A *pied noir* (literally 'black foot') was a European Frenchman living in French North Africa. (Translator's note)
15   Chauvet, *Le Sable et la Neige*, p.253.
16   Béné, *Carnets, Seconde Époque*, p.209.
17   Destrem, *L'Aventure de Leclerc*, p.210.
18   Destrem, *L'Aventure de Leclerc*, p.215. Compagnon, in his work on Leclerc, hypothesises that the choice of positioning the two *DFL*s in Tripolitania was accepted by de Gaulle for logistical reasons, 'only the British 8th Army can continue to support Larminat's group of divisions' (Compagnon, *Leclerc*, p.315).
19   Béné, *Carnets, Seconde Époque*, p.217.
20   *Journal Officiel de la République Française*, jeudi 10 juin 1943, ordonnance du 3 juin 1943.

Tunisian border. Leclerc managed to maintain an administrative centre in Kairouan under the orders of *Commandant* Hausherr to facilitate connections with the *Armée d'Afrique*. Was this city not liberated by his troops? What he did not say in Algiers was that the recruitment office, which was expelled from Tunis, would settle in this administrative centre. Volunteers would thus be able to enlist in Free French units more easily in this Tunisian city rather than in Libyan Tripolitania.

The movement of the *2ᵉ DFL* to Sabratha started on 8 June. The first stage of the journey would take place in Triaga in the suburbs of Sfax, and the second stage in Médenine. Units of the division arrived in the Sabratha region on 10 June. Sabratha is an ancient port founded by the Carthaginians in the fifth century BCE, which came under the control of the Romans in 111 BCE, after the Numidian defeat. The city then became a Roman colony and prospered. 'This magnificent Roman beachside town, coming out of the sands, forum, thermal baths, marble latrines where the seats, arranged in an arc to allow for conversation, are worn down by Roman butts.'[21] Its Roman ruins were impressive: 'Judging by the imposing character of the ancient remains, Sabratha, today a small town, must once have been an grand city.'[22] In 1943, it was nothing more than a 'palm grove close to the sea, dotted with a few beautiful colonial villas.'[23] And Sabratha offered the soldiers no distractions at the time, the Roman remains not inspiring them. Leclerc described it as 'an unattractive town.'[24]

Each unit received an area to set up their encampment. But having been the scene of fighting, it was necessary to clear the region of mines before settling in. No longer having an engineering unit, a surprising system was developed to carry out this dangerous operation without compromising the safety of the men. An unmanned British Bren Gun Carrier, with the hand accelerator engaged, and just enough fuel to cover the desired distance, crisscrossed the terrain to detonate the mines. When it hit a mine, the worst that happened was the vehicle's track was damaged. It was then repaired, and the vehicle relaunched.[25]

Once the areas had been cleared, the units could move in. RTST infantrymen camped in Roman ruins. The *1ᵉʳ RMSM* found a clear area where its vehicles could be parked 5km south of Sabratha. The tanks were stationed east of the ruins, in the Bou Harida oasis. The signals squadron settled on a large farm abandoned by Italian settlers. The artillery was quartered at El Agheila. Leclerc set up his CP 'in a small Italian colonial farm.'[26] This cantonment was no recreation centre. Living conditions were Spartan and the climate very difficult. The water of Sabratha 'was undrinkable. It was excessively salty, and the taste of salt turned up in every dish, including tea and coffee.'[27] The *général's* aide-de-camp noted: 'Blazing heat. Everything is burning hot. Impossible to nap. Shorts and shirt are not suitable for this furnace.'[28] 'The nomads of glory,' as Jean d'Esme would call them,[29] would have to continue to lead this life, in, to say the least, very severe conditions. Fortunately, the British agreed to equip the *2ᵉ DFL* with camp equipment. Each man thus received his 'camp kit' consisting of a collapsible wash basin, a folding bed, and a sleeping bag. The old sheepskin faros of the *méharistes* were quickly abandoned for this more hygienic kit. The bed insulated from the ground and protected from the reptiles which abound in that part of Libya. Concerning hygiene,

---

21   Richard Pranzo, who joined the *2e DFL* in Tunisia in June 1943, wrote an article entitled 'Un été à Sabratha, 1943', *Caravane* No.420, p.32.
22   Dronne, *Carnets de Route,* p.239.
23   Notin, *le Croisé,* p.204.
24   Destrem, *L'Aventure de Leclerc,* p.219.
25   Testimony of *Colonel* Pierre Robédat in 2019.
26   Bergot, *La 2 ème D.B.,* p.15.
27   Robet, Charles, *Souvenirs d'un Médecin de la France Libre* (SIDES, 1994), p.92.
28   Girard, *Journal de Guerre,* p.86.
29   Esme (d'), *Les Nomades de la Gloire, l'Épopée de la Division Leclerc.*

each company was equipped with 'fly proof latrines' fitted with mosquito nets. 'At this time of year the climate is hot and humid and its heaviness weighs terribly. Everything in this country gives off a feeling of desolation and abandonment, everything here agrees with our disappointed hearts.'[30] Fortunately, though, men could go swimming in the sea every evening to cool off.

Dio and his subordinates had to prioritise solving the major problem of the moment, which was personnel in the *RTST*. Now that the fighting was over, it was time to determine who would continue the fight with Leclerc and who would return to Chad. The *RTST* had to continue its mission in this *AEF* territory. Some of the units that made up *Force L* had to return to Chad. Determining who would return to Chad was not easy to manage. For example, the three *groupes nomades*, which had become motorised infantry companies within the *2ᵉ DFL*, had to be remounted on camels and to resume their mission of surveillance and administration of the populations of northern Chad. The selection of the *RTST* cadre who would have to return to Chad was not easy to determine, and it was often a choice from the heart. It is obvious that the early comrades would remain a priority in the choice. They were the ones who had participated in the beginning of the epic, and it would be unjust to deprive them of the rest of it. The Oath of Kufra remained their objective. Leclerc himself had to select from among his direct deputies the one who would return to Chad. He chose Ingold, who would resume his duties as commander of Chad. He made the choice while adding some substance to it. At the end of May, on the seafront in Sousse, he surprised *Colonel* Ingold with the *Croix de la Libération* by pronouncing the ritual phrase: 'We recognise you as our companion for the Liberation of France in honour and through victory.'[31] He could have appointed *Lieutenant Colonel* Dio to get the *RTST* back on its feet, but he was the loyal man whom he would not part with – the two men had remained closely attached ever since Douala. 'Dio is one of the historic leaders of Free France. He played a crucial role in the rallying of Cameroon in 1941 [*sic*], and took part in all of Leclerc's African campaigns (Kufra, Fezzan, Tunisia).'[32] Upon Ingold's departure, Dio became the de facto operational deputy of the *2ᵉ DFL*. *Lieutenant Colonel* Bernard was the chief of staff, the man who effectively managed the division's administrative and technical areas. For the *tirailleurs*, the choice was less difficult. It was done according to their contract; those approaching two years of service had to return to Chad for long-term leave or to return to civilian life, as set out in their contract.

On 18 June, Leclerc organised a ceremony in memory of de Gaulle's 1940 Appeal and took the opportunity to publicise his reorganisation decisions within the *2ᵉ DFL*. First, he dissolved the Flying Column. The *1ᵉʳ RMSM*, under the orders of *Lieutenant Colonel* Rémy, became the reconnaissance regiment of the division. The *1ʳᵉ Compagnie de Chars du Combat*, which was joined by the *2ᵉ Compagnie de Chars du Combat* and the mixed squadron, received the task of training volunteers to form a tank regiment. It would be called the *501ᵉ Régiment de Chars de Combat* (*501ᵉ RCC*) under the orders of *Commandant* Cantarel. It was also at this time that the *1/3ᵉ RAC* was created from the artillery elements present, commanded by *Commandant* Crépin, who would be promoted to *lieutenant colonel*. The division's infantry was grouped into a unit that would be called the *Régiment de Marche du Tchad* (*RMT*). This name, which was inspired by the 'marching battalions' of the *1ʳᵉ DFL*, was different in that it had a regimental and not a battalion structure. Leclerc created a regiment which, like American regiments, comprised several battalions. This would be the case with the *RMT* which comprised three infantry battalions. When he made this decision, Leclerc most certainly received assurances from de Gaulle

30   Béné, *Carnets, Seconde époque*, p.212.
31   Ingold, *Général Ingold*, p.111.
32   Édouard Pellissier, *Le Général Rouvillois ou La Victoire en Chargeant*, préface du Général Dio, (Éditions du Camelot et de la Joyeuse Garde, 1994), p.22.

concerning the future of the *2ᵉ DFL*. In Leclerc's mind, the commander of the regiment could only be *Lieutenant Colonel* Dio: 'As for the command of the *RMT*, it falls to the *général's* right hand man, the former *capitaine* of the Cameroonian night, who likes to arm himself with a club, Louis Dio.'[33] It was a good command, equivalent to a *demi-brigade*, of almost 3,000 men.[34] 'Leclerc had entrusted him with command of the *RMT*, the backbone of the *2ᵉ Division*, which was painfully just seeing the light of day.'[35] Very quickly, the commander of the *2ᵉ DFL* asked for and obtained from de Gaulle Dio's promotion to the rank of *colonel*. He was promoted on a temporary basis on 25 June 1943.[36] More than anything else, Dio was happy to find a command.[37] He had few aspirations for staff work. Leclerc quickly realised that his deputy was above all a hands-on man who thrived in contact with the troops, something his previous actions had repeatedly underlined. Dio had all the units with which he had fought since the beginning of 1941 under his command. He formed the three battalions of the regiment, distributing the units:

- The 1st Battalion under the orders of *Commandant* Vézinet, with the 1st Company (*Capitaine* Wagner), the 12th Company (*Capitaine* Corlu), the *Groupe Nomade du Borkou* (*Commandant* Poletti and then *Capitaine* Sammarcelli), the *1ʳᵉ DC* (*Capitaine* Troadec),
- The 2nd Battalion under the orders of *Commandant* Massu, with the *Groupe Nomade du Tibesti* (*Lieutenant* de Bazelaire), the *Groupe Nomade de l'Ennedi*, a company of *1ᵉʳ Bataillon de Marche*, and the *2ᵉ DC* (*Lieutenant* Eggenspiller),
- The 3rd Battalion under the orders of *Commandant* Barboteu, (formed from *8ᵉ Bataillon de Marche*).[38]

Dio had remarkable leaders for these three battalions, experienced men who were also comrades-in-arms, and with whom he was in perfect agreement. The same was true for the soldiers coming from Chad, as noted in a report on the morale of the 1st Battalion: 'the veterans of Chad have splendid morale; their ideal is unchanged. They form the solid base of the battalion and are characterised by drive and mutual trust.'[39] But the three battalions remained understrength, very short of men. It was even problematic within the 3rd Battalion, formed from *8ᵉ Bataillon de Marche* and commanded by Barboteu. Coming from Garoua in Cameroon, it encountered enormous logistical difficulties in joining *Force L*. In addition, it lacked combat experience. Barely regrouped at Sabratha, the battalion lost all its black soldiers who were transferred to the *1ʳᵉ DFL*. To compensate, it received 200 Europeans from North Africa who turned out to be of poor quality. This was the most pressing problem for the *RMT* commander. He would have to fill the ranks of the battalions by recruiting volunteers. When they arrived, Dio asked his subordinates to carry out the first distribution of the new volunteers at their level. If a candidate did not present any particular problem, he left them the freedom to accept the recruit. But, if the young volunteer was a 'deserter' from the *Armée d'Afrique*, or if he presented problems of any kind, he wanted to receive

---

33   Notin, *le Croisé*, p.218.
34   The name '*BMT*' sometimes appears in works, referring to the *Brigade de Marche du Tchad* as opposed to *Colonel* Malaguti's tank brigade. At the Takrouna cemetery in Tunisia, there are even *BRMT* inscriptions on the graves to indicate *Brigade du RMT*.
35   Bergot, *La 2 ème D.B.*, p.16
36   SHD, Dio, 14 Yd 1759, décret du Général de Gaulle en date du 3 Juin 3 1943.
37   In his Service Record (État Signalétique des Services, Dio, 14 Yd 1759), his assumption of command of the *RMT* dates from 1 June 1943. It was apparently anticipated.
38   Fonds Leclerc, *JMO of the 3e Bataillon du RMT*, boîte L.
39   Fonds Leclerc, boîte K1, dossier 2.

him personally, in a private interview. It was difficult to refuse an application when the need for men was so great. But, at the same time, it was clear to Dio and his subordinates that personnel who were not capable of bearing arms, or those whose motivations were suspect, could not be integrated into the regiment. The terms of the report on morale for the month of September were unambiguous for those:

> …engaged at the end of the Tunisian campaign:
> * 50 percent… Doubtful morale, without discipline and lack of uniformity. A salutary measure was the harsh selection made in Sabratha which resulted in mass eliminations.
> * 50 percent… Good young men, generally very young. They need to be supervised very closely. Most came to us out of sincere enthusiasm, but they do not yet have the basic qualities.[40]

During this time, the British offered the French commanders numerous specialised tactical training courses. For example, the aerial guidance course, which was very popular with officers because it taught them to guide a plane to its target from the ground. Another example was navigation courses using portable sextants. In the more technical field, radio repairmen were sent for training. Operators learnt how to use the new signalling stations using the 'skip distance' technique which allowed clear contacts to be established without the risk of being intercepted.[41] Cavalrymen, artillerymen, and medical personnel received additional training on the British equipment they received.

On 28 June, de Gaulle visited the two Free French divisions at Sabratha. He 'undoubtedly chose that moment to inform Leclerc that the armoured division he promised he would command would be provided with American equipment.[42] Indeed, the leader of Free France, taking advantage of the improvement in his relations with the American military, obtained an agreement in principle for a French division to be integrated into the American forces planning to open the 'second front' that Stalin had been clamouring for. Leclerc told Dio about the new option. The *méhariste*, accustomed to living with meagre resources, was enthusiastic about the prospect: 'from his adventurers, he would be able to make modern soldiers, heroic technicians.'[43] But Leclerc also told him that it was not good news in terms of numbers because the 'black *tirailleurs* were deemed unfit by the American command to serve in an armoured division.[44] This news was devastating to the 'old Chadians' who had been fighting around Dio with the *tirailleurs* for 3 years.[45] 'They are all very attached to the Sara and Adjeraï *tirailleurs*. The separation, though necessary, is painful after the battles fought together in Fezzan, Tripolitania, and Tunisia.[46] Other arguments were found to explain to the *tirailleurs* that the whites were going to part ways with them. 'They would be unable to withstand the extreme cold. And it would take too long to give them armoured unit training, we wouldn't have time.'[47] The number of these *tirailleurs* who had to leave the future 2ᵉ *DB* is

40   Fonds Leclerc, *rapports mensuels sur le moral 1943–1945*, boîte B1, dossier 5, chemise 1.
41   Each shortwave radio frequency travels a 'skip distance' in the ionosphere. It is then a matter of assigning the frequency that corresponds with the distance between two operators who wish to contact each other to prevent being intercepted by the enemy.
42   Levisse-Touzé and Toureille, *Écrits de Combat*, p.457, note 281.
43   Destrem, *L'Aventure de Leclerc*, p.223.
44   Levisse-Touzé and Toureille, *Écrits de Combat*, p.460.
45   The American Army was still segregated at that time. It was not racially integrated until 1948. Black Americans during the Second World War only served in segregated units, commanded by black or white officers.
46   Compagnon, *Leclerc*, p.319.
47   Dronne, *Carnets de Route*, p.242.

estimated at 1,000.[48] 'The youngest and fittest Africans will be transferred to the *Ire DFL*.'[49] Dio convinced Leclerc, despite the shortage in the *2^e DFL*, to let a few of the officers and NCOs to go with them so that they would not be completely disoriented by this forced transfer to another unit. The other *tirailleurs*, who did not volunteer to be assigned to the *Ire DFL*, were sent back to Fezzan and Chad. This decision further complicated the problem of the numbers of the *2^e DFL*, which was far from complete. After the departure of the black soldiers, Chadians or Cameroonians, the *2e DFL* had only 5,000 men, one-third of what was needed to form an armoured division. 'The old *RTST*, which has lost its Senegalese, can only provide a third of the strength that its new name, the *Régiment de Marche du Tchad*, was supposed to give it.'[50] This would be Dio's main challenge for the coming months. He absolutely had to triple the size of his force if he wanted to be able to fulfil the role set for him by Leclerc. Dio set about this priority project, with his ever-present cigarette butt in his mouth, surveying his camp, with the 'heavy gait of a peasant walled in the silence of an old *blédard*' whose 'massive silhouette concealed the power of a wild buffalo in the service of stubborn loyalty.'[51]

On 10 July, the veterans of *Force L* learnt with some emotion that their brothers-in-arms from the British 8th Army had landed in Sicily with Patton's US 7th Army. They were fighting while they had been 'exiled' in Tripolitania for three months, with no official information on the short term. In Russia, the German situation worsened while the Americans in the Pacific began to reconquer, one by one, the islands previously taken by the Japanese. On 14 July, Leclerc organised three parades in Sabratha to celebrate Bastille Day national holiday. After the *spahis* and the artillerymen, he went to the *RMT*, where Dio presented the regiment assembled under arms to him. The ranks were still thin and now completely 'whitened.' This was the first time that the *RMT* paraded without its faithful Saras. At the beginning of August, morale dropped within the *2^e DFL*, primarily due to inaction. Dio knew that was the source of all evil in military units. Leclerc informed Dio that he had a 'stormy interview with Horrocks who 'does justice to our merits in combat but decries our lamentable indiscipline.''[52] The company commanders were no longer able to mobilise the men who had come to join them and wanted to fight as quickly as possible. There was no means, no equipment with which to train them. Morning 'physical culture' sessions were not enough to satisfy these young men. Leaders had to display extraordinary qualities to convince these young men to stay with them, under canvas, in the oppressive heat.

Tripoli, 'a very beautiful city where the Italians had shown through their construction that they were indeed the sons of the Romans,'[53] was only 60 kilometres from Sabratha, and it had not sustained any damage from the recent fighting. The men wanted to go there, but, after some brawls started by a few hotheads among the new arrivals, the British had limited passes to the city. Internal tensions also arose, in particular between *spahis* and colonials who were treated as '*kakalas*, which was not a friendly term.'[54] The command was aware of this situation and tried to organise distractions. The star singer, Germaine Sablon, was invited to Sabratha for a performance. The two divisions came together in the Roman theatre, which had been restored by Italian archaeologists and included a gigantic stage and stands. One afternoon, *Madame* Sablon thrilled the thousands of assembled soldiers with her songs. She was a huge hit when she sang *Mon Légionnaire* after *Java Bleue* and *Les Roses Blanche*. At the end of the performance, the Tahitian guitarists of the

---

48   Notin, *Le Croisé*, p.104.
49   Dronne, R., *Carnets de Route*, p.242.
50   Notin, *Le Croisé*, p.214
51   Bergot, *La 2 ème D.B.*, p.15.
52   Levisse-Touzé and Toureille, *Écrits de Combat*, p.467.
53   Robet, *Souvenirs d'un Médecin de la France Libre*, p.91.
54   Girard, *Journal de Guerre*, p.90. *Kakalas* is military slang for unkempt, poorly educated people.

Bataillon d'Infanterie de Marine du Pacifique were cheered for their song of the canoeists, which was echoed by all the Free Frenchmen upon discovering this captivating Polynesian melody. It was at that performance that the soldiers heard *Chant des Partisans*.[55] 'This song moved us greatly and was etched, forever, in our minds.'[56]

In addition to the distractions and to boost morale, the soldiers were granted leave in North Africa, which had another ulterior goal: 'a damnable idea …. for the understrength *FFL* to increase their numbers. They left with 15, they returned with 30. They were the best propagandists.'[57] The reputation of Leclerc's Chadians was beginning to be known throughout Africa and many young Frenchmen dreamt of joining them.

Leclerc spoke to those closest to him during a dinner on 15 August 1943, to discuss the future. His resentment towards the *Armée d'Afrique* was softening. He realised that he would have to integrate units from it to complete his division. *Capitaine* Girard, his aide-de-camp, reported that in front of his subordinate leaders, he made a point of differentiating the 'big ones [of the *Armée d'Afrique*], those who were responsible for important decisions …. For the others – officers, soldiers …. we must be careful not to be excessively harsh. They were deceived. You have to know how to forget.'[58] Leclerc asked his subordinates to relay his words to the men. Dio once again appreciated this chess player who was always at least one step ahead. He later learnt that Leclerc met with *Colonel* de Langlade on 3 August in Algiers, where Langlade suggested that he bring his armoured regiment, the *12e Régiment de Chasseurs d'Afrique*, to join the division.[59]

On 23 August, *Général* de Gaulle issued the proclamation that the Libyan 'exiles' had longed to hear: 'The unity of the French armies has now been restored. All that remains of the available forces is gathered to march against the enemy. A glorious leader, *Général* Giraud, has received command.'[60] It took two months for the political agreement to be followed by a military agreement, merging the *Armée d'Afrique* with that of the Free French. It meant that the *2e DFL* would certainly finally leave Libya. However, de Gaulle was obliged to give command of the forces to Giraud. In addition, the general staff in Algiers remained in place. Resentments would not be erased overnight and would continue to complicate the life and functioning of Leclerc's troops.

On 24 August, the *2e DFL* was officially transformed into the *2e Division Blindée* or *2e DB*. It would be allowed to leave Tripolitania to go to Morocco.[61] Leclerc chose Morocco, which was dear to his heart, citing the large spaces that would allow him to train. In fact, he wanted to be as far away as possible from the headquarters in Algiers, with whom relations would continue to be strained. On 26 August, a parade was organised to celebrate the third anniversary of the rally of Chad to Free France. Dio's *RMT* 'received two palms for its *Croix de Guerre*.'[62] The memory of Chad was still very present in everyone's minds – a page of two and a half years could not be closed overnight! Dio set the departure of Sabratha for 1 September 1943. Like all his men, he was happy to leave the region but, at the same time, worried about the weakness in the number of his men present in the ranks. There were just 850 of them; three times that many were needed.[63] How could they recruit the 2,500 infantrymen needed to arm the *RMT*? Leclerc entrusted Dio

55   The *Chant des Partisans* was the most popular song among the Free French and the French Resistance. Written in 1943, it called on Frenchmen to stand and fight for their liberty. (Translator's note)

56   Pranzo, 'Un été à Sabratha, 1943', *Caravane* No.420, p.32.

57   Bergot, *La 2 ème D.B.*, p.18.

58   Girard, *Journal de Guerre*, p.93.

59   Levisse-Touzé and Toureille, *Écrits de Combat*, p.466.

60   Béné, *Carnets, Seconde époque*, p.221.

61   Décision ministérielle n° 1682/EMG-G/1/10 du 24 août 1943 de l'état-major général de la guerre à Alger, commandé par le général Giraud.

62   Chauvet, *Le Sable et la Neige*, p.275.

63   Compagnon, *Leclerc*, p.333.

with the mission of forming and commanding the infantry of his future division. Dio would not disappoint him.

On 1 September at 10:00 a.m., *Colonel* Dio gave the departure signal to the column of *RMT* vehicles. The detachment was presented to him at 8:30 a.m. by *Commandant* Vézinet, who had become his deputy since the creation of the *2ᵉ DB*'s infantry regiment.[64] The *RMT* was still equipped with *RTST* vehicles – the old Bedfords and Fords with which they conquered Fezzan and fought the Tunisian campaign with the British. But it was no longer the faithful Cameroonians who drove them. Just like the Chadian *tirailleurs*, they were assigned to the *1ʳᵉ DFL* or repatriated to their country. European soldiers took the wheel. The vehicles were loaded with various and varied loads. It is important to note that the 'epic tramps' who, for three years, had fought in extreme destitution, had learnt to be prepared for difficult tomorrows. In addition to their pack, each person brought objects and materials collected as spoils of war. The *méharistes* kept their *burnous* to protect themselves from the sand or the cold and some, like Dio, kept their *faro* to sleep in. It all made the *RMT* column, with its cabless trucks, look more like a gathering of junk dealers than a military formation. Dio, during his review, was obliged to inject a little order and unload whatever seemed to him to be unacceptable or too cumbersome to transport. Some men even tried to bring with them locals with whom they had become friends.

The departure restored morale in the ranks. The men learnt that the Americans would equip them from top to bottom with the most modern equipment. Everyone was eager to resume combat or to see it for the first time, and the latest arrivals were not the least enthusiastic. The first stage of the trip would not be long, reaching Zuara, which the *1ʳᵉ DFL* had just left to train at Cap Bon near Tunis.[65] The camp left by their sister division of the Free French Army was suitable for a stopover accommodation. The following days, the column would progress via Médenine and Gafsa in Tunisia. On the fourth day, it entered Algeria via the RN10 near Tebessa, from which the penultimate stage would take place. The final stage would take the *RMT* column to Djidjelli on the coast, about 100 kilometres east of Bougie. Before arriving there, passing through the city of Constantine had amazed most of the Free French. For the first time in three years, they felt close to France. This large regional city is similar in many ways to those in the south of metropolitan France. The other units of the *2ᵉ DB* – *spahis*, cavalrymen, artillerymen, and sappers stopped south of Constantine in an area called Ouled Rahmann. There, they left their equipment and vehicles and boarded a train for Morocco.

But the *RMT* did not follow the other units of the division. Dio had one essential goal, which was strengthening his numbers by absorbing units of the *Corps Franc d'Afrique* (*CFA*). He learnt from an officer in this unit that the officers and men no longer tolerated 'the atmosphere that reigns within the *Armée d'Afrique*.'[66] Very interested in this information, Dio inquired about what the *CFA* was. The large unit was created in November 1942 to allow volunteers from North Africa to enlist, 'without distinction of race, religion or nationality. Young or old, active duty [who had been] removed from the cadre, reservists not called up by the depots. The strength of six battalions with depots in Algiers, Oran, Oujda, Fez, Casablanca, was quickly assembled. *Général* de Montsabert commanded the whole unit.'[67] The *CFA* was very quickly the object of ostracism from

---

64   Promoted to *lieutenant colonel* in March 1944, Adolphe Vézinet was Dio's deputy in the future *Groupement Tactique Dio* throughout the French campaign. Then, he became Leclerc's chief of staff in Indochina and North Africa.

65   With the aim of breaking the traditions of this brilliant unit, which (along with the *3e DIA*) remains the most decorated of the Second World War, *Général* Giraud had its name changed in May 1943 to the *1re DMI* (*Division de Marche d'Infanterie*). The Gaullists continued to call it *DFL*.

66   Levisse-Touzé, *Du Capitaine de Hauteclocque au Général Leclerc*, p .284.

67   Fonds Leclerc, Joseph Putz, *Historique sommaire du 3e bataillon du CFA*, boîte L2.

the authorities in Algiers because the majority of the European officers and soldiers claimed to be Gaullists. Poorly armed and poorly equipped, only half of the six battalions were engaged in February 1943 against the Italo-German forces in Tunisia, after only three months of training. Even if some of the men had combat experience, particularly the recruits from the ranks of the Spanish Republicans, this was not the case for the other members of the *CFA*. This was partly the cause of the high losses suffered until May. Some companies lost half of their effective strength during the capture of Bizerte with American troops. At the end of the fighting in Tunisia, Algiers decided to consolidate *CFA* volunteers wishing to serve in Free French units and position them at a water point called Ain Sebti on the road to Philippeville, 38 kilometres from Djidjelli. Giraud's army thus got rid of a unit that it no longer controlled. At the heart of the *CFA*, the only unit that was more or less complete in its establishment was the 3rd Battalion, commanded by *Commandant* Putz. It comprised three combat companies and one headquarters company (*CHR*).[68] The units came from Algeria and Morocco: '9th Company, formed in the Oran region from foreign volunteers (majority Spanish); 10th Company, formed in the Algiers-Bougie region (Kabyles); 11th Company, formed in the Casablanca region and known as 'the Moroccans;' and the *CHR*, formed in the Philippeville-Constantine region.'[69] There were also scattered units of the 6th Battalion of the *CFA*, commanded by *Commandant* Signard. Since May, they had been waiting in this out of the way hole, abandoned by higher command, and treated like lepers ever since they expressed their feelings for de Gaulle.

Dio arrived in Ain Sebti on 5 September 1943, and immediately found *Commandant* Putz. He was eager to get to know this man, whom he had already inquired about. What Dio learnt was a welcome surprise. Of Alsatian stock, Putz was born in 1895. He enlisted in the First World War in 1914, became a front-line officer, and received three citations. Gassed, he was demobilised as a reserve *capitaine* and entered the administrative service. During the Spanish Civil War, he joined the international brigades with his wife, who was a nurse, and very quickly took on leadership responsibilities. As a *coronel*, 'he commanded a brigade during the astonishing victory of Guadalajara.'[70] Promoted to *general*, he then commanded the 1st Republican Division during the defence of Bilbao. Before the end of the civil war, he left Spain for Algeria where he resumed work in the French colonial administration. After the armistice in 1940, he was demobilised without having fought. After the American landing at the end of 1942, he raised a company in Morocco. Integrated into the 3rd Battalion of the *CFA* as commander of the 11th Company, he fought the *Afrika Korps* in Tunisia. 'He was one of the first to enter Bizerte and was promoted to *chef de bataillon*.'[71] Shortly thereafter, he became the commander of the 3rd Battalion of the *CFA*. Such a background story appealed to Dio, who was looking for experienced leaders. The two men hit it off immediately; they were made from the same mould, men of action, not very talkative, simple, having faith in human nature, and hating the Nazis. Now that they knew each other's past, a mutual respect united them. Putz offered to reinforce the *RMT* with his battalion. Dio, as was customary, then asked him to formally present his unit to him. A young non-commissioned officer, Pierre Destray, deserter from the Vichy Army, was there and describes the event:

---

68 A *compagnie hors rang* (*CHR*) is a non-combatant company that includes the support and administrative elements of the battalion such as cooks, maintenance, communication, and medical sections. In the US Army, it is designated Headquarters and Headquarters Company. (Translator's note)

69 Fonds Leclerc, Putz, *Historique sommaire du 3e bataillon du CFA*, boîte L2.

70 Jésus-Maria de Leizaola, 'Autour de la mort d'un grand soldat français, le lieutenant-colonel Putz', *Caravane* No.36, Février 46, pp.11–12.

71 Emmanuel Rigault, *Le Régiment de Marche du Tchad, Koufra 1941 – Sarajevo 1995*, préface du Général Massu, (Imprimerie Sival-Mavit, 1996), p.221.

When *Colonne Leclerc* arrived with its old, yellow-painted trucks, we were stunned; to say that they had crossed the desert seemed incredible to us! For we men from the *Corps Franc d'Afrique*, this junction was a great emotional moment; we were dazzled, admiring in front of these veterans who arrived crowned with the epic of Chad, with their glorious adventure. How proud we would have been to be one of them! One morning we learnt that everyone had to gather in impeccable uniform to be presented to *Lieutenant Colonel* Dio, commanding the *Régiment de Marche du Tchad*. Imagine the situation: we lived with a minimum of clothes. Then the commotion began, everyone got busy, pants or jackets were loaned to each other, 'shoes' were polished. It was a matter of self-esteem, the *Corps Franc d'Afrique* had to make a good impression, and not give the appearance of going around barefoot. So, at the appointed time, the battalion was present and at attention, we awaited with impatience and curiosity the arrival of this famous *colonel*. Then he appeared with *Commandant* Putz at his side. What a surprise for us. We were really stunned, we were expecting to see an officer dressed in a beautiful uniform, and we discovered a kind of giant. Wearing a colonial kepi, worn out by the weather, who spoke to us with authority but very simply. Believe me, he made a sensational impression on us. It's an unforgettable memory. We said to ourselves: this is the man we need; He and Putz go hand-in-hand. We came across admirable and very simple officers who knew how to talk to men and gain their respect.[72]

Dio decided to merge the 3rd Battalion of the *CFA* with his very incomplete 3rd Battalion commanded by Barboteu. By a curious coincidence, the two units had the same company numbers. Keeping their numbering suited everyone, especially the foreigners who had difficulty with the French language. But, for Dio, the most difficult part was to allocate commands between the officers from the *CFA* and those from the *RMT*. He could not dismiss all of Putz's officers, even if many of them had neither the experience nor the abilities of his 'Chadian' leaders. To command the battalion, Dio did not hesitate. Putz won him over as a man and his military past spoke for itself. It was difficult for *Commandant* Barboteu, who had done nothing wrong, but was set aside, nevertheless. For unit command, the distribution was as follows: the headquarters company was commanded by *Capitaine* Florentin (*RMT*), the 9th Company by *Capitaine* Dronne (*RMT*), the 10th Company by *Lieutenant* Marchal (*CFA*), the 11th Company by *Capitaine* Dupont (*RMT*). Dio, in agreement with Putz, entrusted the vast majority of command of the combat units to his former comrades-in-arms, except the 10th Company. But very quickly, *Lieutenant* Marchal would be dismissed and replaced by *Capitaine* Sarazac in command of the company. The 9th Company, which was reputed to be 'difficult' because it was composed mainly of Spanish Republicans, was entrusted to *Capitaine* Dronne. Dio and Putz agreed with his selection. It was Leclerc, passing through Djidjelli, who informed Dronne: "they scare everyone,' he told me. 'They are fine soldiers; you will make do with it. Do you agree?"[73] Dronne understood a little bit of Spanish, which was the language spoken in the company, but the other reason for his selection was his strong personality and his imposing stature. The Spaniards, freedom fighters, only respected courage: woe to the leader who shows fear during the fight. The other *CFA* units were transferred to the other two battalions to supplement the numbers. Thus, the *capitaine* commanding the 2nd Company of the 1st Battalion of the *RMT* noted in his diary 'in Djidjelli, more than thirty officers and men of the *CFA* joined the company.'[74] This first contribution of personnel from the *CFA* was vital for the

---

72   Fonds Leclerc, Pierre Destray, *Les campagnes de France d'Allemagne 1944–1945 de la 2e Division Blindée des Forces Françaises Libres,* p.2, boîte L1.

73   Dronne, *Carnets de Route,* p.242.

74   *De Fort-Lamy à Strasbourg, Historique de la 2ème Cie du RMT* (Paris: Imprimerie Marcel Dart, 1950) p.13.

RMT, although 'the leaders and soldiers show obvious good will, most do not know their job. They have never been trained. Discipline and behaviour need to be perfected.'[75]

The 7th Company of the 6th Battalion of the *CFA* was integrated into the 2nd Battalion of the *RMT* and kept its original number, as well as its unit commander, *Capitaine* Fonde. The Moroccan soldiers would be absorbed into *Capitaine* de Bazelaire's 5th Company and the Algerians into the 6th Company of *Capitaine* Langlois de Bazillac.[76] *Commandant* Signard of the *CFA* was more senior in rank than *Commandant* Massu, so he became the commander of the 2nd Battalion.[77] *Aspirant* Salbaing was section leader of the 7th Company of the *CFA*. A young reservist officer and deserter from a Senegalese *tirailleurs* regiment, he was delighted to be integrated into the *RMT*. He understood that with this unit of the Free French, he would be able to join the fight for liberation. He recounted the ceremony where he met Dio for the first time. 'Dio was a rather extraordinary character who already had his legend …. this colourful officer under whose orders we now found ourselves was nothing but satisfactory, because he was out of the ordinary, and we liked to think that we were, too. His visit made a strong impression on the battalion, particularly among those who did not know him.'[78] Dio was an officer who impressed others, not just by his stature but mainly by the strong charisma that emanated from him.

On 7 September, Leclerc went to Djidjelli to see how the integration of the *CFA* was going. He wrote in his notes: 'Visit to Dio in Djidjelli. He takes his *corps franc* well in hand.'[79] It was certainly on that occasion that he decided with Dio that for 'the infantry regiment ….the amalgamation would be done in the Djidjelli region.'[80] Thus the *RMT* would be the only unit not to reach Morocco directly from Sabratha. On 16 September, the merger between the *RMT* and the *CFA* became official. Dio decided to organise a ceremony to appoint command of the 1st, 2nd, and 3rd Battalions to *Commandants* Farret, Signard, and Putz. The symbol was a Guidon that the *RMT colonel* gave to each commander. It was a sober ceremony, without fanfare. The uniforms in the ranks were still disparate. Regardless, beyond appearances, the symbolism was essential to Dio. It communicated to everyone that their destiny was now linked.

After presenting the Guidons to the three battalion commanders while announcing the standard words of investiture,[81] Dio read his Order of the Day. Very briefly, he announced that the division would soon be engaged in combat and that the regiment would have to hold its own. Consequently, he invited each of the leaders and *marsouins* to perfect their training and work to build a strong cohesion within each battalion. This dual objective set by the regimental commander was favourably received by everyone, each one understanding the significance for themselves. It was with enthusiasm and good humour that the three battalions set to work. They 'organised themselves and took up cantonments far enough apart from each other, so that each had a fairly large area of manoeuvre.'[82] The activities then began at a brisk pace. 'During these five weeks from September to October we did not have a single day of respite.'[83] 'Our schedule was very busy: intensive exer-

75   Fonds Leclerc, *note n°139/2 of 30.9.1943,* boîte K1.
76   Massu, *Sept Ans,* p.88.
77   *Commandant* Signard very quickly realised his shortcomings in relation to Massu and asked Dio on 2 October to relieve him of his position and to replace him with Massu.
78   Jacques Salbaing, *Ardeur et Réflexion* (Paris: Éditions La Pensée Universelle, 1992), pp.83–84.
79   Fonds Leclerc, Leclerc, boîte 10, dossier 1, chemise 3; Levisse-Touzé and Toureille, *Écrits de Combat,* p.474.
80   *Caravane* No.339, 2e trimestre 1983, p.7, 'Témara'.
81   'Officers, non-commissioned officers, and soldiers of X Battalion, from the Leader of Free France, you will henceforth recognise as your leader, *Commandant* X…, present here, and you will obey him in everything he will command you for the good of the service, the execution of military regulations, the observation of the laws and the success of the arms of France.'
82   Salbaing, *Ardeur,* p.75.
83   Salbaing, *Ardeur, p.75.*

cise in the morning – soldier's school. In the afternoon, instruction on weaponry – very detailed explanation of how the machine gun works.'[84] The men had to receive training on 'the new weapons, of which we had received a few examples: American rifles and carbines, American machine guns, and bazooka anti-tank rocket launchers.'[85] Progression exercises with live fire training accustomed the men to the sounds of the battlefield. 'Those soldiers who were too afraid were sent back to the CHR and transferred elsewhere if necessary.'[86]

Unfortunately, accidents sometimes resulted during the training sessions, which were intended to be as realistic as possible. In the 7th Company, there were two hand grenade accidents. More seriously, 'on 22 October, wanting to demonstrate to his company that an anti-tank mine was not dangerous for men, Capitaine de Bazelaire, to demonstrate, stepped on the British mines, which triggered the explosion.'[87] The firing system malfunctioned, as it should have required a weight of more than a ton to trigger the explosion. Dio, shocked by the accident, rushed to the Laveran hospital in Constantine that evening, and helplessly witnessed the agony and terrible suffering of the young méhariste officer. Capitaine de Bazelaire, comrade-in-arms of Dio and Massu in Tibesti, died tragically at the age of 27.[88]

Despite the growing pains among the officers who had come from Chad, everyone was striving to maintain a positive working atmosphere. Dio and his three battalion commanders knew they had to prioritise cohesion. This did not mean relaxing discipline; on the contrary, on Dio's orders, discipline became stricter. Sabratha's experience did not need to be repeated. Given the living conditions in the RMT, standard punishments were not appropriate. For minor offences, the sanction consisted of firing a British anti-tank rifle. The recoil of the weapon was so strong that after firing five rounds, the punished person 'came out with a bruised shoulder for two to three days …. For more serious offences, it was the 'hole:' head shaved to double zero, individual tent, feet and head protruding, and [running the] obstacle course several times during the day.'[89] These non-regulatory punishments had the advantage of serving as training of the soldier while also bringing the strong-willed into line.

To create cohesion among the leaders, Dio believed that nothing was better than setting up a mess hall.[90] It allowed all the leaders of each unit to be grouped around the commander during meals. The 'elders' take the opportunity to 'train' the younger ones by teaching them the traditions and songs of their branch. Sometimes the mess activities were surprising. Massu 'had empty tin cans suspended from wires stretched between the pine trees that surrounded the table. And often, with his encouragement, everyone took out their Colt and emptied a magazine into the boxes which were above the head of their counterpart, as a sort of appetiser for soldiers in the field.'[91]

---

84   Destray, Fonds Leclerc, *Campagne France-Allemagne 44–45*, p.2.

85   Dronne, *Carnets de Route*, p.243.

86   Salbaing, *Ardeur*, p.78.

87   This type of exercise consists of walking on an anti-tank mine as *Capitaine* de Bazelaire did, which was done to show soldiers what is dangerous and what is not. In this specific case, the anti-tank mine was defective. J. Salbaing, *Ardeur*, p.87.

88   Jean de Bazelaire de Ruppierre, from a family of the Lorraine nobility, Saint-Cyrien (Class of 1936–1938), was commanding a *méhariste* platoon in Chad when war was declared. He was part of the camel raid on Tedjéré with Sarazac in 1941. In 1942, he participated in the capture of the Tedjéré Fort with Dio. He was made a Companion of the Liberation (decree of 23 May 1942). In 1943, he played a decisive role in the capture of Gatroun. He was head of a motorised section during the Tunisian campaign. Promoted to *capitaine*, he became commander of the 6th Company of the 2nd Battalion of the RMT. Cited three times, he was made a *Chevalier* of the *Légion d'Honneur*.

89   Salbaing, *Ardeur*, p.79.

90   In the field outside of times of war, the mess hall, or *popote* is a sort of mess where leaders contribute to gather around a rustic meal consisting of standard rations generally improved by local produce.

91   Salbaing, *Ardeur*, p.79.

British officers invited to the mess 'took us for crazy and stubbornly refused to comply.'[92] With Dio's approval, Massu wanted to toughen up his officers, particularly the reservists. This method, which could be described as 'cowboy,' in fact helped to prepare the young officers psychologically for the future battles they would have to fight in a few months. All *RMT* personnel were trained in that same spirit. They would become seasoned infantrymen whose morale would allow them to systematically outperform the Germans in their future battles.

At the beginning of October, Dio received the order to move his regiment to Morocco. The *2ᵉ DB* had difficulty obtaining the green light because the general staff in Algiers was reluctant to see 'the arrival in Morocco of the *Brigade du Tchad*. It seems like they are really afraid to let it come there.'[93] In reality, they were afraid that Dio and his unit would provoke spontaneous rallies of young soldiers wanting to join the Chadians, whose reputation was immense in the ranks of the *Armée d'Afrique*, 'fascinated by the saga of these *FFL* over the past three years, across the desert, from Cameroon to Tunisia.'[94] Leclerc had to go to Algiers himself to lift the blockade against the *RMT*. Dio was happy to join the division now that his regiment had taken a good turn since its merger with the *CFA*. 'Everyone was proud to have achieved this union of minds and hearts in pursuit of the same goal, the same ideal.'[95] All the men were happy to leave the Djidjelli region. 'We didn't know what awaited us, or what we were going to do, but this long trip boded well.'[96] The *RMT* would go to prepare in Morocco, receiving new American equipment and holding its place, within the *2ᵉ DB*, in the fight for the liberation of France.

92   Salbaing, *Ardeur,* p.80.
93   Girard, *Journal de Guerre,* p.102.
94   Destrem, *L'Aventure de Leclerc,* p.214.
95   Destray, Fonds Leclerc, *Campagne France-Allemagne 44–45,* p.2.
96   Salbaing, *Ardeur,* p.90.

Chapter 8

Témara-England,
15 October 1943 to 1 August 1944

The 1st Battalion of the *RMT*, commanded by *Commandant* Farret, left Kabylia in mid-October on the train from Bougie (present day Béjaïa) bound for Morocco. It left all its vehicles, equipment, and weapons behind. The men had a touch of nostalgia as they abandoned their old Bedford and Ford trucks with their 'dented, rusty carcasses, full of bullet holes, scratched by all the rocks, sand, and winds since Kufra…' with which they had made so many memories.[1] They kept only their individual British kit. Arriving in Morocco after three days of a monotonous journey by rail, the 1st Battalion joined the rest of the division 15 kilometres south of Rabat in a large forest by the sea called Témara.[2] This seaside resort with a few 'white villas overlooking a cove, a casino …. backed by a cork oak forest'[3] was chosen by Leclerc 'because it neighbours the ports where the American cornucopia pours out.'[4] The 1st Battalion settled at a place called Rose-Marie. The 2nd Battalion under *Commandant* Massu arrived in Morocco at the end of October following the same route as the 1st Battalion. He reached Skhirat Beach on 3 November. 'The cantonment of the 2nd Battalion was between a dune which separated us from the sea and a small tarmac road… everyone in tents, the soldiers two to a tent, the non-commissioned officers and officers each had the right to their own.'[5] The 3rd Battalion left Djidjelli at the beginning of November. Its assembly area was the ancient fortress of Skhirat on the edge of the beach, in a small bay. 'In the centre and all around these walls, was a large area where the companies were distributed. The small *guitounes*[6] were quickly assembled in a symmetrical and perfect alignment.'[7]

The arrival of the *RMT* battalions in Témara at the end of 1943 provoked comments from among the units of the *Armée d'Afrique* that they joined, some reflecting a type of animosity. 'In a word, some people have trouble imagining former *méharistes* fighting an armoured war in a European theatre. The reports are therefore not yet the best.'[8] Dio also perceived this attitude from his counterparts. *Colonel* Malaguti publicly expressed that the heart of the *2ᵉ DB* was made up of the tank brigade that he commanded. Moreover, at the end of 1943, the *RMT* was called the 'Support Brigade' on the official internal documents of the division, certainly to act as a counterpart to the

---

1   Bergot, *La 2 ème D.B.*, p.14.
2   In the seaside town of Témara there is a casino, a district called Rose-Marie, and the Fort of Skhirat in front of which the military reviews took place. This Moroccan commune was twinned with Saint-Germain-en-Laye in August 1982.
3   Destrem, *L'Aventure de Leclerc*, p.226.
4   Notin, *le Croisé*, p.217.
5   Salbaing, *Ardeur*, p.91.
6   *Guitoune* is military slang for a tent or shelter that derives from Moroccan Arabic. (Translator's note)
7   Destray, Fonds Leclerc, *Campagne France-Allemagne 44–45*, p.3.
8   Massu, *Sept Ans*, p.95.

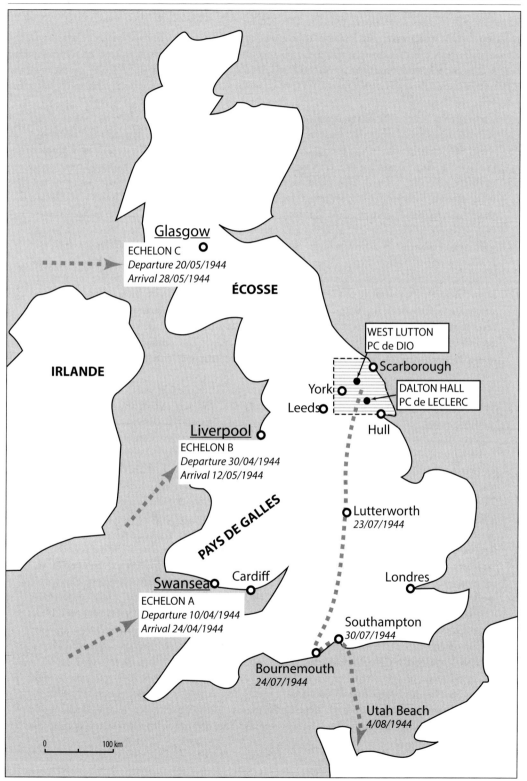

Map 8 The Regrouping in Great Britain.

'tank brigade.'[9] For *Commandant* Massu, this 'shows clearly what role seems to be assigned to the infantry.'[10] Dio was aware, like Leclerc, that it was now time to make peace with the officers of the *Armée d'Afrique*. He also realised that being junior in rank, it was up to him to take the first steps. A few days after his arrival, he introduced himself to *Colonel* de Langlade. The commander of the *12ᵉ Régiment de Chasseurs d'Afrique* (*12ᵉ RCA*) describes his first meeting with Dio in these terms:

I admit that I had a special memory of our first contact. Informed in my tent that a *colonel* wanted to see me, I went out, expecting to find the usual traditional figure in the person of the classic commander in the French Army. I almost ran into a colossus, or at least it seemed that way (in fact he was 1.83 or 1.84 metres, or about 6 feet tall), a very young face of a man of thirty years old, set with direct and hard black eyes, who addressed me thus: '*Mon Colonel*, while passing by your bivouac I stopped by to say hello to you.' I thanked him very much and the frank and direct conversation did not let up for a second. *Colonel* Dio was indeed thirty-two years old at the time. He affected a liberated air and spoke with the pronounced accent specific to Parisians. His conversation was peppered with amusing terms and slang words, and it all formed an infinitely friendly and frank whole. In fact, experience amply demonstrated to me how correct my first impression was. *Colonel* Dio hid, as was proven to me many times later, under this appearance of a brawler from the outer boulevards, an infinitely sensitive and refined soul. Full of heart and as delicate as possible, he was at the same time one of the original comrades of the Free French forces, the most understanding and the most truly eager to remain both objective and benevolent. If I did not fear being misunderstood, I would happily write, in a sense devoid of any irony, that this terrible 'smasher' was gifted with the soul of a young girl.

His story, of which I can only guarantee the broad outlines, is worth summarising here because he portrays a character from this strange era who was one of the highlights of the division at the same time as he made one of the most precipitous climbs experienced by the officers in the service of Free France, and they were formidable champions in this type of competition!

Dio lived in Chad, a modest *capitaine* buried in a bush post and known particularly for the bursts of his thunderous voice and his formidable physique which commanded respect. He even inspired fear because *Colonel* Leclerc, who had not yet been promoted to *général* for the needs of the cause, undertook to seize him and the company of *tirailleurs* he commanded. However, Leclerc thought that before using force, given Dio's stature and violent habits, it was better to talk first, then we would see. That's how, during the course of one meeting, he ordained the career of this officer, who was receptive to *Colonel* Leclerc's presentation and immediately put himself at his service. Had he acted otherwise, the future *Général* Dio would undoubtedly be, at present, a modest, unknown *chef de bataillon* in post. Luck is a woman, you have to grab her by the hair, they say. The future thirty-four-year-old *Général* Dio did not have a second of hesitation, he was a magnificent man who knew his job well. Companion of the *général* throughout Chad and Tripolitania as far as Tunisia, he was a splendid *chef de bataillon* whom it was decided to reward.

At the time of the 'weld' between *Colonne Leclerc* and the *Armée d'Afrique*, the *général* recommended his promotion to *lieutenant colonel*. The Army staff, which was responsible for welding [the two forces together], lacked information at the time and the intelligence reports did not shine with their precision: the fact remains that the office responsible for signing the

9   Fonds Leclerc, *rapport mensuel sur le moral du 1st Battalion*, No. *93/C of 12/20/1943*, boîte K1, dossier 2.
10   Massu, *Sept Ans*, p.96.

promotions proposed *Commandant* Dio for the rank of *colonel* and not for that of *lieutenant colonel*. As soon as he was appointed, the newly promoted man protested very loyally, but could not obtain a demotion!

Everyone gained, the *colonel*'s friends (and he only had friends) were delighted, the Army finally had a commander of men capable of enduring the fatigues of soldiering, and the group of general officers (which was quite saddening overall) was improved three years later in 1946 by the presence of a young man wearing stars at thirty-four years old.[11]

Colonel de Langlade who 'was the first commander in Giraud's *Armée d'Afrique* to join the FFL,'[12] was, along with Dio, one of Leclerc's direct subordinates who, through their open-mindedness, helped prove that the amalgamation could be achieved between the different units. That is what allowed the *2ᵉ DB* to become a first-class operational unit.

The *RMT* battalion commanders were outraged by the attitude of their cavalry counterparts. They also saw the animosity directed towards them and complained to Dio, who calmed them down. To the most virulent of them, he used language similar to that of Leclerc: 'You were right very early on. You must not take any pride in this. You must not despise those who saw clearly later .... we have a common objective: to drive the Germans out of France.'[13] He told everyone that the best response to them would be on the ground. For this, they must have a priority to 'forge highly trained, fierce, manoeuvrable units which, far from following or 'supporting,' will know how to move forward and lead.'[14] It was useless to enter into pointless debates. Furthermore, Dio knew very well that Leclerc, unlike Malaguti, did not consider the infantry as a support branch. Knowing the tense relations between the *général* and this *colonel*, Dio believed that now was not the time to add fuel to the fire. He also understood that his cavalry counterparts could feel the tone of reproach in the claim that 'the *général* is much more colonial than cavalry. Nothing on his uniform recalls his origins as a cavalryman.'[15] It was true that Leclerc still wore the insignia of Chad (which was also that of the *RMT*), as well as colonial buttons on his uniform.[16] Dio admitted that it could cause some jealousy. But he thought, just like the *général*, that time would gradually resolve the resentments. Combat would naturally strengthen the links between the different branches, particularly in the context of the use of *groupements tactiques*, where the units would be mixed. Brotherhood of arms would take precedence over the jealousy of some or the complacency of others.

---

11 This portrait is generally flattering and demonstrates that Dio, far from being a pure and hard-line Free Frenchman, remained understanding and caring. Nevertheless, *Colonel* de Langlade's frustration, which was shared by many of the loyalist leaders, was perceptible in the face of the rapid advancement of Free Frenchmen like Dio. This most certainly led him to write two untruths: Dio was indeed a *lieutenant colonel* from 25 September 1942 to 25 June 1943, and he was named *général* in 1945 at the age of 37 and not in 1946 at the age of 34. Earning his stars at that age remains exceptional considering the regulations of the time and even those of today. In the twentieth century French Army, it seems that Dio's promotion at the age of 37 is a case in point. His classmate, Pierre Billotte, also progressed very quickly but he was 38 years old when he was named *général* in 1944. Leclerc earned his stars at the age of 40, and did not promote himself to *général*, contrary to the writings of Langlade. On the contrary, he only agreed to wear the stars awarded by de Gaulle many months after the decree of his appointment. Paul de Langlade, *En Suivant Leclerc, d'Alger à Berchtesgaden* (Paris: Robert Laffont, 1964), pp.52–55.
12 Destrem, *L'Aventure de Leclerc*, p.226.
13 Destrem, *L'Aventure de Leclerc*, p.232.
14 Massu, *Sept Ans,* p.96.
15 Girard, *Journal de Guerre,* p.168.
16 According to his aide-de-camp, the *général* wore the insignia of Chad until March 1944. That is when the plan for the divisional insignia featuring France stamped with the cross of Lorraine was designed and finalised. Still, Leclerc always continued to wear the badge of Chad on his *fourragère*. Girard, *Journal de Guerre,* p.227.

Once settled in, the three battalions would take turns going to Casablanca to receive their uniforms and equipment. They would cease to be just tramps, becoming instead tramps of hope and victory, as a British officer described them. They were delighted to now be dressed in American uniforms. For equipment, at least three weeks of work was needed to take out and unpack the vehicles and weapons from the large boxes that came off the ships. 'A veritable anthill … a continual coming and going, an intense pace of work.'[17] Italian prisoners helped inventory the equipment. The *marsouins* of the *RMT* were excited to find these ultra-modern vehicles available to them. Those who had sawn the cabs off civilian trucks to make combat vehicles were amazed to discover the half-track which would become the standard armoured vehicle for the infantrymen of the *RMT*. Officers particularly coveted the jeeps, which were excellent ways to get around while being easy to drive.[18] Taking charge of American equipment was not the easiest thing, because the *RMT* was the unit within the division that had the greatest diversity of equipment. As an armoured infantry *demi-brigade*, the *RMT* was organised according to American establishments. At the regimental level, surrounding the commander, there was a headquarters company (*CCR*).[19] The total strength of the *RMT*, consisting of three battalions,[20] was 2,584 men – 175 in the *CCR* and 803 men in each battalion.[21] The *RMT* was equipped with the full range of individual light weapons as well as a wide variety of crew-served and heavy weapons.[22] The range of vehicles was also very

---

17   Destray, Fonds Leclerc, *Campagne France-Allemagne 44–45*, p.3.
18   The half-track was a combat vehicle with wheels in the front and tracks in the back. It had an average weight of eight tons, was armed with heavy and light machine guns, was capable of carrying a group of 8 to 10 equipped infantrymen and could travel at more than 75 kilometres per hour.
19   The headquarters company consisted of:
  • command section
  • services section (administration)
  • protection section (with five groups of infantrymen)
  • the doctor and a chaplain
20   In each of the three battalions, the organisation was:
  • The battalion commander with a small staff, two command and communications sections, and 1 chaplain
  • Headquarters company (CHR) with three sections:
    fuel and ammunition section
    medical section
    maintenance section
  • Support company (CA) including:
    command section (communications, administration, food, maintenance and baggage trains)
    mortar section of three groups on half-track
    howitzer section of three M8 tracked, armoured vehicles
    machine gun section of three groups on half-track
    reconnaissance and observation section on jeep and motorcycle
  • Combat companies, three per battalion, including
    command section ((communications, administration, food, maintenance and baggage trains)
    three combat sections, each of five groups of 10 infantry on 5 half-tracks, or around 50 men.
21   Fonds Leclerc, Tableau des effectifs théoriques de la 2e DB au 1 avril 1944 (*Theoretical staff table of the 2e DB as of 1 April 1944*), boîte 10, dossier 1, chemise 1.
22   The RMT's firepower was enormous:
  • Heavy weapons: 27 each of 75mm howitzers, 60mm mortars, 57mm anti-tank guns
  • Collective weapons: 40 x 12.7mm heavy machine guns, 210 x 7.62mm machine guns, 165 bazookas, 130 grenade launchers, 3,000 anti-tank mines
  • Individual weapons: 600 semi-automatic rifles, 700 M1 carbines, 250 Thompson submachine guns (11.43mm) and 175 automatic pistols
  This was the only time in the history of the French Army that an infantry regiment would have such firepower. Even the mechanised regiments which symbolised the armoured infantry of the 1970s and 1980s would not have such a variety of weaponry.

diverse. For the regiment, this meant a collective of more than 400 vehicles: 100 trucks, 66 jeeps, 215 half-tracks, 15 motorcycles, and 9 M8 armoured self-propelled howitzers.

Dio let the battalion commanders manage the process of receiving the equipment, and very quickly, the companies 'became champions at assembly.'[23] Since taking over command of the regiment, Dio had decided to decentralise his command as much as possible. He had complete confidence in his three *commanders*, Farret, Massu, and Putz. They were, in turn, indebted to him for allowing them great autonomy in the exercise of their responsibilities. Dio naturally applied the principle of command by subsidiarity: not doing what was the responsibility of the subordinate. In addition, he knew that Leclerc would adopt the 'combat commands' that American tacticians recommended for the use of armoured divisions: 'Leclerc adapted to American training directives and organised the division into three 'combat commands.''[24] This involved creating three combined arms groups within the *DB* that Leclerc would call *groupements tactiques*, or tactical groups. Each group would include tanks, infantry, engineers, artillerymen, and support. Leclerc had used this principle of combined arms grouping during the Fezzan campaigns and in Tunisia.[25] They would be autonomous, able to carry out limited operational actions because they had all the tactical components necessary. Dio had no problem with that, he had been in total agreement with Leclerc from the start. *Général* Jean Compagnon wrote: 'At the head of the *GTD* is *Colonel* Dio, linked to the *général* since dawn on 27 August 1940, during the canoe landing in Douala. A very malleable spirit, with devoted and integral loyalty, his communion of thought with the *général* is complete and acquired in advance.'[26] For Dio, this meant his regiment would be split into three. Within *Groupement Tactique Dio (GTD)*, he would tactically command only a third of his own regiment, the first battalion. He retained, of course, administrative responsibilities over all three battalions. He wanted the two battalion commanders, who would be integrated into the other two *groupements tactiques*, to get into the habit of fully assuming their responsibilities in a combined arms environment. By giving them great freedom of action, he prepared them to acquire the autonomy which would be necessary during the French campaign. Later, Leclerc would recognise the merits of this method. His reply to Girard proves it: 'It has become possible since Dio and Crépin did a good job, and they no longer need to have everyone on hand like in the past.'[27]

In mid-November, the 1st Battalion finished collecting the new American equipment, the 2nd Battalion did so at the end of November, and the 3rd at the beginning of December. Dio asked the battalion commanders to immediately begin individual technical training so that each *marsouin* was trained in their position and on their equipment. 'The instruction was carried out at full speed: training of drivers and alternate drivers, training in off-road driving; familiarisation with new weapons, light machine guns and heavy machine guns, bazookas; 57mm anti-tank guns, 60mm mortars, mines, etc.'[28] Previously, American specialists had organised intensive 'train-the-trainer' courses among the cadre of the three battalions of the *RMT*. Those trainers would teach

23   Dronne, *Carnets de Route*, p.244.

24   Jacques Vernet, 'Mise sur pied de la 2e DB, de la diversité à l'unité', in Levisse-Touzé, (ed.), *Du Capitaine de Hauteclocque au Général Leclerc* (Paris: Éditions Complexe, 2000), p.199.

25   *Lieutenant* Leclerc's tactical mastermind in Saumur was *Chef d'Escacrons* du Vigier, who defined the principles of use of mechanised cavalry: organisation in combat into combined arms tactical groups and favouring the tactic of flanking manoeuvres. 'Leclerc puts these principles into effect with the energy and simplifying spirit that characterise him.' (Levisse-Touzé, *Du Capitaine de Hauteclocque au Général Leclerc*, p.215). NB in the armoured cavalry branch, a squadron commander's rank is in the plural (*chef d'escadrons*), which is not the case in the other arms (*chef d'escadron* or *chef de bataillon*).

26   Jean Compagnon, 'Logisticien et Tacticien', in Christine Levisse-Touzé (ed.), *Du Capitaine de Hauteclocque au Général Leclerc* (Paris: Éditions Complexe, 2000), p.217.

27   Girard, *Journal de Guerre*, p.167.

28   Dronne, R., *Carnets de Route,* p.244.

other leaders and *marsouins* in their units how to use which vehicle, which machine gun, which howitzer, et cetera, as swiftly as possible.

Once the individual technical training was complete, the collective tactical training could begin. This training was carried out in phases. In the infantry, it started with the combat group. The sergent, as the group leader, had to teach his 10 men to move and manoeuvre with their half-track. Then, the *lieutenant*, as the section leader, taught his five groups to work together (51 men in the section) and to carry out typical missions: reconnoitre a route, defend a position, and attack enemy positions. Up to this level drill is very important. Finally, the *capitaine*, as the commander of a company, the first tactical organisation in the infantry, brought together his three sections to have them carry out more complex missions.

Small training courses were organised, for example:

1) a shooting competition with the 7.5mm [*sic*, 7.62 or .30 calibre] machine gun on different targets
2) disassembly and reassembly of the machine gun in the minimum time
3) rapid firing of the 57mm gun.[29]

Once the field exercises were completed in accordance with the tactical regulations, they were combined with live fire exercises. The companies carried out small movements using each of the weapons provided, helped by the internal support of the accompanying company. For example, infantry attacked an enemy position while the mortars, howitzers, guns, and the company's machine guns provided supporting fire. At that stage, Dio routinely attended this type of exercise. It was an opportunity for him to control training and maintain contact with his men. At the end of the exercise, he usually addressed the entire unit that had just carried out the manoeuvres to give his assessment. Then, he would hold back the section leaders and set out the areas of progress to be made. At the end, he met with the *capitaine* to tell him what he thought, in the presence of the battalion commander. During those discussions, Dio, always very direct, did not mince his words.[30] But he never upset his men because he always spoke to them in terms of progress and usually ended with a positive remark. They all knew that he never hesitated to congratulate them when it was deserved. They immediately accepted his advice in the field of tactics since his reputation as a military leader had become so strong. During the last months of late 1943, *Colonel* Dio followed the intensive training of his three battalions. The 1st Battalion, the first to be equipped, reached a satisfactory level in mid-December. Dio invited Leclerc to come to watch an exercise of *Capitaine* Perceval's 2nd Company on 21 December. It is worth noting that the *général*, always impatient, harassed his *colonels* to invite him to come into the field to see what they were doing. Dio was not at all worried, he knew that Farret had done a good job of organising the demonstration that the company would deliver in front of the *général*. It was the first exercise by an *RMT* unit with the new American equipment. At the end, Leclerc 'although demanding, gave them only praise.'[31]

During this period, the *RMT* continued to recruit volunteers, mainly among those who had escaped from Nazi occupied France. 'Nearly 2,500 escapees joined the *2ᵉ Division Blindée* training

29   Destray, Fonds Leclerc, *Campagne France-Allemagne 44–45*, p.6.
30   Massu described this way of forging relationships with subordinates: 'following the example of my boss, I camouflage my affection for my subordinates and I leave everyone in constant uncertainty about the esteem I have for them… One must therefore never take my good opinion of someone for granted but one must constantly earn it. Nothing like it for keeping men of duty in suspense.' (J. Massu, *Sept Ans*, p.98).
31   *De Fort-Lamy à Strasbourg*, p.14.

in Témara.'[32] The companies were not yet full, and positions became available. Volunteers, recruited rather quickly in Sabratha or Djidjelli among the *CFA*, sometimes turned out to be mediocre or even unfit soldiers. Dio gave instructions not to keep such men. "The future will sift the good from the bad,' *Colonel* Dio said, with a healthy vision of things.'[33] It was better to be understrength than to have bad apples in the ranks of the regiment. A handwritten letter from *Colonel* Dio to *Général* Leclerc, dated 12 October 1943, demonstrates that Dio personally took charge of the recruitment in respect of the doubtful and undesirable cases. He reported to Leclerc that a *colonel* from the general staff had sent back to him *CFA* personnel 'formerly carried on the roles of the *Corps Franc* and absent for various reasons for several months' whom he had removed. He added 'I need to have my hands completely free to proceed with the purification of the ex-*CFA*.'[34] In contrast, the escapees from France were welcomed without hesitation by Dio and his officers. *Commandant* Vézinet, deputy of the regiment, reported that 'the young men who escaped from France via Spain are physically weak but morally acceptable. A special diet appears to be an essential measure for their complete training.'[35] The 2nd Company, for example, received around 60 young escapees from France who had suffered in Spanish jails. Its commander, *Capitaine* Perceval, noted with insight: 'And it is not one of the least characteristics of the *Régiment du Tchad* to have always had, gathered under its flag, only men who had suffered and who, since 1940, had known no leader other than *Général* de Gaulle, no rallying signs other than the Cross of Lorraine.'[36] This remark, largely justified, would effectively allow the regiment to have motivated and tough men. Dio was aware of this and, while being demanding, always showed his men the greatest humanity in view of the difficulties they encountered in joining the regiment. The *RMT*, like the rest of the division, also recruited North Africans: Tunisians, Moroccans, and Algerians. It was mainly Massu's 2nd Battalion, which absorbed more than 300 of them. But the North Africans were still a minority in the *RMT* even though they represented a quarter of the division's total strength. They were primarily assigned to support units, artillery, and engineers.

Once the *2ᵉ DB* was equipped and had started its training, command inspections became part of the agenda. A few days before Christmas, *Général* Desré, senior commander of the troops in Morocco, accompanied by *Mr* Froment, president of the army commission, inspected the division. Such a shift of authorities was certainly intended to exert control, but also to listen. On that occasion, during the inspection of his regiment, *Colonel* Dio strongly emphasised the unstable condition of his men's accommodations for training. In December, an icy wind blew from the ocean and made life difficult in the tents. Dio was always very concerned about the comfort of his men – he was a soldier's commander, and he stayed close to them. The end of 1943 arrived without activities slowing down. *RMT* leaders and *marsouins* nevertheless celebrated the end of the year fittingly. The New Year's Eve menu had been improved and, with the help of alcohol, the singing of unit songs ended late. The new year of 1944 brought hope to everyone because it would undoubtedly be the year of the fight for the liberation of France.

In the evening of 2 January, *Général* de Lattre, who then commanded Army B, which was intended to succeed the *Corps Expéditionnaire d'Italie*, invited himself for a visit. Leclerc had a dinner prepared to receive him in the presence of his key subordinates. At 6:00 p.m., the first officers arrived at the *général's* villa. Suddenly,

32   Levisse-Touzé, *Du Capitaine de Hauteclocque au Général Leclerc*, 'Leclerc et l'Afrique du Nord, 1943–1944', p.285.
33   Bergot, *La 2 ème D.B.*, p.18.
34   Fonds Leclerc, boîte 9b, dossier 2, chemise 1.
35   Fonds Leclerc, *note 139/2 of September 30, 1943*, boîte K1, dossier 2.
36   *De Fort-Lamy à Strasbourg*, p.13.

...a command to arms rings out and a car with a flag appears on the road – Good God! it's him, exclaims the *général*, who steps out in double time. Everyone follows. Arriving in front of the honour company, the car passes it while slowing down, stops a few metres away and we see *Colonel* Dio get out, confused but laughing. The *général* bursts into laughter.[37]

This anecdote demonstrates the excellent atmosphere reigning between the two leaders. Leclerc forgave Dio everything, even for making him run! De Lattre arrived quite late. At the table, he monopolised the conversation, talking only about himself. Dio, who did not know him, immediately formed a qualified opinion of him, and he noted that Leclerc also did not seem to appreciate the monologue. The next day, the *général* took de Lattre to visit several bivouacs, including that of the 2nd Battalion of the *RMT*. The aim was to show him the difficult living conditions of the soldiers of the *2ᵉ DB*, but the justifiable grievances made no more impact on him than it had on Desré. No measures would be taken at their level to improve the housing conditions of the division's soldiers.[38]

It was not until 3 January that Leclerc came to present his New Year's wishes to the *RMT*. In front of Dio and his leaders gathered in the casino, Leclerc said:

...the year 1944 will be the year of liberation .... those who liberated Gabès and Tunis lived unforgettable hours, but they are nothing compared to those we will experience by delivering the cities of France. The objective that I set for those who left the Congo with me three years ago was Strasbourg. My wish for 1944 is to achieve this goal.[39]

Needless to say, such words coming from the mouth of one whose simple 'presence electrifies our wills and strengthens our efforts'[40] was particularly pleasing to *RMT* officers and *marsouins*.

At the beginning of 1944, the RMT alternated exercises and inspections. The exercises were carried out within the structure of *groupements tactiques*. The cavalry had to learn to work with the infantry and vice versa, and both also had to integrate the engineers and artillerymen into supporting actions and the services into that of support for everyone else. On 21 January, a demonstration was arranged for General Allen F. Kingman, the American officer in charge of the French Training Section of the Joint Rearmament Committee. He had to conduct a technical inspection in mid-February to verify the readiness of the *2ᵉ DB* for combat. Leclerc's aide-de-camp noted, '... very good tank exercise executed by Branet in cooperation with the *3/RMT*.'[41] Putz, commander of the 3rd Battalion, contacted the commander of the *501ᵉ RCC*, *Commandant* Cantarel, to prepare and execute the exercise demonstration. This partnership, started in Morocco, would last 17 months, leading them together into the heart of Nazi Germany.

Command inspections followed one another. The commander of Army B, *Général* de Lattre, returned on 25 January. The *2ᵉ DB* was still under his command, and he had nothing but praise for the division during the inspection. He told the unit commanders 'that judging from postal control,[42] the morale of the division is magnificent.'[43] Dio respected *Général* de Lattre as a military

37   Girard, *Journal de Guerre,* p.115.
38   Reports on morale from this period show that the tentage accommodations took a severe toll on the men because of the cold and the humidity. The November report from the 1st Battalion of the *RMT* proposed raising the tents on wooden platforms to insulate them. Fonds Leclerc, boîte J, dossier 1.
39   Girard, *Journal de Guerre,* p.117.
40   Massu, *Sept Ans,* p.99.
41   Girard, *Journal de Guerre,* p.124.
42   In times of war, soldiers' personal mail was opened and read by a service to verify that secret information such as the name and location of units was not leaked and possibly exploited.
43   Girard, *Journal de Guerre,* p.125.

leader, but did not like him personally, as they were opposites in character. In that sentiment, he adopted the same attitude as Leclerc, who had his 'sullen'[44] look, and who was 'impervious to these praises …. because they are not the most sincere.'[45]

The commander of the *2e DB* and the commander of the *RMT* had another concern at that moment. Part of the Moroccan population had revolted and carried out violent actions against European populations, particularly in Rabat-Salé and Fez. Six French civilians were killed. 'The Moroccans, who had seen the Germans gain the upper hand over the French, and who now saw the Americans masters of the game, were finding it increasingly difficult to tolerate the tutelage of a nation which was itself more or less enslaved.'[46] According to Moroccan sources, 'it seems … that the sultan had received encouragement from the Americans to demand independence.'[47] *Général* Desré asked Leclerc to send detachments to different places in the territory in order to maintain order. Obviously, in these cases, it was the infantry who were sent first. Dio was not happy because the technical inspection was approaching. Furthermore, *Commandant* Farret, commanding the 1st Battalion, reported that, 'the troops did not understand [why they were] being confined and mobilised for weeks to play *gendarmes* without firing a shot.'[48] Facing a crowd that had to be dissuaded while avoiding the use of weapons is a difficult mission for soldiers who are not trained in maintaining order. Managing a crowd is very complex and a tense situation could lead soldiers to use their weapons, which is certainly what the Moroccan nationalist leaders of the Istiqlal Party were hoping for. Fortunately, thanks to their experience and the cohesion of the units, the *RMT* officers managed to control the situation during those days of revolt against the French, and the situation gradually returned to normal.[49]

It was high time, because *Général* Giraud announced on 8 February that he would inspect the division as commander-in-chief. Dio introduced him to the 1st Battalion. 'Everything went well. At the end, he brought the officers together to tell them about what he saw recently in Italy. Above all, it demonstrated that the fight would be tough.'[50] Leclerc wasted no time. The day after this visit, 9 February, he scheduled an officers' communications exercise. This type of training consisted of bringing together all the unit leaders in different rooms of a building, equipping them with radios, giving them fictitious orders on a map to simulate a tactical mission, and asking them to issue their orders over the radio network. It had the advantage of instilling radio discipline and making everyone aware of the environment in which they would have to work. Mainly, it reduced potential maintenance time for the armoured vehicles, which, like planes and ships, had to undergo periodic overhauls. Discussing the exercise, *Général* Leclerc's aide-de-camp noted in his planner: '*Commandant* Vézinet, interim commander of the *Régiment de Marche du Tchad*, is on site almost all the time and is noted for his calm and precision. He speaks calmly, responds to all questions with relevance. Perfect control of himself and his work.'[51] Dio, perhaps in collusion with Leclerc, intentionally took a day off in order to leave his deputy in command. He was keen to empower his direct subordinates so that they could assume command of the unit if necessary. On several occasions in March, Sundays were set aside for those type of leadership exercises 'so as not to interrupt the training programmes specific to each unit.'[52]

44   Girard, *Journal de Guerre*, p.125.
45   Notin, *le Croisé*, p.229.
46   Salbaing, *Ardeur,* p.119.
47   Dronne, *Carnets de Route*, p.247.
48   Fonds Leclerc, *note 35/C of 02/18/1944,* boîte K1, dossier 2.
49   Moroccan nationalists declared independence on 11 January 1944. At the time, Morocco was a French protectorate ruled by Sultan Muhammad V. At the Casablanca conference in January 1943, US President Franklin D. Roosevelt indicated to Muhammad that the US would support Moroccan independence when the war was over. (Translator's note)
50   Girard, *Journal de Guerre*, p.127.
51   Girard, *Journal de Guerre*, p.128.
52   Salbaing, *Ardeur,* p.121.

The technical inspection took place as planned from 12 to 15 February 1944. The *RMT* battalions knew that the inspection was crucial for the future. Everyone redoubled their efforts to not only present their equipment in a state of maximum cleanliness, 'everything was shining and working wonderfully,'[53] but also to study the technical specifications so they could accurately answer the inspectors' questions. Everyone was tested, even senior officers. Massu wrote: 'I myself, a battalion commander mounted on a jeep, am questioned like a student about this 'warhorse,' whose all-terrain operations of the front axle and *crabotage*[54] are fortunately familiar to me.'[55] The technical inspection went very well. The members of the commission emphasised in their report the 'pride of the personnel in using new and quality equipment, in everyone the same desire to learn, the same impatience to fight…'[56] Finally, General A. F. Kingman ended his report with: 'this division will be ready to provide the most real combat services, as soon as the main deficits that I have mentioned have been filled.'[57] The deficits noted were missing equipment that had not yet been delivered to the *2ͤ DB*.

Dio was particularly happy to see that the three battalions of the *RMT* passed their technical inspection without encountering the slightest problem. The units rose to the occasion for the inspection. The regimental commander also wanted to demonstrate to the other units of the division that the *méharistes* from Chad were capable of being retrained on modern mechanised equipment. He believed that this was the best way to respond to certain perfidious remarks heard during the arrival of the *RMT* in Témara in October 1943. The name 'Support Brigade' in reference to the infantry of the *2ͤ DB* would soon disappear from official internal documents. Following the successful inspection, on 2 March 1944, *Colonel* Dio signed regimental Order No.5 in which he delivered 18 testimonials of satisfaction[58] distributed between the three battalions. These awards mainly targeted non-commissioned officers and enlisted personnel. Thus, *Soldat de Deuxième Classe* Maurice Coussot of the 2nd Battalion received his testimonial of satisfaction with the following citation, 'The only mechanic available to the unit, worked tirelessly, thus allowing him to present the vehicles in the best mechanical condition during the Franco-American inspection of 13 February 1944.'[59]

The *RMT* and the other units of the *2ͤ DB* were capable of combat, but no one yet knew with certainty where they would be engaged. 'The unit now considers itself to have passed the test for its departure for operations. Everyone is happy but morale risks dropping quickly if the stay in Morocco is prolonged; distractions will have to be increased.'[60] Leclerc knew that commitment would be easier if cohesion within the division was achieved. But that was hard for units that had been adversaries in the recent past. While certain units still often gave him problems, he confided to his aide-de-camp: 'you see, Girard, the *RMT* and the artillery groups have never given me any trouble. They are commanded by tradesmen, soldiers.'[61] As early as November 1943, to unite the units, the *général* launched the idea of creating a unit insignia badge, which would be painted on all the vehicles. He wanted a strong symbol of belonging to Free France, but he knew that he also had to consider the units of the *Armée d'Afrique*. He let the idea mature. On 22 February, during a meeting with his

---

53   Salbaing, *Ardeur,* p.120.
54   *Crabotage* is a method of engaging the front axle of the vehicle to shift into 4-wheel drive.
55   Massu, *Sept Ans,* p.100.
56   Fonds Leclerc, *Rapport d'inspection de la French Training Section du 23 février 1944,* boîte 10, dossier 3.
57   Fonds Leclerc, *Rapport d'inspection de la French Training Section du 23 février 1944.*
58   A *Témoignage de Satisfaction* (Testimonial of Satisfaction) is a letter from a commander that is used to reward an individual or a unit for excellent conduct or successful action. (Translator's note)
59   Fonds Leclerc, *Rapport d'inspection de la French Training Section du 23 février 1944.*
60   Fonds Leclerc, boîte J, dossier 1, *Rapport n° 35/C du 18 février 1944.* This report also indicates that on Sunday, 6 February when the soldiers were confined, there was 'a sporting and artistic afternoon with basketball games, boxing matches, relay races by company, and crochet session at the soldier's base.'
61   Girard, *Journal de Guerre,* p.166.

principal subordinates, he asked them 'if they thought the time had come to make the Cross of Lorraine obligatory for the entire Division.'[62] Dio and his peers responded in the affirmative but added that the Cross of Lorraine alone was not sufficient. In March, the proposal for a map of France, overlaid with a stylised Cross of Lorraine, was chosen. For the *marsouins* of the *RMT*, a symbolism reminiscent of the Oath of Kufra would have been welcome.[63] Nevertheless, Dio stood behind the simplicity of this final proposal and the beautiful symbol represented by the map of France!

In addition, to cultivate a sense of unit identity, the division decided to name each of its vehicles. Dio let his battalions determine the names of their vehicles themselves. He simply asked them to prescribe guidelines for each company in the choice of names so that there would be a level of consistency. For example, the *RMT* communications section, which had four half-tracks, chose the four aces from a deck of cards. The three battalions managed to find homogeneity in the names assigned to their vehicles. The mortar section of the Support Company of the 1st Battalion (*CA1*) used names starting with *Marguerite* combined with that of a French province; the machine gun section chose names starting with *Chantal* with the same principle. The howitzer section opted for the literature of François Rabelais with *Gargantua, Pantagruel, Picrochole,* et cetera. The 1st Company took the names of French towns. The 3rd Company preferred female first names while *CA2* opted for names of battles from the Libyan theatres. The 5th Company took the names of African cities or regions while the 7th used those of the Tunisian campaign. The howitzers of the *CA3* bore the names of 'the Three Musketeers' and the ammunition half-tracks, the servants of the musketeers. The half-tracks of the 9th Company opted, quite naturally, for places in Spain (*Guernica, Guadalajara…*). Capitaine Sarazac, commanding the 10th Company, chose Chadian names. The 11th Company alternated historic dates (14 July, 11 November, et cetera) with military marches (*Sambre et Meuse, Chant de Départ,* et cetera). When vehicles were later destroyed, some replacement vehicles would be renamed to honour those killed in action or of the locations of battles such as *Grussenheim* or *Croix de Médavi*. In the 10th Company, the half-track *Koro-Toro* became *Soldat Delarue*. The jeep *Sonia* became *Lieutenant Dusehu* in the 11th Company. If this consistency was generally respected in the operational units, it was not always the case with the leaders' vehicles. Thus, Dio himself named his command tank, made available to him by the *12ᵉ Régiment de Cuirassiers, Sainte-Anne d'Auray* in honour of the Breton shrine and the town near Vannes where he was born. Massu chose the name *Moïdo* for his jeep, in memory of a young woman from Tibesti. Dronne named his jeep *Mort aux Cons* (Death to Fools) with the pirate flag. After being chastised by the *général* when he saw that name, he would later call it *Mort aux Boches* (Death to the Germans).[64] *These nicknames given to the vehicles allowed the various leaders and men of the 2ᵉ DB to more easily identify the unit to which these vehicles belonged.*

24 March 1944 was an important day for Dio who commanded his *groupement tactique*, the *GTD*, in the field for the first time. He had to conduct a live fire exercise involving all the group's weaponry. It brought together the commanders of the *12ᵉ Régiment de Cuirassiers*, the 1st Battalion of the RMT, the *3ᵉ Régiment d'Artillerie Coloniale* and the *capitaines* of the 4th Squadron or the *1ᵉʳ Régiment de Marche de Spahis Marocains*, the 2nd Company of the *13ᵉ Bataillon du Génie*, the 2nd Battery of the *22ᵉ Groupement Colonial des Forces Terrestres Antiaériennes* as well as the medical and maintenance units. It consisted of a little less than '4,000 men, mounted on 900 trucks and

---

62   Girard, *Journal de Guerre*, p.140. The Cross of Lorraine, a cross with double horizontal bars, was the symbol of Free France and Gaullism. (Translator's note)

63   One proposal had planned a map of France on which two points would represent Paris and Strasbourg. The symbolism pleased Dio and his officers.

64   When he first saw Dronne's jeep, Leclerc asked him to erase it on the pretext that the division did not have enough ammunition to kill all the fools! Later de Gaulle, seeing the jeep pass in front of him during a parade, is said to have murmured 'enormous task, enormous task!'

armoured vehicles.'[65] They needed to conduct the training exercise with professionalism because live ammunition left no room for guesswork. The exercise also served as a demonstration for the arrival of Russian General Aleksandr Vasiliev. *Lieutenant* Girard noted in his diary: 'Interesting. The fire is very well executed but there are a few blunders, the elements on the ground are not yet dispersed enough, the tanks come into position on the infantry's assembly area, creating excessive concentration, downtime, unnecessary movements.'[66] At the end of the exercise, Dio brought together the *GTD* leaders and told them of his satisfaction despite the imperfections that appeared. He did not expect that the group would already be at such an operational level. He scheduled their next training session to iron out the problems and ended by saying that the 'Boche' would soon regret knowing them. Dio was realistic; he knew very well that he still had work to do. The opposite would have been surprising and even worrying. The demonstration in front of the Russian general mattered little to him. The evaluation of his group was his priority objective. He agreed in advance with any comments that his superiors might have following the imperfections noted during the live fire, but in the end, none were addressed to him.

It was the 2nd Battalion of the *RMT*'s turn to be presented to *Général* Vanier on 5 April. 'During the tour of his units that he gave to Vanier, Leclerc was overjoyed. All the pleasure and all the pride he felt in showing his men and officers to this old friend whom he esteemed was evident. They shone through in the praise he bestowed when presenting Dio, Massu, Langlois, Blasquez, Branet, et cetera.'[67] The *général* remained very attached to his men who had been faithful from the beginning, and they returned the sentiments.

On Thursday, 6 April 1944, the unit commanders gathered by Leclerc learnt 'officially of the embarkation next Monday of a first fraction of the division.'[68] During the meeting, a telex arrived, announcing *Général* de Gaulle's arrival the next day for an inspection. The leader of Free France wanted to see first-hand the division on which he placed so much hope, and which he had succeeded in establishing, despite the many obstacles. Dio, with his pithy comments, simply told his subordinates that 'it smells good,' meaning that the arrival of de Gaulle would surely lead to their departure from Morocco. On the morning of 7 April, for the review at Skhirat in honour of *Général* de Gaulle, Dio presented his assembled regiment. He wanted to send a message to his officers: infantry has a place in an armoured division. *Lieutenant* Girard was impressed by the review:

> At the *RMT*, the presentation is magnificent. On flat, level ground, the battalions, frozen in impressive attention, form a compact block. *Général* de Gaulle goes very slowly, looks for a long time. Dio is in great shape. Personally, I am overwhelmed by the spectacle and when we return to our cars, I cannot take my eyes off this immobile mass, bristling with bayonets which, tomorrow, will raise the honour of France.[69]

Dio also arranged the fine ceremony for his 2,500 men, most of whom had never seen de Gaulle and in particular, 'the young men who …. look with emotion at the large figure who advances slowly in front of them.'[70] 'His size was imposing, even next to Dio, and he impressed with the dignity of his movements.'[71] The young *Aspirant* Salbaing added: 'We would see de Gaulle again

65   Massu, *Sept Ans,* p.101.
66   Girard, *Journal de Guerre,* p.169.
67   Girard, *Journal de Guerre,* p.173.
68   Girard, *Journal de Guerre,* p.174
69   Girard, *Journal de Guerre,* p.175.
70   Massu, *Sept Ans,* p.101.
71   Salbaing, *Ardeur,* p.123.

several times, because he had a particular attachment to us, it seems. We had become, in a way, his '*grognards*,'[72] those on whom he could count in all circumstances…'[73] Dio was satisfied. He knew how to galvanise his men, who presented themselves magnificently to the leader of Free France. That connection flowed… in both directions. He felt that his regiment was ready to go into battle.

In the evening, de Gaulle addressed all the officers of the division gathered in the casino. He finally announced to them: 'You are leaving for England.'[74] That news filled those in attendance with incredible joy. The *2ᵉ DB* would participate in the future Battle of France within an American Army corps. 'It is the only large French unit which will participate in the assault that will be launched from the English coast against the northwest face of Fortress Europe.'[75] Everything would move very quickly then. The embarkation of the 16,000 men equipped with more than 4,000 vehicles was primarily a matter of logistics. The division would be split into three detachments, each under the orders of a *colonel*. Echelon A under *Colonel* de Langlade left Casablanca on 10 April with a large part of the tracked vehicles.[76] Each of the battalions designated a *capitaine* with a dozen other officers, around 20 non-commissioned officers, and 150 *marsouins* to load the *RMT*'s tracked vehicles. The maritime convoy took 14 days to reach Swansea. *Colonel* Malaguti would command Echelon C, composed mainly of personnel. This echelon would wait in a transit centre near Oran. It would not embark until 20 May on two British liners, RMMV *Capetown Castle* and RMS *Franconia*. They reached the port of Glasgow on 29 May, having made a large detour to avoid German submarines.

Dio was responsible for Echelon B, which had to leave Oran with a little less than 3,000 wheeled vehicles but also included the remainder of the half-tracks and the armoured tank destroyers of the *RBFM*. This echelon was the largest in terms of equipment. Dio, at the head of his immense column, left the Témara casino on 12 April. He reached Meknes the first evening. The communications specialist Béné was once again with *Colonel* Dio. He wrote: 'On 13 April, we crossed the Algerian-Moroccan border at Oujda. On 15 April we finally arrived in Oran.'[77] The column was directed to the Hassi-ben-Okhba Camp, about 20 kilometres away, in this 'Staging Area No.1… dominated by inactivity, idleness.'[78] Echelon B was then split in two. The first portion of Echelon B left Oran on 20 April and arrived safely in Swansea on 2 May. Dio, with the bulk of Echelon B had to wait another 10 days in Oran before boarding. Finally, on 30 April 1944, Dio had his column on the docks where the 26 LSTs (Landing Ship Tank) were waiting. 'These strange ships that open like Ali-Baba's caves to let in our vehicles. These are large transport ships, 104 metres long and 16.30 metres wide.'[79] Boarding lasted all day and into part of the evening.

The ships set sail at nightfall. During the day, Radio Paris, a collaborationist radio station, ironically wished a good trip to the detachment that was about to set sail. 'You should know that at the time of departure, Radio Paris had predicted that we were going to go on our cruise at the bottom of the sea. Intelligence was working well, since this same message indicated exactly which units

---

72   A *grognard* is someone who complains, but here it was meant to imply trust and confidence. *Les Grognards* was Napoléon I's nickname for the reliable and capable soldiers of his Old Guard. Although they were loyal and highly competent, they had a tendency to complain, like all soldiers. But as Napoléon's personal guard, they were close enough to complain directly to the Emperor, earning the nickname that Napoléon used as a term of endearment. (Translator's note)

73   Salbaing, *Ardeur,* p.124.

74   Béné, *Carnets, Seconde époque*, p.236.

75   Dronne, *Carnets de Route,* p.248.

76   This included 165 Sherman medium tanks, 95 light tanks, 620 half-tracks, 36 M10 guns and 150 wheeled vehicles, i.e. 1,094 vehicles and 2,560 soldiers. Telex n°2980/EMP-4 of 5 April 1944 SHAT 7P51 dossier 1.

77   Béné, *Carnets, Seconde époque*, p.238.

78   Salbaing, *Ardeur,* p.125.

79   Béné, *Carnets, Seconde Époque*, p.238.

were boarding, as well as the names of the ships.'[80] Dio, imperturbable, cigarette in the corner of his mouth, shrugged his shoulders when one of his officers told him about this radio message. The next day at daybreak, Dio and his officers were able to realise, as they climbed onto the bridge, that the maritime convoy was immense with, 'warships, corvettes, and others circling around the convoy like shepherd dogs around their flock of sheep.'[81] Starting on 4 May, rough seas made transit difficult for passengers because the flat-bottomed LSTs, which did not ride the sea well, pitched and rolled in every direction.

On 11 May, the convoy arrived in the estuary of the River Mersey to dock at the port of Liverpool. Upon landing, the welcome from the British population was fantastic, impressing all the men of the 2ᵉ DB. 'We find tea, chocolate, cigarettes. Nothing is missing! We are amazed and delighted with this friendly and cordial welcome.'[82] The men were able to disembark on 12 May, and in the evening, Dio allowed them free time. This permitted everyone to stretch their legs by wandering the streets and checking out the bars of the large industrial city. The next day, Dio assembled the column of wheeled vehicles at the port. Tracked vehicles would travel by rail, wheeled vehicles by road. The destination was Yorkshire, more precisely the 'East Riding district, Eastern province of the County of York,' located approximately 200 kilometres from Liverpool.[83] They had to cross the north of England from west to east. Progress was slow on the narrow English roads. During the trip, the men of the 2ᵉ DB continued to be welcomed by the British population. 'When we stop near houses or in a village, English women immediately come to us with tea and cake. It is a real comfort for us to see that the fighter is aptly regarded here. What a difference with our passage and our stay in the towns and villages of North Africa.'[84] The same day, Dio arrived with the first elements in Hull, a town in Yorkshire, east of the regional capital. Hull is on the edge of the Humber Estuary on the eastern coast of England, on the North Sea. The area north of the city is rural, far from British industrial centres, which was chosen to allow the 2ᵉ DB to continue training. The area of 40,000 hectares was ideal, and large enough to serve as a field of manoeuvre for a division. 'It was also a landscape exactly similar to those we were going to encounter in France with roads, steep paths, hedges, woods, crops, and villages.'[85] That is where the division set up between Hull and the old City of York. The central point was Dalton Hall Castle where Général Leclerc was based. Dio brought the vehicles together in a transit zone on the outskirts of the town of Hull. From there, the detachments of the units that had already arrived and were quartered in the villages north of Hull, came to collect their vehicles.

The stationing of units in England was organised by groupements tactiques. 'This will strengthen the amalgamation and facilitate joint training.'[86] Leclerc's aide-de-camp noted Dio's arrival on 14 May at his CP 40 miles north of Hull.[87] The GTD commander was clearly not in a good mood when he saw the area that had been planned for his groupement tactique. The 12ᵉ Cuirassiers and the 1st Battalion of the RMT, the two combat arms units of the GTD, were housed in tents at the camp in West Lutton. The same was true of the 3ᵉ RAC which was stationed at Sledmere (5km south of West Lutton), near the RBFM. Girard's diary mentions: 'Colonel Dio has arrived. He went straight to his CP and called, saying that he found it unacceptable. It's understandable. His entire groupement tactique is in tents. Langlade had two very comfortable rooms reserved for him in a very

80   Destray, Fonds Leclerc, Campagne France-Allemagne 44–45, p.8.
81   Béné, Carnets, Seconde Époque, p.239.
82   Destray, Fonds Leclerc, Campagne France-Allemagne 44–45, p.9.
83   Langlade, En Suivant Leclerc, p.102.
84   Béné, Carnets, Seconde époque, p.241.
85   Langlade, En Suivant Leclerc, p.102.
86   Compagnon, Leclerc, p.356.
87   Girard, Journal de Guerre, p.197.

beautiful castle nearby, but Dio would not be able to accept being the only one warm. He asked that his entire staff be housed in 'hard' accommodations so it could work.'[88] Dio did not divulge to his men that they were not in the same conditions as those of the *GTL* whose commander had arrived ahead of them, and had obviously chosen the best locations. Dio wished to assert himself within the *2ᵉ DB*. The message was clear to everyone: he wanted to be on the same footing as his comrades from the *Armée d'Afrique*. Leclerc did not intervene but, deep down, he agreed with Dio: 'the *général* seemed affected that Dio went directly to his CP without going through HQ. But wasn't it normal that he would immediately meet his troops at their cantonment?'[89] *Lieutenant* Girard had also chosen his side and showed his great admiration for Dio. The *colonel* was a strong personality who did not leave others indifferent. Unlike Girard, *Capitaine* Gribius, a cavalry officer assuming the important function of chief of operations on the divisional staff, was not spontaneously an admirer of the *GTD*'s commander. An extract from his book *Une Vie d'Officier* paints an interesting portrait:

> *Colonel* Dio (*GTD*) has been one of the *général*'s companions for a long time. Our first contact leaves me with a mixed impression. His abrupt vocabulary, his sometimes crude manners, initially bother me a little. I would later discover that this gruff facade, this harsh behaviour, is in fact just a way for him to study and judge men. If we stand our ground, don't let ourselves be awed, then we win. Conversely, we lose our means, and we risk being classified among the weak and weak-willed.
>
> In reality, he cultivates dry humour, and sometimes the tricks he invents are particularly studied and developed.
>
> I myself was the victim of one of his pranks: it was in England, and in anticipation of the battles in France, the *général* had asked me to write a note outlining the value he attached to each person being able to live while sleeping as little as possible and eating irregularly.
>
> Invited to lunch at *Colonel* Dio's CP, I notice that we are slow to sit down. Suddenly the *colonel* gets impatient and calls the head waiter.
> - Hurry up and serve, the guests are waiting.
> - But Colonel, today is Tuesday, and in accordance with the note we received, it is a day of training how to fast.
>
> I admit that for a moment I believed it. Until a few minutes later, the dining room opened to an excellent meal.[90]

The colonials often exasperated the cavalrymen by their behaviour, which was the opposite of the orderly world of the armoured cavalry, where dress and good manners, not to mention worldliness, were part of relationships. Leclerc himself, upon arriving at Fort-Lamy, had been shocked by the behaviour and dress of the *RTST* colonials. But Dio, ever since the establishment of the *2ᵉ DB*, had certainly exaggerated his character in order to assert himself in an environment where cavalrymen were the majority. The *général* had long understood Dio's true personality; he knew that he was playing a role and he let him do it. This is also most certainly what irritated the officers of the *Armée d'Afrique* who had only joined Leclerc's epic adventure in the second half of 1943.

On 17 May, Leclerc signed the official note establishing the *groupements tactiques*. The three *GTs* were identical, comprising 'a strength of approximately 4,000 men and 900 trucks and

---

88   Girard, *Journal de Guerre*, p.197.
89   Girard, *Journal de Guerre*, p.198.
90   André Gribius, *Une Vie d'Officier* (Paris: Éditions France-Empire, 1971), pp.98–99.

armoured vehicles.'[91] Dio was then responsible for the units in his *groupement tactique*, but he was still administratively the head of the *RMT*. In England, he performed both functions, which was not easy. Once they landed in France, he would devote most of his time to his role as commander of the *GTD*.[92] The *GTD* had a small staff made up of the headquarters company of the *RMT*. His deputy was still *Lieutenant Colonel* Vézinet with whom he worked well. The chief of the S1 (1st Staff Section – personnel) was *Commandant* Lepointe. S2 (intelligence) was entrusted to *Commandant* Baylon, Dio's classmate who had been his adversary in Gabon.[93] S3 (operations) was under *Commandant* Didelot, while S4 (logistics) was under *Capitaine* Gachet. Dio had a team of excellent officers who would all work together with great cooperation.[94]

Supplies were provided at the level of the *2ᵉ DB*. The *GTD* was a formidable combat tool, and it was important for Dio to learn how to use it. To do so, Dio took advantage of his stay in England to visit the units, to get to know the leaders, and to find out about their specific characteristics and the difficulties they had to resolve. Dio was used to commanding small combined arms detachments in Fezzan, but the *groupement tactique* that Leclerc entrusted to him was of a completely different dimension. The modernity of the weapons, the variety of missions, and the differences in branch culture had to be quickly learnt by the former *méhariste* who had not attended any training school since Saint-Cyr. Thanks to his practical intelligence and his interpersonal skills, he would immediately establish himself at the head of his *GT*, in the same way as Langlade or Malaguti, although they were older than him and graduates of military training schools.

Dio was aware of the need to make all the components of his *GT* work together in order to perfect cohesion. For the moment, the problem was that a large part of the personnel included in Echelon C, under Malaguti's orders, had not yet arrived. Only drivers and some of the leaders were available. That prevented the conduct of even the smallest exercise. Leclerc, who was also growing impatient, summoned his chief subordinates to the dining room of the castle on 22 May. Dalton Hall housed the command post, staff, and the headquarters units that supported and protected

---

91   Langlade, *En Suivant Leclerc*, p.66.
92   The operational units making up the *GTD* were:
   - The 1st Battalion of the *RMT* under *Commandant* Farret, Dio's comrade-in-arms with whom he had fought since the end of 1942, during the Fezzan 2 and Tunisian campaigns
   - The *12e Cuirassiers* tank regiment, commanded by *Lieutenant Colonel* Warabiot, with *Commandant* Noiret as deputy
   - The *3e Régiment d'Artillerie Coloniale* under the orders of *Lieutenant Colonel* Fieschi. This regiment was formed by *Lieutenant Colonel* Crépin from the Chadian artillerymen, some of whom were well known to Dio
   To these three regiments forming the heart of the *GTD*, the following reinforcements were attached:
   - The 4th Squadron of the *1er RMSM*, equipped with armoured cars (AM M8) and jeeps to carry out reconnaissance missions
   - The 3rd Squadron of the *Régiment Blindé de Fusiliers Marins*, sailors equipped with tank destroyers, the only armoured vehicles of the *2e DB* that had guns that could compare to German tanks in terms of ability to penetrate armour
   - The 2nd Battery of the 22e FTA, equipped with Bofors guns, responsible for anti-aircraft defence
   - The 2nd Company of the *13e Régiment de Génie*, responsible mainly for assisting with mobility, primarily with mine clearance and river crossing
   - The 2nd Company of the *13e Bataillon Médical*, with the *Marinette*s as ambulance crews
   - The 3rd Maintenance Squadron of the XV *Groupement d'Évacuation et de Réparation*
93   Baylon would follow Dio throughout the campaign of liberation. He would be his head of services in 1946 at *Groupement Blindé No.2* in Saint-Germain. For six years these two officers worked alongside each other. This demonstrates that Dio remained attached to his subordinates on the one hand and that he was a beloved leader on the other.
94   Staff sections of regiments and battalions use the S-designation (S1, S2, S3, S4) while higher general staff sections are designated with a G (G1, G2, G3, G4). (Translator's note)

the CP. During the meeting, Dio pointedly expressed his dissatisfaction with the poor conditions of his staff's accommodations which, according to him, did not allow him to work properly. A permanent building previously assigned to the artillerymen of the *40ᵉ RANA* was finally made available to them. Leclerc had certainly intervened discreetly with *Colonel* de Langlade.

Echelon C, under the orders of Malaguti and which was the last to leave, rounded the British Isles widely to the west and landed at Greenock in Scotland. This port, on the Clyde Estuary, serves the Scottish economic capital of Glasgow. The welcome given to 'the Frenchies' by the Scots was also very warm. The personnel reached Yorkshire by train in 48 hours. At the beginning of June 1944, the *2ᵉ DB* was finally complete in England, and training could begin at last, and Dio put pressure on his immediate subordinates. It was then a matter of perfecting joint collective training to improve the operational value of the group. At the same time, out of respect and consideration for the British population, each unit of the *GTD* had to ensure their personnel who left the cantonments in the evening were properly dressed. One of the *RMT marsouins* writes: 'our clothes had to be impeccable, the men shaved, their hair done, et cetera because we wanted to give a good impression to our English friends.'[95] Dio was not particularly an Anglophile, but he could not help but admire these people 'where everyone is mobilised, where everyone is working on national defence. Women and young girls work like men. Men aged fifty to sixty-five are mobilised in the Home Gard (*sic*).'[96] The English population called it the 'war effort,' which was 'the abdication of any feeling of personal interest and the total acceptance of the sacrifice of individuals for the general interest of the country in danger.'[97]

On 5 June, Dio and his leaders learnt during dinner that the Allies had entered Rome. The next day, the news of the landing of the Allied forces in Normandy completely stunned them. Then they understood why, 'all night of 5 June, and on 6 June from dawn to dark, the sky resounded with the noise of aeroplane engines which were constantly circling above us…'[98] The first feeling that predominated at the announcement was worry: would the Allies liberate France without waiting for them? After D-Day, the 'radio was religiously listened to and commented on. But, undoubtedly unlike the rest of the world, the men of the *2ᵉ DB* were surely the only ones to be pleased with such a slow advance.'[99] The men of the division were impatient to be engaged in the fight to liberate their country. They were afraid that they would not have the opportunity if they stayed in England too long.

With the *2ᵉ DB* complete again, the pace of inspections could resume. On 7 June, General Cook, commanding the American XII Corps, to which the *2ᵉ DB* would be attached, came for an inspection. The Americans wanted to check on the conditions in which the units were getting back on their feet following their movement from Morocco to England. A dinner was organised in the evening, bringing together all the key officers of the division. Dio was reassured by this first contact with 'This old American general, decorated in 1914 with the *Croix de Guerre* with palm… moved by the idea of commanding, twenty years later, a large French unit.'[100] Their time was approaching, so it was important to bring the *groupement tactique* up to its full operational potential. Dio placed particular emphasis on training and exercises involving tanks and infantrymen. He knew that tanks could not operate without infantry, but he also knew that the infantry would have difficulty keeping up with the armoured vehicles. The infantry needed to be mounted, and only dismount from the half-tracks to deploy at the last moment. The exercises that Dio organised

95   Destray, Fonds Leclerc, *Campagne France-Allemagne 44–45,* p.9.
96   Destray, Fonds Leclerc, *Campagne France-Allemagne 44–45,* p.9.
97   Langlade, *En Suivant Leclerc*, p.87.
98   Salbaing, *Ardeur*, p.135.
99   Bergot, *La 2 ème D.B.,* p.38.
100 Girard, *Journal de Guerre*, p.212.

emphasised the armour-infantry cooperation and relied on the speed of action between the pair. 'The training consisted of jumping from moving vehicles with weapons and baggage, the half-tracks driving along ditches, we had to do combat rolls.'[101] The backbone of the RMT was formed from the two long range reconnaissance and combat companies (DC). Dio had helped design the structure of the *DCs*, which already foreshadowed the principle of a mobile infantryman who, once dismounted, was supported by the weapons of his vehicle. The 'Chadians' compared their half-tracks to their old, converted Bedford trucks.

Under the leadership of Dio and his deputies, the infantry of the *RMT* quickly learnt to work in close cooperation with tanks, favouring speed, which is the hallmark of a large armoured unit such as the *2ᵉ DB*. On the Fylingdales firing range, he had the *3ᵉ RAC* fire as close as possible to the tanks, infantry, and sappers. These combined armour-infantry-artillery exercises allowed each component of the *GTD* to become aware of the environment where they would be called upon to fight and to gain confidence in each other. Thus, like the other *groupements tactiques*, Dio organised, conducted, or participated in numerous training activities: 'subgroup manoeuvres, *groupement tactique* manoeuvres, division manoeuvres, command post exercises, communications exercises, firing ranges of all kinds, day and night.'[102] The pace was intense despite the continuous rains falling in the north of England at the time.

During the training period, *Général* Leclerc had concerns regarding the *RBFM*. This regiment, which arrived late with the division, was not yet operationally ready. Leclerc, who still doubted the abilities of sailors to fight on land with the tank destroyers assigned to the regiment, '25 tank specialist *aspirants*…to supervise the *enseignes de vaisseau*.'[103] In addition, to be the deputy to *Capitaine de Frégate* Maggiar, '*pasha*',[104] of the *RBFM*, he assigned *Chef d'Escadron* Fanneau de La Horie. Leclerc asked *Colonel* Dio to go to 'inspect' this unit. Thus, Dio invited himself to follow the field training of the *RBFM* squadrons for a day. At the end of the exercises, Maggiar invited Dio for dinner, which he accepted. The *pasha*, faithful to the traditions of the navy, pulled out all the stops with china, white tablecloth, and a butler. Dio honoured the meal and said nothing. As soon as he got back, Dio wrote a scathing letter to Maggiar 'in which he is reminded in unequivocal terms that he is preparing for a military campaign and that it is not a question of waging 'war in lace.''[105] This anecdote demonstrates the great trust and agreement between Leclerc and Dio, the two men were on the same wavelength. Dio had great freedom of action by reprimanding the commander of the RBFM, proving that he remained the officer closest to 'the Boss.'

On 10, 11, and 12 June, 'it was the American 'show down' inspection which once again checked the degree of preparation of the division.'[106] It was a complete review, down to the smallest detail, involving all equipment, individual and collective. The French were reluctant, but they submitted. 'What seemed to us to be unnecessarily picky was only a manifestation of order and organisation, so typically American.'[107] On 21 June 1944, all the officers of the *2ᵉ DB* were summoned to Dalton Hall. That day would remain special for them. In the morning, they gathered on the lawn in front of the entrance to the castle. Leclerc addressed them to remind them of their responsibilities and asked them to be ready as quickly as possible. '…You see in life, you only succeed if you are obsessed with one idea. Right now, you must be obsessed with getting back into battle.'[108] At the end of the speech,

---

101 Destray, Fonds Leclerc, *Campagne France-Allemagne 44–45,* p.9.
102 Langlade, *En Suivant Leclerc,* p.106.
103 Jean Mauras, *Souvenirs, 1939–1946* (Lavauzelle, 2010), p.83.
104 The *pasha* in the navy is the commander of a ship, corresponding to the English term 'skipper.'
105 Mauras, *Souvenirs, 1939–1946,* p.96.
106 Compagnon, *Leclerc,* p.359.
107 Salbaing, *Ardeur,* pp.137–138.
108 Levisse-Touzé and Toureille, *Écrits de Combat,* p.512.

Leclerc presented them with the insignia of the *2ᵉ DB*. Everyone received from his hands a small, numbered metal badge of the division. Colonel Dio was given No.6.[109] The unit insignia, whose 'contours were not perfect: Brittany raised its nose a little,'[110] would later be given by the officers to the rest of the personnel in the regiments. 'This distribution of badges makes all *DB* personnel, officers and men, combat arm branches and support branches, united with each other.'[111]

On 23, 24, and 25 June, the three *GTs* were engaged in an Allied exercise that put the *2ᵉ DB* facing the Polish division for three days. Named 'Kestrel,' the exercises took place in the northern region of the East Riding between the village of Thwing in the south and the town of Scarborough on the coast. Its theme was simple: 'the *2ᵉ DB* would be set up in a defensive position and would begin a withdrawing manoeuvre, under attack from the Polish division which would benefit from aviation support.'[112] Girard reported that Leclerc was watching a tank counterattack at the *GTD* headquarters. 'In his CP, Dio, massive and jeering, is surrounded by explosions produced by a phlegmatic British engineer who draws pyrotechnics from a bag hanging around his neck and throws them here and there to create the atmosphere… it's charming.'[113] Dio was clearly having fun during the exercise. He believed that good training could only be done in a good mood. At the end of the exercise, he was satisfied with the units of his *GTD*. The commanders of his units reacted well to orders, cohesion became more and more evident. True to form, Dio had managed to create a good atmosphere within his *GT* that trickled down to the rank-and-file soldier.

On Tuesday, 27 June, they participated in a Z exercise, which is a training scenario dedicated to protective measures against a chemical threat. In all units of the division, specialists surprised the men, usually at breakfast, by releasing tear gas canisters in the buildings. Those who had not carried their protective masks with them, and those who had not taken care to adjust theirs properly to make it airtight, spent the day with irritated eyes. It was an awareness exercise. During the First World War, both sides had used poison gas, and soldiers had to be constantly prepared to protect themselves against a chemical attack. The next day, the commanding general of the 3rd US Army, General Patton, came to inspect the *2ᵉ DB*, which was attached to his Army.[114] Leclerc described him succinctly: 'Handsome head of an old soldier. Student in Saumur[115] in 1912.'[116] Patton did not go unnoticed 'with his copper hair, his light yellow boots decorated with wheeled spurs, his silver-studded belt, his two large calibre automatics which beat his thighs…'[117] He visited all the units. Patton already knew Dio, the US general had worked alongside *Force L* in Tunisia and in particular with *Groupement Dio*. In the Kasserine region, Dio provided Patton with decisive support against German armoured vehicles.[118] The American was impressed at the time by the

109 No.1 was assigned to *Capitaine* Divry, sent to France first, No.2 went to *Général* de Gaulle and No.3 to Winston Churchill. Leclerc granted himself No.5, having given No.4 to his aide-de-camp, Lieutenant Girard. 'Then, it was by seniority of rank and time in service, starting with *Colonel* Dio, then *Colonel* de Langlade, etc…' (G. Lévy-Haussmann, *La 2e D.B. vue par un 2e classe* (Imprimerie Firmin Didot, 2005, p.104.).
110 Destrem, *L'Aventure de Leclerc*, p.242.
111 Vernet, 'Mise sur pied de la 2e DB', p.201.
112 Salbaing, *Ardeur*, p.138.
113 Girard, *Journal de Guerre*, p.221.
114 This American military leader died tragically in December 1945 in a road traffic accident in Luxembourg.
115 Saumur was the location of the French cavalry school, at which Patton had studied fencing as a *lieutenant* following his participation in the modern pentathlon during the 1912 Olympics in Stockholm. Patton returned to Saumur the following year to continue training on advanced fencing techniques. (Translator's note)
116 Fonds Leclerc, Leclerc, *notes manuscrites*, p.9, boîte 10, dossier 1, chemise 3.
117 Destrem, *L'Aventure de Leclerc*, p.243.
118 Testimony of *Colonel* Robédat 'collected from the mouth of *Général* Dio'. Comments made to the author in September 2019.

fighting spirit of the Free French. For their part, Dio's *marsouins* appreciated this general who gave them the same instructions as Leclerc, but in more graphic terms: 'Grab the enemy by the nose with your fire and hit him in the ass with fire from your manoeuvre…'[119]

On 29/30 June and 1 July, a CP exercise was organised, which Leclerc summarised in his notes as follows: 'communications exercise in liaison with the Americans. These manoeuvres teach us how to understand Americans.'[120] Dio did not delegate this exercise to his deputy this time. He wanted to verify for himself that the officers of his *GTD* were capable of applying US radio procedures. He also wanted to review and remember the main American tactical terms. He learnt English during his schooling and officer training, but he was aware that he was more comfortable in Arabic than in the language of Shakespeare. Despite this difficulty in writing and speaking in English, Dio remained calm during the exercise. His aide-de-camp noted that Leclerc went to the *GTD* CP on the morning of 1 July. 'We find Dio there, unperturbed as usual.'[121] Dio's direct subordinates really appreciated that about him because he always remained very calm on all occasions, especially in the presence of higher authorities. Many officers at that time became very nervous when Leclerc arrived, knowing he was demanding. Dio, however, was not stressed around him – he had known him for too long.

On Monday 3 July, a major ceremony was organised for the delivery of the divisional insignia to the units of the *2ᵉ DB*. The regiments, most of them newly created, were not yet supplied with a Standard or a Colours.[122] That day, '*Général* Koenig, commanding the Free French forces, in the name of *Général* de Gaulle, presented to the regiments the Standards and Colours that Leclerc had had made and embroidered in London.'[123] Each flag was 'offered by the Association of Free French of Great Britain.'[124] However, Compagnon mentions the association of 'English friends of the French in London.'[125] For the occasion, Dio resumed command of the three battalions of his regiment. The ceremony began with a parade. At the front of the three battalions presenting arms, he received the first Colours of the *RMT*; it would accompany him throughout the French campaign. *Père* Houchet then proceeded to bless all of the Standards and Colours. Then, at the end of the ceremony, *Colonel* Dio, followed by the colour guard and the three battalions, paraded in front of the French and Allied general officers present. 'The Regiment's parade, with *Colonel* Dio at the head, was impeccable.'[126] The newly created band of the *2ᵉ DB* punctuated the rhythmic step of the 2,500 *marsouins* to the sound of the '*Hymne de la Coloniale.*'

On 5 July, Dio organised a technical training session for the personnel of the *12ᵉ Cuirs*,[127] whose operations log (*Journal de Marches des Opérations* or *JMO*) states 'the *RMT* gave us a mine-clearing demonstration at 11:00 p.m.'[128] The techniques for clearing mines at night were specific

---

119 Destrem, *L'Aventure de Leclerc*, p.244.

120 Fonds Leclerc, Leclerc, *notes manuscrites*.

121 Girard, *Journal de Guerre*, p.225.

122 Depending on the branch of the army, each regiment has a national emblem which can be a Standard or a Colours. Each tricolour Standard or Colours bears the name of the unit and on the obverse the battles in which the unit distinguished itself, along with its decorations. Colours are larger than Standards, the latter is the flag of cavalry, transportation, artillery, et cetera. The battalions have a fanion (a smaller, simpler flag) just like the companies or squadrons. The fanions are not in the form of a tricolour. The number within the regiment determines the colour of the fanion: blue is reserved for the first battalion or company, red for the second, yellow for the third, et cetera. This seniority of hues dates back to the Napoleonic order of 1808!

123 Destrem, *L'aventure de Leclerc*, p.243.

124 Fonds Leclerc, *JMO 1/RMT*, boîte B, dossier 1.

125 Compagnon, *Leclerc*, p.364.

126 Salbaing, *Ardeur*, p.140.

127 The *12e Cuirassiers* is today one of the oldest regiment of cavalry of the French army, created in 1668. It participated in the Battles of Austerlitz and Waterloo.

128 Fonds Leclerc, *JMO 12 e Cuirs*, boîte M1, dossier 1, chemise 2.

and Dio wanted to raise awareness among the tank crews of his *GTD* about the danger of mines. He remembered losing men while advancing at night towards the Djebel Outid in Tunisia. The *12ᵉ Cuirs* changed their commander on 12 July. Leclerc had dismissed *Colonel* Michel Malaguti; *Colonel* Warabiot replaced him in command of the third *GT*, which would become the *GTV*.[129] The deputy of the *12ᵉ Cuirs*, *Lieutenant Colonel* Noiret, succeeded *Colonel* Warabiot in command of the *12ᵉ Cuirs*.

On Saturday, 15 July, Leclerc inspected the *GTD*. His aide-de-camp's diary says: 'Departure at six for an exercise at 1/RMT. Perfect in every detail. The *général* smiles as he sits down at *Colonel* Dio's meal.'[130] Leclerc felt good in the presence of his first combat companions. He wrote to Mrs Ingold on 17 July, 'the old men from Chad, Dio, Guillebon, etc. are doing well. Morale is high.'[131] The exercises concerning the *RMT* very rarely called for any comments from the *général*. Moreover, the other officers of the division noted that 'having retained great freedom of expression in front of Leclerc, who has a deep friendship for him, Dio plays a bit of the role of balancer in the face of the bold initiatives of 'the boss.''[132] As a result, *Colonel* Dio had a certain aura among the other leaders.

On 15 July 1944, Leclerc signed *Colonel* Dio's evaluation as follows: '*Colonel* Dio has been commanding a combined arms *groupement tactique* in the *2ᵉ Division Blindée* for six months. The best description is to say that he gets everything he wants from his subordinates. Combining very firm authority with exceptional moral standards, he is for me a model of a great officer.'[133] Leclerc underlined the adjective 'great' by hand.

On 19 July, Leclerc summoned the commanders of his *groupements tactiques* and their subordinate unit commanders to Dalton Hall. Everyone was afraid of being stuck in England while the fighting raged in France. Leclerc, beaming, reassured them: 'the division must be ready to move towards the ports of England starting the day after tomorrow, 20 July.'[134] He then asked them to write themselves an Order of the Day for their men to announce the *DB*'s commitment to the battle of liberation.[135] He ordered them to 'not forget to specify the total confidence that they had to have in *Général* de Gaulle.'[136] Leclerc thus wanted it to be the unit commanders themselves, and in particular those of the former *Armée d'Afrique*, to show in writing their unambiguous commitment, 'showing the men that they have confidence in de Gaulle.'[137] Dio restrained his joy in front of his subordinates, but he was deeply happy to learn that he would soon be able to set foot on French soil, which he had left six long years earlier. He had no problem writing the Order of the Day. Faithful to his simplicity, he called his men to unity and discipline and expressed his total confidence to them before the fight. His message was 'brief and well put.'[138] The preparations for departure were made with joy. No need to further motivate the men.

The *GTD* left its cantonment area (West Lutton camp) with some relief on 22 August, headed for the south of England. As soon as it left Yorkshire, the division was taken in hand by the

---

129 Like *GTD* for Dio, *GTL* for Langlade, the *GTV* adopted a V for Warabiot, W having been too complicated to pronounce.

130 Girard, *Journal de Guerre*, p.231.

131 Levisse-Touzé and Toureille, *Écrits de Combat*, p.519.

132 Pellissier, *Le Général Rouvillois*, p.22.

133 SHD, Dio, 14 Yd 1759, ESS.

134 Bergot, *La 2 ème D.B.*, p.42.

135 It was General Patton who alone made the decision to land the *2e DB* at the beginning of August instead of at the end of August as initially planned. He had become aware during his inspection that not only was the French division ready but that the men would have difficulty agreeing to stay in England for several more weeks (*Caravane* No.340, 3e trimestre 1983, p.8).

136 Destrem, *L'Aventure de Leclerc*, p.244.

137 Fonds Leclerc, Leclerc, *notes manuscrites*, boîte 10, dossier 1, chemise 3.

138 Girard, *Journal de Guerre*, p.235.

American logistical system. The soldiers then had 'the impression of having entered a mechanical, dehumanised, timed universe where each gesture, undoubtedly studied by specialists in Taylorism, had to be executed within the required time frame or risk disrupting the entire machine.'[139] The tanks of the *12ᵉ Cuirs* moved by train to preserve their mechanics. Their destination was Southampton. The other vehicles took the road towards Weymouth. The movement was carried out in two stages, under the strict control of American guides. On the first day the *GTD* column arrived at Lutterworth. On the second day it reached the waiting area 80km southwest of the large port of Southampton, between Dewlish, Poole, and Bournemouth. On 24 August, the *GTD* was regrouped in the south of England, awaiting its embarkation orders. Divisional insignia were distributed to non-officer personnel on 28 July. Everyone was then wearing the emblem of France with the Cross of Lorraine. It would be a good luck charm for many men before going into battle. The Frenchmen of the *2ᵉ DB* were then completely isolated from the population for security reasons.

Finally, on 30 and 31 July, personnel and equipment were guided to the port of Southampton. They arrived at the 'marshalling area' to undergo American pre-boarding formalities. It was a huge canvas transit camp six kilometres from Southampton. The formal procedures marked all Frenchmen unaccustomed to 'ceasing to being individuals to become registration numbers, passing, one by one, from barrack to barrack following a set agenda, the same for all.' A young French officer, unaccustomed to being treated in this way, quickly described the site as 'a type of American-style concentration camp.'[140] The process of these formalities was sufficiently surprising to the Frenchmen. 'First, they got rid of their personal objects. Then, stark naked, they presented themselves for the medical examination. The big review finished, dressed, helmeted, newly equipped, the men were gathered, by crew, near their vehicles.'[141] Dio and his staff endured more than they liked; these procedures were not usual in the French Army. Finally, the embarkation order arrived on 1 August. The *GTD* units broke up and were distributed across several troop transport boats and liberty ships. Dio did not try to find out what was happening to his units, letting himself be carried along with it all. Like the others, he realised that the *2ᵉ DB* had joined the American Army. In this, planning was all-powerful and the weight of logistics omnipresent. He had to submit to it, which he had done patiently since he had left Yorkshire. He and his men were entirely focused on the fight that awaited them. They were eager to face the Germans. Since Tunisia, they had known that the army of the Third Reich was not superior to them. Their main concern was for France. What state would they find their country in? What had happened to their parents? Some had not received or been able to send any news for several years.

---

139 Bergot, *La 2 ème D.B.*, p.42.
140 Mauras, *Souvenirs, 1939–1946*, p.97.
141 Bergot, *La 2 ème D.B.*, p.42.

Chapter 9

Normandy,
1 August to 22 August 1944

On Wednesday, 2 August 1944, *Colonel* Dio and the officers of the staff of *Groupement Tactique Dio* were on a 'liberty ship'[1] heading for the French coast after having embarked in Southampton the previous evening. Comfort on board was reduced to its simplest form. The few cabins that existed were reserved primarily for the crew. The captain, an American three-striper, had invited Dio to use his cabin. It was the best he could do. The *colonel* had politely declined his offer, preferring to stay with his team. The ship's wardroom was tiny, and there, too, Dio declined because he did not want to be a loner. After a sleepless night crossing the channel, the French coast gradually appeared in the early morning mist. The sea was rough, and the liberty ship positioned itself with other boats south of the mouth of the Vire, opposite Grandcamp. Pointe du Hoc at the end of Omaha Beach stood out to port. The Americans had lost many men there on D-Day, almost two months earlier. Barges approached to transfer men and equipment while the ship anchored, but sea conditions prevented the transfers from taking place. The barges could not come alongside and couple to the liberty ship because the swell was so strong. Dio could tell that the crew was inexperienced. They 'were trained in haste, that's obvious. But .... they scrupulously carry out the instructions they were given and the methods they were taught.'[2] In short, they would not take any risks in landing their cargo of men and equipment as long as the sea was in that state.

Little by little, other liberty ships and LSTs arrived. The ocean was covered with waiting ships. This vast assemblage of anchored boats could constitute a choice target for the *Luftwaffe*. Fortunately, American planes were constantly patrolling the skies above them. In addition, 'The horizon was blocked, as far as the eye could see, by innumerable barrage balloons attached to the ground, from which cables hung, so as to constitute a gigantic net in which any enemy plane trying to dive bomb the landing fleet would have been trapped.'[3] Dio cursed the American logisticians who sent him off in the second wave. He knew that those who embarked on 31 July had been able to disembark on 1 August between Utah Beach and Grandcamp. He tried to be patient. He was seething inside but did not show it to those around him. On the contrary, he reprimanded those who started to complain. He retorted that war is always a matter of long waits, and then pointed out to them that two days were nothing to those who had been dreaming since 1940 of the moment they would be able to set foot on the soil of their homeland again.

Living conditions on board deteriorated quickly. The men were in the hold of the ship, crowded into the vehicles. The ship was not designed to accommodate so many people for several days.

---

1   The American Liberty class of cargo ships comprised around 2,700 ships built from 1941 to 1945, making it the most produced ship model in the world. At 130 metres long, its holds could contain 10,000 tons of materiels. The ship had on-board cranes to quickly unload the materiels.
2   Dronne, *Carnets de Route*, p.272.
3   Salbaing, *Ardeur*, p.157.

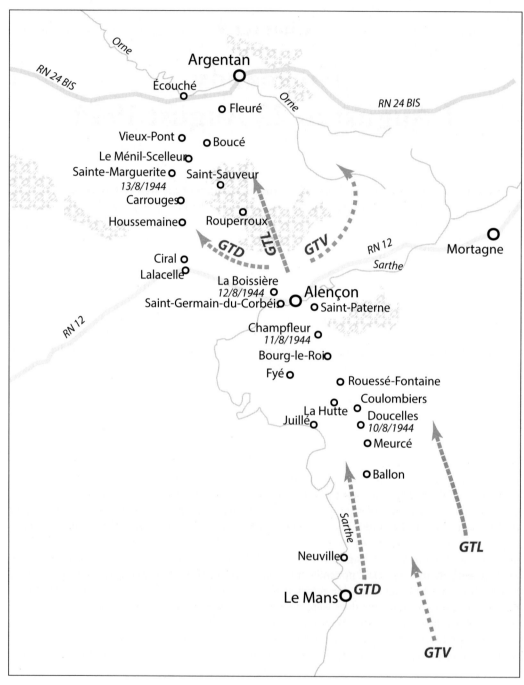

Map 9 The GTD in the Normandy campaign.

'The insufficient number of toilets was becoming worrying, because the men were forced to relieve themselves overboard.'[4] Moreover, each man had received upon embarkation an individual 'K' ration for the crossing. After 24 hours, the liberty ship was resupplied – with more 'K' rations. However, those rations lacked variety: ham and egg or pork and beans, accompanied by small bags of tea, powdered coffee, and 10 cigarettes. In combat, they were convenient because they were compact, were waterproof, and provided sufficient energy. But after three days spent moping around on a ship where there was nothing to alleviate the boredom, the experience quickly became heavy. The men would have preferred the 'C' rations which offered more variety. 'C' rations were opened during calm periods and delivered 'in large cardboard boxes, which contained enough food and cigarettes for ten men.'[5] The officers on each ship tried to find ideas to pass the time for the men. In the 4th Squadron of the *RMSM*, *Capitaine* Savelli 'organised boxing matches with the cargo ship's commander for which a hatch cover served as a ring.'[6]

It was a real relief for everyone to see that the weather had improved considerably on the morning of Friday, 4 August. The barges had reappeared at 8:00 a.m., and the transhipment could begin. The heavy half-tracks were lifted by the cranes and 'waddled like big beetles hanging from a thread.'[7] While the equipment was being transhipped on the port side, DUKW and motor rafts approached on the starboard side.[8] A large landing net was unfolded along the hull. The heavily laden men were invited to cross the railing and to descend on the net along the sides of the ship to disembark. Dio reached the coast in a DUKW, accompanied by the half dozen officers of his staff; when he touched ground, it was 11:00 in the morning. As they set foot on the soil of the homeland, they all felt a pang in their heart but out of modesty they avoided showing it. Some of them shed a silent tear, others bent down to take a little bit of French soil in their hands. It was a fleeting moment, but everyone would remember it for a very long time.

Dio and his troops were directed to a transit camp, allowing the men to recover their equipment. Once the force had recovered its vehicles, it was guided by the American military police, assisted by the division's traffic control police, to the assembly area for the *2e DB*, which was located in the triangle between La-Haye-du-Puits, Vesly, and Lessay, 40 kilometres from Saint Martin-de-Varreville. The small column crossed Sainte-Mère-Église which still bore the scars of the furious fighting that took place there on 6 June. Many of the homes were gutted. Everything was in ruins. In the countryside was the same spectacle of desolation: dead and bloated animals were in the fields. A terrible stench filled the air. German corpses lay on the ground, surrounded by barbed wire to prevent soldiers or civilians from touching them. Some bodies had been booby-trapped, so the order was to leave them there until the situation calmed down. On the Cotentin peninsula, it was clear two months after the landing that 'life had not yet returned to normal.'[9]

The following day, 5 August, Dio asked his staff for an update on the arrival and deployment of his *GT*. The *12e Cuirs* had been stationed in Gerville since 2 August. The *3e RAC*, which also arrived on 2 August, set up in the Lithaire region, five kilometres east of La Haye-du-Puits. The 1st Battalion of the RMT would not arrive until late in the afternoon of 5 August. It would set up along the La-Haye-du-Puits to Lithaire road. In the afternoon, Dio went to meet the population. He noticed during his short trip that the reception from the locals was not very enthusiastic. After engaging in conversation with some of the older men, he learnt that German propaganda,

4   Salbaing, *Ardeur,* p.158.
5   Salbaing, *Ardeur,* p.147.
6   Fonds Leclerc, Jean Guiglini, *Carnet de Route,* p.4, boîte D2.
7   Dronne, *Carnets de Route,* p.273.
8   The DUKW 353, nicknamed 'duck,' was a Chevrolet-GMC amphibious vehicle designed to unload personnel from cargo ships in the absence of ports.
9   Salbaing, *Ardeur,* p.161.

relayed by the collaborating media, had presented Leclerc's army as being fierce communists, ready to settle scores upon arriving in France. In addition, the French population in the region was still traumatised by the violence of the fighting they had endured. Many families had lost loved ones in the bombings. Dio then understood the reserved attitude towards them.

At the end of the afternoon, Leclerc summoned his *groupement* commanders. He explained the Allied tactical situation to them. The Americans were breaking through the German defence lines at Avranches, at the western base of the Cotentin. They were going to be able to attack towards Brittany and Paris. The *2ᵉ DB* was attached to Major General Wade Haislip's US XV Corps. The general direction of march to join the corps was due south.

On 6 August, the *DB* was finally complete; all the units were assembled and ready to depart. The *GTD* set off southward at midday towards Avranches, via Coutances and Grandville. It bypassed Avranches, which had been badly destroyed, and, after having travelled a little over 100km, settled in the northern region of Saint-James, 15km south of Avranches. The *3ᵉ RAC* bivouacked in the Saint-Senier region and the *1/RMT* at Ducey. At the start of the night, the *12ᵉ Cuirs* which was stationed around the Château de Chassily, 4km northeast of Saint-James, noted 'rounds of German planes in the surroundings. Heavy anti-aircraft fire. Sounds of explosions. The earth was shaking.'[10] An aerial bombardment hit the *13ᵉ Bataillon Médical*. The Germans, having lost air superiority to the Allied armadas, could only carry out sorties at night. The medical personnel were the first to be hit. Among the wounded was the student doctor François Jacob, the future Nobel Prize winner for Biology.[11] The *GTD* was unscathed.

7 August was spent in repair and maintenance of equipment. Weapons cleaning in the smallest details was the priority. The cleanliness of the weapons was essential to limit malfunction in combat. Once that was done, the men took advantage of the downtime to rest and sleep. The weather was excellent. Dio passed through the different bivouacs of his units. As a soldier, he also knew that his presence among them was necessary. Many of the men had no experience under fire. He could detect the stress that many were experiencing before going into combat. It was not so much the *fact* of being frightened but rather the *fear* of being frightened – all those who have lived this experience wonder deep down: 'will I be up to it?' The group, cohesion, and fraternity are essential in those moments. The proximity of a leader who has your complete trust and who comes to talk to you while putting his hand on your shoulder helps to relieve the pit in your stomach. Their equipment no longer held any secrets for Dio. When he was in Chad, he always lacked everything and fought with limited means, so he marvelled at the abundance in which his infantry found themselves. What a difference it was from the equipment of his *Groupe Nomade du Tibesti*! The soldiers' clothing also seemed well adapted to him: 'a simple khaki jumpsuit, in one piece, which could be put on or taken off in no time, and had enough pockets to allow us to carry …. both food and ammunition.'[12] One of the major innovations was the heavy khaki canvas belt with straps on which they could hang magazines, grenades, first aid bags, shovels, et cetera.

The half-track was a very well-designed vehicle to carry 10 men, with lockers under the benches allowing them to store their equipment. There was also a reserve of 40 litres of water. The specific set up of the vehicles was left to the initiative of the group leaders, as long as weapons could be accessed immediately. The various half-tracks became quickly differentiated from each other. Those used by the 60mm mortar group and the one towing the 57mm gun (the last vehicle in the

---

10 Fonds Leclerc, *JMO du 12e Cuirs.*, p.19, boîte M1, dossier 1.
11 In his book (Jacob, *La Statue Intérieure*, p.182), he recounts his arm injury at Djebel Garci in May 1943 but not that of 6 August 1944. Hit in the arm and leg by 80 aerial grenade fragments, he was evacuated to the hospital in Cherbourg and then to the Val de Grâce hospital. (https://www.ordredelaliberation.fr/en/node/958) After six months of hospitalisation, he had to give up a career as a surgeon and turn to biology.
12 Salbaing, *Ardeur*, p.151.

section) were adapted to transport ammunition. Most often, the floors of the vehicles were cluttered with weapons and ammunition. A fairly large disorder generally reigned there. How could it be otherwise with each vehicle? They had to consider:

- the individual armament of the group of 10 infantrymen (two rifles, five carbines, two submachine guns, and one pistol)[13]
- weapons such as the bazooka, 7.62mm machine gun, mine detector, grenade launcher, hand grenades, rocket launcher and flame thrower for those who had them,
- ammunition for all the weapons, including anti-tank mines – which were bulky.

The half-tracks had a good range, like the camel. The difference was that after having travelled about 500 kilometres, it could depart again immediately after having filled its tank. Dio did not neglect the cavalrymen of the *12ᵉ Cuirs* assigned to the *GTD*, and in Morocco, he had thoroughly learnt about their primary piece of equipment – the M4 Sherman tank. He even asked to fire the gun to understand what the crews would experience in combat. 'There were five of them in each Sherman, headphones in their ears. In addition to their armament – a gun, three machine guns – and a radio transceiver, they had individual weapons. Each squadron had 17 tanks accompanied by three half-tracks.'[14] The high quality of the *capitaines*, *lieutenants*, and non-commissioned tank commanders made each squadron a formidable operational tool.

On 8 August, Leclerc returned from Haislip's CP, and summoned his *groupements tactiques* commanders to his CP at Chassillé. He informed them that the tactical situation was evolving rapidly. The XV Corps had just taken Le Mans with two divisions, the US 5th Armored Division and the US 90th Infantry Division. The *2ᵉ DB* was to join them as soon as possible. XV Corps had carried out a large outflanking manoeuvre from the south of the positions of the 7th German Army centred around the Domfront region. Patton, with his 3rd Army, wanted to trap the *Wehrmacht* units using a pincer manoeuvre with the XV Corps to the south and the Canadian 1st Army to the north, coming from Falaise. The trap was to be closed at Argentan. The *2ᵉ DB* would begin its movement on 9 August in the early hours of the morning. Leclerc also informed them that *Colonel* Warabiot, who commanded the *GTV*, was being replaced by *Colonel* Pierre Billotte, whom Dio knew well since he was his classmate at Saint-Cyr.[15] Billote, de Gaulle's personal chief of staff, had been warmly recommended, if not imposed, by the head of Free France. Dio did not appreciate this way of doing things where officers were moved around at the whim of 'great leaders'. He naturally reassured *Colonel* Warabiot who, having never been unworthy, had already been replaced at the head of the *12ᵉ Cuirs* in England to take over the *GT* and who now saw himself 'demoted' to become commander of the *501ᵉ RCC*. *Colonel* Warabiot, not being a Free Frenchman, already knew that it would be difficult for him in the eyes of the men of the regiment to replace *Lieutenant Colonel* Cantarel, the titular commander, who therefore found himself his deputy. Moreover, after Paris, Warabiot would leave the command of the *501ᵉ RCC* and the *2ᵉ DB*. Dio knew that Leclerc had to bow to de Gaulle's decision. The commander of the *2ᵉ DB*, exasperated by the changes, kept

---

13   Later, during the fighting, the floors of the half-tracks would be littered with salvaged German weapons such as Beretta submachine guns and sniper rifles, which were highly sought after, as well as *Panzerfausts*, whose penetration power was greater than that of US bazookas.

14   Destrem, *L'Aventure de Leclerc*, p.251.

15   A graduate of Saint-Cyr (1926–1928, Pol Lapeyre promotion), Pierre Billotte (1906–1992) distinguished himself in June 1940 with the *1re Compagnie de Chars* in Mourmelon (Marne) before being captured and interned in Germany. He managed to escape, ending up in the USSR. Following Hitler's attack in June 1941, he became the representative of Free France in Moscow, and then the chief of staff to *Général* de Gaulle.

the name *Groupement Tactique Warabiot* throughout the campaign to continue to designate the third *groupement tactique* of the *DB*. The war had not really started and the *GTV* was already on its third leader!

On the night of 8/9 August, the *GTD* assembled to begin its night movement. 'At 11:00 pm… the *GTD* had barely assembled in a column on the road when about twenty German aircraft came to bomb the main road (D798).'[16] The units were hit hard.[17] The *12ᵉ Cuirs* and the *1/RMT* had 28 and 34 wounded, respectively. The *3ᵉ RAC* suffered its first soldier killed, and 13 more wounded. In total, the *GTD* counted 1 dead and 110 wounded. Equipment and vehicles were destroyed and had to be abandoned. The veterans of Chad realised that the German bombings were of a completely different nature than those of the Italians. Additionally, being bombed at night was more stressful. The German airmen struck while the *GTD* was gathering to form a column before departure – the worst time to be attacked. Girard noted in his diary: 'the *GTD* was badly bombed while passing through the Avranches bottleneck.'[18]

Despite these losses, the *GTD* advanced through Saint-James – Saint-Aubin – Vitré – Cossé-le-Vivien – Château-Gontier – Sablé. The roads at the start were congested by American troops heading towards Brittany. The division was preceded by its 'rows of fuel trucks from the divisional train to carry out …. a resupply two-thirds of the way along the route …. on a long straight line, near Cossé-le-Vivien.'[19] After refuelling, 'around 6:00 p.m. the *GTD* headed for Neuville (4 kilometres northwest of Le Mans).'[20] The bridges over the Sarthe were destroyed. 'On 9 August 1944, on a dark night, with all lights out, the units crossed the Sarthe on two pontoon bridges built by American engineers. Getting to them was difficult…'[21] They were Treadway bridges built in three hours by US engineers. The *GTD* crossed the Sarthe at Neuville downstream from Le Mans, from midnight to 7:00 in the morning, 'in a traffic jam that can only be compared to those of the retreat to Dunkirk.'[22] It was the moment of truth for the 'colonials and *cuirassiers*, [who] are two old units, each with its own combat past. [After a] long time working together in training, it is however the first time that they faced fire together.'[23]

On the morning of 10 August, the US XV Corps attacked from the Le Mans region, heading north, with the *2ᵉ DB* in the lead towards Alençon and the US 5th Armored Division on its right towards Sées. The two US infantry divisions, the 79th and 90th, were in the second echelon. The *GTD* and the *GTL* were ordered to attack in the general direction of Le Mans – Alençon. The *GTD* was to the west on the axis of advance. It would be followed by the *GTV*. The two *GTs* had Alençon as their objective, the west of the city for Dio and the east for Langlade, by seizing the bridges over the Sarthe. The main enemy that the *2ᵉ DB* would have to face in the first days was 'the *9. Panzerdivision*, recently arrived from the Nîmes region to cover the Normandy operations zone facing south.'[24] Colonel Dio's order of operations arrived at the two *GTD* subgroups at 7:00 a.m.[25] Half of the *12ᵉ Cuirs* under the command of the second in command, *Chef d'Escadrons*

---

16 Fonds Leclerc, Guiglini, *Carnet de Route*, p.6.
17 The explanation for this bombing lies, according to Boissieu, in the fact that a jeep of the 2e DB, along with the division's assembly area overlay fell into the hands of the Germans on 6 August. (Alain de Boissieu, *Pour Combattre avec de Gaulle, Souvenirs, 1940–1946* (Paris: Omnibus, 1999), p.234.
18 Girard, *Journal de Guerre*, p.250.
19 Compagnon, *Leclerc*, pp.371–372.
20 Fonds Leclerc, *JMO GTD*.
21 Fonds Leclerc, *JMO 13e BG*, boîte F1, dossier 1, chemise 1.
22 Fonds Leclerc, *JMO du 12e Cuirs*, p.23.
23 Paul Repiton-Préneuf, presented by Georges Buis, *2ème DB: La Campagne de France* (Paris: Éditions Imprimerie Nationale, 1994), p.7.
24 Compagnon, *Leclerc*, p.373.
25 1. Subgroup A: *Commandant* Farret

Rouvillois, was delayed because of the bombardment. It arrived at noon and would be in the second echelon on Axis A.

To conduct his first mission, Dio split his *GT* into two subgroups, which offered the advantage of constituting two solid units with maximum resources. But, in this case, the GT, having no elements in reserve held by its commander, was not able to face an unforeseen threat or to relaunch the action of the first echelon. Subsequently, Dio would organise his group into three subgroups like the *GTV*, while the *GTL* would almost always remain with two subgroups. Each subgroup could, itself, be split into several detachments generally under the orders of an armour or infantry *capitaine*, depending on the mission and the area of action. The *GTD* deployed from the region of La Guierche and began its offensive movement towards the north. At the start, the units of Axis B were blocked by *GTL* vehicles that had mistakenly moved onto their route. The *GTD*'s first contact with the enemy was made by the vanguard of the *12ᵉ Cuirs* on Axis B north of Ballon. The Germans were fighting a defensive battle in depth. They wanted to gain time to allow their 7th Army to get out of the trap at Argentan. They took up positions in all the villages and fired on the first vehicles of the *GTD*. Then they forced Dio's units to manoeuvre. The Germans retreated before being overwhelmed. It was a difficult fight for the attackers. The tension was extreme, where and when was the enemy going to strike? Moreover, this was the first engagement of the *2ᵉ DB*. The armour/infantry coordination was not yet perfect, nor was that with the artillery.

Unfortunately, Dio broke his ankle at Ballon while moving forward to see his first echelon. The timing was extremely inopportune and made the experience particularly unpleasant. The exact circumstances of the accident are unclear. According to his medical records, Dio had a: 'jeep accident in Ballon near Le Mans (Sarthe) on 9 August 1944. Fracture of the external malleolus – intra-articular bar (right foot).'[26] It is possible that in the confused movements at the beginning of the attack, his jeep was damaged in the fighting. The injury came at the worst possible time, it was the day of the first contact with the Germans.[27] Dio refused to be treated, and minimised his injury by calling it a sprain in order to remain at his post. *Lieutenant* Girard wrote in his journal of 10 August that 'Dio has sprained his ankle.'[28] Like him, during this campaign, many personnel of the *2ᵉ DB*, although wounded, resisted their evacuation. This injury was all the more regrettable for Dio as the tactical situation would become difficult during this first day of fighting where the losses would be harshly felt and would have repercussions on morale.

Axis: Neuville – Montbizot – Mareschè – Vivoin – Juillé – La Hutte – Alençon – Lalacelle – Carrouges
1st Bound: Beaumont / 2nd Bound: La Hutte / 3rd Bound: Alençon / 4th Bound: Carrouges
Mission: to reconnoitre the axis and its approaches, possibly pushing back the enemy and the guarding the flank of the division to the west.
Assets: EM 1/*RMT*, 2nd Company *RMT*, *CA1/RMT*, 4th Squadron of the *RMSM* (*Capitaine* Savelli), 1st battery of the *RAC* (*Capitaine* Dubois), 2 platoons of tank destroyers from the Bonnet squadron of the *RBFM*, 2 engineer sections.
2. Subgroup B: *Lieutenant Colonel* Noiret:
Axis: Ballon – Lucé – Meurcé – Coulombiers – Bourg-le-Roi – Champfleur – Alençon – Carrouges
1st Bound: Meurcé / 2nd Bound: Coulombiers / 3rd Bound: Alençon / 4th Bound: Saint-Sauveur
Mission: to reconnoitre the axis and its approaches, possibly push back the enemy, maintain contact with subgroup A to the west and with the GTL to the east.
Assets: *12e Cuirassiers* (minus two squadrons), the 1st and 2nd Companies of the *1/RMT*, 1 platoon of tank destroyers of the *RBFM*, 1 engineer section. Fonds Leclerc, *JMO of the GTD*.
26   SHD, Dio, 14 Yd 1759, ESS.
27   Général Leclerc signed a certificate on 20 August 1944 to declare that 'the injury received by Colonel Dio, commander of the GTD on 10 August in Ballon (Sarthe) is a war injury. Colonel Dio refused to be evacuated.' (Archives of the Ordre de la Libération, note no. 1310/1 of 3, 3 October 1947).
28   Girard, *Journal de Guerre*, p.251.

After the village of Ballon, the vanguard of Subgroup Noiret commanded by *Capitaine* de Laitre of the *12ᵉ Cuirs*, reinforced by the 1st Company of the *RMT* (*Capitaine* Grall), reached Meurcé then continued on to Chérancé. The Germans were firmly waiting for Leclerc's men on the southern outskirts of this village, and the first three light tanks were destroyed. The *capitaine* and a tank commander were killed and three *cuirassiers* wounded. These losses led the vanguard command to waver and then fell back on Meurcé. Having reorganised, the men of the *12ᵉ Cuirs* resumed their advance towards Doucelles where two German tanks were destroyed. At the end of the evening, the hamlet of Coudray, 5km north of Doucelles, was reached.

On Axis A, Farret's subgroup made contact with German light tanks at Boulay, a hamlet on the banks of the Sarthe, and destroyed the leading armoured car. The German units retreated when Farret's subgroup deployed to take them from behind. The villages of Maresché and then Vivoin were taken after an exchange of fire. At the end of the afternoon, the subgroup was stopped near Juillé by a significant German defensive system. At the end of the day on 10 August 1944, the *GTD* had advanced about 20 kilometres to the north and reached a line from Juillé to Doucelles. This was not fast enough to satisfy Leclerc, who was stomping his feet as he followed Subgroup Noiret. But the *GTL* to the east had not done any better, nor had the US 5th Armored Division. This was the first day of combat with the first losses for the *GTD*; there were 8 killed, including 2 officers, and 25 wounded. The *GTD* also lost six tanks and two other vehicles. Dio's men were shaken, especially those who had just experienced their baptism of fire. They were fully aware of the harsh realities of combat. Dio, dealing with his injury, was unable to accompany the first echelon as he would have liked, especially at Chérancé, to relaunch their action. When the unit suffered human and materiel losses, the American support, which seemed very heavy at the beginning for the French, became most appreciated. The US medical service was able to deploy field hospitals as close as possible to the combat line, and the wounded were treated in the minimum of time. Many had their lives saved because of this quality of treatment of the wounded. Others were able to return to combat. And American logistics were incomparable. The fuel supply was of extraordinary efficiency, especially at night on simple request. To replace the vehicles destroyed in combat, the *DB* was over-establishment with tanks, half-tracks, and other equipment. Thus allowing the units to fill the existing gaps in a matter of hours. All *GTD* personnel, including their leader, could only be exceedingly happy with such quality of support.

At the end of this first day, Dio reorganised his system. He had very quickly learnt a lesson from the battle of Chérancé. From now on, his *GT* would always be split into three subgroups, including a reserve element that was capable of relaunching an action to support another element in difficulty. Even if the losses were high and the rate of progress was relatively slow, not everything was negative on that first day of 10 August 1944. It is sufficient to note the toll attributed to the *GTD* among the enemy ranks: 100 killed and 40 prisoners and the destruction of five tanks, three other vehicles, and four anti-tank guns.

11 August 1944 was similar to the previous day. With the first lessons learnt, Dio reinforced Subgroup Farret on Axis A with a squadron of Shermans. That day, he effectively set up the third subgroup under the orders of *Commandant* Rouvillois, the second in command of the *12ᵉ Cuirs*. *Commandant* Farret on Axis A resumed the advance at daybreak. His second bound was the large crossroads of La Hutte, seven kilometres away. The enemy held this important point firmly with 75mm guns. The fighting began fiercely and five French tanks were destroyed. To break through, an infantry company overran from the west, and the crossroads were taken in the early afternoon. The German mobile defence became stronger and stronger, setting up a defensive line at each favourable location, which forced the French troops to manoeuvre. It should be noted that 'the terrain from Le Mans up to Alençon is hedged; high hedges and sunken paths are favourable to a defence staggered in depth. The attacker is forced to continually resume successive efforts against

an adversary who knows his job well, is stubborn and knows how to use the terrain.'[29] The village of Fyé, north of La Hutte, was also firmly held. The infantry had to outflank the resistance to force the German detachments to withdraw after losing three tanks. Subgroup Farret captured the village and established its position to the north of it, at Oisseau-le-Petit at the end of the day. It had advanced only about 12 kilometres.

On Axis B, which was the *GTD*'s axis of advance, Noiret's subgroup had Coulombiers as its first objective, about 10 kilometres away. The enemy had established its position near the road leading to La Hutte. The two leading tanks were destroyed by a German tank. Further north, the village of Rouessé-Fontaine turned out to be firmly held. The four tanks of a platoon of the *12ᵉ Cuirs* were all destroyed. Dio requested air support from the US Air Corps and had the guns of the *3ᵉ RAC* fire. Noiret's subgroup had been severely tested since the start, so Dio relaunched the action on this axis with Rouvillois's subgroup, made up of a squadron of Shermans, a company of the *RMT*, and a platoon of tank destroyers from the *RBFM*. Rouvillois took Bourg-le-Roi using an outflanking manoeuvre in a wooded neck between La Hutte and Rouessé-Fontaine. It was there that *Commandant* Rouvillois[30] called out to Leclerc in his *Tailly* tank (equipped with a dummy gun because the inside of the tank turret had been emptied to allow the *général* to have a small command post with radio equipment and maps): '*Mon Général*, you have just paraded in front of all the German tanks facing you; you have no right to take such risks. If you were killed, who would command the division?'[31] In its momentum, Subgroup Rouvillois seized Champfleur, firmly defended by the Germans, by leading a victorious charge with artillery and air support. The leading units reached Saint-Gilles and Saint-Paterne at nightfall. The town of Alençon was less than five kilometres to the north. The Germans evacuated it in the afternoon. The progress for the day was the same as that of the day before with 20 kilometres covered. But the human and materiel losses of the *GTD* during this second day of combat were worse: 43 killed on the French side against 50 on the German side and 22 French tanks destroyed against only 11 German.[32]

Such an attrition rate, if it were to happen again, would very quickly render the *GTD* combat ineffective, and it would have to be relieved. Dio decided to take measures as quickly as possible to avoid that. At the end of those first two days, he noted, with the officers of his staff, that tanks or armoured cars were not the best choice to be at the head of the column. The majority of losses came from the squadrons of light and medium tanks of the *12ᵉ Cuirs* and the *AMM8* armoured cars of the *RMSM*. Even if it meant bucking the rules of employment of the armoured division, he decided to put the reconnaissance sections at the head, equipped with very light jeeps, to flush out enemy positions. Behind the reconnaissance, the vanguard would be formed with Sherman medium tanks, capable as soon as possible of engaging enemy tanks or 88mm guns. These tanks would also have to work more closely with the infantry, particularly in covered areas or in populated areas. Massu, like Dio, would be a follower of 'the formula 'infantrymen mounted on tanks,' which had not won everyone's approval in Morocco. It reduced the length

---

29   Compagnon, *Leclerc*, p.373.
30   *Commandant* Rouvillois was one of the rare officers in the division to address Leclerc informally because he was from the same Saint-Cyr class as him, the 1922–1924 class named 'de Metz et Strasbourg', i.e. 4 years before that of Dio.
31   Pellissier, *Le Général Rouvillois*, p.28.
32   The *9. Panzerdivision* was 'equipped with Panther and Mark IV tanks but not Tiger tanks. The Tiger was the most powerful tank produced during the war, for its armament (88mm gun) and its armour. It was far superior to the Sherman, a tank which constituted the basic equipment of the American and French tank regiments. The Panther was slightly inferior to the Tiger but remained a formidable adversary for the Sherman.' (Compagnon, *Leclerc*, p.373). Only the *RFBM*'s Tank Destroyer with its 76mm gun could compete in terms of penetrating power with German tanks.

of the vanguard and allowed the rapid intervention of the leading elements. This is the preferred method for the tanks.'[33]

Another lesson would be learnt concerning the connection between the first echelon and the artillery. 'It is appropriate .... to push the batteries as close as possible behind the vanguard so as to crush resistance as soon as it appears.'[34] The infantry assaults would also have to be accompanied by artillery. Dio spoke about it at his CP in the evening to Fieschi, commander of the 3e RAC. The *bigors*'s forward observers (responsible for requesting and adjusting fire) would be positioned with the front-line units from then on. These were radical decisions. The losses within the *GTD* during the future battles of the French campaign would never again be as high as those first two days. Simple tactical principles would gradually be adopted for greater efficiency with a minimum of losses. The *méhariste colonel* very quickly adapted to the mechanisms of armoured combat.

For Dio, 11 August also taught him that *Commandant* Rouvillois was an unparalleled cavalryman at the head of a subgroup. He was a 'go-getter, always ready to masterfully execute the most daring manoeuvres envisaged.'[35] Dio was an infantryman who, by nature, was more balanced, and the two men would sometimes have different opinions on the tactics to use. But in mutual respect and loyalty, they complemented each other well and learnt to respect each other. In addition, the colonial officer gave thanks to the cavalryman who, although older than him, agreed to be under his orders and obeyed him without qualms. In 1945, Dio would designate Rouvillois to succeed him at the head of the *GTD*. The two men remained close after the war.[36]

The attack on Alençon was planned for 6:00 a.m. on 12 August. The *général's* command post was next to Dio's, near Champfleur. They set up in a square, according to *méhariste* custom. The environment was suitable for it. For 36 hours, Leclerc had been following the *GTD* which was on the axis of advance of the 2e *DB* between Le Mans and Alençon. Around 2:00 a.m., the command post took mortar fire. A shot hit a half-track of the *RMT*, burning to death two highly regarded non-commissioned officers of the 1st Battalion (Gabriel Navarro and Georges de Vasita) who were sleeping there, and 'whose ammunition would slowly crackle until morning.'[37] The *général* woke up and asked if the reconnaissance had gone to Alençon. At 3:15 a.m., Leclerc jumped into his jeep and joined Noiret's subgroup, which was at the gates of the city. The *général* led some *marsouins*, *cuirassiers*, and sailors[38] and entered the city with the aim of taking the bridges over the Sarthe intact. A 19-year-old resistance fighter named Raymond Ciroux guided the first elements into the city. This young native of Alençon would immediately enlist in the 2e *DB*. The enemy, who planned to reinvest the city with the German *116. Panzerdivision* to establish a defensive position, was overtaken. Dio, who followed the vanguard, entered Alençon and immediately ordered a defensive position set up to the north of the city, facing Sées, and to the east, towards Mamers, where a *Panzerdivision* was spotted. Despite the continued pain in his ankle, he exerted himself without complaining. He travelled by jeep as much as possible but was sometimes forced to dismount to go and check the position of a unit. To prevent the Germans from reinvesting the city, he rallied Farret's subgroup which joined the main body of the *GTD* in the morning and set

33   Massu, *Sept Ans*, p.316.

34   Crépin, who immediately understood what Dio was asking of him, gave the order to his regiments to push their 'batteries into the very legs of the vanguards'. Jean-René Van der Plaetsen, *La Nostalgie de l'Honneur* (le Livre de Poche, 2018), p.82; Compagnon, *Leclerc*, p.375.

35   Pellissier, *Le Général* Rouvillois, p.24.

36   Dio would agree, as a very exceptional measure, to write a very short preface for the publication of Pellissier's book devoted to *Général* Rouvillois in 1994, in which he wrote: 'In front of Marc Rouvillois, I felt a deep esteem for the man and boundless admiration for the courageous and ardent war leader who led everyone behind him in sound and audacious action...' (Pellissier, *Le Général Rouvillois*, p.11).

37   Repiton-Préneuf, *2ème DB: La Campagne de France*, p.9.

38   In order, Grall's company, forward CP of the *12e Cuirs*, TD platoon, and Gaudet's squadron.

up in Saint-Germain-du-Corbéis, the western district of the city. A company set up in front, at La Boissière, to block access. 'The leading elements of the *116. Panzerdivision* which came to occupy Alençon, were received by our 57 which opened fire on them at 50 metres.'[39]

The *GTL*, blocked by an American bomb line,[40] arrived a little later and took into account the defence facing the east. But it was the *GTD*, launched by the *général*, that seized Alençon and its intact bridges.[41] It was thanks to the German mortars, which woke Leclerc in the middle of the night, that these bridges were taken before the Germans arrived. The prefecture of the Orne was captured and cleared at the end of the day. It was the first major French city liberated by the French, triggering a great popular rejoicing. The liberators were fittingly celebrated. Cider and Calvados flowed freely in the evening. Around 10:00 p.m., the German air force spoiled the party a little by bombing Alençon. The human and materiel toll of the day of 12 August was satisfactory, for the first time since the beginning of the Normandy campaign. In the *GTD*, there were only four soldiers wounded, including *Capitaine* Troadec.[42] On the enemy side, however, there were 140 killed, 200 prisoners, 5 tanks destroyed, and 16 other vehicles destroyed. Dio was relieved. His men had quickly adapted to the directives he had given them. It had taken two days of fighting to take the measure of an enemy who was still among the best German troops.

On 13 August, the enemy, pushed back by the *2ᵉ DB*, took refuge in the forest of Écouves, 10km north of Alençon, between the towns of Carrouges to the west and Sées to the east. The wooded area covered 15,000 hectares, an area 18km long and 10km wide. Leclerc, faithful to his usual tactics, bypassed this forested massif with the *GTD* and the *GTL* from the west and the GTV from the east. The *GTD* was on schedule for the mission it received on 10 August: its fourth bound was for Carrouges, a large town located on a major crossroads, and Saint-Sauveur, a small village 5km to the east. Leaving Alençon, its axis of advance was along the RN12 in a due west direction. Then after 20 kilometres, before the village of Lalacelle, the route branched off due north towards Ciral and Carrouges. To begin the offensive movement on that Sunday, 13 August, Subgroup Rouvillois was at the head of the *GTD* in front of Noiret's subgroup. Farret's subgroup advanced on a parallel axis. Throughout the day, this subgroup, mainly infantry, mopped up the residual German elements of the *116. Panzerdivision,* left in the villages overtaken by the tanks. This was also the case at Ciral, Carrouges, and Le Ménil-Scelleur. Farret also had to guard the flank of the US XV Corps on its west.

Rouvillois's vanguard encountered armoured elements at Lalacelle, destroying three tracked vehicles and two light cars. At that point, the *GTD* advanced north towards Ciral, a village still held by the Germans. The enemy position had to be outmanoeuvred. The infantry in the lead, supported by the tanks, was forced to take the village with great difficulty, slowing down the advance. The Germans who were in the cellars of the houses had to be dislodged. Dio was in his jeep behind the village when he heard the noise of the fighting. He was impatient. He could go there in his vehicle – his broken ankle hurt and prevented him from moving on foot. It was then that, unable to wait any longer, Dio made a somewhat foolhardy decision that his men would discuss with admiration.[43] With his jeep, he went around the village of Ciral to the east across

39   Girard, *Journal de Guerre*, p.254.
40   To avoid friendly fire, a line is identified on the map beyond which friendly bombardment by air or artillery will take place. Ground units are prohibited from moving forward of the line.
41   The name Alençon has appeared on the *RMT*'s Colours ever since.
42   *Capitaine* Troadec had been Leclerc's aide-de-camp in 1941 and 1942. Then he was assigned to *Groupement Dio* for the Fezzan 2 campaign and Tunisia. This reservist officer accompanied Dio when they entered Tunis.
43   Robert Bensaïd, a *marsouin* in the 1st Battalion of the *RMT* in 1944, recounted this feat of arms in 2020 when the author asked him to recall his memories of *Colonel* Dio. This episode is not mentioned in the *GTD JMO, Colonel* Dio refusing, as usual, to talk about it. It is described in the book by Repiton-Préneuf (head

the fields and joined the RN809 five kilometres further north. On the way, he gave the order to a platoon leader of the *12ᵉ Cuirs*, *Lieutenant* Pity, to follow him with his four Shermans.[44] Thus, 'Colonel Dio, who had only a sprain, back in his car, formed an advance guard: two Shermans, his jeep, two other Shermans.'[45] This small detachment headed due north towards 'the Carrouges spur which dominates the whole country,'[46] about 10 kilometres from Ciral.

Near the commune of Houssemaine, Dio and his escort arrived behind a retreating German column, certainly moving to set up a defensive position in Carrouges or to escape the trap set by the Anglo-Americans. Dio then caught up with the column and overtook it while firing his jeep's 30 calibre machine gun, almost at point-blank range. The tanks did the same, sowing panic in the surprised German ranks. 'Dio passes like a great lord, surrounded by his cloud of gun shots and bullets: without a battle, there he is in Carrouges.'[47] The village was heavily occupied. Dio understood that he could not hold the village alone and returned to Ciral to find reinforcements. The detachment then turned around at full speed and set off in the direction from which it came. It thus went back up the German column in the opposite direction for several kilometres. 'This time, the French had a clear view of the devastation caused on the way there. In the midst of this disaster, men wander, mad with terror, overwhelmed with fatigue.'[48] In the meantime, Dio requested support from the American Air Corps, which sowed panic in the German column between Saint-Martin-des-Landes and Carrouges. Nevertheless, some Germans recovered and reacted to the passage of this furious column which owed its salvation only to its great speed. The five vehicles bearing the Cross of Lorraine arrived in front of Ciral where Subgroup Rouvillois regrouped, leaving it to the infantry to clear the village. Dio turned around in front of them and, standing up, shouted at them: 'It's kicking off on all sides… follow me.'[49] Once again, Dio stormed forward at the head of his *GTD* to definitively seize Carrouges.[50] This time, all the Shermans from Capitaine Noël's 3rd Squadron of the *12ᵉ Cuirs* were behind him. The Germans, hearing the dull sound of the tracks coming back towards them once again, fled or threw down their weapons and immediately raised their hands in the air. The senseless action undertaken by Dio, worthy of a still immature *sous lieutenant* of cavalry, not only allowed the capture of Carrouges but created panic in the German ranks whose dead numbered in the hundreds. *Lieutenant* Girard describes the episode:

> The *GTD* charged, all sails out, through a fusillade that cracked everywhere like a fire. It was, in the end, a real charge; Dio, alone in the lead in his jeep, and behind him, launched like racing cars and firing in all directions, were Noël's Shermans. This whirlwind pushed everything up as far as Carrouges. It had fallen on the flank of an armoured division that was heading towards Sées. The carnage was terrible. The machine guns were white. Countless prisoners, some of whom were crying, it seems, with fear.[51]

---

of the division's intelligence office), Erwan Bergot, and especially Girard, Leclerc's aide-de-camp. Only the *JMO* of the *13e Bataillon du Génie* very briefly mentions *Colonel* Dio's role in the capture of Carrouges.

44   The town of Carrouges named a square and a stele after *Sous Lieutenant* Michel Pity, leader of the 1st platoon of the 4th squadron of the *12e Régiment des Cuirassiers*. It is located on the D909. This 24-year-old officer was killed during the fighting at Le Bourget on 27 August 1944.

45   Repiton-Préneuf, *2ème DB: La Campagne de France*, p.15.

46   Repiton-Préneuf, *2ème DB: La Campagne de France*, p.11.

47   Repiton-Préneuf, *2ème DB: La Campagne de France*, p.15.

48   Bergot, *La 2 ème D.B.*, p.98.

49   Fond Leclerc, *JMO of the 13e BG*, p.35.

50   Compagnon, *Leclerc*, p.378.

51   Girard, *Journal de Guerre*, pp.254–255.

The enemy that was then facing the *GTD* were from the *2. Panzerdivision*. 'At Carrouges, beaming, Dio passed a message to Leclerc to announce his position. He added, 'We're continuing.' It was 11:30 a.m. Leaving Corlu (deputy of the 1st Battalion of the *RMT*) to finish mopping up the city, Dio sent Rouvillois towards the northeast, by the D2.'[52] In his momentum, Rouvillois advanced to Ménil-Scelleur, seven kilometres north of Carrouges. He pushed on to La Perdrière, five kilometres to the east on the edge of the forest of Écouves. The enemy was more and more aggressive. A platoon of TDs destroyed several tanks around what appeared to be a headquarters, and they took prisoners, who were from the SS. 'Dio would learn in the evening that Rouvillois's vanguard had clashed hard with the elements guarding the advance of the *2. SS Panzerdivision*.'[53] The *GTD JMO* mentions that 'The Headquarters of the *2. SS Panzer* is destroyed.'[54] It seems rather that it was actually 'the *2. Panzer* [Division], its counterpart from the *Wehrmacht*.' as Repiton-Préneuf specified and the confusion was certainly coming from the uniforms of the German tankers.[55]

Meanwhile, Dio sent Noiret's subgroup to the east of Carrouges in the direction of Chahains. It was near the village of Rouperroux that the *GTD* units met those from the *GTL*. Massu's subgroup was in the lead. Dio ran to meet his *méhariste* companion from Zouar. The friendship between the two men was strong. They were in the process of telling each other their latest exploits when a jeep arrived with *Lieutenant* de Valence, the liaison officer from the *GTL*. He had come to ask *Colonel* Dio, on behalf of Langlade, to move the *GTD* back, because his leading elements were in Massu's zone.[56] It was not an easy task for Valence who, surprisingly, did not get too much of a telling off from Dio, which was often the case when liaison officers came to carry out this kind of mission with him. Guy de Valence was born in Vannes, which did not make the *GTD* commander indifferent. Once he had relayed his message, the *lieutenant* approached the fighting taking place 200m ahead. 'Suddenly, a violent shock knocked him to the ground. As soon as he got up, he realised that he no longer had a right arm. It had just been shot clean off at the shoulder by an 88mm round from a German tank.'[57] The young cavalry officer, nonchalant, got back into his jeep[58] and, turning to the astonished *marsouins*, said to them: 'Well, that's not bad for a staff officer. Come on, make them pay for that arm.'[59]

At the end of the afternoon, Dio gave the orders to seize the villages surrounding Carrouges to widen the security zone to avoid surprises during the units' resupply operations. Thus, the villages of Sainte-Marguerite-de-Carrouges to the northwest and Saint-Sauveur-de-Carrouges to the northeast were held by *GTD* units. Access to important crossroads was firmly defended. No German could approach them. The *GTD* commander, who set up his CP on the church square in

---

52 Bergot, *La 2 ème D.B.*, p.90.

53 Bergot, *La 2 ème D.B.*, p.92.

54 Fonds Leclerc, *JMO GTD*, p.5.

55 Repiton-Préneuf, *2ème DB: La Campagne de France*, p.15. German tankers wore black coveralls with a skull on the collar of their jackets or overalls

56 In military terms, a zone or zone of action is an area of land assigned to a unit, that has very precise boundaries to prevent interference and friendly fire.

57 Langlade, *En suivant Leclerc*, p.165.

58 *Lieutenant* de Valence recovered very quickly, the shell having cauterised the wound. He received the *Médaille Militaire* for his courage and his astonishing morale. The citation awarding him the *Médaille Militaire* ends as follows: 'by his extraordinary attitude and composure, he astonished and inspired the infantry elements present.' (Decree of 21 November 1944, published in the *Journal Officiel* of 3 December 1944). It was he whom Leclerc chose to succeed Girard as aide-de-camp. Valence accompanied him to Indochina. He was still his aide-de-camp when the *général* died in 1947. Langlade adds that it is unfortunate that Valence was not on Leclerc's fatal flight, because if 'Valence, who had enough character and independence to resist the *général's* anger and make him see reason, had been present, perhaps this tragedy would have been avoided.' (Langlade, *En suivant Leclerc,* p.167).

59 Bergot, *La 2 ème D.B.*, p.93.

Carrouges, was particularly satisfied with the day. The report presented to him at the end of the day was telling. The group had only 5 killed and 10 wounded, including his deputy *Lieutenant Colonel* Vézinet and two officers from his staff, *Capitaine* Revault d'Allonnes and *Capitaine* Deveaux. The latter was wounded in the fighting at Carrouges while he was in Dio's command Sherman, the *Sainte-Anne d'Auray*. On the equipment side, there were only two tanks and two vehicles destroyed. This was very light in comparison to the enemy losses: 1,022 killed, 1,417 prisoners, 12 tanks, 11 guns, and 190 vehicles destroyed. Several times during the day, Dio called in air support for his units. After having experienced the battle of Ksar Rhilane in Tunisia, he knew at what point in the battle it was necessary to call in US aircraft. His experience in that area had most certainly helped to limit losses within his units.

Personally, Dio was amused by the outburst he had during the day when he rushed towards Carrouges in a jeep. He sometimes liked to provoke luck. It was like at Kufra, where he had jumped on the Italian *capitano*'s horse and taunted the Italian machine guns in the fort. At Tedjéré, he had not hesitated to mount the assault and he had his cap shot through. At the evening briefing, he felt that even Rouvillois was looking at him with a certain admiration. He, the *biffin*[60] *méhariste*, rather balanced in his tactical choices, showed all these cavalrymen that he was capable of leading a charge and that panache was not only taught in Saumur. This bold move would make him, in spite of himself, a legendary figure among the *GTD* officers and soldiers. For the time being, after two days of combat and three sleepless nights, the *GTD*, firmly established in Carrouges, could take a restorative break during the night of 12/13 August 1944.

On the evening of 13 August, the Germans were at bay. Having lost control of the sky, their columns were continually pounded by ground attack aircraft such as the Douglas Invader with its 12 x 12.7mm machine guns or the Hawker Typhoon with its rockets. On the ground, the pressure was also very hard on them. The three tactical groups of the *2ᵉ DB* were able to take Argentan in stride, so bold and clear had been their successes throughout the day. However, General Omar Bradley forbad the *2ᵉ DB* from crossing the Orne and entering Argentan.[61] Leclerc and his *GT* commanders did not understand this decision. They were ready to sound the death knell, and the American command forbad them from victory. *Colonel* de Langlade described the situation:

> …crushed between the two claws of the Anglo-American pincer, twenty German divisions madly kept on site in the defence of the 'Atlantic Wall' were struggling to escape to the east. The English were at Falaise, the French and the Americans were at Argentan. Only a bottle-neck of 23 kilometres which was tightening by the hour, allowed this totally defeated army to withdraw by a single and mediocre road, the N1816.[62]

As a result, on 14 August, even if its losses were considerable, the 7th German Army avoided anni-hilation. The Allied air forces and artillery struck relentlessly at these columns trying to escape the trap, causing real massacres in places, such as at Chambois which 'will remain in our memory the typical mass grave, the one where, to open a passage for vehicles, the American, conveniently, cleared the corpses with bulldozers.'[63]

---

60 *Biffin* is pejorative military slang for infantryman.
61 This decision would remain one of the most controversial of the entire war. It seems to have been the result of a misunderstanding between Montgomery, who commanded the Anglo-Canadian Army Group in the north, and Bradley, commanding the American Army Group with the *2e DB* in the south. It seems that the two generals had previously defined a boundary between them to prevent the two army groups from mixing.
62 Langlade, *En Suivant Leclerc*, p.169.
63 Repiton-Préneuf, *2ème DB: La Campagne de France*, p.22.

Leclerc set up his CP in Fleuré, a village on elevated ground with views of the town of Argentan. The *GTD* was in second echelon in Carrouges, ready to support either the *GTV*, which held Écouché on the banks of the Orne, or the *GTL*, which was set up in the Mortrée-Montmerrei region. The *GTD* had experienced three intense days of manoeuvre and fighting. It would finally experience a calmer period which it would use for maintenance and resupply. On 14 August, Dio ordered his units to carry out offensive reconnaissance missions to locate enemy presence in the surrounding area. These actions had the advantage of reducing residual resistance in remote areas. The *GTD* captured many prisoners, 315 in total for the day, and it destroyed the German equipment it found. On 15 August, the *GTD* bounded forward 10 kilometres to the north and settled in the area of Boucé, a village 15 kilometres south of Argentan, just behind Leclerc's CP. Dio pushed reconnaissance in the village of Vieux-Pont to its west and on Chantelou to its northeast. The *GTD* units linked up with the American 3rd Armored Division, which had come from Mayenne. These limited actions led to the capture of about 50 prisoners and the destruction of more than 60 vehicles and a dozen anti-tank guns. During that time, the artillery group of the *2ᵉ DB* under the orders of *Lieutenant Colonel* Crépin joined the American artillerymen to pound the last German convoys as they tried to make their way north of Argentan. Within the *DB*, the artillerymen were the most active during those days of mid-August.

16 August was the calmest day since the landing. Still in Boucé, the *GTD* took advantage of the lull to replace its damaged or destroyed equipment. Young local Frenchmen were recruited to replace those who had been killed or seriously injured.[64] The prestige of the '*Division Leclerc*' was already high in France. Once uniformed and equipped, those young men would learn on the job how to become soldiers, guided and advised by the veterans.

On 17 August, the *GTD* moved into the Fleuré region, approaching Argentan. It set up strong-points, defensive positions that blocked the exits from the city. In short order, they dug themselves in to fight with no thought of retreat. The American command was clearly concerned about a German counterattack coming from Argentan. The *GTD*'s CP was at Meigné-le-Vicomte, which has views of the southern exits of Argentan, allowing it to direct the fire of the *3ᵉ RAC*. A strong-point under Rouvillois's orders was established in Mauvaisville. The position overlooked the River Orne less than a kilometre away to the southeast. A second strongpoint, under Noiret was set up at Tanques, to the west of Fleuré. The third strongpoint, under *Capitaine* de Boissieu, who was the head of the *général's* protection squadron, was set up at Fleuré, near the division's CP. Only the strongpoint at Mauvaisville would be called upon to intervene against enemy elements trying to escape from Argentan. The situation remained unchanged on 18 August. Only the *bigors* of the *GTD* intervened with barrage fire on a German counterattack in the sector of the US 80th Infantry Division. The *3ᵉ RAC* fired at more than 10 kilometres onto the German convoys. 19 August looked a lot like the previous day. The *3ᵉ RAC* fired in support of the US 80th Infantry Division, which was engaged with German units. The deputy of the 1st Battalion's escort company, *Capitaine* Schrimpf, was killed while conducting a liaison mission with the American division.

By 20 August the fighting in Argentan had almost ceased; it was a pivotal day. Dio had just been warned by Leclerc to prepare to move east towards Paris. Why would Paris suddenly have become the objective of the *2ᵉ DB*? It was a matter of timing. Indeed, as early as September 1943, the leader

---

64   Thus the young Guy Merle, after having served as a guide to the Canadian troops in Caen, ran after the *2e DB* to join it. He managed to catch up to it in Carrouges. He was assigned to the 2nd Section of the 3rd Company. He would fight the entire French campaign in the half-track 'Marie-Hélène.' He later followed Leclerc to Indochina. He then had a great career in civilian life before becoming the president of the 1st Battalion Association and then president of the *RMT Association*, which had finally been reunited. He would be the founder and editor of the *Chamelier*, a publication responsible for ensuring the link between the former *RMT marsouins*.

of Free France had warned Leclerc that, in his mind, the *2ᵉ DB* was created to liberate Paris. This is what he had also expressed to Eisenhower at the end of December of that year.[65] The American military realised at that time that they needed not only French forces but also the assistance of their leaders and the support of the population.[66] Leclerc had received a very secret personal letter from de Gaulle on 15 December 1943, designating him 'as interim military governor of Paris.'[67] It was certainly in August that Leclerc revealed to his direct assistants this mission of a political-military nature that the de Gaulle had entrusted to him. De Gaulle absolutely wanted the French to liberate the capital, not only in regard to the Allies, but also for the domestic front where the communists with the *FTP* (*francs-tireurs partisans*) were agitating. Moreover, the latter, with the *FFI*, had launched the insurrection in Paris the day before, after the strikes that had begun on 13 August. On the 19th, police officers seized the police prefecture and turned it into a stronghold. The German troops in Paris were largely not operational units. Instead, the German garrison of Paris was mainly made up of service units and general staff. The insurgents quickly controlled a third of the city, but they lacked sufficient firepower and ammunition, so their situation was going to become more and more precarious. The German command assembled a division stationed in the Lille region to enter Paris and crush the insurrection, and then set up a defence of the city. Leclerc harangued his American military superiors, whose orders he was under, to obtain their agreement for him to go to Paris. He learnt from Haislip that two American divisions had already left for Dreux. Dio understood. He gave the orders for his units to regroup and carry out the final preparatory operations before departure.

The 1st Battalion of Farret's subgroup settled in Mauvaisville. The *12ᵉ Cuirs* regrouped in the village of Tanques. The *3ᵉ RAC* settled in La Maladrerie. There were no changes for the *GTD* on 21 August as the units continued to replace their damaged equipment. They were all resupplied with ammunition and fuel to the maximum extent possible and weapons maintenance was emphasised. The cavalrymen and artillerymen cleaned their guns. The infantry cleaned their individual weapons and the machine guns of the half-tracks. Meanwhile, Leclerc wrote to de Gaulle. He told him of his incomprehension at having been ordered to stop in front of Argentan. 'Due to a lack of communication between the two armies, the Allied command let 250,000 *Boches* escape.'[68] He reported the human losses suffered by his division, 160 killed and 550 wounded. He informed him that he had decided, without the agreement of the Americans, to send a reconnaissance detachment under Guillebon's command towards Paris. The latter, at the head of a column composed of a squadron of light tanks, two platoons of armoured cars, and two infantry sections, left the Fleuré region on the 21st at 11:00 a.m. The *GTD* provided *Capitaine* Perceval's 2nd Company of the *1/RMT* to constitute the infantry component of Guillebon's column and the two platoons of *spahis* of the 4th Squadron of the *1ᵉʳ RMSM*.

On 22 August, Leclerc flew in a Piper Cub to General Bradley's CP and waited there for his return for more than half a day. In doing so, he went around General Leonard Gerow, the commander of the US V Corps, the new commander under which he had been placed.[69] Leclerc

---

65   De Gaulle sent a memorandum on 18 September 1943 to Churchill and Roosevelt concerning French participation in the operations to liberate Europe. He requested that French troops land with the Allies in the south of France but also in the North-West coming from England. On 27 December 1943, he made the participation of the entire French Army in the South conditional on the integration of at least one armoured division with the Allied troops, 'otherwise, we could not give our agreement, nor our troops.' (Compagnon, *Leclerc*, p.389).

66   Jean Edward Smith, *The Liberation of Paris: How Eisenhower, de Gaulle, and von Choltitz Saved the City of Light* (Simon & Schuster, 2019), p.43.

67   Compagnon, *Leclerc*, p.389.

68   Girard, *Journal de Guerre*, p.261.

69   The message that Gerow then sent to Leclerc hinted at the future tensions between the two *généraux*: 'I desire

wanted to act, but he could see that the Americans were hesitant to enter Paris. The prospect of urban combat, which would be costly in human lives, certainly dissuaded them. Additionally, they did not want to be responsible for feeding and supplying a population of seven million people, which represented a logistics requirement of 3,000 tons of supplies per day. For them, 'the most appropriate tactic is therefore to flank from the north and the south and to pick Paris like a ripe fruit.'[70] Moreover, by that date, American units had already reached the Seine, at Mantes in the north and Melun in the south. De Gaulle and Leclerc did not see things the same way as the Americans. They could not take the risk of letting the insurrection be harshly repressed. At the end of the day on the 22nd, Leclerc finally obtained the green light from General Bradley to enter and liberate Paris under the command of General Gerow, with the US 4th Infantry Division in support. The commander of the *2e DB* immediately returned to his command post, and he had barely landed in his Piper Cub as night fell. He summoned his three *GT* commanders upon arriving at Fleuré to give them instructions on the movement that would be carried out the following morning. Hearing this, Dio and his two fellow *colonels* looked at each other and smiled. After these last few days where they had remained static, they would be able to resume movement and combat. Their men were waiting for exactly that.

The Normandy campaign ended after 22 days of operations since the landing. 'The Battle of Normandy is over. The *2e DB* fought it offensively from Le Mans to Argentan, from the morning of 10 August to midday of 14 August, then statically from 15th to 20th.'[71] The fighting of the first two days was difficult, the time to perfect the cohesion between the units, in particular the armour/infantry liaison down to the lowest level and the artillery-first echelon liaison to improve the responsiveness of the support fire. Following this short breaking-in period, soldiers of the *GTD* were animated with confidence. They had taken the measure of the Germans. Dio also followed the behaviour of the other two battalions of his regiment. The second battalion with Massu and the third with Putz had become, respectively, the spearhead subgroups of the *GTL* and the *GTV*. The men of the *RMT* behind their leader were proud to learn, according to the first reports circulating, that the Germans lost in the battle of Normandy '450,000 men, including 200,000 killed, and left behind 1,500 tanks, 2,000 guns, and 20,000 vehicles.'[72] Some historians compare this German rout to that suffered at Stalingrad in 1943. The toll inflicted by the *2e DB* alone on the German troops is difficult to ascertain. Girard mentions: '7,000 killed or prisoners, 600 vehicles, 70 Panthers, 10 Tigers destroyed, plus about 40 guns of various calibres.'[73] Morale was at its highest in the French ranks. The welcome from the population upon their arrival in each village overwhelmed all Leclerc's men, who became aware of the significance of their role. Never had a French soldier had the privilege, like them, of participating in the liberation of their homeland. The leaders and the men of the *GTD*, confident in the future, were in a hurry to leave Normandy. Another chapter opened up to them, which would be about driving the Germans out of the capital of their country.

Dio was excited by his mission. At times, he forgot about his ankle which, despite treatment, would sometimes painfully remind him of the injury, especially when he wanted to move around

to make it clear to you that the 2d Armored Division (French) is under my command for all purposes and no part of it will be employed by you except in the execution of missions assigned by this headquarters.' (Martin Blumenson, *United States Army in World War II, Breakout and Pursuit,* Center of Military History, United States Army, Washington DC, 1993, p.600.)

70   Compagnon, *Leclerc*, p.390.
71   Jean Compagnon, 'Paris en ligne de Mire,' *Armées d'Aujourd'hui*, May 1994, 190, pp.128–132.
72   Compagnon, *Leclerc*, p.383.
73   Girard, *Journal de Guerre*, p.256.

on foot. *Colonel* Dio would be cited in the Army Orders, with the award of the *Croix de Guerre* with palm, accompanied by the following citation:

> Despite very serious difficulties, from the beginning of the engagement of his *groupement tactique*, managed to push back the enemy resistance defending Alençon. At the capture of Carrouges, led his troops with a magnificent élan, causing a veritable carnage in the enemy columns.[74]

---

74   Décision Ministérielle No.105, *JORF* of 19.11.1944.

Chapter 10

Paris and the Paris Region, 22 August to 7 September 1944

Colonel Dio was a busy man on 22 August 1944. Returning to Fleuré early in the evening from Leclerc's headquarters, the commander of *Groupement Tactique Dio* summoned all the officers of his staff as well as the subgroup commanders and department chiefs, to his headquarters in Meigné-le-Vicomte. Once all the leaders had arrived, Dio gave his verbal instructions. The *GTD* would advance about 200km on Route 1 in echelon behind *Groupement Tactique Langlade* (*GTL*). The objective was Saint-Cyr-l'École and to take up a battle position in preparation for entering Paris. The tactical group was arrayed south of Argentan, divided into two parts.[1] According to the plan, the two parts of the *GTD* would meet in Mortrée. Movement would begin on the afternoon of 23 August with a pause for refuelling at Maintenon.[2] A written movement order reached the units the next day. The units of the *GTD*[3] *departed around 4:00 p.m. on 23 August,*[4] *and refuelling took place at midnight in Maintenon as planned. It was a very dark night, and the advance was chaotic as drivers inched their way along congested routes with their lights turned off. Accidents dotted the course and slowed progress. Arriving in the Paris region in the early morning of 24 August, the GTD* crews had hardly slept after having covered the 200 kilometres in about 10 hours.

The division's operations order was written the day before at 6:00 p.m.[5] An extract from the order reads:

MISSION
1. Seize Paris
2. Hold Paris by occupying the roads between Ivry-sur-Seine and Neuilly-sur-Marne
   - push elements into the region northeast of Paris
   - keep a reserve element in Paris

---

1   In the area of Tanques – Le Breuil – Meigné-le-Vicomte were the headquarters, with the *12e Cuirs*, the Engineer units, the *RMSM*, the *RBFM* and the *13e Bataillon Médical*. Distributed in the area of Mauvaisville – St-Martin-des-Champs – La Maladrerie were the *1/RMT*, the 3e RAC and Maintenance Group 15 (*GER XV*) with combat trains.

2   Fonds Leclerc, *Ordre de Mouvement n°223/3 du 23 août 1944*, boîte K1.

3   They followed the route Mortrée – Sées – Mortagne-au-Perche – Longny-au-Perche – Digny – Châteauneuf-en-Thymerais – Maintenon – Épernon.

4   Fonds Leclerc, *JMO du GTD*, boîte K1.

5   Leclerc had this order read to de Gaulle, who had joined him in Rambouillet. The leader of the Free French stated: 'It's all the same, Leclerc, liberating Paris with an armoured division; no French leader has ever had a greater chance, but no one has deserved it better. The luck of *générals* in time of war is the happiness of governments and peoples.' (Alain de Boissieu, 'La Libération Capitale,' *Armées d'Aujourd'hui* No.190, numéro spécial (mai 1994), pp.190–193.

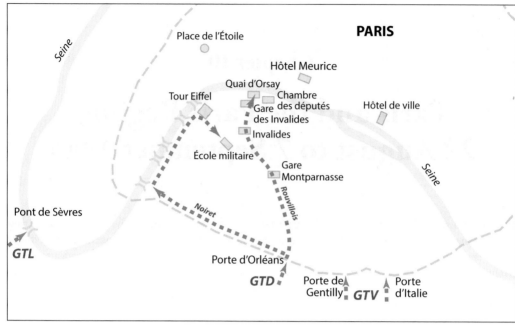

Map 10a The GTD in the fight to liberate Paris (25 August 1944).

....

Groupement Tactique 'D'

a) Make the *3ᵉ RAC* available to *GTV*, prepared:
- Either to support that group with all available means
- Or to support *GTL* by pushing a subgroup in the direction of the Pont de Sèvres

b) Clear the centre of Paris of enemy forces

c) In the event of immediate success of the various operations of *Groupements Tactiques* V and L, push elements towards Pantin, north of Paris.

Command Post: Town Hall in Pantin

The *GTD* was to be in the second echelon entering Paris, behind the *GTV*. Ultimately, the tactical group had to clear the centre of Paris, which required storming the German bastions and then setting up defensive positions facing north of the capital.[6] In fact, intelligence confirmed the imminent arrival of the German *47. Infanterie-Division*, coming from Pas-de-Calais to suppress the Parisian insurrection. Since *Général* de Gaulle had recommended *Colonel* Billotte to Leclerc, the *GTV* was in the lead on the division's axis of advance: Arpajon – Longjumeau – Antony and Porte d'Orléans, moving almost due north along the Route Nationale 20. After entering the capital, the *GTV* had to hold the exits east of Paris in the direction of Gare d'Austerlitz – Bois de Vincennes

---

6   The German military presence in Paris in 1944 consisted of:
- Von Choltitz's command post at the Hôtel Meurice (rue de Rivoli)
- the main staff headquarters at the Hôtel Majestic (Avenue Kléber)
- three army barracks: Vincennes, Latour-Maubourg, and Place de la République,
- a few strongholds located at the Senate, the Chambre des Députés, the Quai d'Orsay, the École Militaire, and the École des Mines.

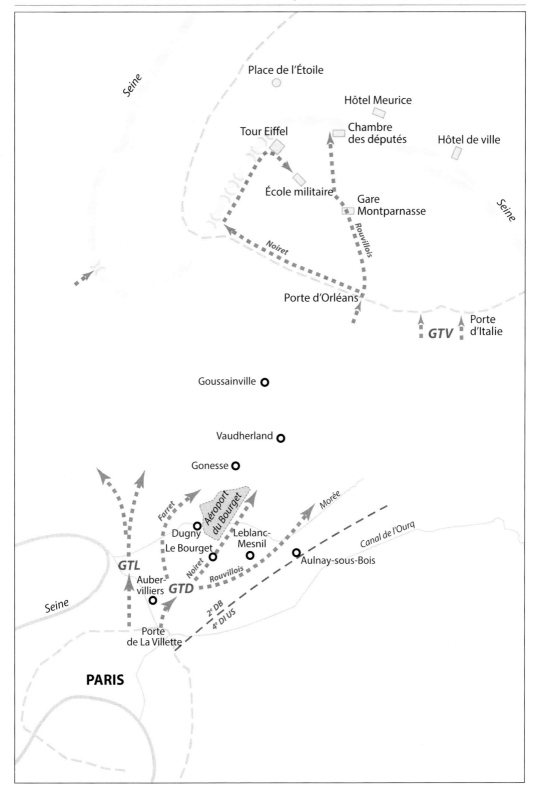

Map 10b The GTD in the fighting to the North of Paris (26-28 August 1944).

in coordination with the 4th US Infantry Division,[7] which was advancing on its right. The *GTL* was on the division's secondary axis, coming from Rambouillet, forcing it to use the Chevreuse valley to enter Paris by the Pont de Sèvres and to take up positions at the Place de la Concorde as a mobile reserve.

The *Wehrmacht* had established a defensive system outside Paris that was particularly strong in the area south of the city.

> The [German] 1st Army has been pulled up from Bordeaux and had been ordered to gather the remnants of the 7th Army that had escaped from Normandy. It had established a defensive zone running from Villeneuve-Saint-Georges to Versailles which covers the bridges of the Seine in Paris and those below the city. Those troops are very well equipped with 88mm anti-aircraft guns, which are very effective in an anti-tank role...[8]

At 8:00 a.m. on 24 August, *Colonel* Dio formed a subgroup under the orders of *Commandant* Rouvillois to support the *GTV*, which had launched the assault from Arpajon towards the Porte d'Orléans along the N20. Subgroup Rouvillois took the route of Rambouillet, Clairefontaine, Rochefort-en-Yvelines, Limours, Fontenay-lès-Briis, Villejust, and Longjumeau. When they linked up around 10:00 a.m., Rouvillois found the *GTV* blocked at Longjumeau. The weather was bad and visibility low. Dio accompanied Rouvillois's advance guard so he could be as close as possible to the fighting and to gain a first-hand understanding of the terrain. He ordered Rouvillois to reduce the enemy resistance in Champlan, a town to the west of the main axis that threatened the flanks of the *GTV*. The rest of the *GTD* under Vézinet's orders arrived at 1:00 p.m. Dio ordered them to mop up the remaining enemy resistance between Longjumeau and Saulx-les-Chartreux during the afternoon. At 8:00 p.m., the *colonel* consolidated his tactical group in the region of Saulx-les-Chartreux. As the division reserve, he prepared to advance, should he be ordered to do so. He gave instructions to immediately refuel and rearm the tanks so the crews would be ready for action on the following day.

Early that evening, Dio was summoned to Leclerc's headquarters in a quarry in Croix-de-Berny. The *2ᵉ DB* had not accomplished its mission of taking Paris by the evening of the 24th. Leclerc, stopped in the Parisian suburb of Antony, was frustrated when he discovered that Billotte had persisted in reducing the enemy defensive positions on the main axis of the N20 when he had told him to avoid serious enemy contact by taking alternate routes. As a result, the *GTV* was stopped in the southern suburbs and could not enter Paris, with the exception of Dronne's detachment. Contrary to planning assumptions, the southern axis proved to be the most strongly defended by the Germans. Therefore, while Dio was delayed, the *GTL* on the secondary axis arrived at the Pont de Sèvres during the evening of the 24th. At the head of the column, Massu was dismayed when he was denied permission to continue into Paris, which was primarily due to logistical reasons. He insisted that it was urgent he entered the city as quickly as possible before things got out of control among the communist resistance fighters. Indeed, 'the infantry of the *RMT* were surprised to see that among the enthusiastic crowds in Boulogne red banners were flying alongside the tricolour in equal numbers.'[9]

While meeting with his commanders, Dio learnt that *Capitaine* Dronne's detachment had entered Paris a few minutes earlier.[10] From out in the southern suburbs, had he then had the privi-

7   The US 4th Infantry Division, under the command of General Raymond Barton, had stormed Utah Beach on 6 June. The insignia of this division was four green ivy leaves.
8   Compagnon, *Leclerc*, p.397.
9   Compagnon, *Leclerc*, p.402.
10   Dronne's detachment, infiltrating from Antony in the southern suburbs, entered Paris through the Porte

lege of hearing the bells of all the Parisian churches announcing the arrival of Leclerc's men in the capital? Dio was happy that the honour fell to his friend Dronne, the colonial administrator of Cameroon. He remembered their shared memories of Yaoundé, Gabon, Fezzan, and Tunisia where Dronne had been seriously injured. This reservist officer was, like him, one of the very first to rally to Leclerc. His full temperament, his gruff manner of speech, and his sometimes out of control reactions certainly kept him from advancing in rank, but he was one of the few officers capable of commanding the 9th Company of the *RMT*, made up of a majority of Spanish Republicans. It was to him that Leclerc entrusted the mission of entering Paris first to reassure the Parisian insurgents.

Dio was saddened to learn of the death of *Capitaine* Emmanuel Dupont, the commander of the 11th Company of the 3rd Battalion of the *RMT*, in front of the Fresnes prison.[11] Despite this bad news, the commander of the *GTD* was rather satisfied with the events of 24 August. After a night of sleepless driving, his men had performed well, and it had been a successful day. The *GTD* suffered only six wounded in its ranks, but in exchange, the *groupement tactique* had inflicted more than 100 German casualties (43 killed and 60 wounded) and taken 247 prisoners, while destroying two guns and six German vehicles. The staff was able to rest a little before daybreak. During the night, drawing on the lessons of the day as well as those provided by Dronne's infiltration, Leclerc modified his initial order. The *GTV* would rush into Paris through the Porte d'Italie and the Porte de Gentilly. Its objective would be the Hôtel Meurice, headquarters of *General* Dietrich von Choltitz. The *GTL*'s mission remained unchanged, with the Place de la Concorde as its objective after moving through the Place de l'Étoile. The *GTD* had to take the main axis towards the Porte d'Orléans. 'At half past four, Leclerc called together Dio, Noiret, and Vézinet and gave them his instructions.'[12] After returning to his command post, Dio summoned his immediate subordinates to give them his orders. Despite the continued pain in his ankle, he formed two subgroups under his direct command, with a reduced staff:

- Subgroup Rouvillois, made up of the 1st Company of the *RMT*, the 2nd squadron of the *12ᵉ Cuirs*, Marles' battery of the *3ᵉ RAC* (3 x 105mm guns),[13] an engineering section, and a platoon of the *RMSM*. 'Subgroup Rouvillois will advance to the German centres of resistance at Les Invalides – La Tour-Maubourg and the National Assembly – Quai d'Orsay.'[14]
- Subgroup Noiret, consisting of the 4th Squadron of the *12ᵉ Cuirs*, the 2nd Company of the *RMT*, Magna's battery of the *3ᵉ RAC*, two engineering sections, and a platoon of the *RMSM*. 'Subgroup Noiret will advance along the outer boulevards to reach the Seine, secure its bridges as far as the Champ de Mars and take as its objective the German centre of resistance at the École Militaire.'[15]

---

d'Italie and reached the Hôtel de Ville (city hall) at 9:22 p.m. The detachment was composed of a section from the 9th Company of *3/RMT*, two sections of infantry, a platoon reduced to three tanks from the *501e RCC* and a section of the engineers of the *13e Bataillon du Génie*. Upon the news of the arrival of this detachment, all the church bells of Paris started ringing, including 'the loud voice of the great bell of Notre-Dame' (Dronne, *Carnets de Route*, p.335).

11   This Saint-Cyrien, who joined up in Narvik, rejoined in England and Cameroon. With his company, he became part of the *RMT* in Sabratha. He never left the *2e DB* again. A strong Christian believer, his companions nicknamed him 'Ponpon the Saint.' He left behind greatly spiritual writings.

12   Girard, *Journal de Guerre*, pp.270–271.

13   In the city, to support the progress of the subgroup, the guns of the artillery could fire effectively only in direct fire mode at a range between 400 and 1,200 metres, roughly the same as that of a tank.

14   Fonds Leclerc, Compagnon, boîte 12, dossier 2, chemise 4, p.86.

15   Fonds Leclerc, Compagnon.

- The 3rd Company of the *RMT* was detached as reinforcement to the *GTV*.[16]
- The rest of the units of the *GTD* remained under *Lieutenant Colonel* Vézinet, Dio's deputy.

The forecast for Friday, 25 August promised mild weather. The rising morning mist would soon give way to the sun. The day would forever remain etched in the memory of Leclerc's men: 'For all those who took part in it, the liberation of Paris will forever be an unforgettable memory.'[17] They were going to fight to liberate the capital of their country in a manner recalling the storming of the Bastille on 14 July 1789. It was not going to be easy, and the losses were going to be heavy, and in addition, the *GTD* had the task of reducing the German strongpoints on the left bank, as well! Yet, despite the danger, every one of them was eager for the fight.

The tanks and half-tracks of the *GTD* moved out at 7:00 a.m. and began their advance towards the capital. In front of them, the civilian population aided the *FFI* and *FTP* resistance fighters as they busily cleared the road of barricades and filled in holes.[18] Surrounded by a joyfully delirious crowd, the progress was slow. 'We had trouble moving through the crowd, which, despite our tanks, constantly closed in around us. As soon as we'd stop, a swarm of people descended on us, pull us out of our seats, kiss us, offer us flowers, drinks, et cetera. All of Paris was going crazy.'[19] Leclerc's men, knowing that they were headed into Paris, had taken extra care to clean themselves up that morning. 'The faces that were so thoroughly washed this morning and already blackened are covered in lipstick…'[20]

The *GTD*, with Rouvillois in the lead, entered Paris through the Porte d'Orléans. 'The advance into Paris is a mixture of popular jubilation and combat, as was the case yesterday in the suburbs. This type of war is dangerous for the soldiers of the *2ᵉ DB*.'[21] Dio and Leclerc's vehicles followed behind the commander of the subgroup. Dio decided to directly command the two subgroups so he could coordinate their actions. He was accompanied by his three staff section chiefs (for intelligence, operations, and logistics), acting as an advanced command post. Leclerc, who followed behind Dio, wanted to meet up with the resistance as quickly as possible. He held a paper signed by de Gaulle appointing him the provisional military governor of Paris, and he needed to set up his headquarters to command all the various operations being carried out against the Nazis in Paris. Passing through Denfert-Rochereau, Rouvillois branched off along Boulevard Raspail towards the Montparnasse train station, which he seized without firing a shot.[22] Leclerc, who picked up the young *Général* Chaban-Delmas in Denfert, immediately set up his command post at the station to take advantage of the telephone facilities there. Dio established his advanced headquarters at

---

16   The 3rd Company of the *RMT* would actively participate in the attack of the Ministère de la Marine on the Place de la Concorde, then the Tuileries, and then in the seizure of the Hôtel Meurice, where *General* von Choltitz and his staff were captured. 'It was *Lieutenant* Karcher with his 1st Section who obtained the surrender of *General* von Choltitz, *Kommandant* of *Gross-Paris* in the Hôtel Meurice.' (Fonds Leclerc, Gambourg, *'le destin de la 3e Cie'*, p.3.).

17   Massu, *Sept Ans*, p.157.

18   According to historians, there were about 600 barricades set up in Paris between 20 and 25 July. They became quite a hindrance to the *2e DB* and the US 4th Infantry Division entering Paris.

19   Guy Merle, *L'Assaut, avec la 2e D.B.*, (Paris: Brive la Gaillarde, Ver Luisant, 2003), p.27.

20   Fonds Leclerc, Roger Loison, *Moteurs En Route, Récit, 1944–1945*, 2004, (not catalogued), p.12.

21   Compagnon, *Leclerc*, p.406.

22   Today, one is reminded of this historical route of the commander of the *2e DB* by a statue of *Général* Leclerc at the Porte d'Orléans, by the avenue that took his name between the Porte d'Orléans and the Place Denfert-Rochereau, and finally by the Musée du Général Leclerc de Hauteclocque et de la Libération de Paris – Musée Jean Moulin located in the Pavillons d'Octroi to the left and right of the Place Denfert-Rochereau, on either side of the statue of the Lion of Belfort.

the station as well, so he could lead his two subgroups. He found a table in one of the rooms of the station where he and his officers could track their movements around a map of Paris.[23]

Subgroup Rouvillois continued its progress towards the Seine by taking Avenue du Maine and the Boulevards of Montparnasse and Invalides. At the Church of Saint François Xavier, Rouvillois formed combined arms detachments of tanks and infantry under the orders of a *capitaine* to attack first the Invalides train station,[24] then the barracks at La Tour-Maubourg, and then the Quai d'Orsay and the Assemblée Nationale. The first two objectives fell quickly in the beginning of the afternoon, but the resistance at the Assemblée Nationale was determined. 'The Assemblée was set on fire on the orders of *Commandant* Rouvillois to force the Germans who were there to surrender.'[25] At 4:00 p.m., the capitulation of *General* von Choltitz, the German military governor of '*Gross-Paris*,' was announced on the radio. The units then received the order to cease offensive operations to prevent unnecessary loss of life. The remaining strongholds of German resistance would have to be dealt with through negotiation. Mixed teams of German and French officers (with leadership provided by the support company of the 1st Battalion of the *RMT* for the *GTD*) were formed to present von Choltitz's act of capitulation to each pocket of German resistance and to negotiate the terms of their surrender.

Meanwhile, Subgroup Noiret entered Paris through the Porte d'Orléans at 10:58 a.m. It took the outer boulevards which at that time formed the beltway encircling the capital.[26] After following the rue Balard towards the Seine, Noiret seized five important bridges in succession: Mirabeau, Grenelle, Passy,[27] Iéna, and Alma. He arrived at the Eiffel Tower at 11:58 a.m. His soldiers cleared the base of the tower and the Champ de Mars, and at 12:13 p.m., resistance fighters from the *FFI* hoisted a French flag at the top of the Eiffel Tower. *Capitaine* Gaudet, commanding the 4th Squadron of the *12e Cuirassiers*, reinforced by a platoon of armoured cars, received the order to attack the École Militaire, where a German garrison of 200 men had decided to obstinately continue fighting. The tanks were greeted 'by heavy fire from blockhouses and windows. They responded immediately and the entire squadron deployed in front of the building, concentrating fire on all the loopholes.'[28] The fire from both sides was intense, evidence of which can be found in the numerous bulletholes that still scar the main facade of the École Militaire today. After the *capitaine* requested reinforcement from an infantry unit, the tanks smashed the entrance gate of the École and penetrated inside the enclosure. An engineer section and two *FFI* sections from the *maquis de l'Eure*[29] entered the buildings to dislodge the Germans. The German commander at the École Militaire, *Major* Neumann, then decided to surrender with 150 men. The prisoners were quickly evacuated on the turrets of the tanks to save them from the vindictiveness of the Parisian crowd.

---

23   An anecdote from this period deserves to be mentioned: During a reunion, the sister of a soldier from the *13e Bataillon du Génie* entered the room asking around if anyone knows a certain Terver, a forester in Cameroon. 'Dio, who knew me well, lifted his head in hearing my name. Gruff as usual, he eyed her without amenity, then, amused, he gave a hint of one of his soft and soothing smiles, that revealed his true nature: 'Terver, he is currently at the Étoile (Arc de Triomphe)' he barked…
    'But he didn't even warn me, he could have called me when he got here…'
    Patiently, it was one of his good days, he explained to her that I [Terver] had more pressing things to do, that I had just arrived after a very tough day for me and for my unit.' Pierre Terver, *Soldats de Leclerc* (Paris: Lavauzelle, 1997), pp.137–138.
24   Today the RER C train station and the Air France Terminal are located there.
25   Fonds Leclerc, *JMO du GTD*.
26   These outer boulevards are now called the Boulevards des Maréchals, named mostly for the *maréchals* who served Napoléon I.
27   Now Pont Bir Hakeim.
28   Fonds Leclerc, *JMO du 12e Cuirs*, boîte M1.
29   *Maquis*: originally used to describe the areas where the Resistance fighters were hiding in Southern France, the term became synonymous with the French underground movement: the Resistance.

At 4:30 p.m., Subgroup Noiret prepared to move to the aid of the *GTV*, which was caught up in an intense fight raging at the Luxembourg Palace. However, movement stopped around 6:00 p.m. to allow surrender talks to begin. At the same time, *Capitaine* Perceval's 2nd Company of the RMT was responsible for forming a detachment. After crossing the Pont d'Iéna, the company attacked the Invalides train station, forcing the surrender of the German unit defending it. Perceval continued to advance along the Seine, seized the Pont de la Concorde, and crossed the river to the right bank. '*Lieutenant* Jourdan blew up two roadblocks on avenue Kléber, attacked the block-house in the Hôtel Baltimore with rockets, and captured more than 100 prisoners. Blanchard sent him to the Arc de Triomphe where he joined the elements of *Groupement Tactique Langlade* that had taken the [Hôtel] Majestic.'[30]

At the end of the afternoon, as surrender talks began with the pockets of German resistance, the *GTD* had largely accomplished its mission by having 'mopped up' a large part of the left bank of the capital and assisting the *GTL* and the *GTV* in their fight on the right bank. The *GTD* seized eight bridges over the Seine, from the Pont de Mirabeau to the Pont de la Concorde. It reduced all the enemy strongholds, the École Militaire, the Invalides train station, Quai d'Orsay, Palais Bourbon, and the barracks of La Tour-Maubourg. On 25 August at 6:30 p.m., the *2ᵉ DB* and the 4th US Infantry Division controlled the Paris metropolitan area south of the line passing through the Madeleine, the Grands Boulevards, and the Place de la République. The northern and north-eastern part of the city had not yet been liberated. At the beginning of the evening, Leclerc decided to temporarily suspend the division's *groupements tactiques* organisation and to pull the regiments back together in one place, under the orders of their commanders. This was done to prepare for the events of the following day. '*Général* de Gaulle had decided to come at 2:00 p.m. to salute the Unknown Soldier at the Arc de Triomphe, to relight the Flame, then to walk down the Champs-Élysées and attend a thanksgiving mass at Notre-Dame.'[31] Leclerc had to be responsible for the safety of the Head of the Provisional Government of France. He decided to render honours to de Gaulle all along the route, which could best be accomplished if the division was reorganised into its organic regiments.

The *12ᵉ Cuirs* set up in the École Militaire, while the *3ᵉ RAC* gathered in the Parc Montsouris. The 1st Battalion of the *RMT* was quartered in the Jardin du Luxembourg. Dio set up his command post at the École Polytechnique, which was then located on the heights of the Montagne Sainte Geneviève on rue Descartes, in the 5th Arrondissement. Once the fighting stopped, popular jubilation erupted and the entire population expressed its gratitude to the men of the *2ᵉ DB*, who were covered in kisses by the women and children of Paris.[32] The men brought out bottles of alcohol and toasted the victory with Leclerc's men. Many of the soldiers were invited to eat with families. That first night of the liberation was wild, and Dio and his officers let the soldiers go along with it. How could they prevent these young men, some of whom had suffered so much, from joining in the general euphoria? 'Visits from women are quite numerous, and our officers closed their eyes, 'it is the warrior's rest."[33] The officers were simply asked to ensure that events did not get too far out of control and that detachments could be quickly formed to counter any threats arising in the capital.

The *GTD*'s balance sheet during the day of Parisian liberation was heavy. Among the Germans, 230 were killed, 40 wounded, and 2,601 prisoners were taken, including 189 officers. The French

30   *De Fort-Lamy à Strasbourg*, p.18.
31   Compagnon, *Leclerc*, p.410.
32   Father Cordier, chaplain of the Division, could not resist from noting the fickleness of the French population, which, in June, had accompanied in large numbers the coffin of Philippe Henriot, a collaborationist who had been executed by the Resistance, to his funeral at Notre-Dame Cathedral with *Maréchal* Philippe Pétain in attendance.
33   Destray, Fonds Leclerc, *Campagne France-Allemagne 44–45*, p.18.

sustained 18 killed and 78 wounded, evidence of the bitterness of the fighting. Five Sherman tanks were destroyed. In urban combat, the primary burden falls on the infantry, which has to use rifles and grenades to dislodge enemy snipers from the buildings. It is gruelling combat where threats can be anywhere: the corners of upstairs windows or balconies, cellar windows, or from the roof tops. Tanks lay in ambush at the corners of the streets supporting movements with guns and machine guns. Accordingly, it was the *marsouins* of the *RMT* who paid the heaviest price in these urban fights for the liberation of the capital.

Having reorganised as complete units, the regiments were gradually being reconstituted on the morning of 26 August. Many of the men that morning had throbbing headaches from the excessive drinking the night before. Patrols were soon formed to crisscross Paris. 'Starting at noon, preparations began for the parade in honour of *Général* de Gaulle, president of the provisional government of France.'[34] Leclerc laid out the following plan:

- The *RMT* under the orders of *Colonel* Dio with his three battalions renders honours to *Général* de Gaulle on his arrival at the Arc de Triomphe[35]
- The four armoured formations at the Place de la Concorde (including *RBFM*)
- The three artillery formations at Notre-Dame
- The *RMSM* at the Hôtel de Ville

Leclerc and Dio waited for *Général* de Gaulle at the Place de l'Étoile in front of the Arc de Triomphe at 2:00 p.m. The moment is forever captured in a well-known photograph: Leclerc in his dress uniform leaning on his cane and Dio in battle fatigues with canvas webbing, tie, pistol at his side, and kepi on his head, standing with his hands on his hips. Behind them is *Commandant* Massu, commanding the 2nd Battalion, on a howitzer from his supporting battery. *Général* de Gaulle reviewed the units of the *RMT*, and then proceeded down the Champs Élysées on foot to the Place de la Concorde in an atmosphere of indescribable jubilation. *Capitaine* Dronne had the honour to follow the procession with his half-tracks deployed on the right and left as security. That highly-photographed and filmed walk descending down the incline of the Champs-Élysées was an unforgettable moment for everyone present.

As the afternoon came to an end, the regiments reformed into their previous *groupement tactique* organisation. That evening, Leclerc gathered his subordinate commanders at his new command post at La Tour-Maubourg to brief them on the next day's operation. Intelligence reported the German *47. Infanterie-Division* would shortly arrive by forced march in the northern suburbs to counterattack into Paris. Additionally, German anti-aircraft forces that had withdrawn from the south of the capital had dug in near Le Bourget, northeast of the city. Earlier in the day, Leclerc had sent the newly formed *Groupement Tactique Rémy* (*GTR*) to carry out reconnaissance northwards to the vicinity of Enghien. Rémy confirmed that German troops had arrived at Le Bourget airport in the northern suburbs: 'The same evening its advanced elements moved into the towns previously liberated by the *FFI*: Gonesse, Herblay, and as far south as Raincy. They [the Germans] took hostages, whom they shot without trial. After foolish hope, anguish.'[36]

---

34   Fonds Leclerc, *JMO du 12e Cuirs*.
35   The *RMT* participation was: Farret's *1/RMT* was represented by the 1st (*Capitaine* Boussion) and the 2nd (*Capitaine* Perceval) Companies, Massu's *2/RMT* by the 5th (*Capitaine* Rogier) and 6th (*Capitaine* Langlois de Bazillac) Companies. Putz's *3/RMT* by the 9th Company (*Capitaine* Dronne) which was given the honour of providing security during de Gaulle's descent, on foot, of the Champs Élysées while the 10th Company (*Capitaine* Sarrazac) provided security around the Place de l'Étoile.
36   Bergot, *La 2 ème D.B.*, p.164

While 26 August was essentially devoted to establishing *Général* de Gaulle's authority, there was nevertheless still some localised fighting in Paris and its suburbs. The *JMO* of the *GTD* for the 26th includes the following assessment:

- Enemy: 48 killed, 311 prisoners, 12 vehicles destroyed
- Friendly Forces: two killed and six wounded.

Despite the parade and ceremony, Paris had not yet been completely liberated. During the night of 26/27 August, German shells fell on the east of Paris, continuing to inflict casualties on the *3ᵉ RAC*.[37] The evening of Saturday, 26 August closed with Leclerc's soldiers preparing for continued combat. The last carousing soldiers found their units, although some, like Hannibal in Capua, were still enjoying the pleasures of the city the next day when their units departed.[38] Eventually they caught back up later in the morning in the northern suburbs.

After the relatively calm day of the 26th, the division resumed the offensive on Sunday 27th. Leclerc's operations order reached the four *groupements tactiques* the previous day, assigning tasks to each of them. The main effort north of Paris would be carried out by *GTD* and *GTL*, moving in the direction of Blanc-Mesnil and Montmorency, respectively. The *GTV*, meanwhile, was ordered to secure the west of Paris. The *GTR*, which was already deployed in the northern suburbs, would be relieved and become the division reserve. Thus, as he had done in the Sarthe at the beginning of the campaign in August, Leclerc put his two tactical groups in the lead, and 'launched Dio and Langlade, two impressive men, the first more popular, with a thunderous voice and a working-class accent, and the second more aristocratic, with the elegance and seduction of a classical cavalryman.'[39] Dio was responsible for leading the attack against the German *47. Infanterie-Division* [40] with Langlade to his left and the US 4th Infantry Division to his right. In typical fashion, Dio formed three subgroups.

- That of *Commandant* Farret commanding the 1st Battalion, consisting of his 3rd Company and his *CA1*, the Tank Destroyer squadron of the *RBFM*, an engineering company and a platoon of the *RMSM*.
- That of *Lieutenant Colonel* Noiret, consisting of the 4th Squadron of the *12ᵉ Cuirs*, the 1st Company of the *RMT*, a 3 gun artillery section (*Lieutenant* Juif) of the 3rd Battery and a platoon of the *RMSM*.
- Finally, that of *Commandant* Rouvillois, consisting of a squadron of the *12ᵉ Cuirs*, the 2nd Company of the *RMT* and a 3 gun artillery section (*Lieutenant* Watson) of the 2nd Battery of the *3ᵉ RAC*.

---

37   As a sort of revenge for the capture of the capital by the *2e DB*, the Allies, and the Resistance, the Germans twice sent their planes to blindly bomb the north and east of Paris, as well as the 12e, 13e, and 14e arrondissements, destroying the Bichat hospital and the depots of the Halle aux Vins, resulting in nearly 200 killed and 900 wounded. The *3e RAC*, bivouacking in the park Montsouris, suffered one killed and four wounded.

38   A *GB2* officer and Dio would, a few years later, discuss the 3,000 babies born in Paris nine months after the division passed through (Mauras, *Souvenirs, 1939–1946*, p.223).

39   Dansette, *Leclerc*, p.180.

40   The *47. Infanterie-Division*, created on 1 February 1944, in Calais, included three *Grenadier-Regiments* (103, 104, and 105), each made up of three infantry battalions, and the *Artillerie-Regiment 147*. It was commanded by *Generalmajor* Karl Wahle, an experienced officer who held several similar commands, most notably in Russia.

Commandant Farret's predominantly infantry subgroup had the most resources because it was expected to fight against dug-in infantry in a suburban area. His first objective was the commune of Dugny on the western edge of Le Bourget airport. As Subgroup Farret approached the bridge into Dugny, it came up against a strong German position between the road to Soissons (currently the N2) and the River Vieille Mer. Despite a tenacious metre-by-metre defence from the *Grenadier-Regiment 105* of the *47. Infanterie-Division, Capitaine* Sammarcelli's 3rd Company, along with the *spahis'* armoured cars and *Enseigne de Vaisseau* Philippe de Gaulle's platoon of naval troops, managed to seize Dugny. Having achieved initial success, Farret then continued the attack towards Le Bourget airport, oriented on the hangars bordering the field. As the fighting raged on, the Chadian infantrymen took heavy casualties. *Lieutenant* Kirch of 1st Heavy Weapons Company and *Capitaine* Sammarcelli were both wounded. *Commandant* Corlu,[41] deputy commander of the 1st Battalion, and *Lieutenant* Humbert de Waziers, *Général* Leclerc's cousin, were both mortally wounded. At 6:00 p.m., the Germans withdrew and *Commandant* Farret set up company strong-points at the airport to consolidate the positions they had taken. That action enabled him to repel a dogged German counterattack from the 3rd Company of the *Grenadier-Regiment 103* at 11:30 p.m. It took the support of the division's two artillery groups (*40ᵉ RANA* and *3ᵉ RAC*), hastily assembled together under *Lieutenant Colonel* Crépin, and the mortars and howitzers of the *CA1*, to repel the enemy, who left their numerous dead scattered across the ground.

Meanwhile, Noiret's subgroup attacked on Farret's right towards Pantin-Bobigny. Noiret 'also experienced a hard afternoon against the left wing of the *Grenadier-Regiment 105* and the right wing of the *Grenadier-Regiment 103*. His mission was to seize Le Bourget's airstrip and then to establish a position on its northern edges.'[42] Noiret reached the south-eastern edges of the airport by midday. Despite excellent cooperation at every level between *Capitaine* Gaudet's *cuirassiers* (4th Squadron) and the naval troops of *Capitaine* Boussion (temporarily acting for *Capitaine* Grall at the head of the 1st Company), Subgroup Noiret stalled at the River Morée. In response, *Lieutenant* Pity's platoon of Sherman tanks bypassed the enemy position to the west, taking advantage of Farret's battle, and took the enemy position from behind. Fierce hand-to-hand combat continued until the Germans finally surrendered. Some of the cuirassiers, including *Lieutenant* Pity,[43] then climbed down from their tanks and were shot by the Germans. 'With rage in their hearts, the 4th Squadron of the *12ᵉ Cuirassiers*, reinforced by the remnants of the *RMT*'s infantrymen, and grouped under the command of *Capitaine* Gaudet, launched a particularly bloody final attack.'[44] After more than six hours of combat, at 7:30 p.m., the Germans withdrew and Subgroup Noiret was able to set up on the north bank of the Morée. The mission had been accomplished.

Finally, three kilometres to the east of Le Bourget airport, Subgroup Rouvillois attacked towards Blanc-Mesnil. 'Thanks to the information provided by the resistance, and with their support, it was able to seize the town without a fight, and then to continue the attack across the Morée.'[45] Then with the help of Crépin's artillery, the subgroup cleared the German strong-points that had been bypassed. At the end of the evening, Rouvillois established a position north of the River Morée, in line with Noiret. At nightfall on Sunday 27 August, the *GTD* had not

---

41 Corlu died from his wounds three days later, at the age of 30. Saint-Cyrien, class of 1931–1933, *Commandant* Corlu had already been injured in Kufra with Dio in the attack on the Italian bastion. He had covered himself with glory in Fezzan, Tunisia, and in the west of France, notably in Alençon.

42 Philippe Duplay, *Soldats de* Leclerc (Paris: Lavauzelle, 1997), p.156.

43 *Sous Lieutenant* Michel Pity was a Saint-Cyrien from the class of 1941–1943. He reached Africa via the Spanish prisons of Franco. He stood out by leading the charge on Carrouges with *Colonel* Dio. He had received a second citation for his bravery during the battles of the École Militaire.

44 Duplay, *Soldats de Leclerc*, p.157.

45 Duplay, *Soldats de Leclerc*, p.158.

quite 'reached the Arnouville – Gonesse line, the objective set by the V Army Corps.'[46] It had nevertheless pushed strongly into the defensive positions of the *Grenadier-Regiments 103 & 105*. *Groupement Tactique Dio* had killed 420 German soldiers, taken 943 prisoners, and destroyed 2 tanks and 11 other vehicles. Unfortunately, Dio had lost 12 killed and 54 wounded from his ranks. The death of *Commandant* Corlu hit Dio particularly hard, and the serious wounding of *Capitaine* Sammarcelli, commanding the 3rd Company of the *RMT*, deprived this unit of experienced leadership.[47] *Général* Leclerc was also very affected by his losses. He wrote to *Général* de Gaulle on the evening of 27th: 'Situation this evening: the airfield at Le Bourget was taken by Dio after a serious fight … some of our best officers from the earliest days fell there (*Commandant* Corlu seriously injured, *Capitaine* Sammarcelli…), one of my first cousins,[48] who was a *lieutenant* in the *Régiment du Tchad*, was killed north of Le Bourget.'[49] The three officers all belonged to the 1st Battalion of the RMT.

Groupement Tactique Dio spent the night of 27/28 August on reconquered territory. Général Leclerc set up his headquarters at Porte de La Chapelle to be closer to the action but did not interfere when Dio gave his orders for 28 August to Farret and Noiret. It was essentially a matter of continuing the attack towards Gonesse, a few kilometres north of Le Bourget's runway, and then further north towards Vaudherland and Roissy-en-France. For *Groupement Tactique Dio*, unlike *Groupement Tactique Langlade* on the left, the day was calmer than the day before. The Germans retreated north of Gonesse, yielding the town to the French without a fight. Leclerc's men were met only with mortar fire as they entered. Division orders on the afternoon of the 28th called for a return to the initial strongpoints, signalling an imminent relief by the US 28th Infantry Division. Dio pushed out patrols to the north to avoid being surprised by an unexpected enemy attack. Additionally, *Lieutenant Colonel* Crépin, 'commanding the divisional artillery, was to recon the area with Piper Cub aircraft for possible enemy incursions.'[50] After the losses of the previous day, Leclerc wanted to limit any further casualties. His precautions proved unnecessary, though, since the Germans were overwhelmed to the south and north by the American advance and were forced to withdraw. With the threat to Paris eliminated, Leclerc and Dio considered the mission accomplished. Activity on the 29th was limited to further patrolling. At 6:45 p.m., the *3ᵉ RAC*, reinforced by two US artillery battalions (the 955th equipped with 155mm guns and the 196th with 105mm guns), fired on some Germans reported north of Gonesse. *Groupement Tactique Dio* was relieved by units of the US 28th Infantry Division at the end of the day and withdrew from the front line. From 30 August to 1 September 1944, the *GTD's JMO* records that the tactical group was busy 'reorganising by unit in the Dugny, Le Bourget, Blanc-Mesnil region and conducting equipment repair.'[51] Gathering units together in a single location made it easier to maintain and repair equipment, especially for the tanks and armoured vehicles.

The enemy threat to the capital was finally eliminated. Although the Parisian population did not realise it, 'Leclerc really won the battle of Paris and liberated it during the battle of 27–30

---

46   Duplay, *Soldats de Leclerc*, p.185.

47   Magistrate in the *AEF*, Sammarcelli became a reserve officer of the *RTST* in 1940. Participating in all of the battles of Kufra, Fezzan, and Tunisia, he took command of the 3rd Company when the *2e DB* was formed, a company formed in large part of young Corsicans. He would later serve in the National Assembly as the representative of Corte (in Corsica) from 1958 to 1962. He was made a Companion of the Liberation in September 1945.

48   Humbert van der Cruisse de Waziers, only son of Pierre de Waziers, brother of Leclerc's mother, Saint-Cyrien, *lieutenant* in the 1st Battalion of the *Régiment de Marche du Tchad*, was killed on 27 August at Le Bourget.

49   Levisse-Touzé and Toureille, *Écrits de Combat*, p.546.

50   Fonds Leclerc, *Instruction 2e DB du 28 août 1944, 14h40*.

51   Fonds Leclerc, *JMO du GTD*, boîte K1.

August.'[52] Without a doubt, the Parisian uprising would have been suppressed in a bloodbath if not for the *2ᵉ DB*. 'It is certain that if Leclerc's division had not entered Paris in time to prevent the arrival of enemy reinforcements, the situation could have turned out very badly for the Resistance and the inhabitants of the capital. Within a day or two, von Choltitz could have restored the situation to his advantage and inflicted tremendous damage.'[53]

The *GTD* was one of the main players in this victory north of the capital and it paid a heavy price. The 1st Battalion of the *RMT* lost the most men killed in action during the battles for the liberation of Paris, sustaining 20 percent of the *2ᵉ DB*'s 146 deaths at the end of August 1944. For the *2ᵉ DB*, and for *Groupement Tactique Dio* in particular, 31 August was, a 'sadly moving' day as they buried 'Cerlu (*sic*), Dupont, so many others…'[54] They now rest in the Pantin Cemetery in Paris.

On 2 September, Dio decided to regroup the 1st Battalion of the *RMT* and the *12ᵉ Cuirs* at Blanc-Mesnil, 'to give the troops some rest and facilitate maintenance on their equipment.'[55] The *1/RMT* set up in the Groupe Scolaire Jean-Jaurès[56] where it remained until 8 September, when it moved out again to the east. The *12ᵉ Cuirs* established its CP on the rue du Plateau and Dio kept his headquarters at Le Bourget. The *JMO* describes the activities of 3–6 September as: 'Day devoted to the instruction of new recruits, the collection of equipment and the reorganisation of units.'[57] The fighting in and around Paris was barely over, and the *GTD* was already looking to the future. After taking so many casualties, personnel losses had to be replaced as quickly as possible. Volunteers flocked to the ranks. *Commandant* Massu distinguished two categories among them: the 'pure' and those with 'sins to redeem.'[58] Only those with some military experience or whose skills were essential joined the ranks immediately, learning from the veterans through on the job training. The rest were sent to Saint-Germain-en-Laye for intensive training before later joining the division. It was around that time that Leclerc asked Dio to bring his 18-year-old eldest son, Henri,[59] into the 2nd Battalion of the *RMT*. Henri was entrusted to *Commandant* Massu, who took it as an honour: 'The choice of the *2ᵉ Bataillon du Tchad* made by his illustrious father means more to me than the highest award.'[60]

Thirty percent of the men were allowed to take leave in Paris each evening. Leclerc's men could see that the attitude of the Parisians towards them had changed. *Capitaine* Branet of the *501ᵉ RCC* wrote that they felt like they were becoming unwelcome intruders in the capital. 'We expect someone to say to us one day: 'why are you still here?''[61] Nevertheless, those few days offered the men of the *GTD* a refreshing rest after three hard weeks of combat. During that period of respite, *Colonel* Dio was able to devote some time to his duties as the commander of the *RMT*. Although he was a *groupement tactique* commander like Langlade and Billotte, he also had to take care of a

---

52   Croidys, *Notre Second Bayard*, p.185.
53   Philippe de Gaulle, *Mémoires* (Bouquins, 2022), p.395.
54   Girard, *Journal de Guerre*, p.277.
55   Fonds Leclerc, *JMO du GTD*.
56   The 'groupe scolaire Jean-Jaurès' in Levallois-Perret is now the Collège Jean-Jaurès.
57   Fonds Leclerc, *JMO du GTD*.
58   Massu, *Sept Ans*, p.153.
59   Henri de Hauteclocque was assigned to the *CA2* under *Capitaine* Eggenspiller, who took charge of his training. The young man showed bravery. He was shot in the neck in Contrexéville shortly after his enlistment. He was wounded again on 20 November 1944, in Dabo. He would be cited in the Order of the Army as a *caporal*. He entered Saint-Cyr at the end of the war and became an officer. He then joined Massu's *4e Batallion de Marche* in Indochina, where he commanded the jeep scout section and was seriously injured. In 1947 he was a *méhariste* in Chad. He died on the field of honour on 4 January 1952, during a second tour in Indochina at the head of a company. He was 26 years old. He would be made an *officier* of the *Légion d'Honneur*.
60   Massu, *Sept Ans*, p.153.
61   Notin, *le Croisé*, p.282.

regiment of nearly 3,000 men. The administrative tasks were numerous. He had to replenish the losses and write letters to the families of the dead and wounded from the three battalions. He was also responsible for writing awards citations, knowing that it is important to remember and reward each act of bravery and valour. Additionally, he had to identify and appoint new section leaders and unit commanders to replace those who had been killed or injured. In doing so, he needed to consider the unique needs of each of his units, which he alone truly understood. To succeed *Capitaine* Dupont, who had been killed in front of Fresnes prison while commanding the 11th Company, he appointed *Capitaine* Dubut, one of the 'Chadians.' In *Commandant* Corlu's place, and with Leclerc's consent, he appointed *Commandant* Fosse. He pulled *Capitaine* Joubert from the *CCR* to succeed *Capitaine* Sammarcelli in command of the 3rd Company. Only Dio could lend legitimacy to a future unit commander. He was both the *colonel* of the regiment and the operational leader recognised by his men.

Dio also took advantage of those quieter few days to finalise the project of restructuring the organisation of his battalions. Ever since landing in France, the lack of infantry within the *2ᵉ DB* was evident. Tanks had occasionally found themselves isolated in urban areas without infantry support. In addition, losses among the naval troops were high, due to their vulnerability on land. As a result, Dio decided to add a fourth company to each of the *RMT* battalions, the 4th for the *1/RMT*, the 8th for the *2/RMT* and the 12th for the *3/RMT*. This fourth company would be similar in composition and equipment to the other companies. The reorganisation became official on 2 October 1944 and provided 500 additional infantry to the division. These extra personnel came primarily from the ranks of the *FFI* who had gained some basic operational experience during the fight for liberation. Some of the *FFI* units such as the 'Vaugirard Squadron' which became the 8th Company, already had a military structure. Expected US equipment had not yet arrived when the *groupement tactique* departed Paris, so the RMT set up three 'mounted *FFI* squadrons,' which would become the future companies of the three battalions.[62] Equipped with a variety of weapons and makeshift means of transport, these three *FFI* squadrons followed their battalion as they moved east. The American equipment and materiel finally arrived at the beginning of October. Without disrupting the 'old' companies, the battalion commanders appointed experienced leaders to strengthen the leadership of the new companies. Unfortunately, it soon became evident in their first engagements with the enemy that their training had been insufficient. The new companies suffered disproportionately high casualties in Lorraine and Alsace, forcing battalion commanders to take their inexperience into account when assigning future combat missions. By 1945, though, their operational effectiveness had much improved. With this new organisation, the *RMT* became a 'big shop' within the *2ᵉ DB*. One final act taken by Dio in Paris was to make the insignia badge for the *RMT*, enlarging a version which had been worn by the Chadians since 1942. The son of the Parisian medal maker Arthus-Bertrand was among the naval troops in the *RMT*, so Dio asked him to contact his father to make a larger badge. Since Arthus-Bertrand lacked sufficient metal to make the new badges, Dio sent over three trucks filled with 105mm shell casings from the *3ᵉ RAC*.

On 6 September, *Colonel* Dio signed a casualty statement tallying the *GTD*'s losses since landing in Normandy: 93 killed, 371 wounded, 9 missing, 37 tanks and 18 other vehicles destroyed.[63] Losses inflicted on the Germans by the *GTD* were: 2,201 killed, 4,184 taken prisoner; 42 tanks, 429 vehicles, and 39 guns destroyed. It should be noted that these numbers are for the territory assigned to Dio. The number of enemy killed, for example, is partly attributable to units that

---

62   In the French system, a squadron is the equivalent of a company for the cavalry. They were still called by their old name so as not to assimilate them into companies because they were not yet equipped or trained. They would then become the 4th Company in the three *RMT* battalions.

63   Fonds Leclerc, Annexe du *JMO du GTD* du 8 au 30 août 1944.

supported the *GTD*, such as the supporting artillery and aircraft. Nevertheless, the ratio between the losses of the *GTD* and those inflicted on the enemy was very high and it is a measure of *Colonel* Dio's efforts to preserve the lives of his personnel as much as possible through well-planned operations. It also signifies, in part, the quality of medical assistance from which the wounded of the *GTD* benefited. This was not the case for the German soldiers who, particularly in Normandy, had to withdraw in great disorganisation. On the other hand, the destruction record of tanks was quite similar. Subjected to an almost permanent air threat, the losses of the German armour crews and their equipment rivalled that of the French.

For his contribution to the liberation of Paris, *Colonel* Dio received a citation[64] signed by de Gaulle:

> On the recommendation of the Minister of War, the President of the Provisional Government of the French Republic and Chief of the Armed Forces recognises Louis-Joseph-Marie Dio, *colonel*, commanding *Groupement Tactique 'D':* A senior officer of exceptional bravery, who accepts great personal risk and embodies the finest military virtues. After having brilliantly led his tactical group in Normandy, he contributed to the liberation of Paris, notably by taking part in the battles in the Luxembourg Gardens, the Tuileries, and at the Ministry of Foreign Affairs. Then, leading his group boldly and decisively, he seized Aubervilliers, Gonesse, and Blanc-Mesnil in a spectacular fashion.[65]

On 7 September 1944, *Groupement Tactique Dio* finally received orders from Leclerc to move out the following day. On the 2nd, the head of Free France had notified General Eisenhower that 'now that order and calm have returned to Paris, it is no longer necessary to keep the *2ᵉ DB* there.'[66] The *GTD* was sent south to the region of Troyes with an advance detachment from the 5th Squadron of the *RMSM* in the lead. Dio learnt that the *2ᵉ DB* would be once again attached to General Haislip's XV Corps, which was welcome news because he recognised that Haislip clearly understood the French better than General Gerow did.

The men of the *GTD* were glad to leave the Paris region and head towards the east of France. 'Paris is only one step. The Oath of Kufra has only been partially fulfilled and our eyes remain fixed towards the east.'[67]

---

64   The citation included the award of the *Croix de Guerre* with palm and the appointment to the rank of *Officier* in the *Légion d'Honneur*.

65   Décret du 08.02.1945, JORF du 02.03.1945 – page G 221.

66   Notin, *le Croisé*, p.282.

67   Massu, *Sept Ans*, p.157.

Chapter 11

From Paris to Strasbourg,
8 September to 23 November 1944

On the morning of 8 September 1944, *Colonel* Dio, at the head of the *GTD*, prepared to leave the Paris region towards the east of France. He wanted to be at the front of the division, but it was unfortunately, for logistical reasons, decided otherwise. On that date, the division was short of fuel. American logistics was having difficulty supplying the Allied units because the Belgian and Dutch ports had not yet been liberated. The distances from Normandy, where the fuel supplies were arriving, were becoming significant. Yet, the daily consumption of the 4,200 vehicles of the *2ᵉ DB* was 300,000 litres of fuel. The *GTD*'s rate was around 75,000 litres per day. It was therefore the *GTL*, whose vehicles had the best potential in terms of fuel levels, which was chosen to be the first to leave Paris on the morning of 8 September.[1]

Returning to the supervision of General Haislip's XV Corps, the *2ᵉ DB* was on the right of the American forces advancing eastward. Paired with the US 79th Infantry Division, it was responsible for protecting the southern flank of the American 3rd Army, from the towns of Auxerre to Chaumont. The German *1. Armee* faced Patton's army to the west and blocked access to the Rhine 'with, no doubt, advanced defences on the Moselle and the Vosges.'[2] Behind the *GTL*, which had set off in the lead, the *GTV* provided southern cover for the corps, while the *GTD* followed in second echelon in a central position, ready to reinforce one or other of the *GT*s. The *DB*'s first bound was set in an area southeast of Troyes. The *GTD* was preceded by a detachment under the command of *Capitaine* Revault d'Allonnes, from the 5th Squadron of the *RMSM* of *Capitaine* Troquereau. It was tasked with providing all the useful information for the move. The *GTD* with its thousand vehicles was a heavy organism. Once launched, it could not change direction on short notice, so it was necessary to anticipate and know where to engage the wheeled and tracked vehicles, taking into account the obstacles that the Germans would most certainly create, particularly by blowing up the bridges. The *GTD*'s route was Saint Maurice – Joinville – Bry Torcy – Lagny – Coulommiers – Chailly – Choisy – Provins – Nogent – Romilly – La Belle Étoile – Mery – Troyes – Vendeuvre-sur-Barse – Arsonval – Bar-sur-Aube.

The leading elements of the *GTD* arrived south of Romilly at 2:00 p.m., having covered 150 kilometres. The units set up camp and proceeded with resupplying operations. The 1st Battalion of the *RMT* had integrated the *FFI* squadron of *Capitaine* Bonhomme into its ranks. On Dio's instructions, *Commandant* Farret kept it under his thumb, using it, the time being, as a unit to protect the CP and taking that opportunity to toughen it up.[3] At the end of the afternoon, the division sent a supplement to the movement order. The enemy had been reported 48 hours earlier

---

1   Levisse-Touzé, *Du Capitaine de Hauteclocque au Général Leclerc,* p.210.
2   Bergot, *La 2 ème D.B.,* p.168.
3   Bergot, *La 2 ème D.B.,* p.169.

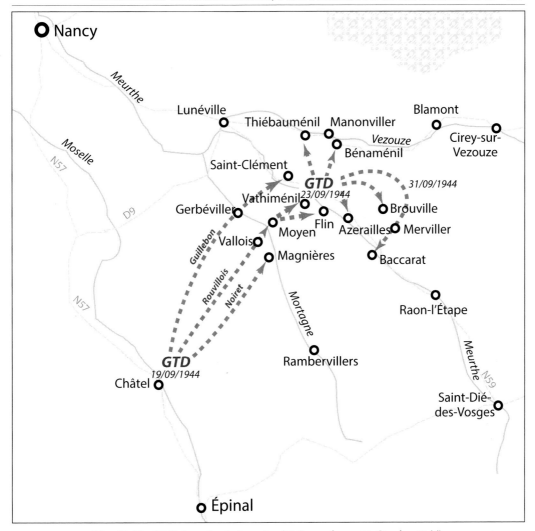

Map 11 The GTD in action in Lorraine (19 September to 31 October 1944).

at Chaumont, about 50 kilometres east of Bar-sur-Aube. Dio took no risks, asking *Lieutenant Colonel* Noiret to go to the head of the column to open the *GTD* route by force. On 9 September, the advance was made without problem. At 2:00 p.m., the leading units of the *groupement tactique* arrived in the Villars-en-Azois region, 30km west of Chaumont. Having received the order to cover itself facing east and south, Dio adopted a formation with infantry and engineers facing Chaumont and armoured vehicles with *spahis*, facing Châtillon-sur-Seine.

On 10 September, the *GTD* received the order for the following day to seize:

- From the village of Chateauvillain to a point 15km to its east where a German company was reported. This village was on the western edge of a large wooded area and the access roads were mined.
- From the town of Châtillon-sur-Seine to a point 25km to its south, which was an important road junction.

In the afternoon, the *GTD* received the order to provide assistance to an *FFI* detachment struggling with 400 Germans in the area. The engagement took place east of Châtillon-sur-Seine in a village called Maisey-le-Duc. Dio sent the *capitaine* of the 5th Squadron of the *RMSM* with two platoons. On 11 September, Dio formed two detachments that departed at 7:00 a.m.:

- One on Chateauvillain, with *Capitaine* Germain commanding the 3rd Company of the *13ᵉ BG*, with the mission of seizing the town and clearing mines from the roads. He had his company, a platoon of the *12ᵉ Cuirs*, and a howitzer from the *3ᵉ RAC*,
- The other on Châtillon-sur-Seine, with *Capitaine* Perceval of the *RMT*, composed of his 2nd Company, an engineering section, a platoon of Shermans, and a 105mm howitzer, with the mission of taking the city and then covering itself facing south and east. The 5th Squadron of the *RMSM* had to join them after resolving the intervention with the *FFI*.

These two actions were carried out successfully, with little resistance from the Germans. The obstacles of abatis and mines were neutralised by the sappers. However, the action of the *FFI* did not achieve the desired result; their commander hesitated, thus allowing the Germans to escape.

The *GTD*'s tally on 11 September was: 17 prisoners including 3 officers, 53 vehicles captured, along with 2 heavy machine guns and 2 mortars. Early in the evening, a surprising order reached the group's headquarters. *Commandant* Farret,[4] commanding the 1st Battalion since October 1943, and *Capitaine* de Biéville, of the *12ᵉ Cuirs*, had to leave the *GTD* without delay. They were selected to go to the Paris region to supervise the *FFI* there. *Commandant* Quilichini took command of the 1st Battalion of the *RMT* the next day.

On 12 September 1944 the *2ᵉ DB* linked up with the *1ʳᵉ DFL* of the *1ʳᵉ Armée Française* coming from the south. It was an historic day for the French Army, merging the two operations of OVERLORD (Normandy) and DRAGOON (Provence). The *GTD* had the honour of ensuring this contact with the sister division of the Free French.[5] The *JMO* of the *GTD* records: '*Capitaine* Gaudet of the *12ᵉ Cuirs* meets *Capitaine* Queyrat of the *1ʳᵉ DB* south of Châtillon – first meeting of the division made with the army of the south.'[6] It appears that this meeting took place at Nod-sur-Seine, a small village south of Châtillon-sur-Seine. But the junction was also made by other units on the same day. *Capitaine* Perceval of the *RMT* learnt at Châtillon-sur-Seine that the *1ʳᵉ Armée* had liberated Dijon the day before. He then decided to send his deputy, *Lieutenant* Jourdan, accompanied by *Lieutenant* Marson, leader of the 1st Section, towards Dijon on the

---

4   The question arises as to why Dio agreed to exchange one of his battalion commanders during operations. This is a surprising event in military practice. In such circumstances, only serious facts justify such a change. *Commandant* Farret was certainly a cold person, but that had been true since 1943! Farret was a veteran of Chad and the ties between the two men were strong. He did not disgrace himself in Normandy nor in Paris. Had there been a dispute between them since then? *Colonel* Robédat testified that in the 1970s and 80s, Farret visited Dio in Toulon and that their friendship was visible. Was it Koenig who forced the *2e DB* to provide him with senior officers capable of commanding *FFI* battalions in training? Did Leclerc impose *Commandant* Quilichini on Dio so he could in turn hold an operational command? In fact, Quilichini had been languishing since 1943 at the head of the division's personnel office (G1). It should be recalled that having deserted his unit in Dahomey, *Lieutenant* Quilichini arrived in Cameroon by canoe with *Colonel* Leclerc in August 1940. That created a connection. Much later, Quilichini would also be one of the faithful who came to visit Dio in Toulon.

5   There is a very beautiful monument today that commemorates this 12 September 1944 junction of the two units. It is located near the village of Nod-sur-Seine, on the edge of the road. This village is three kilometres from Aisey-sur-Seine. Each year, the Maréchal Leclerc de Hauteclocque Foundation and the Free France Foundation co-organise a ceremony to commemorate the event. The half-track next to the monument is named 'Tchad' in honour of *Lieutenant* Marson.

6   Fonds Leclerc, *JMO GTD*, boîte J, chemise 1.

(present day) D971. The junction 'will be made at the presbytery of Aisey-sur-Seine between *Lieutenants* Marson and Jourdan and a *capitaine* of the *1ʳᵉ Armée*. A few kilometres further south, Marson and Jourdan met with the famous *Général* Brosset who, at the wheel of his jeep, preceded his units. They arrived around 5:00 p.m. at Sainte-Seine-l'Abbaye, occupied by our comrades of the *1ʳᵉ DFL*.'[7] In addition to this historic meeting, the 12 September entry in the *JMO* of the *GTD* also records an important change within the leadership since a subgroup under the orders of *Lieutenant Colonel* de Guillebon[8] received the mission of 'setting up in Andelot after capture by the *GTV*, and guarding the crossroads, to ensure the southern flank guard of the division.' It consisted of a squadron of Shermans, a company of the *RMT*, and a battery of the *3ᵉ RAC*.[9] Andelot was about 20 kilometres northeast of Chaumont. The *GTD* was still in second echelon with the *GTV*, behind the *GTL*, which was at the forefront. *Colonel* Langlade avoided the resistance and dug 'like a wedge into the enemy camp for nearly 100km.'[10] True to his tactics, Leclerc led a real charge to disorganise the enemy, emphasising audacity and speed. This is why he asked the *GTD* to cover his flanks, which were also those of Patton's 3rd Army, and to 'mop up' the resistance that had been bypassed by the first echelon.

Also on 12 September, the *GTL* with Massu had just taken Vittel and, maintaining its momentum, reached Dompaire in the evening. The day before, it had liberated Contrexéville while inflicting heavy losses on the enemy. The infantrymen of Chad fought like lions in the street battles where superior morale is the main guarantor of success. During the briefing at the division's CP, Dio was proud to learn of these feats of arms achieved by his 2nd Battalion, even if his joy was tempered by the announcement of the death in Vittel of *Lieutenant* Gauffre, a veteran of Chad.[11] The same day, the *GTV* took the town of Andelot, which had been bypassed by the *GTL*, with great difficulty. Subgroups La Horie, Cantarel, and Putz overcame the German resistance. On 13 September, the *GTD*'s units were split at several points. The 5th Squadron of the *RMSM* occupied Chaumont after it fell. The engineering company cleared mines at Chaumont and then went to Andelot to join Subgroup Guillebon. Part of the *GTD* remained in Villars-en-Azois on surveillance facing south. In the evening, Dio received the order to send a subgroup to Vrécourt to establish a strongpoint there. The village of Vrécourt is 20km west of Vittel, at the entrance to the Département des Vosges. For this mission, he chose *Commandant* Rouvillois and reinforced him with the light squadron and the 105mm platoon from the *12ᵉ Cuirs*, an infantry company, and an artillery battery. During the day of 13 September, Subgroup Massu was engaged in Dompaire

---

7   *De Fort-Lamy à Strasbourg*, p.18.
8   It is surprising to note that Guillebon's name appears for the first time in the *GTD*'s *JMO* without it having announced a prior assignment, as is the rule and as was done for *Commandant* Quilichini, for example. Furthermore, the *GTD* had the required number of senior officers likely to take command of a subgroup. Finally, this operational assignment would usually be entrusted to a member of a unit that was part of the *GTD*, which Guillebon was not. It seems that here too, this officer, who had worked since 1940 alongside *Colonel* and then *Général* Leclerc, asked for and received an assignment to an operational command. It is also likely that Leclerc, anticipating the departure of *Colonel* Billotte and, having planned for *Lieutenant Colonel* de Guillebon to replace him, wanted to give the latter prior operational experience. He entrusted this particular mission to Dio, within the framework of the very closed circle of 'Chadians.'
9   Fonds Leclerc, *JMO GTD*, boîte J, chemise 1.
10   Destrem, *L'Aventure de Leclerc*, p.304.
11   Paul Gauffre, born in 1910, began his career in the colonial infantry. He was a non-commissioned officer in 1940 when the *RTST* rallied the entirety of Chad to *Général* de Gaulle. He took part in the victory of Kufra and then the Fezzan 1 campaign, at the end of which he became an *aspirant* in April 1942. After Fezzan 2, he was assigned to the *Groupe Nomade de l'Ennedi*, a unit that became the 7th Company of the *RMT* when the *2e DB* was created. Promoted to *lieutenant* in June 1944, he commanded the 3rd Section of the 5th Company during the landing. He fought brilliantly in Normandy and Paris, his calm demeanour admired by all. He was made a Companion of the Liberation (decree of 29 December 1944).

with the *112. Panzerbrigade* and its 90 tanks, Mark V Panthers and Mark IVs. Commanded by *General* Hasso von Manteuffel, this brigade was a shock element of the German Army.[12] With the support of the 19th Tactical Air Command, Massu overcame it. Unfortunately, once again, a first-class officer was killed in action – *Lieutenant* Guigon, commander of the 1st Section of the 7th Company.[13]

On 14 September, Rouvillois left early in the morning for Vrécourt. During the advance, he received an order at 2:00 p.m. to reduce enemy resistance at Bourmont, consisting of infantry and anti-tank guns. He carried out the mission in the afternoon and then continued towards Vrécourt, which he captured at 7:00 p.m. Subgroup Guillebon left Andelot and moved to the village of Brainville-sur-Meuse to flank from the north. Early in the evening the *GTD* units that had remained in their position were ordered to be ready to move during the following day. Also on 14 September, the remaining units moved to the Rimaucourt region, to the east of Andelot. Only a squadron of medium tanks and the *FFI* squadron of *Capitaine* Bonhomme remained in Villars-en-Azois as the southern flank guard of the 3rd US Army. Subgroup Rouvillois received the order to set up at Dombrot-le-Sec and then to occupy Vittel, which it accomplished by 2:00 p.m. In the afternoon, Dio's CP moved to Rimaucourt and the units to the surrounding towns. The tally for the day was 70 German prisoners taken, but the number of killed could not be estimated. On the *GTD* side, it was 11 wounded including 4 officers.

On 15 September, the *GTD* moved to the region of Bulgnéville, to the west of Vittel and 50km from Rimaucourt. Rouvillois was in Vittel. The day's toll was 10 prisoners on the enemy side, with friendly losses amounting to 2 killed and 4 wounded. On 16 September, Guillebon held Contrexéville, while Rouvillois was still in Vittel and placed at the disposal of the *GTV*. The toll was 9 German prisoners and 4 wounded from the *GTD*. On 17 September 1944, the two units that had been left on the southern flank rejoined the group. Subgroup Rouvillois, under the orders of the *GTV*, moved during the night to Derbamont, northeast of Dompaire. Enemy movements having been reported north of Épinal on the west bank of the Moselle, the light tanks were replaced by medium tanks; the Sherman M4s. Subgroup Guillebon left Contrexéville to go to Hymont, northwest of Dompaire. On 18 September, Leclerc wanted to continue the action towards the east and decided to modify the disposition of the *DB*. The mission of the division was to 'cross the Moselle at Nomexy-Châtel-sur-Moselle and continue the mission of protecting the southern flank of the 3rd US Army in a first bound to the Mortagne River (not to be crossed without orders) while scouting up to the River Meurthe.'[14] Leclerc intended to cross the Moselle in force at Nomexy-Châtel on 19 September and then use that conquest to continue his advance towards the next river – the Mortagne.[15] The distance separating the Moselle from the Meurthe is approximately 35km, with the Mortagne halfway between. These three rivers, oriented north-south, are significant obstacles for an armoured division advancing towards the east.

The *GTV* was responsible for the Moselle, and the *GTD* for the exploitation towards the Mortagne. Dio, trailing the other *groupements tactiques* since Paris, finally passed to the front of

12   Bergot, *La 2 ème D.B.*, p.188.
13   Roger Guigon was born in 1921. A graduate of Saint-Cyr, he chose the colonial army. He was serving in the RICM in Morocco when the war broke out. Assigned to the *Corps Franc d'Afrique*, he joined the RMT in Djidjelli in 1943. He earned the admiration of his men and his leaders during the battles in Normandy and Paris. He was one of the officers that the men of the 2nd Battalion of the RMT mourned the most. 'It was that day, in Dompaire, that he would 'fall with a smile on his face.' He was 23 years old.' (Fonds Leclerc, J. Salbaing, Allocution prononcée le 11 septembre 1994 à Dompaire devant la stèle du Lieutenant Guigon, boîte 37, dossier 1, chemise 3)
14   *JMO du 12e Cuirs,* Fonds Leclerc, boîte M1, dossier 1, chemise 1.
15   Compagnon, *Leclerc*, p.430.

the division. The information on the enemy certainly led Leclerc to put the group that had been least tested by the fighting to that point in the lead.

On 19 September, the *GTD* crossed the Moselle at around 9:30 a.m. on bridges built by the *13ᵉ Génie* and set off in a south-easterly direction: Moriville, Hallainville, Damas-aux-Bois, Saint-Boingt, Vennezey, Giriviller. Three subgroups were formed. Rouvillois arrived at Vallois, a village on the Mortagne, at 2:00 p.m. He continued towards the Meurthe and captured Moyen. Light elements were sent to Vathiménil on the Meurthe.[16] Guillebon occupied Gerbéviller, a village on the Mortagne to the north of the *GTD*'s zone of action. Noiret, meanwhile, arrived at Magnières at around 6:00 p.m. and captured the village from German infantry. At the end of the day, Dio had fulfilled his mission. He held all the points on the Mortagne between Gerbéviller and Magnières and even beyond, since a subgroup was at Vathiménil. The crossings of the Mortagne were made by ford because the bridges had been destroyed. It is noteworthy that 'the *FFI* squadron which moved in the recovery vehicles could not cross the Moselle and it bivouacked at Nomexy.'[17] There were only three wounded among the *GTD*'s ranks. There were 32 German soldiers taken prisoner, but it had not been possible to record the number of their dead.

On 20 September, Dio sent a reconnaissance to Flin to examine the state of the bridge over the Meurthe.[18] The Germans had abandoned the village, but the bridge was destroyed and the Germans firmly held the northern heights. The commander of the *GTD* then laid out his plan:

- Rouvillois would hold Moyen and Vathiménil and position a unit at Flin.
- Guillebon would occupy Vallois and hold the eastern exits of Giriviller.
- Noiret would hold Magnières and Mattexey.
- The *2ᵉ Compagnie de Génie* would be responsible for establishing two crossings over the Mortagne, at Vallois and Magnières.

Enemy artillery fire killed 4 *GTD* soldiers and wounded 10, while 15 Germans were taken prisoner. On 21 September, the situation was unchanged. Heavy artillery fire rained down on the elements in Flin, killing a *spahi* officer, *Lieutenant* Matheeh. The *3ᵉ RAC* carried out 'counter-battery fire with the American group on positions reported by the air force. A German battery was silenced.'[19]

After only nine days with the *GTD*, *Lieutenant Colonel* de Guillebon departed.[20] Leclerc appointed him to take command of the *GTV*, replacing *Général* Billotte who left to take over the command of the *10ᵉ Division FFI*, which was forming in Paris. For Leclerc, *Lieutenant Colonel* de Guillebon was 'the kind of officer he likes, one of the rare *colonels* of the division, along with Dio, with whom he does not need long sentences to be understood.'[21] *Commandant* André Gribius, who could not be suspected of immoderate sympathy for the Free French, later wrote: 'In the eyes of the whole division, such a selection could not be better.'[22] Dio was very satisfied with Guillebon's selection to lead the third *groupement tactique*. Except for Langlade, the principal leaders around Leclerc were now all Free French. 'Fortunately, all Free French sectarianism had disappeared from

---

16   *Caravane*, No.12 supplément, 5 février 1945, 'De la Marne à la Meurthe', p.6.
17   Fonds Leclerc, *JMO du 1/RMT.*
18   The village, initially taken by the Americans, was retaken by the Germans who, decided to punish the inhabitants for having brought out the French flags and hastily celebrating their liberation by setting fire to the houses and the church with around 50 inhabitants, including the priest, locked inside.
19   Fonds Leclerc, *JMO du 3e RAC.*
20   Fonds Leclerc, Note de service No. 284/3 du GTD du 20 Septembre 1944 signée Dio, boîte J, dossier 1, chemise 1.
21   Bergot, *La 2 ème D.B.*, p.204.
22   Gribius, *Une Vie d'Officier*, p.101.

the division in the face of the necessity of fighting' wrote Leclerc to d'Argenlieu.[23] Dio, with Crépin and Guillebon, was the leader of a united and efficient team 'which sees with only one eye and beats with only one heart,'[24] welded behind their leader. That led Compagnon to say: 'unity of thought was then completely achieved at the level of the divisional high command.'[25] The command of the three *groupements tactiques* remained unchanged until Berchtesgaden.[26]

Within the *GTD*, *Commandant* Quilichini succeeded Guillebon at the head of the subgroup. The man who had previously held staff positions (G1, personnel section) was able to prove his worth as an operational leader. On 22 September, the *GTD* was tasked with establishing a bridge-head on the Meurthe near Flin with a view to resuming the advance towards the Vezouze River, 10km further north. Dio divided up the missions as follows (*GTD* order 285/3):

- Subgroup Rouvillois, reinforced with the 2nd Company of the *RMT* would seize the Flin bridgehead by force, starting at 12:00 pm,
- Subgroup Noiret would exploit from 2:00 p.m. towards Buriville and Bénaménil,[27]
- Subgroup Quilichini would exploit towards Thiébauménil,
- The *3ᵉ RAC*, part of an artillery group comprising the 975th Group of 155mm and the 276th Group of American self-propelled 105mm, would support the three subgroups.

Rouvillois, with two companies of the *RMT*, a squadron of tanks, and an artillery battery, attempted to cross the Meurthe via a ford 500 metres west of the destroyed bridge. The armoured vehicles got bogged down and the first Sherman coming out of the river was destroyed by a *Panzerfaust*. The infantry then crossed the river at another ford downstream to take the enemy positions from behind. Rouvillois requested and obtained artillery fire to support the advance of his men. He benefited 'at 3:30 p.m. from a 600-metre smoke screen lasting 10 minutes in front of the SW edges of Ménil-Flin.'[28] The manoeuvre succeeded, causing the Germans to withdraw. It was 5:00 p.m. A few tanks were then able to cross at the first ford to reinforce the infantrymen and extend the bridgehead to Saint-Clément and Laronxe.[29] The exploitation phase was postponed until the following day. On 23 September, Subgroup Noiret crossed the Meurthe at 6:00 a.m., followed by Subgroups Quilichini and Rouvillois, which 'advanced into the forest of Mondon. Rouvillois occupied the north-eastern and eastern edges, opposite the last villages protecting Baccarat: Azerailles, Hallainville, Bénaménil. Quilichini rushed into the middle of the forest, emerging north of the Vezouze where he occupied Thiébauménil.'[30] Dio asked that the first-echelon units prepare the terrain to create strongpoints to be able to oppose any return of the Germans and protect themselves from indirect fire. Indeed, the Germans, who held the heights, pounded the French troops with artillery and mortar fire, causing higher losses than those of the morning.[31] The *3ᵉ RAC*, aided by US artillery, conducted counter-battery fire which reduced the pressure. The rainy weather prevented the intervention of air support. The toll was 5 killed and 23 wounded in the ranks of the *GTD*. The number of killed on the German side was 'high but impossible to

23   Destrem, *L'Aventure de Leclerc*, p.309.
24   Fonds Leclerc, Jean Cocteau, *Salut à la Division Leclerc*, boîte 30, dossier 2, chemise 1.
25   Compagnon, 'Logisticien et Tacticien', p.218
26   Bergot, *La 2 ème D.B.*, p.204.
27   Exploit, in a military mission, means taking advantage of a breakthrough to take as much ground as possible, translating tactical success into an operational advantage and reinforcing enemy disorganisation and confusion.
28   Fonds Leclerc, *JMO du 3e RAC*.
29   Pellissier, *Le Général Rouvillois*, p.58.
30   *Caravane*, No.12, supplément, 'De la Marne à la Meurthe'.
31   Fonds Leclerc, *JMO du GTD*.

assess;' 51 prisoners were taken. There was no change at the operational level on 24 September. *Colonel* Dio went in person to all the units and 'verbally gave them the following order 'Don't show yourself to the enemy, and continue to monitor the villages by observations and patrols. The artillery will take on any enemy movement.'[32] Since the German artillery was still effective, Dio did not want to lose any more men unnecessarily. In fact, the daily loss report of the JMO noted nine wounded by artillery fire for that day.

The following day, 25 September, would be the last dynamic day for several weeks. Dio was woken up at 5:00 a.m. by the *général* who came to verbally give his orders for the day. Leclerc enjoyed meeting up in Dio's CP to have a coffee and chat with him. Dio was the only one in his entourage who told him his problems or his feelings about the situation without any fear. It was in this capacity that he had become 'one of the pillars of the division.'[33] The two men valued those moments of brotherhood-in-arms. The *GTD* had taken the villages of Bénaménil and Thiébauménil on the Vezouze. But in Manonviller, a small village to the rear, on the ridge line between the two towns, there was a fort dating from the First World War which had blocked the advance of the French army in 1915. Thirty years later, the enemy was once again occupying the village and the fort in strength, holding the ridges overlooking the Vezouze.[34] The commander of the 2ᵉ *DB* ordered the *GTD* 'to test the enemy resistance to try to capture the village of Manonviller.'[35] Dio entrusted two subgroups with the mission of carrying out a simultaneous attack at noon from their positions: Rouvillois from Bénaménil and Quilichini from Thiébauménil. Unfortunately, Rouvillois could not cross the Vezouze.[36] Quilichini had two sections of infantry ford the river. Then they advanced into the village of Manonviller, taking prisoners belonging to the *Panzergrenadier-Regiment 104*. However, after the first vehicle got stuck in the mud, the tanks of Noël's squadron were unable to cross the river. Suffering heavy losses, without tanks, Quilichini ordered his infantry to withdraw. The attack caused 15 dead and 26 wounded in the ranks of the *GTD* as well as the loss of a Sherman, the recovery tank, and two half-tracks.[37]

During lunch, *Général* de Gaulle arrived unexpectedly at Leclerc's CP in the village of Moyen. Dio was summoned to the CP with the other commanders of the *groupements tactiques*. He left Vézinet to direct operations from his CP in La Féculerie. The head of the provisional government was in a good mood and relaxed. He had come to assess the operational situation. He knew Dio well by then and appreciated his candour.

At the end of the day on 25 September, *Groupement Tactique Dio* had regrouped on the Vezouze in the first echelon of the 2ᵉ *DB*. 'On this date, two armoured detachments of the GTD crossed the forest of Mondon, one due north, the other towards the east; the first reached the Vezouze, at the foot of the fort of Manonviller held by the Germans; the other stopped at the edge of the forest facing the occupied villages…'[38] Its advance had unintentionally created a sort of salient in the forward disposition of the 2ᵉ *DB*. It was the only unit to have crossed the right bank of the Meurthe. The *GTR*, *GTL*, and *GTV* in that order, were to the south of its position but on the left bank of the river. It was therefore in a perilous situation, with no one on its right facing south. Dio

32   Fonds Leclerc, *JMO du GTD*.
33   Pierre Bourdan, *Carnet de Retour avec la Division Leclerc* (Paris: Éditions Pierre Trémois, 1945), p.205.
34   Fonds Leclerc, *JMO du 3e RAC*.
35   Fonds Leclerc, *JMO du GTD*.
36   The river is more than 20 metres wide with a depth between 0.7 and 1 metre. (Fonds Leclerc, JMO de la 2e Compagnie du 13e BG).
37   *Lieutenant* Ferrano, leader of the 2nd Section of the 3rd Company, 'who rejoined his company that morning after leaving the hospital, was wounded by shrapnel in the afternoon and evacuated.' (Fonds Leclerc, JMO du 1/RMT.) This demonstrates the intensity of the artillery fire that fell on the combatants on both sides.
38   Compagnon, *Leclerc*, p.440.

recovered Noiret's subgroup which was in reserve at Saint-Clément with the *FFI* squadron. He deployed all of his resources to face not only the east but also the south. All night long, the *GTD* units were subjected to intense artillery fire.

From 25 September to the end of October, the *2e DB* remained in its positions and did not cross the old 1915 border.[39] The offensive was then stopped on the orders of the Americans. Eisenhower, the supreme commander of the Allied troops, gave priority to the supply of fuel and munitions to Montgomery's British forces. Their mission was to liberate Belgium, particularly Antwerp, to quickly make it the primary port for the supply of Allied troops in 1945. The aim was also to 'neutralise the deployment bases of the V1 and V2 which were bombarding England.'[40] Unfortunately, the Germans took advantage of this period of respite to organise their line of defence. They would 'constitute a defensive position in the Vosges, the *Vogesen Stellung,* around the ridges and passes. They created an advanced position, called *Vorvogesen Stellung,* in front of the towns of Réchicourt – Blamont – Badonviller – Senones, at the western foot of the massif. Even further forward of this advanced position, the Baccarat road junction was firmly held, protected by relatively important strongpoints, at Azerailles, Hablainville, Ogéviller, Herbéviller, the forest of Mondon.'[41] *General* von Manteuffel was the local German commander.[42] 'Opposite, the *2e DB* held the front extending from the Vezouze to Rambervillers. To its right, the US 45th Infantry Division secured the flank facing the south-east along the road from Épinal to Saint-Dié. To its left, the US 79th and 44th Infantry Divisions ensured the front in front of the forest of Parroy, east of Lunéville.'[43]

26 September brought no change at operational level. The weather was atrocious, and air support was grounded. Artillery fire continued to hit the *GTD* units on the Vezouze, killing two during the day. In Nancy, *Général* de Gaulle presided over an important ceremony where he presented a number of decorations. Dio was among those decorated with officers from his regiment, including Massu, Putz, and Dronne.[44] The commander of the *GTD* was elevated to the rank of *Officier* in the *Légion d'honneur.* Massu, the architect of Dompaire's success, was promoted to *lieutenant colonel* and he too was made an *Officier* of the *Légion d'honneur.* The commander of the 2nd Battalion of the *RMT* was astonished because he had never been made a *Chevalier* of the *Légion d'honneur,* which is normally a mandatory step before being made an *Officier.* Later in the evening, it would be a laughing matter between Dio and all the decorated officers of the *RMT* gathered to celebrate this among themselves. Dio took advantage of these occasions to keep in touch with the officers of the three battalions of his regiment.

Starting on 27 September, *Colonel* Dio asked his subgroups to adopt a deliberate defensive system with the laying of mines and the construction of bunkers.[45] His CP moved to Laronxe north of Saint-Clément. The enemy artillery continued its firing, killing two sappers of the *13e BG* and wounding 11 more in 24 hours. On 28 September, the artillery fire was violent during the day on Thiébauménil and Bénaménil, followed at night by harassing fire. The American XV Corps, commanded by General Haislip, was detached from Patton's 3rd Army and came

39   Pellissier, *Général Rouvillois,* p.60.
40   Compagnon, *Leclerc,* p.440.
41   Compagnon, *Leclerc,* pp.440–41.
42   A general with a predestined name, since in German Mann means man and Teufel means devil, so 'Manteuffel' could be translated as 'devil man!'
43   Bergot, *La 2 ème D.B.,* p.207.
44   Dio had been made a *Chevalier* on 18 March 1941 at the Fort-Lamy hospital. The decree formalising this promotion would not appear in the *Journal Officiel* until 15 April 1945, while that for the rank of *Officier* would appear on 2 March 1945. In times of war, the administrative process is often disrupted.
45   Fonds Leclerc, *JMO du GTD.*

under the command of General Alexander Patch, commanding the US 7th Army. This army was part of General Jacob Devers' 6th Army Group, a group which also included de Lattre's *1re Armée Française*.

On 29 September, the enemy, who held the northern ridges of the Vezouze, began to patrol. He left his positions and approached the strongpoints set up by the *GTD* to assess their strength.[46] Those two days, operationally static, were used to conduct training. The *FFI* squadron of the 1st Battalion of the *RMT* was the first to train. This was also the case for the 'individuals,' the replacements who were designated to fill the vacancies in the units. On 30 September, Dio, aware that the situation was likely to drag on, took a measure to allow the units to continue in their combat positions. He assigned each of the three subgroups two positions, one on the front line and the other, several kilometres back, to allow them to recover while being less subject to artillery fire. The leaders of each subgroup could thus rotate their personnel in halves, which would allow everyone to take turns to catch their breath and to endure. The system planned for three days on the front line followed by three days of semi-rest with one afternoon leave per week in Lunéville, to take a hot shower.[47] *Lieutenant Colonel* Noiret's subgroup was the furthest north. It included Perceval's 2nd Company of the *RMT*, Gaudet's 4th Squadron of medium tanks, Lenoir's 1st Squadron of light tanks and the *2e Compagnie du Génie* of *Capitaine* Germain. It held Thiébauménil on the Vezouze and Saint-Clément on the Meurthe, six kilometres to the south. Quilichini's subgroup was in the centre. It held Bénaménil and Chenevières with Joubert's 3rd Company, Bonhomme's *FFI* mounted squadron, Lavergne's *CA1*, *Lieutenant* Bonnet's[48] 3rd Squadron of the *RBFM*, and a platoon of medium tanks provided by *Lieutenant Colonel* Noiret. This subgroup was the most well equipped, because it was intended to be able to reinforce either of the other two subgroups. Rouvillois's subgroup was set up in Ménil-Flin to the south and on the northern edges of the forest overlooking the Vezouze. It had Boussion's 1st Company, Noël's 3rd Squadron, the *général's* protection squadron commanded by *Capitaine* de Boissieu, and the *4e Compagnie du Génie*. The *GTD* CP remained in Laronxe with Orgeix's 2nd Squadron in reserve and the *CCR* of the *RMT*. Each strongpoint prepared the terrain to build underground bunkers and surrounded itself with anti-personnel and anti-tank mines to secure them.

The implementation of the rotation plan began on 30 September. Unfortunately, *Lieutenant* Maurel, head of the reconnaissance section of the support company of the 1st Battalion of the *RMT*, stepped on a mine in the vicinity of Thiébauménil and was killed. The bad news would pile up for Dio, on that 30 October, he also learnt of the death of two officers of the 3rd Battalion of the *RMT* who had been in Kufra with him, *Capitaines* Dubut[49] and Geoffroy,[50] 'two heroes of the

---

46   Fonds Leclerc, *JMO du GTD*.

47   Loison, R., *Moteurs en Route*, p.23.

48   Dio and his men were aware of the valuable contribution of the *RBFM*'s tank destroyers in the anti-tank fighting. This is why everyone was happy to read Order of the Day No.53, of 16 September 1944, in which Leclerc recognised the merit of the sailors of the *DB* and authorised them from that point on to wear again the red *fourragère* of the *Légion d'honneur*, which he had forbidden them to wear in Témara. Raymond Maggiar, *Les Fusiliers Marins dans la Division Leclerc* (Éditions Albin Michel, 1947), p.152.

49   René Dubut was a graduate of Saint-Cyr. He was Massu's deputy in Bardaï in Tibesti in Chad when the war broke out. He was in all of the battles of Leclerc's African epic. In Kufra, he commanded the mortars and received a citation. The capture of Gatroun during Fezzan 1 earned him a second citation. Serving on the staff of the 1st Battalion until then, he had taken command of the 11th Company 10 days before being killed near the village of Doncières. He was 32 years old.

50   André Geoffroy was also a graduate of Saint-Cyr. He commanded a company of Senegalese *tirailleurs* in Yaoundé when Leclerc landed in Douala. He placed his unit at Dio's disposal when he seized the Cameroonian capital. Then he participated with his company in the capture of Libreville. He played a key role in Kufra, being one of the two platoon leaders who, under the direct orders of *Colonel* Leclerc, routed the *Sahariana*. He was made a companion of the Liberation by decree of 14 July 1941. He took command of

African campaigns, killed by a burst of fire from a lone soldier perched in a tree.'[51] Their battalion, acting within the *GTV*, was fighting in the Rambervillers region, as part of the support provided to the American 45th Infantry Division. This loss of the two young officers was felt bitterly by the entire *DB*. The *général's* aide-de-camp wrote:

> Geoffroy is killed by a burst of machine gun fire while carrying out reconnaissance in a wood that seemed deserted and the rumour is going around that Dubut is seriously wounded. Another bad series. The *général* is deeply affected by it. Why must fate be so relentless on his old and dear team. Tonight in Roville, say goodbye to poor Geoffroy. We learnt that Dubut was also dead. Three bullets in the head. What losses and what quality![52]

The toll of September's losses within the *GTD* was heavy, with 41 men killed, 134 wounded, and four declared missing. Since the landing, the *GTD* had lost 93 men and had 371 wounded. The losses inflicted on the Germans by the *GTD* were estimated at 2,201 killed and 4,184 prisoners with the destruction of 42 tanks, 429 vehicles, and 39 guns.

The period of relative stability that the *2ᵉ DB* and the *GTD* would experience in front of Baccarat allowed them to replenish the troops with new blood and to welcome the return of some of the wounded from Normandy and Paris who rejoined their units. The training battalion of Saint-Germain-en-Laye could send specific profiles of individual volunteers on request. At the end of October, 'the troops are once again at the desired level.'[53] The same was true for the equipment. The destroyed tanks and half-tracks were replaced. Rather than taking back their original baptismal name, some of them were renamed in homage to those killed, such as, the half-track *Lieutenant Gauffre* of the *RMT* or the Sherman *Lieutenant Spaniel* of the *3ᵉ RAC*.

Starting on 1 October, the *GTD* experienced difficult weeks devoted to the defence. The men were subjected to constant enemy artillery fire and the danger of mines during patrols, all with very rainy weather that seriously complicated their living conditions. This relative forced immobility ended up creating a certain gloom within the units. 'It is not a question of inaction, because the daily task is made up of local missions, day and night, patrols and ambushes …. we must accept losses.'[54] This state of mind was also fuelled by the news coming from the liberated part of the country, which had fallen back into the quarrels and political manoeuvres of the pre-war period.[55] The men perceived through the information they received that the war no longer seemed to be the priority for a majority of Frenchmen. Many of the officers of the *2ᵉ DB* were reservists. They naturally asked themselves where their place was in the reconstruction of the country. By continuing to fight, were they not going to let opportunists take all the posts? Finally, at the level of the private soldier, operational information was not always sufficiently explained. The private does not understand why he remained stuck in the mud and the cold so long when the division had favoured the advance ever since their landing. Dio noted these drops in morale in Chad during the summer months of 1941 and 1942 when future operations on Fezzan were being prepared. The

---

the *2e Compagnie de Découverte et de Combat* and seized the post of Uigh-el-Kébir during Fezzan 1. He was with Dio during Fezzan 2 still at the head of the *2e DC*. When the *RMT* was created, he was Putz's deputy at the *3/RMT*. He distinguished himself in Paris by actively participating in the capture of the Hôtel Meurice. He was ambushed in Doncières, a village north of Rambervillers. Cited six times, he was 34 years old when he was killed.

51   Bourdan, *Carnet de Retour*, p.214.
52   Girard, *Journal de Guerre*, p.297.
53   Bergot, *La 2 ème D.B.*, p.208.
54   Compagnon, *Leclerc*, p.436.
55   Compagnon, *Leclerc*, p.436.

JMOs of the *GTD* units mention the same reports throughout this month of October: the number of artillery and mortar shells and bombs, the patrols carried out, the reliefs, the daily losses, the few instruction and training activities, et cetera. What was new was the flight of Messerschmitt 109s over the positions of the units, searching for the French artillery. The 2nd Battery of the *22ᵉ GCFTA* was called upon to intervene several times with its Bofors anti-aircraft guns, deployed as protection around the battery positions of the *3ᵉ RAC*.

The first day of October was dedicated to completing the reorganisation of the *GTD*'s defensive system between the Vezouze, the line of contact with the Germans, and the right bank of the Meurthe, six to seven kilometres further south. In order to facilitate the movement of the units, *Lieutenant Colonel* Fieschi, commanding the *3ᵉ RAC*, on Dio's orders, carried out an intense artillery fire on the German positions that day. For this mission, he was reinforced by three US artillery battalions, two of which had 155mm guns, with a more powerful effect than the 105mm of the *3ᵉ RAC*. He was thus able, through the intensity of the fire, to make the Germans keep their heads down. In the afternoon, the mayor of Laronxe organised a ceremony in tribute to those killed in the *2ᵉ DB*, by laying a wreath at the war memorial. 'After this ceremony, a wine of honour presided over by *Colonel* Dio and the mayor of Laronxe was offered to the notables of the country and to the officers.'[56] *Colonel* Dio was very keen to build good relations with the local population, especially those whose villages had suffered from the bombing. He missed no opportunity to meet with the notables when he could, and he asked his officers to do the same, each in his own area.

On 2 October, the *FFI* squadron, which followed the 1st Battalion as best they could in buses requisitioned from the *TCRP* (Public Transport Company of the Paris Region), became the 4th Company of the 1st Battalion. Equipment, vehicles, and weapons were provided by American logistics. Some leaders from other companies were selected to accompany this gradual increase in strength in order to provide their combat expertise and technical know-how. Little by little, the use of the half-tracks and the modes of action of the combat groups and sections would be instilled in these young men who were eager to learn and were aware that their lives depended on this learning. Over the months, the *FFI* would become fully-fledged soldiers within the battalion. On 6 October, the 4th Company thus appeared for the first time in the *JMO* of the 1st Battalion: 'The 4th Company has a section in the forest of Mondon in 209-947 responsible for security patrols. The other two sections are in Chenevières resting and training.'[57] With this additional creation of the 4th, 8th, and 12th Companies within the three battalions, the *RMT* now had 12 companies of *fusiliers-voltigeurs*.

The operational situation changed little. On 10 October, the Germans left the village of Manonviller, leaving behind countless booby-traps. On 12 October, the Americans of the 79th Infantry Division occupied the Thiébauménil strongpoint. This allowed the *GTD*, whose front line was relatively wide, to tighten its forces and man its lines with more infantry. In mid-October, the threat of a German counterattack led Dio to strengthen his defence. Additional small forts were built on the strongpoints, men dug in, additional mines were laid, and barbed wire put in. The *13ᵉ Bataillon du Génie* accomplished a tremendous job and 'all this work earned our sappers the congratulations of *Colonel* Dio and *Commandant* Rouvillois, who carried out an inspection tour in the sector.'[58]

Around 23 October, news spread through the division that the static and defensive period would soon end.[59] Indeed, *Général* Leclerc, who could wait no longer, convinced General Haislip

---

56   Fonds Leclerc, *JMO du 12e Cuirs.*
57   Fonds Leclerc, *JMO du 1/RMT* ou sont inclues les coordonnées (longitude/latitude) de la carte d'État-Major (where the coordinates (longitude/latitude) of the General Staff map are included)
58   Fonds Leclerc, *JMO du 13e BG.*
59   Compagnon, *Leclerc*, p.438

and the American high command to launch an offensive to seize Baccarat. The town, which was an important crossroads, constituted a salient in front of the *Vorvogesen Stellung*. The Americans finally give their approval to Leclerc.

The German *General* von Manteuffel commanded the *Wehrmacht* troops in the area. He knew Leclerc and his division, which the Germans called the *Blitzpanzer*.[60] An expert in armoured vehicles, he assumed that the tracked vehicles would not risk being deployed off road, given the weather conditions at the time. So, he waited for the French on the roads and placed his formidable 88mm guns on all axes coming from the west and south and leading to Baccarat. He built strong defensive positions based on the villages. The Germans had a month to get organised, using forced labour from the inhabitants. The German positions were buried, anti-tank ditches dug, and mines laid. The German line of defence on the right bank of the Meurthe was built around three strong points, the villages of Azerailles, Hablainville, and Ogéviller; 'these three strong points were connected by a screen of infantry, without any depth.'[61]

On the other side, the staff of the *DB* was actively preparing, under Leclerc's leadership. First, the intelligence section collected a wealth of vital information from the local population and the resistance fighters. This was the first time the *DB* would realise 'the tactical effectiveness of the resistance fighters for the immediate benefit of the battle.'[62] This information most often concerned the enemy but also the terrain, buildings, observation positions, overrunning axes, et cetera. All very useful information before planning a manoeuvre. *Commandant* de Tarragon, head of the *GTD* intel section, received the order to contact the resistance and collect information in the zone of action. He reached out to the resistance networks, and the *FFI* spontaneously came to introduce themselves. They increasingly served as guides for the patrols of the units in the forest of Mondon. The best known of these resistance fighters in the zone was Father Stutzman, also called the 'priest of Domèvre.'[63] Dio befriended him. Stutzman, in a cassock, crisscrossed the zone on a bicycle, moving through the German positions. He brought back vital information on the exact position of the enemy's heavy weapons and crew-served weapons (machine guns, mortars and artillery). All this information was gathered and then brought to *Colonel* Crépin, chief of the divisional artillery. In the area of Rouvillois' subgroup, 'a young woman from Baccarat, Marcelle Cuny arrived, bringing with her two English airmen she had been hiding for three months,' and then she stayed with the French outposts.[64] This young woman would play an important role in the capture of 'the Crystal City.'[65]

In parallel with this intelligence effort, the divisional artillery meticulously prepared its fire plan. The Americans promised to significantly reinforce the division's three artillery regiments. Crépin, as a good *polytechnicien*, allocated all the German objectives (called 'poles' in military terminology) according to a detailed timeline, in coordination with the operations section. The operations staff knew that Manteuffel was waiting for the division on the main axes on either side

---

60   The Germans phonetically translated Leclerc's name as '*l'éclair*' (or 'lightning'), hence the nickname given to his division, '*Division l'Éclair*' (lightning division) in French, or *Blitzpanzer Division* in German.

61   EM 2e DB, *Caravane* No.5 (29 octobre au 6 novembre 1944), 'La Prise de Baccarat'.

62   Compagnon, *Leclerc*, p.441.

63   Henri Stutzman, born in Alsace, was the priest of Domèvre-sur-Vezouze in 1940. Chaplain of the *279e Régiment d'Infanterie*, he was cited twice for his courage. Taken prisoner by the Germans, he was released to resume his duties in Domèvre. He became chief of the zone of resistance (*FFI* sector number 414) at the beginning of 1944. Receiving parachute drops of weapons, he organised several attacks on the Paris-Strasbourg line and on electrical transformers. He narrowly escaped a roundup by the Gestapo at the end of August. He joined the *DB*, providing valuable information in the Baccarat and Cirey sectors. He would be cited by Leclerc. He died in 1984 and is buried in Brin-sur-Seille.

64   *Caravane* No.5, 'La Prise de Baccarat'.

65   Baccarat is famous for its glassworks and crystal factory. (Translator's note)

of the Meurthe, either on the right bank where the *GTD* was located, or on the left bank with the *GTL* and the *GTV*. In front of Baccarat on the right bank was the forest of Mondon, not very suitable terrain for tanks. The axes of the left bank seemed more appropriate. Obviously, Leclerc, as a tactician who favoured speed and surprise, asked his operations section to prepare an attack plan on the right bank off the main roads. Thus, he wanted to seize Baccarat from the zone held by the *GTD*. But the plan of attack through the forest of Mondon required preparations so that the armoured vehicles could cross it. Starting on 20 October, the *13ᵉ Génie* entered into action in the forest of Mondon, supported by 'an American engineer regiment with 120 GMC dump trucks and all its equipment, a four-kilometre roadway was paved in four days: the whirlwind of trucks turned night and day without attracting the attention of the enemy.'[66] They had to make three routes through the forest in order to reach its eastern edges, requiring the greatest discretion to prevent alerting the Germans. The wet, foggy October weather was favourable for *Commandant* Gravier's sappers to work in. 'The exit will be from the eastern edges of the forest of Mondon, but the last part of the movement, by the three routes set up in recent days by the engineers through the forest, will only take place immediately before deployment on the morning of the 31st, to maintain the maximum surprise.'[67]

The *GTV*, as well as part of the *GTL*, had to discreetly switch to the right bank. When the time came, the remaining units of the *GTL* would feign an attack from the south. Manteuffel would not see anything coming and, until the last moment, would not be able to anticipate the manoeuvre of the *2ᵉ DB*. The division deployed 'on the right bank of the Meurthe on 30 October, on a foggy day that hid the views and sounds perfectly.'[68] Attacking in a south-easterly direction, the *GTD* kept the Meurthe as a guardrail. To its left, the *GTV* was in the centre, and Massu's subgroup of the *GTL* to the north. All the men scanned the sky anxiously. The ground was very wet, and the soldiers tested the ground to see how the tanks and half-tracks handled off road. It was close. Fortunately, the sun, with cold weather, appeared on the morning of 31 October.[69] Leclerc and his men were lucky. To initiate the attack, a formidable cannonade rang out and woke up the entire region. From 8:30 to 8:50, Crépin, supported by all the artillery of the American corps, which represented the total firepower of the division multiplied by 10,[70] pounded the enemy targets, crushing them under a deluge of fire.[71] The Piper Cubs attached to the divisional artillery had taken to the air, with the weather now allowing their flight, and they were responsible for adjusting the fire. Simultaneously, the sappers of the *13ᵉ BG* cleared the mine belts they had set up at Buriville, Hablainville, and Ménil-Flin on the three routes which were going to be used by the *2ᵉ DB*.

The *GTD* was ready. Having received the division's Operations Order No.150/3 on 29 October, Dio was able to comment on it on the 30th in the presence of all his operational leaders. Then he issued the *groupement* order.[72] True to his habit, Dio organised three subgroups for the attack, Quilichini and Rouvillois in the lead, Noiret in reserve. The axis of advance for the attack from Ménil-Flin would pass through Azerailles, Gélacourt, Brouville, Merviller then Baccarat and the Grammont farm (located 3km east of Baccarat, on the western edge of the forest of Grammont). On 31 October 1944, Dio launched his two subgroups.

66   Fonds Leclerc, *JMO du 13e BG*.
67   Fonds Leclerc, *JMO du 13e BG*.
68   *Caravane* No.5, 'La Prise de Baccarat'.
69   *Caravane* No.5, 'La Prise de Baccarat'.
70   Compagnon, *Leclerc*, p.441.
71   P. Purson, gunner on the tank *Brive* of the *12e Cuirs*, mentions no fewer than 400 guns. Fonds Leclerc, Pierre Purson, *Itinéraire Suivi par le Troisième Escadron du 12e Cuirs, Peloton Krebs*, 1994, p.18.
72   Fonds Leclerc, *no.363/3 du GTD en date du 10/30/44*, boîte J.

Quilichini came out of the Hauts Bois unexpectedly, taking Azerailles from the flank: the company and the anti-tank units that were holding the village were almost entirely taken prisoner, an operation in which one of their own soldiers, a Russian who had come over the day before to give us his intelligence and knowledge of minefields, participated brilliantly: he had little trouble convincing his former comrades, machine gun in hand, that after all, 'it was indeed he who was right!' Rouvillois in turn emerged from Ménil-Flin by the N59, which he immediately dominated, and rushed towards Gélacourt. Quilichini, who had become available again, simultaneously took Joubert's detachment to Merviller, which was held by the *GTV.* And, from Gélacourt and Merviller, both acting on Baccarat, Rouvillois neutralised the 88 and the position reinforced with Flak guns in the Bois des Aulnes. Guided by a young girl from Baccarat, Marcelle Cuny, he then left the road, avoiding the obstacles set up by the Germans at the entrance to the town.[73]

The key, and priority, objective was the town's main bridge over the Meurthe. The detachment led by Joubert (commanding the 3rd Company) of Quilichini's subgroup, guided by the *gendarme* Calamai,

reached the Sainte Catherine Quarter (north of Baccarat) around 6:00 p.m. *Sous Lieutenant* Lucchési, the first Frenchman to enter the city, made contact with the leading elements of Rouvillois's subgroup .... the sections of Lucchési and Mac Clenahan then entered the town. The main bridge over the Meurthe in the centre of the city was taken intact, even though it was mined, thanks to the decisiveness of *Lieutenant* Mac Clenahan, who killed the German officer just as he was preparing to blow up the bridge.[74]

The 3rd Section of the *2e Compagnie du Génie* assigned to the *GTD* was tasked, along with the sections of the *RMT,* with taking it intact at all costs and confirmed the previous sequence of events: 'arrival at the Baccarat bridge at 6:45 p.m.: after the death of the German officer in charge of ignition (Mac-Lénan's [*sic*] section), demining of the bridge on the instructions of a non-commissioned officer prisoner.'[75] The bridge was heavily mined. The non-commissioned officer PoW was Polish.[76] 'He then told the engineers how they should get rid of the imposing bombs that were littering that area: two charges from four Stuka bombs each and three shells of three bombs of around 50kg.'[77] If the Germans had been able to blow up the bridge, the concentration of explosives was such that part of the town would have been destroyed. This action is what led the municipality of Baccarat to subsequently name the bridge after *Lieutenant* Mac Clenahan.

It is noteworthy that the units of the two subgroups acted in concert to take the town during the attack. Lucchési's section (*RMT*) was part of Noël's detachment of the *12e Cuirs* of Quilichini's subgroup while that of *Lieutenant* Mac Clenahan (*RMT*) was part of Joubert's detachment of the *RMT* of Rouvillois' subgroup. In the early evening, the two subgroups held the strongpoints

---

73   *Caravane* No.5, 'La Prise de Baccarat'.
74   Fonds Leclerc, *JMO du 1/RMT.*
75   Fonds Leclerc, *JMO du 2e Compagnie du 13e BG.*
76   In 1944, German units often included many men from Eastern Europe. Very often these Poles, Russians, Ukrainians, and others had been forced to join the ranks of the *Wehrmacht,* their families remaining hostages. These soldiers tended to desert during this period. Subsequently, the Germans did not hesitate to tie them up to force them to fight. During the fighting at Badonviller, for example, Leclerc's men were surprised to see that the Ukrainian crew of the 88mm guns were chained to their gun (*JMO du 3e RMT*). These guns, initially Russian 85mm, had been rebored to 88mm.
77   Fonds Leclerc, *JMO du 13e BG.*

from which they proceeded to 'mop up' the city, with the help of the population. The Germans were hunted down and surrendered en masse. On the evening of 31 October, the *GTD* seized the crystal city without breaking anything fragile! The *GTL* and *GTV* simultaneously seized the villages north of Baccarat. Those of Ogéviller, Mignéville, Herbéviller, and Vacqueville fell on 1 November. The *GTD*, responsible for expanding the position around Baccarat, seized the village of Bertrichamps, five kilometres to the southeast, on the road to Saint-Dié the same day. On 2 November, Dio's men reconnoitred the road due south leading to Rambervillers and towards Sainte-Barbe, and linked up with elements of the American 117th Cavalry.[78]

The following days were used to secure the region around Baccarat and to stabilise the positions. On 4 November, the *2ᵉ DB* was relieved in its positions by American units from VI Corps. The *GTD*'s movement order stipulated that once the units had been relieved by the Americans, the regiments would regroup organically on 5 November in R&R quarters. As was the case after Le Bourget, it was a matter of reconditioning, repairing, and taking a breather. On 5 November, the day the units were to leave, 'the municipality of Baccarat and the management of the crystal factory offered a reception at 11:30 a.m. to *Général Leclerc, Lieutenant Colonel* Vézinet, *Commandant* Rouvillois, and a few officers and men, chosen from among those who had contributed the most to the liberation of the city.'[79] The *général* then made a short speech. He said very simply that Baccarat represented, for him, one of his finest operational achievements. Historians would later speak of the 'Baccarat minuet.' Like a conductor, Leclerc led the operation meticulously and without a false note. The town was taken by surprise and was not destroyed. The *GTD* was the cornerstone of the conquest of the town and the seizure of the intact bridge. Subgroups Rouvillois and Quilichini were the actors in this success, without underestimating, of course, the role of the other *GT*s as well as that of the artillery and intelligence.

At the end of the reception, the *GTD*, like the other *GT*s, began its movement towards the rest area. The attached units of *spahis*, sappers, and navy *fusiliers*, assigned to reinforce the *GTD*, would rejoin their respective regiments. The group's command post and the health and logistics services were centred around the village of Moyen. The *1/RMT* moved to the left bank of the Meurthe and was spread out in the villages of Xaffévillers and Roville-aux-Chênes, north of Rambervillers. The men took advantage of the proximity of this town to go to take a shower, something they had not done for many weeks. On 11 November, the *1/RMT* organised a ceremony in Roville-aux-Chênes to proceed with a 'roll call of the 75 officers and soldiers of the battalion who had fallen on the field of honour since the beginning of the French campaign.' Dio presided over the ceremony and attended the mass celebrated by Father Blondeau, chaplain of the *1/RMT*. The *12ᵉ Cuirs* settled in Magnières and Saint-Pierremont, villages close to those of the *1/RMT*. During this period, the regiment changed leadership. *Lieutenant Colonel* Noiret was assigned to a cavalry command in Paris. *Lieutenant Colonel* Rouvillois, promoted at the beginning of November, officially became the regimental commander during a ceremony on 12 November in Magnières in the presence of *Général* Leclerc and *Colonel* Dio. *Commandant* Didelot, who had until then served on the *GTD* staff, became second in command of the regiment.

The *3ᵉ RAC* was the only unit to remain on the right bank of the Meurthe, setting up in Saint-Clément, Laronxe, and Azerailles. This was because the *3ᵉ RAC* would continue to fire on previously identified enemy positions during the rest period.[80] Artillery fire was most often planned at the corps level. The American artillery supported the division during its attack on Baccarat; it was

---

78   Fonds Leclerc, *JMO du 12e Cuirs*.
79   *Colonel* Dio was absent on this date, for an unknown reason – mission, health? Fonds Leclerc, *JMO du 12e Cuirs*.
80   Fonds Leclerc, *JMO du 3e RAC*.

normal that in return the divisional artillery could support the American troops who had moved to the first echelon. The *3ᵉ RAC* would be the only unit of the *GTD* not to be able to go into its rest quarters.

During this period, the units that needed replacements welcomed the young recruits trained in the reinforcement battalion (*BR No.2*) of Saint-Germain-en-Laye. This training unit remained, through special exception, subordinate to the *2ᵉ DB*, allowing the training to be adapted to the specific needs of the division.[81] The replacement operation mainly concerned the *1/RMT* and the *12e Cuirs* who had lost men since Paris. Dio asked his officers to ensure that each of these incorporations be carried out within a system of close and progressive sponsorship: a veteran taking charge of the new arrival and taking advantage of every opportunity to complete the training on the job.

The rest period soon ended, and the fighting resumed under the leadership of the American corps. The Baccarat salient had been erased, but the Germans were firmly established on the Pré-Vosgienne Line (*Vervogesen Stellung*), a line of defence based on the foothills of the Vosges Massif. It 'relies on the marshes of Fénétrange and the Haute-Meurthe …. to join the foothills of La Schlucht above Gérardmer to the south: its strong points in our corridor are Blamont, Ancerviller, Sainte-Pôle, Neufmaisons, which are connected by continuous networks of trenches and anti-tank ditches heavily protected by mines.'[82] Further east, the Vosgienne Line (*Vogesen Stellung*) was based on the southern heights of the Vosges Massif with Le Bonhomme, La Schlucht, Le Donon, then on the Red Saar and the White Saar, and finally the Saverne Gap between Mittelbronn and Phaslbourg.[83] The enemy line was occupied by two infantry divisions, 'the 553rd in the gap backing onto Réchicourt and Blamont, and the 708th backing onto Badonviller.'[84] This last division partly included units of *Gebirgsjäger*, light mountain infantry, that were particularly suited to a delaying fight in the Vosges.

Leclerc and his group commanders had learnt that the Germans lacked sufficient troops to hold both lines simultaneously. A large part of the troops planned for the Vosgienne Line had to come from the units that had withdrawn from the Pré-Vosgienne Line. This was crucial information that would be decisive for future operations, particularly on the pace at which the attack would be carried out.

General Haislip, commander of the American XV Corps, had two infantry divisions, the 44th and 79th, and the *2ᵉ DB*. He intended to attack the Pré-Vosgienne Line with the two infantry divisions, supported and covered by the *2ᵉ DB*. After breaking through the German defence line, he planned to launch the *2ᵉ DB* to seize the eastern exits of the Saverne Gap. For Leclerc and his subordinates, this tactic made sense because the German defence lines were built in areas cut by large ponds, two canals (the Marne-Rhine Canal and the Sarre Coal Mine Canal), and were densely wooded. This was more favourable terrain for infantry than for armoured vehicles.

On 12 November, Leclerc summoned his group and subgroup commanders to the Baccarat crystal factory exhibition hall to discuss Operation Order No.376/3. He explained to them that his intention was to exploit eastward as soon as the Americans broke through the first defensive line (the Pré-Vosgienne). The distribution of missions was as follows: the *GTD* and the *GTL* were in the first echelon, the *GTR* and *GTV* in cover and reserve. The *GTD* was to the north of the *2ᵉ DB*'s zone of action, along the main axis of Route Nationale 4. 'This was the most difficult mission, because the Germans had concentrated as many resources as possible there and were certainly blocking this corridor, a veritable obligatory passage, with a series of obstacles that would have to

81   Compagnon, *Leclerc*, p.448.
82   Repiton-Préneuf, *2ème DB: La Campagne de France*, p.89.
83   The Saverne Gap is a pass connecting the Lorraine Plateau and the Alsace Plain.
84   Repiton-Préneuf, *2ème DB: La Campagne de France*, p.92.

be removed by force.'[85] 'The Boss' requested that liaison teams be formed as quickly as possible with the US divisions. 'This liaison and intelligence mission is extremely important, since its aim is to prepare the future engagement of the *GTD*.'[86] Dio sent *Capitaine* Revault d'Allonnes to the American 44th Infantry Division, which was in front of the *groupement*. The *GTD* had been working alongside this division for several weeks. Their men knew each other well and personal ties had been established between the leaders. *Groupement Dio* would have two axes for the exploitation phase:

- Axis A: Avricourt – Réchicourt – Gondrexange – Héming – Haut-Clocher – Oberstinzel – Rauwiller – Schalbach – Metting – Eschbourg – Zinzel Valley – Dossenheim.
- Axis B: Igney – Saint-Georges – Lorquin – Bebing – the north of Sarrebourg – Sarraltroff – Lixheim – Mittelbronn – Phalsbourg – Saverne Pass – Saverne.

Dio and his commanders realised that Axis A was more of a bypass route while Axis B was more direct, even if it used parallel secondary axes before reaching the RN4 before Phalsbourg. In fact, the *GTD* had to carry out a double action in the zone assigned to it: 'Saverne, the first objective assigned by the Corps, outflanked to the south by Dabo, was therefore simultaneously attacked from the north and from the centre. This double task was carried out by *Groupement Dio*.'[87] They understood the diabolical manoeuvre of 'the Boss.' He set up a pincer movement with two branches to take the German system from behind near the Saverne Gap. Axis A of the *GTD* was the branch on the northern flank of the enemy. Axis D of the *GTL* was the southern branch. Axis B was the centre of the 2ᵉ *DB*'s attack, responsible for fixing the enemy who was waiting for the *Blitzpanzer* in this direction.

Dio organised three subgroups to carry out its mission:

- Rouvillois, on Axis A: a squadron of medium tanks (d'Orgeix), the 3rd Company (Joubert) and the 4th Company (Leroy) of the *RMT*, an artillery battery, an engineering section, a tank destroyer platoon of the *RBFM*, a platoon of light tanks, a platoon of armoured cars from the *RMSM*, and support,
- Quilichini, on Axis B: a squadron of medium tanks from the *12ᵉ Cuirs* (Noël), the 1st Company (Boussion) and the *CA 1* (Lavergne), an artillery battery, an engineering section, a tank destroyer platoon, a light tank platoon and an armoured car platoon,
- Didelot, in reserve: a squadron of medium tanks (Gaudet), the 2nd Company (Perceval), the 5th Squadron of the *RMSM* (minus two platoons), the 3rd Squadron of the *RBFM* (minus two platoons), the 2nd Company of the *13ᵉ Génie* (minus two sections), a platoon of light tanks, the protection platoon of the *CCR* of the *RMT*, the *3ᵉ RAC* (minus two batteries).

The Subgroups of Rouvillois and Quilichini were made up of mobile elements, capable of advancing on secondary axes, with two companies of infantry each. Their attention was 'drawn to the fact that the planned operations must be carried out without loss of time, speed being of primary importance.'[88] Dio, moreover, favouring tank-infantry coordination, made sure to always associate the same pairs of *capitaines* from the *12ᵉ Cuirs* and the *RMT*: d'Orgeix with Joubert,

85   Bergot, *La 2 ème D.B.*, p.218.
86   Fonds Leclerc, *JMO du 12e Cuirs*.
87   Repiton-Préneuf, *2ème DB: La Campagne de France*, p.99.
88   Fonds Leclerc, *JMO du 12e Cuirs*.

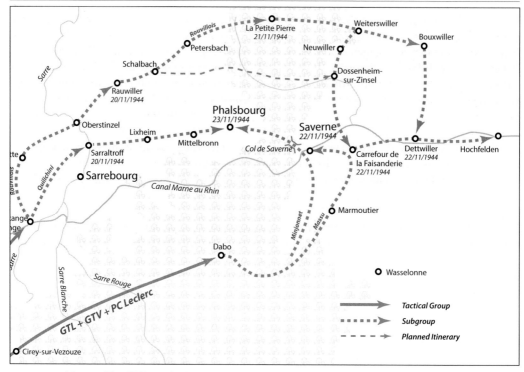

Map 12 The GTD in the Saverne Gap operation (19 November to 23 November 1944).

Noël with Boussion, and Gaudet with Perceval. These young officers had been working together since Normandy. The pairing was also carried out quite naturally at the lower level of the platoon-sections and often even went down to the level of the tank and the combat group. In Lorraine and Alsace, offensive charges were increasingly carried out with the infantry riding on the rear decks of the tanks. Only great confidence and a lot of experience made it possible to carry out this non-regulation combat procedure.

On the morning of 13 November, the men of the *GTD* were awakened by the distant but distinct sound of artillery. Operations were about to resume. Everyone was getting ready. On 13, 14, 15, and 16 November, the American infantry came up against the defensive positions of the Pré-Vosgienne Line, around Blamont and Réchicourt-le-Château.[89] Leclerc was impatient. He knew that the arrival of winter would complicate operations if the attack did not succeed. On 17 November, he launched the subgroup of La Horie, his classmate, who had 'the build of a jockey and the heart of an elite',[90] on the eastern flank of the US 79th Infantry Division. The 79th, took the Pré-Vosgienne strongpoint at Badonviller by surprise, and then immediately exploited towards the north. A detachment of *spahis*, under the command of Morel-Deville, infiltrated and took the bridges of Cirey-sur-Vezouze intact. From that moment on, the entire German system began to fall apart.

The next day, La Horie wanted to relaunch his action towards Bréménil. During a meeting with his *capitaines*, he was mortally wounded by artillery fire. *Capitaine* Maziéras, commander of the 11th Company of the *3/RMT*, was also killed at his side. This young colonial officer was Dio's deputy in Cameroon and Gabon. His journey ended in Lorraine, much to Dio's dismay.

---

89   Compagnon, *Leclerc*, p.458.
90   Bourdan, *Carnet de Retour*, p.214.

On 17 November, Dio wrote Movement Order No.385/3 so that the three subgroups, as they approached the area of operations, could reorganise into their combat formation. The planned positioning was located north of Baccarat on the right bank. Dio's CP was in Brouville, Rouvillois's in Reherrey, Gélacourt for Quilichini, and Fontenoy-le-Château for Didelot. Meanwhile, the US 44th Infantry Division was advancing. It managed to break through the Pré-Vosgienne Line at Avricourt. The *GTD* would be able to pass through it to attack when it reached the Gondrexange-Lorquin line. On 19 November, Dio decided to move closer to the 44th Infantry Division. Intelligence on the enemy indicated that the German units were beginning to withdraw. They were gradually leaving the Pré-Vosgienne Line to settle on the Vosgienne Line. This period of reorganisation, when the German units would be vulnerable, was an unmissable opportunity. Dio was ready to ensure that the German withdrawal would not be carried out at leisure.[91] Subgroup Rouvillois had reached Réchicourt-le-Château and spent the night at the forward CP of the 324th US Infantry Regiment. Quilichini's column crossed Blamont and spent the night on the road near the village of Saint-Georges. Subgroup Didelot settled in Blamont. The *3e RAC*, which was stationed near Blamont, was reinforced by the US 59th Armored Field Artillery Battalion, which was bivouacked in Foulcrey. Thus, the *GTD*, isolated from the rest of the *DB*, doubled its firepower by having a second artillery unit.

Dio planned to launch the attack on the morning of 20 November. Leclerc's order was: 'push the maximum of your resources on the axis to your front. Cross the Vosges and fall back on Saverne, which I intend to attack from the south.'[92] During the night, each officer of the group prepared the conditions at his echelon for the next day's passage through the lines, making physical contact with the officer of the American unit that they would pass through.[93] In the early morning, Dio's main concern was to understand the possibilities of the crossing of the Marne-Rhine Canal. He was less than 5 kilometres from that obstacle. He could not engage the 900 vehicles of the *GTD* on such a shallow depth at the risk of finding himself blocked. Dio then decided to give only Subgroup Quilichini the mission of finding a bridge to cross the canal. After having passed through the Americans at Landange, the commander of the 1st Battalion sent his detachments towards the canal. Favouring speed, the detachment led by Krebs (deputy commander of the 3rd Squadron of the *12e Cuirs*) 'rushes towards Xouaxange and succeeds in seizing the bridge over the Marne-Rhine Canal.'[94] The column of vehicles from the entire *GTD* immediately rushed into the crossing point.[95] Quilichini outflanked the town of Sarrebourg, which was held by strong resistance, to the west, and the Americans of the 44th Infantry Division, who followed behind the *2e DB*, reduced it. Without delay, the leading subgroup rushed north towards the Saar, another obstacle to cross. Krebs's detachment, in the lead once again, was unable to take the Sarraltroff bridge, which had been blown up shortly before its arrival. The infantry crossed the ford and seized the village. In order to consolidate the bridgehead with a few tanks, the engineers carried out 'a crossing with three sets of Treadway [pontoon bridges] resting on an abutment that seemed firm, the other being destroyed. The bridge was completed at midnight.'[96] Unfortunately, this bridge collapsed under the weight of the first medium tank that tried to cross it. As the rain fell in torrents, the advance on Axis B was stopped. The subgroup spent the night in and around the village.

91   Repiton-Préneuf, *2ème DB: La Campagne de France*, p.100.
92   Compagnon, *Leclerc*, p.462.
93   Leaders at all levels down to the lowest met. The leader of the unit being passed through gave the position of his units, the possible axes of advance through his position, and the latest situation of enemy positions.
94   Fonds Leclerc, *JMO du 1/RMT,* boîte B1, dossier 1, chemise 1.
95   Some historians attribute the capture of the bridge to the Americans of the 44th ID.
96   Fonds Leclerc, *JMO du 13e BG.*

Subgroup Rouvillois only began its advance on Axis A at 1:00 p.m. because it had to cross the canal at Xouaxange behind Quilichini. Taking the smaller roads, it crossed Langatte and pushed the enemy back at Haut-Clocher and Dolving. It found, to its surprise, the bridge over the Saar at Oberstinzel intact. The explanation was comical. A team of German sappers had undertaken to mine the bridge during the day to destroy it. The miller, living nearby and fearing the destruction of his mill in the explosion, had invited the sappers to join him to drink Mirabelle brandy, and he kept them drunk until Rouvillois's cavalry arrived. In the evening, the latter held the large crossroads of Rauwiller. On the evening of 20 November, Subgroup Rouvillois, which had left in second position, had advanced more than 25 kilometres in only half a day. All night long, retreating German convoys fell into the French formation, which turned into a real trap for them. Didelot's subgroup was tasked with accounting for this unexpected mass of prisoners. The enemy was in total confusion. 'Around 8:00 p.m., the commander of the Drulingen *Gestapo* called to ask if the Americans were in Rauwiller. He was told (there were Alsatians in the *2e DB*!) that the gunfire that had been heard in the region was fired by drunken German soldiers. The [*Gestapo* officer] came the next morning to assess the situation. At the sight of a tank emerging from Rauwiller, he quickly fled into the woods, abandoning his Mercedes-Benz intact.'[97] Axis A seemed to be the most favourable to accomplish the mission. Dio was not mistaken. He would follow Rouvillois.

On 21 November, the commander of the *GTD* arrived at Rauwiller at 8:30 a.m. After direct consultation with *Lieutenant Colonel* Rouvillois, he ordered him 'to push on Petersbach, and possibly on Petite-Pierre – Weiterswiller, leaving flank guards at Rauwiller – Schalbach – Siewiller, and a strong detachment at Petersbach.'[98] This part of the JMO of the *12e Cuirs* explains the future success of Subgroup Rouvillois in seizing the eastern exits of the Saverne Gap. Remember that Axis A planned to bypass the Saverne Gap by taking a shorter route, via Dossenheim, along the Zinzel valley. This new option, taken by Dio in consultation with Rouvillois, to outflank more widely than planned to the north, would be decisive. Rouvillois knew the region well. Considering then that the passage through the Zinzel valley was too risky, he convinced his chief to modify the plan of operations by going through a less dense forest where the tanks would be able to manoeuvre better.[99] Dio had shoulders wide enough to validate this initiative at his level. In any case, he was not in contact with Leclerc who was on the side of the Dabo Pass. The choice to modify the planned route was perhaps also based, in part, on information concerning enemy positions passed on by the population. At daybreak, *Lieutenant Colonel* Rouvillois sent two detachments forward. Lenoir's detachment (1st Squadron of the *12e Cuirs*) took Lixheim after a vicious skirmish, and that of Briot de la Crochais (deputy of Compagnon's 2nd squadron) seized the village of Schalbach despite a barricade held by infantry armed with *Panzerfausts*.[100] 'With 75s, the Shermans neutralised the anti-tank guns, then, through the soaked fields, the infantrymen overran and attacked the Germans from behind. About 30 *feldgrau*[101] corpses littered the pavement.'[102] At midday, Lenoir was at Siewiller where the fighting was heavy, while Josse's detachment (*RBFM*) was already at Petersbach, having travelled 15km since the morning. The enemy, although disconcerted, was very numerous in the area, trying to fall back to reach the Vosgienne Line. The German artillery units were surprised while on the move. Rouvillois's columns, following their instructions,

---

97 Fonds Leclerc, *JMO du 12e Cuirs,* boîte M1, dossier 1, chemise 2.

98 Fonds Leclerc, *JMO du 12e Cuirs.*

99 Bergot, *La 2 ème D.B.,* p.235.

100 *Sous Lieutenant* Corap of Lenoir's squadron fell gloriously at Lixheim. He was the son of André Corap, the '*général* [who was] unjustly made a scapegoat for the defeat at Sedan by Paul Reynaud in May 1940.' (Compagnon, *Leclerc,* p.462.).

101 German uniforms were *Feldgrau* (Field Grey) in colour. (Translator's note)

102 Bergot, *La 2 ème D.B.,* p.235.

favoured speed and outflanked the resistance without delay. The Germans, seeing themselves taken from behind, surrendered by the hundreds. Around 2:30 p.m., *Lieutenant Colonel* Rouvillois launched the detachments of Compagnon (*12ᵉ RC*) and Joubert (*RMT*) on the village of Petite-Pierre located on a 340-metre-high pass, separating the Lorraine Plateau from the Alsace Plain. Compagnon's tanks were engaged at the entrance to the village by the *361. Volksgrenadiers.* The *3ᵉ RAC* 'carried out several very effective shots on Petite-Pierre … in particular a burst of fire on the village…'[103] Joubert's infantry outflanked the enemy through the forest. The trench network was taken by *Lieutenant* Lucchési's men with grenades. The village was taken at 4:30 p.m. At 8:00 p.m., Rouvillois had two detachments at La Petite-Pierre, two at Petersbach, and one at Siewiller. He was spread out over more than 10km, forced to hold the important villages in which a large number of German prisoners were being held.

Meanwhile, Quilichini's subgroup, blocked in front of the Saar at Sarraltroff, finally crossed the river at Oberstinzel on Axis A. Around 10:00 a.m., it returned to Axis B towards Mittelbronn. Boussion's company, which was advancing in the vanguard, was attacked at the entrance to the village. The *capitaine* was mortally wounded by a bullet to the head.[104] *Lieutenant* Py, head of the howitzer section, took command of the unit and launched his infantry to attack three successive lines of trenches. The fighting was fierce. Two section leaders, Djambekoff and Mac Clenahan, were wounded. Quilichini finally captured Mittelbronn. Leclerc's intelligence chief then made the observation: '*General* Bruhn, who commands the 553rd *Volksgrenadier* Division …. is hypnotised by this charge. He only thinks about garrisoning his defences and facing it …. He will no longer have the freedom of mind necessary to look north or south and he will concentrate all his equipment, which is still significant, around Phalsbourg.'[105] When Quilichini relaunched his action towards the town of Phalsbourg, his leading elements were stopped by powerful fire coming from fortified works to the west of the town. The trap had worked. The pincer manoeuvre could be carried out under good conditions. Night was falling. Quilichini decided to postpone the attack on this important German defence until the next day. Wary, he organised his detachments into strongpoints around Mittelbronn. It was a good thing for him because the enemy in Phalsbourg launched a night counterattack, without success. The third subgroup of the *GTD*, that of *Commandant* Didelot in a second echelon, reduced the resistance (Bettborn, Baerendorf, Veckersviller), relieved the first echelon, and regrouped with the hundreds of prisoners.

At the end of the day of 21 November, *Colonel* Dio was particularly satisfied. Present as close as possible to the first attack echelon despite his ankle, which kept reminding himself of it, he made sure to force a rapid pace of advance on his two leading subgroups. Pressed everywhere, the enemy did not have time to recover. Throughout the day, he followed Rouvillois because he sensed that Axis A would allow him to outflank Saverne. 'Dio spread wide to the north' wrote the intelligence chief.[106] This was the right choice. In the evening the pass was held by the *GTD*.[107] The descent towards the Alsace Plain could take place the following day. The northern branch of the pincer movement was in place and would be able to take the German defensive system from behind. Quilichini, for his part, was in front of Phalsbourg. He had fulfilled his role as a decoy.

---

103 Fonds Leclerc, *JMO du 3e RAC.*

104 Boussion joined *Colonne Leclerc* in Tunisia. He commanded the *CHR* and replaced *Capitaine* Grall at the head of the 1st Company after 30 September.

105 Repiton-Préneuf, *2ème DB: La Campagne de France*, p.101.

106 Repiton-Préneuf, *2ème DB: La Campagne de France*, p.99.

107 General Patch, commanding the US 7th Army wrote in his Order of the Day: 'One of your armored columns, by a brilliant maneuver and remarkable audacity, has annihilated the main enemy defensive organisations to the west of Phalsbourg, completely routing the enemy forces which protected the Saverne Pass to the North.' (A. M. Patch, 'Ordre du Jour No.113', *Caravane* No.7).

The German garrison of Phalsbourg, obsessed with the defence of the Saverne Pass, did not realise the *GTD* was flanking them from the north.

22 November was a decisive day for *Groupement Tactique Dio*. The *colonel* was with Rouvillois and had not been able to establish contact with the *général*. He did not know whether the southern branch of the pincer movement, planned through the Dabo Pass, had succeeded or not. After having been partially resupplied, Dio resumed the action at daybreak, sticking to the terms of his initial mission: to take the Saverne Gap from the east. In the second part of the night *Lieutenant Colonel* Rouvillois had launched his *spahis* towards Weiterswiller, which was the first village on the Alsace Plain coming down from the Vosges Massif. *Lieutenant* Bompard reported at 7:15 a.m. that the village was not held by the enemy. The path was clear for Rouvillois. 'At 7:30 a.m., the *colonel* commanding the *GTD* gave me the order to push on Dettwiller via Bouxwiller and Steinbourg.'[108] Having left the forest, Dio could then fall back towards the south to arrive east of Saverne. The objective was the large crossroads of Dettwiller including the River Zorn and the Marne-Rhine Canal. To have a better chance of quickly seizing that strongpoint, he set two axes of advance for Subgroup Rouvillois. On the westernmost axis, strong enemy resistance was reported at Neuwiller-lès-Saverne by Compagnon. Rouvillois asked that the infantry of the detachment flank through the forest to take the enemy defences from behind. That is what they did, the village was taken and the advance could resume. Meanwhile, the units of the western axis advanced through Bouxwiller. Lenoir's detachment pushed back German artillery units and reached Steinbourg. Further south on the airfield, *Capitaine* Lenoir established contact with *Capitaine* Vandière of Massu's subgroup.[109] 'The pincer will close towards the assigned point.'[110] The pincer manoeuvre succeeded just before noon. But it almost turned into a tragedy. Indeed, the infantry of the 2nd Battalion of the *RMT*, considering that the German MG 34 and 42 machine guns had a better rate of fire than the US Brownings, had equipped their half-tracks with them. When the two subgroups found themselves face to face, 'the American tracers and the light yellow German tracers curiously mixed together…'[111] The tank turrets began to turn… shouts: Stop! Cease fire! Don't shoot! It's Massu! Stop!'[112]

The Germans in Saverne were trapped, no longer able to withdraw towards Strasbourg. Together, the two subgroup commanders, Massu and Rouvillois, arrived at the Brasserie Crossroads,[113] east of Saverne,[114] around 2:15 p.m. They coordinated their action so that their units did not cross paths. Rouvillois was asked to stay 5km east of Saverne. His subgroup was divided between the two villages of Dettwiller and Steinbourg. Saverne would mainly be the *GTL*'s concern. Subgroup Minjonnet entered the town from the south and dislodged the enemy hiding in the western districts with flamethrowers. The subgroup just crossed through the town; its objective was the Saverne Pass. Massu, for his part, finished clearing the central and eastern parts of the town. *Capitaine* Rogier, commanding the 5th Company of the *RMT*, intercepted a camouflaged/disguised Mercedes and captured *General* Johannes Bruhn, commanding the *553. Volskgrenadier Division*.[115] Meanwhile, Rouvillois pushed his leading elements to Wilwisheim, 15km east of

108 Fonds Leclerc, *JMO du 12e Cuirs.*

109 Fonds Leclerc, *JMO du 12e Cuirs.*

110 Repiton-Préneuf, *2ème DB: La Campagne de France*, p.102.

111 Dio prohibited the use of recovered German machine guns in order to avoid friendly fire.

112 Loison, *Moteurs en Route*, p.31.

113 Compagnon mentions 'the crossroads of La Faisanderie, 5km east of Saverne' as a junction point: Compagnon, *Leclerc*, p.463.

114 Pellissier, *Le Général Rouvillois*, p.82.

115 This version (Bergot, *La 2 ème D.B.*, p.239) is taken up by Dr Robet (*Souvenirs d'un Médecin de la France Libre*, p.93) and, without being as precise, is implied by Massu (J. Massu, *Sept Ans*, p.196) and Compagnon (Compagnon, *Leclerc*, p.464). However, *Commandant* Maggiar wrote that it was *Aspirant* Bastolet, deputy

Saverne. He set up his CP at Dettwiller. Leclerc arrived there at the end of the afternoon. Didelot's subgroup followed Rouvillois's advance in a second echelon. As with the day before, it reduced the resistance and took German prisoners. At the beginning of the afternoon, it was tasked with ensuring the northern flank guard of the units of the *2ᵉ DB* that were arriving on the Alsace Plain. It held the villages of Dossenheim-sur-Zinzel and Bouxwiller. As for Quilichini's subgroup, it was ordered not to launch an assault on the fortified works west of Phalsbourg – the pincer manoeuvre having succeeded, there was no point in losing soldiers unnecessarily. The German system would be attacked by Subgroup Minjonnet which, from Saverne, went towards Phalsbourg to take it from behind. The positions of the enemy 88s had been dug in to face the west. Therefore, they were unable to oppose a threat coming from behind them. With humour, the commander of the *RBFM*, wrote: 'the Boches are outraged! the French have not played the game! We don't enter through an exit door.'[116]

At the end of the afternoon of 22 November, Leclerc could see that the enemy was helpless. According to him, the Germans were not in a position to defend the access to Strasbourg in the next 24 hours. Moreover, Alsatian resistance fighters confirmed that the routes to Strasbourg were currently not defended. It was essential to take advantage of this period to launch the attack on the Alsatian capital before the *Wehrmacht* recovered. But, despite Rouvillois' requests, Leclerc refused to rush immediately to Strasbourg. The reason was simple: Leclerc could not abandon the Saverne Pass and Phalsbourg, where the situation was still confused. The Americans were not in a position to relieve the *GTD* units there for several hours. He was counting on American logistics for his supplies and medical support. The fuel and ammunition trucks needed a secure logistics route to be able to support the units at the front. The opening of the *RN 4* between Phalsbourg and Strasbourg was vital for the armoured vehicles of the *2ᵉ DB*. Furthermore, Leclerc could not engage his men in urban fighting without having the deployment of American military hospitals behind him. Additionally, he knew that to hold a metropolis like Strasbourg in the long term, he would need the participation of the two American infantry divisions. Yet *Général* Leclerc would have liked to liberate Strasbourg on the anniversary of its liberation in 1918 by the French Army, and what is more, on his 42nd birthday. With Haislip's agreement, he decided to lead the attack on Strasbourg the next day. But he had to leave a group on site in order to complete the securing of the logistics route. For that task, not ignoring the frustrating aspect that it entailed, Leclerc asked Dio 'to completely clear out the German elements that remained isolated between the Saverne Pass and Phalsbourg in order to completely free the Corps' supply axis.'[117] Indeed, the area 'was teeming with Germans still capable of offensive reactions against convoys and isolated individuals.'[118] In addition, Dio had to provide a flank guard facing north so that the other two *GTs* that were going to rush towards Strasbourg were protected from any threat coming from that direction, the threat from the south being taken into account by the *GTR*. Leclerc reorganised his system to gain time. He swapped the command of two subgroups. Rouvillois was detached to the *GTL* for the 23 November while Minjonnet moved to the *GTD*.[119] Leaving Dio on the evening of 22 November, Leclerc ordered Dio to join him in Strasbourg as soon as he had handed over the Saverne Pass to the Americans and had been relieved of his flank guard mission.

of the 2nd Platoon of the 4th Squadron of the *RBFM*, detached within Subgroup Minjonnet, who took *General* Bruhn prisoner, the spelling of whose name varies between Brühn, Brunhes (Maggiar), or Brusch (Compagnon).

116 Maggiar, *Les Fusiliers Marins dans la Division Leclerc,* p.199.
117 Langlade, *En Suivant Leclerc,* p.312.
118 Compagnon, *Leclerc,* p.464.
119 From a military point of view, such a change in the middle of combat is commendable. It required exceptional cohesion within the *DB* to envisage and succeed in it.

Dio would have preferred to participate in the seizure of Strasbourg, whose cathedral had haunted his mind, as well as that of his men, since Kufra. He told himself that fate was cruel to him. He did not witness the capture of the Fort of El Tag, having been wounded and evacuated a few days before. As a result, he did not hear Leclerc issue the oath. And he would not participate, three and a half years later, in the capture of the city, which he sensed would certainly remain the most important day in the history of the *2ᵉ DB*. But Dio knew that personal feelings could not prevail over his current responsibilities. So, on that evening of 22 November, he resolutely prepared for his new mission. It certainly seemed secondary, but it would enable the continuation of the *2ᵉ DB*'s fight in the near term. Dio consoled himself by telling himself that he had a large degree of autonomy to carry out the mission, which proved all the confidence Leclerc had in him.

The next day, 23 November 1944, Subgroup Rouvillois, no longer temporarily under Colonel Dio's orders, would play a major role in the capture of the Alsatian capital. Dio would be proud to note that one of the *GTD* subgroups, detached for the benefit of the GTL, would be honoured. He was thus consoled for not having been able to participate personally in the last stage of the Oath of Kufra. For his historic attack on Strasbourg, *Lieutenant Colonel* Rouvillois had a reinforced subgroup.[120]

For the attack on Strasbourg, Leclerc planned five routes. The one furthest north was assigned to Rouvillois. The 7:15 departure included everyone, like a car race. The weather was rainy and visibility was limited, which would facilitate the first part of the offensive.

Rouvillois received help from an Alsatian named Robert Fleig, who would guide the subgroup to infiltrate into Strasbourg. With half the distance covered, the route followed the Zorn River. Rouvillois passed through the villages of Wilwisheim, Hochfelden, and Schwindratzheim without any problems. Enemy elements were in Mommenheim. The vanguard of the subgroup, commanded by Compagnon's deputy, *Lieutenant* Briot de la Crochais, pushed the enemy back and continued the advance. It then encountered a German convoy at Brumath, surprising the enemy troops, who were very quickly taken prisoner. The bridge was not mined. Then heading due south, the columns of *Lieutenant Colonel* Rouvillois arrived in Vendeheim just before the bridge was to be blown up. Fortunately, *Lieutenant* de La Brousse's sappers had time to cut the ignition charges intended to destroy it.

The objective set was now Schiltigheim, on the northern outskirts of the Alsatian urban area. The vanguard pushed German infantry back at the crossroads of the Mundolsheim-Reichstett road. The second echelon took them prisoner. At 9:00 a.m., the column arrived at Schiltigheim without further incident.[121] Briot de la Crochais was assigned the first bridge over the Ill at the entrance to the city as his objective. At 9:15 a.m., he reached the Place de Haguenau.[122] The

---

120 It consisted of:
>   the 2nd Squadron of the *12e RC* under the command of *Capitaine* Compagnon
>   the 1st Squadron of light tanks of the *12e RC* of *Capitaine* Lenoir, minus two platoons
>   The staff squadron (support) of the *12e Cuirs* of *Lieutenant* Besnier
>   the 3rd Company of the *RMT* of *Capitaine* Joubert
>   the 4th Company (ex-*FFI*) of the *RMT* of *Capitaine* Leroy
>   the 1st Battery of the *3e RAC* of *Capitaine* Dubois
>   a section of the 2nd Company of the *13e BG* of *Lieutenant* de La Brousse
>   a platoon of TDs from the *RBFM*, of *Enseigne de Vaisseau* Josse
>   the 1st Bompard platoon of the 5th Squadron of the 1st *RMSM*.

121 Rouvillois' column crossed the belt of forts around Strasbourg between Fort Rapp to the east and Fort Desaix to the west. Why did the Germans let them pass unchallenged? The other subgroups coming from the west were aggressively attacked from Forts Foch, Frère, and Kléber. This success could partly be attributed to Robert Fleig who knew the flaws in the German defensive system.

122 Pellissier, *Le Général Rouvillois*, p.85.

column of tanks and half-tracks 'entered Strasbourg at high speed, causing panic, firing guns and machine guns at all the German vehicles and isolated individuals.'[123] It was the morning commute time when civilians and military personnel were heading to their places of work. The two bridges over the Ill were crossed via the Avenue des Vosges without resistance.

A little before 10:00 the column regrouped. Rouvillois gave his orders to the leaders of the detachments. The ultimate objective was the Kehl Bridge. On Fleig's advice, he split the subgroup into two columns to approach the Rhine, one directly by taking the Avenue de la Forêt Noire, the other passing by the cathedral and the Bourse. It was during that stop that Rouvillois had his radiomen send his famous message: '*Tissu est dans iode*' (Cloth is in iodine).[124] Leclerc received it at 10:30 in his CP in Birkenwald. *Colonel* Langlade, in response to Rouvillois' announcement of his entry into Strasbourg, reminded him of the priority objective with the message: 'Bravo, the Bridge, the Bridge .... a cross, three medals for officers and first non-commissioned officers at Kehl.'[125] This was, of course, the Kehl Bridge.

Briot de la Crochais crossed the city centre by the direct route and reached the bridge over the Vauban Canal at 11:00. But he was stopped at that point by fire from an '88'. Indeed, the Germans had pulled themselves together and reacted from the five barracks located in the south-eastern part of the city. From there, they attacked the vehicles of the subgroup that arrived. Violent clashes took place. The infantry disembarked and, supported by tanks, engaged in street fighting. Meanwhile, with Lenoir's light tanks and Leroy's company, Rouvillois headed towards the *Kommandantur* (German military headquarters) in the *Kaiserpalast*[126] to try to obtain the capitulation of the city commander. The Germans, noting the weakness of the French troops present on the square, initially refused to surrender. Rouvillois instructed *Capitaine* Roussel, commanding the head-quarters squadron, to bring the German general staff to capitulate. Rouvillois then joined his two detachments whose mission was to take the Kehl bridge. The one on the southern route had been blocked since 11:00 a.m. on the bridge over the Vauban Bassin. The one on the northern route reached the Petit Rhin Bridge at 12:00 p.m. But the two detachments could not break through in the face of the German fire. Early in the afternoon, Rouvillois launched Compagnon's detachment, which had been relieved in town by Massu's men. The objective was to cross the Petit Rhin Bridge and then seize the one under the railway. Compagnon reached it after clearing the approaches which were guarded by German infantry armed with *Panzerfausts*. He tried to advance to get a view of the Kehl Bridge, about 600 metres away. Manoeuvring with the infantry of Lucchési's section, the detachment was the target of heavy fire. Despite reaching the end of the road, it was still 100 metres from the objective. It was during this phase that the *Cherbourg Tank,* a 105mm Sherman, was destroyed along with the *Meknès*. The tank commander of the first, *Maréchal des Logis* Zimmer, an Alsatian born in La Wantzenau, was killed. The infantry of Lucchési's section lost *Sergent Chef* Gallo and *Caporal* Corvisier. The chaplain of the *2e DB*, *Père* Houchet, was mortally wounded while helping his driver. Finally, Robert Fleig, the civilian guide who was always in the thick of the fighting, fell in turn, a victim of his patriotism.[127] Compagnon

---

123   Fonds Leclerc, *JMO du 12e Cuirs.*
124   Langlade, *En Suivant Leclerc,* p.313.
125   Fonds Leclerc, *JMO du 12e Cuirs.*
126   Present day Palais du Rhin on the Place de la République.
127   Each year, the Strasbourg ceremonies begin at the 'Zimmer tank' and at the steles dedicated to *Père* Houchet and Robert Fleig. Zimmer was born in La Wantzenau, a village located about 10 kilometres north-east of Strasbourg. He went a few kilometres from his home in the morning without being able to warn his family. Rvd Père Houchet of the brotherhood of the Pères du Saint Esprit was a missionary in Kindamba in the Congo when war was declared. He joined the *2e DB* and took part in the African epic, never hesitating in the thick of the fighting to go forward to give the wounded and the dying moral support and also religious help to those who wanted it. Leclerc personally decorated Robert Fleig's daughter in 1945, in recognition of

was forced to retreat. At the end of the day, Subgroup Rouvillois was on the island between the Petit and Grand Rhin in a precarious defensive position.[128] It would remain there for four days, unable to reach the Kehl Bridge.

Early in the afternoon, the *spahis* of the 1st Platoon of the 5th Squadron of the *RMSM*, the unit attached to the *GTD* since Paris, patrolled the streets of the city centre. At 1:00 p.m., they decided to erect a flag on top of the cathedral. They wanted to find a large one. '*Madame* Lorentz, the friendly wife of the pork butcher on Place Saint-Etienne, made us the most beautiful flag with her blue apron, a white shirt, and a red *spahi* belt.'[129] The *spahis* drew a Cross of Lorraine on it with the inscription: *RMSM, 5ᵉ Escradon, 1ᵉʳ Peleton*. The platoon leader, *Lieutenant* Bompard, selected a vehicle commander, *Brigadier Chef* Maurice Lebrun, with his team, to go to hang the flag on the spire of Strasbourg Cathedral. Barehanded, in the cold, without any safety equipment, the young NCO succeeded in the feat. It was 2:30 p.m.[130] The French flag flew 142 metres above the square and it was a man from the *GTD* who hung it. THE OATH OF KOUFRA HAD BEEN KEPT.

At the end of the day on 23 November, all the soldiers of the *2ᵉ DB*, as well as the population, could see the blue, white, and red flag flying over the cathedral. 'In a tactical paradox, almost the entire division had penetrated into the city, while the external defence works – the forts – had not yet been neutralised.'[131] True to its tradition, *Division Leclerc* favoured manoeuvre over a frontal assault.

During 23 November and the liberation of Strasbourg, *Colonel* Dio was still in the vicinity of Saverne. He had three subgroups: Quilichini, Didelot, and Minjonnet attached from the *GTL*.[132] The day before, Subgroup Minjonnet crossed the western part of Saverne, creating panic among the German troops. Then it climbed the pass, reducing the resistance it encountered, especially at the foot of the pass, on the Lorraine side. With 'concrete blockhouses bristling with heavy guns and *PAK* batteries,'[133] it was the strongpoint of the German defensive system.[134] Arriving in the rear of the positions made it easier to reduce the defences. On the evening of 22 November, Minjonnet held both sides of the pass. On the morning of 23 November, under the orders of the *GTD*, Subgroup Minjonnet advanced towards Phalsbourg. It reached the village of Quatre Vents two kilometres east of the city. Dio then ordered it to stop and wait for the American infantry to arrive. The link up, which was always a problematic operational phase, was organised by Piper Cub to avoid friendly fire. At 1:30 p.m., the Americans relieved the French and took control of the pass. Minjonnet and his men were then able to return to Saverne to enjoy a little rest as well as the Alsatian wine that the inhabitants spontaneously offered them.

As for Subgroup Quilichini, Dio asked it to let the GIs of the 44th Infantry Division seize Phalsbourg. This was easily accomplished in the morning. The Germans, taken from behind, surrendered en

---

128   Compagnon, *Leclerc*, p.465.

129   Bompard, 'Comment notre drapeau fut hissé sur la cathédrale', *Soldats de Leclerc* (Paris: Lavauzelle, 1997), pp.221–222.

130   In his famous letter on *Kommandantur* letterhead addressed on 24 November to his friend Pleven, Leclerc mentioned the 4:00 p.m. time. He also reported it in the letter written the same day to his wife. But, the register of the Strasbourg Cathedral containing the 4 signatures of the *spahis* who climbed the bell tower says, 'at 2:30 p.m., the tricolour was hoisted by the *Spahis*.'

131   Bourdan, *Carnet de Retour*, p.225.

132   Lieutenant-Colonel Minjonnet was the commander of the *12e RCA*. 'Béarnais and small in stature .... he showed throughout the campaign, great humanity, courage and firmness in his command, which earned him our affection and respect.' (Salbaing, p.168). Dio appreciated this discreet and efficient officer who never went anywhere without his pipe.

133   *PAK* (or *Panzerabwehrkanone*) is anti-tank in German. The 88mm guns were originally an anti-aircraft weapon that also proved very effective in the anti-tank role.

134   Bergot, *La 2 ème D.B.*, p.234.

masse. Meanwhile, Quilichini 'received the order to ensure the security of the northern route and to guard the division's flank to the north.'[135] He reached Axis A, taken by Rouvillois, and set up his CP at La Petite-Pierre. Positioning one detachment at Petersbach and the other at Weiterswiller, the subgroup held the Vosges Massif north of Saverne. On 23 November, Subgroup Didelot carried out the same flank guard mission facing north, east of Quilichini's position.

On the evening of 23 November, the men of the *GTD* all felt they had been left behind compared to the rest of the division, which had just taken Strasbourg.[136] But their feeling of frustration was alleviated by seeing the columns of fuel tankers descend from the Lorraine Plateau at the end of the afternoon and head towards the Alsatian capital to resupply the *DB*'s armoured vehicles. They also saw the ambulances passing in the opposite direction, testifying to the fierceness of the fighting. 'We were at least certain that we had been useful, because it was hard to imagine such traffic and such rapid transport to the field hospitals, via the winding and narrow path of the Dabo Pass!'[137] Thanks to them, the Saverne Pass would become, for several weeks, the umbilical cord of the Allied units in Alsace. Soon their frustration would be nothing more than a distant memory. The three subgroups had just received the order to move from the *GTD* headquarters to join the division the following day.

On the morning of 24 November, Subgroup Didelot was the first to leave its positions. From Bouxwiller, it went straight to Strasbourg. It received the order to secure the northern and north-eastern part of the city by stationing itself in the Jardin de l'Orangerie. Subgroup Minjonnet left Saverne in the morning and also headed directly to Strasbourg via Brumath. It joined the *GTL*. Subgroup Quilichini had to wait to be relieved in its positions by the GIs before heading to Strasbourg. It arrived there early in the afternoon. The subgroup was entrusted with the defence of the area northwest of the city, including the train station and Place d'Haguenau. Quilichini settled into the Carlton Hotel, on Place de la Gare. In the evening, he offered champagne to the officers to celebrate the capture of Strasbourg.[138] While also maintaining their security mission, the personnel of the two *GTD* subgroups who had just arrived made arrangements to take turns enjoying the amenities offered by the city. Only Subgroup Rouvillois remained in operational mode, facing the bridgehead that the Germans had managed to maintain on the left bank of the Rhine near Kehl.

Dio returned to Strasbourg in the middle of the day and inquired about the *général*'s location. Guided, he headed towards the *Kaiserpalast* where Leclerc had set up his CP after the surrender of the German general staff. A direct witness to the scene recounted what would remain a strong moment between Leclerc and Dio. *Général* Leclerc,[139] with Girard and his chief of intelligence, Repiton-Préneuf, was 'having lunch in a corner of the *Kaiserpalast* lounge. At dessert, there's *Colonel* Dio. The *général*'s face lights up. 'Hey, my old Dio! Here we are, this time! Now we can both croak!"[140] At that very moment, the *Kaiserpalast* was subjected to a German bombardment of heavy artillery from the other side of the Rhine. The enormous chandelier smashed to the floor with a terrible crash and the room filled with smoke. When it cleared, the extent of the damage became apparent.[141]

---

135 Fonds Leclerc, *JMO du 1/RMT.*
136 Salbaing, *Ardeur,* p.317.
137 Salbaing, *Ardeur*, p.318.
138 Fonds Leclerc, *JMO du 3e RAC.*
139 This is how Général Leclerc would tell this anecdote during his speech in Strasbourg in 1946: 'A few hours later, at the Palais du Rhin, I was joined by *Colonel* Dio, one of our comrades in combat from the very beginning. We fell into each other's arms and I expressed our feelings to him in these words that I apologise for reproducing: 'So my dear Dio, now we can croak!" (Fonds Leclerc, boîte 21B, dossier 1, chemise 1).
140 Repiton-Préneuf, *2ème DB: La Campagne de France*, p.111.
141 Compagnon, *Leclerc,* p.467.

Behind the desk, stripped bare by the blast, the window was in pieces, and its torn off frame had fallen on the armchair. The curtains hung lamentably against a background of flames and smoke. Cars were burning. *Colonel* Dio was the first to stand up, putting his hand to the back of his neck. The général cried out:

"Dio are you hurt?"
"No, no, mon Général, I have nothing, nothing."

He took a few steps, turned around and muttered in surprise:

"A funny thing."[142]

This shout out from Leclerc to the man who had given him unwavering support from Cameroon, who had fought alongside him to subdue Gabon and who, above all, was his deputy in Kufra, demonstrates the feelings that bound the two men. Leclerc, seeing Dio join him, had a sort of surge of affection that was not usual for him. He realised that the Oath of Kufra for which they had given everything during the previous three and a half years had been kept. It was a joy and a pride at the same time. Nothing for them could then equal the feeling of accomplishment that they felt. 'We can both croak!' shouted Leclerc to his comrade-in-arms, with the awareness of duty accomplished. The German artillery had come close to immediately realising this aphorism from Leclerc which was only meant to signify the fulfilment in which he found himself. But, since 1940, the two officers had had '*la Baraka.*' Later, in the citation in the Order of the Army that he issued to him, *Général* Leclerc summarised the actions carried out by his subordinate between Paris and Strasbourg:

> *Colonel* of the 2ᵉ *Division Blindée.* Commanding a *groupement tactique* in the Battle of the Vosges, he carried out a remarkable operation through the use of his subgroups and the judicious use he made of them, not hesitating to push resolutely and boldly into the enemy positions, where enemy resistance seemed weakest. Crossed the Vosges on 22 November via the Petite-Pierre Gap, despite the terrain difficulties deemed insurmountable by the enemy. Charged, from 23 November, with participating in the operations to clear the main axes of the Saverne Gap, through the speed of the actions undertaken, he enabled the infantry divisions to quickly reach the Alsace Plain to support and thus achieve the total success of the corps' operations on the Alsace Plain.[143]

---

142 Girard, *Journal de Guerre,* pp.318–319.
143 Decision No. 363 – JORF de 04.03.1945.

Chapter 12

From Strasbourg to Berchtesgaden, 24 November 1944 to 8 May 1945

At the beginning of the afternoon of 24 November 1944, Leclerc and Dio quickly left the *Kaiserpalast,* which had become the target of German artillery. They were lucky not to have been injured by the 240mm shell that exploded on the roof of the building in which they were having lunch. There was no point in tempting fate a second time, and the command post of the *2ᵉ DB* was to be set up in a more discreet building, namely the *NSDAP*[1] hotel located on Rudolf-Hess-Strasse. Leclerc wrote a proclamation to the inhabitants of Strasbourg:

> During the gigantic four-year struggle, waged behind Général de Gaulle, the spire of our cathedral remained our obsession. We had sworn to once again display the national colours there. It is done… Inhabitants of Strasbourg! France and its allies will not repeat yesterday's mistake, the invader will not return.[2]

Then he addressed his men in Order of the Day No.73:

> 'Officers, Non-Commissioned Officers, and Soldiers of the *2ᵉ Division Blindée*, in five days you have crossed the Vosges, despite enemy defences, and liberated Strasbourg. **The Oath of Kufra is kept!** Finally, and above all, you have chased the invader from the capital of our Alsace, thus restoring to France and its army its prestige of yesterday. Our fallen comrades died as heroes. Let us honour their memory!'[3]

Dio set up his CP at the Hôtel Lutétia and in the building next door, at No.7 Christophstrasse. His *groupement tactique* had not yet recovered Subgroup Rouvillois which had remained protecting the Kehl bridge, facing the German bridgehead on the left bank of the Rhine. The Germans would blow it up in a few days, withdrawing their forces to the right bank. Subgroup Quilichini still had the mission of ensuring the defence of the northwest of the city, the district around the train station, and in the quadrilateral bordered by the Place d'Haguenau, Steinstrasse, the River

---

1   National Socialist German Workers' (Nazi) Party. Béné, the radio operator, wrote that Leclerc's CP was 'installed for security reasons in the Esca building, on the left bank of the Ill' (C. Béné, *Carnets de Route 2,* p.287) *ESCA* is the acronym of a financial company created in 1923 in Strasbourg by Maurice Burrus, an Alsatian industrialist and politician who had received the *Croix de Guerre* during the First World War and whose Germanophobia was notorious.

2   The last sentence of this proclamation was prophetic. In a few weeks, Leclerc would undoubtedly think about it, when the Americans wanted to abandon Strasbourg by withdrawing their force to the Vosges Massif to oppose von Rundstedt's counterattack in the Ardennes. *Caravane* No.7, 17 Novembre au 7 Décembre 1944.

3   Jean Compagnon, *Leclerc*, p.468.

Ill, and Wissenburgerstrasse. The mission of Subgroup Didelot remained unchanged. Its various detachments were responsible for holding the bridges over the Ill and over the canal, and then searching the houses, street by street. Didelot's men took prisoners throughout the day. Around 10:00 p.m., the area was subjected to an artillery bombardment. On 25 November, Subgroup Didelot's zone of action was modified, re-centring it beyond the Avenue des Vosges. Didelot was given the mission of reconnoitring Fort Pétain to the northwest of the city. The fort was empty. During that day, *Colonel* de Langlade seized Fort Ney, in which *Generalmajor* Vaterrodt, military governor of Strasbourg, had taken refuge with 1,000 men.

The next day, 26 November, the *GTD* issued Operations Order No.401/3. The 5th Squadron of the *RMSM* under the command of *Capitaine* Troquereau was attached to the *GTD*, which was still not the case for Subgroup Rouvillois. Dio sent his two other subgroups to explore the area 20km north of the city to reduce small isolated pockets of resistance. No significant enemy presence was detected during these patrols. In the afternoon of 26 November, a ceremony took place on the central square of Strasbourg, which had had its pre-occupation name of Place Kléber[4] restored,[5] bringing together a tank company and two infantry companies with the band of the *12ᵉ Cuirs*. *Lieutenant Colonel* Rouvillois, with the Standard of the *12ᵉ RC* was the commander of the troops. Leclerc wanted to celebrate the capture of the Alsatian capital by honouring the one who entered it first. Subgroup Quilichini detached three infantry sections. Didelot designated a detachment on foot and a detachment of tanks. A small parade in the streets of the city closed the ceremony. The city had not yet been completely cleared of residual enemy elements. Despite the risks, Leclerc sent a special message to the population of Strasbourg,[6] telling them that they had nothing more to fear. The ceremony seemed reassuring and, little by little, the population ventured out into the streets with flags and applauded the French troops.[7] The Alsatian display of flags in the streets demonstrated their attachment to France. They had defied the *Gestapo* for four years, aware that possession of a French flag meant immediate death for them. Alsace 'unable to resist physical force, has victoriously resisted all forms of moral annexation.'[8]

The US infantry divisions were settling into Strasbourg, and the *2ᵉ DB* was going to be relieved. On the orders of General Devers, the division left General Haislip's XV Corps to be attached to the US VI Corps.

During 27 November, Leclerc had his staff draw up the operations order prescribing the resumption of the offensive towards Colmar to meet the *1ʳᵉ Armée* and drive the *Wehrmacht* from the Alsatian Plain. The two armoured divisions of the *1ʳᵉ Armée* to the south were ready. *Général* Touzet du Vigier's *1ʳᵉ DB* had taken Mulhouse on 20 November; alongside it was Vernejoul's *5ᵉ DB*. To close the Colmar Pocket, de Lattre had only to launch the attack along the Rhine towards the north, in coordination with the *2ᵉ DB* and General Dahlquist's 36th US Infantry Division to the north. General Wiese's German *19. Armee* would be trapped between the Vosges and the Rhine. *Général* Leclerc told Dio and the other *colonels* that 'the Battle of Alsace was only a matter of days.'[9] Indeed, 60 kilometres then separated Leclerc's tanks from those of du Vigier and Vernejoul. The

---

4   Named in 1840 in honour of Jean-Baptiste Kléber, originally from Strasbourg, it kept its name during the period of the German Annexation of Alsace from 1871 to 1918, only losing it in 1940 when it was renamed Karl-Roos-Platz, to commemorate a pro-German Alsatian executed for espionage in February 1940.

5   Repiton-Préneuf, *2eme DB. La Campagne de France*, p.110.

6   'This meeting marked the beginning of a friendship between the *général* and the people of Strasbourg, the loyalty and warmth of which was never to fail to show itself in the future.' (Maggiar, *Les Fusiliers Marins dans la Division Leclerc*, p.226).

7   Repiton-Préneuf, *2eme DB. La Campagne de France* p.111.

8   Bourdan, *Carnet de Retour avec la Division Leclerc*, p.232

9   Destrem, *L'Aventure de Leclerc*, p.325.

fight for the definitive liberation of the Alsace Plain would thus begin for Leclerc's men. It was the *GTD*'s turn to be in the lead as the division's main effort. The small *GTD* staff drew up Operations Order No.405/3, intended for the three subgroups. The departure from Strasbourg towards the south was set for the following day. Subgroup Quilichini on Axis D and Didelot on Axis C would be at the front of the group. Subgroup Rouvillois, which had just rejoined the *GTD*, remained in reserve behind Didelot. The two fixed routes were:

Route D: Route Nationale 68 – Erstein – Osthouse – Matzenheim – Sand – Herbsheim – Rossfeld – Witternheim – Bindernheim – Wittisheim – Sundhouse – Richtolsheim, around 50km from Strasbourg,

Route C: Route Nationale 83 – Schaeffersheim – Westhouse – Benheld – Huttenheim – Riedhof – Hilsenheim – Wittisheim – Ohnenheim – Mutzenheim – Widensolem, around 70km from Strasbourg.

Their mission was to outflank enemy resistance with speed and surprise, engaging only on orders. The enemy, seeing itself outflanked and taken from behind by the first combat echelon, would most probably lay down its arms when the second echelon arrived. Dio had adopted this tactic which combined efficiency and the preservation of the lives of personnel. On 28 November at 7:00 a.m., Subgroup Didelot set off on Route C, heading south along the RN83. Delayed by destroyed bridges at Fegersheim and Lipsheim, its leading elements were stopped by heavy fire coming from the northern and western edges of the town of Erstein, which was held by a battalion of German infantry. Perceval's detachment comprising three sections of infantry (150 men) from the 2nd Company and a reduced platoon of Shermans (3 tanks out of 5) infiltrated Erstein and dislodged the German defenders block-by-block. The losses were heavy, 1 killed and 17 wounded were evacuated on the allied side. With the help of *Capitaine* Da's detachment of the *1er RMSM*, the town of Erstein was seized at 7:00 p.m.[10] Gaudet's detachment from the *12e Cuirs* captured the lightly held village of Schaeffersheim and then crossed Bolsenheim, which was unoccupied. At the end of the afternoon, it reached the village of Osthouse, south of Erstein. At 6:30 p.m., it was strongly counterattacked by German tanks and infantry, and it had to fight hand-to-hand for part of the night, but with reinforcements, it managed to push the Germans back. It was 2:30 a.m. when Gaudet finally became master of the situation. The losses were high, with 3 killed including an officer and about 10 wounded. Two tanks of the *12e RC* were destroyed by *Panzerfausts*.

Subgroup Quilichini left Strasbourg at 7:30 a.m. on Axis D. The village of Plobsheim was held with mined defences. The order was given to bypass it to the west. The state of the waterlogged ground made any off-road flanking manoeuvre difficult, even with tracked vehicles. Two kilometres south of the village, the bridge over the supply canal had been blown up, so the engineers had to erect a footbridge. There were long delays. The German artillery, from the right bank of the Rhine, continually harassed the units of the *GTD*. Night fell, and Quilichini received the order to halt.

On 29 November, a shocking piece of news arrived in the CPs of the *2e DB*. *Général* de Lattre suddenly decided to stop the south-north attack of his tanks on the Alsace Plain.[11] He completely

---

10   A document No.167/2 dated 29 November from the GTD intelligence office informs us that suspects among the population were arrested in Erstein. The document is signed by *Colonel* Vézinet, acting commander of the *GTD*. Where was *Colonel* Dio on that date? He may have been sent to Paris to carry out a mission on behalf of *Général* Leclerc with an important person in Paris, or be 'missing' for medical reasons.

11   De Lattre's decision has not found any real justification among the many historians who have questioned it. It is notable that de Lattre did not like armour, which he used in a dispersed manner to support the infantry.

changed his plans. The offensive would involve his infantry divisions attacking from west to east via Kaysersberg from the Vosges. This decision would unfortunately give the Germans time to recover and hold on to the terrain. Taking advantage of the many obstacles that crossed the Alsatian Plain along a north-south axis, the terrible weather that prevented the intervention of US aircraft, and the many villages that were as many strong points for the defensive, the German infantry and artillery would now dearly defend every metre taken by the *Ire Armée*. It would be necessary to wait until the second week of February 1945 for the Colmar Pocket to be reduced. 'The two days of lightning campaign still possible on 30 November, *Général* de Vernejoul, commander of the 5e DB, would allege after the war, became two months of killings and ruins after 3 December.'[12]

Leclerc had to bow to events. The division would experience two and a half difficult months in Alsace, interrupted in January by a return trip to Lorraine to oppose *Generalfeldmarshall* Gerd von Rundstedt. The first phase would last the entire month of December, and could be described as 'participation in the Battle of Alsace by continuous pressure exerted on the northern flank of the pocket in the regions of Friesenheim – Witternheim – Ebermunster – Sélestat, under the orders of the *Ire Armée Française*.'[13] On 29 November 1944, Subgroup Didelot received the order from the *GTD* to resume its advance towards the south to seize Sand (9km south of Erstein) then to cross the Ill and advance on the Herbsheim – Rossfeld – Bindernheim and Wittisheim axis (15km from Sand), located between the River Ill and the Rhône-Rhine Canal. The advance resumed at daybreak, but quickly proved difficult because the *route nationale* was obstructed by abatis. The German artillery was aggressive. In addition, it was not possible to outflank the enemy because of the floods between the River Ill and the canal. A light tank of the *RMSM* collapsed a wooden footbridge, drowning two soldiers. Subgroup Didelot was then ordered to set up a defensive position in the villages of Osthouse – Schaeffersheim – Bolsenheim and transfer over to *Groupement Tactique Rémy*, which was tasked with guarding the flank of the current stationing area. Dio's staff asked Rouvillois to take Quilichini's Route D, which then became the *GTD*'s sole axis as well as the division's axis of effort.

Subgroup Quilichini resumed its advance at daybreak on its route between the Rhine and the Rhône-Rhine Canal. Its vanguard seized the north of the village of Krafft but the destroyed bridge on the Ill discharge canal stopped the column: the span was 50 metres wide. Infantrymen established a bridgehead to allow the engineers to lay bridges across this canal. *Commandant* Fosse, deputy of the 1st Battalion, took command of the Krafft strongpoint. Enemy artillery hit the *GTD*'s units with heavy fire, killing *Lieutenant* Spaniel, artillery observer from the *3^e RAC*.[14] On 30 November, the *GTD* CP was set up in Plobsheim. Subgroup Didelot returned to the *GTD*'s command and Quilichini resumed the advance at dawn. *Capitaine* Lavergne's accompanying company, in the vanguard, took the firmly held village of Gerstheim by force, inflicting severe losses on the enemy, including two Mark V tanks, an 88mm gun, and six armoured vehicles.

It seems, in fact, that he did not want to accept the possibility of seeing Leclerc arrive first at Colmar, while the *2e DB* was only about 30 kilometres from that city (Jean-Christophe Notin, *Leclerc,* p.300). *Général* de Montsabert wrote in his Operations Order No.75: 'It would be in the moral interest of the *1re Armée Française* to be the first to enter Colmar.' (Destrem, *L'Aventure de Leclerc,* p.327).

12 Notin, *Leclerc,* p.300

13 Compagnon, *Leclerc,* p.476.

14 Yvan Spaniel was a Czech student who joined Free France in England in 1940 and then in Chad in 1941. He took part in the Fezzan 2 Campaign and then in all the battles led by Leclerc. Artillery observers were generally young officers or senior non-commissioned officers; they followed the vanguard of the unit that they were responsible for supporting with artillery fire. Their mission was to call for artillery fire over the radio, indicate the nature and locations of the enemy on the ground, so that the guns, which were several kilometres behind, could fire on those targets. Observers had an essential role in supporting the advance of the infantry and tanks.

Girard wrote in his journal, 'The *général* is completely refreshed. This is because Quilichini pulled off a very fine coup on Gerstheim, taking four tanks and 300 prisoners to his credit.'[15]

Noël's detachment of the *12ᵉ Cuirs* relaunched the action towards Obenheim. An enemy tank was destroyed and the village taken at 4:00 p.m. after street fighting; 100 Germans were taken prisoner. The *GTD* then asked Subgroup Rouvillois to move to the front. Rouvillois passed through Subgroup Quilichini and rushed towards Boofzheim. The German artillery conducted particularly effective blocking fire, causing losses in the ranks of the *GTD*. The border with Germany was only four kilometres east of the allied positions. The configuration of the terrain on which the German artillery was firing was familiar to them; on the other side of the Rhine, still relatively sheltered, and they were very effective. The bridge over the Westergraben Creek was destroyed. Night fell and the attack had to be postponed until the following day.

On 1 December, Dio, whose CP was in Gerstheim, very close to the fighting, decided to reinforce Rouvillois with infantry to take the large village of Boofzheim. He assigned *Capitaine* Perceval's 2nd Company of the *RMT*, from Didelot's subgroup, as reinforcements. The manoeuvre was simple. *Capitaine* Lenoir's armoured detachment arrived from Obenheim from the north, distracting the enemy's attention. Meanwhile, Perceval's detachment, based around infantry reinforced by three Shermans, infiltrated from the east. Despite the mines, the presence of four Mark IVs, and 200 Germans, the village was entered by force.[16] It was cleared at 10:30 a.m. in a thick fog where the aggression of the French infantry got the upper hand over the enemy, which also included Russian soldiers from the Vlasov Army.[17] The losses were heavy: 9 killed, including one officer of the *12ᵉ RC* (*Aspirant* Lecornu), 13 wounded, and a tank destroyed. The enemy artillery relentlessly bombarded the village, preventing the population from leaving the cellars to welcome their liberators.

2 December would be a particularly difficult day of battle for the *GTD*. Perceval's 2nd Company had been in the vanguard for two days because the terrain forced the infantry to act. The tanks could only support, having to stay on the roads because of the flooding. Some spoke of 'a lake battlefield.'[18] The infantry were forced to confront the enemy entrenched on the northern outskirts of the village of Friesenheim head-on. Reinforced by the 3rd Company, Perceval launched an assault and reached the first houses at midday. It would take the whole afternoon to drive the enemy out of the village after fierce street fighting. The human and materiel losses within the *GTD* were significant, particularly for the infantry and the sappers who were called upon to clear mines.

Progress on a single axis became difficult for the *GTD*. The floods prevented the manoeuvring that the *DB* was accustomed to. 'Straight ahead, with no possible manoeuvre, the tanks and infantry charged the villages. The lead tank was almost certainly sacrificed.'[19] The half-tracks, with even weaker armour, were also exposed not only to direct fire but also to indirect fire from artillery and mortars. For the first time since the landing, Dio and his subordinates had to accept high losses to fulfil the assigned missions. Nevertheless, the men maintained their morale and wanted to continue to fight it out even though they were stuck on the flooded plain. The cold became intense. In addition, the damnable German artillery created a climate of permanent tension with random strikes, day and night. The shells sometimes came from the south, from the 'pocket,' but more regularly from within German territory. Among this shelling, the most feared were those from the 'blue train,' also called *la vache* (the cow), a particularly

---

15   Girard, *Journal de Guerre,* p.326.

16   Loison, *Moteurs en Route,* p.35.

17   The Vlasov Army, the so-called *Russische Befreiungsarmee* (Russian Liberation Army) was formed of volunteers equipped by the *Wehrmacht* during World War II.

18   Bourdan, *Carnet de Retour avec la Division Leclerc,* p.226.

19   Repiton-Préneuf, *2eme DB. La Campagne de France,* p.117.

effective six-barrel German mortar,[20] the predecessor of today's multiple rocket launcher. These self-propelled munitions make a shrill noise as they spin around, like a sort of howl that makes your head drop into your shoulders. The six 90kgm shells explode, saturating the surface the size of half a football field with each salvo.[21] Fortunately, the German shots were met with counter-battery fire[22] coming from the *3ᵉ RAC* and the two other groups of the division, and sometimes even from the American artillery. The Germans were forced to reposition, allowing Dio's men to breathe.

On the orders of the commander of the 6th Army Group, General Devers, the *2ᵉ DB* left Patch's 6th Army on 2 December, and came under the command of the *1ʳᵉ Armée Française*, along with General Dahlquist's 36th US Infantry Division. While de Lattre was still stumbling around the Colmar region, the 'Americans, who are preparing to pounce on Germany, now have their eyes fixed on the north of Alsace.'[23] Leclerc saw this as a lost opportunity to cross into Germany,[24] and had to resolve to come under the direct orders of *Général* de Montsabert, commander of the *2ᵉ Corps d'Armée*. As someone close to 'the Boss,' Dio understood that this attachment caused concern for the commander of the *2ᵉ DB*: leaving the Americans meant returning to French procedures, which were still poorly adapted to the needs of an armoured division. But above all, it meant no longer benefiting from American logistical support: for example, destroyed vehicles were not replaced within the *1ʳᵉ Armée*. Dio also understood that two profound tactical differences divided Leclerc and de Lattre. First of all, this concerned the use of armoured vehicles. The *général* commanding the *1ʳᵉ Armée* 'although originally a cavalryman, did not appreciate large armoured *chevauchées* (attacks); he tended to use his dispersed armoured vehicles in support of large infantry units, according to a method that Leclerc considered outdated.'[25] There was also a tactical opposition on the fight to be waged in Alsace. For Leclerc, 'Alsace must be taken in the natural direction of its rivers,'[26] meaning by leading attacks in a north-south or south-north direction, rather than having to cross the natural obstacles. However, 'de Lattre's tactical intention to lead the main effort against the Colmar Pocket from the west, from the Vosges towards the Rhine,'[27] became known. Dio fully agreed with his leader. Like Leclerc, he knew that such concepts, inherited from the First World War, risked causing losses in the ranks of his *groupement tactique*. That was what happened with the capture of Friesenheim, which cost the *GTD* 15 killed, including 9 infantrymen of the RMT and 3 sappers of the *13ᵉ Bataillon de Génie*, and several dozen wounded. On 3 December, Subgroup Didelot launched the 4th Company of the *RMT* on Rhinau, a village two kilometres southeast of Boofzheim, on the banks of the Rhine. Three infantrymen were killed in the failed effort.

On 4 December, the 4th Company relieved the exhausted 2nd and 3rd Companies in Friesenheim. The units remained in their positions in the captured villages. German planes attacked and the anti-aircraft gunners of the *22ᵉ GCFTA*, who were primarily protecting the artillery batteries,

20   Mauras, *Souvenirs, 1939–1946*, p.141.
21   *Colonel* Robédat testifies that 'the blue train' made an 'apocalyptic' noise. In Italy, when his rifle section suffered this kind of fire for the first time, he had to control the beginnings of panic, his soldiers claiming that the noise came from a demon.
22   Counter-battery fire consists of hitting the estimated location of enemy artillery with one's own artillery fire. In 1944, the position of the enemy battery was estimated through observation. Now there are very precise trajectory radars which, by calculating the starting position of the trajectory, force the gunners to move after each shot.
23   Notin, *Leclerc*, p.301.
24   Leclerc feared that the Allies would seek to push the French out of the Rhineland. Girard, *Journal de Guerre*, p.325.
25   Compagnon, *Leclerc*, p.485.
26   Compagnon, *Leclerc*, p.483.
27   Compagnon, *Leclerc*, p.483.

responded, scoring a direct hit, and downing a Messerschmitt 109.[28] The next day, the village of Rhinau was finally occupied after the Germans withdrew. Rouvillois was wounded in the leg by a mine and evacuated to Strasbourg, so *Commandant* Fosse of the *RMT* took command of Subgroup Rouvillois. This interim commander demonstrated the very great cohesion existing within the *GTD*. The officers of the *12ᵉ Cuirs* and the 1st Battalion of the *RMT* fought side by side for almost five months, almost without interruption, and sometimes died together. An infantryman replaced a cavalryman on short notice and vice versa, with no impact on the operational plan of the subgroup.

The 6 and 7 December saw no change for the units of the *GTD*. This region of France usually commemorates Saint Nicholas on 6 December, and was that the reason for the relative calm? Leclerc took the opportunity to come to see for himself.

> This morning at the *GTD*, the *général* chatted with non-commissioned officers and men. All told him, with a broad smile, about their participation in the recent fighting. On returning, the *général* concluded: 'No, we can't deprive these guys of going to Berlin.'[29]

On 7 December, the Germans in Colmar received a visit from Heinrich Himmler. He arrived accompanied by 20 battalions, more than 10,000 men. These fresh battalions would relieve the front lines, and the pocket would become a real fortress. *General der Infanterie* Wiese's German *19. Armee* clung on inch-by-inch to this part of Alsace. With only the Neuf-Brisach bridge connecting them to their home country, their obstinacy was astonishing. In a few days, the men of the *GTD* would understand the reason.

The operational situation did not change during the next two days. Leclerc took advantage of this lull to sign Dio's annual report on 9 December, writing about his subordinate:

> Since the beginning of the French campaign, Colonel Dio has commanded a combined arms *groupement tactique* including tanks, infantry, artillery, engineers, and frequently reinforced by additional American units. He has given full satisfaction, taking in particular a leading part in the capture of Alençon, the manoeuvre on Carrouges, and that of the Saverne Gap. Already trained in Africa in motorised warfare, he now knows armoured warfare perfectly well, which makes him a complete leader, particularly conscientious in his command and capable of taking on the greatest responsibilities. His great character and his record of service for four years make him a leader undisputed by all. Must be promoted.[30]

When he wrote *Colonel* Dio's evaluation, Leclerc had most certainly already formed the idea of making him his successor. He emphasised his combined arms skills and his expertise in the field of armoured combat – a general officer must indeed know the use of all arms. Leclerc ended by asking that he be promoted into the general officer ranks. He would evaluate his *colonel* twice more and his evaluation would have no other purpose than to make him a *général* so that he could succeed him. In terms of career management, it was nevertheless unusual to promote to général a colonel who was only 36 years old. Yet, that was Dio's age in 1944.

No change in the situation was reported during 10, 11, 12, 13 December. The German artillery was still very active 'the shells continued to fall on the villages, which gradually collapsed.'[31]

28   Fonds Leclerc, *JMO de la 2e Batterie du 22e GCFTA*, boîte E2, dossier 1, chemise 2.
29   Girard, *Journal de Guerre,* p.329.
30   SHD, ESS de L. DIO.
31   Fonds Leclerc, *JMO du 12e Cuirs*.

Patrols were carried out to monitor the German positions. Dio decided to rotate his units, as he had done in October on the Vezouze. He even instituted a system of leave. The men, in small groups, rotated out to Strasbourg to rest and relax. The division, with the help of Strasbourg's civil authorities, organised these short stays. Dio had perceived that his soldiers 'felt forgotten, now that the country was liberated!'[32] Indeed, in the national media, the fighting taking place in that part of Alsace was relegated to second place. This naturally had a negative impact on the morale of the troops. During this period, the *GTV* seized the village of Witternheim with difficulty and with heavy losses within the *3/RMT*, particularly for the 9th and 10th Companies. Dio followed this closely, especially since the fighting was taking place near the *GTD* positions in the western zone.

Suddenly, on 16 December, *Generalfeldmarschall* von Rundstedt attacked in the Ardennes with 30 divisions and 200,000 men, beginning what was to become known as the Battle of the Bulge. The immediate objective was the city of Bastogne in Belgium and then, finally, the port of Antwerp to cut the Allied front in two. This offensive explains why the Germans under *General* Wiese clung to the Colmar Pocket. For them, it was a question of pinning down as many enemy troops as possible, hoping to benefit from the attack in Lorraine to enable them to retake Strasbourg while reaching out to von Rundstedt's troops. 'By calling upon the Allied reserves, the Ardennes salient diluted the rest of the front.'[33] This attack initially took place in the zone held by American troops. At first, Dio and his officers were not too worried about it. They had confidence in the Americans, especially in their considerable resources.

Following the meeting of 19 December, which took place at the division's CP, the *GTD* received the order to seize the villages of Diebolsheim and Zelsheim two kilometres south. The attack would be coordinated with that of the *GTV* to the west. In his Operations Order No.427/3 of the *GTD*, Dio planned to establish an attacking subgroup under the orders of his deputy, *Lieutenant Colonel* Vézinet. It included the *1er Régiment de Chasseurs Parachutistes* of the *1re Armée*, Perceval's 2nd Company, Noël's Squadron, the *2e Compagnie de Génie* with bridging assets, and two platoons of tank destroyers. Dio also obtained infantry reinforcements. The 1st Battalion of the *RMT* suffered losses in December that had not yet been replaced. The mission would involve storming the German positions through minefields. The tanks, which would not be able to keep up with the infantry, prepared to fire indirectly, as if they were artillery. It is an uncommon method of firing, but the cavalry had to know how to do it. The *3e RAC*, with reinforcements from the *40e RANA*, had to support the attack. Subgroup Quilichini was tasked with ensuring the defence of Boofzheim – Obenheim – Daubensand – Rhinau by guarding the flank of the *GTD* facing the Rhine. Ultimately, the rather risky attack, which was scheduled for 20 December, was cancelled. Indeed, 'we can only advance at the cost of excessive losses,'[34] which was contrary to what the *2e DB* was used to doing.

During 21, 22, and 23 December, patrol activities continued to be carried out from each of the points held while random German artillery fire persisted.[35] Rhinau was the target of violent mortar fire. Half the village was destroyed and the civilian population, which suffered many casualties, was evacuated.[36] Dio, aware of the pressure his men were under, had units of the first echelon relieved whenever possible. The entire division was put to work. The *général's* protection platoon and the anti-aircraft gunners of the *22e Groupe Colonial FTA* relieved the sections that had been hard pressed for 48 hours. The Americans also contributed to these reliefs. The *3e RAC* received reinforcements from the American 975th Field Artillery Battalion. Additionally, 'a battalion of

---

32   Maggiar, *Les Fusiliers Marins dans la Division Leclerc,* p.230
33   Fonds Leclerc, *JMO du 13e BG,* boîte F1, dossier 1, chemise 3.
34   Maggiar, *Les Fusiliers Marins dans la Division Leclerc,* p.228.
35   During the period from 16 to 31 December, Pierre Purson of the *12e Cuirs* (Fonds Leclerc, *Itinéraire suivi par le Troisième Escadron,* p.22) noted a shell on average every 90 seconds over 24 hours.
36   Fonds Leclerc, *JMO of 1/RMT.*

300 men from the 'Alsace-Lorraine brigade' was placed at the disposal of the *colonel* commanding the *GTD* for the defence of the rear of the sub-sector.'[37] They were resistance fighters from eastern France, who had volunteered to enlist and thus be able to participate in the fighting alongside the regular troops. All these reinforcements gave Dio's men a break. The solidarity within the *2ᵉ DB* strengthened its cohesion. All the units were combined arms units. There was no longer a '*guerre des boutons*' (war of buttons)[38] between those who fought on the front line (infantry and cavalry), those in support units (engineers, artillery, military police), and those troops in logistical support (logistics, maintenance, and medical).

On 24 December, each of the *GTD* units celebrated Christmas in the positions they held. The *GTD*'s CP was in Obenheim, Didelot's in Gerstheim, Fosse's in Erstein, and Quilichini's in Friesenheim. Leclerc's men were experiencing the positional war that their fathers had experienced in the trenches 30 years earlier. Everyone tried to find comfort to celebrate New Year's Eve. The CP of the *12ᵉ Cuirs* invited the *Marinettes*[39] to spend New Year's Eve together. Each soldier received two packages, one from a Strasbourg family containing local pastries and sweets, the other from the Red Cross. 'It was neither the volume of the packages nor their contents that were most appreciated, but rather the intention.'[40] At 3:00 p.m., *Général* de Gaulle arrived unexpectedly at Leclerc's CP in Erstein to spend Christmas with the *2ᵉ DB*. Relations had been strained recently between the two men. The commander of the *2ᵉ DB* did not want to be placed under de Lattre's orders and had made this known in writing to de Gaulle. De Gaulle, in turn, was annoyed by his young divisional commander's stubbornness.[41] With Leclerc, he 'attended a midnight mass said at 4:00 p.m., in the freezing cold, but fortunately without bombing.'[42] Then he spent Christmas Eve in the Villa Vogel in Erstein.[43] He would not be bothered by the noise of nearby battle since the German and French artillery remained quiet that night. The Christmas truce was respected. The next day, 25 December, 'a review took place by *Général* de Gaulle in a field some two kilometres from Erstein … It was armoured elements of Colonel Dio who rendered the honours.'[44] De Gaulle presented some decorations, including the *Légion d'honneur* to *Lieutenant Colonel* Fieschi, the commander of the *GTD* artillery.[45] *Lieutenant* Nouveau, the youngest and only Free Frenchman of the *12ᵉ RCA*, received the *Croix de la Libération*.[46] During the day, German artillery sent shells containing

---

37   Fonds Leclerc, *Note 439/3 du GTD du 23 décembre 1944, boîte J, dossier 1, chemise 1.*

38   A '*guerre des boutons*' is a branch rivalry; for example, between the infantry and the cavalry. (Translator's note)

39   When they were created, the ambulance drivers called '*Marinettes*' came from the Women's Fleet Service (*Service Féminin de la Flotte*, or SFF) and were assigned to the *RBFM*. They had the ranks of the French Navy and wore the famous red pompom on their headdress. The *Enseigne de Vaisseau* (equivalent to a *lieutenant* in the army) Carsignol, a famous woman aviator and parachutist, was their commander. At the start of the French campaign, the *Marinettes*, 12 in number, were detached to the 2nd Company of the *13e Bataillon Médical*, the one assigned to the *GTD*. The ambulance drivers evacuated all the wounded, French or German, from the front line to the rear aid stations. This consisted of carrying stretchers, giving first aid, loading the casualties into ambulances, and ensuring their transport. Another group, the *Rochambelles* was assigned to the GTV, while the *GTL* was supported by British Quakers.

40   Salbaing, *Ardeur et Réflexion*, pp.352–353.

41   De Gaulle went to see de Lattre after his stay with the *2e DB* and gave him the *Croix de la Libération*. He was one of the rare recipients of this order who was not a Free Frenchman. Dio and many of his companions did not understand the decision. Leclerc, for his part, must have appreciated it even less, given the circumstances.

42   Compagnon, *Leclerc*, p.482.

43   Notin, *Leclerc*, p.306.

44   Langlade, *En suivant Leclerc*, p.335.

45   Fonds Leclerc, *JMO du 3e RAC.*

46   This young officer, a Sherman platoon leader, distinguished himself near Mortain, on the Place de la Concorde in Paris, at Voyer-en-Moselle, and at Royan. He volunteered for Indochina where he became aide-de-camp to *Colonel* Massu. He made a second trip to Indochina with the *1er REC*. Cited 8 times, he was made *Commandeur de la Légion d'honneur*. He died in 1991. See full article in *Caravane* 2020, No.487, p.7.

leaflets over the front lines. These double-sided printed leaflets invited French soldiers to surrender, claiming a powerful German offensive was underway and would reverse the course of the war.[47]

There was no change to the situation from 26 to 31 December. The *JMO* reports only mention the patrolling activities with their share of losses to mines and German artillery. The artillery of the *GTD* was not left out. The *3ᵉ RAC* fired several hundred shells daily, 336 rounds on 28 December and 436 on 30th.[48] On intelligence received from the division, the *GTD* sent Defence Order No.449/3 to its units on 27 December 'anticipating an enemy attack between the Ill and the Rhine, and, in that event, the establishment of a line on the Ill to be defended by all the means of the division.'[49] Dio formed a strong infantry subgroup under Quilichini to hold the ground, and two subgroups, under *Capitaine* Joubert and *Commandant* Didelot, that could intervene to support Quilichini. Minefields were planned and the destruction of the bridges was prepared. The order was only two pages and was a model of its kind. It was thoroughly detailed, considering all scenarios while remaining clear. It demonstrated, if it needed to be, the high level of expertise of the *GTD* to manage its subgroups according to the mission, the terrain, and the enemy. The companies and squadrons continually changed organisation and leaders without problems. The *GTD* had become a formidable combat tool within the *2ᵉ DB*, due certainly to the experience acquired during combat, but especially to the value of its leaders and the high morale of its troops.

The *GTD* was informed on 28 December that all the available American reserves had been committed to contain von Rundstedt's offensive in the Ardennes. The *2ᵉ DB* was called in as a reinforcement. While the movement orders were being drafted, the units were warned to prepare for a wide-ranging movement. Yet the command could not abandon their dearly won positions. Also at the end of the year, the *GTD* saw the arrival on its positions of the advance elements of Général Garbay's *1ʳᵉ DFL*,[50] which had just been designated as their replacement. It was with a certain pleasure that the colonials of the *2ᵉ DB* saw the arrival of 'Chadian' officers, whom they knew and had left at Sabratha more than a year earlier. Dio liked Garbay who was the deputy of Colonna d'Ornano at Faya-Largeau when he himself commanded the *Groupe Nomade du Tibesti*. Within the 2nd Brigade of the *1ʳᵉ DFL*, most of the officers came from the *AEF* with the *BM4*, *BM5*, and *BM11*. The 1st Brigade was composed exclusively of the *13ᵉ demi-brigade* of the Foreign Legion with *Colonel* Delange at their head. Delange was a *méhariste* who commanded the *Groupe Nomade de l'Ennedi* when Dio commanded its counterpart in Tibesti. The 3rd Brigade was composed of troops from *AOF*. In 1943, after Sabratha, the *1ʳᵉ DFL* was engaged in Italy, and then landed in Provence in August 1944. Advancing with the *1ʳᵉ Armée* along the Rhône, it had to carry out the forced 'whitening' of its troops, near Autun. The African soldiers, poorly equipped, suffered too much in the cold. They were replaced by French resistance fighters and gendarmes, for example, for the *4ᵉ Bataillon de Marche*.

The *1ʳᵉ DFL* was participating in the fighting in the Vosges in mid-December when it was suddenly transferred by rail to Montendre near Bordeaux to be engaged against the pockets of German forces of the Atlantic. It had just enough time to engage the Germans at Saint-Ciers-sur-Gironde for 24 hours when it received the order to return urgently to Alsace, this time by road. This large sister unit of the *2ᵉ DB* comprised around 15,000 men but was predominantly infantry. There was only one anti-tank company and one 105mm short battery per brigade. Its reconnaissance regiment was the *1ᵉʳ Régiment de Fusiliers Marins* equipped with M3 light tanks and M5 howitzers. Arriving via Sainte-Marie-aux-Mines, the *1ʳᵉ DFL* descended from the Vosges between

---

47   Salbaing, *Ardeur et Réflexion*, p.354.
48   Fonds Leclerc, *JMO du 3e RAC*.
49   Fonds Leclerc, *JMO du 3e RAC*.
50   Officially, it was renamed *1re Division de Marche d'Infanterie* in Algiers in 1943. But the officers and troops never accepted it and continued to call themselves by their original name, *1re Division Française Libre*.

31 December 1944 and 1 January 1945 on an icy road leading to numerous exits from the route. From Sélestat, the different battalions would relieve the units of the three *groupements tactiques* of the *2ᵉ DB*. This large infantry unit, completely outclassed in heavy weapons, would have to hold on to the terrain to resist the next German armour attacks. It would consent to yield ground, but only at the cost of hard fighting that would exhaust the *Wehrmacht* and break its offensive. The *1ʳᵉ DFL* would thus prevent the recapture of Strasbourg by the Nazis.[51]

For the *2ᵉ DB*, the second phase of the campaign would take place 'at the beginning of January 1945, in Lorraine, west of the Vosges, in the region of Bitche-Sarre Union, covering action within the US XV Corps (General Haislip) of the 7th US Army.'[52] Indeed, on 31 December, at midnight, a new German counter-offensive began. *General* von Rundstedt's objective was to seize the Saverne Gap from the Lorraine side of the Vosges and thus cut off the Allies' essential logistical axis in Alsace. On 31 December, the *GTL* departed urgently for Lorraine. The German attack took place in the XV Corps' sector. Although the 16 December attack towards Bastogne had certainly been defeated, 'their game would consist of attacking non-stop, sometimes here, sometimes there, constantly forcing the Americans to draw on their reserves and preventing them from mounting a major operation.'[53]

Still in Alsace, the *GTD* issued a preparatory Movement Order No.461/3, dated 31 December. Dio, like his leader, was anxious about the city of Strasbourg. The bulk of the American forces had left the city to reinforce the Lorraine theatre. Fortunately, before leaving, he learnt that the *1ʳᵉ Armée Française* had designated *Général* Guillaume's *3ᵉ Division d'Infanterie Algérienne* to occupy Strasbourg and, if necessary, 'make it a Stalingrad there.'[54] Dio was also satisfied to serve in General Haislip's XV Corps again. Working relations were better with the Americans and the *2ᵉ DB* was treated better. Subgroup Quilichini was relieved by elements of the *1ʳᵉ DFL* on 1 January, as was Subgroup Didelot, which left 'to the poor and badly equipped *1ʳᵉ DFL* the guard of the sector'[55] that it occupied. On the same day, the *GTD* sent its units Regrouping Order No.462/3, dated 1 January 1945. The *groupement*, once relieved by the *1ʳᵉ DFL* in its combat locations, left Alsace to go to Lorraine. During this second phase, as part of the operational rotation within the *2ᵉ DB*, the *GTD* would remain in second echelon. It had been responsible for the division's main effort throughout the month of December, suffering heavy losses, and it had not yet been able to replace its losses. Some tank platoons and infantry sections had fallen to less than 70 percent of their human and materiel strength. On 2 January, the division began movement towards Fénétrange, the destination point assigned in Movement Order No.463/3 of 2 January. Dio's men retraced the route taken in November during the attack on Strasbourg. But this time, the population, which felt it was being abandoned, did not celebrate them. On the contrary, in some villages, the soldiers received hostile gestures from civilians who believed they were fleeing before the German advance.

The weather conditions had deteriorated, with the thermometer showing -15° Celsius (5° Fahrenheit). Even the tracked vehicles were slipping on the icy road. Fénétrange was located 25 kilometres northeast of Phalsbourg. But, after crossing the Saverne Pass, the subgroups received a counter-order (Order No.465/3) ordering them to head towards Ottwiller, redirecting their advance towards the north at Phalsbourg. This route, passing through Metting – Schalbach – Siewiller and Lohr was well known to the three subgroups of the *GTD*.[56]

51   Testimony in 2019 from *Colonel* Pierre Robédat, section leader in *BM4*.
52   Compagnon, *Leclerc*, p.476.
53   Girard, *Journal de Guerre*, p.340.
54   Massu, *Sept Ans*, p.210.
55   Fonds Leclerc, *JMO du 12e Cuirs*.
56   The subgroups were distributed in the following villages:
      Quilichini in Bettwiller, Durstel, Adamswiller, and Rexingen

The GTD was staggered in three lines over a depth of 15 kilometres, an arrangement that allowed Dio to maintain manoeuvre capabilities. He set up his CP at Asswiller, behind Quilichini. The Americans seemed to be suffering serious checks. At Phalsbourg, the *groupement* crossed paths with elements of the 117th Cavalry Squadron, which seemed to be retreating.[57] On the morning of 3 January, the *Wehrmacht* and SS troops of von Rundstedt's left wing recaptured Achen and Gros-Réderching, two towns about 10 kilometres southeast of Sarreguemines. The situation became tense for the Americans, who no longer had any reserves to contain the German advance. Eisenhower even considered realigning his force on the Vosges, which meant abandoning Strasbourg. Leclerc and his officers were appalled when they learnt of such a possibility. Leclerc sent Dio's deputy, *Lieutenant Colonel* Vézinet, to personally deliver a letter to *Général* de Gaulle. In it, Leclerc wrote that 'if such a decision were ever taken, the *2e DB* would die on the spot but would not leave.'[58] Fortunately, de Gaulle had already convinced Eisenhower at his Versailles headquarters to call off the planned withdrawal. To do so, he reportedly threatened 'the Americans with depriving them of the use of French railways if Strasbourg was abandoned.'[59]

The same day, *Colonel* Dio sent Operations Order No.470/3 to his three subgroups. Quilichini was detached and placed at the disposal of the *GTL*. At Rahling it took the place of Subgroup Massu, which was tasked with retaking Achen and Gros-Réderching. Didelot took Quilichini's position and firmly held Tieffenbach and Adamswiller facing northeast and east. Josse, who would be replaced by *Commandant* Fosse during the day, occupied Didelot's position; from Petersbach, he was able to intervene to support the US 66th Infantry Division, which was in contact. Given the persistent snow, Dio gave the order to paint the vehicles white to blend into the environment. The soldiers' helmets were also painted and sheets found to cover their uniforms. An internal note from the *GTD* headquarters in Ottwiller, dated 4 January, reported the capture of Gros-Réderching the day before by Subgroup Massu. During the night, Germans, disguised as Americans and in US tanks and vehicles, entered the *GTL*'s positions by surprise. Furious fighting lasted all night with significant losses on the allied side: six killed in the 6th Company of the *RMT* and two killed in the 2nd Squadron of the *12e RCA*. *Capitaine* Langlois,[60] commanding the 6th Company, was taken prisoner.[61] On the German side, the *JMO* of the *2/RMT* mentions 200 killed and 62 prisoners taken.

On 5, 6, and 7 January, orders and counter-orders followed one another. The position occupied at Rahling by Subgroup Quilichini proved to be completely useless given the number of Americans in the sector.[62] The batteries of the *3e RAC* were also subject to a series of orders and counter-orders. Dio did not appreciate this disorganisation, which was mainly due to the lack

---

Didelot in Petersbach and Tieffenbach, Struth and Ottwiller

Josse in Vescheim and Vilsberg

The *3e RAC* at Lohr with the 2nd Battery of the *22e FTA* which systematically deployed to provide anti-aircraft protection for the batteries.

57   Fonds Leclerc, *JMO du 12e Cuirs.*
58   Girard, *Journal de Guerre*, p.337.
59   Notin, *Leclerc*, p.309.
60   *Capitaine* Langlois de Bazillac was a former Chadian who commanded the 6th Company of the 2nd Battalion of the *RMT*. Adored by his officers and his men, he was captured by the Germans while trying to reorganise his sections' positions in the confusion of night fighting. He was interrogated bare-chested in the freezing cold. Only by the beginning of May, would he manage to escape from the Oflag in Germany, where he was held prisoner. He joined the *2e DB* in Bavaria, deeply affected by those terrible weeks. He became Leclerc's orderly officer after the war. Suffering from an incurable disease, he died sometime later. J. Salbaing, *Ardeur*, pp.369–370.
61   Fonds Leclerc, *note 474/3 du GTD en date du 4 janvier 1945*, boîte J, dossier 1, chemise 1.
62   Fonds Leclerc, *JMO du 1/RMT.*

of coordination of the Americans who had been badly shaken by the German offensive. On 8 January, Subgroup Didelot deployed again in the Wintersbourg region. The *GTD* set up its CP in Lixheim, a village taken on 21 November by Lenoir's detachment. Finally, the *3ᵉ RAC* was placed at the disposal of the US 156th Field Artillery Battalion of the 44th Infantry Division. It was the only unit of the *GTD* that intervened operationally after that date, firing 358 rounds in Lorraine on 9 January, 106 rounds on the 10th, and 376 on the 12th. The offensive in Lorraine ended in failure for the Germans, and even if they persisted for a few more days, Sarrebourg was out of danger. So, they shifted their forces towards Alsace with the energy of desperation and essentially to maintain morale among the German population.[63]

On 9 January, the *GTD* learnt that the *1ʳᵉ DFL* was facing violent attacks south of Strasbourg. A new German mountain division had been engaged against the French, news that worried the men of the *GTD*. 'We learnt that the villages in Alsace that we had departed from had been retaken by the Germans, who were said to be at Pont de Sand.'[64] The *24ᵉ BM*, surrounded in Obenheim, lost 772 men in 48 hours.[65] Against the German tanks, Garbay's infantry could do nothing. The Americans refused Leclerc's proposal to send the *GTV* as reinforcements. The *GTD* shifted towards the south on 10 January. Subgroup Quilichini withdrew from Rahling, replaced by Massu to settle in Schmittviller, 4 kilometres to the northwest. Subgroup Didelot occupied the villages of Vescheim and Wintersbourg, 30 kilometres further south. Subgroup Fosse defended the eastern part of Mittelbronn, 3 kilometres west of Phalsbourg.

As the situation stabilised at the operational level, Dio asked his subgroups to resume training, in particular target practice. A temporary firing range was found near the village of Pfalzweyer. The squadrons of the *12ᵉ Cuirs* practised firing the main guns of their tanks. The US 36th Infantry Division reported the arrival of 100 German paratroopers in the Fénétrange region. All activities on 13 January were suspended until the following day. *Lieutenant Colonel* Massu sent a letter to Leclerc to inform him 'that his unit needs rest, that it needs a month to recover and that if the situation continues, it will be combat ineffective.'[66] At first, Leclerc was annoyed by the letter. He turned to Dio during a meeting the next day to discuss this surprising paper, especially coming from Massu. But Dio immediately and bluntly confirmed that the physical and nervous state of the men in Quilichini's battalion, as well as in Putz's, was becoming worrying. Dio, as the division's infantry commander, was waiting for the end of the operation in Lorraine to report it to the *général*. Massu had beaten him to it. A section leader of the *RMT* wrote:

> Never since Normandy had we felt such a need to rest, even if only for a moment. Whole days and nights spent in the ever-harsher wet and cold, fighting almost daily since 1 November, basic food and sleep that was too often cut short, had somewhat exhausted us physically and nervously. This was reflected in the behaviour of the men, who openly complained of always being on the go.[67]

The cavalry was certainly in the same state. But only the 'Chadians' could so directly draw Leclerc's attention to such a disturbing situation. The commander of the *2ᵉ DB*, particularly attentive to Dio's analyses, took his report into account and spared his units, when possible, during the last battles in Alsace. In particular, Subgroup Massu would remain in reserve and would no longer be

---

63   Fonds Leclerc, *JMO du 13e BG.*
64   Fonds Leclerc, *JMO du 12e Cuirs.*
65   Notin, *Leclerc,* p.311.
66   Girard, *Journal de Guerre,* p.345.
67   Salbaing, *Ardeur et Réflexion,* p.339.

engaged in the first echelon. Leclerc would subsequently want to 'spare the armoured infantry: it is few in number and takes a long time to train.'[68]

On 15 January, Dio decided to regroup the *GTD* around Phalsbourg. Cantonments to accommodate the units were found. As he did after Baccarat, this regrouping would be done by organic unit. It would allow each unit to catch its breath and recondition itself in terms of personnel and equipment. The subgroups broke up and the different units joined their original regiments on 16 January. The *1/RMT* was cantoned to the northwest of Phalsbourg in the villages of Zilling – Mittelbronn – Vescheim – Metting. The *12e Cuirs* settled to the south of the *RMT* in the villages of Brouwiller – Lixheim and Saint-Jean-Kourtzerode. Until the departure from Lorraine, the *JMO* makes no further mention of anything interesting; instead, reports of the 'monotonous life of rest' or 'calm and monotonous life in the snow'[69] appear. One of the rare activities enjoyed by the soldiers were the showers in Sarrebourg, which were organised by unit.

Everything sped up on 17 January with the arrival of General Devers, the army group commander, at Leclerc's CP in Drulingen. He came to announce that the *2e DB* would leave the XV Corps to join the *1re Armée Française*. The situation was becoming critical not only to the south of Strasbourg but also, recently, to the north of the city. This was news that pleased no one within the *GTD*. These comings and goings of the *2e DB*, like a unit of firefighters, irritated the officers and the soldiers. Nevertheless, the prospect that Strasbourg could be retaken by the *Wehrmacht* restored the motivation of all of Leclerc's men. The *GTL*, whose cantonments were the closest to Alsace, and was in divisional reserve, departed again in the direction of Strasbourg, via Wasselonne, on 18 January.

On 19 January, the *GTD* sent its units Movement Order No.502/3, which was to take them to Alsace, via the following route: N61 – Phalsbourg – Saverne – N4 – Marmoutier – Wasselonne. Before setting off once again towards the Alsatian Plain, it was to be relieved in place by the American 101st Airborne Division. The *GTD* carried out its movement at night, leaving at 8:00 p.m. on 20 January. The night advance was very difficult due to a heavy snowstorm on a slippery road. The return of the *2e DB* towards the east began the third phase of the Battle of Alsace. This period, from the end of January to the end of February 1945, consisted essentially of an 'offensive participation in the Battle of Colmar, including scattered actions in support of different divisions of the *1re Armée Française*.'[70] During this third phase, the division would no longer be grouped under the orders of Leclerc, who had been given responsibility for the northern sector of Montsabert's *2e Corps d'Armée*. Its *groupements tactiques* were spread out between the *3e Division Algérienne* (*3e DIA*) to the north and the *1re DFL* to the south. It should be noted that the weather and the condition of the terrain limited the use of armoured vehicles, leaving them only a secondary role to the infantry. After being transferred to Alsace, the *2e DB* received the order to approach the River Ill from Sélestat to Strasbourg to support Montsabert's future offensive on Marckolsheim.

On 21 January, upon arrival in Alsace, Dio gave the order to reconstitute the subgroups:

> Subgroup Quilichini, with the 1st Company, *CA1*, and the 2nd Squadron of the *12e Cuirs*, settled in the village of Truchtersheim. Subgroup Fosse, with the 2nd and 4th Companies, the 3rd Squadron, occupied Behlenheim and Wiwersheim. Finally, Subgroup Person (successor to *Commandant* Didelot) was in Ittenheim with the 3rd Company and the 1st Squadron of Shermans. The *3e RAC* was detached to the *1re Armée* from 21 to 22 January to support *Groupement Raynal* of the *1re DFL* in front of Sélestat and Ebersheim as well as the 2nd Battalion

---

68   Compagnon, *Leclerc*, p.494.
69   Fonds Leclerc, *JMO du 12e Cuirs*.
70   Compagnon, *Leclerc*, p.476.

of the *4ᵉ Régiment de Tirailleurs Tunisiens* (*4ᵉ RTT*) of the *3ᵉ DIA* in front of Kogenheim and Sermersheim. On 23 January, the *GTD* artillery fired 2,000 rounds to support an offensive by the *1ʳᵉ DFL* and the American 3rd Infantry Division towards Marckolsheim.[71] On 22 January, part of the *GTL* was engaged in Kilstett. This town, located less than 10 kilometres from the north-eastern suburbs of Strasbourg, was held by a battalion of the *3ᵉ DIA*, which was surrounded. Subgroup Gribius[72] was engaged to loosen the grip and neutralise the threat to Strasbourg. Dio apprehensively followed from afar these last battles, which turned out to be very deadly once again for his *marsouins*. The 7th and 8th Companies suffered significant losses on the ground. But the Battle of Kilstett was a success and the city of Strasbourg could breathe; it would no longer be threatened by an attack coming from the north.

The attack of the *1ʳᵉ Armée* on Colmar began on Tuesday, 23 January 1945. The French forces were exhausted while the German resistance was very strong. The River Ill proved to be a serious obstacle preventing any progress. The *GTD* was in reserve behind the *3ᵉ DIA*, to the west of it, in the Stotzheim region. Leclerc 'wanted to keep it in reserve so that it could ensure the defence of Strasbourg in case the lines actually gave way.'[73] The Alsatian capital remained the object of the greatest attention, for Leclerc as for Dio. On 25 January, the commander of the *GTD*, whose CP was in Valff, sent Operations Order No.520/3. The first step was to wait, at night, for the establishment of a bridgehead at Huttenheim by the *3/RMT* reinforced by the 3rd Battalion of the *4ᵉ RTT*. Once the engineers built the bridge, Subgroup Quilichini had to emerge on the right bank of the Ill the next day.[74]

The operations order required Quilichini to seize Rossfeld, 4 kilometres southeast of Huttenheim. Then after a flanking manoeuvre, Subgroup Fosse had to attack and seize Witternheim (3km to the south). As for Person's subgroup, it had to seize the village of Neunkirch, 2 kilometres east of Witternheim. Unfortunately, the attack on the morning of 26 January did not take place under optimal conditions. The condition of the terrain prohibited any deployment and manoeuvre. 50 centimetres (20 inches) of snow covered the ground and the weather was terrible. In addition, enemy artillery pounded the site. The pneumatic tubes supporting the decks of the Treadway bridges were punctured, so the attack had to be cancelled. The *3ᵉ RAC*, reinforced by the *67ᵉ RA*, fired smoke rounds to conceal Subgroup Quilichini's withdrawal, which was moving back to the west of the River Ill. This aborted attack cost the *1/RMT* five killed and 18 wounded. The *3/RMT* lost 100 men out of action. Leclerc realised, following the warning from Dio and Massu in Lorraine, that the men[75] were truly physically and mentally exhausted. The next day, the same

---

71   Fonds Leclerc, *JMO du 3e RAC*.

72   *Commandant* Gribius was the chief of the operations section (G3) of the *2e DB* staff, serving to everyone's satisfaction. Having asked the *général* for the possibility of an operational command, Leclerc entrusted it to *Général* de Langlade who had been his commander in Senegal from 1941 to 1943. Gribius succeeded *Lieutenant Colonel* Minjonnet at the head of the subgroup. The latter remained at the *GTL* as Langlade's deputy.

73   Girard, *Journal de Guerre*, p.349.

74   The subgroup included:
   2nd Squadron,
   Capitaine Leroy's 1st Company
   Capitaine Lavergne's CA1
   A company of the *4e RTT*
   A platoon of light tanks from the *12e Cuirs*
   A Tank Destroyer platoon reduced to two Tank Destroyers
   A section of the 2nd Company of the *13e BG*

75   Fonds Leclerc, *JMO du 1/RMT*.

kind of operation[76] was to be carried out by Subgroup Fosse at the village of Sand, 5 kilometres further north of Huttenheim. This operation was finally cancelled by the *2ᵉ DB* at the end of the evening. On 28 January, the three GTD subgroups occupied the following villages:

- Subgroup Quilichini: Barr – Andlau – Mittelbergheim
- Subgroup Fosse: Heiligerstein
- Subgroup Person: Niedernai – Meistratzheim

28 January 1945 would remain a tragic day for Dio as commander of the *RMT*, with the engagement of Putz's 3rd Battalion at Grussenheim. Like the *GTD* further north, the *GTV*, south of Sélestat, was responsible for supporting the *1ʳᵉ DFL* and the American 3rdInfantry Division during the crossing of the Ill, and then to exploit towards the east by 'taking the three bottlenecks of Grussenheim, Elsenheim, and Ohnenheim, covering the Rhône-Rhine Canal near Marckolsheim.'[77] Grussenheim was the strongpoint of the German system. The movement from west to east was carried out in fits and starts, the waterways being oriented north-south. Confronting that type of obstacle, the infantry had to cross it by swimming, and then seize a sufficient bridgehead on the other side of the bank so that the engineers could work on building a bridge. The delays were then significant. The day of 27 January was devoted to crossing the Blind, a small stream to the west of Grussenheim. The weather was terrible. Many of the infantry had frozen feet and hands. In addition, it was very difficult to dig an individual foxhole in the icy ground to protect oneself. On the morning of the 28th, Subgroup Putz, reinforced by a battalion of the Foreign Legion, arrived in front of the village and prepared to attack it. The enemy, due to the slowness of the advance, was able to react effectively with artillery fire. Early in the afternoon, a shell fell on a group of officers, killing *Lieutenant Colonel* Putz[78] and *Commandant* Puig, serving on the *GTL* staff. *Commandant* Debray, Putz's deputy, took command and, at the cost of heavy losses, seized the town by an outflanking manoeuvre from the south. The capture of the village of Grussenheim came at an exorbitant human cost for the *2ᵉ DB*, with 66 killed and 260 wounded. The 3rd Battalion of the *RMT* alone lost 34 men including 4 officers. The *GTV* lost more killed in this village than the entire division during its ten-day campaign between Baccarat and Strasbourg.[79]

Dio was revolted. Usually calm and measured in his judgements, the commander of the *GTD* made known to Leclerc his opposition to being under the orders of certain leaders of the *1ʳᵉ Armée*. He knew that Leclerc was as enraged as he was. Leclerc also immediately contested the orders of *Général* de Montsabert[80] by refusing to engage the *GTV* in the attack on the village of Elsenheim.

76   Fonds Leclerc, *Ordre No. 523/3, 27 janvier 1945, JMO du Sous-groupement Fosse*, boîte J, dossier 1, chemise 2.

77   Rigault, *Le Régiment de Marche du Tchad, Koufra 1941 – Sarajevo 1995*, p.117.

78   The funerals of *Lieutenant Colonel* Putz, *Commandant* Puig, *Lieutenant* Dusehu, and *Marsouin* Thorez took place in Sélestat, their coffins resting on a machine gun car. Putz has since been buried in the military square of Grussenheim, surrounded by 34 brothers-in-arms. To succeed him at the head of the 3rd Battalion, Dio suggested to Leclerc the name of Fernand Barboteu, who was in his class at Saint-Cyr. Barboteu was part of Leclerc's Chadian phalanx. As leader of the *Groupe Nomade de l'Ennedi*, he participated in the victory of Kufra. At the end, *Capitaine* Barboteu was entrusted with the defence of the oasis and Fort El Tag. By a curious twist of fate, in September 1943 in Djidjelli, Barboteu, then a *commandant*, had to turn over command of the 3rd Battalion to *Commandant* Putz. In 1945, *Commandant* Barboteu's subgroup had the honour of being the first to arrive at Hitler's Eagle's Nest.

79   Destrem, *L'Aventure de Leclerc*, p.332.

80   Excerpt from the dialogue between Leclerc and Montsabert, who, persisting with his order of attack, was answered by Leclerc:
      'When one of my subordinates tells me that the order I give him is bull**it, I think about the arguments he presents to me.

The commander of the *2e DB* had a very stormy meeting with *Général* de Lattre in Molsheim three days later. On the morning of 31 January, information circulated that the enemy had broken contact during the night and had withdrawn beyond the canal and even beyond the Rhine.[81]

At the end of January in Alsace, 'it was the thaw, this thaw in the literal sense seemed to be accompanied by a debacle among the enemy, whose resistance seemed to suddenly collapse.'[82] Subgroup Fosse went to Sand and, without waiting for the engineers to complete the bridge under construction, made the river crossing with Ferrano's company, which entered Obenheim on foot at 4:00 p.m. The subgroup crossed the Ill in the middle of the afternoon but was slowed down by the numerous booby-trapped obstacles left by the Germans. The engineer section suffered losses while clearing mines. Then Fosse reached Rossfeld on 1 February at 3:00 a.m. Perceval's company had set up for the night in Boofzheim. Then the two companies, still on foot, took over Diebolsheim (Perceval) and Friesenheim (Ferrano) during the day. History recorded that Perceval's company liberated Boofzheim and Friesenheim twice, once in early December 1944 and then definitively in early February 1945.[83] In 36 hours, Subgroup Fosse recaptured most of the ground that the *GTD* had taken in December 1944. During the day, *Colonel* Dio was delighted to see *Lieutenant Colonel* Rouvillois return, taking over command of the *12e Cuirs*. In the evening, his mood deteriorated when he learnt that the *1re Armée* had requested that the wounded of the *2e DB* no longer be subject to the procedures specific to American personnel, because the men of the *1re Armée* could not benefit from them. The leaders of the *2e DB*, including Dio, found this request contemptable. Subgroup Fosse remained in its positions, proceeding to clear mines from the region. The other two *GTD* subgroups returned to their initial positions west of the Ill. Subgroup Fosse in turn moved to the west of the river on 4 February.

The next day, *Colonel* Dio ordered the various components of the three subgroups to rejoin their organic units. The *1/RMT* was divided across the three villages: Barr – Mittelbergheim – Andlau. The *12e Cuirs* settled in the villages of Bischoffsheim – Niedernai – Meistratzheim. From 6 to 14 February, the *GTD* units recovered and rested. The vehicles were cleaned and returned to their original colour. But the final battles continued. The *GTL* liaised with the elements of the *1re DB* in Fessenheim on 8 February. The Colmar Pocket was collapsed, thus ending the operations in Alsace. The 2nd Company of the *RMT* celebrated this victory by saying: 'Alsace is completely liberated. The old veterans are few and far between, but the spirit of Chad remains and inspires the young people who have come to raise up the dead and support the living. Soldiers of the *Armée d'Afrique*, combatants of the *Corps Franc*, escapees from France via Spain, enlisted from Normandy and Paris, *Marsouins* and cavalrymen, sappers, artillerymen, and sailors, with the veterans of Chad, kept the oath of Leclerc on the evening of one of the first victories of Free France.'[84] But the war was not over for the *2e DB*. While waiting for operations to resume, the division's units were able to lick their wounds, train reinforcements and repair their equipment. These periods of relative calm were also used to update administrative and management tasks such as evaluations. On 8 February, Leclerc signed Dio's evaluation in which he wrote:

You mean I'm full of bull**it.
Precisely.
Would you like to put this in writing for me?
If you want.' (Girard, *Journal de Guerre,* p.351)
When he learnt of this exchange, Dio agreed with Leclerc and did not hide his support for Leclerc's position.

81 Fonds Leclerc, *JMO du 1/RMT.*
82 Fonds Leclerc, *JMO du 13e BG.*
83 *From Fort-Lamy to Strasbourg,* p.25.
84 *From Fort-Lamy to Strasbourg,* p.25.

Colonel Dio has taken part in all the operations under my command since 1940. For over a year, he has commanded a *groupement tactique* that distinguished itself in Normandy, Lorraine, and Alsace. Very good character, enjoying undisputed prestige among all, an excellent organiser, *Colonel* Dio has remarkable combat experience. He fully deserves his stars. Some of his classmates, with far fewer war honours than he, already have them. The objection of age should therefore not be raised.[85]

As in the previous evaluation, Leclerc supported promoting Dio to the rank of *général* to help achieve the idea he had certainly formed of having Dio succeed him. To make it happen, he put pressure on the decision-maker, in this case *Général* de Gaulle, by mentioning, without naming him, the fact that Billotte was appointed *général* at the end of 1944. The latter was in fact from the same Saint-Cyr class as Dio, but he was two years older. He was therefore 38 years old when he was promoted. Dio was only 37 years old in 1945, which is why Leclerc ended by saying that the objection of age should not be raised because Dio was also deserving.

The *GTD* was on the front line during the first phase of December. It was called on much less during the following two phases in January. Nevertheless, *Colonel* Dio, who was also the commander of the *RMT*, suffered an emotional blow with the 2nd Battalion in Gros-Réderching and with the 3rd Battalion in Grussenheim. In that village of the Haut-Rhin, he lost one of his three battalion commanders. With *Lieutenant Colonel* Putz, who was much older than him, he had established a relationship based on a great mutual respect. When this former Spanish Republican *general*, who became a battalion commander in the *Corps Franc d'Afrique*, introduced himself to Dio in Djidjelli in Algeria, the connection between the two men was instantaneous.

To celebrate the return of Alsace to France, de Gaulle came to preside over a ceremony in Colmar on 10 February 1945. He presented the star of a *Grand Officier* of the *Légion d'honneur* to *Général* Leclerc, the fourth rank in the *Légion*. The following day, the *2ᵉ DB* left the *1ʳᵉ Armée* and came once again under the command of the US XV Corps, which Leclerc had requested for several weeks. The division was able to join the American corps which was still stationed in Lorraine. While waiting for the departure, the *12e Cuirs* took the opportunity to organise a ceremony at its level on 12 February in Niedernai in the presence of *Général* Leclerc and *Colonel* Dio. A certain number of officers of the regiment were raised to the rank of *Chevalier* of the *Légion d'honneur*. *Lieutenant Colonel* Rouvillois received the rosette of *Officier* of the *Légion d'honneur* for his first-class campaign at the head of a subgroup of the *GTD*.

The *groupement* left Alsace on 15 February at 11:00 a.m. with the *2ᵉ DB*, to become the reserve of the XV Corps in the area of Morhange. This 180km movement was carried out without incident. The villages in this area of Lorraine were partly destroyed, limiting their capacity to house the troops. This forced the units to disperse widely to find lodging with the inhabitants. After seven months of almost uninterrupted operations, the *groupements tactiques* were able to rest and recover. The *GTD* needed it like the others. The last three months were very difficult in part due to the weather, but mainly because of the positional fighting that was imposed on them, which was poorly suited to an armoured division. It was a war of attrition. The bodies and nerves subjected to permanent stress under constant artillery fire were put to the test. The stay in Lorraine was not the most pleasant in the almost deserted villages. The piles of manure in front of the houses made the men long for Alsace.[86] Leisure time was rare, but he soldiers sought to improve their daily lives. There were many fish ponds in the area, and with a grenade and a boat, fishing always turned out wonderfully, especially when catching perch and pike.

---

85 SHD, L. Dio file, *Notes et Appréciations.*
86 Salbaing, *Ardeur et Réflexion*, p.399.

Colonel Dio took advantage of the period to send officers and soldiers on leave. Some of his *mars-ouins* had not seen their families for several years. The period of leave was restorative to those who could take advantage of it. At the same time, it allowed them to become aware of the atmosphere in French society at the beginning of 1945. Those returning from leave painted a confusing picture of the situation within the country to their comrades. The occupation had changed mentalities and created great divisions between the French people. Some had taken advantage of the purge to settle disputes that often had nothing to do with the occupation. The last-minute resistance fighters were especially making their own law in 'corners' of the provinces. The extreme left and the communist party supported these movements, some of which were evolving towards a kind of anarchy. On leave in Auch, *Lieutenant* Salbaing reported the presence of armed groups that had appropriated administrative buildings 'with the very definite intention of controlling and operating all the cogs of the administration for their own benefit.'[87] What was alarming was that the population remained passive, visibly no longer interested in the fate of the country. In Toulouse, a man named Ravanel, head of the *FTP*,[88] ruled over the city with the Spaniards.[89] France could potentially slide into a form of anarchy.

Within the *GTD*, *Commandant* Quilichini departed command of the 1st Battalion on 23 February – designated to take over the personnel section of the *3ᵉ Corps d'Armée Français*, which was then forming. Dio and the battalion's officers were all sad to see him leave. During a simple farewell drink bringing together a large number of officers from the three *RMT* battalions at the 1st Battalion CP in Riche, Dio thanked him for his service within the *GTD*. Quilichini spent only five months at the head of the 1st Battalion. He, the human resources expert, demonstrated outstanding operational leadership qualities at the head of his subgroup. Dio reminded him of Vezouze, Baccarat, Phalsbourg, and then the villages of Kraft, Gerstheim, and Obenheim, seized in a hard-fought struggle at the end of the year. His subgroup, along with that of Rouvillois, was the spearhead of the *GTD*. Quilichini's deputy, *Commandant* Fosse, took over command of the 1st Battalion.

On 24 February, Leclerc organised a parade in Marimont during which he presented the *Croix d'Officier* of the *Légion d'honneur* to his superior, General Haislip. Dio, who also liked the American officer, with whom he had excellent relations, made the trip. The 1st Battalion provided two companies of 160 men for the event. During the ceremony, Dio heard Leclerc urging Haislip to ensure that the *2ᵉ DB* was kept in his corps with a view to returning to Germany. Unfortunately for the commander of the *2ᵉ DB*, his wish would not be granted. Indeed, 'It is not for the east that the *2ᵉ DB* is designated, but for the west, for the Atlantic front.'[90] The Parisian military leaders convinced the head of government to respond to Général de Larminat's pressing request. Larminat, commanding the *FFO* (*Forces Françaises de l'Ouest*) was unable, with his FFI division, to reduce the isolated resistance, including that at Royan.[91]

In the meantime, Leclerc was offered command of a corps that he would have to establish. The général thought about his succession at the head of the division. Girard wrote in his diary on 25 February: 'The problem also arose of who would replace the général at the head of the division. Dio? Langlade? A third party? Opinions were divided and there were some unexpected ones.'[92]

---

87   Salbaing, *Ardeur et Réflexion,* p.397.
88   The *Francs-Tireurs et Partisans* was a communist resistance organisation. (Translator's note)
89   Destrem, *L'Aventure de Leclerc,* p.337.
90   Notin, *Leclerc,* p.319.
91   'It is a rectangular pocket formed by Royan – l'Aiguillon – La Tremblade and the tip of La Conche, which, until now, has resisted the assaults of the FFI of the Gironde Division, formed of the Oléron and Médoc Brigades.' (Gribius, *Une Vie d'Officier,* p.179).
92   Girard, *Journal de Guerre,* p.362.

Dio's name came first. Apparently he was Général Leclerc's favourite choice. However, the most logical option would be to designate Général de Langlade. He was a cavalryman, already promoted to the rank of général, with sufficient seniority in service, and having proven his merits at the head of a *groupement tactique*. It was a difficult choice for Leclerc.

The move westward was becoming clearer and, on 25 February, the *GTD* sent a preparatory movement order to its units (No. 554/3 GTD of 25 February). The planned destination was Châteauroux. Only armoured vehicles would be transported by train from Sarrebourg station (Order No. 557/3 of the *GTD* of 27 February). The half-tracks and wheeled vehicles took to the road. Dio wondered why he was going to the centre of France. It seemed that de Gaulle had told Leclerc that sending the *2ᵉ DB* was necessary to restore calm to the regions in the grip of disorder. 'The *2ᵉ DB* will instil in the country the certainty of a strong state.'[93] In Loches, the *12ᵉ Cuirs* put an end to the actions of an *FFI* (or *FTP*) leader who was ruling the region by 'raising taxes, causing numerous exactions and, where necessary, not hesitating to kill.'[94] The confused situation of the immediate post-war period in certain regions of France was consistent with what the soldiers on leave had said on their return. Nevertheless, Colonel Dio was not far from thinking that it was a pretext to distance *Division Leclerc*, which created a lot of envy and jealousy around it. Following its troubles with the *1ʳᵉ Armée*, the *2ᵉ DB* seemed to have been put in 'penance,' far from the operational front.

On 27 February, the advance elements left Lorraine, some to prepare the stage lodgings during the move, others to organise the cantonments on arrival. In the afternoon, Colonel Dio in turn organised a ceremony, at his CP in Vergaville, to present the RMT insignia to General Haislip[95] and make him an honorary corporal of the colonial troops. It is a tradition of the branch, as well as in the Foreign Legion, to make the great leaders honorary corporals of another branch or another army, as a sign of appreciation.

The next day, the *GTD* units began the 700km move, which would take three days, passing through Nancy, Chaumont, Tonnerre, Auxerre, Nevers, Bourges, and Châteauroux. The rail convoy also took three days; the tanks were on flatcars while the soldiers were crammed into 3rd class passenger cars. The *2ᵉ DB* reached its cantonment areas on 2 March. The GTD column broke up at Châtillon-sur-Indre, 50km northwest of Châteauroux. Dio wanted to regroup his three battalions. He set up his CP at the Château de Coudray southeast of Loches. The 1st Battalion occupied the area between Châtillon-sur-Indre and Loches. The 3rd Battalion settled in Valencay, and the 2nd Battalion in the area around Châtillon-sur-Indre. The *12ᵉ Cuirs* were stationed in Loches and its surrounding area. The *3ᵉ RAC* took possession of Beaulieu and the villages north of the Loches national forest.[96] Its planes (Piper Cubs) were in Beaulieu at the gates of the town of Loches.

Dio resumed command of the three battalions of his regiment. He asked the three battalion commanders to reconnect with the rules of life and discipline that the fighting had stretched. The men's uniforms left something to be desired. They would also have to work on their driving because there had been too many accidents with their vehicles. Very quickly, the *colonel* ordered his battalions to organise training platoons at their level to train *aspirants* from among those who had distinguished themselves in combat, as well as junior officers. During this period, the battalion strengths were largely supplemented by young recruits trained at Saint-Germain-en-Laye. With

93 Notin, *Leclerc*, p.319.
94 Loison, *Moteurs En Route*, p.48.
95 This American general officer, whom Dio and all his men appreciated for his calm demeanour, his tactical sense, and his pragmatism, ended his career in 1951 as Vice-Chief of Staff of the US Army, the second highest position of the entire American Army.
96 Mauras, *Souvenirs, 1939–1946*, p.178.

the return of the wounded, some battalions were even overstrength, with nearly 1,200 men (*JMO of the 3/RMT*). Redistribution was carried out at the regimental level. Dio ensured that his men rested and relaxed, initiating a leave rotation. For the *marsouins* of the *RMT*, this stay in the Indre was like a vacation. Massu wrote that it was two months of idleness.[97] The 2nd Battalion's mess hall was recreated as it had been in Témara.

The spring of 1945 was wonderful. The men had trouble realising that only a month earlier they had been playing with death and cold. Football matches against civilians were organised. It must be said that the population of Tours gave Leclerc's men a very warm welcome. They organised festivities in honour of the *2ᵉ DB* and the 'waltz musette' was on the agenda.[98] There were many distractions, and the men rediscovered the pleasure of sleeping in beds.[99] The stay was humorously called by some 'the wine campaign.'[100] In the support units, 'life in Châteauroux was nothing but evenings, galas, balls, and parties. Everyone was keen to forget the last few years, and especially the months spent since Paris.'[101] During this period, the *RMT* saw many officers promoted: *Capitaines* Dronne (9th), Fonde (7th), Joubert (3rd), and Florentin became *commandants*; *Commandant* Fosse was promoted to *lieutenant colonel*. These promotions were an opportunity to get together for a drink organised in each battalion followed by a lunch, presided over by *Colonel* Dio.

On 2 March, *Général* Leclerc considered the possible composition of his future corps. He wrote to de Gaulle: 'Dio, promoted to *général*, would be perfectly capable of taking an infantry division, *Général* de Langlade then taking the *2ᵉ DB*.'[102] Leclerc wanted to make Dio a *général* and wanted to keep him within his corps. For the moment it was logical that the cavalryman Langlade would command an armoured division and the *méhariste* Dio an infantry division. It should be noted that Leclerc wanted to give his faithful deputy command of a division, without going through the intermediate level, which would be a brigade. But in the immediate future, the *2ᵉ DB* had a mission to fulfil: reduction of the pockets of the Atlantic.

Leclerc did everything he could to be sent as quickly as possible to Germany where the Allies were pushing forward to meet the Russian Army. Various arguments were then presented to him to confirm his mission – the Picard was not a man to let himself be shifted around without being convinced of the merits of what he was being asked to do. He sent *Colonel* Dio to Royan, asking him to make the most complete assessment possible of the situation. Dio was indeed available. And it was he, and he alone, who had the necessary weight with *Général* de Larminat, as a Free Frenchman, to go and carry out this kind of mission within the *Forces Françaises de l'Ouest*. He did not have an official mandate, but he would know how to use his prestige and diplomacy to have the possibility of understanding the situation without appearing too intrusive. In addition, Leclerc had great confidence in Dio's analyses. Dio knew the troops perfectly and was capable of gauging the operational value of a unit in a few minutes. *Colonel* Dio carried out the assessment mission in the first half of March, leaving command of the *RMT* and the *GTD* to his deputy, *Lieutenant Colonel* Vézinet.

When Dio's report reached Leclerc, it was uncompromising. First, he dismantled one of the main arguments put forward by Leclerc to justify the urgent reduction of the Royan pocket. His report began: 'It does not seem that the Royan operation would have a direct and immediate effect on the use of the port of Bordeaux.' He proved it in the following lines. Then, he discovered that the reduction of the pocket had no other objective than a moral one: the Germans of Royan must

97   Massu, *Sept Ans,* p.217.
98   Fonds Leclerc, *JMO du 3/RMT.*
99   Fonds Leclerc, *JMO du 12e Cuirs.*
100 Rigault, *Le Régiment de Marche du Tchad, Koufra 1941 – Sarajevo 1995,* p.121.
101 Mauras, *Souvenirs, 1939–1946,* p.177.
102 SHAT 1K239.8; Notin, *Leclerc,* p.319.

not return to Germany undefeated. However, after examining the question, Dio asserted that success could not be assured under the conditions in which the operation was currently being mounted. The reasons for his reservations about future success were based on several observations. The Germans had high morale, were well armed and prepared, and had powerful artillery. On the other hand, on the French side, he noted serious shortcomings concerning the aptitude of the officers, *FFI* in particular, in communications assets, in the arming of the troops, and in the low levels of ammunition. On the operational level, of the 15 battalions present, only five seemed to him capable of being engaged against the enemy. To make this kind of assessment, Dio went straight to the men and spoke directly with them, as was his habit.

Before going to deliver his report to Leclerc, Dio referred it to *Général* de Larminat. They knew each other well from Cameroon. Dio did not hesitate to share with him his assessment that demonstrated that the operation, as it was currently set up, was likely to fail. According to Dio, it was necessary to revise the plans and to implement other means. He easily convinced Larminat who, certainly poorly supported, then offered Dio command of the Northern attack column. Dio refused before even speaking to his chief. *Général* Leclerc was very interested in the report and, of course, informed *Général* Juin, who was Chief of the General Staff of the National Defence. Juin even asked to speak with *Colonel* Dio on 3 April in Paris. Leclerc also met with American military leaders to try to be relieved of this secondary mission. But nothing worked. At the end of March, *Général* de Gaulle and General Devers, operational commander-in-chief, confirmed the mission of the *2ᵉ DB* in support of the *FFO*.

The work carried out by Dio would prove important insofar as the plan of operations would be resumed, reinforcements were added with colonial units, and better American involvement was added, bringing additional artillery and, crucially, air support. The operation was called INDEPENDENCE. The *2ᵉ DB* put its guns at the disposal of *Général* de Larminat. All the artillery, the armoured vehicles of the *12ᵉ RCA*, the *12e Cuirs*, and the *RBFM*, the 1st Company of the *13ᵉ Génie*, and the communications assets were integrated into a super group, placed under the orders of *Général* de Langlade.

The entire *RMT*, the *501ᵉ RCC*, the *1ᵉʳ RMSM*, the *13ᵉ BG*, and the *22ᵉ GCFTA* remained in the centre of France. Seeing this, Dio's idea that this mission entrusted to the *2ᵉ DB* was in fact a pretext to move it away from the real German operational theatre was strengthened. An armoured division was not the best suited unit to attack the fortified redoubt of Royan. Internally, this distribution within the *DB*, between those engaged in Royan and those remaining in the centre of France, gave rise to reflections and often criticism. Indeed, the units engaged in Operation INDEPENDENCE were almost all the former units of the *Armée d'Afrique* while those that remained 'hot' were the 'Free French' units, with the exception of the *3ᵉ RAC*. Not without a certain irony, *Commandant* Gribius,[103] who commanded a subgroup, wrote: 'If Operation 'Germany' were launched unexpectedly, it was fitting that the old comrades would be the first to be called upon to attack the enemy.'[104] Old frustrations resurfaced and, in this specific case, they seemed justified. It is true that Leclerc was loyal to those who had served him since Chad. Despite the merger with the *Armée d'Afrique* in which remarkable men emerged like Langlade and Minjonnet, as well as his classmates Rouvillois and La Horie, to name only the most senior, Leclerc would always favour those from Chad. He considered that those who were with him from the start deserved to be 'served'

---

103 *Commandant* Gribius was seriously wounded in the face on 15 April near Fondebeau. He became one of the *gueule cassée* (those with a broken face), the name given since the First World War to soldiers wounded in the face. He was not able to return to combat with the *2e DB* before the end of the war. He ended his career with the stars of a *général*.

104 Gribius, *Une Vie d'Officier*, p.180.

first in operational terms. Entering Germany represented for his 'Chadians' a just reward after four years of effort with him.

There was also certainly a more pragmatic reason for this choice to spare the Free French units. They 'had not stopped being in the breach for nearly five years, and were thus deserving of leave and rest.'[105] In mid-March, activities intensified for the units that were going to be engaged, while for the others, rest and relaxation continued. On 16 March, the 2nd Battalion of the *RMT* organised a ceremony, presided over by Leclerc and Dio, to present a large number of decorations to the officers and soldiers who had distinguished themselves. On the list of recipients, Leclerc saw the name of his son, Henri, for the award of a *Croix de Guerre*. He turned to Massu in a gruff tone: 'Why this cross for my son? I don't agree.' *Lieutenant Colonel* Massu immediately retorted, to Dio's great joy, with, 'Excuse me, *Mon Général*, but this does not concern you. This soldier deserves to be rewarded. That is the point of view of his *capitaine*, and it is mine, as well. Whether he is your son or not changes nothing.' Massu wrote that, 'Young Henri, his eyes shining with joy, was decorated by his father, who was as happy as he was. The traditional embrace was not purely a formality, and we were all moved.'[106]

During that period when the *GTD* was put into hibernation, Dio nevertheless kept an eye on the units that it was composed of. On 22 March, for example, he inspected the cantonments of the *3ᵉ RAC*.[107] Before the advance towards Royan, a large ceremony took place at the Loches Stadium on 28 March, followed by a parade, bringing together the entire *GTD*. Each battalion of the *RMT* provided 14 sections of 30 men each. *Général* Leclerc reviewed the units alongside *Colonel* Dio. The commander of the *2ᵉ DB* decorated the *RMT* Colours with the *Croix de Guerre* with palm. Dio, in summer dress, firmly presented the Colours to Leclerc who pinned the *Croix de Guerre* on the streamer. All the *marsouins* of the *RMT* were thus honoured, particularly those who had given their lives since Utah Beach. During the ceremony, many individual decorations were awarded by the division commander to the men of the *GTD*. *Lieutenant Colonel* Fieschi received the *Croix de Guerre* with palm for the formidable support provided by his *bigors* during the Battle of Alsace.

The operations order concerning the engagement towards the Atlantic reached the *GTD* on 31 March. On 4 April, the *12ᵉ Cuirs* and the *3ᵉ RAC*, included in Operation INDEPENDENCE, began their movement towards Cognac and Saintes. The tracked vehicles embarked on the trains on 4 and 5 April at Villedieu. The wheeled movement by road started on 5 April. Once it arrived on site, *Super Groupement de Langlade* was organised into combat order and prepared for the attack. Colonel Dio would be part of the movement, with two regiments of his *GTD* engaged. He followed the operations with the headquarters of the *2ᵉ DB*.[108] On the morning of 14 April, hundreds of bombers[109] dropped tons of bombs on Royan and the Arvert peninsula, and the land attack was launched shortly after. The tanks of the *12ᵉ RC* and the *12ᵉ RCA* attacked with Larminat's infantry, supported by the division's artillery, reinforced with US artillery battalions. The offensive, preceded by aerial bombardments, continued over the next two days. The fighting was fierce. The presence of the tanks was decisive and allowed the pockets of enemy resistance to be gradually reduced, particularly the German concrete bunkers. The triple minefields in front of the German positions were crossed aggressively but at the cost of several tanks destroyed. *Commandant*

---

105 Salbaing, *Ardeur et Réflexion,* p.400.

106 Massu, *Sept Ans,* p.217.

107 Fonds Leclerc, *JMO du 3e RAC.*

108 The service record (ESS) mentions Colonel Dio's participation in the Royan operations.

109 As many as 1,450 B-24 Liberators and B–17 Flying Fortresses pounded the outer defences of Royan. Unfortunately, a large part of the bombs fell instead on the city of Royan, which was almost entirely destroyed.

de Person, Rouvillois's deputy, was killed by a burst of shells from the German artillery. On 17 April, all that remained to be reduced was the fort of Coubre where the German commander, *Konteradmiral* Hans Michahelles, had taken refuge.[110] The final assault was being prepared, but finally, after some negotiations, the Germans surrendered on 18 April.

A guard of honour was formed when the Germans departed their stronghold to salute the courage of the fighters who fought so ferociously.[111] Dio witnessed the end of the fighting. He accompanied his faithful *12e Cuirs* and his no-less-faithful friend Rouvillois, the regimental commander.[112] The Gironde estuary was not yet completely liberated, but *Général* de Larminat returned the elements of the *2e DB* to *Général* Leclerc. Before leaving, a ceremony to celebrate the end of the fighting in the Atlantic pockets brought together all the troops who had participated. On 22 April, at Les Mathes, *Général* de Gaulle came to review them. The Royan pocket was reduced in four days, a shorter period than expected. By allowing the operation to be undertaken in better conditions than those initially planned, *Colonel* Dio played an important role in Royan that has not been previously acknowledged. Nevertheless, he proved essential for the *2e DB*.

The rapid resolution of this battle would allow the *2e DB* to transfer its units to Germany before the fighting of the Second World War ended in Europe. Indeed, since mid-April, the commander of the *2e DB* had been harassing his superiors for the green light to push his troops into Germany. He noted that the Allied units had already pushed far into Germany. A race against time was underway with the Russians. The *1re Armée Française*, for its part, had crossed the Rhine, passed through Württemberg, emerged in Baden, and was arriving from the north in Bavaria.[113] Leclerc absolutely wanted his division to participate in the conquest of Germany, weapons in hand – he considered that it was a right for those who were the first, those who had been fighting against the Axis forces for more than four years. Anxiety was growing in the ranks of the *2e DB*, 'as the waiting in Indre continues. The German Army is cracking on all sides. The Russians are under the walls of Prague, Vienna, Berlin.'[114] Leclerc had *Groupement Tactique Guillebon*, minus its artillery, the *40e RANA*. The order was given to reform the *GTV*, starting at the beginning of April, with the 3rd Battalion of the *RMT* under the command of *Commandant* Barboteu, the *501e RCC* of *Commandant* Delpierre (who had replaced Cantarel), and the reinforcement units. The three subgroups under the command of *Commandant* Sarazac, *Commandant* Delpierre, and *Commandant* Barboteu were reconstituted to be able to leave without delay. However, the green light would not be given to Leclerc until after the success at Royan.

The train for the tracked vehicles of the *GTV* was loaded on Sunday, 22 April; the convoy of wheeled vehicles left the same day. After crossing the Rhine at Frankenthal, the *2e DB*, which was attached to General Milburn's US XXI Corps on 25 April, was given Salzburg in Austria via Berchtesgaden as its objective. Leclerc and his group commanders were ultimately happy to receive this objective. They knew that they would not be able to go to Berlin because the Red Army had beaten them to it. However, Berchtesgaden, in the heart of the Bavarian Alps, was considered a strong symbol of Nazism. It was Hitler's birthplace. His summer residence, the Berghof, which Bormann built for him at the top of the Kehlstein spur for his 50th birthday on 30 April 1939 was there. The summer residences of the main Nazi leaders were places that seemed impregnable, guarded by the SS Praetorian Guard. Hitler received his allies there with pomp, as well as the submissive leaders, to show them his power.[115] Leclerc's men were happy to go and seize, in a final

110 Michahelles is often spelled Michaelis.
111 Fonds Leclerc, *JMO du 12e Cuirs*.
112 Pellissier, *Le Général Rouvillois*, p.114.
113 Fonds Leclerc, *JMO du 13e BG*.
114 Fonds Leclerc, *JMO du 3/RMT*.
115 Ambassador François-Poncet had given a precise description of it in 1939 with photos published in

challenge, the place where Hitler had promised to deliver the most stubborn fight with his SS.[116] They were ready to fight these Nazis, whom they so hated.

In the last week of April, Colonel Dio, still in Indre, was impatient. Without waiting for the missing elements of his *GTD* – namely the *12e Cuirs* of Rouvillois, the *3e RAC* of Fieschi, as well as the 3rd Squadron of the *RBFM* – he reassembled near Châteauroux those who had not participated in the fighting of Royan. The 1st Battalion of the *RMT*, the 2nd Company of the *13e BG*, the 5th Squadron of the *1er RMSM* and the 2nd Battery of the *22e GCFTA*, as well as the *2e Compagnie Médicale* of the *13e Bataillon Médical* and the *3e Escadron de Réparation* of the *GER XV* were ready. To save time, he sent the wheeled vehicles on 24 April, prioritising the 1st Battalion. The tracked vehicles loaded the train at Châteauroux and headed towards Alsace. Similarly, all the *RMT*'s half-tracks were in the first rail convoy. Dio's goal was to reconstitute his infantry unit as quickly as possible so that it could be engaged in combat. The armoured vehicles of the *12e Cuirs* were loaded at Saintes on 25 April. Thus the *GTD*, with its 1,000 vehicles, would be stretched out between the Bordeaux region and the German border for several days. The units, spread out on the road or on the train, would then try to regroup. It would be a real obstacle course for them to find each other while moving. Indeed, rather than proceeding with a general regrouping at a given point and to avoid wasting any time, Dio decided to advance into Germany with his CP and his 1st Battalion, asking the other units to follow him and to latch on to him whenever they could. Thus, the *12e Cuirs* and the *3e RAC* ran after their *groupement tactique* leader. To measure the scale of the task, it should be noted that the state of the roads in Germany at that time was catastrophic. Most of the major bridges had been destroyed. To get across the rivers, it was necessary to find the rare small bridges that had been forgotten. American troops had priority on the bridges built by their own units, so the units of the *GTD* had to wait. In addition, the roads were clogged by columns of prisoners that continued to grow as the advance towards the east continued.

As for the *GTV*, its two elements, those moving by road and those moving by rail, managed to reassemble in Germany on 28 April. The next day, the *groupement* entered Swabia, a region west of Munich between Baden-Württemberg and Bavaria. The commanding general of the US XXI Corps placed Guillebon under the command of General Roderick Allen's 12th US Armored Division. This allowed the French to be looked after by the American logistics, particularly for fuel supplies. Guillebon crossed the Danube at Dillingen on 30 April, and the next day, south of Augsburg, crossed the Lech, a river running south-north on the Bavarian border. The *GTV* then moved from a travelling formation to a combat formation. During its advance, it came up against a few organised defences, particularly near the bridges. But the German morale had collapsed, and they very quickly surrendered as soon as the French demonstrated their willingness to fight. While the *GTV* was pushing into southern Germany, the rest of the *2e DB* was still in France. As for the *GTD* units, all the tracked vehicles transported by train disembarked at Brumath, north of Strasbourg, during the last days of April, and they crossed the Rhine on a pontoon bridge west of Rastatt on 27 April. The *GTD* column advanced into Germany, via Karlsruhe, which had been completely destroyed, and then Heilbronn, Dillingen on the Danube, then Augsburg, and Munich.[117] Spring had not yet arrived there, and it was still winter, with snow and wind. Despite a colossal effort to cover these 1,200 kilometres in a minimum of time, the *GTD* was not able to regroup for several days. Dio decided to continue moving with his vanguard, consisting largely of Fosse's 1st Battalion. The regrouping of the *12e Cuirs* between armoured vehicles and wheeled vehicles did not happen until 2 May in Germany, and not until the next day for the *3e RAC*.

---

l'Illustration. Darlan and Laval had gone there.
116 Compagnon, *Leclerc,* p.505.
117 Merle, *L'Assaut, avec la 2e D.B.,* p.66.

The *GTV* reached the Inn River at Nussdorf on 3 May and left the 12th Armored Division, which had stopped. There, the objective of Berchtesgaden was confirmed for Guillebon. The advance continued without a halt, only slowed down by the destroyed bridges. They drove day and night.

Meanwhile, the *GTD* elements, including the CP, departed first, crossing the Danube at Dillingen along the same route taken by the *GTV*. On 3 May, Dio arrived in Bad Tölz, on the Isar. He knew that this town had hosted the officers' training school of the *Waffen SS* for 10 years. That sanctuary had 'sheltered the elite of the master race, produced fanatical cadres armed with intransigence and discipline.'[118] The buildings had been pulverised by the Allied air forces. Justly deserved, thought all the men of the *GTD* as they passed in front of the ruins. On Dio's recommendation, Leclerc agreed that the 1st Battalion of the *RMT* should be pushed forward to form the second echelon of the *GTV*. In such a mountainous region, on narrow roads, half-tracks were more agile than tanks and could advance faster. Leclerc resumed command of the *GTV* and the *GTD* battalion which followed at a forced march.

The regrouped *12ᵉ Cuirs* set up their cantonment in the region of Obermülhausen, a small village 55 kilometres west of Munich. 'We control traffic on the roads …. where groups of isolated Germans with weapons circulate.'[119] As it advanced, the *GTD* column came across small groups of freed French prisoners trying to return to France. It also came across groups of *Wehrmacht* soldiers marching with white flags. Many were terrified and adopted a servile and obsequious attitude that struck Leclerc's men. In Normandy or the Vosges, their behaviour was quite different. 4 May would remain a historic day. The French *GTV* column arrived at Bad Reichenhall, a town leading to the Berchtesgaden salient. Elements of the *2ᵉ DB* entered into competition with General John O'Daniel's 3rd US Infantry Division. O'Daniel understood the importance for his division to arrive first at Berchtesgaden, and he had the engineering resources to build bridges. The bridge over the River Saalach, which blocked the entrance to the Berchtesgaden salient, had been destroyed. After having re-established a crossing point on the river, O'Daniel launched his units and gave instructions to block the French who were waiting behind, for several hours, giving him a head start. Behind him, Subgroup Barboteu reached Berchtesgaden at 5:00 p.m., a few hours after the Americans. A small mountain resort nestled in a circle, it was located south of the Austrian city of Salzburg, 140 kilometres southeast of Munich. It should be noted that the objective assigned to the 3rdInfantry Division was initially the Austrian city of Salzburg, rather than the small resort in Tyrol. As a result, the US leaders were most certainly unaware of the topography of the place. This explains why, although the first to arrive in Berchtesgaden, they would be the second to make it to the lair of Nazism. 'These people, we will never know why, neglected the Obersalzberg where the houses of Hitler and Göring are built and above, the famous 'Eagle's Nest.'"[120]

Capitaine Touyeras of the *64ᵉ RADB* went up for the first time in a jeep with Brigadier Borg to the Obersalzberg, located at an altitude of 900 metres. Then, having come back down, he went there a second time with *Lieutenant* Messiah's 2nd Section of the 12th Company.[121] The small

---

118 Bergot, *La 2e D.B*, p.267.
119 Fonds Leclerc, *JMO du 12e Cuirs*.
120 Fonds Leclerc, *JMO du 3/RMT*.
121 The 12th Company of the 3rd Battalion of the *RMT* was formed after the liberation of Paris with a very large majority of *FFI*. They acquired, during the hard fighting of the end of 1944 and the beginning of 1945, the experience of the old troops. Young in age, their particularity was their hatred of the Germans after four years of occupation and a great skill for System D (the ability to make do and be resourceful in adversity). They were driven by revenge, their *lieutenant* more than any of them, because Messiah was Jewish. Bergot, *La 2e D.B.*, p.268.

detachment then visited this group of summer residences of the Nazi regime, which had been destroyed during the aerial bombardment of 24 April – the Berghof, Hitler's house, was even burning. This was the work of the last SS men who, before fleeing, tried to save the Nazi sanctuary from the desecration of the victorious Allied forces.[122] All the buildings were connected by a maze of underground passages that were filled with objects of art looted or stolen by the Nazis, as well as all sorts of miscellaneous objects and materials. A Dutch flag was found in the rubble.[123] No worry, by flipping it around 90 degrees, it became a French flag! It 'covers the retaining wall, the one that supports the terrace of the Berghof, on top of which so many pretentious silhouettes have strutted.'[124] The unfurled flag marked the primacy of the French army. Then the men of Messiah's section settled in at the Platterhof (the hotel for visitors) to spend the night there.[125] Only 48 hours after the capture of Berlin by the Russians, the French seized the other symbolic site of Nazism.

Meanwhile, on the same day, the *3ᵉ RAC* and the 2nd Battery of the *FTA* only reached the southwest region of Munich, where the *12ᵉ Cuirs* and the central portion of the *GTD* had just settled. The artillerymen settled around the town of Landsberg. The *GTD* staff, finally complete, ordered the *12ᵉ Cuirs* and the *3ᵉ RAC* to stay put.

On the morning of the 5th, Leclerc finally arrived in Berchtesgaden. He asked *Capitaine* Touyeras to take him to the Obersalzberg. There, Leclerc ordered that the French flag be hung on the Eagle's Nest, Hitler's famous tearoom overlooking Berchtesgaden at an altitude of 1,834 metres.[126] It was a detachment commanded by *Sous Lieutenant* Catelain of the 12th Company of the *RMT* with two officers from the *64ᵉ RADB* and filmmakers from the Army Communication Services, who succeeded in climbing to the summit. It took them nine hours to reach it, the lift to the top having been destroyed. The building on the rocky spur was of modest size, with only two rooms with large windows overlooking the magnificent Königsee lake. A large French flag, brought all the way from Cairo and provided by *Lieutenant Colonel* Barboteu, was hung on the edge of the terrace.[127] It was 5:00 p.m.[128] 'At this poignant moment, all eyes fill with tears; this French flag with the Cross of Lorraine floating so high in the German sky, over the spiritual redoubt of

---

122 Langlade, *En Suivant Leclerc,* p.411.
123 Destrem, *L'Aventure de Leclerc,* p.341.
124 Gribius, *Une Vie d'Officier,* p.138.
125 This version is the most widely accepted among French historians. It is contested by the American side, which claims that it was the GIs of the 7th US Infantry Regiment who were the first at the Berghof, with photos to support this. The paratroopers of the 101st Airborne also use the same kind of photos to claim primacy. Internally, the *2e DB* also had different versions. *Capitaine* Touyeras claimed to have been the first to arrive at the Berghof with his jeep and driver. Some soldiers from the 12th Company disputed this version, saying that it was Messiah's section that arrived first. Others claimed that Touyeras and Messiah met at the entrance. The accounts contradicted each other, particularly regarding the timetables, the presence of SS men on site, the conditions of access, and *Général* Leclerc's schedule. In 1945, based on the reports of the time, Leclerc would only acknowledge *Capitaine* Touyeras' version, with a citation to support his claim. In conclusion, not everything is very clear about the Obersalzberg.
126 Compagnon, *Leclerc,* p.505.
127 Raymond Dronne, *L'Hallali de Paris à Berchtesgaden, Août 1944–Mai 1945*, (Paris: Éditions France-Empire, 1985, p.242.
128 This version is also questionable regarding the conditions in which it took place. On 5 May, Leclerc returned from Augsburg (250km from Berchtesgaden), where he met General Patch, commander of the 7th US Army. In his diary, Girard recorded the arrival of the *général* at Berchtesgaden on 6 May and the visit to Obersalzberg on 7 May (Girard, *Journal de Guerre,* pp.367–368). Therefore, it does not seem that the version according to which Leclerc himself would have given the order to plant the flag on the Eagle's Nest on 5 May is proved. The testimonies, several years after the events, must be taken with caution. However, there is no doubt about the Eagle's Nest – it was indeed Leclerc's men who first hung the French flag there, on 5 May. Photos attest to this, this version not being contested by the Americans. The flag still exists and is in the *Salle d'Honneur* of the *RMT* in Meyenheim.

Nazism, is truly the symbol of our victory and the defeat of Germany's excessive pride.'[129] The *2ᵉ DB* had once again entered the military history of this second global conflict. 'Providence allowed Leclerc and his division to finish it in the symbolic high place of Hitler's power, Berchtesgaden.'[130] Thus ended *Général* Leclerc's epic, which began in August 1940 in Cameroon and consisted only of victories. The episode of Berchtesgaden can be considered as a sort of reward granted by fate to the *2ᵉ DB*. Politically, it placed France and its army in the spotlight for having participated in this final act of the war while the negotiations between the Allies and the Russians were about to begin.

The same day, after having driven at night, the 1st Battalion and Dio's forward CP settled in the area of Bergen, a town 50 kilometres northwest of Berchtesgaden. At 3:00 p.m., the notice of capitulation of the German *Heeresgruppe G* (Army Group G), which was in their zone, arrived.[131] Dio and his men then understood that they would not have to fight. They would simply be tasked with surveillance and control missions so that the operations to neutralise the *Wehrmacht* would take place under good conditions. Unfortunately, that day, the head of the reconnaissance section of the *3/RMT*, *Aspirant* Peters,[132] was killed in Hirschbischl, west of Berchtesgaden, in a mountain encounter with a group of German fugitives. He was the last man from the *RMT* and the *2ᵉ DB* to die in combat during the Second World War. The vanguard of the *GTD* resumed its advance on 6 May, with Berchtesgaden as its objective. The 1st Battalion of the *RMT* arrived there at midday. Berchtesgaden was in a sort of cul-de-sac, and there were many US troops there. The Americans were quite annoyed at having been overtaken on the Obersalzberg at the last moment by the French. So, the *GTD* elements received the order in the afternoon to turn back to the area around Diessen, a small tourist resort stuck to the south of the large 16-kilometre-long Lake Ammersee.

Before leaving, Dio had time to go up to see the summer residences of the Nazi leaders. He received from his men a host of 'souvenirs' from these highly symbolic places. He said nothing because he was so moved. His friend Crépin was with him – what a long way the two officers had travelled since Douala, and so many deaths to get here! Having only 400 men for Kufra, then 2,500 for Fezzan, they found themselves at 16,000-strong to take Paris and Strasbourg and, finally, a few thousand in the very lair of Nazism. Their feelings were mixed; pride but also resentment. Certainly, Hitler and his clique were largely responsible for all this disaster. But this should not exonerate those who did nothing when there was still time, particularly in France at the end of the 1930s, and those who collaborated – those authorities would have to be held accountable. The next day, the *GTD*, which had taken the opposite route, was stationed in the region of Bad Reichenhall. It was there, a few steps from the Austrian border, that Dio and his men learnt of the signing of Germany's unconditional surrender in Reims on 7 May at 2:41 a.m. At 3:00 p.m. on 8 May, the official proclamation of the end of the conflict reached the entire *2ᵉ DB*. To celebrate, the soldiers let off steam with their American allies by firing their weapons into the air. All night long, the sky was lit up by fireworks consisting of parachute flares and tracers of all calibres, amidst the smoke from incendiary and smoke grenades. Both banks of the lake were completely lit up.[133] The *GTD*'s CP was set up about 10 kilometres from Diessen around the town of Reichling. The

---

129   Dronne, 'Le drapeau à croix de Lorraine sur le nid d'aigle d'Hitler', *Soldats de Leclerc* (Paris: Lavauzelle, 1997), p.256.

130   Jean Compagnon, *Leclerc*, p.505.

131   Fonds Leclerc, *JMO du 1/RMT.*

132   This reserve officer joined the *RMT* on 28 August 1944 at the age of 25. Assigned to Dronne's 9th Company, he was wounded on 17 November and refused to be evacuated. His behaviour earned him the *Croix de Guerre* with palm and the *Médaille Militaire*. At the start of 1945, he took command of the reconnaissance and observation section of the support company of the 3rd battalion. He was posthumously made a *Chevalier* of the *Légion d'Honneur* and cited a second time in the Orders of the Army. In 1981, the 103rd promotion of reserve officer cadets at the infantry school chose to take the baptismal name '*Aspirant* Peters.'

133   Fonds Leclerc, *JMO du 12e Cuirs.*

GTV remained in Berchtesgaden until 8 May, at the express and renewed request of the American command.[134]

The German Campaign left *Colonel* Dio with a taste of unfinished business. His tactical group had not been engaged as such, just like Langlade's. 'Indeed, two-thirds of the division, the *GTL* and *GTD*, would be deprived of participating in the German Campaign.'[135] Like Leclerc, he did not understand why *Général* de Gaulle had required the *2ᵉ DB* to resolve the secondary problem of Royan instead of participating in the death knell in Germany. The Chadian soldiers, those who rallied first and had shown themselves to be the most loyal to the leader of Free France, had not had the honour of actually fighting in Germany. Of course, he personally was able to make it with his two *RMT* battalions as far as Berchtesgaden. It was his *marsouins* who planted the French flags on the Obersalzberg and the Eagle's Nest. It was a strong symbol and a just reward for the unit that, in Chad in 1940, served as the launching pad for Leclerc's epic. Dio's initial feeling of frustration faded quickly, he had to celebrate the final victory with his men, as it should be. The underground passages, particularly the cellars, of the Obersalzberg had been visited by the *marsouins*. They were full of great vintages of champagne and Bordeaux wine. Raising their crystal glasses, engraved with the initials AH,[136] Dio and his subordinates joyfully toasted the cessation of hostilities and the victory over Nazi Germany. They deserved it!

134 Girard, *Journal de Guerre,* p.369.
135 Compagnon, *Leclerc,* p.503.
136 Adolf Hitler.

Chapter 13

Commander of The 2ᵉ DB, 8 May 1945 to 25 September 1946

On 8 May 1945, the *2ᵉ DB* was regrouped in the area between Lake Ammersee and the River Lech, west of Munich. The end of the war was fittingly celebrated. The joy was general and the officers let the troops celebrate the victory perhaps more than was reasonable. Général Leclerc sent the following daily order to all the personnel of the division: 'The enemy has capitulated; from Chad to Berchtesgaden, everywhere you have beaten him. In the name of France I thank you, and I ask you to show in the service of the country, the same energy tomorrow in peace, as yesterday in war.'[1] The war had barely ended, and Général Leclerc was already focused on the reconstruction of liberated France.

The next day, having found the units of his *groupement*, Dio visited Rouvillois' *12ᵉ Cuirs* and Fieschi's *3ᵉ RAC*, who were unable to participate in the death blow because they had just arrived from Royan. They simply conducted surveillance operations on the main roads before the end of hostilities, as well as the support and disarmament of German soldiers wanting to surrender. The region was beautiful; spring had finally arrived with the peace. The German population was surprisingly welcoming. Dio and his men were very circumspect in the face of this enthusiasm. They wondered where the Nazis had gone, as if there had never been any in this country! They were stunned by the fickleness of the German people,[2] leading them to meditate on the fragility of human destinies and ambitions.[3] In any case, the behaviour of Leclerc's soldiers towards the German civilian populations remained dignified on all occasions. At the *GTD*, Dio was uncompromising towards the few proven transgressions that were brought to his attention following complaints from locals. That was not always the case with other occupying armies. However, the men of the *GTD* were less conciliatory with the countless unarmed German soldiers walking along the roads to return to their homes. At the time, many French prisoners were also on the roads to reach France under their own means. For Leclerc's men, it was a sad spectacle, these Frenchmen who still represented a defeated France to them. These ex-prisoners of war were often destitute of everything and very poorly equipped.[4] Leclerc's men did not hesitate to take shoes, equipment, bicycles, et cetera from German soldiers for the benefit of their fellow citizens.[5]

During that period of about 10 days, the *GTD* was on holiday. Taking advantage of the weather, the command organised leisure activities for the soldiers. Dio knew that idleness among soldiers

---

1   Merle, *L'Assaut, avec la 2e D.B.,* p.68.
2   The American press unanimously pointed out in its editorials the responsibility of the entire German people, 'guilty of the crimes committed by the Nazis…we must admit the fact of a national and collective guilt.' (*Caravane* No.20, 20 May 1945, p.20).
3   Salbaing, *Ardeur et Réflexion,* p.405.
4   Salbaing, *Ardeur et Réflexion,* p.405.
5   Destray, *Les Campagnes de France d'Allemagne 1944/1945,* p.38.

always leads to trouble. Already, fights were breaking out with the Americans in the bars. So, boat trips on the lake and swimming were offered to them. Visits to the city of Munich and the resort of Innsbrück were organised.[6] The units that had not made it to Berchtesgaden were authorised to go there. Thus the 2nd Battery of the *22ᵉ GCFTA* sent two trucks full of soldiers to visit Berchtesgaden and make the climb to the Eagle's Nest.[7]

The attention of the officers of the *2ᵉ DB* was soon drawn to the Dachau concentration camp, located only 20 kilometres northwest of Munich, or 40 kilometres from Lake Ammersee. They learnt that the camp was administered by the American Lieutenant Colonel Martin Joyce,[8] who rightly imposed very strict quarantine measures on the deportees to avoid the risk of contamination. There were still around 30,000 deportees in the camp and its annexes. On 12 May, Leclerc directed Langlade to contact the authorities at Dachau. Langlade went there accompanied by a doctor and with trucks of medicine and food. The commander of the *GTL* returned in shock. Like many, he thought that a concentration camp was a camp for hard labour, not an extermination camp. Following Langlade's story, Dio decided to go there, too. It became increasingly difficult to enter the camp. Dio and his subordinates managed to gain access only through long negotiation, and only through access annexes.

Once inside, they were horrified by what they saw. There were still several thousand deportees inside. They were mostly walking corpses, suffering from typhus, tuberculosis, and dysentery. The entire *GTD* team asked itself the same question: how is it possible to behave like this towards other human beings? Dio headed towards the barracks reserved for the French.[9] He asked to see their leader. A skeletal character arrived. His eyes were striking in the middle of his gaunt face. He introduced himself with dignity: 'My name is Edmond Michelet.'[10] He was an admirable man, entirely devoted to others and fired with great willpower. He showed the *GTD* officers the barracks occupied by his compatriots. A pestilential smell emanated from the wooden frames where 4,000 Frenchmen were lying one on top of the other. A thousand others were in the *Kommando* annex of Allach. They all asked to be allowed to get out of that hell as quickly as possible. But many were contaminated and required special treatment to be cured before their release. In addition, they had to relearn how to feed themselves by taking small portions of food regularly. Upon leaving that infernal place, Dio was seized with a cold rage towards the German people, whom he believed were guilty of this crime against humanity perpetrated by their government. In its great majority, 'this

6   Loison, *Moteurs En Route,* p.58.
7   Fonds Leclerc, *JMO de la 2e Bie du 22e GCAFTA.*
8   Lieutenant Colonel Martin Joyce was a veteran of the First World War and a Massachusetts State Policeman. Called to active duty after the attack on Pearl Harbor, he served in the Pacific, North African, and European Theatres. After the US Army liberated the Dachau Concentration Camp, Joyce served as its commander from April to July 1945. In 2012, Joyce's papers, including around 250 documents and a photo album from Dachau, were discovered in a briefcase in Wayland High School, in Massachusetts. Students at the school digitised the collection and have made it available online: https://www.ltcoljoycepapers.org/. The originals have been donated to the United States Holocaust Memorial Museum. (Translator's note)
9   As a condition of *Maréchal* Pétain's armistice in 1940, anti-Jewish laws were enacted in both German occupied France and in Vichy-controlled territory. Between 1942 and 1944, around 75,000 French Jews were deported to Nazi concentration and extermination camps, where 73,500 of them were subsequently murdered. In addition, many Frenchmen who resisted the German occupation were arrested and deported to concentration camps, such as Dachau. (Translator's note)
10 Less than a year later, Dio welcomed Edmond Michelet, a fervent Gaullist, to Paris, at the headquarters of the *Maison des Anciens de la 2e DB*. Minister of the Armed Forces from 1945 to 1946, Michelet then became Minister of Justice from 1959 to 1961, Minister of State for the Civil Service from 1967 to 1968, and finally Minister of Cultural Affairs from 1969 until his death in October 1970. His beatification process was initiated in 1976.

people who knew, covered this accumulation of horrors with their silence and their tacit approval, by shouting 'Heil Hitler' with a frenzy that never weakened.'[11]

Back in Etting, at the division's headquarters, Dio reported to Leclerc about what he saw and the requests of the deportees who complained of feeling abandoned. Leclerc visited the camp a few days later and succeeded in gaining the approval of the health service officials to release the first 600 French deportees, including Edmond Michelet, on 16 May. Among them, the Jesuit priest Michel Riquet agreed to speak in front of an audience of officers gathered at the division's head-quarters about his deportation to Mauthausen and then to Dachau.[12] His testimony provoked a great moment of emotion among the assembly. The faces of the participants tensed as the priest's story progressed, revealing the rise of a cold anger. Dio thought that it was ultimately better that such atrocities were known now that the fighting was over. Otherwise, there would not have been many SS men left alive. Dio decided to send some of his men to visit Dachau while respecting health constraints. Like Massu, he thought 'that we must see and show what justified the tragedy of a new war, what gives meaning to all the sacrifices of our comrades.'[13] The support of the 2ᵉ DB to speed up the release of the French deportees was necessarily limited given the limitations of its resources. The support was mainly moral, even if the entire divisional medical service made itself available to the American authorities. Medicines and food were sent there until the last moment of the 2ᵉ DB's presence in Germany.[14] Fortunately, American logistics very quickly succeeded in largely providing for the needs of the survivors. Thus, the thousands of deportees were evacuated little by little while respecting the prescribed health standards. As for the evacuation of all the French from the camp, the 1ʳᵉ Armée would fulfil this mission to everyone's satisfaction.

Apart from the first euphoric days following 8 May, Dio noted that, despite the activities offered, a certain gloom was beginning to set in among the ranks. The war was over, and many of the personnel were asking themselves questions about their future, the 'dread of tomorrow. Separation first. The men have fought, suffered, hoped, waited together… The beautiful adventure is coming to an end.'[15] They will have to part ways and readjust to civilian life.

Soon, news reached the units that an intervention force in the Far East was being formed. Leclerc would command it and would ask for volunteers. For some, it was an opportunity to pursue the fight against the Japanese together. In mid-May, another piece of news arrived that 'rekindled the flame in everyone and put the heart back in place.'[16] It was announced that Général de Gaulle would preside over a parade on German soil on 19 May to honour the 2ᵉ DB and celebrate the military victory, a resounding revenge for the shameful disaster of 1940. On this Saturday of Pentecost, the entire division was reunited in full, for the first time since the landing, on the immense Klosterlechfeld airfield 20 kilometres south of Augsburg. It was a former Luftwaffe airfield and the bodies of Messerschmitts, manufactured in neighbouring factories, were still visible, birds with swastikas nailed to the ground before they could take off. Very early in the morning, the division moved to form up in a square of impeccable alignment. All the vehicles and machines were present, their names telling the glorious epic of Leclerc, from Kufra via Libya, Tunisia, Morocco, Normandy, Paris, Baccarat, Saverne, Strasbourg, Royan, and finally Berchtesgaden, the Berghof, and the Eagle's Nest. The division waited to be reviewed by Général de Gaulle. Finally at 5:30 p.m. 'Le Grand Charles' arrived, accompanied by American generals Patch and Brooks,[17] the Minister

11   Langlade, *En Suivant Leclerc*, p.415.
12   Notin, *Le Croisé*, p.334.
13   Massu, *Sept Ans*, p.219.
14   Fonds Leclerc, *JMO du 3e RAC*.
15   Bergot, *La 2 ème D.B.*, p.271.
16   Massu, *Sept Ans*, p.221.
17   General Edward H. Brooks commanded the 2nd US Armored Division. Landing on 9 June, he participated

of War, André Diethelm, *Général* Sevez,[18] and *Général* Leclerc. The commander of the troops was *Général* de Langlade. Dio was at the head of his *GTD*. De Gaulle slowly reviewed from a vehicle, passing in front of the troops, whose formation stretched almost 3 kilometres. He slowly saluted Standards and Colours, unfurled in the wind. The weather was magnificent. The moment was solemn and the presenting of arms of the troops was flawless. 'The great figure advances for one last time in front of these men, who have proven that France 'had not lost the war.''[19]

At the end of the review of the troops, de Gaulle presented decorations, starting with Leclerc, whom he elevated to the dignity of *Grand-Croix* of the *Légion d'honneur*. It is the fifth and final rank of the highest national order, the most prestigious, and Leclerc was only 43 years old. It rewarded the commitment and loyalty of the man to the leader of Free France and the exceptional career of the great French military leader, consistently victorious in command. After Leclerc, he decorated deserving officers with the order of the *Légion d'honneur*, including Bernard, Guillebon, Rémy, Delpierre, Barboteu, Repiton-Préneuf, Touyeras, and Lucchési. Then, 19 non-commissioned officers and other ranks were decorated with the *Médaille Militaire*. After which, de Gaulle honoured the *Régiment de Marche du Tchad* with the *Croix de Guerre* with Palm. Dio presented the Colours to the head of government who pinned the decoration on the streamer of the Colours. Other regiments of the division would subsequently receive the same medal, but the *RMT* remained the first in de Gaulle's mind, quite simply because it was the first to join him. During his speech, de Gaulle thanked those who followed him from the start as well as those who did so later.

At the end of the parade, the 1,160 combat vehicles of the division – tracked and half-tracked armoured vehicles, as well as wheeled vehicles – set off in columns of six in a triumphant parade 'with a deafening roar, rolling its steel waves in a sparkling river… An unforgettable moment.'[20] Standing in his tank, the *Sainte-Anne d'Auray*, Dio at the head of his *groupement tactique* felt a sense of power in the dust and smoke of the engines that he had never known before. Saluting the platform of leaders, he noted that *Général* de Gaulle seemed pensive as he watched the grandiose spectacle. He must certainly have been thinking of 1940, when at the head of a few dozen tanks of the *4ᵉ Division Blindée*, he had managed to stem the German advance for a few hours at Montcornet. If the great military leaders of the time had accepted the then *Colonel* de Gaulle's proposal to create several divisions like the one that was now parading before his eyes, the fate of the war would most certainly have been different.

The parade, which lasted more than an hour, was followed by a small dinner offered by Leclerc to his hosts aboard the barge *Le Diessen* on Lake Ammersee. Only six guests surrounded de Gaulle and Leclerc: *Ministre* Diethelm, *Général* Sevez, and the four *groupements tactiques* commanders. Dio was on Leclerc's left, almost facing *Général* de Gaulle. The atmosphere was relaxed, with no formal speeches. As soon as dinner began, the head of government began a soliloquy, with everyone drinking in his words. He told them how proud he was to be among them on German soil, a few days after the victory. He told them of the comradely affection he had for the *2ᵉ DB*, which included his first companions in its ranks. 'He assured all those who had joined him of his affection, adding in a deep and strong voice that always, in the future, whatever might happen, each of the leaders and soldiers who had belonged to it could be assured of his special affection and

---

in all the battles fought in France. Commanding the US VI Corps, he distinguished himself during the Battle of Heilbronn, between Stuttgart and Heidelberg, from 4 to 12 April.

18   *Général* François Sevez was *Général* Juin's deputy at the time. He had the honour of being the representative of France to countersign the German surrender in Reims on 7 May 1945.

19   Massu, *Sept Ans*, p.221.

20   Destrem, *L'Aventure de Leclerc*, p.342.

loyalty.'[21] Dio would long remember this long monologue in which de Gaulle expressed his gratitude and affection to them, a term used several times during the evening and which the great man nevertheless very rarely used. He thought back to the words that de Gaulle had said to them in Témara: '*Général* Leclerc's Armoured Division is marked by destiny to accomplish great things.'[22] The leader of Free France had helped shape the destiny of the *2ᵉ DB*; Dio was deeply convinced of that. He was grateful to him. That evening, de Gaulle, surrounded exclusively by soldiers, with the exception of the minister, felt good among his faithful, and he spoke from the heart. At the end of the meal, he even teased Leclerc by mentioning the latter's propensity to carry out orders that he did not like only with difficulty. The day remained an unforgettable moment for all, but it also meant that the page had been turned. Nothing would ever be the same compared to everything they had experienced.

The *2ᵉ DB*, which had arrived late in Germany, was not intended to remain long in the defeated country. The officers agreed: 'This period of ad hoc occupation is neither pleasant nor healthy. It should not last.'[23] They needed to return to France quickly. The orders arrived accordingly, and the division had to leave Germany before the end of the month. It would begin its move to France on 24 May. Leclerc had left by car the day before. The final destination of the *2ᵉ DB* was set for the Fontainebleau region. The move from Lake Ammersee to eastern France was made by road in small stages. The *GTD* left Bavaria on 24 May. Taking the *Reich Autobahn,* the column arrived in Karlsruhe via Pforzheim, two cities that had been completely 'Coventryised,'[24] whose large buildings no longer had ceilings or floors, the rest having been blown out and burnt. From there, it reached Rastatt then Kehl where it crossed the Rhine. On the Alsatian side, a sign reading, 'Here begins the land of freedom' welcomed Dio and his men.[25] Once in France, the units reached the stations to load the armoured vehicles onto the train. The Alsatian population always showed the same affection towards their liberators. During the movement to load the tanks and half-tracks in Strasbourg, Leclerc's men were the object of much attention from the population. The detachments of wheeled vehicles continued by road, so the division's column left Alsace on 28 May.

It took two days to reach its destination in the south-east of the Paris region. Shortly afterwards, the armoured vehicles disembarked from the trains. Little by little, the units of the *2ᵉ DB* settled in the area inside a widened quadrilateral around Fontainebleau, including the towns of Malesherbes – Provins – Melun. The division's CP was set up in Marlotte, 9km south of Fontainebleau[26] in the villa of Chiappe, a former police prefect. The *GTD* established its CP in Nangis. The *1ᵉʳ Bataillon* set up around Nogent-sur-Seine and the *12ᵉ RC* at Donnemarie-en-Montois.[27] The *13ᵉ Bataillon de Génie* grouped in the Melun region,[28] while the *3ᵉ RAC* set up around Provins. The *2ᵉ Bataillon* of the *RMT* occupied Malesherbes (CP), Puiseaux, Briare-sur-Essonne, Boigneville, and Nanteau. The CP of the GTL was in Nemours. The *GTV* was located further east, between Nemours and Sens, its CP being in the Yonne at Villeneuve-la-Guyard. The *3ᵉ Bataillon* of the *RMT* was in the Chéroy-Voulx-Vallery and Saint Valérien quadrilateral. The *501ᵉ RCC* was deployed north of Sens while the *64ᵉ RADB* was centred on Courlon-sur-Yonne. The *GTD*'s armoured vehicles arrived by

21 Langlade, *En Suivant Leclerc,* p.419.
22 Perceval, *Sur les Chemins de l'Audace,* p.194.
23 Massu, *Sept Ans,* p.221.
24 The British bombarded Pforzheim for 45 minutes with phosphorus. It was a bit of revenge: in November 1941, the German air raids had concentrated on the industrial city of Coventry, which was 75 percent destroyed. Albert Altfeld and Huguette Serri, *Le Pont de Tardets, un Anciens de Leclerc Raconte,* inédit, p.186.
25 Merle, *L'Assaut, avec la 2e D.B.,* p.73.
26 Loison, *Carnets de Route,* p.52.
27 JMO du *1/RMT.*
28 JMO du *13e Génie.*

train on 31 May; the *groupement* was finally complete and in the designated locations. The same was also true for the rest of the *2ᵉ DB*. The return to France was ultimately carried out in a very short time. De Gaulle's political situation had not yet stabilised at the time, and the remark of a non-commissioned officer of the *12ᵉ Cuirs* is perhaps well-founded: 'it seems that the government feared an imminent communist putsch and that it needed 'something' to count on.'[29] This could explain the positioning of the *2ᵉ DB* at the gates of the capital.

On 7 June 1945, the *RMT* and Dio were cited in the Orders of the Army:

> The *Régiment de Marche du Tchad* – Magnificent regiment, heir to the finest traditions of the Colonial Army which has already acquired many titles of glory during the expeditions of Kufra, Fezzan, Tripolitania, and Tunisia. Already cited for its recent successes in Normandy and Paris, continued, under the command of Dio, in the Vosges and in Alsace with the same enthusiasm and the same spirit of sacrifice, to accumulate the most glorious feats of arms. After fierce battles on the Moselle, the Mortagne, the Meurthe, and the Vezouze, fighting on foot in difficult, wooded and flooded terrain, seized the town of Baccarat by a skilful manoeuvre that was masterfully executed. Continuing the series of successes in close liaison with the armoured elements of the Division, it covered itself with glory in the Vosges and in Alsace, operating on three axes under the orders of the three battalion commanders, throwing disorder into the enemy's rear, killing or capturing a considerable number of Germans, destroying a significant quantity of equipment and penetrating with the lead tanks into the city of Strasbourg.[30]

The citation rewarded the merits of the *RMT* and its leader for the Vosges and Alsace campaigns. During that period when the infantry remained the preferred operational actor because of the weather and the terrain, the regiment suffered heavy casualties. The same day, Leclerc, promoted to *général de corps d'armée* on 25 May, was officially tasked by the Provisional Government of the Republic to organise and train an expeditionary force destined for the Far East.[31] On 8 June in Marlotte, Leclerc organised a command meeting bringing together the *GT* commanders, service directors, unit commanders, and office department heads of the general staff. During the meeting, he intended to inform them of his next assignment. But before addressing that point, he wanted to announce the name of his successor himself. In a slightly hoarse voice filled with emotion, the *général* explained the reasons that justified the choice of *Colonel* Dio to succeed him when *Général* de Langlade should naturally have been selected.[32] 'However, *Général* de Gaulle considered that because of the traditions of this division from the Free French forces, and to maintain the symbolic tradition, it was necessary that this command be placed in the hands of one of our first companions, unanimity was reached around *Colonel* Dio.'[33] This appointment was certainly difficult to make. Appointing an infantry *colonel* who was only 37 years old to head an armoured division contravened the usual administrative rules within the military. For the writer Notin, it was 'A choice that was necessary for all the *grognards* of Africa, but a whim for the officers of the *Annuaire*.'[34]

---

29   Loison, *Carnets de Route*, p.52.
30   SHD, ESS of L. Dio, décision no. 649 – JORF du 07.06.1945, p.4679.
31   Destrem, *L'Aventure de Leclerc*, p.343.
32   Massu, *Sept Ans*, p.223.
33   Langlade, *En suivant Leclerc*, p.423.
34   Within the French armed forces, the *Annuaire* is an annual document summarising the list of all officers by rank according to the date of their promotion and their age. The dual categories of 'age/date of promotion' are strictly followed. It is the document which serves as a reference to establish the order of precedence.

A strong-willed man, Dio was only 37 years old. Of course, he would soon wear his stars, but, the first problem for commanding an armoured division was that he came from *la Coloniale* (the colonial army), 'a society as foreign to the graduates of [the Cavalry School in] Saumur as the provincial bourgeoisie was to the Parisian aristocracy.'[35] *Capitaine de Frégate* Rémy Maggiar, commanding the *Régiment Blindé de Fusiliers Marins*, recognised the legitimacy of this choice by writing: 'He is the leader of the colonials and *méharistes* who formed the core of the division. Through the simplicity of his life, the mysticism of his thinking, his ruggedness as a soldier, he exerts a profound influence on the division. He also carries the général's legacy on his robust shoulders.'[36] At the same time, the division had an extraordinary history, and it was somewhat usual that the successor should be 'the one who ensured Leclerc's first success for *Général* de Gaulle.'[37] Leclerc benefited from an exceptionally accelerated promotion to be able to lead the operations that contributed to the liberation of France. Dio was the only officer who had completed every single one of the stages of Leclerc's incredible epic, from Douala to Berchtesgaden. He, too, could legitimately be the subject of special consideration to succeed Leclerc. Leclerc himself justified the seniority issue as follows: 'It is true that most of these officers are young,' he argued. 'They owe the benefit of their advancement to having followed Général de Gaulle for years, having fought for France while others waited in a prudent attitude until their position vis-à-vis the enemy could be taken without risks.'[38]

Dio was proud of the consideration that de Gaulle and Leclerc had for him. At the same time, command of the division would prevent him from having the option of leaving with Leclerc for the Far East. For his part, *Général* de Langlade, who had never performed poorly while serving in Leclerc's division, was selected to command the *3ᵉ Division Blindée*. But his disappointment at not having been chosen remained immense and he would not attend the transfer of command of the *2ᵉ DB* between Leclerc and Dio.[39]

Leclerc informed his officers that the *2ᵉ DB* would provide a sort of vanguard for the expeditionary force that was being formed for Indochina, a *groupement de marche* composed of volunteers designated by him, from all the regiments and services. Leclerc then asked his subordinates who wanted to leave with him to raise their hands. Among the unit commanders, only Massu volunteered. It was therefore he who would command the *groupement de marche*, the backbone of which would be formed from a newly created unit that would be called the 4th Battalion of the *RMT*. Senior officers from the general staff or from the branch directorates[40] also opted to continue their collaboration with 'the Boss' in the Far East.[41] Among the lower ranks and soldiers, a certain number of them, notably those from the 2nd Battalion of the *RMT*, would decide to continue to serve, not only with Leclerc, but also with '*le Roi des Nazes*' (the King of the Suckers), the nickname given to Massu by his men. In the 1st Section of the 7th Company of the 2nd Battalion, for example, 34 men out of 50 volunteered for Indochina.[42] All units of the *2ᵉ DB* provided more or less volunteer soldiers to serve within the *groupement de marche* of the *2ᵉ DB*.

Shortly after this meeting, Leclerc signed Dio's annual appraisement review, having written:

35   Notin, *le Croisé*, p.341.
36   Maggiar, *Les fusiliers marins dans la Division Leclerc*, p.47.
37   Compagnon, *Leclerc*, p.508.
38   Notin, *le Croisé*, p.342.
39   Langlade, *En suivant Leclerc*, p.424. He said goodbye to his *GTL* on 15 June.
40   Among the volunteers to follow Leclerc to Indochina, were Guillebon, Crépin, Repiton-Préneuf, Quilichini, Dronne, Sarazac, Mirambeau, Langlois, Compagnon, Sorret, Grall, Fonde, Podeur, Duplay, Peschaud, Valence, la Brousse, Vésy, Torrès S., Ferrano, as well as others.
41   Massu, *Sept Ans*, p.224.
42   Salbaing, *Ardeur et Réflexion*, p.411.

As I hand over command of the division to *Colonel* Dio, I can only confirm the previous notes. His qualities of command and tact, the general esteem he enjoys, mark him out for the command of this unit in a particularly delicate period. *Colonel* Dio's value was demonstrated during the Carrouges manoeuvre and during the operations that preceded the capture of Strasbourg. His total disinterestedness allows him to judge objectively; his great modesty must attract the attention of our leaders. He deserves to be promoted to general officer.[43]

For the third time, Leclerc requested Dio's promotion as part of his annual review. It was the last time that Leclerc would rate his loyal deputy. In this assessment, as in the previous ones, Leclerc always returned to three points that, according to him, characterised Dio: he was an exceptional operational leader, with the particularity of being esteemed and followed by his subordinates, while demonstrating selflessness and humility.

The last public military ceremony of *Division Leclerc* took place in Paris on 18 June 1945. To commemorate the first anniversary of de Gaulle's Appeal to be celebrated in a liberated France, de Gaulle selected the *2ᵉ DB* for a mounted parade. The head of government wanted to honour those who had followed him since 18 June 1940, so that 'Whatever happens, the Flame of the French Resistance must not and will not be extinguished.'[44] He also wanted to establish his political legitimacy in a period when the political parties were resuming their scheming. For this, the ceremony, which promised to be grandiose by the number of participants under arms, would also mark the end of the war, the victory and the rebirth of the French Army.

The regiments of the *2ᵉ DB* left their respective *groupements tactiques* to reconstitute themselves into their organic units before moving to Paris. The stay in the capital would be brief. Dio, at the head of his three battalions, had arrived the previous afternoon and had set up the regiment in Nanterre. From the morning of the 18th, the *RMT*'s half-tracks, lined up in rows of six, stretched as far as the eye could see on the Avenue de la Grande Armée.[45] The vehicles were cleaned and sprayed with diesel to revive the paint. They looked like new – from a distance! An enthusiastic crowd was present, and many tricolour flags hung from the balconies of the Haussmannian buildings. But the crowds were not the same as those who had gathered on the Champs-Élysées on 26 August 1944. It must be said that 18 June 1945 fell on a Monday and was not a holiday. Not all Parisians would have the opportunity to see this deployment of several thousand armoured vehicles in the capital, something that had never been done before, and certainly has not been done since. The parade was opened at 9:30 a.m. by *La Garde Républicaine*[46] on horseback. The foot parade lasted one and a half hours and included units from seven infantry divisions. At 11:00 a.m., Leclerc opened the mounted portion of the parade, aboard his *Tailly* tank. He was followed by the *1ᵉʳ RMSM*. The *RMT* was in second position, and was presented as being 'the mounted assault infantry brigade.' The regiment, with Dio in the lead, drove down the Champs-Élysées. The *colonel* was followed by the half-track carrying the *RMT* Colours. Just behind, the 200 tracked vehicles of the three battalions paraded in rows of six. The crowd cheered, '*Vive les Leclercs!*'[47] Arriving at Place de la Concorde, the columns split in two in front of the official platform where *Général* de Gaulle and the Sultan of Morocco waited. Dio regrouped his regiment in the Bois de Vincennes,

---

43   SHD, Dossier L. Dio.

44   Appeal of 18 June 1940.

45   Merle, *L'Assaut, avec la 2e D.B.*, p.74.

46   *La Garde Républicaine* is the unit of the National Gendarmerie that serves as the guard of honour at official ceremonies in Paris and also provides security for the President of the Republic and other key members and locations of the French government. (Translator's note)

47   Merle, *L'Assaut, avec la 2e D.B.*, p.75.

and then, after a rudimentary meal, the *CCR*[48] guided the columns of vehicles to their cantonment locations southeast of Paris.

Three days later, Dio entrusted command of the *GTD* to *Lieutenant Colonel* Rouvillois, himself replaced by *Chef d'Escadron* de Viéville at the head of the *12ᵉ Cuirs*.[49] The ceremony must have taken place in relative privacy because no JMO mentions it. Rouvillois' appointment was unanimously popular among the officers as well as the men. He had demonstrated outstanding professional and human qualities at the head of his unit. Dio wanted him for the job because Rouvillois had become his friend during the months of fighting. Additionally, Rouvillois had not expressed the desire to leave for the Far East and was therefore available to assume the new position. As for the command of the *Régiment de Marche du Tchad* with its three battalions, Dio would have no successor. He would be the only commander of the *RMT* in its battalion structure, copied from the American Army. Each battalion became a regiment in its own right with a commander at its head, which was more in line with the usual organisation of the French Army.

The ceremony for Leclerc's departure and Dio's assumption of command took place in Fontainebleau on 22 June 1945. Even if the objective was primarily to ensure the transfer of command, it remained, within the *2ᵉ DB*, as that of the *'Adieux de Fontainebleau.'*[50] That Friday morning in June 1945 was very hot, announcing an early summer. The Hippodrome de la Solle at Fontainebleau had been chosen to bring together the entire division for a dismounted parade, without vehicles. The rustic and natural setting suited this ceremony, which was intended to be simple, and without an audience, a family reunion of sorts. All the officers and soldiers of the *2ᵉ DB* were gathered for the last time in front of the 'Boss.' There was contemplation tinged with sadness in everyone's hearts: they would soon have to say goodbye.

At the time set for the start of the ceremony, *Colonel* Dio was at the centre of the formation that gathered all the units of the division. He greeted Leclerc with a 'powerful present arms' followed by the 'clashing of several thousand palm slapping several thousand rifle butts.'[51] Accompanied by Dio, *Général* Leclerc passed one last time in front of all the units for the review of the troops, saluting Standards and Colours. At the end of this inspection, a large presentation of decorations began. Leclerc started that part of the ceremony by handing over the Standard of the *22ᵉ Groupe de FTA* to *Chef d'Escadron* Lancrenon. Until then, this anti-aircraft artillery unit had not been considered as a separate unit. In the process, all the Standards and Colours of the division gathered in the centre of the formation. The outgoing division commander decorated all the emblems of his large unit. The first to be decorated was the *RMT*. Leclerc approached and gave the formulaic address: *'Régiment de Marche du Tchad,'* he pronounced with a deep and emotional voice, 'in the name of *Général* de Gaulle, we recognise you as our Companion in the fight for the Liberation for the Fatherland, in Glory, and through Victory.' He pinned the *Croix de la Libération* to the streamer of the Colours.[52] The *RMT* was the first regiment of the *2ᵉ DB* to be honoured with the cross that made it a Companion unit. Three other regiments of the *2ᵉ DB* would be honoured later by decree of 7 August 1945: the *501ᵉ RCC*, the *1ᵉʳ RMSM*, and the *3ᵉ RAC*.

---

48   This was the *397e Compagnie de Circulation Routière* (traffic company).
49   Dio's service and personnel records indicate that he left command of the GTD and RMT on 21 June 1945.
50   'Farewells of Fontainebleau.' Historically, this name is generally reserved for the farewell ceremony that the Emperor Napoléon held on 20 April 1814 for his Old Guard in the Cour du Cheval Blanc of the Château de Fontainebleau.
51   René de Berval, 'Á Fontainebleau. Les Adieux du Général', *Caravane* No.23, Juin 25, 1945, p.3.
52   Decree of 12 June 1945. Initially the plan was for de Gaulle to pin the *Croix de la Libération* to the *RMT* Colours during the ceremony of 18 June in Paris. An honour battalion composed of units from the three battalions had been formed for that purpose. (JMO of the *1/RMT*) For unknown reasons, this presentation of the decoration was cancelled at the last moment.

The citation of the *RMT* in the Order of the Army, accompanying the presentation of the *Croix de la Liberation* read:

'The *Régiment de Marche du Tchad*, an elite regiment formed by *Colonel* Dio with elements of the former *Corps Franc d'Afrique* and the former *Forces Françaises Libres*, who came from Chad, after having covered themselves with glory in Kufra – in Fezzan – in Tripolitania, and in Tunisia, participated in the liberation of the Fatherland in Normandy, in Paris, and in the Vosges, manoeuvring and defeating the enemy everywhere thanks to its offensive spirit and the technical ability of its officers. Has to its credit the destruction of about 800 enemy vehicles of all kinds, killed and taken prisoner a very high number of Germans, lost a third of its personnel. Can be cited as an example to all as representing the perfect type of armoured infantry regiment, thus bringing honour to the Colonial Army.'[53]

De Gaulle wanted to give primacy to this regiment because he had not forgotten that the *RTST*, from which the *RMT* came, was the first and only unit to have rallied in its entirety to Free France, as early as 26 August 1940. It was also the one that suffered the most losses during the four years of combat, having had, proportionally, the most killed and wounded in its ranks.[54] Finally, it had the honour of having, among the personnel who served it, a total of 106 Companions of the Liberation. As at Klosterlechfeld in May, it was *Colonel* Dio who, as regimental commander, had the honour of presenting the Colours to *Général* Leclerc so he could pin the *Croix de la Liberation* on the streamer of the Colours, which already bore the *Croix de Guerre*. This decoration would allow the officers and *marsouins* serving in the unit to wear, from 18 June 1996, the *fourragère* in the colours of the *Croix de la Liberation*.

Then Leclerc decorated all the other Colours and standards of the division with the *Croix de Guerre*. The ceremony was long because, at each presentation, the citation awarding the unit was read in full. When the Colours returned to the ranks, 61 recipient officers then stepped out to line up in front of him. Leclerc presented 38 medals of the *Légion d'honneur* to officers and non-commissioned officers, two medals of the *Croix de la Liberation*, and 21 *Médailles Militaires* to officers and non-commissioned officers. The first, *Colonel* Dio, was decorated with the highest decoration of the day, the neck ribbon of a *Commandeur* of the *Légion d'honneur*. The former *méhariste* went from *chevalier* in 1941 and *officier* in 1944, to *commandeur* in 1945. This exceptional progression of three ranks in only four years, in the order of the highest French decoration, was due above all to his record of service. It also rewarded his loyalty and fidelity to his leader. *Lieutenant Colonel* Rouvillois, the new commander of the *GTD*, also received the ribbon of *Commandeur* of the *Légion d'honneur*. *Lieutenant Colonel* Verdier, commander of the *GTL* and *Commandant* Lantenois, head of the logistics section, were made Companions of the Liberation.

After the presentation of decorations, Leclerc approached the microphone to address his men. He asked them 'to give the same satisfaction to my successor, *Colonel* Dio. For nearly five years at my side, and often my adviser, he is the model of a French leader in all his uprightness and nobility.'[55] In these three lines where he spoke of his successor, Leclerc evoked the role of adviser

---

53   Perceval, *Sur les Chemins de l'Audace*, p.197.
54   For example, the losses of the 7th Company of the *RMT*: '82% of the nominal strength was killed or wounded, and for the 1st Section alone… 11 killed and 37 wounded out of a nominal strength of 51 men.' (Salbaing, *Ardeur et Réflexion*, p.18). Within the *12e Cuirs* of the GTD, the 3rd Squadron lost 44 percent of its strength (Fonds Leclerc, Purson, *Itinéraire suivi par le Troisième Escadron du 12e Cuirs*, p.31). These casualty rates, enormous by today's standards, prove that the French campaign was no walk in the park and how fierce the fighting was.
55   Berval, 'À Fontainebleau. Les Adieux du Général', *Caravane* No.23, p.4.

played by his companion from the beginning. This advice was most often formulated spontaneously during command meetings. Dio was the only one to dare to express a judgement that
sometimes diverged or provided nuance to Leclerc's operational intentions. Even though the two
officers had the same tactical approach, there were sometimes differences of opinion in the way of
carrying out the mission. In training schools, the cavalry officer learns to reason quickly, at the
speed of his machine. The tactical approach of the *méhariste* was completely different because he
moved on foot, at best at the speed of his camel. As a result, the ex-*méhariste* who had retained
great freedom of speech 'plays a bit of a role of balancer, in the face of the bold initiatives of the
Patron.'[56] The *général* often sought his subordinate's advice before deciding. It even reassured him
to have this complementarity of thought with Dio. He did it all the more willingly because he
knew that once the decision had been made, everyone, including Dio, would show the greatest
discipline in carrying out his orders.

Then, in the rest of his speech, Leclerc thanked all the categories of men who made up the division. The words of his farewell went straight to the hearts of each of the participants. As he left,
he gave them one last mission: 'tomorrow, like yesterday, maintain an active patriotism...' then
he ended with a recommendation: 'Find your comrades again, your leaders, and carry on...' This
invitation prefigured the upcoming creation of the association of the *Maison des Anciens de la 2ᵉ
DB*. The ceremony ended with a pass in review. Dio, at the head of the troops, followed by the
standard bearer of the *2ᵉ DB*, arrived in front of the small stand on which Leclerc had taken his
place. Opposite him, on the other side of the route of march, he stopped and faced him. 'Thus
the two leaders, the old and the new, would together see parading before their eyes these troops,
whom they made what they are, and whom they loved, these magnificent troops who, from Chad
to Berchtesgaden, while covering themselves in glory, contributed so powerfully to the Liberation
of France and the crushing of the enemy, and who avenged, in front of the world, the shame of
the Armistice.'[57]

The farewells at Fontainebleau marked the end of Leclerc's epic. The men felt that they were
living the apogee of their adventure on the Hippodrome of Fontainebleau.[58] Nothing would be
able to surpass what they had lived. After the ceremony, nothing would ever be the same again.
Within the *2ᵉ DB*, the personnel then experienced what can be called 'an end of an era, each
one worrying about his personal future.'[59] The large unit would be deeply affected by the mass
departures of its personnel. Very quickly, three groups would form: those who would ask to be
demobilised by choosing to return to the civilian world, those who would leave for the Far East,
and finally those who, by remaining within the *2ᵉ DB*, wanted to make a career in the army. Many
of the men in the division were those who would leave the military profession. The main reason
comes from the conditions of its creation. It was formed in stages, from disparate elements coming
mainly from the civilian world. In Africa, they were reservist officers and volunteers from England.
In Morocco, they were young Frenchmen who had made their way through Spain. After Paris, it
was the *FFI*, young resistance fighters, who integrated into the different units. Most of these men
had signed up to fight Nazism, but not for a military career. During that time, many prepared
for their demobilisation. They wanted to return to the civilian life they had left behind, before it
was too late. The students wanted to finish their studies. For many others, the peacetime military
life did not appeal to them. Salaries were low and working conditions had deteriorated considerably. The country was rebuilding, and the military was no longer the priority. Training could not

---

56   Pellissier, *Massu, le Croisé*, p.22.
57   Berval, 'Á Fontainebleau. Les Adieux du Général', *Caravane* No.23, p.5.
58   Massu, *Sept Ans*, p.225.
59   Salbaing, *Ardeur et Réflexion*, p.410.

really resume due to lack of infrastructure or resources; there was no fuel even to train new drivers! In addition, food, since the division was no longer supported by its American ally, had become a source for universal complaints from officers and soldiers.[60] Finally, relations with the civilian population, with whom the units were housed, deteriorated. In Nogent-sur-Seine, incidents multiplied because cohabitation became difficult for everyone. All of these shortcomings, noted since the end of the fighting, did not encourage the undecided to stay in the army.

Demobilisation operations were to begin quickly and take place throughout the summer. *Colonel* Dio had each of them given a cardstock certificate framed in three colours, entitled '*DÉMOBILISÉS DE LA 2ᵉ DB.*' The text of this document read:

> You will leave your division after several years of effort and combat. Whether in Morocco, during the period of preparation and training, in England where our preparation was ending, or on the battlefields of Normandy, Paris, the Vosges, Alsace, or Germany, united in the same ideal around your esteemed leader, *Général* LECLERC, you have given yourselves without counting the cost. The sacrifice of those among you who died or who were wounded, your suffering and your daily trials have allowed the liberation of the Fatherland. Your glorious victories of Alençon, Paris, Baccarat, Strasbourg, Royan, and Berchtesgaden have allowed France to not die. Those who led you into combat and the entire country thank you. But the effort is not over; this France which thanks to you is not dead, depends on you so that it continues to live. On the threshold of this civilian life, which you await, and which will allow you to return to your homes and your former occupations, remember that you are veterans of the glorious *Division LECLERC* and that as such you are bound by the obligation to remain united in effort, in work, which alone will allow France to rise again and resume its true place in the world. This taste for effort, this self-denial, this spirit of sacrifice, this enthusiasm that you had in combat, may your new life be imbued with it. You owe it to those of your comrades who have fallen and to yourselves. I am sure that you will not forget it, and before you leave, I want to tell you that your memory will remain alive in this Division which owes you much; we will ensure that your spirit, your merit, animate the young soldiers who now have the honour of serving in your place in your regiments.
>
> 20 July 1945. Signed: Colonel DIO,
Commanding the 2ᵉ Division Blindée.[61]

Dio took up the theme so dear to Leclerc, according to which any former member of the *DB*, on becoming a private citizen must strive to promote patriotism in the country. He also wanted to create among these newcomers a particular esprit de corps based on pride in victories and the memory of those who died in combat. These were the two levers that would lead to many of them gathering within the future association of the *Maison des Anciens Combattants de la 2ᵉ DB*.

As the new commander of the *2ᵉ DB*, Dio was faced with a dilemma concerning those who chose the Far East. He had to help Massu's *groupement de marche* by assigning to it the best officers and soldiers. But he also had to be careful not to completely strip the division entrusted to him. Massu was fully aware of this when he described the difficulties of 'the mother division, dismantled by my withdrawals of personnel and equipment.'[62] Dio knew that Massu needed to skim, that is, to select the best of the *capitaines* and *lieutenants*, many of whom volunteered to continue serving in the

---

60   Fonds Leclerc, *Rapport sur le moral n° 946 du 1/ RMT, 29 juin 1945,* boîte B1, chemise 1, dossier 5.
61   Fonds Leclerc, 'Démobilisés de la 2e DB par le Colonel Dio,' boîte 29, chemise 3, dossier 3.
62   Massu, *Sept Ans,* p.224.

Far East: 'the most fervent supporters, and practitioners of the Leclerc method, are up for it.'[63] At the same time, his role was to preserve the operational capacity of his division. Fortunately, there were those who chose to stay. One of the solutions, to increase the leadership ratio, was to relaunch training. Dio encouraged soldiers and non-commissioned officers with the potential, and who had behaved well under fire, to join the officers' training school in Coëtquidan.[64] The curriculum for the first post-war promotion focused mainly on academic training for officers who had proven their operational value and lasted only six months. Yet, in the short term, that decision further impoverished the level of leadership within the division's units.

Dio was perfectly aware of the difficulties he would have to face following the profound reorganisation that affected his large unit. This new *2ᵉ DB* would not outlive the spirit of that of the battles of liberation. The life of peacetime service with its ups and downs would make it fall into line with the other large units of the French army. But Dio did not give up. He knew that his immediate mission would be to preserve the operational capacity of the division after the war, despite losing men who departed for civilian life, or to the Far East, and to training schools. He also knew that the majority of the military leaders of the post-war French Army were not Free French and would not give him any special consideration. He wanted to avoid future inspections, which would not be long in coming, that might recommend the dissolution of the *2ᵉ DB* by noting its operational weakness.

The first order of battle of the *2ᵉ DB* commanded by *Colonel* Dio was dated 26 June. Oddly enough, the division remained organised into *groupements tactiques*. But it was subjected to a major overhaul, particularly in its leadership, which was reinvigorated. For the position of chief of staff, *Lieutenant Colonel* Fieschi, former regimental commander of the *3ᵉ RAC*, was called upon to replace *Colonel* Bernard. The staff section chiefs were reduced to the rank of *capitaine*. The divisional artillery was commanded by *Lieutenant Colonel* Tranié, the engineers by *Commandant* Delage, communications by *Commandant* Lamure, medical by *Médecin-Colonel* Richet, and logistics by *Commandant* Payan. The *GTD* was under the orders of *Lieutenant Colonel* Rouvillois, replaced by *Lieutenant Colonel* de Viéville at the head of the *12ᵉ Cuirs*. The *1/RMT* was commanded by *Lieutenant Colonel* Fosse and the *3ᵉ RAC* by *Commandant* Demarle. The *GTL* was under the command of *Lieutenant Colonel* de Gonfreville, with Minjonnet at the head of the *12ᵉ RCA*, Massu, who had not yet left for Indochina, at that of the *2/RMT* and *Commandant* Devaux at the *40ᵉ RANA*. The *GTV* was under the command of *Colonel* Rémy with Delpierre at the head of the *501ᵉ RCC*, Barboteu for the *3/RMT* and *Commandant* Dovin at the *64ᵉ RADB*. The *1ᵉʳ RMSM* was under the command of *Lieutenant Colonel* de Soultrait. The *RBFM* of *Capitaine de Frégate* Maggiar was quickly returned to the navy. The tank destroyers were handed over to the *9ᵉ Cuirs* of *Lieutenant Colonel* Roy, a new unit within the *2ᵉ DB*. The *13ᵉ Bataillon du Génie* was commanded by *Capitaine* Durcos and the *22ᵉ Groupe Colonial de FTA* by *Commandant* Jeger.[65] The three *GT* commanders were swapped, as were most of the department heads and staff section chiefs of the general staff. The various command functions of the division were lowered by one rank level.

Many departures were recorded, particularly among company officers of the rank of *lieutenant* and *capitaine*. Many of them were reservists. They preferred to resume their civilian lives rather than opt for a career in the army, which was looking to be more than problematic in the aftermath of the war. Their departure would deprive the division of their combat experience accumulated

---

63   Notin, *Le Croisé*, p.342.

64   Among the 285 sent to Coëtquidan, (*Caravane* No.26, p.25) we can mention Mademba Sy of the *1/RMT* and Maurice Courdesses of the *2/RMT*. They were part of the first post-war class, or promotion, named 'Victoire 1945,' which provided 1,747 officers.

65   The ranks of this new leadership of the *2e DB* only mentions the new leaders or those who had changed position.

during the operations to liberate France. There was no training capable of replacing it. As for those who chose a career in the army, many opted to serve in the Far East. They were those who, still young, wanted to continue the adventure with Leclerc and Massu. They were among the best junior officers of the former *2ᵉ DB*.

Personally, *Colonel* Dio was to experience difficult weeks. Two weeks after being named by Leclerc to command the *2ᵉ DB*, he had still not received the official document confirming this assumption of command. On 5 July 1945, he sent a letter to the Minister of War explaining that his situation was becoming difficult and asked him to remedy it:

> This situation, if it continues, risks harming my prestige, vis-à-vis the personnel of the *2ᵉ Division Blindée* and external formations. I respectfully point out to you that having never sought this command, having never stooped to solicit any advancement or any honour whatsoever, I am the last officer on whom such a humiliation could be inflicted.[66]

At last, the official decree appointing him commander of the *2ᵉ DB* came out on 28 July 1945, more than a month after he had actually assumed command. But Dio still held the rank of *colonel*, which was unheard of at the head of a division. In 1945, he was the only one in that situation. It was true that, through its successes, its uniqueness, its status as a beloved unit, the personality of its former leader, the *2ᵉ DB* aroused extreme jealousy within the French Army.

On 1 August 1945, Dio presided over his first major ceremony as commander of the *2ᵉ DB*. During a parade at Fontainebleau, wearing the stripes of a *caporal honoraire* of the *RMT* on his left sleeve, General Wade Haislip, newly appointed commander of the US 7th Army, presented the Presidential Unit Citation to the *2ᵉ DB* on behalf of the President of the United States. *Général* Leclerc was present, but it was *Colonel* Dio who held and handed the division Colours to the American general so that he could pin the prestigious decoration on it. It was to recognise the division for the charge of Strasbourg that the *2ᵉ DB* was awarded this American distinction, which was awarded only to units for exceptional battlefield feats. The text of the citation is:

> The *2d Armored Division, French Army*, assigned the mission, in the campaign to liberate Saverne and Strasbourg, of supporting the attack of the XV American Corps on the enemy's double fortifications in the Vosges Mountains and of exploiting any breakthrough by capturing the eastern exits of Saverne, from 16 to 24 November 1944, constantly alert to the opportunity and acting with powerful, determined shock action and audacious speed, breached the initial line, the Vorvosgen Stellung, by capture of Badonviller on 17 November. Continuing its spirited, relentlessly sustained attack, with skillful maneuver, it breached the second line, the Vosgen Stellung, by forcing a crossing of the Sarre Blanche River at St Michel on the 20 November. Currently, it seized the opportunity afforded by the capture of Blamont by American forces to attack Saverne from the northwest. In a masterful maneuver characterised by audacity, high courage, and resistless speed, the *2d Armored Division, French Army*, operating over terrain which was considered almost impassable to armor and against carefully prepared and strong enemy defenses, converged on the eastern exit of Saverne in columns from both north and south. The defenses of Montbronn were rapidly reduced, the fortifications of Phalsbourg neutralised, the enemy garrison of Saverne captured, and the northern entrance to the Alsace Plain secured by the seizure of the strategic Saverne gate. Ordered to attack Strasbourg, the Division, scarcely pausing overnight, struck in multiple columns on 22 November over a distance of 50 kilometres in a swift, stunning attack which occasioned

---

66   Fonds Leclerc, *lettre 1070/1-CPO du 5 juillet 1945*, boîte 34, dossier 1, chemise 1.

the fall of the city in 48 hours. In the course of this magnificent operation, the *2d Armored Division, French Army,* destroyed the combat effectiveness of four enemy divisions, opened the gateway to the Alsatian Plain, liberated the capital of Alsace, and contributed greatly to the success of Allied Arms.'[67]

This Presidential Unit Citation was presented in the form of a small blue ribbon enclosed in a gold border. Even today, it is worn, individually, by soldiers who serve in one of the historical units of the *2ᵉ DB*. When American officers see this distinction on the uniforms of French soldiers, it is easy to realise what it represents for the soldiers of their country. Officers who graduate from the US Military Academy at West Point know about the charge of the *2ᵉ DB* on Strasbourg because it is taught as part of their tactical training. They also know that 'outside of official documents, Patch called Leclerc's men 'crack troops.'[68]

Leclerc embarked for Indochina on 18 August. He had the opportunity to participate in the first anniversary of the liberation of Alençon on 12 August, accompanied by 'his comrades-in-arms, including the oldest and most faithful, *Colonel* Dio, his current successor...'[69] For the occasion, the Avenue du Général Leclerc and Place de la Division Leclerc were inaugurated in the city. As a token of their gratitude, the citizens of Alençon presented Leclerc with a star of *Grand-Croix* of the *Légion d'honneur* set with diamonds.

On 6 and 10 August, the two atomic bombs on Hiroshima and on Nagasaki put an end to the conflict with Japan. But the Indochinese problem remained very complex and the *groupement de marche* of the *2ᵉ DB* remained in place. *Lieutenant Colonel* Massu's unit included a little more than 2,000 men. It was called upon to serve within the *Corps Expéditionnaire Français en Extrême-Orient*, a role similar to that of the *RMT* within the *2ᵉ DB*. As a result, *Colonel* Dio would remain very close to the unit. When the *groupement de marche* left, Dio sent them General Order No.124, dated 29 August 1945:

> As *Lieutenant Colonel* Massu's group is about to leave the metropolis to go to Indochina, the *colonel* commanding the *2ᵉ DB* sends him his warm greetings. He regrets not having been able, due to the rapid establishment of this group, to visit the units that make it up before their departure. The *2ᵉ DB* will keep the memory of this select element, which will perpetuate in the Far East a tradition to which we are all unfailingly attached.'[70]

The *Ville de Strasbourg*, an old cargo ship of the *Messageries Maritimes*, left Marseille on 9 September with a first detachment of 1,000 men under the orders of *Lieutenant-Colonel* Massu, seconded by two faithful men, *Commandants* Dronne and Sarrazac.[71]

In Paris, on 21 August 1945, Paul Bellon made the declaration creating an association bearing the name *Association de la Maison des Anciens Combattants de la 2ᵉ DB*, whose head office was located at 12 Rue François 1ᵉʳ in the 8ᵉ Arrondissement of the capital. This declaration was inserted in the *Journal Officiel* of 25 August 1945, Mr Gentin being designated as the secretary general of the association. The goal of this new association was to bring together all those who belonged to the 2ᵉ DB in order to:

67   War Department, Washington DC, 6 June 1945, General Orders No.44.
68   Destrem, *L'Aventure de Leclerc,* p.318.
69   *Caravane* No.26, du 25 août 1945, p.5, '12 août 1944: Libération d'Alençon'.
70   Fonds Leclerc, *Général Dio – Juin 1945 au 3 Août 1947,* boîte 4, chemise 1, dossier 1.
71   *Caravane* No.27, 20 Septembre 1945, p.23. 'Ils sont partis…'.

- provide its members with… mutual aid and assistance in all forms that they may need for themselves, their families, and the families of their comrades who died for France,
- support, with all means, their moral and material interests,
- represent its members to the public authorities for all matters relating to the activity of the association.

Its objective was twofold. First of all, it was social. The command of the *2^e DB* had anticipated the difficulties that some of its soldiers would face when returning to civilian life, particularly foreigners. On 10 January 1945, Leclerc had created the social service of the *2^e DB* to help the wounded (600 at the beginning of 1945) as well as their families, and to help the widows and orphans.[72] Around 20 social workers would be employed to resolve difficult social cases. The second aim was to allow all the veterans, scattered throughout France, to maintain the spirit of the division by finding in the *Maison* 'a common point, a centre of attraction…where this fraternity, this spirit of the DB, are found stronger and more firm.'[73] The name '*Maison*' (house), which Leclerc wanted, was important, because it meant that the association should be considered as a second home by the veterans. To this end, under the action of the editor-in-chief of *Caravane*, Louis Tournebize, chapters of the *Maison des Anciens* were created throughout France. Soon, 23 chapters were listed in France and five in North Africa.

On 18 September, Dio organised the constitutive assembly to define the statutes of the Association and appoint the executive committee of 30 members who would hold an office. Unsurprisingly, *Colonel* Louis Dio was the first president of the Association. Leclerc was the founding president while *Colonel* Vézinet and a soldier by the name of Vilgrain were vice presidents. Dio was not naturally drawn to this kind of associative function. But, most certainly, he accepted this position at *Général* Leclerc's request to demonstrate the involvement of the command behind the establishment of the Association. In this, he remained consistent with the recommendation that Leclerc made to his men at Fontainebleau: 'look for your leaders and find your comrades.' Only those who served in the *RTST* after 26 August 1940, then in the *2^e DB* until 8 May 1945, could claim to become members of the Association. The *Maison* would thus provide the relay allowing the former members to keep in touch with each other. Its director was *Commandant* de Boissoudy. The cramped nature of the first headquarters, in the premises of the HQ of the *2e DB* at 12 Rue François 1er, did not meet the ambitions that Dio and his team wanted to give to the *Maison*. So, at the beginning of 1946, they decided to move to 118 Rue de Grenelle to occupy the small Hôtel du Maréchal de Villars. Very close to the town hall of the 7e Arrondissement, the building offered a magnificent setting. Dio had to have used his connections to find such location.

25 August 1945 marked the first anniversary of the liberation of Paris. Curiously, *Caravane* does not mention any special ceremony. In April, Paris had received the *Croix de ville Compagnon de la Libération* (Companion City of the Liberation) from the hands of de Gaulle. Issue 26 of *Caravane*[74] offered a page to *Général* Chaban-Delmas, national military delegate in the occupied territories, to share his memories of the day of the liberation of the capital in 1944. Issue 27 devoted a major article to the commemoration of the battles of Le Bourget and Blanc-Mesnil. These battles, the day after the liberation of Paris, involved the *GTD* and the *GTL*. Many officers and soldiers lost their lives there. A large ceremony involving all the communes of the region took place in Blanc-Mesnil. The *2e DB* was present with detachments of the *12e Cuirs*, *RMT*, *3e RAC*, and *13e BG*. After a review of the troops, *Colonel* Dio presented decorations. He first presented the *Croix de*

---

72   *Caravane* No.36, 10 Février 1946, p.20, 'Assistantes sociales'.
73   *Caravane* No.36, 10 Février 1946, p.20, 'Assistantes sociales'.
74   It is on the front page of the 25 August 1945 issue (p.3).

la Libération to the son of *Adjudant Chef* René Quantin,[75] who died in August in Mézières-sous-Ballon. A photo shows *Colonel* Dio carrying the young boy in his arms to hug him, in front of the boy's mother dressed all in black. He also pinned *Croix de Guerre* on the chests of resistance fighters. After the parade, there was a mass, with an altar erected on the turret of Dio's Sherman tank, *Sainte-Anne d'Auray*. A banquet was offered to the officers while the soldiers were invited to lunch at the homes of the inhabitants of Blanc-Mesnil.

The *2ᵉ DB* was still stationed in the Fontainebleau region, and the units were still housed in local homes and cohabitation was becoming increasingly difficult. Operational activities were de facto reduced, and diversionary activities had to be found. The general staff, on Dio's instructions, organised divisional challenges for the units. For example, a competition that included events such as commando marching, shooting, drawing, cross-country running, river crossing, and singing took place on 28 August 1945. *Colonel* Dio presented the winner's cup to the team from the *12ᵉ RCA* and 'in a few words, highlighted the need for everyone to maintain their morale and physical fitness at all costs.'[76] In this immediate post-war period, the *2ᵉ DB*, along with the entire French Army, suffered from unsuitable living and working conditions.

At the end of the month, a visit brightened up the lives of the soldiers and officers of the *2ᵉ DB*. On 30 August, Dio welcomed the famous singer Lily Pons into the garden of his villa in Marlotte. Lily Pons was a Frenchwoman who had become a naturalised American and had supported Free France since 1940. She sang many times in the United States during the war for the benefit of French Relief (an association providing relief for the French). She ended each of her performances with the *Marseillaise*. Dio declared her the godmother of the *2ᵉ DB*. He gave her the rank of *Spahi de 1ʳᵉ Classe* and gave her the red cap of the *spahis*. He invited her to climb into an armoured car named after her. Then there were many photos taken of the global celebrity.

At the urgent request of the armoured branch management, the *2ᵉ DB* set up an internal working committee on 30 August. The aim was to draw up the main lessons learnt from the war. These were to be used in studies aimed at designing the structures of the future French armoured division. Dio entrusted this committee to *Lieutenant Colonel* Rouvillois, who brought together officers representing all the units. To prepare their work, a questionnaire was distributed to them. Two working sessions taking place at Nangis, the headquarters of the *GTD* commander, were sufficient. On 11 September, *Colonel* Dio sent the study to the army staff. It was accompanied by a document requesting approval of the personnel tables of the *2ᵉ Division Blindée*.[77] This letter was quite surprising on two counts. First, in terms of form. Dio had received the request from the branch management, but he sent the response directly to the army staff, bypassing a hierarchical level. Second, in substance. If the document agreed to make some savings in personnel and equipment, it recommended a general reinforcement of resources, particularly armoured ones. What was Dio's tactic? Sensing that the branch headquarters wanted to reduce the number of units, he sent a document to central headquarters for approval, which he presented as temporary. By placing the study's proposals at a high level, he hoped to limit the announced reductions. It was a risky tactic, but the aura of the *Division Leclerc* in the operational domain was still strong among the military leaders.

All of these uncertainties did not prevent *Colonel* Dio from carrying out his duties rigorously – quite the contrary. Thus, on 4 September, the 'commander of the *2ᵉ DB* informed the troops under

---

75   Serving in 1940 within the *BM1*, this non-commissioned officer participated in the Gabon campaign and then Syria. Joining *Colonne Leclerc* in 1942, he participated in the Fezzan 2 campaign, then Tripolitania, and then finally Tunisia. Section leader within the 2nd Battalion of the *RMT*, he was killed in his half-track, hit by a shell. *Chevalier* of the *Légion d'Honneur*, he was made a Companion of the Liberation by decree of 24 March 1945.

76   *Caravane* No.27, 20 Septembre, 1945, 'La Coupe du G.T.L.', p.29.

77   Fonds Leclerc, *No. 72/SC du 11 Septembre 1945*, boîte 34, dossier 1, chemise 1.

his command of some convictions handed down at the sessions of the Military Tribunal of the *2ᵉ DB*.'⁷⁸ Reading this document, it appeared that military justice at that time was not lax: three months in prison for a *marsouin* of the *RMT* for falling asleep while on guard duty. Two years in prison for a sapper of the *13ᵉ Génie* for assault on a superior. Two years in prison for embezzling postal packages. Three years in prison for a *cuirassier* of the *12ᵉ Cuirs* for assault and battery. Five years in prison for a *bigor* of the *3ᵉ RAC* for desertion. Ten years in prison for an artilleryman of the *64ᵉ RADB* for indecent assault with violence. It should be noted that a certain number of volunteers, recruited during the campaign, joined for reasons other than patriotic ones. 'Others may have sins to atone for and prefer not to wait for the settling of scores.'⁷⁹ The command, aware of that, did not tolerate any fault and issued harsh punishments to set an example. This iron discipline was one of the hallmarks of the *2ᵉ DB* under Leclerc. This explains the generally exemplary behaviour of the men of the *2ᵉ DB* during the occupation in Germany. Dio adopted the same rules without weakening, especially since, with peace restored, the French Army had to be irreproachable.

On 6 September, the commander of the *2ᵉ DB* signed an Order of the Day for the departure of *Colonel* Bernard. He was a man in the shadows, but he had been very useful as Leclerc's chief of staff since 1943.⁸⁰ Dio ensured that those leaving were honoured according to their merit and *Colonel* Bernard was one of them. Like Dio, he cultivated discretion and humility, always putting the general interest before his own.

Finally, on 1 October 1945, the commander of the *2ᵉ DB* was promoted to *général de brigade*. This promotion would above all allow Dio to more easily carry out the implicit mission that Leclerc had entrusted to him by designating him as his successor: to integrate the *2ᵉ DB* into the organisation of the French Army, despite jealousies.

At the end of November, the first anniversary of the liberation of Strasbourg took on particular importance, especially since Leclerc was absent. The commander of the *2ᵉ DB* was present with *Colonel* Rouvillois on that day of 23 November 1945. *Général* de Langlade, who was to become military governor of the city in a few days, was also there. Dio had brought detachments from the entire division. Former members of the *2ᵉ DB* living in the region had been invited to attend in large numbers. The ceremony therefore retained the *Division Leclerc* stamp. *Général* de Montsabert, commander-in-chief in Germany, made the trip. *Mr* Frey, mayor of Strasbourg, inaugurated the statue of Jean-Baptiste Kléber that the Germans had removed and which, for its return to the square that bears his name, was flanked by two tanks from the *12ᵉ Cuirs*. His speech was addressed to:

> The officers and soldiers of the *Division Leclerc*! Please accept our heartfelt thanks for all that you have done for us, and rest assured that the memory of your extraordinary feat of arms will never fade from our memories, but will be faithfully transmitted from generation to generation.⁸¹

Mr Frey realised that the speed and audacity of the men of the *2ᵉ DB* in liberating his city had saved it from the terrible destruction and large numbers of civilian deaths that had happened in Alençon and Paris. During the official lunch, '*Général* Dio, Leclerc's companion, spoke on behalf of his comrades-in-arms, rightly noting that the struggle was continuing and that France had to

78   Fonds Leclerc, *Ordre Général No.126, E-M.-1er bureau en date du 4 Septembre 1945,* boîte 34, dossier 1, chemise 1.
79   Massu, *Sept Ans,* p.153.
80   Fonds Leclerc, *Ordre du Jour No.127, 1er bureau, du 6 Septembre 1945*, boîte 34, dossier 1, chemise 1.
81   Louis Forest, 'Le Rendez-vous de Kléber' *Caravane* No.32, 5 Décembre 1945, p.8.

be put back on its feet.'[82] The commander of the *2ᵉ DB* took up Leclerc's important theme of the reconstruction of the country. The first anniversary of the liberation of Strasbourg and the fulfilment of the Oath of Kufra was celebrated with pomp and warmth by the Alsatians. Returning to Marlotte in his car, Dio remembered the jubilation of this population, who had not forgotten. He wrote a note to Leclerc to tell him about it.

At the beginning of 1946, the division lost one of its officers, *Commandant* de Marcilly, following a long illness. This senior officer had supported Massu throughout the campaign and had even succeeded him as head of the 2nd Battalion of the *RMT*. All the officers under Dio attended the funeral in Saint Cloud on 4 January. '*Général* Dio …. retraced in a few words the brilliant career of the deceased and addressed him a moving farewell.'[83] In the days following Marcilly's burial, Dio chaired the general meeting of the *Association de la Maison des Anciens de la 2ᵉ DB*, which took place on 19 January 1946 at the new headquarters on Rue de Grenelle, in the Salle des Horticulteurs. '*Général* Dio, in his particularly thunderous voice that was so well known to the veterans, addressed the assembly: gentlemen, come closer, so as not to force *Commandant* de Boissoudy to bellow like a jackass.'[84] In his always colourful and extemporaneous language, Dio launched the first general assembly of the *Maison des Anciens de la 2ᵉ DB* in a good mood. It defined the activities to be carried out and established a budget to do so. From that date, the *Maison des Anciens* got its bearings. Dio, always very pragmatic, let the ideas flow and redirected the debates. He did not intervene often but, when he did, his opinion counted.

Fortunately, life as a division commander also brought entertainment to the young *général*. Jean Nohain, who was a veteran of the division, known under the name of Jaboune, wrote a two-act play at the time called *Le Bal des Pompiers* (The Firefighters' Ball). The first performance at the Théâtre Verlaine was reserved for veterans of the *2ᵉ DB* and took place on 14 February 1946. A photo of the event[85] shows Dio with his kepi, cigarette in his lips, deep in discussion with Jean Nohain and Claude Dauphin.[86]

In this transitional period after the war, many studies, lasting nearly six months, were conducted by the Parisian general staff to restructure the army units. These restructurings were aimed primarily to reduce the size of the forces, which was no secret to anyone. Politicians had an eye for the army budget, which they wanted to reduce now that peace had returned. Dio was of course very well informed, and he was rightly concerned with respect to the results of the studies. On 20 January 1946, Général de Gaulle resigned. The army budget that the head of the provisional government had proposed was not voted on by the Chamber of Deputies. The return of the parties to French political life dissuaded de Gaulle from remaining in command. He considered that he was no longer able, under those conditions, to carry out the reforms that the country needed. Dio was aware that his departure would weaken the future of the *2ᵉ DB*. He wrote to Leclerc on 23 February: 'I don't know if the *2ᵉ DB* will ever be set up; I don't even know whether I'll be thrown out soon like the garbage. Now that the Big Boss has retired to his tent, anything could happen.'[87]

82   Forest, 'Le Rendez-vous de Kléber' *Caravane* No.32, 5 Décembre 1945, p.9.
83   *Caravane* No.35, 25 Janvier 1946, 'Le Chef de Bataillon de Marcilly', p.31.
84   *Caravane* No.36, 10 Février 1946, 'Assemblée Générale des Anciens de la 2e DB', p.21.
85   *Caravane* No. 38, 10 Mars 1946, 'Le Bal des Pompiers', p.18, photo at the top of the page.
86   Claude Dauphin, whose real name was Claude Marie Eugène Legrand, was the brother of Jean Nohain, also a former member of the 2e DB. He became a well-known film actor in the post-war period. The 2e DB welcomed many global personalities to the show. Among the best known were Jean Marais, Jean-Claude Pascal, and Jean Gabin.
87   Fonds Leclerc, *Correspondance Leclerc et Dio: Lettre Dio à Leclerc du 23 Janvier 1946,* boîte 17 a, chemise 1, dossier 2.

An official document arrived in Saint-Germain to inform the forces of the decisions taken regarding the new format envisaged for the French Army. The term used was 'compression of the army.' Three divisions were planned to remain in Germany: the *5ᵉ DB* and two infantry divisions. The 9 divisions stationed in metropolitan France had to be transformed into *groupements tactiques*. That meant that from a size of 15,000 men, these large units would be reduced to around 5,000 men. The divisions would therefore become brigades. Before responding to the general staff, *Général* Dio turned again to Leclerc, the only protector whose aura was still powerful among politicians and the military. On 14 February 1946, Dio wrote a manuscript letter to his former commander in Indochina.[88] He informed him of the plan to reduce the *2ᵉ DB*. 'If this happens, there is nothing to say,' he wrote, because the actual strength of the *2ᵉ DB*, after all the departures, barely amounted to more than 4,000 men. Dio 'no longer saw the possibility of putting it back on its feet in its original form.' But he feared, 'manoeuvres directed against you and everything connected to you and that the high command will take advantage of this to oust from the future *2ᵉ DB* everything that recalls *Général* Leclerc and Free France.' He then asked Leclerc 'to write personally to the minister to obtain satisfaction on the following points:

1. Keep the integrity of the *2ᵉ DB*: this maximum demand was necessary to ensure minimum satisfaction.
2. Designate the GT formed from the *2ᵉ DB* by the name *2ᵉ Brigade Blindée* or *Brigade Blindée du Tchad*.
3. Maintain the insignia of the *2ᵉ DB*.
4. Command of the armoured brigade and the units of this brigade exercised by former members of the *2ᵉ DB* (practically a choice to be exercised by myself).
5. Composition of this armoured brigade based on former FFL units, namely:
    a. Infantry: *Régiment de Marche du Tchad*
    b. Artillery: *3ᵉ RAC*
    c. Tanks: *501ᵉ*.'[89]

What did Leclerc do after receiving Dio's letter? Certainly, he intervened. But at what level? It is unknown. In his official response to the Chief of the General Staff on 12 March 1946,[90] Dio made his suggestions concerning the compression of the *2ᵉ DB* into a 'Combat Command.'[91] To compose the new unit, he recommended keeping the three Free French units, arguing for his choice. For the infantry, the *RMT* could provide one battalion out of the three existing ones. For the artillery, the choice was more difficult. According to Dio, it should be the *3ᵉ RAC* for reasons of seniority within the historic *2ᵉ DB*. The same principle should lead to favouring the *501ᵉ RCC* for the tank regiments. Finally, for reconnaissance, the choice should fall on the *RMSM*, also a historic regiment. As for the designation of the commander of this Combat Command, Dio favoured *Colonel* Rémy over *Lieutenant Colonel* Rouvillois. Here too, despite his friendship for the latter, he remained consistent in the preference he believed should be given to those who had chosen Free France. As for the geographical location to station the units, he recommended Versailles for the infantry, engineers, and the maintenance unit, Rambouillet for the tanks, Fontainebleau for the artillery and the anti-aircraft artillery. The CP could be established in Saint-Germain with the

---

88   During this period, Leclerc reconquered Northern Tonkin under very difficult circumstances, fighting with the Chinese Army and having to face the Communists led by Ho Chi Minh.

89   Fonds Leclerc, *Correspondance Leclerc et Dio: Lettre Dio à Leclerc du 14 Février 1946*, boîte 17 a., chemise 1, dossier 2.

90   Fonds Leclerc, *Courrier du Général Dio au Chef d'État-Major Général en date du 12 Mars 1946*, boîte 34.

91   Combat Command is a term borrowed from the American Army which designates a *groupement tactique*.

communications, transportation, and medical. For the name, he recommended either the *Brigade Blindée du Tchad* or the *2ᵉ Brigade Blindée* to maintain the traditions of the *Division Leclerc*.

In the midst of these studies, vital for the future of the *2ᵉ DB*, Dio also had to invest in the operation of the *Maison des Anciens*. After the developments that were agreed following the installation at 118 Rue de Grenelle, the time had come to make the new location for the headquarters official. On Friday, 15 March, the club was inaugurated, the part that included the bar, the restaurant, and the library of *the Maison des Anciens* of the *Division Leclerc*. *Général* Dio presided over it in the presence of Edmond Michelet, Minister of the Armed Forces, *Générals* de Lattre, Larminat, Legentilhomme, Revers, and many military and civilian personalities such as Maurice Schumann, the voice of London.[92] Issue 40 of *Caravane* gives a photographic summary of this inauguration which was a real Parisian socialite soirée. The photos allow us to see Maurice Schumann 'telling a good story' to a group of officers including *Général* de Larminat.[93] *Général* Dio is next to the broadly-smiling *Général* de Lattre.[94] Everything was organised down to the smallest detail. The reception was a high-quality affair. The drinks were served in glasses 'straight from the Baccarat crystal factory which, in opening its doors, wanted to honour its liberators.'[95] This inaugural evening was important because it brought together the main civil and military leaders of French defence, and positioned the *2ᵉ DB*, through its *Maison des Anciens*, as a dynamic unit that had its place in a peacetime army. The next day, Saturday, 16 March, the first evening open to members of the *Maison* took place. From that date on, the restaurant and bar would welcome veterans and friends of the *2ᵉ DB* throughout the year. The *Maison* would serve as a stopover, a point of contact, even a refuge, for all those who fought under Leclerc's orders. Dio had succeeded in the mission entrusted to him in this area.

The decision of the military high command concerning the reorganisation measures was made on 28 March 1946.[96] It took effect on 1 April. Dio's proposals were partly accepted. The official name was *Groupement Blindée de la 2ᵉ DB* or *GB2*. The composition of the units was in line with Dio's suggestions. However, his proposals concerning the garrisons where the units were stationed underwent changes. While the CP of the *GB2* was located in Saint-Germain, the *501ᵉ RCC* was located in Alençon, the *1/RMT* in Melun, and the *3ᵉ RAC* in Vernon. The *RMSM*, the *12ᵉ Cuirs*, the *12ᵉ RCA*, and the *40ᵉ RA* were assigned to other units. The two battalions of the *RMT* were dissolved as well as the *64ᵉ RADB*. As for the appointment of the officers, it was in line with the recommendations, *Colonel* Rémy would be Dio's successor when he left his command.[97] For the command of the units, *Lieutenant Colonel* de Soultrait was appointed to the *501ᵉ RCC*, *Commandant* Lavergne to the *1/RMT*, and *Commandant* Demarle to the *3ᵉ RAC*.

---

92   Maurice Schumann was the one who spoke regularly on the 'Honneur et Patrie' programme on Radio London between July 1940 and May 1944, and who was known as the voice of London to all who listened to him, at their own risk, in occupied France.

93   *Caravane* No. 40, 'Le Club des Leclerc', pp.16–17.

94   In a letter to Leclerc, Dio mentioned the smiles of *Général* de Lattre who 'sincere or not, assured in the presence of a gathering of *générals* that the 2e DB is the first division that he would put back on its feet as soon as circumstances allowed.' (Fonds Leclerc, *Courrier Manuscrit en Date du 10 Avril 1946*, boîte 17a, dossier 1, chemise 2.) Dio had known de Lattre since 1943 in Morocco. He was very wary of him, aware of the liabilities accumulated with the boss of the 2e DB.

95   As soon as they reopened after the liberation of Baccarat, the Cristalleries de Baccarat wanted to honour their liberators by offering them this gift. Charles d'Ydewalle, 'Notre Maison', *Caravane* No. 42, 10 mai 1946, p.23.

96   Fonds Leclerc, *Note No. 04032 EMA/1, Objet: Dissolution des 1re D.B., 2e D.B., 1re D.M.I., 2e D.M.I.,* boîte 34, chemise 3, dossier 3.

97   Ultimately, it was *Colonel* Rouvillois who succeeded Dio in September 1946.

Général Dio was generally satisfied because the three main units came from Free France, including two units from the ex-*GTD*, the *1/RMT* and the *3ᵉ RAC*. *Commandants* Lavergne and Demarle, the unit commanders, were from the faithful of Chad. The spirit of the *2ᵉ DB* would be maintained with the reorganisation. That is what mattered most in the mind of *Général* Dio and, most certainly, also in that of *Général* Leclerc. Dio led this 'compression' with great commitment and tactical sense, demonstrating an excellent ability to move in the political-military spheres. He proved his adaptability and the accuracy of his reasoning outside the operational domain. Personally, he was satisfied to have succeeded in establishing the CP of *GB2* in the city of Saint-Germain. Historically, it was in that garrison that the reinforcement battalion of the *2ᵉ DB* was created in 1944. Dio liked the city, at once both close to and far from Paris, located on the edge of an immense forest. In addition, the Grammont district had a military riding centre, allowing him to practice the sport that he enjoyed. His ankle was healed by then, and he could once again wear his riding boots.

On 1 April 1946, *Général* Dio officially took command of *GB2*. It was not a promotion since he was downgrading his responsibilities: from a division, he now commanded a brigade. Prioritising above all the survival of the historic *2ᵉ DB*, he accepted this personal downgrade knowing that, unfortunately, there were very few Free French to defend him within the Parisian general staff.[98] He wrote to Leclerc: 'I was deeply affected by this dissolution, but I believe in all conscience that I have not done badly in the management of your legacy.'[99] For Dio, the main thing was to have been able to save part of the *2ᵉ DB* and preserve its traditions, which had not been the case for the *1ʳᵉ DFL*. He also knew that his promotion to the rank of *général officier* aroused very strong jealousy among those who, once peace had returned, demanded that the rules of advancement respect the usual age limits for each rank. *Général* Dio, who fortunately had some allies in place, had been warned that he would very soon have a posting outside the metropolis. That is what he wanted most.

On the occasion of the dissolution of the *2ᵉ DB*,[100] the commanding *général* duly organised a military ceremony on 6 April 1946. It was an opportunity to bring together for the last time the units that had served gloriously during the campaign to liberate France and to honour their 1,600 dead during the fighting. It was also an opportunity to thank, before their departure, those who would not remain within the *GB2*. He sent an official telegram to Leclerc:

> On the final *prise d'armes* (ceremony) in which all units and standards participated today in Saint-Germain at the time of the dissolution of the *2ᵉ DB*, we shared with emotion in the memory of the glorious stages covered under your illustrious command Stop The tradition and the spirit with which you have marked us for the good of the Fatherland will persist in the units resulting from our dear *DB* Stop We hope that they will be worthy of the valiant *groupement de marche* of the Far East which has the honour of continuing to serve under your orders and whose brilliant operations, which have returned Indochina to France, we have not ceased to follow Stop Accept, mon *Général*, the expression of the entire affectionate devotion of your former companions, soldiers, non-commissioned officers, officers, and of me End Dio

---

98   The other Free French division, the *1re DFL*, was curiously dissolved on 15 August 1945, while *Général* de Gaulle was still in office. Many of the personnel from that division did not understand the decision.

99   Fonds Leclerc, *Correspondance Leclerc et Dio: Courrier Manuscrit en date du 10 Avril 1946*, boîte 17a, chemise 1.

100 The *2e Division Blindée* was recreated on 1 July 1979, 33 years after this dissolution. The first commanding *général* was *Général* du Payrat, a *marsouin*. It was again dissolved in 1999, with *Général* d'Anselme being its last commander. The traditions were then taken up by the *2e Brigade Blindée*, created as a replacement, whose first commander was *Général* Cuche, who would assume the presidency of the association of the *Maison des Anciens de la 2e DB* for several years afterwards. Since its creation in 1943, the *2e DB* has existed twice, for a period of three years and then 20 years. Twice, in the flow of the reforms of the French Army, it was reduced to a brigade.

Leclerc answered:

> Very moved to learn of the dissolution of the *2ᵉ DB* and the final *prise d'armes* Stop Firmly hope that this will not mark a separation between the veterans of the division but that they will always maintain the same spirit in the service of the country Stop My affectionate remembrance to all and for you my dear Dio my faithful friendship End Général Leclerc[101]

Dio assumed his new role as commander of *GB2* without any qualms. He did so all the more easily since, during this period, his personal life had just undergone a major transformation. At 38, an old bachelor, on 27 February 1946 he married a young woman named Denise Wagener at the town hall of the 7th Arrondissement. The religious marriage took place the same day in the church of Saint-Pierre du Gros-Caillou, at 92 Rue Saint Dominique.[102] *Caravane* specifies that the ceremony took place, 'in the strictest privacy' and the name of his wife mentioned in the review was Madame Bouchet.[103] How did Louis Dio meet this young woman? Particularly discreet about his private life, his correspondence does not provide any information on the circumstances of their meeting. In any case, the photos of Général Dio, in the period 1945 and 1946, reveal a certain physical transformation. On 22 June 1945 in Fontainebleau, when he took command of the *2ᵉ DB*, Dio was a strong and imposing man. Leclerc seemed tiny next to him when he hugged him after placing his neck ribbon as a *Commandeur* of the *Légion d'honneur*. Six months later, during the Christmas celebrations for the children of the *2ᵉ DB*, at the end of December 1945, '*Général* Dio was there, smiling (and he did not smile often) and as young as a young *lieutenant*.'[104] The staff who knew him noted this change. Indeed, at the beginning of 1946, Dio's silhouette had become more refined, as had his face. His moustache was finely trimmed. The old bachelor had transformed into a future husband who was visibly more attentive to his appearance. These photos may suggest that this was a happy period in Louis Dio's personal life. In this context, it was certainly easier for him to accept professional turpitudes. Unfortunately, this marriage would not be without its problems for him in the long term.

The dissolution and reorganisation operations monopolised Dio's energy during the spring of 1946. He kept Leclerc informed by letter: 'the compression of the DB is practically finished and I hope that GB2 will soon be operating at full capacity.'[105] The transition took a long time for the simple reason that it concerned personnel, many of whom had families: the transfers had to be carried out with the greatest care. Dio continued to inform Leclerc of the atmosphere in which this reorganisation at the national level continued, 'in an atmosphere of demagogy, incoherence and high fantasy.' In this letter, Dio also mentioned the rumour of Leclerc's return to France during the month of July. He had even learnt that the command of North Africa would be reserved for him. At the end of his missive, Dio informed him that his wish to be assigned to Madagascar would not happen. He added that he could then ask him for a 'drop-off point' in North Africa under his orders. The former *méhariste* was visibly disappointed with his current job. With the reorganisation complete, he no longer hid his impatience to be posted overseas. The colonial soldier that he was had never really served in mainland France until now. Due to his proximity to the capital,

---

101 Fonds Leclerc, *Télégrammes en date du 9 Avril 1946*, boîte 34, dossier 1, chemise 1.

102 The religious ceremony is mentioned on the baptismal certificate in the collection of the Diocesan Archives of Vannes.

103 *Caravane* No.38, 10 Mars 1946, p.27, 'Quelles Nouvelles'.

104 Louis Forest, 'Le Coin du Râleur', *Caravane* No.34, 10 Janvier 1946, p.30.

105 Fonds Leclerc, *Courrier Manuscrit en Date du 22 Mai 1946*, boîte 17a, dossier 1, chemise 2. The letterhead of the correspondence card on which Dio wrote was still marked with the *2e DB* insignia. This shows that, for many veterans, the dissolution of the division had not yet truly sunk in.

he was a privileged observer of the Parisian general staff; they were clearly not part of his world or his tastes. His only consolation remained command. He continued to live in contact with his men, surprising them with unexpected visits to the workplace and chatting with them. It was true that he knew how to adapt his language and speak to them in a familiar manner. The men adored this 'colourful character, this magnificent warrior worthy of Leclerc'[106] who did not hesitate to smoke a cigarette with them or even share their lunch in the mess hall. For the time, in his style of command Général Dio was completely atypical. But that is how he saw his command, and he did not care about being 'in tune with the times' now that the war was over.

On 20 July 1946, Leclerc was appointed inspector of land forces in North Africa. Coming from Saigon, he landed in Paris on 26 July to take up his new duties. Dio was in Villacoublay to welcome him. In the meantime, Dio's future had become clearer. A decree signed on 22 July assigned him to command the territories of southern Tunisia. Did Leclerc intervene for his assignment? There is a strong chance because normally the assignment to North Africa was reserved for metropolitan troops, not for colonials, who were typically sent to Asia or Sub-Saharan Africa. Leclerc kept a close eye on those who served him. 'If Leclerc was loyal to his suzerain (de Gaulle), he was loyal to his own vassals …. Leclerc wanted and obtained for his subordinates from the first day that the greatest missions be entrusted to them.'[107]

A few days later, on 1 August 1946, Général Leclerc spent the day with Dio. The two men met in Saint-Germain-en-Laye, where the GB2 and its staff were based. Photos show this meeting: Leclerc was still in light tropical uniform with a short-sleeved shirt while Dio was in regulation uniform with a jacket. They were probably taking stock of the situation together regarding the reorganisation of the French Army in the immediate post-war period. After his year spent in Indochina, Leclerc needed to get back to the course of metropolitan affairs. They discussed together the difficulties concerning the management of personnel who had belonged to the 2^e DB. The former officers and soldiers knew that their superiors had not abandoned them and they did not hesitate to ask for their support. Leclerc and Dio followed the careers of their subordinates and intervened whenever necessary. They thus ensured their assignments but also their promotions and decorations.

During the day, the two general officers went to Paris to the *Maison des Anciens*. Dio showed Leclerc the new premises that he had inaugurated on 15 March 1946. The director, *Commandant* de Boissoudy, was there with the members of the executive committee and all the staff. The association, under the presidency of Dio, had found its cruising speed. The half dozen social workers seconded to the *Maison des Anciens de la 2^e DB* were not idle. In addition to social work, the association helped maintain contact between the former demobilised soldiers who had returned to all regions of the country. They could, as Leclerc had asked them, be active patriots. Their line of conduct was defined thus by this former member of the *DB*: 'we must not – and we do not want to – be veterans of committees and *cafés du commerce*, profitlessly rehashing old stories from times gone by, but we must remain fighters, fighting in peace today to rebuild our country, as we fought yesterday in the war to liberate our country.'[108] The visit ended with a very pleasant meal. 'There was no speech – that is not the style of the *Maison* – but in a few frank and simple words, *Général* Dio expressed all our joy at having among us the man who was the soul of the 2e DB and repeated to him how happy we were with this reunion.'[109] Leclerc was pleased with what he saw and congratulated Dio 'for having found a lively and welcoming *Maison*, worthy of our ideal, this

106 Mauras, *Souvenirs, 1939–1946*, p.223.
107 Bendjebbar, Levisse-Touzé, ed., 'Leclerc, Soldat de Légende', *Du Capitaine de Hauteclocque au Général Leclerc* p.414.
108 *Caravane* No.41, 25 Avril 1946, p.1, 'Adieux à la 2e DB'.
109 *Caravane* No.48, 25 Août 1946, p.21., 'La Visite du Général Leclerc'.

'spirit of the *2ᵉ DB*.'[110] It was he who, as the first president, created the framework, the organisation, and the dynamics of the association. The Maison is a specificity of the *2ᵉ DB*. No other division created such a structure at the end of the war, which partly explains why more than 75 years later, the association is still very much alive.

The summer of 1946 saw many ceremonies take place along the route of the *2ᵉ DB* to celebrate the second anniversary of the liberation. Leclerc, present in France, was invited to the locations of combat by the towns liberated by the division. Dio accompanied Leclerc in the Departments of Sarthe and Orne. Alençon would become an unmissable event. Then, at the end of August, it was the ceremonies in the Paris region that took up the agenda of the two *généraux*. Their presence was desired everywhere. They were the object of a real cult. Streets, avenues, and squares were inaugurated in number all along the route followed by the *2ᵉ DB*. Popular jubilation and joy were the order of the day.

Sometimes, certain ceremonies reminded the veterans of sad memories. That was the case for Dio in the summer of 1946 at Le Bourget. Rare for him, he agreed to deliver a brief but poignant speech to pay tribute to *Commandant* Corlu.

> To evoke the memory of *Commandant* Corlu is to evoke the memory of Free France from the very beginning in all its nobility, purity, and selflessness. Corlu was one of those young and ardent men in love with the highest ideals who, before the tragedy of the world war, had deliberately turned their backs on the easy life of the metropolis to seek fulfilment in the simple and harsh grandeur of Saharan life. Corlu was certainly one of the men I loved the most: to his qualities of heart and mind, to his qualities as a leader and soldier, were added such frankness, such moral honesty, such purity of soul allied to the toughness of strength that his personality radiated intensely, even unknowingly, to all his comrades in combat. Wounded side by side at Kufra, evacuated on the same plane, bed neighbours at Largeau, we had been able to get to know each other better during those long days of boredom and suffering, and, slowly, tacitly, without outward manifestations, one of those solid and deep human friendships had been created between us that nothing can shake. I was able to experience the depth of this friendship when Corlu, mortally wounded at Le Bourget, succumbed to his wounds; we were all cruelly affected by this loss, but we did not pity him because, as a Christian, he fell asleep with his soul in peace in the bosom of the God of Armies; as a soldier, he fully realised himself by falling before the enemy in full youth and glory, leaving us the imperishable memory of an upright life and an example to follow ... Happy are those who died in a just war.[111]

Dio's throat tightened with emotion as he spoke his words.

At the beginning of September, *Général* Dio received his transfer orders. He was officially designated to take command of the territories of southern Tunisia[112] from 25 September 1946. He then prepared his succession. On the associative side, taking advantage of a board of directors meeting, he had *Colonel* Rouvillois appointed to succeed him as president of the *Maison des Anciens de la 2ᵉ DB*. Before he left, Dio had a few days of leave to prepare for his departure to Tunisia. With his wife, he selected the personal items that would be transported in a custom-made crate to the Tunisian residence that would be assigned to him. Although housed in a furnished official residence, he had the opportunity to take dishes, decorations, books, and other small items. He took

---

110 *Caravane* No.48, 25 Août 1946, p.21., 'La Visite du Général Leclerc'.
111 Dio, 'Commandant Corlu', *Caravane* No. 48, 25 Août 1946, p.3.
112 At that time, the Fezzan was placed under the responsibility of this command.

advantage of this period to go to Brittany to visit his mother who lived alone in Ménimur, a new district located north of the city of Vannes. He passed through Pontivy to see his brother Daniel, a philosophy teacher at the private lycée Saint-Ivy, where he would become Superior in 1947. He also devoted his last days in Saint-Germain to preparing his successor, setting him up in the best conditions. The high command had selected *Colonel* Rémy to succeed him. What had happened in the meantime? It seems that *Colonel* Rémy preferred the command of a mobile group in North Africa, and the successor designated in September was *Colonel* Marc Rouvillois. This ultimately suited *Général* Dio, although Rouvillois was not a Free Frenchman. The former commander of the *12e Cuirs* had fought within the *GTD* throughout the campaign of liberation, and it was Rouvillois who took command of the *GTD* when Dio became the commander of the division. A solid friendship united the two men. Instructions from leader to leader are easier to pass on when there is mutual esteem. The change of command ceremony took place on 22 September 1946 in Saint-Germain. *Général* Leclerc was not present, and was probably in North Africa. The next day, Dio sent him a handwritten letter to inform him that 'Rouvillois has definitively taken command, in excellent materiel and moral conditions …. I am leaving quite happy for Gabès because I know that there is good work to be done in Tunisia.'[113] Then he expressed his emotion at leaving the division and the comrades of all ranks with whom he had served since 1938. He ended his letter by hoping he would be able to see Leclerc again soon during one of the future inspections in Tunisia.

Dio was satisfied to have been able to hand over his command in good condition. His successor was an officer unanimously recognised and appreciated within the new *GB2*. He was also happy to leave the metropolis to return to the African Continent. This post-war France did not suit him. The five years of war did not seem to have brought changes in the governance of the country. In politics, pettiness between parties had resumed in full swing. The interests of the country seemed to come after group and individual interests. Everyone wanted to make the most of the funds allocated to reconstruction.

After five years of war and a difficult year of command, *Général* Dio aspired to a less hectic and more fulfilling life, and he was delighted to soon show Tunisia to his wife. It would be all the easier since he knew the region of southern Tunisia that he would command. The staff of the *18e RTS*, where he was assigned in 1928, was based in Gabès. The 6th Company, in which he served as a *sous lieutenant*, was garrisoned in Médenine. In the spring of 1943, he had quickly crossed the region again during the Tunisian campaign. He was eager to return. He was happy and full of hope at the idea of taking command of the territories of southern Tunisia.

---

113   Fonds Leclerc, *Lettre de Dio à Leclerc en date du 23 Septembre 1946,* boîte 17a, chemise 1, dossier 2.

Bibliography

Archives

Centre Historique et Études des Troupes d'Outre-Mer (CHETOM)
Jacques Chauderon, 18H296, dossier 2
Jacques Fourneau, *Témoignage d'un administrateur en poste*, 18H42
Jean de Pange, lettre au colonel Dronne, 18H283 n°31, p.16
Monographie du poste militaire d'Agades – juin 42, box 18H149
L.V. Bertarelli, *Libia* (Milano, TCI, mars 1937)

Musée de la Libération de Paris, Musée Général Leclerc, Musée Jean Moulin (MLM/Paris Musées)
Archives du fonds historique du Général Leclerc (Fonds Leclerc)
Boîte 2: CORRESPONDANCE GENERAL de GAULLE – GÉNÉRAL LECLERC 1940–1947
Dossier1, chemise 1: Correspondance de Gaulle-Leclerc
Boîte 5a: FRANCE LIBRE 1940–1942
Dossier 2, chemise 1: Colonel Denise
Dossier 2, chemise 2: Mémoires du colonel Tutenges
Dossier 3, chemise 1: Note de service n°359 du 16.03.40
Boîte 6a: CORRESPONDANCE 1940
Dossier 2, chemise 2: Roger Ceccaldi, *Causerie du 4 octobre 1997 à Rambouillet*
Dossier 2, chemise 2b: Rapport d'opérations Koufra, 15 mars 1941
Dossier 2, chemise 3: Rapport concernant l'activité des FFL du Tchad en janvier et février 1941, signé Leclerc du 10 mars 1941
Boîte 7
Dossier 1, chemise 1: Ordre du Jour 7 mars 1941
Dossier 2, chemise 1: Aperçu sur la dissidence (Extrait du Bulletin d'information n°3) Mai 1941
Dossier 2, chemise 3: Procès-verbal d'une conférence à Kano le 22 juillet 1941
Boîte 8a
Dossier 1, chemise 1: Correspondance 42 entre Leclerc et Dio, 21 août 1942
Boîte 9a
Dossier 1, chemise 2: Correspondance 1943, Dio
Dossier 1, chemise 5: Lettre Massu à Farret
Boîte 10: 2ème D.B. au MAROC 1943–1944
Dossier 1, chemise 1: Tableau des effectifs théoriques de la 2e DB au 1 avril 1944
Dossier 1, chemise 3:
Leclerc, notes manuscrites
Rapport d'inspection de la French Training Section du 23 février 1944
Boîte 12
Dossier 2, chemise 4: Jean Compagnon, *La 2ème DB dans la Libération de Paris*

Boîte 13b: NORMANDIE – PARIS – OPERATIONS (suite)

Dossier 3, chemise 1: Duplay n°3. Opérations des unités de la 2e D.B. les 26–27–28 août 1944 au nord de Paris (R.H.A.)

Boîte 15: AMBIANCE, COLONIES, A.F.N., FRANCE, INDOCHINE, DECOLONISATION

Dossier n°1, chemise 6: Ambiance Cameroun 1940–41 – Documents André Rogez

Boîte 17a: CORRESPONDANCE 1946–1947

Dossier 1, chemise 2, correspondance Leclerc:

Lettre de Dio à Leclerc du 14 février 1946

Lettre de Dio à Leclerc du 23 février 1946

Lettre de Dio à Leclerc du 10 avril 1946

Lettre de Dio à Leclerc du 22 mai 1946

Lettre de Dio à Leclerc du 23 septembre 1946

Boîte 21b: CONFÉRENCES, ALLOCUTIONS du GÉNÉRAL LECLERC –

Dossier 1, chemise 1, Conférences de Leclerc: *Causerie Léopoldville du 9 juin 1942*

Boîte 29: COMPAGNONS DE LA LIBERATION – TUES AUX COMBATS – MEDAILLES

Dossier 3, chemise 3, « Démobilisés de la 2e DB par le Colonel Dio »

Boîte 30: POEMES-FILMS-CHANSONS –

Dossier 2, chemise 1, Jean Cocteau, *Salut à la Division Leclerc*

Boîte 34

Dossier 1, chemise 1: Général Dio – juin 1945 au 3 août 1947

Lettre n°1070/1-CPO du 5 juillet 1945

Ordre du jour n°127, 1er bureau, du 6 septembre 1945

Télégrammes en date du 9 avril 1946

Dossier 3, chemise 3: Organisation d'une D.B., Articulation au combat 1944–1947

Lettres du général Dio: Courrier du général Dio au Chef d'État-Major Général en date du 12 mars 1946. Le terme emprunte à l'armée américaine de Combat-command désigne un groupement tactique

Dissolution de la 2ème DB

Boîte 37: ORGANISATION 2ème D.B.

Dossier 1, chemise 3: Jacques Salbaing: *allocution prononcée le 11 septembre 1994 à Dompaire devant la stèle du Lieutenant Guigon*

Boîte A: AIDES-DE-CAMP (TROADEC ; GIRARD ; LANGLOIS)

Dossier 2, chemise 1: René Troadec, *Journal du capitaine Troadec du 10 mars 42 au 1er novembre 42* (51 pages)

Boîte B1: REGIMENT DE MARCHE DU TCHAD (1/R.M.T.)

Dossier 1, chemise 1: *JMO du 1/RMT*

Dossier 3, Chemise 1: André Gambourg, *Le destin de la 3ᵉ compagnie du Tchad*

Dossier 5, chemise 1: *Rapport mensuel sur le moral n°946 du 1/RMT en date du 29 juin 1945*

Boîte D1: 1ᵉʳ REGIMENT DE MARCHE DES SPAHIS MAROCAINS

Dossier 1, chemise 1: *JMO du 1ᵉʳ RMSM du 07/06/1941 au 02/01/1946*

Boîte E2: 22ème G.C.F.T.A. – TRANSMISSIONS – B.R.1 – B.R.2

Dossier 1, chemise 2: 2ᵉ batterie du *22ᵉ F.T.A.*

Boîte F1: 13ème BATAILLON DU GÉNIE

Dossier 1, chemise 1: *JMO du 13ᵉ BG*

Dossier 1, chemise 3: *JMO 2ᵉ compagnie (GTD)*

Boîte I: SERVICE SANTE DE LA DIVISION – *13ᵉ* BATAILLON MEDICAL

Dossier, 2, chemise 3: Charles Mauric, *Souvenirs du docteur Charles Mauric*

Boîte J: GROUPEMENT TACTIQUE DIO (G.T.D.)

Dossier 1, chemise 1: *JMO du GTD*

Ordre de mouvement n°223/3 du 23 août 1944

Note de service n°284/3 du GTD du 20 septembre 1944 signée Dio

Note de service n°363/3 du GTD en date du 30.10.44

Note n°439/3 du GTD du 23 décembre 1944

Dossier 1, chemise 2: JMO du sous-groupement Fosse

Boîte K1: GROUPEMENT TACTIQUE DIO (G.T.D.)

Dossier 2: *rapport mensuel sur le moral du 1ᵉʳ Bataillon,* No. *93/C of 12/20/1943*

Boîte L1: REGIMENT DE MARCHE DU TCHAD – *13ᵉ* R.M.T.

Dossier 1, chemise 1: *JMO du 3ᵉ bataillon RMT*

Dossier 1, Chemise 6: Pierre Destray, *Les campagnes de France d'Allemagne 1944/1945 de la 2eme Division Blindée des Forces Françaises Libres*

Boîte L2: REGIMENT DE MARCHE DU TCHAD – *13ᵉ* R.M.T.

Dossier 2, chemise 1: Joseph Putz, « Historique sommaire du 3ᵉ bataillon du CFA »

Boîte M1: 12ème CUIRASSIERS

Dossier 1, chemises 1 et 2: *JMO 12ᵉ Cuirs*

Boîte O1: 3ème REGIMENT d'ARTILLERIE COLONIALE (*13ᵉ* R.A.C.)

Dossier 2, chemise 1: *JMO 3ᵉ RAC du 1/01/44 au 11/11/48*

Boîte R: ÉCRITS, CONFÉRENCES, ALLOCUTIONS du général de GUILLEBON, de GAULLE et l'INDOCHINE, dossier Gal MASSU

Dossier 2, chemise 1: *Note 46/6 signée Leclerc du 10 décembre 1941 sur les principes de manœuvre*

Boîte U: PRESSE DU CAMEROUN

Gaulle, C. (de), Journal Eveil du Cameroun du 7 sept. 1940

Fondation Maréchal Leclerc de Hauteclocque: unclassified archives**

Jean Guiglini, *Carnet de route.*

Roger Loison, *Moteurs en Route, récits 1944–1945* (2004)

Roger Loison, *Carnets de Route, 1943–1945* (2005)

Pierre Purson, *Itinéraire suivi par le Troisième Escadron du 12ᵉ Cuirs, Peloton Krebs,* 1994.

Dossier Robédat.

Journal Officiel de la République Française (JOFR)

Décision ministérielle n°105, JORF du 19.11.1944

Décret du 08.02.1945, JORF du 02.03.1945

Décision n°363 – JORF du 04.03.1945

Fondation de la France Libre (FFL)

Note du commandement militaire du Cameroun Français/ 3° bureau n°74/3 'opérations menées en zone forestière par les troupes du Cameroun signée Lieutenant-Colonel de Tournadre, Commandant militaire.'

Raymond Dronne 'La douloureuse affaire du Gabon en 1940', *Carrefour*, 1965.

Ordre de mission n°1.278/3 de la 14e demi-brigade de Légion étrangère du 27 octobre 1940, signé colonel Monclar, de son vrai nom Magrain-Verneret.

TO n°79 du 5.11.40 du Commandant Parant au Gouverneur général Brazzaville.

Ordre de la Libération

Note n°1310/1, 3 October 1947

Jesus Maria de Leizaola, dans La Voix des Basques, 28.02.1945

Dossier Dio

Service historique de l'armée de Terre (SHAT) see SHD
Service historique de la Défense (SHD)
    Folder 14 Yd 1759: DIO, Louis, Joseph, Marie, GÉNÉRAL D'ARMÉE, décédé le 15 Juin
        1994
    SHAT, 1K239.4 étude de l'état-major des colonies du 25 septembre 1939
    SHAT 1K239.8
    SHAT, 7P51, dossier 1 Telex n°2980/EMP-4 of 5 April 1944

Published Works

Anonymous, *Le Général Leclerc, vu pas ses Compagnons de Combat* (Paris: Éditions Alsatia, 1948)
Anonymous, *Le Général Leclerc et l'Afrique Française Libre, 1940–1942, Actes du Colloque International* (Paris: Fondation Maréchal Leclerc de Hauteclocque, 1987)
Anonymous, *Soldats de Leclerc, Récits et Anecdotes 1940–1946,* Fondation Général Leclerc de Hauteclocque, Maréchal de France (Paris: éditions Lavauzelle, 1997)
Anonymous, *De Fort-Lamy à Strasbourg, historique de la 2ème cie du RMT* (Paris: Imprimerie Marcel Dart, 1950)
Bendjebbar, André, 'Leclerc, Soldat de Légende', *Du Capitaine de Hauteclocque au Général Leclerc* (Paris: Éditions Complexe, 2000), pp.409–427
Béné, Charles, *Carnets de Route d'un 'Rat du Désert', Alsacien de la France Libre, Première époque, 1940–1942* (Raon-l'Étape: Imprimerie Fetzer S.A., 1991)
Béné, Charles, *Carnets de Route d'un 'Rat du Désert', Alsacien de la France Libre, Seconde époque, 1942–1945* (Issy-les-Moulineaux: Elsevier Masson, 1999)
Bergot, Erwan, *La 2ᵉ D.B.* (Paris: Presses de la Cité, 1980)
Berntsen, Christian et Soulat, Robert, *Un viking chez les Bédouins* (Paris: Gallimard, 1957)
Bimberg, Edward L., *Tricolor over the Sahara, The Desert Battles of the Free French, 1940–1942* (Westport, CT: Greenwood Press, 2002)
Boissieu, Alain de, *Pour combattre avec de Gaulle, Souvenirs, 1940–1946* (Omnibus, 1999)
Bourdan, Pierre, *Carnet de retour avec la Division Leclerc* (Paris: Éditions Pierre Trémois, 1945)
Chauvet, Michel, *Le Sable et la Neige, 'Mes carnets dans la tourmente', 1939–1945* (Paris: Éditions du Petit Véhicule, 1996)
Clayton, Anthony, *Histoire de l'Armée Française en Afrique, 1830–1962* (Paris: Éditions Albin Michel, l994)
Compagnon, Jean, *Leclerc, Maréchal de France* (Paris: Flammarion, 1994)
Corbonnois, Didier, en collaboration avec Godec, Alain, *L'Odyssée de la Colonne Leclerc, Les Français Libres au combat sur le front du Tchad, 1940–43* (Paris: Histoire & Collections, 2003)
Cordier, Maurice & Fouquer, Roger, *Le Général Leclerc, ou se Commander à soi-même* (Paris: Éditions Desclée de Brouwer, 1990)
Croidys, Pierre, *Notre Second Bayard, le Général Leclerc – Grand Soldat – Grand Chrétien,* (Paris: Éditions Spes, 1950)
Dansette, Adrien, *Leclerc* (Paris: Éditions J'ai Lu, Flammarion, 1952)
Dejouy, Jacques, *Les Grandes Certitudes* (Saint-Brieuc: Éditions Vu de France, 1993)
Destrem, Maja, *L'Aventure de Leclerc* (Paris: Éditions Fayard, 1984)
Di Martino, *Scenari Sahariani Libia, 1919–1943, la Via Italiana alla Guerra nel Deserto* (Roma: Ufficio Storico Stato Maggiore Difesa, 2021)
Dronne, Raymond, *Le Serment de Koufra* (Paris: Éditions du Temps, 1965)
Dronne, Raymond, *Carnets de Route d'un Croisé de la France Libre* (Paris: Éditions France-Empire, 1983)

Dronne, Raymond, *L'Hallali de Paris à Berchtesgaden, Août 1944-Mai 1945* (Paris: Éditions France-Empire, 1985)

Esme, Jean d', *Les Nomades de la Gloire, l'Épopée de la Division Leclerc* (Paris: Les publications techniques et artistiques, 1944)

Etchegoyen, Philippe, *Une Ombre dans la Nuit* (Paris: Les Éditions la Bruyère, 1992)

Eymard, Alain, *2ᵉ DB* (Paris: Éditions Heimdal, 1990)

Fisher, Raymond, *325 Jours avec les Spahis de Leclerc* (Issy-les-Moulineaux, Muller édition, 1999)

Frison-Roche, Roger, *La Piste Oubliée* (Paris: Éditions Arthaud, 1951)

Faure-Biguet, Jacques-Napoléon, *Le Général Leclerc* (Paris: Librairie Plon, 1948)

Fonde, Jean-Julien, *J'ai vu une Meute de Loups, avec la 2ᵉ D.B. du Maroc à Berchtesgaden* (Paris: Fernand Nathan, 1969)

Fonde, Jean-Julien, *Les Loups de Leclerc* (Paris: Librairie Plon, 1982)

Forget, Dominique, *L'Épopée de Leclerc et de ses Hommes* (Mundolsheim: Éditions du Signé, 2011)

Gaulle, Charles de, *Mémoires de Guerre. L'Appel, 1940–1942* (Paris, Éditions Plon, 1961)

Gaulle, Philippe de, *Mémoires* (Paris: Bouquins, 2022)

Girard, Christian, *Journal de Guerre, 1939–1945, Témoignage de l'Aide de Camp du Général Leclerc de Hauteclocque* (Paris: L'Harmattan, 2000)

Giraud, Victor, *Leclerc, Maréchal de France* (Paris: Éditions Spes, 1952)

Gribius, André, *Une Vie d'Officier* (Paris: Éditions France-Empire, 1971)

Guillebon, Jacques (de), *Leclerc le Victorieux, 1902–1947* (Paris: Fondation du Maréchal Leclerc de Hauteclocque, 1954)

Heitzler, Jeanne, *Souvenirs de Grussenheim et des Environs* (la Défense de Strasbourg et Libération de la poche de Colmar Nord, 6e édition, 1995)

Hettier de Boislambert, Claude, *Les Fers de l'Espoir* (Paris: Plon, 1978)

Ingold, François (Gal), *Ceux de Leclerc en Tunisie, Février-Mai 1943* (Paris, Office Français d'Édition, 1945)

Ingold, François (Gal), *L'Épopée Leclerc au Sahara, 1940–1943* (Paris, Éditions Berger-Levrault, 1948)

Ingold, François, & Mouilleseaux, Louis, *Leclerc de Hauteclocque* (Paris: Éditions Littéraires de France, 1948)

Ingold, Gérard, *Général Ingold, Figure de la France Libre* (Paris: Challenges d'Aujourd'hui, 1995)

Jacob, François, *La Statue Intérieure* (Paris: Éditions Odile Jacob, 1987)

Jennings, Éric T., *La France Libre fut Africaine* (Paris, Perrin, Ministère de la Défense, 2014)

Lacouture, Jean, *De Gaulle. 1. Le Rebelle, 1890–1944* (Paris: Éditions du Seuil, 1984)

Langlade, Paul de, *En Suivant Leclerc, d'Alger à Berchtesgaden* (Paris: Robert Laffont, 1964)

Larminat, Edgard de, *Chroniques Irrévérencieuses* (Paris: Éditions Plon, 1962)

Leclerc, (Gal), *La 2 DB, combattants et combats en France* (Paris: Éditions Arts et Métiers Graphiques, 1945)

Levisse-Touzé, Christine, sous la direction de, *Du Capitaine de Hauteclocque au Général Leclerc* (Bruxelles: Éditions Complexe, 2000)

Levisse-Touzé, Christine, et Toureille, Julien, *Écrits de Combat,* avec préface du Général Cuche (Paris: Sorbonne Université Presses, 2023)

Lévy-Haussmann, Gilbert, *La 2ᵉ D.B. vue par un 2ᵉ classe* (Paris: Imprimerie Firmin Didot, 2005)

Lormier, Dominique, *C'est Nous les Africains, l'Épopée de l'armée française d'Afrique 1940–1945* (Paris: Calmann-Lévy, 2006)

Maggiar, Raymond, *Les Fusiliers Marins dans la Division Leclerc* (Paris: Éditions Albin Michel, 1947)

Malraux, André, *Oraisons Funèbres* (Paris: Gallimard, 1971)

Martel, André, *Leclerc, Le Soldat et le Politique* (Paris: Éditions Albin Michel, 1998)

Massu, Jacques, *Sept Ans avec Leclerc* (Paris: Librairie Plon, 1974)

Maule, Henry, *Out of the Sand* (London: Corgi Books, 1996)

Mauras, Jean, *Souvenirs, 1939–1946* (Paris: Éditions Lavauzelle, 2010)

Mengone, Barthélémy Ntoma, *La Bataille de Libreville* (Paris: ed. L'Harmattan, 2014)

Merle, Guy, *L'Assaut, avec la 2ᵉ D.B.* (Brive la Gaillarde: Ver Luisant, 2003)

Messmer, Pierre, *Après tant de Batailles…, Mémoires* (Paris: Albin Michel, 1992)

Minella, Alain-Gilles, *Entretiens avec le Général Massu* (Paris: Éditions Mame, collection 'Trajectoire', 1993)

Moore, William Mortimer, *Free France's Lion, the Life of Philippe Leclerc, De Gaulle Greatest General* (Havertown, PA: Casemate Publishers, 2011)

Mouchet, Jean, *Leclerc. Débuts Méconnus de son Historique Épopée – Londres-Cameroun 1940* (Toulon: Les éditions du Midi, 1978)

Moynet, Paul, *L'Épopée du Fezzan* (Office français d'Éditions, Alger, 1944)

Notin, Jean-Christophe, *Leclerc, le Croisé de la France Libre* (Paris: Éditions Perrin, 2015)

Ollandet, Jérôme, *Brazzaville, capitale de la France Libre, 1940–1944* (Paris: L'Harmattan, 2013)

Pellissier, Édouard, *Le Général Rouvillois ou La Victoire en Chargeant,* préface du Général Dio (Ed. Du Camelot Et De La Joyeuse Garde, 1994)

Pellissier, Pierre, Massu (Paris: Perrin, 2003)

Perceval, André, *Joseph Perceval, Compagnon de la Libération* (Paris: Presses du Groupe Cilaos, 2000)

Quillet, Pierre, *Le Chemin le plus Long. Chronique de la Compagnie de chars de combat du Général de Gaulle, 1940–1945* (Paris: Maisonneuve et Larose, 1997)

Repiton-Préneuf, Paul, présenté par Buis, Georges, *2ᵉᵐᵉ DB. La Campagne de France* (Paris: Éditions Imprimerie Nationale, 1994) (première édition, Général Leclerc, 1945)

Rigault, Emmanuel, *Le Régiment de Marche du Tchad, Koufra 1941 – Sarajevo 1995,* préface du Général Massu (Carcassonne: Imprimerie Sival-Mavit, 1996)

Robet: Charles, *Souvenirs d'un Médecin de la France Libre* (Paris: Sides, 1994).

Rosset, Geoffroy, *Itinéraire d'un Compagnon de la Libération, Geoffroy de Bagneux, duc de Ghadamès* (Paris: L'Harmattan, 2018)

Salbaing, Jacques, *Ardeur et Réflexion* (Paris: Éditions La Pensée Universelle, 1992)

Salbaing, Jacques, *La Victoire de Leclerc à Dompaire, 13 Septembre 1944* (Issy-les Moulineaux: Muller Éditions, 1997)

Smith, Jean Edward, *The Liberation of Paris, How Eisenhower, de Gaulle and Von Choltitz Saved the City of Light* (New York: Simon & Schuster, 2019)

Van der Plaetsen, Jean-René, *La Nostalgie de l'Honneur* (Paris: le Livre de Poche, 2018)

Vernejoul, Henri de, et Durlewanger, Armand, *Autopsie d'une victoire morte* (Colmar-Ingersheim: SAEP, 1970)

Vézinet, Adolphe, *Le Général Leclerc,* (Paris: Éditions J'ai Lu, 1982)

Villeminey, R. et Marquet, J. J., *Insignes et Historiques des Formations Indigènes de l'Infanterie Coloniale* (Château-Chinon: Presses de l'Établissement d'Impression de l'Armée de Terre, 2004)

Vincent, Jean-Noël, *Les Forces Françaises Libres en Afrique, 1940–1943* (Service Historique Armée de Terre, 1983)

Watson, John and Jones, Louis, *3 Squadron at War* (D.A.F. Squadron Association, Carlingford, New South Wales, 1959)

Articles, Essays, Chapters

Caravane: Many of the articles in *Caravane* do not include the author's name and were likely written by the editorial board. The ones quoted in this study were published in the following issues: 1944 (Nos 5, 7), 1945 (Nos 20, 26, 27), 1946 (Nos 35, 36, 38, 40, 41, 48), 1983 (No.340), 2020 (No.487)

Bendjebbar, André, 'Leclerc, Soldat de Légende', *Du Capitaine de Hauteclocque au Général Leclerc* (Paris: Éditions Complexe, 2000), pp.409–427

Berval, René de, 'Á Fontainebleau. Les Adieux du Général', *Caravane*, 23, 25 Juin 1945

Berval, René de, 'Le Colonel Dio', *Caravane* No. 26, 1945, pp.31–32

Boissieu, Alain de, 'La Libération capitale' in *Armées d'Aujourd'hui* No. 190, numéro spécial (mai 1994), pp.190–193

Bompard, 'Comment notre drapeau fut hissé sur la cathédrale', *Soldats de Leclerc, Récits et Anecdotes 1940–1946,* Foundation Général Leclerc de Hauteclocque, Maréchal de France, (Paris: Éditions Lavauzelle, 1997), pp.221–222

Ceccaldi, Roger, 'Koufra, Souvenir de l'Artilleur', special issue, *Revue Historique des Armées –* n°151-*(1983),* Les troupes de Marine, pp.40–49

Ceccaldi, Roger, 'Témoignage de l'Artilleur de Koufra', *Le Général Leclerc et l'Afrique Française Libre, 1940–1942,* Actes du Colloque International, Fondation Maréchal Leclerc de Hauteclocque (Paris, 1987), pp.297–300

Ceccaldi, Roger, 'Koufra, Souvenir de l'Artilleur', *Le Général Leclerc et l'Afrique Française Libre, 1940–1942,* Actes du Colloque International, Fondation Maréchal Leclerc de Hauteclocque (Paris, 1987), pp.423–442

Chaban-Delmas, Jacques, 'Libération de Paris', *Caravane* No.26, p.3

Chauliac, Guy, 'Souvenirs du Tchad', *Le Général Leclerc et l'Afrique Française Libre, 1940–1942,* Actes du Colloque International, Fondation Maréchal Leclerc de Hauteclocque (Paris, 1987), pp.259–266

Compagnon, Jean, 'Instructeur et formateur', pp.165–176; 'Logisticien et Tacticien' pp.205–224, in Christine Levisse-Touzé (ed.), *Du Capitaine de Hauteclocque au Général Leclerc* (Paris: Éditions Complexe, 2000)

Compagnon, Jean, 'Paris en ligne de Mire,' *Armées d'Aujourd'hui*, May 1994, 190, pp.128–132.

Corlu, Jean-Marie, 'Causerie', *Eveil du Cameroun* (26 mai 1941)

Cunningham, Harry, 'Sahara, The Fighting French March to Tripoli', *Infantry Journal*, October 1943, pp.32–37

Delmas, Jean, 'Le Général Leclerc et la contribution de l'Afrique Française Libre aux opérations', *Le Général Leclerc et l'Afrique Française Libre, 1940–1942,* Actes du Colloque International (Paris: Fondation Maréchal Leclerc de Hauteclocque, 1987), pp.147–172

Dio, Louis, 'Commandant Corlu', *Caravane* No. 48, 25 Août 1946, p.3

Dio, Louis, 'L'Audace Raisonnée du Général Leclerc', *Caravane* No.89, avril 1949, pp.13–14

Dio, Louis, 'Quand le Général Leclerc Dédicaçait des Photographies à Raspoutine', *Caravane* No.89 avril 1949, p.26

Dronne, Raymond, 'Le Drapeau à Croix de Lorraine sur le nid d'Aigle d'Hitler', *Soldats de Leclerc,* Fondation Général Leclerc de Hauteclocque, Maréchal de France (Paris: Éditions Lavauzelle, 1997), pp.255–256

Dubois, Robert, 'Raid Logistique au Soudan Anglo-Égyptien', *Soldats de Leclerc,* Fondation Général Leclerc de Hauteclocque, Maréchal de France (Paris: Éditions Lavauzelle, 1997), pp.55–60

Duplay, Philippe, '26, 27 et 28 août 1944: combats au nord de Paris', *Soldats de Leclerc, Récits et Anecdotes 1940–1946,* Fondation Général Leclerc de Hauteclocque, Maréchal de France (Paris: éditions Lavauzelle, 1997) pp.147–162

Etat-Major 2e DB, *Caravane* No. 5 (29 octobre au 6 novembre 1944), 'La Prise de Baccarat'

Fonde, Jean-Julien, 'Koufra: la victoire d'une volonté', *La Cohorte,*78 & 79, (avril & juillet 1983) pp.13–21 & 6–9

Forest, Louis, 'Le Rendez-vous de Kléber', *Caravane* No. 32, 5 Décembre 1945, pp.8–9

Forest, Louis, 'Le Coin du Râleur', *Caravane* No. 34, 10 Janvier 1946, p.30

Grognier, Gilberte, 'Extraits du journal tenu à Douala', *Le Général Leclerc et l'Afrique Française Libre*, Actes du Colloque International, (Fondation Maréchal Leclerc de Hauteclocque, Paris, 1987), document n°8, pp.575–581

Lansdowne, Georges Mercer Nairne, Lord, 'Leclerc, Chef de Guerre', *Le Général Leclerc et l'Afrique Française Libre, 1940–1942,* Actes du Colloque International (Paris: Fondation Maréchal Leclerc de Hauteclocque, 1987), pp.237–240

Leizaola, Jésus-Maria de, 'Autour de la mort d'un grand soldat français, le lieutenant-colonel Putz', *Caravane,* No. 36 Février 46, pp.11–12

Martel, André, 'L'A.F.L. support de guerre français et allié' in *Le Général Leclerc et l'Afrique Française Libre, 1940–1942,* Actes du Colloque International (Fondation Maréchal Leclerc de Hauteclocque, Paris, 1987) pp.87–105

Massu, Jacques,'Souvenirs du Général Dio', *Caravane*, No.384, 1994, p.3

Michel, Marc, 'Leclerc et l'Afrique Noire', *Du Capitaine de Hauteclocque au Général Leclerc* (Paris: Éditions Complexe 2000), pp.253–273

Michel, Marc, 'L'AFL, support de guerre français et allié', *Le Général Leclerc et l'Afrique Française Libre, 1940–1942,* Actes du Colloque International (Paris: Fondation Maréchal Leclerc de Hauteclocque, 1987), pp.87–105

Mveng, Engelbert, S. J., 'L'œuvre de Leclerc au Cameroun et la contribution des Camerounais à l'effort de guerre', *Le Général Leclerc et l'Afrique Française Libre*, Actes du Colloque International (Paris: Fondation Maréchal Leclerc de Hauteclocque, 1987) pp.59–72

Pons, Roger & Lucchési, Jean, 'Le Général Louis Dio, ancien président national de l'AFL', *Revue de l'AFL,* 288 (4e trimestre 1994), p.60

Pranzo, Richard, 'Un été à Sabratha, 1943', *Caravane* 2003, No.420, p.32.

Rainero, Romain H., 'L'Italie et la Campagne Saharienne de Leclerc' in Christine Levisse-Touzé (ed.), *Du Capitaine de Hauteclocque au Général Leclerc* (Paris: Éditions Complexe, 2000), pp.333–344

Sancy, Alain de, 'Mon ami Commeinhes' in *Soldats de Leclerc, Récits et Anecdotes 1940–1946,* Foundation Général Leclerc de Hauteclocque, Maréchal de France (Paris: éditions Lavauzelle, 1997), pp.210–211

Terver, Pierre, 'Paris', *Soldats de Leclerc, Récits et Anecdotes 1940–1946,* Fondation Général Leclerc de Hauteclocque, Maréchal de France (Paris: Éditions Lavauzelle, 1997), pp.137–138

Touzé (ed.), *Du capitaine de Hauteclocque au Général Leclerc* (Éditions Complexe, 2000), pp.191–203

Troadec, René, 'Extraits du Journal', *Le Général Leclerc et l'Afrique Française Libre, 1940–1942,* Actes du Colloque International, (Paris: Fondation Maréchal Leclerc de Hauteclocque, 1987), pp.584–595

Verdier, Henri, 'Le rôle du Colonel Leclerc dans la Constitution de l'Afrique Française Libre' in *Le Général Leclerc et l'Afrique Française Libre, 1940–1942,* Actes du Colloque International (Paris: Fondation Maréchal Leclerc de Hauteclocque, 1987), pp.43–57

Vernet, Jacques, 'Mise sur pied de la 2e DB, de la diversité à l'unité', in Christine Levisse-Touzé (ed.), *Du Capitaine de Hauteclocque au Général Leclerc* (Paris: Éditions Complexe, 2000)

Vézinet, Adolphe, *La 2ème DB, Gal Leclerc* (Paris: Arts et Métiers Graphiques,1945), pp.167–174

Unpublished

Altfeld, Albert & Serri, Huguette, *Le Pont de Tardets, un Ancien de Leclerc Raconte*
Létang, Géraud, *Mirages d'une rébellion. Être Français libre au Tchad (1940 – 1943)*, Thèse de
   doctorat en histoire, Institut d'Études Politiques de Paris (2020)

The *Établissement de communication et de production audiovisuelle de la Défense*, is a centre of leading audiovisual archives and production. In this respect, it retains an exceptional collection of audiovisual and photographic archives on all contemporary conflicts in which the French Army was engaged since 1915, or 15 million photos and 94,000 hours of films. These collections are constantly enriched by the work of military reporters, payments from defence organisations and donations from individuals. ECPAD is a real-time witness of the engagement of French armed forces in all operational theatres with its reporting teams trained in filming under operational conditions. A true cultural actor, ECPAD showcases its collections through film co-production, co-publishing of works, the creation of exhibitions and participation in festivals. The establishment is also an actor in education and research with schoolchildren, students, and teachers, and is a training centre thanks to its *École des métiers de l'image*.

**The *Fonds Leclerc* is now housed at the *Musée de la Libération de Paris, Musée du Général Leclerc, Musée Jean Moulin*.

Index